The New Form 990

The New Form 990

Law, Policy, and Preparation

Bruce R. Hopkins
Douglas K. Anning
Virginia C. Gross
Thomas J. Schenkelberg

WILEY

John Wiley & Sons, Inc.

Library of Congress Cataloging-in-Publication Data:

The new form 990 : law, policy, and preparation / Bruce R. Hopkins . . . [et al.].
    p. cm.
  Includes index.
  ISBN 978-0-470-37505-1 (cloth)
  1. Nonprofit organizations–Taxation–Law and legislation–United States. 2.   Tax exemption–Law and legislation–United States–Forms. 3.   Tax returns–United States.   I. Hopkins, Bruce R.
  KF6449.N49 2009
  343.7305'2668–dc22   2008040277

Contents

CONTENTS

■ vii ■

About the Authors

BRUCE R. HOPKINS is a senior partner in the law firm of Polsinelli Shughart, practicing in the firm's Kansas City, Missouri, and Washington, D.C., offices. He specializes in the representation of tax-exempt organizations. His practice ranges over the entirety of law matters involving exempt organizations, with emphasis on the formation of nonprofit organizations, acquisition of recognition of tax-exempt status for them, the private inurement and private benefit doctrines, the intermediate sanctions rules, legislative and political campaign activities issues, public charity and private foundation rules, unrelated business planning, use of exempt and for-profit subsidiaries, joint venture planning, tax shelter involvement, review of annual information returns, Internet communications developments, the law of charitable giving (including planned giving), and fundraising law issues.

Mr. Hopkins served as chair of the Committee on Exempt Organizations, Tax Section, American Bar Association; chair, Section of Taxation, National Association of College and University Attorneys; and president, Planned Giving Study Group of Greater Washington, D.C.

Mr. Hopkins is the series editor of Wiley's Nonprofit Law, Finance, and Management Series. He is the author of *The Law of Tax-Exempt Organizations, Ninth Edition; Planning Guide for the Law of Tax-Exempt Organizations: Strategies and Commentaries; IRS Audits of Tax-Exempt Organizations: Policies, Practices, and Procedures; The Tax Law of Charitable Giving, Third Edition; The Law of Fundraising, Fourth Edition; The Tax Law of Associations; The Tax Law of Unrelated Business for Nonprofit Organizations; The Nonprofits' Guide to Internet Communications Law; The Law of Intermediate Sanctions: A Guide for Nonprofits; Starting and Managing a Nonprofit Organization: A Legal Guide, Fifth Edition; Nonprofit Law Made Easy; Charitable Giving Law Made Easy; Private Foundation Law Made Easy; 650 Essential Nonprofit Law Questions Answered; The First Legal Answer Book for Fund-Raisers; The Second Legal Answer Book for Fund-Raisers; The Legal Answer Book for Nonprofit Organizations; The Second Legal Answer Book for Nonprofit Organizations;* and *The Nonprofit Law Dictionary;* and is the coauthor, with Jody Blazek, of *Private Foundations: Tax Law and Compliance, Third Edition;* also with Ms. Blazek, *The Legal Answer Book for Private Foundations;* with Thomas K. Hyatt, of *The Law of Tax-Exempt Healthcare Organizations, Third Edition;* and with David O. Middlebrook, of *Nonprofit Law for Religious Organizations: Essential Questions and Answers.* He also writes *Bruce R. Hopkins' Nonprofit Counsel,* a monthly newsletter, published by John Wiley & Sons.

Mr. Hopkins earned his J.D. and L.L.M. degrees at the George Washington University National Law Center and his B.A. at the University of Michigan. He is a member of the bars of the District of Columbia and the State of Missouri.

Mr. Hopkins received the 2007 Outstanding Nonprofit Lawyer Award (Vanguard Lifetime Achievement Award) from the American Bar Association, Section of Business Law, Committee on Nonprofit Corporations. He is listed in *The Best Lawyers in America, Nonprofit Organizations/Charity Law,* 2007, 2008.

DOUGLAS K. ANNING, is a shareholder of Polsinelli Shughart, and is vice-chair of the firm's Nonprofit Organizations Practice Group. Mr. Anning advises clients on their general tax and corporate law needs, navigates family foundations through complex IRS requirements and regulations, serves as general advisor and counselor to a number of nonprofit organizations, and consults with healthcare organizations regarding myriad regulatory requirements (including tax-exemption, bond issues, HIPAA, anti-kickback, Stark self-referral, EMTALA, FTC/DOJ Antitrust, Joint Commission, and nonprofit governance). He also counsels, government entities, schools and universities, churches, trade associations and other nonprofit organizations. In addition, he has substantial experience in mergers and acquisitions, transactional matters, and structuring joint ventures. Mr. Anning is listed in *The Best Lawyers in America* in the category of Nonprofit/Charities Law for 2009.

VIRGINIA C. GROSS is a shareholder of Polsinelli Shughart. Ms. Gross concentrates her practice in the fields of tax and nonprofit law. She represents a variety of nonprofit clients, including public charities, educational organizations, private foundations, associations, supporting organizations, medical research and other healthcare organizations, and social welfare organizations. She works with all aspects of nonprofit law, such as issues regarding the structure, operations, fundraising, unrelated business income planning, and joint venturing and partnering of tax-exempt entities, and use of supporting organizations and for-profit subsidiaries by exempt organizations. Ms. Gross is a frequent writer and speaker on nonprofit issues. She was named one of the Best Lawyers in America for nonprofit/charities law for 2008 and 2009.

THOMAS J. SCHENKELBERG is a shareholder in the law firm of Polsinelli Shughart. He is also the chair of the firm's Nonprofit Organizations Practice Group. Drawing on his experience as both an attorney and a certified public accountant, Mr. Schenkelberg's practice specializes in the areas of tax, nonprofit, and healthcare law.

Clients include national hospital systems, research organizations, private foundations, colleges, universities, associations, social welfare organizations, political action committees, and governmental entities.

Clients turn to Mr. Schenkelberg for structuring mergers and acquisitions, guiding corporate reorganizations, qualification for tax exemption, joint ventures of nonprofit and for-profit entities, nonprofit governance issues, compliance with private foundation rules, unrelated business income planning, fundraising programs, for-profit subsidiary planning, public charity qualification, and use of supporting organizations. His practice also involves planning for various hospital/physician joint ventures, integrated delivery systems, whole-hospital joint ventures, medical service organizations, and planning to avoid private inurement/intermediate sanctions. He is a frequent writer and speaker on nonprofit law topics. He has written for many publications and is coauthor of the Tax Management Portfolio's "Private Foundations—Distributions (Sec. 4942)" published by the Bureau of National Affairs.

Preface

It is not often that one has the opportunity to write a book about a government form. (This is a good thing.) As discussed in the book, the redesigned Form 990, however, is no ordinary government document. The promulgation of this return is one of the most extraordinary developments affecting the nonprofit community in recent times. Although there are defects with this form and many nonprofit organizations are unhappy that it exists, it cannot be credibly denied that the new return is a work of art.

Most government forms are based on law, usually statutory law. The new Form 990 has this basis, with a considerable portion of the underlying law enacted in the last three or four years. The new Form 990, however, goes far beyond that foundation and has created, and is creating, much new law. This is demonstrated, for example, in the various policies, procedures, and protocols stressed by the IRS in its new return. Moreover, the new Form 990 is designed to induce and/or modify practices of tax-exempt organizations by the nature of the questions and the way they are to be answered (all those enticing—sometimes terrifying—"yes" boxes). Thus, the IRS has stated that the new Form 990 is now its governance enforcement tool and the governance portion of it is the "crown jewel" of the return.

When the revised Form 990 was published in draft form, we immediately saw its enormous implications and suspected that far too many nonprofit organizations were unprepared for what is coming their way (indeed, did not even realize what was coming). The solution to this problem, as we saw, was the writing of this book. Then, working with Professional Education Systems, Inc., we designed a series of seminars and webinars to help sound the alarm and spread the word in the interim.

The principal purpose of this book is to summarize the law—both preexisting law and the law created by promulgation of the return—that nonprofit organizations and their return preparers need to know to properly and effectively (this is, after all, a public document) prepare the new return. In addition, the book focuses on line-by-line analysis of the return to help in the preparation of the Form 990 and provides many checklists of steps to take to be in the best possible position to prepare the return.

As to this matter of the law, a development occurred that came too late to be incorporated into the book text: the promulgation by the IRS of the proposed, temporary, and final regulations to implement the new Form 990 (T.D. 9423, REG-142333-07). The temporary regulations revise the preexisting regulations to allow for new threshold amounts for reporting compensation, require that compensation be reported on a calendar-year basis, modify the scope of organizations subject to information-reporting requirements on a substantial contraction, eliminate the advance ruling process for new organizations, change the public support computation period for publicly supported charities, and clarify that support must be reported using the organization's overall method of accounting.

The size of this volume is a testament to what the IRS has wrought and the massive impact this formidable Form 990 is having on the management, operations, and governance of most exempt organizations. We hope the book will be of assistance as organizations struggle to revamp their operations and upgrade their practices in order to complete this capacious return.

Bruce R. Hopkins
Douglas K. Anning
Virginia C. Gross
Thomas J. Schenkelberg

The New Form 990

CHAPTER ONE

Part I—Overview of New Form 990

The annual information return filed by most tax-exempt organizations with the Internal Revenue Service (IRS) is the Form 990. This return was issued in dramatically redesigned form on December 19, 2007, for the 2008 tax year (returns filed in 2009). In its altered form, the new Form 990 has enormous implications for exempt organizations. A copy of this return, including its many schedules, is in Appendix A.

At the time the revised Form 990 was issued as a discussion draft (on June 14, 2007), the Acting Commissioner of Internal Revenue said: "The tax-exempt sector has changed markedly since the Form 990 was last overhauled more than a quarter of a century ago. We need a Form 990 that reflects the way this growing sector operates in the 21st century. The new 990 aims to give both the IRS and the public an improved window into the way tax-exempt organizations go about their vital mission."

The Director of the IRS's Exempt Organizations Division, on that occasion, added: "Most organizations should not experience a change in burden. However, those with complicated compensation arrangements, related entity structures and activities that raise compliance concerns may have to spend more time providing meaningful information to the public."

When the new Form 990 was released in final form, the Commissioner, Tax Exempt/Governmental Entities, said: "When we released the redesigned draft form this past June, we said we needed a Form 990 that reflects the way this growing sector operates in the 21st century. The public comments we received in response to our draft form helped us develop a final form consistent with our guiding principles of transparency, compliance and burden minimization."

The new Commissioner of Internal Revenue said:

> Tax-exempt organizations provide tremendous benefits to the people and the communities they serve, but their ability to do good work hinges upon the public's trust. The new Form 990 will foster this trust by greatly improving transparency and compliance in the tax-exempt sector. Public comment on the draft instructions will help the IRS to minimize the reporting burden on tax-exempt organizations, which is another important goal.

On the occasion of issuance of the final instructions for the 2008 Form 990, on August 19, 2008, the Commissioner said:

> These instructions are the final step in a tremendous effort to bring the Form 990 up to date and to reflect the diversity and complexity of the tax-exempt community.

The revised form will give the IRS and the public a much better view of how exempt organizations operate. The improved transparency provided by these changes will also benefit the tax-exempt community.

On the day after the draft of the revised Form 990 was issued, the executive director of a large public charity said: "If this is the Form 990 we will have to file, we don't want to be tax-exempt anymore."

The return to be filed by small tax-exempt organizations (Form 990-EZ) has also been revised (see § 1.9). Many of the schedules that accompany the Form 990 (see § 1.8) may have to be filed with this small exempt organizations return. (The Form 990-PF filed by private foundations has not been revised as part of this process.)

§ 1.1 FORM 990 BASICS

Nearly every organization that is exempt from federal income taxation must file an annual information return with the IRS. This return generally calls for the provision of much information, some of it financial and some in prose form. This document, being an *information return* rather than a *tax return*, is available for public inspection (see § 1.1(e)).

(a) Various Forms

For most tax-exempt organizations, the information return that must be filed annually is Form 990. Private foundations, however, file an information return that is uniquely styled for them: Form 990-PF. Small organizations (other than private foundations)—that is, entities that have gross receipts that are less than $100,000 and total assets that are less than $250,000 in value at the end of the reporting year—file Form 990-EZ. Other forms in the 990 series are Form 990-N, 990-T, and 990-W.

(b) Filing Exceptions

The requirement for the filing of an annual information return does not apply to:

- Churches (including interchurch organizations of local units of a church)
- Integrated auxiliaries of churches
- Conventions or associations of churches
- Financing, fund management, or retirement insurance program management organizations functioning on behalf of the foregoing organizations
- Certain other entities affiliated with a church or convention or association of churches
- Most religious orders (to the exclusive extent of their religious activities)
- State and local institutions
- Certain schools and mission societies
- Governmental units
- Affiliates of governmental units (which can include nonprofit, tax-exempt organizations)

- Organizations (other than private foundations) that have gross receipts that normally are not in excess of $25,000 annually

- Foreign organizations (other than private foundations) that normally do not receive more than $25,000 in gross receipts annually from sources within the United States and that do not have any significant activity (including lobbying or political activity) in the United States

(c)   Filing Due Dates

The annual information return is due on or before the 15th day of the 5th month following the close of the organization's tax year. Thus, the return for a calendar-year organization should be filed by May 15 of each year. One or more extensions may be obtained. These returns are filed with the IRS service center in Ogden, Utah.

The filing date for an annual information return may fall due while the organization's application for recognition of tax-exempt status is pending with the IRS. In that instance, the organization should nonetheless file the information return (rather than a tax return) and indicate on it that the application is pending.

(d)   Penalties

Failure to timely file the annual information return, without reasonable cause or an exception, can generally give rise to a $20-per-day penalty. The organization must pay for each day the failure continues, up to a maximum of $10,000. For larger organizations (those with annual gross receipts in excess of $1 million), the per-day penalty is $100 and the maximum penalty is $50,000.

An additional penalty can be imposed, at the same rate and up to the same maximum, on the individual(s) responsible for the failure to file, absent reasonable cause. Other fines and even imprisonment can be imposed for willfully failing to file returns or for filing fraudulent returns and statements with the IRS.

(e)   Disclosure Requirements

The IRS, in its instructions, observes: "Some members of the public rely on Form 990, or Form 990-EZ, as the primary or sole source of information about a particular organization. How the public perceives an organization in such cases may be determined by the information presented on its returns."

A tax-exempt organization's completed Form 990 or Form 990-EZ is available for public inspection and disclosure. Schedule B (see § 1.8(b)) is generally not available for public inspection, although it is available in the case of political organizations that file either return (and private foundations). Form 990-T filed by a charitable organization after August 17, 2006, to report unrelated business income, is also available for public inspection and disclosure.

(1) Availability through IRS.   Form 4506-A may be filed to request (1) a copy of a tax-exempt organization's return, report, notice, or application for recognition of exemption, and/or (2) an inspection of a return, report, notice, or application at an IRS office.

(2) Availability through Exempt Organization. In general, a tax-exempt organization must:

- Make its application for recognition of exemption and its annual information returns available for public inspection without charge at its principal, regional, and district offices during regular business hours

- Make each annual information return available for a period of three years, beginning on the date the return is required to be filed or is actually filed, whichever is later

- Provide a copy without charge, other than a reasonable fee for reproduction and actual postage costs, of all or any part of any application or return required to be made available for public inspection to any individual who makes a request for such copy in person or in writing

A tax-exempt organization must:

- Provide copies of required documents in response to a request made in person at its principal, regional, and district offices during regular business hours

- Provide these copies to a requester on the day the request is made, except for unusual circumstances

In the case of an in-person request, where unusual circumstances exist so that fulfilling the request on the same business day causes an unreasonable burden to the tax-exempt organization, the organization must provide the copies no later than the next business day following the day that the unusual circumstances cease to exist or the fifth business day after the date of the request, whichever occurs first. *Unusual circumstances* include requests received (1) that exceed the organization's daily capacity to make copies, (2) shortly before the end of regular business hours that require an extensive amount of copying, or (3) on a day when the organization's managerial staff capable of fulfilling the request is conducting special duties, such as student registration or attending an off-site meeting or convention.

A tax-exempt organization may charge a reasonable fee for providing copies. Before the organization provides the documents, it may require that the individual requesting the copies pay the fee. If the organization has provided an individual making the request with notice of the fee, and the individual does not pay the fee within 30 days, or if the individual pays the fee by check and the check does not clear, the organization may disregard the request.

A tax-exempt organization is not required to comply with a request for a copy of its application for recognition of exemption or an annual information return if the organization has made the requested document widely available. (It must nonetheless comply with the public inspection rules.) This *widely available* requirement is satisfied by posting the document on a Web site that the exempt organization maintains or on a Web site maintained by another organization where:

- The Web site clearly informs readers that the document is available and provides instructions for downloading it.

- The document is posted in a format that, when accessed, downloaded, viewed, and printed in hard copy, exactly reproduces the image of the application for recognition of exemption or annual information return as it was originally filed with the IRS (except for any information permitted by statute to be withheld from public disclosure).

- An individual with access to the Internet can access, download, view, and print the document without special computer hardware or software required for that format and without payment of a fee to the exempt organization or another entity maintaining the Web site.

If the Director, Exempt Organizations Examination (or a designee) determines that a tax-exempt organization is being harassed, the organization is not required to comply with any request for copies that it reasonably believes is part of a harassment campaign. Whether a group of requests constitutes a harassment campaign depends on the relevant facts and circumstances, such as a sudden increase in requests, an extraordinary number of requests by form letters or similarly worded correspondence, hostile requests, evidence showing bad faith or deterrence of the organization's exempt purpose, and a demonstration that the organization routinely provides copies of its documents on request. An exempt organization may disregard any request for copies of all or part of any document beyond the first two received within a 30-day period or the first four received within a one-year period from the same individual or the same address, irrespective of whether the IRS has determined that the organization is a victim of a harassment campaign.

§ 1.2 IRS GUIDING PRINCIPLES

The IRS said that its retooling of this annual information return was based on these guiding principles:

- Enhancing transparency by providing the IRS and the public with a realistic picture of the filing organization and its operations, along with the basis for comparing the organization to similar organizations

- Promoting compliance, by designing a return that accurately reflects the organization's operations and use of assets, thereby enabling the IRS to more efficiently assess the risk of any noncompliance by the organization

- Minimizing the burden on filing organizations, by asking questions in a manner that makes it relatively easy to prepare the return and not impose unwarranted record-keeping or information-gathering burdens to obtain and substantiate the reported information

§ 1.3 IMPORT OF NEW FORM 990

The redesigned Form 990 is no ordinary information return and, for that matter, is no ordinary government form. This is a significant, complex, and extraordinary document. It is, in many ways, a work of art, in that it captures the requirements of a large amount of statutory law, much of it recently enacted. At the same time, because of its size and complexity, many organizations will be engaging in considerable effort (time and money) to create needed documents, maintain records, and properly prepare and timely file the return.

From a law perspective, the new return has, as noted, enormous implications for tax-exempt organizations, for two reasons.

1. The form in various places and ways has the effect of creating much new law. A dramatic example of this fact is the portion on governance (see Chapter 5).

2. The form is designed to induce certain behavior by the management of non-profit, tax-exempt organizations by in essence forcing organizations to check "yes" boxes (or avoid checking "no" boxes). The import of this "shaming technique" can be seen, for example, in the requirements as to development of various policies and dissemination to the public of various documents.

§1.4 NEW FORM 990 INTRODUCTION

The introduction to the new Form 990 requests this information:

Item A. The tax year of the organization, which is either the calendar year (2008) or a fiscal year (a year that began in 2008).

Item B. An indication, by checking one or more boxes, as to whether there has been an address change, a name change, the return is the initial return, the organization has been terminated (so that the return is the final return), the return is an amended return, and/or the filing organization's application for recognition of exemption (usually Form 1023 or 1024) is pending with the IRS.

Item C. The name of the organization, any other name in which it is doing business, and the organization's address where mail is delivered.

Item D. The organization's employer identification number.

Item E. The organization's telephone number.

Item F. The name and address of the organization's principal officer.

Item G. The amount of the organization's gross receipts.

Item H. Information as to any group exemption, namely, whether the Form 990 is a group return for affiliates; whether all affiliates are included in the return; if all affiliates are not included, a list of those that are included (as an attachment); and the group exemption number.

Item I. Identification of the organization's tax-exempt status, by reference to the appropriate section of the Internal Revenue Code.

Item J. The organization's Web site address.

Item K. The type of the organization, such as a corporation, a trust, or an unincorporated association. This inquiry may cause some confusion, in that an incorporated association may indicate that it is an "association."

Item L. The year the organization was formed.

Item M. The state in which the organization is legally domiciled.

If the organization has changed its name and it is a corporation, it should attach to the Form 990 a copy of the amendment to the articles of incorporation and proof of filing with the state of incorporation. If there was a name change and the entity is a trust, a copy of the amendment to the trust agreement or declaration of trust, signed by the trustee, should be attached. If there was a name change and the entity is an unincorporated association, a copy of the amendment to the organizing document (such as a constitution or articles of association), with the signatures of at least two officers and/or members, should be attached.

An organization that checks the box in the case of a termination is required to attach Schedule N to the return. If the organization checks the amended return box, it should attach Schedule O, stating in that schedule which part(s) and schedule(s) of the return are being amended, and a description of the amendment(s). If a change of address occurs after the return is filed, the organization should use Form 8822 to notify the IRS of the new address.

As to the telephone number (item E), the organization should enter a telephone number of the organization that members of the public and government personnel may use during normal business hours to obtain information about the organization's finances and activities. If the organization does not have a telephone number, it should enter the telephone number of an organization official who can provide that information.

As to the name and address of a principal officer (item F), the address provided must be a complete mailing address to enable the IRS to communicate with the officer if necessary. If the officer prefers to be contacted at the organization's address (item C), the entry should be: "Same as C, above." For this purpose, the term *principal officer* means an individual who, regardless of title, has ultimate responsibility for implementing the decisions of the organization's governing body, or for supervising the management, administration, or operation of the organization.

As to *gross receipts*, that amount is equal to the amount derived by adding the amounts on lines 6b (both columns), 7b (both columns), 8b, 9b, 10b, and 12, Column A of the new Form 990, Part VIII. Some organizations, because of the amount of their gross receipts, are not required to file Form 990 (see § 1.9).

If the Form 990 is a group return (item H), so that the organization answers "yes" in response to the question on line H(a), but it answers "no" to the question on line H(b), the organization should attach a list (not using Schedule O) showing the name, address, and employer identification number of each subordinate organization included in the group return. This list should (1) show the form number (Form 990) and tax year, (2) show the organization's name and employer identification number, (3) show the group exemption number, and (4) be on a piece of paper that is the same size as the Form 990 pages.

The group exemption number should be entered on line H(c) if the organization is (1) filing a group return or (2) a central or subordinate in a group exemption arrangement and is filing a separate return. The IRS's instructions caution organizations to not confuse the group exemption number (four digits) with the employer identification number (item D, consisting of nine digits).

As to the Web site address (item J), if the organization does not have a Web site, the IRS's draft instructions instruct the filing organization to enter "N/A." (This is inconsistent with several instructions accompanying the new Form 990 where, if a line or question is not applicable, the instructions state that the line is to be left blank.)

As to the type of organization (item K), the draft instructions provide that the organization should check the box referencing the organization's "legal entity form." The choices are corporation, trust, unincorporated associations, and "other." The instructions state that *other* includes partnerships and limited liability companies. This is a bit inconsistent with the Form 1023 (*Application for Recognition of Exemption*) filed by organizations seeking recognition as charitable entities; that form allows only corporations, trusts, unincorporated associations, and limited liability companies to file it. A partnership that elects to be treated as a corporation for federal tax purposes presumably would apply for recognition of exemption as a partnership.

As to the state of legal domicile (item M), the draft instructions state that an organization should, if it is a corporation, enter the state of incorporation or, if a foreign corporation, the country of incorporation. If the organization is a trust or other entity, it should enter the state the law of which governs the organization's internal affairs or, if a foreign entity, the foreign country the law of which governs the organization.

§ 1.5 SUMMARY OF PARTS OF NEW FORM 990

The redesigned Form 990 includes an 11-page "core form." There is a one-page summary of the organization (Part I), followed by 10 additional parts (II–XI). Part II is the signature block. This core return is accompanied by 16 schedules. (See § 1.8.)

(a) Part I (Summary)

The summary requests, in line 1, a brief description of the organization's mission or most significant activities. The organization has the choice as to which it wishes to highlight. This summary asks for the number of voting members of the organization's governing body (line 3), the number of these board members who are independent (line 4), the number of employees (line 5), and the number of volunteers (line 6). Other questions concern the amount of contributions and grants (line 8), program service revenue (line 9), investment income (line 10), other revenue (line 11), total gross unrelated business income (line 7a), total revenue and expenses (lines 12 and 18), grants and similar amounts paid (line 13), compensation (line 15), professional fundraising expenses (line 16a), other expenses (line 17), and total assets and liabilities (lines 20 and 21). (See §§ 1.6, 1.7.)

A box is to be checked (line 2) if the organization discontinued its operations or disposed of more than 25 percent of its assets. That is, this box is to be checked if the organization answered "yes" to lines 31 or 32 of Part IV (see § 3.1(ll), (mm)) and thus completed Schedule N, Parts I or II (see § 20.2(a), (b)).

As to volunteers (line 6), the organization is required to provide the number of volunteers, full time and part time, who provided services to the organization during the reporting year. Organizations that do not keep track of this information in their books and records or report this information elsewhere (such as in annual reports or grant proposals) may provide a "reasonable estimate [of this number], and may use any reasonable basis for determining this estimate." Organizations may, but are not required to, provide an explanation on Schedule O as to how this number was determined as well as the types of services or benefits provided by their volunteers.

As to unrelated business taxable income (line 7b), if the organization is not required to file a Form 990-T for the tax year, it should enter "0." If the organization has not yet filed Form 990-T for the tax year, it should provide an estimate of the amount it expects to report on that return (line 34) when it is filed.

Lines 8 to 19 require reporting of prior-year (2007) revenue and expense amounts. This list should be used to determine what to report on these lines for prior-year revenue and expense amounts from the 2007 Form 990:

- Contributions and grants (line 8) (2007 Form 990, Part I, line 1e)
- Program service revenue (line 9) (2007 Form 990, Part I, lines 2 and 3)
- Investment income (line 10) (2007 Form 990, Part I, lines 4, 5, and 7, less any royalties reported on line 7, and 8d)
- Other revenue (line 11) (2007 Form 990, Part I, lines 6c, 9c, 10c, and 11, plus any royalties reported in line 7)
- Total revenue (line 12) (2007 Form 990, Part I, line 12)
- Grants and similar amounts paid (line 13) (2007 Form 990, Part II, lines 22a–23, column (A))
- Benefits paid to or for members (line 14) (2007 Form 990, line 24, column (A))
- Salaries, other compensation, employee benefits (line 15) (2007 Form 990, Part II, lines 25a–28, column (A))
- Professional fundraising expenses (line 16) (2007 Form 990, Part II, line 30, column (A))
- Other expenses (line 17) (2007 Form 990, Part II, lines 29 and 31–43g, column (A))
- Total expenses (line 18) (2007 Form 990, Part II, line 44, column (A))
- Revenue less expenses (line 19) (2007 Form 990, Part I, line 18)

The IRS, in its instructions, advises organizations that, because Part I generally reflects information reported elsewhere in the new Form 990, completion of this part (Summary) should be deferred until completion of the other parts of the return. (See the sequencing list in § 1.11.)

(b) Part II (Signature Block)

To make the new Form 990 complete, an officer of the filing organization authorized to sign the return must sign it in the space provided. For a corporation or unincorporated association, this officer may be the president, vice president, treasurer, assistant treasurer, chief accounting officer, or other corporate or association officer, such as a tax officer. A receiver, trustee, or assignee must sign any return her or she files for a corporation or an association. For a trust, the authorized trustee(s) must sign the return.

Generally, anyone who is paid to prepare the return must sign in the Paid Preparer's Use Only area. The paid preparer must (1) sign the return in the space provided for the preparer's signature, (2) enter the preparer information (other than the preparer taxpayer identification number and the employer identification number blocks, except as described next), and (3) provide a copy of the return to the organization.

The paid preparer, however, must enter the preparer taxpayer identification number and the preparer's firm's employer identification number only if filing the Form 990 for a nonexempt charitable split-interest trust that is not filing Form 1041. The paid preparer's space is to be left blank if a regular employee of the filing organization prepared the return.

On the last line of Part II, the organization should check the "yes" box if the IRS may contact the paid preparer who signed the return to discuss the return. By checking this box "yes," the organization is authorizing the IRS to contact the paid preparer to discuss any matter relating to this return. The "no" box is to be checked if the IRS is to contact the organization or its principal officer (listed in item F of the introduction (heading) (see § 1.4)) rather than the paid preparer.

(c)   Part III (Program Service Accomplishments)

Part III of the redesigned Form 990 concerns the filing organization's program service accomplishments. It is required to describe its mission, new significant program services, any significant changes in the way it conducts a program, a cessation of any activity, and the exempt purpose achievements for each of its three largest programs services by expenses. Charitable and social welfare organizations are required to report the amount of grants and allocations to others, total; expenses; and any revenue for each program service reported. (See Chapter 2.)

(d)   Part IV (Schedules)

Part IV of the redesigned Form 990 is a checklist of (potentially) required schedules. This schedule references 44 questions and 16 schedules. (See Chapter 3.)

(e)   Part V (Other IRS Filings)

Part V of the Form 990 pertains to a variety of activities and IRS filings. As to activities, there are questions about unrelated business income, involvement in a prohibited tax shelter transaction, use of supporting organizations, use of donor-advised funds, and payments with respect to personal benefit contracts. As to IRS filings, there are questions about the filing of seven forms (990-T, 1096, 1098-C, 8282, 8886-T, W-2G, and W-3). (See Chapter 4.)

(f)   Part VI (Governance)

Part VI of the Form 990 concerns governance, management, policies, and disclosure. As to the governing body and management (Section A), questions concern the number of the voting members of the governing body and the number of board members who are "independent." Inquiry is made as to whether the organization has conflict-of-interest, whistleblower, and document retention and destruction policies, as well as policies governing the activities of chapters, affiliates, and "branches" (Section B). Additional questions pertain to various disclosures (Section C). (See Chapter 5.)

(g)   Part VII (Compensation)

Part VII of the Form 990 focuses on compensation of insiders and independent contractors. The persons currently in their positions must be listed (irrespective of compensation), along with a list of the organization's five highest-compensated employees (other than insiders) who received compensation of more than $100,000 from the organization and any related organizations during the year; the organization's former officers, key employees, or highest-compensated employees who received more than $100,000 of compensation from the organization and any related organizations during the year; and the organization's former directors or trustees who received (in that capacity) more than $10,000 of compensation from the organization and any related organizations during the year. (See Chapter 6.)

(h) Parts VIII to XI (Financial Information)

Part VIII of the Form 990 is a revenue statement, Part IX is a statement of expenses (including functional reporting), Part X is a balance sheet, and Part XI concerns financial statements. (See Chapter 7.)

§1.6 LAW AND POLICY AS TO SUMMARY

As is discussed throughout (indeed, is the central message of this book), the new Form 990, while creating much new law, is also predicated on much preexisting law and policy. The Summary (Form 990, Part I) alone requires knowledge, to properly prepare it, of at least nine discrete bodies of law.

(a) Mission Statements

The Summary requests a description of the filing organization's *mission* or *most significant activities* (line 1). Mission and activities are totally different concepts. An organization's mission is essentially equivalent to its *purpose* or *purposes*. Activities are the organization's undertakings engaged in to accomplish the mission or purpose. Thus, whether an activity is an exempt function is dependent on the context in which it is conducted. An activity can be an exempt program in one setting and a nonexempt function in another.

The federal tax law, which focuses on an organization's purpose or purposes, is silent as to the *mission statement* of a tax-exempt organization. (Or at least the law was until the advent of the new Form 990.) Most exempt organizations are creatures of state law; that body of law normally expects a nonprofit organization to have a *statement of purpose* (or purposes). A statement of purpose, however, tends to be a short, perhaps technical, rendition of what the objectives of an organization are. A mission statement, by contrast, can be lengthier and less technical in nature.

The IRS issued a draft of good governance principles for charitable organizations in early 2007. In the aftermath of adoption of the new Form 990, the IRS jettisoned that draft of governance principles, stating (on its Web site) that the current IRS positions on nonprofit governance "are best reflected in the reporting required by the revised Form 990." (That alone is ample evidence of the considerable significance of the new return.) Thus, in early 2008, the IRS replaced it with a new document as part of the agency's Life Cycle educational tool.

This new statement encourages charitable organizations (and to a lesser extent other tax-exempt organizations) to establish and regularly review the organization's mission. A clearly articulated mission statement, adopted by the organization's governing board, serves, the IRS has stated, to explain and popularize the charity's purpose and guide its work. It also addresses why the charity exists, what it hopes to accomplish, and what activities it will undertake, where, and for whom.

(b) Governing Instruments

An organization must have governing instruments to qualify for tax exemption, if only to satisfy the appropriate organizational test. This is particularly the case for charitable organizations, as to which the federal tax law imposes specific organizational requirements (see § 1.6(c)). The document by which an organization is created is known generically, in the federal tax law, as the *articles of organization*.

If the corporate form is used, the governing instruments are articles of incorporation and bylaws. An unincorporated association will have articles of organization, most likely in the form of a constitution, and undoubtedly also bylaws. If the entity is a trust, the basic document is a declaration of trust or a trust agreement. A mission statement may be embedded in the articles of organization or may be in a separate document.

(c) Organizational Test

An organization, to be tax-exempt as a charitable entity, must be both organized and operated exclusively for one or more of the permissible exempt purposes. This requirement is reflected in an *organizational test* and an *operational test*. If an organization fails to meet either test, it cannot qualify for exemption as a charitable entity. (These tests are also available with respect to other types of exempt organizations but are not as well articulated in the law.)

An organization is organized exclusively for one or more tax-exempt, charitable purposes only if its articles of organization limit its purposes to one or more exempt purposes and do not expressly empower it to engage, otherwise than as an insubstantial part of its activities, in activities that in themselves are not in furtherance of one or more exempt purposes.

(d) Statement of Purposes

In meeting the organizational test, the charitable organization's purposes, as stated in its articles of organization, may be as broad as or more specific than the particular exempt purposes recognized in the law, such as charitable, educational, scientific, or religious ends. Articles of organization of charitable entities may not authorize the carrying on of nonexempt activities (unless they are insubstantial), even though the organization is, by the terms of its articles, created for a purpose that is no broader than the specified charitable purposes.

In no case will an organization be considered to be organized exclusively for one or more tax-exempt charitable purposes if, by the terms of its articles of organization, the purposes for which the organization is created are broader than the specified charitable purposes. The fact that the actual operations of the organization have been exclusively in furtherance of one or more exempt purposes is not sufficient to permit the organization to meet the organizational test.

An organization is not considered organized exclusively for one or more exempt charitable purposes if its articles of organization expressly authorize it to (1) devote more than an insubstantial part of its activities to attempting to influence legislation; (2) directly or indirectly participate in, or intervene in (including the publishing or distributing of statements), any political campaign on behalf of or in opposition to any candidate for public office; or (3) have objectives and engage in activities that characterize it as an *action organization* (see Chapters 9–10). The organizational test, however, does not require that references be made in the organizational document to the prohibitions on private inurement, substantial private benefit, substantial lobbying, and political campaign activities.

A statement of purposes and a mission statement can be the same text in the same document. Or a mission statement can be a separate document. If the latter, the phraseology of the mission statement should not be inconsistent with the more formal statement of purposes.

(e)   Primary Purpose Rule

A basic concept of the law of tax-exempt organizations is the *primary purpose rule*. This rule is one of the fundamental bases for determination of the appropriate category of tax exemption (if any) for an organization. The principle is formally explicated in the law by the use of words such as *exclusively* and *substantially*. These words are generally subsumed, in this context, in the word *primary*. This principle of the federal tax law is generally applicable to all categories of exempt organizations.

The primary purpose of an organization is not taken into account only when determining whether it qualifies for tax-exempt status. This purpose can also be a critical factor in application of the unrelated business rules.

Development and review of a mission statement for a tax-exempt organization should be undertaken in a manner consistent with the requirements of the primary purpose test.

(f)   Independent Members of Governing Body

The federal tax law does not generally impose a requirement on a tax-exempt organization that some or all of the members of its governing body be *independent*. Special rules for hospitals, supporting organizations, and charities that are publicly supported by reason of the facts-and-circumstances test apply in relation to the composition of their governing boards. These rules, however, tend to focus more on whether board members are reflective of the community or whether board members who are not independent (i.e., are insiders, disqualified persons, or have a conflict of interest) control the organization. The IRS ruled that an organization with a board of two individuals could not qualify as a charitable entity because the board structure amounted to inherent private benefit.

Nonetheless, the filing organization must report the number of the voting members of its governing body that are *independent* (line 4).

(g)   Unrelated Business

The Summary requires that the filing organization report its gross unrelated business income and net unrelated business taxable income (line 7). The reporting of these amounts necessitates an understanding of the unrelated business rules. This body of law envisions a tax-exempt organization as a cluster of businesses, some of which are related to the organization's exempt purposes and some of which are unrelated to exempt purposes. A variety of exceptions is available for various activities and forms of income.

(h) Program Service Revenue

Program service revenue (line 9) pertains to forms of income that are generated by a tax-exempt organization as the result of the sale of services or goods. Contributions and grants (line 8) thus are treated separately. There may be an issue as to whether an item of revenue is derived from a *grant* or a *sale of services*. Synonyms for program service revenue are *exempt function income* and *related business income*.

(i) Professional Fundraising Expenses

The Summary must include a reporting of the organization's *professional fundraising expenses* (line 16a). There is no federal tax law definition of this term. It is, however, used at the state level where, in the administration of their *charitable solicitation acts*, the states define the term. Unfortunately, the states are inconsistent in the definition of the term *professional fundraiser*; some states employ the term to mean the same as *professional solicitor* and/or *professional fundraising consultant*, while others do not. (See Chapter 19.)

§ 1.7 PREPARATION OF NEW FORM 990, PART I

Organizations that are required to file Form 990 may describe their mission in Part I, line 1, and are required to describe their mission in Part III, line 1.

The Summary (Part I) poses 8 questions about an organization's activities and governance:

1. The organization is asked to briefly describe its mission or most significant activities (line 1). This is an unusual choice, because, as noted, the mission pertains to the organization's purposes, while activities, of course, mean actual operations. These are two different matters entirely. The filing organization gets to choose.

2. The organization must indicate (by checking a box) if it, during the filing year, discontinued its operations or disposed of more than 25 percent of its assets (line 2).

3. The number of voting members of the governing body (line 3) (see Form 990, Part VI, line 1a) (see § 5.2(a)(1)).

4. The number of independent voting members of the governing body (line 4) (see Form 990, Part VI, line 1b) (see § 5.2(a)(1)).

5. The total number of employees (line 5) (see Form 990, Part V, line 2a).

6. The total number of volunteers (if necessary, an estimate will suffice) (line 6).

7. The total amount of gross unrelated business revenue (line 7a) (see Form 990, Part VIII, line 12, column (C)) (see § 7.1(b)).

8. The net amount of unrelated business taxable income (line 7b) (see Form 990-T, line 34) (see § 7.1(b)).

The summary poses 10 questions about revenue, 5 of which concern the current year and 5 of which concern the prior year:

1. The amount of contributions and grants (line 8) (see Form 990, Part VIII, line 1h).

2. The amount of program service revenue (line 9) (see Form 990, Part VIII, line 2g).

3. The amount of investment income (line 10) (see Form 990, Part VIII, lines 3, 4, and 7d).

4. The amount of other revenue (line 11) (see Form 990, Part VIII, lines 5, 6d, 8c, 9c, and 10c of column (A), and 11e).

5. The amount of total revenue (line 12, which is the sum of the amounts on lines 8–11) (see Form 990, Part VIII, line 12, column (A)).

The summary poses 16 questions about expenses, 8 of which concern the current year and 8 of which concern the prior year:

1. The amount of grants and similar amounts paid (line 13) (see Form 990, Part IX, lines 1–3, column (A)).

2. The amount of benefits paid to or for members (line 14) (see Form 990, Part IX, line 4, column (A)).

3. The amount of salaries, other compensation, and employee benefits (line 15) (see Form 990, Part IX, lines 5–10, column (A)).

4. The amount of professional fundraising expenses (line 16a) (see Form 990, Part IX, line 11e, column (A)).

5. The total amount paid for fundraising, calculated on the basis of functional accounting (line 16b) (see Form 990, Part IX, line 25, column (D)).

6. The amount of other expenses (line 17) (see Form 990, Part IX, lines 11d, 11f–24f).

7. The amount of total expenses (line 18, which is the sum of the amounts on lines 13–17) (see Form 990, Part IX, line 25, column (A)).

8. The amount of revenue less expenses (line 19, which is the amount on line 12 minus the amount on line 18).

The summary poses 6 questions about net assets or fund balances, 3 of which concern the amounts at the beginning of the year and 3 of which concern the amounts at the end of the year:

1. The value of total assets (line 20) (see Form 990, Part X, line 16).

2. The amount of total liabilities (line 21) (see Form 990, Part X, line 26).

3. The value of net assets or the fund balance (line 22, which is the amount on line 20 minus the amount on line 21).

§1.8   SUMMARY OF NEW FORM 990 SCHEDULES

As noted, the new Form 990 includes 16 schedules.

(a) Schedule A

Schedule A of the Form 990 is used by charitable organizations to report their public charity status. Specific questions about supporting organizations include identification of the organization's type, a certification as to lack of control by disqualified persons, contributions from disqualified persons, and information about supported organizations.

There are separate public support schedules for the basic types of publicly supported charitable organizations. The public support computation period has been lengthened to five years, which makes it consistent with the advance ruling period public support test. An organization can claim public charity status on the basis of the facts-and-circumstances test on this schedule. (See Chapter 8.)

(b) Schedule B

Schedule B is the schedule used to report charitable contributions and grants. It is the same as the preexisting Schedule B.

(c) Schedule C

Schedule C comprises questions concerning political campaign and lobbying activities, principally by charitable organizations. Filing organizations are required to describe their direct and indirect political campaign activities, including the amounts of political expenditures and volunteer hours. There are separate parts for lobbying charitable organizations that are under the substantial part test and the expenditure test. Certain other types of tax-exempt entities must prepare additional parts of this schedule. (See Chapters 9 and 10.)

(d) Schedule D

Schedule D is used to report supplemental financial information, such as for investments, liabilities, conservation easements, donor-advised funds, art collections, trust accounts, and endowment funds. (See Chapter 11.)

(e) Schedule E

Schedule E is filed by organizations that constitute tax-exempt private schools. Most of this schedule relates to the requirement that the organization cannot, to be tax-exempt maintain a racially discriminatory policy. A question inquires as to whether the organization receives any financial aid or other assistance from a governmental agency. (See Chapter 12.)

(f) Schedule F

The essence of Schedule F is the reporting of activities outside the United States. These activities, such as program services, grantmaking, and fundraising, are reported on a per-region basis. Grant makers are required to describe their procedures for monitoring the use of grant funds. Information must be supplied if a grantee or other recipient of assistance is related to any person with an interest in the grant-making organization. Additional details are required in instances of grants or other assistance to organizations or individuals. (See Chapter 13.)

(g) Schedule G

Schedule G largely concerns fundraising activities. The filing organization indicates the type or types of fundraising in which it is engaged and provides information about any fundraising contracts (including those with insiders). The organization is required to list the jurisdictions in which it is authorized to solicit funds. A part of this schedule focuses on fundraising events; another part solicits details about gaming activities. (See Chapter 14.)

(h) Schedule H

Schedule H is filed by tax-exempt hospitals. The first part of this schedule (Part I) is a "community benefit report." The filing hospital indicates whether it provides free or discounted care to low-income individuals or those who are "medically indigent." The hospital reports on its charity care (such as care at cost, unreimbursed Medicaid services, and other unreimbursed costs in connection with government programs) and other community benefits (such as health improvement services, health professions education, subsidized health services, and research). The organization is asked whether it prepares an annual community benefit report and to describe its charity care policy.

The second part of this schedule (Part II) inquires as to the hospital's "community building" activities. These activities include physical improvements and housing, economic development, community support, environmental improvements, leadership development and training for community members, coalition building, community health improvement advocacy, and workforce development.

Another part (Part III) pertains to bad debt, Medicare, and collection practices. A fourth part asks questions about the use of management companies and involvement in joint ventures. A fifth part (Part V) seeks information about the hospital's facilities. The schedule (Part VI) requests a description of how the organization assesses the health care needs of the communities it serves and how the organization informs patients about their eligibility for assistance under federal, state, or local government programs or under its charity care policy. (See Chapter 15.)

(i) Schedule I

Schedule I is used to solicit information about the organization's domestic grant and other assistance programs. For example, the organization is asked whether it maintains records to substantiate the amount of its assistance and about the organization's selection criteria and grantees' eligibility. Information is required for grants of more than $5,000 to organizations and all grants to individuals. (See Chapter 16.)

(j) Schedule J

Schedule J is used to solicit supplemental information about compensation. The organization must indicate (in Part I) if it provides to its insiders payments or items in forms such as first-class or charter travel, a discretionary spending account, a housing allowance, or health or social club dues; it is asked whether it follows a written policy in connection with such payments (or reimbursements) or items. The organization is asked how it determines certain executive compensation and, in the case of charitable and social welfare organizations, whether it provided any form of nonfixed payments.

The organization reports information concerning compensation paid to trustees, directors, officers, key employees, and highly compensated employees (Part II). There is a breakdown as to base compensation, bonus and incentive compensation, deferred compensation, and nontaxable benefits. (See Chapter 6.)

(k) Schedule K

Schedule K is used to solicit information about tax-exempt bond issues (Part I) and the use of the proceeds (Part II). There are questions about the private use rules (Part III) and arbitrage (Part IV). (See Chapter 17.)

(l) Schedule L

Schedule L concerns excess benefit transactions and loans to and from interested persons. Information sought includes the name of the debtor/creditor, original principal amount, balance due, the purpose of the loan, and whether there is a written agreement. Questions are also asked about grants or other forms of assistance benefiting, and business transactions involving, interested persons. (See Chapter 18.)

(m) Schedule M

The focus of Schedule M is on noncash contributions. Thus, information is sought about gifts of art (including fractional interests), books, clothing and household goods, automobiles, airplanes, boats, intellectual property, securities, qualified conservation property, real estate, collectibles, food inventory, drugs and medical supplies, taxidermy, historical artifacts, scientific specimens, and archeological artifacts.

This schedule inquires as to the number of Forms 8283 received by the organization for contributions for which the organization completed the donee acknowledgment portion (see § 19.2(r)); whether the organization received any property that it must hold for at least three years from the date of its contribution, which is not required to be used for exempt purposes during the entire holding period; whether the organization has a gift acceptance policy that requires the review of nonstandard contributions; and whether the organization used third parties or related organizations to solicit, process, or sell noncash distributions. (See Chapter 19.)

(n) Schedule N

Schedule N pertains to liquidations, terminations, dissolutions, and significant dispositions of assets. Questions include a description of the assets involved, their value, the method of determining the value, the date of the distribution, and the name and address of the recipient. Other questions concern the involvement of an insider with the successor or transferee organization, notification of one or more state officials, and other compliance with state laws. Additional information is sought concerning transfers of more than 25 percent of the organization's assets. (See Chapter 20.)

(o) Schedule O

Filing organizations use Schedule O to provide additional information for responses to specific questions in the Form 990 and/or its schedules and to provide additional information.

(p) Schedule R

Schedule R has as one of its purposes the identification of disregarded entities and related tax-exempt organizations. Related organizations taxable as a partnership and as a corporation or trust must also be identified. A series of questions about transactions with related organizations and unrelated organizations taxable as partnerships is posed. (See Chapter 21.)

§1.9 FORM 990-EZ

To alleviate the annual reporting burden for smaller tax-exempt organizations, the IRS promulgated a less extensive annual information return. This is the two-page Form 990-EZ. As noted, the Form 990-EZ for 2008 was released in late 2007.

Under current law, this return may be used by tax-exempt organizations that have gross receipts that are less than $100,000 and total assets that are less than $250,000 in value at the end of the reporting year.

§1.10 TRANSITION RULES

The IRS announced a graduated three-year transition period for annual information return filings. For the 2008 tax year (returns filed in 2009), organizations with gross receipts of more than $1 million or total assets in excess of $2.5 million are required to file the Form 990. For the 2009 tax year (returns filed in 2010), organizations with gross receipts over $500,000 or total assets over $1.25 million are required to file the Form 990. Tax-exempt organizations below these thresholds are allowed to file the Form 990-EZ (with the option to file the new Form 990).

The filing threshold will be permanently set, beginning with the 2010 tax year, at $200,000 in gross receipts and $500,000 in total assets. Starting with the 2010 tax year, the filing threshold for organizations required to file the Form 990-N (the e-postcard) (see § 1.11) will be increased to $50,000 (from $25,000).

§1.11 INSTRUCTIONS

The IRS, on April 7, 2008, issued draft instructions to accompany the new Form 990 for 2008. The IRS, on April 19, 2008, provided final instructions to accompany the Form 990 for 2008 (subject to approval of the Office of Management and Budget). These instructions provide guidance that is specific to each part and schedule of the new Form 990, plus an appendix of law and a 24-page glossary. The elements of these instructions are interspersed throughout this book.

The instructions include a *sequencing list*, to assist an organization in completing the form and its schedules. As is noted, "certain later parts of the form must first be completed in order to complete earlier parts." According to this list, here is the way to approach the new Form 990:

1. Complete lines A to F and H(a) to M in the heading of the return.

2. Determine the organization's related organizations for which reporting will be required (see Schedule R).

3. Determine the organization's officers, directors, trustees, key employees, and five highest compensated employees (to be listed in Part VII, Section A).

4. Complete Parts VIII, IX, and X (revenue and expense statements, and balance sheet).

5. Complete line G in the heading (gross receipts).

6. Complete Parts III, V, VII, and XI.

7. Complete Schedule L (concerning transactions with interested persons) (if required).

8. Complete Part VI. (Transactions reported in Schedule L are relevant to determining the independence of members of the governing body (Part VI, line 1b).)

9. Complete Part I (on the basis of information derived from other parts of the return).

10. Complete Part IV.

11. Complete remaining applicable schedules (for which "yes" boxes were checked in Part IV). (Schedule O is used to provide required supplemental information and other narrative explanation.)

12. Complete Part II (signature block).

Another unique feature of these instructions is the appendix, which provides information about:

- Types of tax-exempt organizations (a reference chart)
- Steps for determining various levels of gross receipts (such as the $25,000 filing threshold)
- Public inspection of returns
- Group exemption returns
- Disregarded entities and joint ventures
- Excess benefit transactions

The Director of the Exempt Organization's Division said: "We were immensely gratified by the amount and quality of public comments we received on the Form 990 redesign. Public input resulted in a form that meets the needs of tax-exempt organizations, the public and tax administrators."

CHAPTER TWO

Part III—Program Service Accomplishments

In Part III of the new Form 990, the organization is required to, and has the opportunity to, explain its program service accomplishments. In response to comments in connection with the draft of the revised Form 990, the IRS moved this part up from the rear of the return to follow the Summary (Part I).

§2.1 LAW AND POLICY

Nearly all types of tax-exempt organizations are required to file the Form 990. The nature of the filing organization's program services are, therefore, obviously dictated by the type of exempt entity it is.

(a) Primary Purpose Rule

The appropriate category of tax exemption (if any) for a nonprofit organization is dictated by application of the *primary purpose rule*. Also, an organization's primary purpose can change; this development may cause the organization to evolve into a different type of exempt entity (or, in rare cases, to lose exempt status). The law, however, tolerates incidental nonexempt purposes.

The general rule, as stated by the Supreme Court, is that the "presence of a single . . . [nonexempt] purpose, if substantial in nature, will destroy the exemption regardless of the number or importance of truly . . . [exempt] purposes." A federal court of appeals held that nonexempt activity will not result in loss or denial of tax exemption where it is "only incidental and less than substantial" and that a "slight and comparatively unimportant deviation from the narrow furrow of tax approved activity is not fatal." In the words of the IRS, the rules applicable to charitable organizations in general have been "construed as requiring all the resources of the organization [other than an insubstantial part] to be applied to the pursuit of one or more of the [allowable] exempt purposes."

There is no definition of the term *insubstantial* in this context. Thus, application of these rules is an issue of fact to be determined under the facts and circumstances of each case. In some instances, this is a matter of weighing the relative importance of purposes. For example, an organization with some charitable and educational purposes will not qualify for exemption as a charitable organization if its predominant purposes are social and recreational; an organization in this situation will be classified as a social club.

Nonprofit organizations should, therefore, frame their statement of purposes with care. Also, it is prudent to revisit the statement from time to time to be certain that it accurately reflects the entity's contemporary activities and objectives.

(b) Articles of Organization

Generically, the document by which a tax-exempt organization is created is known, in the parlance of the federal tax law, as the *articles of organization*. There usually is a separate document containing rules by which the organization conducts its affairs; this document is most often termed *bylaws*. The organization may develop other documents governing its operations, such as various policies and procedures, an employee handbook, a conflict-of-interest policy (although that may be part of the bylaws), and/or a code of ethics.

The types of articles of organization for each of the principal types of tax-exempt, nonprofit organizations are:

- Corporation: articles of incorporation
- Unincorporated association: constitution
- Trust: declaration of trust or trust agreement

(c) Operational Test

In theory, every type of tax-exempt organization must adhere to an *operational test*. As the name implies, this test looks to the manner in which the entity is operated; concerns whether the organization is in fact operated for exempt purposes. The elements of an operational test are the most developed in the case of charitable organizations. Generally, defects in an entity's articles of organization cannot be cured by complete adherence to the operational test.

Charitable organizations, to be tax-exempt, must, of course, have charitable purposes and engage in the appropriate activities to advance those purposes. These purposes must, at a minimum, be the organization's primary purposes. There are basically 18 discrete ways an organization can serve charitable purposes (see § 2.1(e)).

(d) Mission Statement

The IRS's draft instructions provided that a tax-exempt organization's *mission statement* "may address why the organization exists, what it hopes to accomplish, who it intends to serve, and what activities it will undertake and where." This definition does not, however, appear in the final instructions.

(e) Charitable Purposes and Activities

The federal tax law recognizes 18 *charitable* (using that term in its most expansive sense) purposes and activities:

1. Relief of the poor
2. Relief of the distressed

3. Promotion of health

4. Lessening the burdens of government

5. Promotion of social welfare

6. Advancement of education

7. Advancement of science

8. Advancement of religion

9. Promotion of the arts

10. Protection of the environment

11. Promotion of patriotism

12. Promotion of sports for youth

13. Prevention of cruelty to children or animals

14. Certain forms of economic development

15. Operation of formal educational institutions (such as schools, colleges, universities, and museums)

16. Operation of scientific organizations, including research entities

17. Operation of religious organizations (such as churches, conventions or associations of churches, and religious orders)

18. Operation of certain cooperative investment entities or charitable risk pools

(f) Other Exempt Purposes and Activities

The federal tax law recognizes 32 ways to be tax-exempt, other than as a charitable entity (§ 2.1(e)):

1. Corporations organized under an act of Congress

2. Title-holding corporations

3. Social welfare organizations

4. Labor organizations

5. Agricultural organizations

6. Horticultural organizations

7. Business leagues

8. Social clubs

9. Fraternal beneficiary organizations

10. Domestic fraternal societies

11. Voluntary employees' beneficiary associations

12. Teachers' retirement fund associations

13. Mutual and cooperative entities

14. Cemetery companies

15. State-chartered credit unions

16. Certain insurance companies

17. Crop financing organizations

18. Supplemental unemployment benefit trusts

19. Certain employee funded pension trusts

20. Veterans' organizations

21. Black lung benefit trusts

22. Withdrawal liability payment funds

23. Multiparent title-holding entities

24. Health coverage organizations for high-risk individuals

25. Workers' compensation and insurance organizations

26. Apostolic organizations

27. Cooperative hospital service organizations

28. Cooperative organizations for educational institutions

29. Child care organizations

30. Charitable risk pools

31. Political organizations

32. Units of government

(g) Recognition of Exemption

The IRS may recognize an organization's tax-exempt status; this is done by issuance of a determination letter or ruling, following the filing by the organization of an application for recognition of exemption. As a general rule, a charitable organization must, to be tax-exempt, have its exemption recognized by the IRS; the application to be filed in this regard is Form 1023. Private foundations and supporting organizations must, to be exempt, have their exemptions so recognized, as must certain credit counseling organizations and employee benefit funds. Churches and certain small organizations are exempt from this requirement.

(h) Program Service Accomplishments

An organization achieves its tax-exempt purposes by means of the program or programs it conducts. The purpose of Part III of the new Form 990 is to provide the organization with the opportunity (although it is required) to summarize its programs. This is done by having the organization first explain its mission and then provide summaries of what it has done by means of the programs engaged in to achieve those purposes. On the Form 990, these summaries are known as *program service accomplishments.*

The IRS's instructions to accompany the new Form 990 state that a *program service* is an "activity of an organization that accomplishes its exempt purpose." The instructions continue:

Examples of exempt purpose achievements may include providing charity care under a hospital's charity care policy, providing higher education to students under a college's degree program, making grants or providing assistance to individuals who were victims of a natural disaster, and providing rehabilitation services to residents of a long-term care facility.

The description of program service accomplishments should include specific measurements, such as clients served, days of care provided, number of sessions or events held, or publications issued. The organization should describe the activity's objective, for the reporting time period and the longer-term goal, if the output is intangible, such as in a research activity. It should provide reasonable estimates for any statistical information if exact figures are not readily available; the organization should indicate that the information is estimated when that is the case. The IRS's instructions urge the organization to be "clear, concise, and complete" in these descriptions. Schedule O is to be utilized if additional space is needed.

An organization may report the amount of any donated services, or use of materials, equipment, or facilities it received or used in connection with a specific program service, on the lines for the narrative description of the appropriate program service. These amounts, however, should not be included in revenues, expenses, or grants reported.

A tax-exempt public interest law firm must include a list of all of the cases in litigation or that have been litigated during the year. For each case, the organization should describe the matter in dispute and explain how the litigation will benefit the public generally. Further, the organization must report the fees sought and recovered in each case.

The instructions admonish a tax-exempt organization not to report a fundraising activity (see Chapter 14) as a program service accomplishment unless it is substantially related to the accomplishment of the organization's exempt purposes (other than by raising funds).

§ 2.2   PREPARATION OF NEW FORM 990 PART III

The essence of Part III of the new Form 990 is to cause the filing organization to report as to its mission, any significant changes in its program services, and details as to its three largest program undertakings.

(a)   Statement of Mission

The question in Part III, line 1 of the new Form 990 calls on the filing organization to briefly describe the organization's *mission* (or, more technically, its purposes) (see § 2.1(e), (f)). Although the question contains the word *briefly*, the organization should make an effort to fully and accurately describe why it exists and what it is trying to accomplish. The specific answer to this question may be "See attached statement."

For some organizations, the mission statement is captured in the explanation of the organization's purposes as found in the governing instrument by which the entity was established (as noted, known in tax law parlance as the *articles of organization*). Most organizations, however, will find that language too stilted or filled with legalese to serve as a proper mission statement, causing the organization to prepare a separate and fuller mission statement. Two recommendations in this regard: The organization should (1) have the mission statement approved by its governing board, and periodically revisited, and (2) be certain that the statement is not inconsistent with its statement of purposes in its articles of organization or with the elements of its operational test.

If an organization does not have a mission statement that was adopted by its governing body, it should state "None".

(b) Changes in Program Services

The question in Part III, line 2 inquires as to whether the organization undertook any significant program services during the filing year that were not listed on the organization's prior annual information returns (Form 990 or 990-EZ). A "yes" or "no" box must be checked. If the answer is "yes," a suitable description must be provided on Schedule O.

The question in Part III, line 3 inquires as to whether the organization ceased conducting or made significant changes in how it conducts, during the filing year, its program services. A "yes" or "no" box must be checked. If the answer is "yes," a suitable description must be provided on Schedule O.

These two questions obviously are intended to derive information as to whether the organization made any material changes in its operations during the filing year. It should be noted, however, that the second question contains the phraseology "not listed on the prior" annual information return. An organization may find itself in the position of not making any significant program changes in the filing year but engaging in a significant program activity that was not "listed" on a prior return. The prior and current (new) Form 990 had a question as to whether an organization made any changes in its program operations, but that question is frequently glossed over and answered "no" without anyone involved in preparation of the return paying any attention to it. The new Form 990 thus forces filing organizations to be much clearer in reporting changes in program operations.

(c) Program Service Accomplishments

Line 4 of the new Form 990 requires the filing organization to describe the *exempt purpose achievements* (a synonym for *program service accomplishments*) for each of the organization's three largest program services by expenses. If there were only one or two of these activities, they are to be described. Public charities, exempt social welfare organizations, and nonexempt charitable trusts are required to report the amount of any grants and other allocations to others, the total expenses, and any revenue generated for each program service so reported. For all other filing tax-exempt organizations, the entering of these amounts is optional.

The total expenses to be reported are those reflected in Part IX, line 25, column (B). Total grants and allocations (if any) are those items included within the total expenses that were reported on lines 1–3, column (B) of Part IX.

These three (or fewer) program services are reported on lines 4a, 4b, and 4c. Each program will, in the future, be assigned a code (to be found in the instructions); the code system is not in effect for 2008. There are discrete spaces for reporting expenses, grants, and revenue. The word *briefly* is not used in connection with this question; the filing organization may wish to answer one or more of the three questions by referencing an attached statement.

For each program service activity, the organization is to report any revenue derived directly from the activity, such as fees for services or from the sale of goods that directly relate to the listed activity. This revenue includes program service revenue reported in Part VIII, line 2, column (A), and includes other amounts reported in lines 3–11 of Part VIII as related or exempt function revenue. Also to be included is unrelated business revenue from a business that exploits an exempt function, such as advertising in an exempt function journal.

For this purpose, charitable contributions and grants (including the charitable contribution portion, if any, of membership dues) reported in line 1 of Part VIII are not considered revenues derived from program services.

Public charities, social welfare organizations, and split-interest trusts must report the total expenses and the total grants and allocations reported in Part IX, column (B) that are attributable to these other program services on line 4d. Total program service expenses (from lines 4a–4d) are reported on line 4e. This line 4e amount must be the same as that reported on the new Form 990, Part IX, line 25, column (B) (see § 7.2(b)(36)). For other filing tax-exempt organizations, the entry of these amounts is optional.

These other program services are to be listed in Schedule O; the total revenue derived directly from these other program services is to be reported. The detailed information required for the three largest program services need not be provided for these other program services.

§ 2.3 NEW FORM 990 COMPLIANCE TASKS

A tax-exempt organization that is preparing Part III of the new Form 990 should be attending to these nine tasks:

1. **Articles of Organization.** The organization should locate a copy of its articles of organization and review the statement of purposes in it.

2. **Bylaws.** The organization should locate a copy of its bylaws and be certain that there is nothing in that document that is inconsistent with the statement of its purposes in the articles.

3. **Mission Statement.** The organization should develop or review its statement of its mission (including approval by its governing board), for use in responding to the new Form 990, Part III.

4. **Program Operations.** The organization should carefully review its program operations to ascertain whether any changes should be reported on Schedule O and, if so, carefully prepare the appropriate response(s).

5. **Major Program Services.** The organization should carefully prepare descriptions of its three largest program services.

6. **Related Expenses.** If necessary, the organization should accurately identify and report the expenses, grants, and revenue associated with these programs.

7. **Other Programs.** The organization should carefully prepare a description of its other programs (if any) for purposes of reporting on Schedule O.

8. **Matching of Amounts.** The organization should be certain that the amounts on the new Form 990, Part III, line 4e and on Part IX, line 25, column (B) are identical.

9. **Telling the Story.** The organization should, mindful of the fact that this document will be in the public domain (see § 1.1(e), review not only the entire return but particularly this part, to be certain that the return properly and fully (and accurately) captures and reflects the nature of the organization and "tells the story" of the organization the way the organization wants it told.

CHAPTER THREE

Part IV—Checklist of Schedules

The redesigned Form 990 is sufficiently intricate as to warrant a table of contents. This feature, in Part IV, was added by the IRS following the receipt of comments on the point in response to public review of the draft of the return. This text is a daunting part of the new Form 990, yet it also is helpful in enabling organizations to determine which schedules they must prepare.

Part IV poses 44 questions, spanning nearly all of the law of tax-exempt organizations, each of which must be answered "yes" or "no" by the filing organization, by checking a box in the right-hand column.

§3.1 LAW AND POLICY

Part IV of the new Form 990 requires an understanding of 44 discrete bodies of federal tax law. Most of this law is described in the chapters of this book discussing each schedule.

(a) Line 1 (Public Charities and Split-Interest Trusts)

The answer to the question posed in line 1 of the new Form 990 requires the organization to prepare and file with the return a schedule if it is a public charity or a split-interest trust. (See § 3.2(a), Chapter 8.)

(b) Line 2 (Contributors)

The answer to the question in line 2 requires the organization to know if it is required to prepare and file with the return a schedule of contributors. The answer is "yes" if:

- A charitable organization met the one-third public support test of the donative publicly supported organization rules and received from a contributor, during the reporting year, a contribution of the greater of $5,000 (in money or property) or 2 percent of the amount on Form 990, Part VIII, line 1h.

- A charitable organization did not meet this public support test and received, during the year, one or more contributions of $5,000 or more.

- A social club or fraternal organization that received, during the year, contributions of any amount for use exclusively for charitable purposes or contributions of $5,000 or more not exclusively for charitable purposes from one or more contributors.

- Any other tax-exempt organization that received, during the year, contributions of $5,000 or more from one or more contributors. (See §§ 3.2(b), 14.2.)

(c) Line 3 (Political Campaign Activities)

The answer to the question in line 3 requires the organization to prepare and file with the return a part of a schedule if it engaged, directly or indirectly, in political campaign activities on behalf of or in opposition to a candidate for public office. (See § 3.2(c), Chapter 10.)

(d) Line 4 (Lobbying Activities)

The answer to the question in line 4, which is addressed to public charities, requires the organization to prepare and file with the return a part of a schedule if it engaged in lobbying activities. (See § 3.2(d), Chapter 9.)

(e) Line 5 (Notice, Reporting, Proxy Tax)

The question in line 5 is addressed to tax-exempt social welfare organizations, labor organizations, and business leagues (associations). The answer to this question requires an organization of this type to prepare and file with the return a part of a schedule if it engaged in certain lobbying and/or political activities and thus is subject to certain notice and reporting requirements, and perhaps the proxy tax. (See § 3.2(e), Chapters 9, 10.)

(1) Exempt Social Welfare Organizations. Tax exemption is available for civic leagues or other organizations operated exclusively for the promotion of social welfare. The term *social welfare* is, in the parlance of the tax regulations, commensurate with the "common good and general welfare" and "civic betterments and social improvements." An exempt social welfare organization is to be operated for the benefit of a *community*. Some social welfare organizations are advocacy groups; there is no limit on social welfare organizations as to allowable lobbying (as long as it is for an exempt purpose), and political campaign activity is permissible as long as it is not the organization's primary activity.

(2) Exempt Labor Organizations. Tax exemption is available for labor organizations, which are entities that engage in collective action to better the working conditions of individuals engaged in a common pursuit. The most common type of labor organization is the union. There is no limit on labor organizations as to allowable lobbying (as long as it is for an exempt purpose), and political campaign activity is permissible as long as it is not the organization's primary activity.

(3) Exempt Business Leagues. Tax exemption is available for *business leagues*, which are associations of persons having some common business interest, the purpose of which is to promote that interest. The activities of a business league must be directed to the improvement of business conditions of one or more lines of business, as distinguished from the performance of particular services for individual persons. It must be of the same general class as a chamber of commerce, board of trade, or the like. There is no limit on business leagues as to allowable lobbying (as long as it is for an exempt purpose), and political campaign activity is permissible as long as it is not the organization's primary activity.

(f)   Line 6 (Donor-Advised Funds)

The answer to the question in line 6 requires the organization to prepare and file with the return a part of a schedule if it maintains one or more funds or any other accounts where donors have the right to provide advice on the distribution or investment of amounts in the funds or accounts (usually donor-advised funds). (See §§ 3.2(f), 11.1(a).)

(g)   Line 7 (Conservation Easements)

The answer to the question in line 7 requires the organization to prepare and file with the return a part of a schedule if it received or held, during the year, a conservation easement. A *conservation easement* is an easement or similar legally enforceable restriction on the use of real property that is established for the purpose of conservation or preservation. It includes easements that are qualified real property interests, including façade easements. (See §§ 3.2(g), 11.1(b).)

(h)   Line 8 (Works of Art, etc.)

The answer to the question in line 8 requires the organization to prepare and file with the return a part of a schedule if it maintains collections of works of art, historical treasures, or other similar assets. (See §§ 3.2(h), 11.1(c).)

(i)   Line 9 (Credit Counseling, etc.)

The answer to the question in line 9 requires the organization to prepare and file with the return a part of a schedule if it provides credit counseling, debt management, credit repair, or debt negotiation services, or services as a custodian for certain amounts. (See §§ 3.2(i), 11.1(d)(2).)

The term *credit counseling services* includes the provision of information to the public on budgeting, personal finance, and saving and spending practices, or assisting individuals and families with financial problems by providing them with counseling. *Debt management*, *credit repair*, and *debt negotiation services* are services related to the repayment, consolidation, or restructuring of a consumer's debt, and include the negotiation with creditors of lower interest rates, the waiver or reduction of fees, and the marketing and processing of debt management plans.

The phrase *custodial accounts* includes:

- Amounts held in a trust account or an escrow account for other organizations or individuals that the organization has signature authority over and that have been reported on the new Form 990 (Part X, line 21)

- Amounts held in a trust account or an escrow account for other organizations or individuals that the organization has signature authority over but does not report the assets or liabilities on the Form 990 (Part X, line 21)

■ 31 ■

(j) Line 10 (Endowments)

The answer to the question on line 10 requires the organization to prepare and file with the return a part of a schedule if it holds assets in term, permanent, or quasi-endowments. (See § 3.2(j); Chapter 7.)

(k) Line 11 (Assets and Liabilities)

The answer to the question on line 11 requires the organization to prepare and file with the return one or more parts of a schedule if it reports amounts on the balance sheet (Part X) pertaining to land, buildings, and equipment; investments (other than publicly traded securities); program-related investments; other assets; and/or other liabilities. (See § 3.2(k); Chapter 7.)

(l) Line 12 (Audited Financial Statements)

The answer to the question on line 12 requires the organization to prepare and file with the return parts of a schedule if it received an audited financial statement for the year for which it is completing the Form 990 that was prepared in accordance with generally accepted accounting principles. (See § 3.2(l); Chapter 7.)

(m) Line 13 (Schools)

The answer to the question in line 13 requires the organization to prepare and file with the return a schedule if it is a school. (See § 3.2(m); Chapter 12.)

(n) Line 14a (International Activities)

The answer to the question in line 14a requires the organization to state whether it maintains an office, employees, or agents outside the United States. (See § 3.2(n); Chapter 13.)

(o) Line 14b (International Revenues, Expenses)

The answer to the question in line 14b requires the organization to prepare and file with the return a part of a schedule if it has aggregate revenues or expenses of more than $10,000 from grantmaking, fundraising, business, and program service activities outside the United States. (See § 3.2(o); Chapter 13.)

(p) Line 15 (International Grantmaking to Organizations)

The answer to the question in line 15 requires the organization to prepare and file with the return a part of a schedule if it is reporting more than $5,000 of grants or assistance to an organization located outside the United States. (See § 3.2(p); Chapter 13.)

(q) Line 16 (International Grantmaking to Individuals)

The answer to the question in line 16 requires the organization to prepare and file with the return a part of a schedule if it is reporting more than $5,000 of aggregate grants or assistance to individuals located outside the United States. (See § 3.2(q); Chapter 13.)

(r) Line 17 (Fundraising Activities)

The answer to the question in line 17 requires the organization to prepare and file with the return a part of a schedule if it is reporting more than $15,000 in fees for professional fundraising. (See § 3.2(r); Chapter 14.)

(s) Line 18 (Fundraising Events)

The answer to the question in line 18 requires the organization to prepare and file with the return a part of a schedule if it is reporting more than $15,000 in revenue from fundraising events. (See § 3.2(s); Chapter 14.)

(t) Line 19 (Gaming)

The answer to the question on line 19 requires the organization to prepare and file with the return a part of a schedule if it is reporting more than $15,000 in gross income from gaming activities. (See § 3.2(t); Chapter 14.)

(u) Line 20 (Hospitals)

The answer to question 20 requires the organization to prepare and file with the return a schedule if it operates one or more hospitals. (See § 3.2(u); Chapter 15.)

(v) Line 21 (Domestic Grants to Organizations)

The answer to the question on line 21 requires the organization to prepare and file with the return parts of a schedule if it is reporting more than $5,000 in grants and other assistance to governments and organizations in the United States. (See § 3.2(v); Chapter 16.)

(w) Line 22 (Domestic Grants to Individuals)

The answer to the question on line 22 requires the organization to prepare and file with the return parts of a schedule if it is reporting more than $5,000 in grants and other assistance to individuals in the United States. (See § 3.2(w); Chapter 16.)

(x) Line 23 (Compensation of Former Officers, etc.)

The answer to the question on line 23 requires the organization to prepare and file with the return a schedule if it listed former officers and the like in the compensation portion of Form 990 (Part VII, Section A), where compensation for any individual from the organization and related organizations is in excess of $150,000, or where any person received compensation from an unrelated organization for services rendered to the organization (Part VII, Section A, lines 3–5). (See § 3.2(x); Chapter 16.)

(y) Line 24a (Outstanding Bond Issues)

The answer to the question on line 24a requires the organization to prepare and file with the return a schedule, and answer questions 24b–24d, if it had a tax-exempt bond issue with an outstanding principal amount of more than $100,000 as of the last day of the year and that was issued after December 31, 2002. (See § 3.2(y); Chapter 17.)

(z)   Line 24b (Tax-Exempt Bonds Investments)

The answer to the question on line 24b requires the organization, if it answered "yes" to question 24a, to report whether it invested any proceeds of tax-exempt bonds beyond a temporary period exception. (See § 3.2(z); Chapter 17.)

(aa)   Line 24c (Tax-Exempt Bonds Defeasements)

The answer to the question on line 24c requires the organization, if it answered "yes" to question 24a, to report whether it maintained an escrow account, other than a refunding escrow, at any time during the year to defease any tax-exempt bonds. For this purpose, an organization is treated as maintaining an escrow account if a trustee maintains the account with respect to tax-exempt bonds issued for the benefit of the organization. (See § 3.2(aa); Chapter 17.)

(bb)   Line 24d ("On Behalf of" Issues)

The answer to the question on line 24d requires the organization, if it answered "yes" to question 24a, to report whether it acted as an "on behalf of" issuer for bonds outstanding at any time during the year. The criteria for the issuance of these bonds are in Revenue Ruling 63-20. This question also pertains to outstanding qualified scholarship funding bonds and bonds of a qualified volunteer fire department. (See § 3.2(bb); Chapter 17.)

(cc)   Line 25a (Excess Benefit Transactions)

The question on line 25a is addressed to public charities and tax-exempt social welfare organizations. A "yes" answer to question 25a requires an organization of this type to prepare and file with the return a part of a schedule if it engaged in an excess benefit transaction with a disqualified person during the year. (See § 3.2(cc); Chapter 18.)

(dd)   Line 25b (Prior-Year Excess Benefit Transactions)

The question on line 25b is addressed to public charities and tax-exempt social welfare organizations. A "yes" answer to question 25b requires an organization of this type to prepare and file with the return a part of a schedule if it became aware that it had engaged in an excess benefit transaction with a disqualified person from a prior year. (See § 3.2(dd); Chapter 18.)

The IRS's instructions observe that an excess benefit transaction "may have serious implications for the disqualified person that entered into the transaction with the organization, any organization managers that knowingly approved of the transaction, and the organization itself." An exempt charitable or social welfare organization that "becomes aware that it may have engaged in an excess benefit transaction should obtain competent advice regarding" the intermediate sanctions rules, "consider pursuing correction of any excess benefit, and take other appropriate steps to protect its interests with regard to such transaction and the potential impact it could have on the organization's continued tax-exempt status." This matter of an impact on exempt status pertains to potential application of the doctrine of private inurement (see § 6.1(a)).

(ee) Line 26 (Loans to Interested Persons)

The answer to the question on line 26 requires the organization to prepare and file with the return a part of a schedule if a loan to or by a current or former officer, director, trustee, key employee, highly compensated employee, or disqualified person was outstanding as of the end of the organization's reporting year. (See §§ 3.2(ee), 18.1(b).)

(ff) Line 27 (Assistance to Interested Persons)

The answer to the question on line 27 requires the organization to prepare and file with the return a part of a schedule if it provided a grant or other form of assistance to an officer, director, trustee, key employee, or substantial contributor, or to a person related to such an individual. (See § 3.2(ff); Chapter 18.)

(gg) Line 28a (Business Relationships)

The answer to the question on line 28a requires the organization to prepare and file with the return a part of a schedule if, during the year, any person who is a current or former officer, director, trustee, or key employee had a direct business relationship with the organization (other than as an officer, director, trustee, or employee) or an indirect business relationship through ownership of more than 35 percent in another entity (individually or collectively with other interested persons). (See § 3.2(gg); Chapter 18.)

(hh) Line 28b (Business Relationships)

The answer to the question on line 28b requires the organization to prepare and file with the return a part of a schedule if, during the year, any person who is a current or former officer, director, trustee, or key employee had a family member who had a direct or indirect business relationship with the organization. (See § 3.2(hh); Chapter 18.)

(ii) Line 28c (Business Relationships)

The answer to the question on line 28c requires the organization to prepare and file with the return a part of a schedule if, during the year, any person who is a current or former officer, director, trustee, or key employee served as an officer, director, trustee, key employee, partner, or member of an entity (or a shareholder of a professional corporation) doing business with the organization. (See § 3.2(ii); Chapter 18.)

(jj) Line 29 (Noncash Contributions)

The answer to the question on line 29 requires the organization to prepare and file with the return a schedule if the organization received more than $25,000 in noncash contributions. (See § 3.2(jj); Chapter 19.) The concept of noncash contributions does not include contributions of services or contributions to the capital of an organization.

(kk) Line 30 (Noncash Contributions)

The answer to the question on line 30 requires the organization to prepare and file with the return a schedule if the organization received contributions of art, historical treasures, or other similar assets, or qualified conservation contributions. (See § 3.2(kk); Chapter 19.) Again, the concept of noncash contributions does not include contributions of services or contributions to the capital of an organization.

(ll) Line 31 (Dissolutions, etc.)

The answer to the question on line 31 requires the organization to prepare and file with the return a part of a schedule if the organization terminated, or dissolved and ceased operations. (See § 3.2(ll); Chapter 20.)

(mm) Line 32 (Substantial Contractions, etc.)

The answer to the question on line 32 requires the organization to prepare and file with the return a part of a schedule if the organization sold, exchanged, disposed of, or transferred more than 25 percent of its net assets or underwent a substantial contraction. (See § 3.2(mm); Chapter 20.)

(nn) Line 33 (Disregarded Entities)

The answer to the question on line 33 requires the organization to prepare and file with the return a part of a schedule if the organization owned 100 percent of a disregarded entity. (See § 3.2(nn): Chapter 21.)

(oo) Line 34 (Related Entities)

The answer to the question on line 34 requires the organization to prepare and file with the return parts of a schedule if the organization was related to a tax-exempt or taxable entity. (See § 3.2(oo); Chapter 21.)

(pp) Line 35 (Controlled Entity)

The answer to question 35 requires the organization to prepare and file with the return a part of a schedule if a related organization is a controlled entity. (See § 3.2(pp); Chapter 21.)

(qq) Line 36 (Transfers to Noncharitable Organizations)

The answer to the question on line 36, which is addressed to public charities, requires the organization to prepare and file with the return a part of a schedule if it made any transfers to a tax-exempt noncharitable related organization. (See § 3.2(qq); Chapter 21.)

(rr)   Line 37 (Use of Entities Taxed as Partnership)

The answer to the question on line 37 requires the organization to prepare and file with the return a part of a schedule if it conducted more than 5 percent of its exempt activities through an entity that is not a related organization and that is taxed as a partnership. This 5 percent test is applied on a partnership-by-partnership basis, although direct ownership by the organization and indirect ownership through disregarded or tiered entities is aggregated for this purpose. (See § 3.2(rr); Chapter 21.)

For purposes of this question, the filing organization need not report the conduct of activities by an entity the sole purpose of which is to make passive investments or the conduct of activities through an organization treated as a taxable or tax-exempt corporation for federal income tax purposes.

§3.2   PREPARATION OF NEW FORM 990 PART IV

These 44 questions relate to the potentiality of preparation of as many as 16 schedules.

(a)   Line 1 (Public Charities and Split-Interest Trusts)

If the answer to the question in line 1 of Part IV is "yes," because the organization is a public charity or a split-interest trust, the organization must prepare and file Schedule A. (See Chapter 8.) All other organizations answer this question "no."

(b)   Line 2 (Contributors)

If the answer to the question in line 2 of Part IV is "yes," the organization must prepare and file Schedule B. (See § 14.1(m).)

(c)   Line 3 (Political Campaign Activities)

If the answer to the question in line 3 of Part IV is "yes," the organization must prepare and file Schedule C, Part I. All filing organizations must answer this question, even if they are not charitable entities subject to the prohibition against political campaign participation. This question should be answered "yes" even if the campaign activity is conducted through a disregarded entity or a joint venture or other arrangement that is taxed as a partnership and in which the organization is an owner. (See Chapter 10.)

(d)   Line 4 (Lobbying Activities)

If the answer to the question in line 4 of Part IV is "yes," because the filing organization is a public charity, the organization must prepare and file Schedule C, Part II. (See Chapter 9.) All other organizations must leave this line blank.

(e)   Line 5 (Notice, Reporting, Proxy Tax)

If the answer to the question in line 5 of Part IV is "yes," the organization must prepare and file Schedule C, Part III. This question must be answered "yes" if the filing organization is a tax-exempt social welfare organization, labor organization, or business league. All other organizations should leave this line blank. (See Chapters 9, 10.)

(f) Line 6 (Donor-Advised Funds)

If the answer to the question on line 6 of Part IV is "yes," the organization must prepare and file Schedule D, Part I. This question must be answered "yes" if the organization maintained a donor-advised fund (or account) at any time during the year. (See Chapter 11.)

(g) Line 7 (Conservation Easements)

If the answer to the question on line 7 of Part IV is "yes," the organization must prepare and file Schedule D, Part II. The answer to this question is "yes" if the organization received or held any conservation easement at any time during the year, irrespective of how the organization acquired the easement or whether a charitable contribution deduction was claimed by a donor of the easement. (See Chapter 19.)

(h) Line 8 (Works of Art, etc.)

If the answer to the question on line 8 of Part IV is "yes," the organization must prepare and file Schedule D, Part III. This question is answered "yes" if, at any time during the year, the organization maintained collections of works of art, historical treasures, or other similar assets, regardless of whether the organization reported revenues and assets relating to such collections in its financial statements. (See Chapter 19.) Organizations that answer "yes" to this question often will answer "yes" to the question on line 30, Part IV.

(i) Line 9 (Credit Counseling, etc.)

If the answer to the question on line 9 of Part IV is "yes," the organization must prepare and file Schedule D, Part IV. This question is to be answered "yes" if the organization has an escrow account liability, holds funds in custodial accounts for other organizations or individuals, or provides credit counseling, debt management, credit repair, or debt negotiation services. (See Chapter 11.)

(j) Line 10 (Endowments)

If the answer to the question on line 10 of Part IV is "yes," the organization must prepare and file Schedule D, Part V. This question is to be answered "yes" if the organization, a related organization, or an organization formed and maintained exclusively to further one or more exempt purposes of the organization (such as a foundation formed to hold an endowment) held assets in term, permanent, or quasi-endowment funds at any time during the year. (See Chapter 11.)

(k) Line 11 (Assets and Liabilities)

If the answer to the question on line 11 of Part IV is "yes," the organization must prepare and file Schedule D, Parts VI, VII, VIII, IX, or X, as applicable. The answer to this question is "yes" if the organization reported an amount for land, buildings and equipment, investments (including program-related investments), other assets, or other liabilities. (See Chapter 11.)

(l)   Line 12 (Audited Financial Statements)

If the answer to the question on line 12 of Part IV is "yes," the organization must prepare and file Schedule D, Parts XI, XII, and XIII. This question is answered "yes" if the organization received an audited financial statement prepared in accordance with generally accepted accounting principles for the year for which it is completing the Form 990. (See Chapter 11.) An organization that answers "no" may (and is not required to) provide the reconciliation contained in Schedule D, Parts XI to XIII.

(m)   Line 13 (Schools)

If the answer to the question on line 13 of Part IV is "yes," because the organization is a school (Form 990, Schedule A, Part I, line 2), the organization must prepare and file Schedule E. (See Chapter 12.)

(n)   Line 14a (International Activities)

If the answer to the question on line 14a of Part IV is "yes," the organization need only check the "yes" box. The answer is "yes" if the organization maintained an office, or had employees or agents, outside the United States. A schedule is not required simply because the answer to this question is "yes." (See Chapter 13.)

(o)   Line 14b (International Revenue, Expenses)

If the answer to the question on line 14b of Part IV is "yes," the organization must prepare and file Schedule F, Part I. (See Chapter 13.)

(p)   Line 15 (International Grantmaking to Organizations)

If the answer to the question on line 15 of Part IV is "yes," the organization must prepare and file Schedule F, Part II. (See Chapter 13.)

(q)   Line 16 (International Grantmaking to Individuals)

If the answer to the question on line 16 of Part IV is "yes," the organization must prepare and file Schedule F, Part III. (See Chapter 13.)

(r)   Line 17 (Fundraising Activities)

If the answer to the question on line 17 of Part IV is "yes," the organization must prepare and file Schedule G, Part I. An organization that answers "no" to this question is advised by the IRS, in the draft instructions, to consider completing Schedule G nonetheless in order to report its fundraising for state or other reporting purposes. (See Chapter 14.)

(s) Line 18 (Fundraising Events)

If the answer to the question on line 18 of Part IV is "yes," the organization must prepare and file Schedule G, Part II. An organization that answers "no" to this question is advised by the IRS, in the draft instructions, to consider completing Schedule G nonetheless in order to report its fundraising for state or other reporting purposes. (See Chapter 14.)

(t) Line 19 (Gaming)

If the answer to the question on line 19 of Part IV is "yes," the organization must prepare and file Schedule G, Part III. An organization that answers "no" to this question is advised by the IRS, in the draft instructions, to consider completing Schedule G nonetheless in order to report its gaming activities for state or other reporting purposes. (See Chapter 14.)

(u) Line 20 (Hospitals)

If the answer to the question on line 20 of Part IV is "yes," the organization must prepare and file Schedule H. This question is to be answered "yes" if the organization, directly or indirectly through a disregarded entity or joint venture taxed as a partnership, operated any facility that at any time during the years was, or was required to be, licensed or certified by a state as a hospital. Except in the case of a group return, the organization should not take into account facilities operated by another organization that is treated as a separate taxable or tax-exempt corporation for federal income tax purposes. In the case of group returns, this question is to be answered "yes" if any affiliate (subordinate) within the group operated such a facility. (See Chapter 15.)

(v) Line 21 (Domestic Grants to Organizations)

If the answer to the question on line 21 of Part IV is "yes," the organization must prepare and file Schedule I, Parts I and II. An organization that answers "no" to this question is advised by the IRS, in the draft instructions, to consider completing Schedule I nonetheless in order to report its grantmaking activities in the United States for state or other reporting purposes. (See Chapter 16.)

(w) Line 22 (Domestic Grants to Individuals)

If the answer to the question on line 22 of Part IV is "yes," the organization must prepare and file Schedule I, Parts I and III. An organization that answers "no" to this question is advised by the IRS, in the draft instructions, to consider completing Schedule G nonetheless in order to report its grantmaking activities in the United States for state or other reporting purposes. (See Chapter 16.)

(x) Line 23 (Compensation of Former Officers, etc.)

If the answer to the question on line 23 of Part IV is "yes," the organization must prepare and file Schedule J. All organizations are required to complete Part VII of the new Form 990 (pages 7 and 8). The organization must answer "yes" to this question if it (1) listed in Part VII a former trustee, director, officer, key employee, or highest-compensated employee, or (2) reported for any person listed in Part VII more than $150,000 of reportable or other compensation. The answer to the question also is "yes" if, under the circumstances described in the instructions to Part VII, Section A, line 5 (see § 6.4(a)(9)), the organization had knowledge that any person listed in Part VII received or accrued compensation from an unrelated organization for services rendered to the filing organization. (See Chapter 6.)

(y)   Line 24a (Outstanding Bond Issues)

If the answer to the question on line 24a of Part IV is "yes," the organization must answer questions 24b 24d and prepare and file Schedule K. All organizations must answer this question. An organization that answers "no" may proceed to line 25.

The answer to this question is "yes" if the organization had any tax-exempt bond liabilities outstanding at any time during the tax year. Schedule K must be completed and attached for each tax-exempt bond issued after December 31, 2002, including refunding bonds, with an outstanding principal amount of more than $100,000 as of the last day of the tax year. (See Chapter 17.)

(z)   Line 24b (Tax-Exempt Bonds Investments)

If the answer to the question on line 24b of Part IV is "yes," the organization need only check the "yes" box. A schedule is not required. For purposes of this question, the organization need not include the following as investments of proceeds: any investment of proceeds relating to a reasonably required reserve or replacement fund, any investment of proceeds properly characterized as replacement proceeds, and any investment of net proceeds relating to a refunding escrow. (See Chapter 17.)

(aa)   Line 24c (Tax-Exempt Bonds Defeasements)

If the answer to the question in line 24c of Part IV is "yes," the organization need only check the "yes" box. A schedule is not required. (See Chapter 17.)

(bb)   Line 24d ("On Behalf of" Issues)

If the answer to the question on line 24d of Part IV is "yes," the organization need only check the "yes" box. A "yes" answer is required if the organization meets the conditions for issuing tax-exempt bonds as set forth in Revenue Ruling 63-20, has outstanding qualified scholarship funding bonds, or bonds of a qualified volunteer fire department. A schedule is not required. (See Chapter 17.)

(cc)   Line 25a (Excess Benefit Transactions)

The question on line 25a of Part IV must be answered by tax-exempt charitable and social welfare organizations. If the answer to this question is "yes," because the organization engaged in an excess benefit transaction with a disqualified person during the year, the organization must prepare and file Schedule L, Part I. (See Chapter 18.) All other exempt organizations leave line 25a blank.

(dd) Line 25b (Prior-Year Excess Benefit Transactions)

The question on line 25b of Part IV must be answered by tax-exempt charitable and social welfare organizations. If the answer to this question is "yes," because the organization became aware that it had engaged in an excess benefit transaction with a disqualified person in a prior year, the organization must prepare and file Schedule L, Part I. (See Chapter 18.) All other exempt organizations leave line 25b blank.

(ee) Line 26 (Loans to Interested Persons)

If the answer to the question on line 26 of Part IV is "yes," the organization must prepare and file Schedule L, Part II. (See Chapter 18.)

(ff) Line 27 (Assistance to Interested Persons)

If the answer to the question on line 27 of Part IV is "yes," the organization must prepare and file Schedule L, Part III. (See Chapter 18.)

(gg) Line 28a (Business Relationships)

If the answer to the question on line 28a of Part IV is "yes," the organization must prepare and file Schedule L, Part IV. (See Chapter 18.)

(hh) Line 28b (Business Relationships)

If the answer to the question on line 28b of Part IV is "yes," the organization must prepare and file Schedule L, Part IV. (See Chapter 18.)

(ii) Line 28c (Business Relationships)

If the answer to the question on line 28c of Part IV is "yes," the organization must prepare and file Schedule L, Part IV. (See Chapter 18.) The IRS, noting in the draft instructions that all organizations must answer the questions on lines 26 to 28, advises the filing organization to carefully review the instructions accompanying Schedule L, Parts II to IV, before answering these questions and completing Schedule L.

(jj) Line 29 (Noncash Contributions)

If the answer to the question on line 29 of Part IV is "yes," the organization must prepare and file Schedule M. All organizations are required to answer "yes" to this question if they received, during the year, more than $25,000 in value of contributions or grants of property other than cash, irrespective of whether they reported these amounts as noncash contributions in Part VIII, line 1g. (See Chapter 19.)

(kk) Line 30 (Noncash Contributions)

If the answer to the question on line 30 of Part IV is "yes," the organization must prepare and file Schedule M. All organizations are required to answer "yes" to this question if they received, during the year, as a contribution or grant (1) a work of art, historical treasure, historical artifact, scientific specimen, archeological artifact, or similar asset, including a fractional interest, irrespective of amount or whether the organization maintains a collection of the items, or (2) any conservation easements regardless of whether the contributor claimed a charitable contribution deduction for the gift. (See Chapter 19.)

(ll)   Line 31 (Dissolutions, etc.)

If the answer to the question on line 31 of Part IV is "yes," the organization must prepare and file Schedule N, Part I. (See Chapter 20.) An organization that answered "yes" to this question must also check the box on line 2 of Part I.

(mm)   Line 32 (Substantial Contractions, etc.)

If the answer to the question on line 32 of Part IV is "yes," the organization must prepare and file Schedule N, Part II. (See Chapter 20.) An organization that answered "yes" to this question must also check the box on line 2 of Part I.

(nn)   Line 33 (Disregarded Entities)

If the answer to the question on line 33 of Part IV is "yes," the organization must prepare and file Schedule R, Part I. (See Chapter 21.)

(oo)   Line 34 (Related Entities)

If the answer to the question on line 34 of Part IV is "yes," the organization must prepare and file Schedule R, Parts II, III, IV, and V, line 1. (See Chapter 21.)

(pp)   Line 35 (Controlled Entity)

If the answer to the question on line 35 of Part IV is "yes," the organization must prepare and file Schedule R, Part V, line 2. (See Chapter 21.)

(qq)   Line 36 (Transfers to Noncharitable Organizations)

If the answer to question 36 of Part IV is "yes," the organization must prepare and file Schedule R, Part V, line 2. This question is to be answered only by public charities; all other tax-exempt organizations are to leave this line blank. (See Chapter 21.)

(rr)   Line 37 (Use of Entities Taxed as Partnership)

If the answer to the question on line 37 of Part IV is "yes," the organization must prepare and file Schedule R, Part VI. This question is to be answered "yes" if at any time during the year, the organization conducted more than 5 percent of its activities, measured by total gross revenue or total assets of the organization, through an unrelated organization that is taxed as a partnership for federal income tax purposes. (See Chapter 21.)

§3.3   NEW FORM 990 COMPLIANCE TASKS

A tax-exempt organization filing the new Form 990 should carefully review the 44 questions of Part IV to be certain that it is filing all of the required schedules.

CHAPTER FOUR

Part V—Other IRS Filings and Tax Compliance

Part V of the new Form 990 is intended to capture and report on the organization's need to file other forms with the IRS and engage in aspects of tax law compliance not addressed elsewhere in the new annual information return.

§ 4.1 LAW AND POLICY

Part V of the new Form 990 pertains to 20 filing requirements and bodies of the federal tax law.

(a) Form 1096 Rules

An organization is required to use Form 1096, titled *Annual Summary and Transmittal of U.S. Information Returns,* to transmit to the IRS four information returns reporting certain amounts paid or received by the organization: Forms 1098, 1099, 5498, and W-2G (see § 4.1(b)). Examples of payments requiring Form 1099 reporting include certain payments to independent contractors for services rendered.

(b) Form W-2G Rules

Form W-2G pertains to certain gambling winnings.

(c) Backup Withholding Rules

Information on backup withholding for missing or incorrect names or taxpayer identification numbers is available in IRS Publication 1281.

(d) Form W-3 Rules

Form W-3 is titled *Transmittal of Wage and Tax Statements.*

(e) Federal Employment Tax Returns

The federal unemployment tax returns are Forms 940 and 941. Information about federal employment taxes is available in IRS Publication 557.

(f) Electronic Filing Requirements

A mandatory annual information return electronic filing program took effect in 2005, for certain tax-exempt organizations that file at least 250 returns during the course of the calendar year involved:

- Exempt organizations with assets of at least $100 million that are required to file Form 990 were required to file electronically beginning with tax years ending on or after December 31, 2005.

- Exempt organizations with assets of at least $10 million that are required to file Form 990 must file electronically beginning with tax years ending on or after December 31, 2006.

- Charitable split-interest trusts (and private foundations) that are required to file must file electronically (irrespective of asset size) beginning with tax years ending on or after December 31, 2006.

The IRS developed procedures by which exempt organizations can request a waiver of the requirement to electronically file annual information returns.

(g) Form 990-T Rules

A tax-exempt organization is required to file a Form 990-T (unrelated business income tax return) if its total gross income from all of its unrelated businesses is at least $1,000 for the year. The term *gross income* means the amount of gross receipts less the cost of goods sold.

Tax-exempt organizations must pay estimated taxes with respect to their unrelated business income if they expect their unrelated business income tax liability to be at least $500. These estimated taxes are computed and reported on Form 990-W.

(h) Form TD F 90-22.1 Rules

Form TD F 90.22.1, titled *Report of Foreign Bank and Financial Accounts*, must be filed with the Department of the Treasury if:

- At any time during the calendar year ending with or within the organization's tax year, the organization had an interest in, or signature or other authority over, a financial account in a foreign country (such as a bank account, securities account, or other financial account), and

  ○ The combined value of all of these accounts was more than $10,000 at any time during the calendar year, and

  ○ The accounts were not with a U.S. military banking facility operated by a U.S. financial institution.

- The organization owns more than 50 percent of the stock in a corporation that must answer "yes" to the foregoing item.

This form must be filed by June 30 following the end of the calendar year. The form should not be filed with the IRS, either independently or as an attachment to a Form 990.

(i) Prohibited Tax Shelter Transactions

An excise tax is imposed on most tax-exempt organizations (including private foundations) and/or organization managers that participate in prohibited tax shelter transactions as accommodation parties. This tax can be triggered in three instances: (1) an exempt organization is liable for the tax in the year it becomes a party to the transaction and any subsequent year or years in which it is such a party; (2) an exempt organization is liable for the tax in any year it is a party to a subsequently listed transaction; and (3) an exempt organization manager is liable for the tax if the manager caused the organization to be a party to a prohibited tax shelter transaction at any time during a year and knew or had reason to know that the transaction is such a transaction.

A *prohibited tax shelter transaction* is of two types: a listed transaction and a prohibited reportable transaction. A *listed transaction* is a reportable transaction that is the same as, or is substantially similar to, a transaction specifically identified by the IRS as a tax avoidance transaction. A *reportable transaction* is a transaction as to which information is required to be included with a tax return or statement because the transaction is of a type that the IRS determined has a potential for tax avoidance.

A *prohibited reportable transaction* is any confidential or otherwise contractually protected transaction that is a reportable transaction. A *subsequently listed transaction* is a transaction to which a tax-exempt entity is a party and which is determined by the IRS to be a listed transaction at any time after the entity has become a party to the transaction.

An organization that files Form 990 and is a party to a prohibited tax shelter transaction must file Form 8886-T, titled *Disclosure by Tax-Exempt Entity Regarding Prohibited Tax Shelter Transaction*. The organization may also have to file Form 4720 and pay the excise tax.

(j) Nondeductible Contributions

A fundraising solicitation by or on behalf of a tax-exempt organization that is not eligible to receive contributions that are deductible as charitable contributions for federal income tax purposes must include an explicit statement with the solicitation that contributions to it are not deductible as charitable contributions. The statement must be in an easily recognizable format, irrespective of whether the solicitation is a written or printed form, by television or radio, or by telephone. This rule is applicable only to organizations that normally have annual gross receipts in excess of $100,000.

Failure to disclose that contributions are not deductible could result in a penalty of $1,000 for each day on which a failure occurs. The maximum penalty for failures by any organization, during any calendar year, may not exceed $10,000. In cases where the failure to make the disclosure is due to intentional disregard of the law, more severe penalties apply. A penalty will not be imposed where a failure to disclose is due to reasonable cause.

(k) Quid Pro Quo Contributions

If a donor makes a payment in excess of $75, where the payment is partly a contribution and partly consideration for goods or services provided by a tax-exempt organization—a *quid pro quo contribution*—the organization generally must notify the donor of the value of the goods or services provided. Here is an illustration of this rule:

> **Example.** A donor pays a charitable organization $100 and receives in exchange a concert ticket with a value of $40. Of the transferred amount, $60 is a charitable contribution. Because this donor's payment is in excess of $75, the organization must furnish the requisite disclosure statement. This is the case even though the charitable gift element is not more than $75.

Separate payments of $75 or less made at different times of the year for separate fundraising events are not aggregated for purposes of this $75 threshold.

(l) Form 8282 Rules

Form 8282 is used by donee tax-exempt organizations to report information to the IRS and to donors about dispositions of certain contributed property that occur within three years after the date on which the donor contributed the property. (See Chapter 19.)

(m) Personal Benefit Contracts

Charitable split-dollar insurance plans, whereby life insurance was the underpinning for forms of endowment-building investment vehicles for charitable organizations, have been effectively outlawed by the federal tax law. That is, the federal tax law denies an income tax charitable contribution deduction for, and imposes excise tax penalties on, transfers associated with use of these plans.

Specifically, there is no federal charitable contribution deduction for a transfer to or for the use of a charitable organization, if, in connection with the transfer, (1) the organization directly or indirectly pays, or has previously paid, any premium on any personal benefit contract with respect to the transferor; or (2) there is an understanding or expectation that any person will directly or indirectly pay any premium on this type of a contract with respect to the transferor. A *personal benefit contract*, with respect to a transferor, is any life insurance, annuity, or endowment contract, if any direct or indirect beneficiary under the contract is the transferor, any member of the transferor's family, or any other person (other than a charitable organization) designated by the transferor.

The organization must report on Form 8870 the premiums it paid and the premiums paid by others but treated as paid by the organization. The organization must report and pay the excise tax, equal to the amount of premiums paid, on Form 4720.

(n) Contributions of Intellectual Property

Contributions of most forms of intellectual property are among the list of types of charitable gifts that give rise to a charitable contribution deduction that is confined to the donor's basis in the property, although in instances of gifts of intellectual property there may be one or more subsequent charitable deductions. Form 8899, titled *Notice of Income from Donated Intellectual Property*, must be filed by certain organizations that received a charitable contribution of qualified intellectual property that produces net income. (These rules are discussed more fully in § 19.1(h).)

(o) Contributions of Vehicles

The federal tax law contains rules as to deductibility and substantiation in connection with contributions to charity of motor vehicles, boats, and airplanes—collectively termed *qualified vehicles*. These requirements supplant the general gift substantiation rules where the claimed value of the contributed property exceeds $500. (These rules are discussed in § 19.1(g).)

Pursuant to these rules, a federal income tax charitable contribution deduction is not allowed unless the donor substantiates the contribution by a contemporaneous written acknowledgment of it by the donee organization and includes the acknowledgment with the donor's income tax return reflecting the deduction. The IRS issued Form 1098-C to be used by donee charitable organizations to report to the IRS contributions of qualified vehicles and to provide the donor with a contemporaneous written acknowledgment of the contribution. A donor of a qualified vehicle must attach Copy B of this form to the donor's income tax return in order to take a deduction for the contribution of the vehicle where the claimed value is in excess of $500. Generally, the donee must furnish Copies B and C of the form to the donor either no later than 30 days after the date of sale or 30 days after the date of the contribution, depending on the circumstances. Copy A of this form is to be filed with the IRS, Copy C is for the donor's records, and Copy D is retained by the charitable donee.

(p) Excess Business Holdings Rules

A sponsoring organization or a supporting organization must disclose in Part V of the new Form 990 whether it had, at any time during the reporting year, *excess business holdings*. The concept of excess business holdings was originally developed in the private foundation law context.

(1) Basic Rules.   The basic rule is that the combined ownership, of a foundation and those who are disqualified persons with respect to it, of a business enterprise in any form—corporation, limited liability company, partnership, joint venture, sole proprietorship, or other type of unincorporated entity—may not exceed 20 percent. The law enables foundations to, without penalty, receive and dispose of excess holdings when the enterprise or business interests were acquired by the foundation by means of a contribution or inheritance.

These rules came into being (in 1969) out of concern that foundations were being used as holding companies of commercial enterprises, with owners of the businesses obtaining a charitable contribution deduction for transfer of ownership from one entity they controlled (the business) to another entity they controlled (the foundation). A collateral worry was that these business enterprises did not produce much income to be used for charitable purposes. Further, there was trepidation that foundation managers would concentrate on maintaining and improving the business, to the detriment of their charitable duties. Moreover, when a business is held in this fashion (by a tax-exempt foundation), it may operate in a way which unfairly competes with other similar businesses whose owners must pay taxes on the income they derive from the enterprise.

(2) Definition of *Business Enterprise.* The term *business enterprise* is broadly defined in the federal tax law to include the active conduct of a trade or business, including any activity that is regularly carried on for the production of income from the sale of goods or the performance of services and that constitutes an unrelated trade or business. Where an activity carried on for profit is an unrelated business, no part of it may be excluded from classification as a business enterprise merely because it does not result in a profit.

Thus, just as is the case with the unrelated business rules, a threshold determination must be made as to whether the *business* involved is a *related* or *unrelated* one. For example, a private foundation proposed to build, maintain, and lease a public ice arena. This facility, which was planned to conform to National Hockey League and college rink specifications, was expected to include a pro shop, coffee shop, concession area, day care center, and cocktail lounge; other contemplated facilities were conference, gymnastics, and athletic medicine facilities. The foundation proposed to lease this arena at fair rental value rates. On the face of it, this undertaking might appear to be a commercial (unrelated) one. The IRS, however, concluded that the development, ownership, and leasing of the arena would promote the health and welfare of the community and lessen the burdens of local government. Thus, this bundle of activities was held to not constitute a business enterprise for purposes of the excess business holdings rules.

A bond or other evidence of indebtedness is not a holding in a business enterprise unless it is otherwise determined to be an equitable interest in the enterprise. Thus, an ostensible indebtedness will be treated as a business holding if it is essentially an equity holding in disguise. A leasehold interest in real property is not an interest in a business enterprise, even if the rent is based on profits, unless the leasehold interest is an interest in the income or profits of an unrelated trade or business.

The term *business enterprise* does not include a functionally related business, a program-related investment, or a trade or business that is a passive income business.

(3) Passive Income Businesses. For purposes of the excess business holdings rules, exempted from the concept of the *business enterprise* is a trade or business of which at least 95 percent of the gross income is derived from passive sources. Thus, stock in a passive holding company is not considered a holding in a business enterprise, even if the company is controlled by the foundation. The foundation, however, is treated as owning its proportionate share of the interests in a business enterprise held by the company. Tax-exempt title-holding companies can be utilized to house passive business operations.

The notion of *passive source income* is derived from the unrelated business rules. Consequently, passive income includes items considered passive in nature for purposes of these rules, including:

- Dividends, interest, and annuities
- Royalties, including overriding royalties, whether measured by production or by gross or taxable income from the property

- Rental income from real property and from personal property leased with real property, if the rent attributable to the personal property is incidental (less than 50 percent of the total rent)

- Gains or losses from sales, exchanges, or other dispositions of property (other than stock in trade held for regular sale to customers)

- Income from the sale of goods, if the seller does not manufacture, produce, physically receive or deliver, negotiate sales of, or keep inventories in the goods

The fact that the unrelated debt-financed income rules may apply to an item of passive income does not alter the character of the income as passive for purposes of the excess business holdings rules.

(4) Percentage Limitations. As noted, the excess business holdings rules generally limit to 20 percent the permitted ownership of a corporation's voting stock or other interest in a business enterprise that may be held by a private foundation and all disqualified persons combined. Thus, as a general rule, a foundation and its substantial contributors, managers, their family members, and related organizations cannot collectively own more than 20 percent of an active business enterprise.

Usually, ownership of a corporation is determined by means of voting stock. For these purposes, the percentage of voting stock held by a person in a corporation is normally determined by reference to the power of stockholders to vote for the election of directors, with treasury stock and stock that is authorized but unissued disregarded.

Where all disqualified persons with respect to a private foundation together do not own more than 20 percent of the voting stock of an incorporated business enterprise, the foundation can own any amount of nonvoting stock. Equity interests that do not have voting power attributable to them are classified as nonvoting stock. Stock carrying contingent voting rights is treated as nonvoting stock, for this purpose, until the event triggering the right to vote occurs. (An illustration is preferred stock that can be voted only if dividends are not paid.)

If effective control of a business of a business enterprise can be shown to the satisfaction of the IRS to be elsewhere (i.e., other than by a private foundation and its disqualified persons), a 35 percent limit may be substituted for the 20 percent limit. The term *effective control* means possession of the power, whether direct or indirect, and whether or not actually exercised, to direct or cause the direction of the management and policies of a business enterprise. Effective control can be achieved by means such as ownership of voting stock, use of voting trusts, and/or contractual arrangements. It is the reality of control that is decisive, rather than its form or the ways in which it may be exercisable. For this 35 percent rule to apply, a private foundation must demonstrate by affirmative proof that an unrelated party, or group of parties, does in fact exercise control over the business enterprise involved.

A private foundation must, however, directly or indirectly hold more than 2 percent of the voting stock or other value of a business enterprise before either of these limitations becomes applicable. The holdings of related foundations are aggregated for the purpose of computing this 2 percent amount. This aggregation rule exists, of course, to preclude the use of multiple foundations as a means of subverting the law by converting this de minimis rule into a method of evading the excess business holdings rules.

(5) Applicability of Rules to Supporting Organizations. Only certain supporting organizations (in general, see § 8.1(h)) are subject to the excess business holdings rules. They are (1) Type III supporting organizations that are not functionally integrated and (2) Type II supporting organizations that accept any contribution from a person who, alone or in conjunction with a related party, controls an entity that is a supported organization of that supporting organization.

(q) Donor-Advised Funds

One of the most controversial entities in the realm of charitable organizations is the *donor-advised fund*. These funds are created and maintained within public charities, such as community foundations, colleges and universities, churches, and charitable gift funds. Indeed, these funds were invented by community foundations, which have existed for nearly 100 years. Today, there are billions of dollars in money and other assets reposing in donor-advised funds.

While this giving vehicle has been a part of the U.S. charitable giving scene for nearly a century, only recently has it become the subject of considerable scrutiny, criticism, and law. Several federal tax law issues are triggered by these funds, all resting on the fundamental fact that the donor-advised fund is an alternative to the private foundation. Some choose to state the matter somewhat differently, regarding these funds as a means of sidestepping or inappropriately avoiding the private foundation rules.

A donor-advised fund is not a separate legal entity. Rather, as noted, it is a fund within an organization that is classified as a public charity. This type of fund is often referred to as an *account* or sometimes as a *subaccount* of the host organization. These accounts usually are named, reflecting an individual, family, corporation, private foundation, or cause. A donor-advised fund can appear to be a legal entity—seemingly a charitable organization with many of the attributes of a private foundation.

The donor-advised fund should be contrasted with the donor-directed fund. In the case of a *donor-directed fund*, the donor or a designee of the donor has the *right* to direct the investment of the fund's assets and/or to direct grants from the fund for charitable purposes. By contrast, with the donor-advised fund, the donor or a designee of the donor has the mere *ability* to make *recommendations* (proffer advice) as to investment policy and/or the making of grants.

In recent years, commercial investment companies have created donor-advised funds as charitable entities. That is what triggered the furor. As long as use of these funds was confined to community foundations, there was no controversy. The attention accorded these funds, including criticism, started when other types of public charities began generating gifts by means of donor-advised funds. The new statutory law was enacted in 2006.

This legislation enacted in 2006 introduced a statutory definition of the term *donor-advised fund*. Essentially, it is a fund (or account) that is (1) separately identified by reference to contributions of one or more donors, (2) that is owned and controlled by a sponsoring organization, and (3) as to which a donor or a donor advisor has, or reasonably expects to have, advisory privileges with respect to the distribution or investment of amounts held in the fund by reason of the donor's status as a donor. A *sponsoring organization* is a public charity that maintains one or more donor-advised funds.

A donor-advised fund does not include funds that make distributions only to a single identified organization or governmental entity, or certain funds where a donor or donor advisor provides advice as to which individuals receive grants for travel, study, or similar purposes. The IRS has the authority to exempt a fund from treatment as a donor-advised fund under certain circumstances. Exercising this authority, the IRS announced that employer-sponsored disaster relief assistance funds do not constitute donor-advised funds.

A distribution from a donor-advised fund is taxable if it is to an individual or any other person for a noncharitable purpose, unless expenditure responsibility is exercised with respect to the distribution. A tax, in the amount of 20 percent of the amount involved, is imposed on the sponsoring organization for making a taxable distribution. Another tax, of 5 percent, is imposed on the agreement of a fund manager to the making of a taxable distribution, where the manager knew that the distribution was a taxable one. The tax on fund management is subject to a joint and several liability requirement. This tax does not apply to a distribution from a donor-advised fund to most public charities (but not including a nonfunctionally integrated Type III supporting organization), the fund's sponsoring organization, or another donor-advised fund.

If a donor, donor advisor, or person related to a donor or donor advisor with respect to a donor-advised fund provides advice as to a distribution that results in any of these persons receiving, directly or indirectly, a benefit that is more than incidental, an excise tax equal to 125 percent of the amount of the benefit is imposed on the person who advised as to the distribution and on the recipient of the benefit. Also, if a manager of the sponsoring organization agreed to the making of the distribution, knowing that the distribution would confer more than an incidental benefit on a donor, donor advisor, or related person, the manager is subject to an excise tax equal to 10 percent of the amount of the benefit. These taxes are also subject to a joint and several liability requirement. A *related person* is any family member or 35-percent controlled entity of the donor or donor advisor.

A grant, loan, compensation, or other similar payment (such as reimbursement of expenses) from a donor-advised fund to a person that, with respect to the fund, is a donor, donor advisor, or related person automatically is treated as an excess benefit transaction for intermediate sanctions law purposes. This means that the entire amount paid to any of these persons is an excess benefit. Donors and donor advisors with respect to a donor-advised fund, and related persons, are disqualified persons for intermediate sanctions law purposes with respect to transactions with the donor-advised fund (although not necessarily with respect to transactions with the sponsoring organization).

The private foundation excess business holdings rules (see § 4.1(p)) apply to donor-advised funds. For this purpose, the term *disqualified person* means, with respect to a donor-advised fund, a donor, donor advisor, member of the family of either, or 35-percent controlled entity of any such person.

A donor must obtain, with respect to each charitable contribution to a sponsoring organization to be maintained in a donor-advised fund, a contemporaneous written acknowledgment from the sponsoring organization that the organization has exclusive legal control over the funds or other assets contributed.

A sponsoring organization is required to disclose on its annual information return the number of donor-advised funds it owns, the aggregate value of assets held in the funds at the end of the organization's tax year involved, and the aggregate contributions to and grants made from these funds during the year. When seeking recognition of tax-exempt status, a sponsoring organization must disclose whether it intends to maintain donor-advised funds. As to this latter rule, the organization must provide information regarding its planned operation of these funds, including a description of procedures it intends to use to:

- Communicate to donors and donor advisors that assets held in the funds are the property of the sponsoring organization, and

- Ensure that distributions from donor-advised funds do not result in more than incidental benefit to any person.

The Department of the Treasury was directed by Congress to undertake a study on the organization and operation of donor-advised funds, to consider whether (1) the deductions allowed for income, estate, or gift taxes for charitable contributions to sponsoring organizations are appropriate in consideration of the use of contributed assets or the use of the assets of these organizations for the benefit of the person making the charitable contribution, (2) donor-advised funds should be required to distribute for charitable purposes a specified amount in order to ensure that the sponsoring organization with respect to the funds is operating in a manner consistent with its tax-exempt or public charity status, (3) the retention by donors to donor-advised funds of "rights or privileges" with respect to amounts transferred to these organizations (including advisory rights or privileges with respect to the making of grants or the investment of assets) is consistent with the treatment of these transfers as completed gifts, and (4) these issues are also issues with respect to other forms of charitable organizations or charitable contributions.

(r) Social Clubs

Federal income tax exemption is available for qualified social clubs; these clubs are organized for pleasure, recreation, and other comparable purposes. Generally, tax exemption is extended to nonprofit social and recreational clubs that are supported primarily by membership fees, dues, and assessments. To be exempt, a club must have an established membership of individuals, personal contacts, and fellowship; a commingling of the members must play a material part in the life of the organization.

A tax-exempt club generally can receive as much as 35 percent of its gross receipts, including investment income, from sources outside of its membership without losing exempt status. Within that 35-percent amount, generally no more than 15 percent of the gross receipts can be derived from the use of the club's facilities or services by the public.

(s) Mutual Organizations

Federal income tax exemption is available for qualified benevolent life insurance associations of a purely local character, mutual ditch or irrigation companies, mutual or cooperative telephone companies, and like organizations. In general, at least 85 percent of the gross income of these entities must consist of amounts collected from members for the sole purpose of meeting losses and expenses. For this purpose, the term *gross income* means gross receipts without reduction for any cost of goods sold.

Gross income for mutual or cooperative electric companies is determined by excluding any income received or accrued from (1) qualified pole rentals; (2) any provision or sale of electric energy transmission services or ancillary services if the services are provided on a nondiscriminatory, open-access basis under an open access transmission tariff, approved or accepted by the Federal Energy Regulatory Commission (FERC) or under an independent transmission provider agreement approved or accepted by the FERC (other than income received or accrued directly or indirectly from a member); (3) the provision or sale of electric energy distribution services or ancillary services if the services are provided on a nondiscriminatory, open-access basis to distribute electric energy not owned by the mutual or electric company (a) to end users who are served by distribution facilities not owned by the company or any of its members (other than income received or accrued directly or indirectly from a member), or (b) generated by a generation facility not owned or leased by the company or any of its members and which is directly connected to distribution facilities owned by the company or any of its members (other than income received or accrued directly or indirectly from a member); (4) from any nuclear decommissioning transaction; or (5) from any asset exchange or conversion transaction.

For a mutual or cooperative telephone company, *gross income* does not include amounts received or accrued from (1) another telephone company for completing long-distance calls to or from or between the company's members, (2) qualified pole rentals, (3) the sale of display listings in a directory furnished to the company's members, or (4) the prepayment of certain loans.

(t) Nonexempt Charitable Trusts

Nonexempt charitable trusts are trusts that are not tax-exempt but are treated as private foundations for federal tax law purposes. These trusts are funded and operated in nearly identical fashion as exempt private foundations. This type of trust has exclusively charitable interests; donors to them are allowed to claim a tax deduction for charitable contributions. Unlike private foundations, nonexempt charitable trusts are required to pay an annual tax on income that is not distributed for charitable purposes.

If a nonexempt charitable trust does not have any taxable income, its filing of Form 990 may be used to meet its income tax return filing requirement. That is, in this circumstance, the filing of Form 1041 is not required.

§4.2 PREPARATION OF NEW FORM 990 PART V

Part V of the new Form 990 poses a battery of questions.

(a) Various Information Returns

Line 1a of Part V of the new Form 990 requires the filing organization to supply the number of information returns reported in Box 3 of the Form 1096. If the organization has transmitted any of these returns electronically, the number of them should be added to the total reported on line 1a. If this question is inapplicable, the organization should enter "0."

Line 1b of Part V requires the filing organization to enter the number of Forms W-2G included in the answer to the line 1a question. If this question is inapplicable, the organization should enter "0."

The question on line 1c inquires as to whether the organization complied with the backup withholding rules for reportable payments to vendors and reportable gaming winnings to prize winners. This question is to be answered by checking a "yes" or "no" box.

Line 2a requires the organization to enter the number of employees it reported on Form W-3 filed for the calendar year ending with or within the year covered by the new (2008) Form 990. If at least one employee is reported in the response to line 2a, the organization is required by line 2b to indicate if it filed all required federal employment tax returns. This line 2b question is to be answered by checking a "yes" or "no" box.

If the sum of lines 1a and 2a is greater than 250, the organization may be required to file the new Form 990 electronically. (See § 4.1(f).)

(b) Unrelated Business Income

The line 3a question asks if the organization had unrelated business gross income of at least $1,000 during the year covered by the new Form 990. This question is to be answered by checking a "yes" or "no" box. If the answer to this question is "yes," the organization must report, in response to line 3b, whether it filed a Form 990-T for the year; this question is to be answered by checking a "yes" or "no" box. If the answer to the line 3b question is "no," the organization must provide an explanation in Schedule O. This explanation must be carefully crafted because a Form 990-T is *required* under these circumstances.

(c) Foreign Bank Account(s)

Line 4a poses the question as to whether, at any time during the calendar year (2008), the organization had an interest in, or a signature or other authority over, a financial account in a foreign country (such as a bank account or securities account). This line 4a question is to be answered by checking a "yes" or "no" box. If the answer to this question is yes," the name of the country must be reported on line 4b. The filing of Form TD F 90-22.1 may be required.

(d) Prohibited Tax Shelter Transactions

The filing organization is asked, in the line 5a question, whether the organization was a party to a prohibited tax shelter transaction at any time during the tax year. The organization is also asked, in the line 5b question, whether a taxable party notified the organization that it was or is a party to this type of transaction. These questions are to be answered by checking "yes" or "no" boxes. If the answer to either of these questions is "yes," the organization is asked in line 5c if it filed a Form 8886-T; this question is to be answered by checking a "yes" or "no" box.

(e) Nondeductible Contributions

The organization is required, by the line 6a question, to report whether it solicited any contributions that were not tax-deductible. If the answer to this question is "yes," the organization is required, via the line 6b question, to indicate whether it included with every solicitation an express statement that the contribution was not tax-deductible. These questions are to be answered by checking "yes" or "no" boxes. A charitable organization, however, should answer question 6a "no."

(f) Quid Pro Quo Contributions

An organization that is eligible to receive tax-deductible charitable contributions is required to report, by the line 7a question, whether it provided any goods or services in exchange for any contribution of $75 or more. If the answer to this question is "yes," the organization must indicate, in response to the line 7b question, whether it notified the donor in this circumstance of the value of the goods or services provided. These questions are to be answered by checking "yes" or "no" boxes. Organizations that may not receive deductions contributions should leave these two lines blank.

(g) Form 8282

An organization that is eligible to receive tax-deductible charitable contributions is required to report, by the line 7c question, whether it sold, exchanged, or otherwise disposed of tangible personal property for which it filed Form 8282. This line 7c question is to be answered by checking a "yes" or "no" box. If the answer is "yes," the filing organization must indicate, on line 7d, the number of these forms filed during the year. (See § 19.1(v).)

(h) Personal Benefit Contracts

An organization that is eligible to receive tax-deductible charitable contributions is required to report, by the line 7e question, whether it, during the year, received any funds, directly or indirectly, to pay premiums on a personal benefit contract. The organization is also asked, by the line 7f question, whether it, during the year, paid premiums, directly or indirectly, on a personal benefit contract. These questions are to be answered by checking "yes" or "no" boxes.

(i) Contributions of Intellectual Property

An organization that is eligible to receive tax-deductible charitable contributions is required to report, by the line 7g question, whether, if it received one or more contributions of qualified intellectual property, it filed Form 8899. This question is to be answered by checking a "yes" or "no" box. An organization should check the "yes" box if it provided all required Forms 8899 for the year for net income produced by contributed qualified intellectual property. (See § 19.1(h).)

(j) Contributions of Vehicles

An organization that is eligible to receive tax-deductible charitable contributions is required to report, by the line 7h question, whether, if it received one or more contributions of cars, boats, airplanes, and/or other vehicles, it filed Form 1098-C. This question is to be answered by checking a "yes" or "no" box. (See § 19.1(g).)

(k)   Excess Business Holdings

Supporting organizations and organizations that maintain donor-advised funds (sponsoring organizations) are asked, by the line 8 question, whether they had any excess business holdings at any time during the year. This question is to be answered by checking a "yes" or "no" box. All other organizations should leave this line blank.

If the answer to this question is "yes," the organization may be subject to the excess business holdings excise tax and thus required to file Form 4720.

(l)   Donor-Advised Funds

Charitable and other sponsoring organizations (see § 11.1(a)) are asked, in the line 9a question, whether they made any taxable distributions (presumably during the filing year). These organizations are also asked, in the line 9b question, whether they made a distribution to a donor, donor-advisor, or related person. These questions are to be answered by checking "yes" or "no" boxes. Organizations that are not sponsoring organizations should leave these two lines blank.

Those that are liable for the excise tax imposed in this context must file a Form 4720 to calculate and pay the tax.

(m)   Social Clubs

Tax-exempt social clubs are required, pursuant to line 10a, to report the amount of initiation fees paid and capital contributions to them. (If, however, the organization is a college fraternity or sorority that charges membership initiation fees but not annual dues, the initiation fees should not be included on this line.) These organizations are also required, in accordance with line 10b, to report the amount of gross receipts received for public use of the club's facilities. (These amounts are also reported in Part VIII, line 12.) The purpose of these questions, of course, is to determine if the filing organization is staying within the bounds of the 15-percent limitation on receipts derived from public use of the club.

The amount that is reported on line 10a should also be reported on Form 990-T. If the filing organization is not a tax-exempt social club, these two lines should be left blank.

(n)   Mutual Organizations

Tax-exempt mutual organizations are required, by line 11a, to report the amount of their gross income from members or shareholders. Line 11b requires these organizations to report their gross income from other sources. These questions are being asked, of course, to determine if the filing organization is in compliance with the 85-percent gross income threshold.

When ascertaining these gross amounts, these organizations are not to net amounts due or paid to other sources against amounts due or received from them. If the filing organization is not a tax-exempt mutual organization, these two lines should be left blank.

(o)   Nonexempt Charitable Trusts

Nonexempt charitable trusts must, in accordance with line 12a, indicate whether they are filing the Form 990 in lieu of Form 1041. This question is to be answered by checking a "yes" or "no" box. These trusts are also required, by line 12b, to report the amount of tax-exempt interest they received or accrued during the year. If the filing organization is not a nonexempt charitable trust, these two lines should be left blank.

§4.3   NEW FORM 990 COMPLIANCE TASKS

A tax-exempt organization that is required to prepare Part V of the new Form 990 should be attending to one or more of these 21 tasks:

1. **Form 1096.** Ascertain the number reported in box 3 of Form 1096.

2. **Form W-2G.** Ascertain the number of Forms W-2G filed that are included in the number in task no. 1.

3. **Backup Withholding.** If applicable, prepare the answer to the backup withholding question.

4. **Form W-3.** Ascertain the number of employees reported in the Form W-3.

5. **Employment Tax Returns.** If applicable, prepare the answer to the question about federal employment tax returns.

6. **Electronic Filing.** Determine if the organization is required to file the new Form 990 electronically.

7. **Form 990-T.** Ascertain whether the organization is required to file Form 990-T for 2008.

8. **Form 990-T.** If the organization is required to file Form 990-T for 2008 and is not doing so, prepare the explanation to be provided on Schedule O.

9. **Foreign Bank Accounts.** If applicable, prepare the answer(s) to the question(s) concerning foreign bank accounts.

10. **Tax Shelter Transactions.** If applicable, prepare the answer(s) to the question(s) concerning participation in a prohibited tax shelter transaction.

11. **Nondeductible Contributions.** If applicable, prepare the answer(s) to the question(s) about solicitation of nondeductible contributions.

12. **Quid Pro Quo Contributions.** If applicable, prepare the answer(s) to the question(s) about quid pro quo contributions.

13. **Form 8282.** If applicable, prepare the answer(s) to the question(s) concerning the filing of Form(s) 8282.

14. **Personal Benefit Contracts.** If applicable, prepare the answer(s) to the question(s) about personal benefit contracts.

15. **Form 8899.** If applicable, prepare the answer to the question about the filing of Form 8899.

16. **Form 1098-C.** If applicable, prepare the answer to the question about the filing of Form 1098-C.

17. **Donor-Advised Funds.** If applicable, prepare the answer(s) to the question(s) about maintenance of donor-advised funds.

18. **Social Clubs.** If the organization is a tax-exempt social club, prepare answers to the two questions posed of those clubs.

19. **Mutual Organizations.** If the organization is a tax-exempt mutual organization, prepare answers to the two questions posed of those entities.

20. **Mutual Organizations.** In connection with the preceding question, if the organization cannot satisfy the 85-percent gross income test, it should seek the services of legal counsel.

21. **Nonexempt Charitable Trusts.** If the organization is a nonexempt charitable trust, prepare answers to the two questions posed of those trusts.

CHAPTER FIVE

Part VI—Corporate Governance

Part VI of the Form 990 is designed to solicit information from a tax-exempt organization about its corporate governance, policies, and disclosure practices. By requesting the information, the IRS will likely conform the practices of exempt entities to its own view of good governance principles. Many of the questions asked in Part VI do not reflect legal requirements to which exempt organizations are subject, but instead are designed to determine whether an exempt entity is engaging in practices that are closely aligned with principles of good corporate governance.

The IRS believes the "existence of an independent governing body and well-defined governance and management policies and practices increases the likelihood that an organization is operating in compliance with federal tax law." In Part VI, the IRS is requesting information about the organization's board composition and independence, its governance and management structure and policies, and whether (and if so, how) the organization promotes transparency and accountability to its constituents and beneficiaries. An IRS representative characterized Part VI as the "crown jewel" of the Form 990. The IRS states that, while many of the Part VI questions address policies and procedures that are not required by the Internal Revenue Code, the IRS considers such policies and procedures generally to improve tax compliance. Further, the IRS states that the "absence of appropriate policies and procedures may lead to opportunities for excess benefit transactions, inurement, operation for non-exempt purposes, or other activities inconsistent with exempt status."

§5.1 LAW AND POLICY

Generally, the body of law applicable to the governance of a tax-exempt organization is state, not federal, law. The nature of governance of a nonprofit, exempt organization depends mainly on the form of the entity. Exempt organizations are generally of three types: a nonprofit corporation, an unincorporated association, or a trust. In addition, a nonprofit organization may be organized as a limited liability company. The state act governing the creation and operation of a nonprofit entity will address matters relating to the organization's governance. The IRS and other interested organizations are working to conform the governing practices of exempt organizations despite their lack of any apparent legal authority for taking these actions.

(a) Creation and Governance of a Tax-Exempt Organization

A nonprofit corporation is generally created by filing articles of incorporation. An unincorporated association is typically formed using articles of organization or a constitution. A nonprofit trust is created in a trust instrument or in a will. These documents characteristically contain language governing the organization and operation of the nonprofit entity. In addition, the organization usually has bylaws that also govern the operation of the organization.

Tax-exempt organizations that are corporations are typically governed by either a board of directors or a board of trustees. If the exempt organization is a trust, it may have a board of trustees or be governed by a single, sometimes corporate, trustee. How the nonprofit organization is organized determines how its directors are selected. Some nonprofit organizations are established with a self-perpetuating board of directors, meaning that the directors elect their successors. In other instances, the members of the nonprofit organization elect the directors. In the rare instance of a nonprofit corporation organized as a stock corporation, which is allowable only in a few states, the stockholders elect the directors. With trusts, the trust document often appoints the trustees. Certain director positions may be ex officio, with the individual serving as a director because of a position held in another entity. However selected, the governing board of a nonprofit organization is responsible for overseeing its affairs.

A nonprofit organization's officers are usually elected by the governing body or by the organization's members. The election process is typically governed by the organization's bylaws.

(b) Board Size

State law typically mandates at least three individuals serve as the governing body, although some states require only one. Some nonprofit corporations have very large boards of directors; state law generally does not set a maximum on the number of directors of nonprofit organizations. Some agencies and organizations suggest a minimum of three or five directors in their good governance guidelines, and at least one suggests a 15-person maximum. The IRS, in its "Life Cycle" educational document regarding governance found on its Web site (see § 5.1(g)(2).), states:

> Very small or very large governing boards may not adequately serve the needs of the organization. Small boards may run the risk of not representing a sufficiently broad public interest and of lacking the required skills and other resources required to effectively govern the organization. On the other hand, very large boards may have a more difficult time getting down to business and making decisions.

The document further cautions that if an organization's "governing board is large, the organization may want to establish an executive committee with delegated responsibilities or advisory committees." The Panel on the Nonprofit Sector, in its "Principles for Good Governance and Ethical Practice," states that a board of a charitable organization should establish its own size and structure and review its size periodically, and further that a board "should have enough members to allow for full deliberation and diversity of thinking on governance and other organization matters." The Panel on the Nonprofit Sector, in its 2005 report to Congress, states that "[i]n the end, each charitable organization must determine the most appropriate size for its board and the appropriate number and responsibilities of board committees to ensure that the board is able to fulfill its fiduciary and other governance duties responsibly and effectively."

(c)   Board Composition

The composition of a nonprofit organization's governing board is generally a matter of state law. Currently, there are four exceptions to this general rule: (1) tax-exempt healthcare organizations are required to satisfy a community benefit test, which includes having a community board; (2) organizations qualifying as a publicly supported charity by reason of the facts-and-circumstances test may need to have a governing board that is representative of the community, as a community board is one of the factors considered in meeting the test; (3) organizations that qualify as supporting organizations are subject to certain requirements as to their board composition and/or selection; and (4) entities qualifying as exempt credit counseling organizations are subject to board composition requirements regarding financial independence from the organization.

IRS agents, when reviewing initial applications of exempt organizations, often try to impose their own views on board compositions, such as requiring the addition of independent directors; such views are not correct assertions of the law. One IRS representative stated publicly that "outside of the very smallest organizations, or possibly family foundations," an active, independent, and engaged board of directors is the "gold standard" of board composition.

(d)   Independent Board Members

There is no general requirement that a nonprofit organization have a certain number of independent board members. The inclusion of independent directors on the board of a nonprofit entity, however, is considered a good governance practice. In 2007, the Panel on the Nonprofit Sector released its Principles for Good Governance and Ethical Practice, which suggest that two-thirds of a charity's board should be composed of independent members, that is, members who (a) are not compensated by the organization as employees or independent contractors, (b) do not have their compensation set by individuals who are compensated by the organization, (c) do not receive, directly or indirectly, material financial benefits from the organization except as a member of the charitable class served by the organization, or (d) are not related to anyone described in (a) through (c), or reside with a person so described. This recommendation represents an increased proportion of independent board members over the Panel's earlier recommendation. In the Panel on the Nonprofit Sector's 2005 report to Congress, the Panel recommended that public charities be legally required to have independent board members because charities are not subject to the self-dealing rules to which private foundations are subject and therefore have a heightened need for independence on their boards. In this report, the Panel suggests that at least one-third of a charity's board members be independent.

Independent members of a governing body are generally those members with no financial or family connections to the organization. The recommendation of independent directors stems from the notion that a board of directors will be less conflicted, and more mindful of the organization's mission, if independent from the other members of the governing body and from the organization itself. Directors who are related through family and business relationships, or whose compensation is set by the other directors, may be less inclined to exercise independence in their decision making.

A member of the governing body is considered *independent* for Form 990 reporting purposes only if all three of these circumstances applied at all times during the organization's tax year:

1. The member was not compensated as an officer or other employee of the organization or of a related organization, except for the religious exception discussed in the next list.

2. The member did not receive total compensation or other payments exceeding $10,000 for the year from the organization or from related organizations as an independent contractor, other than reimbursement of expenses or reasonable compensation for services provided in the capacity as a member of the governing body. For example, a person who receives reasonable expense reimbursements and reasonable compensation as a director of the organization does not cease to be independent merely because he or she also receives payments of $7,500 from the organization for other arrangements.

3. Neither the member, nor any family member of the member, was involved in a transaction with the organization, directly or indirectly through affiliation with another organization, that is required to be reported on Schedule L for the organization's tax year or in a transaction with a related organization of a type and amount that would be reportable on Schedule L if required to be filed by the related organization.

A member of the governing body is not considered to lack independence merely because of any of the following circumstances:

- The member is a major donor to the organization, regardless of the amount of the contribution.

- The member has taken a bona fide vow of poverty and either (i) receives compensation as an agent of a religious order or of a religious and apostolic organization, but only under circumstances in which the individual does not receive taxable income or (ii) belongs to a religious order that receives sponsorship or payments from the organization that do not constitute taxable income to the member.

- The member receives financial benefits from the organization solely in the capacity of being a member of the charitable or other class served by the organization in the exercise of its exempt function, such as being a member of a trade association, so long as the financial benefits comply with the organization's terms of membership.

Example 1. B is a voting member of the organization's board of directors. B is also a partner with a profits and capital interest greater than 5% in a law firm, C, that charged $120,000 to the organization for legal services in a court case. The transaction between C and the organization must be reported on Schedule L because it is a transaction between the organization and an entity of which B is a more than 5%

owner, and because the payment from C to the organization exceeded $100,000. Accordingly, B is not an independent member of the governing body, because the $120,000 payment must be reported on Schedule L as an indirect business transaction with B. If B were an associate attorney (an employee) but not an officer, director, trustee, key employee, or owner of the law firm then the transaction would not affect B's status as an independent member of the organization's governing body.

Example 2. D is a voting member of both the organization's governing body and the governing body of C, a related organization. D's daughter, E, received $40,000 in taxable compensation as a part-time employee of C. D is not an independent member of the governing body, because E received compensation from C, a related organization to D, and the compensation was of a type (compensation to family member of a member of C's governing body) and amount (over $10,000) that would be reportable of Schedule L if the related organization, C, were required to file Schedule L

The filing organization need not engage in more than a reasonable effort to obtain the necessary information to determine the independence of members of the governing body and may rely on information provided by such members. For instance, the organization may rely on information it obtains in response to a questionnaire sent annually to each member of the governing body that includes the name, title, date, and signature of each person reporting information and contains the pertinent instructions and definitions to determine whether the member is or is not independent.

(e) Board Functions and Fiduciary Responsibility

The board of a tax-exempt organization is collectively responsible for developing and advancing the organization's mission; maintaining the organization's tax-exempt status and (if applicable) its ability to attract charitable contributions; protecting the organization's resources; formulating the organization's budget; hiring and evaluating the chief executive; generally overseeing the organization's management; and supporting and fundraising that the organization undertakes. According to the Panel on the Nonprofit Sector, a charitable organization must have a governing body "that is responsible for reviewing and approving the organization's mission and strategic direction, annual budget and key financial transactions, compensation practices and policies, and fiscal and governance policies." In addition, the board should "meet regularly enough to conduct its business and fulfill its duties" and "establish an effective, systematic process for educating and communicating with board members to ensure that they are aware of their legal and ethical responsibilities, are knowledgeable about the programs and activities of the organization, and can carry their oversight functions effectively."

Embodied in state law are fiduciary duties for members of the governing body of a nonprofit organization. Fiduciary duties arose out of the charitable law of trusts and impose on directors and trustees standards of conduct and management. One of the principal responsibilities of board members is to maintain financial accountability and effective oversight of the organization they serve. Board members are guardians of the organization's assets, and are expected to exercise due diligence to see that the organization is well managed and has a financial position that is as strong as is reasonable under the circumstances. Fiduciary duty requires board members of non-profit organizations to be objective, unselfish, responsible, honest, trustworthy, and efficient. Board members, as stewards of the organization, should always act for the organization's good and betterment rather than for their personal benefit. They should exercise reasonable care in their decision making and not place the organization under unnecessary risk.

The distinction as to legal liability between the board as a group and the board members as individuals relates to the responsibility of the board for the organization's affairs and the responsibility of individual board members for their actions personally. The board collectively is responsible and may be liable for what transpires within and what happens to the organization. As the ultimate authority, the board should ensure that the organization is operating in compliance with the law and its governing instruments. If legal action ensues, it is often traceable to an inattentive, passive, and/or captive board. Legislators and government regulators are becoming more aggressive in demanding higher levels of involvement by and accountability of board members of tax-exempt organizations; this is causing a dramatic shift in thinking about board functions, away from the concept of mere oversight and toward the precept that board members should be far more involved in policy-setting and review, employee supervision, and overall management of the organization. Consequently, many boards of exempt organizations are becoming more vigilant and active in implementing and maintaining sound policies and procedures.

In turn, the board's shared legal responsibilities depend on the actions of individuals. Each board member is liable for his or her acts (commissions and omissions), including those that may be civil law or even criminal law offenses. In practice, this requires board members to hold each other accountable for deeds that prove harmful to the organization.

(f) Duties of Directors

The duties of the board of directors of a tax-exempt organization essentially are the duty of care, the duty of loyalty, and the duty of obedience. Defined by case law, these are the legal standards against which all actions taken or not taken by directors are measured. They are collective duties adhering to the entire board; the mandate is active participation by all of the board members. Accountability can be demonstrated by showing the effective discharge of these three duties.

(1) Duty of Care. The duty of care requires directors of a tax-exempt organization to be reasonably informed about the organization's activities, participate in decision making, and act in good faith and with the care of an ordinarily prudent person in comparable circumstances. In short, the duty of care requires the board—and its members individually—to pay attention to the organization's activities and operations.

The duty of care is satisfied by attendance at meetings of the board and appropriate committees; advance preparation for board meetings, such as reviewing reports and the agenda prior to meetings of the board; obtaining information, before voting, to make appropriate decisions; use of independent judgment; periodic examination of the credentials and performance of those who serve the organization; frequent review of the organization's finances and financial policies; and compliance with filing requirements, particularly annual information returns.

(2) Duty of Loyalty.   The duty of loyalty requires board members to exercise their power in the interest of the tax-exempt organization and not in their personal interest or the interest of another entity, particularly one with which they have a formal relationship. When acting on behalf of the exempt organization, board members are expected to place the interests of the organization before their personal and professional interests.

The duty of loyalty is satisfied when board members disclose any conflicts of interest; otherwise adhere to the organization's conflict-of-interest policy; avoid the use of corporate opportunities for the individual's personal gain or other benefit; and do not disclose confidential information concerning the information.

Conflicts of interest are not inherently illegal. Indeed, they can be common because board members often are simultaneously affiliated with several entities, both for-profit and nonprofit. The important factor is the process by which the board handles these conflicts. A conflict-of-interest policy (see § 5.1(i)(1)) can help protect the organization and its board members by establishing a procedure for disclosure and voting when situations arise where a board member may potentially derive personal or potential benefit from the organization's activities.

(3) Duty of Obedience.   The duty of obedience requires that directors of a tax-exempt organization comply with applicable federal, state, and local laws; adhere to the organization's governing documents; and remain guardians of the organization's mission. The duty of obedience is complied with when the board endeavors to be certain that the organization is in compliance with applicable regulatory requirements, complies with and periodically reviews all documents governing the operations of the organization, and makes decisions in advancement of the organization's mission and within the scope of the entity's governing documents.

(g)   National Developments in Nonprofit Governance

In recent years, Congress, the IRS, and other groups have been attempting to exercise more influence and control over the governance of tax-exempt organizations, especially charities. For example, in early 2007, the IRS published a draft of its "Good Governance Practices for 501(c)(3) Organizations," which was later replaced with the IRS Life Cycle Governance Document (see § 5.1(g)(2)). Other groups and organizations, such as the Panel on the Nonprofit Sector, have published similar guidelines.

At this time, however, there is little federal law applicable to the governance of tax-exempt organizations. Although a few provisions of the Sarbanes-Oxley Act apply to nonprofit organizations, Congress has not yet enacted laws that affect the governance, oversight, and management of nonprofit organizations to any significant degree. This is still a matter that is impacted principally by state law. As a result of the redesigned Form 990, however, the IRS is attempting to conform the governance practices of tax-exempt organizations, by virtue of the questions posed on the Form 990 and the anticipated reluctance by nonprofit organizations to repeatedly answer these questions "no."

(1) Sarbanes-Oxley Act.   The Sarbanes-Oxley Act was enacted in 2002. The act is principally focused on publicly traded companies and large accounting firms, and imposes many standards and requirements on these entities.

Two provisions of the Sarbanes-Oxley Act are applicable to all organizations, including tax-exempt organizations. These are the provisions of the act regarding protection of whistleblowers and the criminal law concerning the destruction of documents with the intent to impede, obstruct, or influence a federal investigation or matter. As a result, all exempt organizations are advised to have a whistleblower policy and a document retention and destruction policy. Other than these two noted exceptions, Sarbanes-Oxley does not apply to exempt organizations. Even so, many nonprofit organizations are choosing to voluntarily adopt some of the act's provisions, even if not specifically applicable to tax-exempt organizations. In addition, many of the Sarbanes-Oxley principles have worked their way into good governance guidelines for nonprofit organizations issued by various organizations and agencies, as discussed below. These principles include rotating auditing firms, separating auditing and accounting functions, and establishing audit and compensation committees.

(2) Best Practices Guidance by the IRS and Other Organizations. Many groups, in recent years, have drafted their own versions of "best practices" guidelines for nonprofit organizations. One such organization is the BBB (Better Business Bureau) Wise Giving Alliance, which developed its "Standards for Charity Accountability" to assist donors with making "sound giving decisions and to foster public confidence in charitable organizations." These Standards for Charity Accountability include having at least five board members, having no more than the greater of one or 10 percent of the board members be compensated, engaging in no transaction in which board or staff members have material conflicting interests with the charity as a result of any relationship or business affiliation, spending at least 65 percent of total expenditures on program activities, spending no more than 35 percent of related contributions on fundraising, and avoiding the accumulation of funds that could be used for program activities.

The Panel on the Nonprofit Sector, convened by the Independent Sector at the encouragement of the Senate Finance Committee, has issued many reports and publications since its creation in 2004. The Panel issued its first report to Congress in 2004 and issued a final report in 2005. The reports contained many recommendations to amend federal law applicable to tax-exempt organizations. Some, but not all, of these recommendations were enacted into law through the Pension Protection Act of 2006, such as changes in the laws regarding supporting organizations and donor-advised funds. Many of the Panel's recommendations for disclosure on the Form 990 were incorporated into the redesigned Form 990, such as disclosure of independent governing body members and of whether an organization has a conflicts-of-interest policy.

More recently, the Panel published "Principles for Good Governance and Ethical Practice," setting forth 33 principles to advance the state of governance and self-regulations. According to the Panel, the principles "should be considered by every charitable organization as a guide for strengthening its effectiveness and accountability." The 33 principles are divided into four main categories: legal compliance and public disclosure, effective governance, strong financial oversight, and responsible fundraising. Among the effective governance principles are recommendations that a board of directors have no less than five members (except for very small organizations), that two-thirds of the board be independent, and that organizations with paid staff ensure that the positions of chief staff officer, board chair, and board treasurer are held by separate individuals.

The Independent Sector also published a Checklist for Accountability to serve as a self-examination for charitable organizations. The Checklist for Accountability, among its many recommendations, encourages charitable organizations to develop a culture of accountability and transparency, adopt a statement of values and a code of ethics, adopt conflicts-of-interest and whistleblower policies, conduct financial reviews and audits, and remain current with the law. Although the checklist is directed at charitable organizations, it can provide guidance to all types of nonprofit organizations.

In early 2007, the IRS posted a preliminary discussion draft of the agency's "Good Governance Practices" for charitable organizations. In February 2008, the IRS replaced its draft document with a new educational governance document in its "Life Cycle" educational tool for public charities entitled "Governance and Related Topics—501(c)(3) Organizations," (referred to herein as the IRS Life Cycle Governance Document), which can be found on the IRS's Web site at www.irs.gov/pub/irs-tege/governance_practices.pdf. The IRS states that its current positions on nonprofit governance are best reflected in reporting requirements of the new Form 990 and in the IRS Life Cycle Governance Document posted on its Web site. In this latter document, the IRS expresses its view that governing boards of charitable organizations "should be composed of persons who are informed and active in overseeing a charity's operations and finances." If a governing board "tolerates a climate of secrecy or neglect, [the IRS is] concerned that charitable assets are more likely to be diverted to benefit the private interests of insiders at the expense of public and charitable interests." According to the IRS, successful governing boards "include individuals who not only are knowledgeable and engaged, but selected with the organization's needs in mind (e.g., accounting, finance, compensation and ethics)." In the IRS Life Cycle Governance Document, the IRS focuses on six areas: mission, organizational documents, governing body, governance and management policies, financial statements and Form 990 reporting, and transparency and accounting. The IRS states that although the Internal Revenue Code does not require charities to have governance and management policies, the IRS will review an organization's exemption application and Form 990 to determine whether the organization "has implemented policies relating to executive compensation, conflicts of interest, investments, fundraising, documenting governance decisions, document retention and destruction, and whistleblower claims."

Many in the nonprofit community are questioning the IRS's authority to regulate the manner in which nonprofit organizations are governed. Most believe the IRS is effectively trying to make law by virtue of the questions it asks on the new Form 990 and through the exempt organization application process. The IRS, however, has stated that it has no intentions of backing away from the issue of nonprofit governance and will continue to "educate, engage, and indeed irritate" in the area of nonprofit governance.

(3) American Red Cross Modernization Act of 2007. Another development of which all nonprofit organizations should take note is Congress's passing of the American Red Cross Modernization Act of 2007. The purpose of the act was to amend the congressional charter of the American Red Cross to modernize its structure and enhance the ability of the board of governors to support the mission of the Red Cross. The act was passed after an investigation into the American Red Cross following Hurricane Katrina, which brought to light an unwieldy, arguably ineffective 50-person board structure and a need for governance changes. Although the American Red Cross operates in corporate form, it is a congressionally chartered organization that must have Congress approve changes to its charter.

The main functions of the act were to reduce the board size of the Red Cross, cause the board members to have staggered terms, impose term limits on board members, authorize an executive committee, establish an advisory committee, and disallow proxy voting by directors. In addition, the act outlines the board's responsibilities, which can serve as a checklist for all nonprofit boards:

- Reviewing and approving the mission statement for the American National Red Cross
- Approving and overseeing the corporation's strategic plan and maintaining strategic oversight of operational matters
- Selecting, evaluation, and determining the level of compensation of the corporation's chief executive officer
- Evaluating the performance and establishing the compensation of the senior leadership team and providing for management succession
- Overseeing the financial reporting and audit process, internal controls, and legal compliance
- Holding management accountable for performance
- Providing oversight of the financial stability of the corporation
- Ensuring the inclusiveness and diversity of the corporation
- Ensuring the chapters of the Red Cross are geographically and regionally diverse
- Providing oversight of the projection of the brand of the corporation
- Assisting with fundraising on behalf of the corporation

(h) State Acts on Charitable Accountability

Certain states have enacted laws regarding the accountability of nonprofit organizations. Most of these provisions involve the requirement of audited financial statements for nonprofit organizations with revenues in excess of a certain threshold. Many states require charitable organizations to file audited financial statements as part of the charitable solicitation registration process.

The state of California has the most extensive set of rules concerning governance and accountability of nonprofit organizations, mainly due to the state's enactment of the Nonprofit Integrity Act in 2004. Among other provisions, the California statutes requires charitable corporations with gross revenues of at least $2 million, and which are required to register and file reports with the state's attorney general, to establish and maintain an audit committee. The audit committee members must be independent, meaning they cannot be members of the organization's staff or receive any compensation from the charity aside from compensation for services as a director and cannot have a material financial interest in any entity doing business with the corporation. The audit committee must be separate from the finance committee. The chair of the finance committee cannot serve on the audit committee, and finance committee members must constitute less than one-half of the members of the audit committee.

The statute requires that executive compensation must be reviewed and approved by a nonprofit organization's governing body or an authorized committee. Educational organizations, hospitals, and religious organizations are specifically exempted from these statutes.

(i) Corporate Policies

With a few noted exceptions, a nonprofit entity is not legally required to have corporate policies. In fact, the IRS states this on the new Form 990. However, the prevailing view by the IRS and watchdog organizations in the nonprofit community is that a well-governed nonprofit organization is more effective and more compliant, and that policies and procedures are an indication of a well-governed entity. As a result, tax-exempt organizations should consider implementing policies that are applicable and relevant to their organization both as a matter of good governance and to demonstrate that they are effectively governed in the event of an audit or investigation.

A discussion of policies mentioned in Part VI of the Form 990 follows. Other parts and schedules of the Form 990 request information on additional policies, and those policies are discussed in the relevant sections. Note that the IRS discusses four policies in the IRS Life Cycle Governance Document that are not specifically mentioned in the Form 990: an executive compensation policy, an investment policy, a fundraising policy, and a code of ethics.

(1) Conflicts-of-Interest Policy. A conflicts-of-interest policy is recommended for all nonprofit organizations, even though a nonprofit organization is generally not required to have such a policy. The IRS Form 1023, Application for Recognition of Exemption, requests a copy of an organization's conflicts-of-interest policy, and the redesigned Form 990 asks whether an organization has one. The law applicable to nonprofit organizations in many states has certain conflicts-of-interest provisions with which an organization's policy should comply.

According to the "Principles for Good Governance and Ethical Practices" published by the Panel on the Nonprofit Sector, a conflicts-of-interest policy should require full disclosure of all potential conflicts of interest within an organization and should apply to every person who has the ability to influence decisions of the organization, including board members, staff, and persons related to them. The IRS, in its IRS Life Cycle Governance Document, "encourages a charity's board to adopt and regularly evaluate a written conflict of interest policy that requires directors and staff to act solely in the interest of the charity without regard for personal interest; includes written procedures for determining whether a relationship, financial interest, or business affiliation results in a conflict of interest; and prescribes a course of action in the event a conflict of interest is identified." A conflicts-of-interest policy should also contain a requirement that decisions made regarding conflicts of interest should be documented in writing. A sample conflict of interest policy can be found in the instructions to IRS Form 1023.

For purposes of Form 990 reporting, a *conflict-of-interest policy* defines conflicts of interest, identifies the classes of individuals within the organization covered by the policy, facilitates disclosure of information that may help identify conflicts of interest, and specifies procedures to be followed in managing conflicts of interest. A *conflict of interest* arises when a person in a position of authority over an organization, such as an officer, director, or manager, may benefit financially from a decision he or she could make in such capacity, including indirect benefits such as to family members or businesses with which the person is closely associated. For this purpose, a conflict of interest does not include questions involving a person's competing or respective duties to the organization and to another organization, such as by serving on the board of directors of both organizations, that do not involve a material financial interest of, or benefit to, such person.

Disclosure of conflicts of interest, actual or potential, is necessary for board members to carry out their fiduciary duty of loyalty to an organization. An important element of a conflicts-of-interest policy is an annual disclosure statement signed by each board member, officer and key employee, disclosing all relationships, family and business, that could give rise to a conflict. The IRS, in the IRS Life Cycle Governance Document, encourages organizations to require the individuals covered by the conflicts-of-interest policy to make periodic, written disclosures of any known financial interest that the individual, or member of the individual's family, has in entities transacting business with the nonprofit. These statements should be periodically reviewed by the organization to determine instances of potential conflicts.

Conflicts of interest are not inherently illegal or unethical, but they must be handled appropriately. The person with the actual or potential conflict of interest should disclose the conflict and then recuse himself or herself from further participation in any decision making involving the conflict. Nonprofit organizations should maintain records, such as minutes from meetings, documenting any noted conflicts and the method in which the conflict was handled.

(2) Whistleblower and Document Retention and Destruction Policies. As discussed, the whistleblower and document destruction provisions of Sarbanes-Oxley are applicable to all organizations, not only publicly traded entities. Consequently, all nonprofit organizations are advised to have a whistleblower policy and a document retention and destruction policy. The IRS recommends adopting these policies in the IRS Life Cycle Governance Document.

A *whistleblower policy* encourages staff and volunteers to come forward with credible information on illegal practices or violations of adopted policies of the organization, specifies that the organization will protect the individual from retaliation, and identifies those staff or board members or outside parties to whom such information can be reported. A whistleblower policy typically covers suspected incidents of theft or misappropriation, financial information that is intentionally misleading, improper or undocumented financial transactions, improper use of assets, and violations of the organization's conflicts-of-interest policy. A *document retention and destruction policy* identifies the record retention responsibilities of staff, volunteers, board members, and outsiders for maintaining and documenting the storage and destruction of the organization's documents and records. The policy should address the length of time specific types of documents must be retained as well as when it is permissible or required to destroy certain types of documents. The policy should contain specific procedures to ensure that document destruction is halted immediately if any official investigation of the organization is under way or anticipated.

(3) Policy Regarding Participation in Joint Venture Arrangements.   Nonprofit organizations are increasingly participating in joint venture arrangements with other nonprofit, and sometimes for-profit, entities. Sometimes these joint ventures are organized as separate legal entities (typically as partnerships or limited liability companies taxed as partnerships), or less formally as joint ventures. For Form 990 filing purposes, the IRS refers to all these arrangements as joint ventures.

Typically, a joint venture with a nonprofit entity that has the same tax-exempt status does not pose a concern with an organization's own exempt status, as both parties will need to operate the joint venture in a manner that protects each member's tax-exempt status. With a joint venture between a tax-exempt organization and a for-profit entity or an individual, both parties will not necessarily be concerned with operating the joint venture in furtherance of tax-exempt purposes. If not structured carefully, these arrangements can jeopardize an organization's tax-exempt status or, less severely, result in unrelated business income to the nonprofit organization. Recent decisions and rulings in this area provide that a nonprofit organization can protect its tax-exempt status by maintaining a controlling position in the joint venture and taking steps to ensure that the joint venture will be conducted solely in furtherance of the nonprofit organization's exempt purposes. For a discussion on joint ventures and revenue sharing, see § 21.1(f).

The Form 990 requests information on whether a tax-exempt organization is participating in a joint venture and, if so, has it adopted a written policy or procedure requiring the organization to evaluate its participation in joint venture arrangements under applicable federal tax law and taken steps to safeguard the organization's exempt status with respect to such arrangement. Some examples of safeguards include control over the venture or arrangement sufficient to ensure that the venture furthers the exempt purposes of the organization; a requirement that the venture or arrangement give priority to exempt purposes over maximizing profits for the other participants; a requirement that it not engage in activities that would jeopardize the organization's exemption; and a requirement that all contracts entered into with the organization be on terms that are arm's length or more favorable to the organization.

A *joint venture* or similar arrangement means any joint ownership or contractual arrangement through which there is an agreement to jointly undertake a specific business enterprise, investment, or exempt purpose activity without regard to (1) whether the organization controls the venture or arrangement, (2) the legal structure of the venture or arrangement, or (3) whether the venture or arrangement is taxed as a partnership or as an association or corporation for federal income tax purposes. Certain joint ventures entered into principally for investment purposes are disregarded. More specifically, organizations may disregard joint ventures or arrangements that meet both of these conditions:

1. 95 percent or more of the venture's or arrangement's income for its tax year ending with or within the organization's tax year is passive income excludable from the unrelated business income tax as certain types of income (including unrelated debt-financed income); and

2. The primary purpose of the organization's contribution to, or investment or participation in, the venture or arrangement is the production of income or appreciation of property.

(4) Policy Regarding Branches, Chapters, and Affiliates/Group Exemptions. Some tax-exempt organizations are organized in a manner where there is a national or regional organization, with local chapters or affiliates. In some instances, the local organizations are legally part of the national or regional organization; in other instances, the local organizations are separate, legal entities. In the former case, the national organization is liable for the acts of the local organizations, because they are all part of the same legal entity. For this reason, exempt organizations often encourage chapters and affiliates to be organized as separate entities.

Certain organizations, such as a chapter or affiliate of a larger exempt organization, may be tax-exempt solely on the basis that they are affiliated with and subject to the general supervision or control of a central organization (typically a state, regional, or national organization). A central organization can file for a *group exemption* for all the affiliates or chapters (called *subordinate organizations*). With a group exemption, the subordinate organizations are recognized as exempt organizations without each having to file a separate application for recognition of exemption.

A central, or parent, organization must seek a group exemption letter on behalf of its subordinates. The central organization must first obtain its own recognition of exemption before filing for a group exemption for its subordinates. As part of the group exemption filing, the central organization must establish that all subordinates to be included in the group are affiliated with the central organization and subject to its general supervision or control, have the same tax-exempt status (although not necessarily the same tax-exempt status as the central organization), and not private foundations or foreign organizations. In addition, all subordinates must be on the same accounting period as the central organization if they will be included in a group information return and must be formed within the requisite time period prior to the date of submission of the group exemption application, otherwise the exemption will not relate back to the formation date of the subordinates. Each subordinate must authorize, in writing, the central organization to include it in the group exemption application.

Once the group exemption letter is issued, the parent organization must make an annual filing with the IRS listing its qualifying tax-exempt subordinate organizations and providing certain information relating to them. Because the central organization is attesting to the qualification of the subordinate organizations, it is important that the central organization conduct an evaluation of its subordinates. The central organization can make additions to and deletions from the group from year to year.

Regardless of whether the chapters or affiliates are organized as separate entities, a tax-exempt entity with branches, chapters, or affiliates should have some standardization and consistency regarding the branches, chapters, and affiliates, given their common mission and goals as well as the public perception that the organizations are all part of one entity, despite what may otherwise be legally true. In addition, a tax-exempt organization that is a central organization in a group exemption must ensure that its chapters and affiliates are generally subject to its control and do not engage in activities that jeopardize their tax-exempt status. The Form 990 asks a filing organization whether it has written policies and procedures governing the activities of chapters, branches, and affiliates to ensure their consistency with activities of the organization; such documents are used by the organization and its local units to address the policies, practices, and activities of the local unit. These policies and procedures may include required provisions in the chapter's articles of organization or bylaws, a manual provided to chapters, a constitution, or similar documents.

Organizations with affiliates may also wish to address standards of conduct, permissible activities, and approved use of the national or parent organization's name in the policy.

The central organization of a group can file a Form 990 on behalf of the entire group. In addition, it can file a Form 990 for only some of the subordinates in the group, but it must attach a statement to the Form 990 designating the subordinates for which the return is being filed. The central organization must file a separate Form 990; it cannot include itself on the group return.

(j)   Document Disclosure Rules

One of the nonprofit buzzwords of the day is *transparency*. Most good governance guidelines have, as one of their tenets, a principle that a nonprofit organization should make information regarding the entity widely known and available to the public, including information about its mission, activities, finances, board, and staff. Some of these matters are already part of the law applicable to tax-exempt organizations. Others represent opinions on good governance, but are not legal requirements.

Generally, a tax-exempt organization must make its IRS application for recognition of exemption (including documents submitted in support of the application and any letter or other document issued by the IRS regarding the application) and its three most recent annual information returns (Form 990) available for public inspection. Exempt organizations other than private foundations and political entities are not required to disclose the names and addresses of their donors, and may redact this information prior to providing copies or otherwise making information returns available. Beginning with tax returns filed after August 17, 2006, public charities are required to make their Forms 990-T available for public inspection. The IRS has also established a procedure for requesting copies of these documents and returns from the IRS using IRS Form 4506-A, Request for Public Inspection or Copy of Exempt or Political Organization IRS Form.

Documents required to be disclosed must be made available for inspection at the organization's principal office and certain regional and/or district offices during regular business hours, and organizations are required to provide copies of these documents to those who request them, either in person or in writing. Copies must be provided without charge, other than a reasonable fee for reproduction and mailing costs.

A tax-exempt organization is not required to comply with the requests for copies of its application for recognition of exemption or annual information returns if the organization has made the document widely available. For this purpose, making the documents widely available is satisfied if an organization posts the documents on a web page that the organization establishes and maintains, or if the documents are posted as part of a database of similar documents by other exempt organizations on a web page established or maintained by another entity, provided certain other criteria are met. The rules for public inspection of the documents will continue to apply, even if the organization makes the documents widely available to satisfy the requirements regarding copies.

If the IRS determines that a tax-exempt organization is the subject of a harassment campaign and that compliance with the requests would not be in the public interest, the tax-exempt organization does not have to fulfill a request for a copy that it reasonably believes is part of the campaign. The document disclosure rules apply to the notice that must be filed by political organizations to establish their tax-exempt status and to the reports they must file.

In the IRS Life Cycle Governance Document, the IRS encourages all charities to adopt and monitor procedures to ensure that its Form 1023, Form 990, Form 990-T, annual reports, and financial statements are complete and accurate, that these documents are posted on their Web sites and are made available to the public upon request. In addition, the Panel on the Nonprofit Sector, in its "Principles for Good Governance and Ethical Practice," recommends that all charities publish an annual report and post copies of the charity's annual report, Forms 990, and financial statements on the organization's Web site. The BBB Wise Giving Alliance's "Standards for Charity Accountability" include standards that an organization makes available to all, on request, complete annual financial statements and an annual report. Even though the IRS and others make these comments, at this time, there is no legal requirement that a tax-exempt organization produce its annual report and financial statements to the public. Appendix D to the Form 990 instructions contains a detailed description of the document disclosure requirements for tax-exempt organizations.

(k) Reporting Material Changes to the IRS

An organization's tax-exempt status remains in effect as long as the organization does not materially change its character, purposes, or methods of operation. A tax-exempt entity should report material changes in its character, purposes, or methods of operation to the IRS as soon as possible after the change is made or becomes effective. Other changes that are not material, but that are not insubstantial, should be reported to the IRS on the organization's Form 990.

While there is no automatic IRS sanction for failure to report a material change, a tax-exempt organization may not rely on a determination letter or ruling recognizing its exempt status if there has been a material change in the organization's character, purposes, or methods of operation.

If an organization changes its form, the IRS generally regards this change as the creation of a new legal entity. This includes the conversion of a trust to a corporation, the incorporation of an unincorporated association, and the reincorporation of a non-profit corporation in another jurisdiction. In these instances, the organization should file a new application for recognition of exemption with the IRS.

The IRS, in the Form 990 instructions, provides these examples of significant changes to the organizing or enabling document or bylaws, such as changes in the:

- Number, composition, qualifications, authority, or duties of the governing body's voting members
- Number, composition, qualifications, authority, or duties of the organization's officers or key employees
- Role of the stockholders or membership in governance
- Distribution of assets upon dissolution
- Provisions to amend the organizing or enabling document or bylaws
- Quorum, voting rights, or voting approval requirements of the governing body members or the organization's stockholders or membership

- Organization's exempt purposes or mission

- Policies or procedures contained within the organizing document or bylaws regarding compensation of officers, directors, trustees, or key employees, conflicts of interest, whistleblowers, or document retention and destruction

- Composition or procedures contained within the organizing document or bylaws of an audit committee

A change to a policy that is not contained within the entity's organizing document or bylaws does not need to be reported. Insignificant changes made to organizing or enabling documents or bylaws, such as changes to the organization's registered agent with the state or the required or permitted number or frequency of governing body or member meetings, are not required to be reported. Organizations are instructed not to report changes to policies described or established outside of the organizing or enabling document and bylaws, such as the adoption of, or change to, a policy adopted by resolution of the governing body that does not entail a change to the organizing document or bylaws. For example, if an organization revises its written conflicts-of-interest policy by board resolution and the policy is not within the organization's articles of incorporation or bylaws, then the change does not need to be reported on the Form 990.

(l) Filing a Copy of the Form 990 with State Authorities

Federal income tax law requires private foundations, but not public charities and other tax-exempt organizations, to file a copy of their information return with the state attorneys general. In the case of a private foundation, the organization must file a copy of its federal information return with the attorney general of the state in which the foundation's principal office is located, the state in which the foundation was incorporated or created, and certain other states. Even though the IRS does not require tax-exempt organizations other than private foundations to file their information returns with state officials, some states require tax-exempt organizations to make such filings for other purposes, such as state charitable solicitation registration.

§5.2 PREPARATION OF NEW FORM 990, PART VI

Part VI is designed to solicit information on a tax-exempt organization's governance structure, management, corporate policies, and disclosure practices. Generally, organizations are instructed not to take into consideration joint ventures and partnerships in responding to Part VI, other than for line 16, which specifically requests information on joint ventures. With respect to disregarded entities, Appendix F to the Form 990 instructions states that members of the governing body, officer, directors, trustees, and employees of a disregarded entity are not treated as governing body members, officers, directors, or trustees of the filing organization, but such persons may constitute key employees or highest-compensated employees of the filing organization by virtue of compensation paid by the disregarded entity, or the persons' responsibilities and authority over operations of the disregarded entity when compared to the filing organization as a whole.

Part VI is divided into three sections, as set forth next.

(a) Section A (Governing Body and Management)

Section A is designed to solicit information regarding a tax-exempt organization's governing structure, composition of its governing body, and governing body procedures.

(1) Line 1 (Voting Members of the Governing Body). Line 1 is designed to determine the size of the organization's governing body (i.e., its board of directors or trustees) that is entitled to vote and the number of members of the governing body that are independent. Line 1(a) asks the organization to enter the number of voting members of its governing body, as of the end of the year. *Voting members* are members with the power to vote on all matters that may come before the governing body (other than when a conflict of interest disqualifies the member from voting). If the members of the governing body do not all have the same voting rights, the organization is instructed to explain material differences in voting rights on Schedule O. Line 1(b) asks the organization to enter the number of voting members that are independent, as of the end of the year.

If the organization's governing body delegated authority to act on its behalf to an executive committee or similar committee with broad authority to act on behalf of the governing body, and the committee held such authority at any time during the organization's tax year, describe in Schedule O the composition of the committee, whether any of the committee's members are not on the governing body, and the scope of the committee's authority. (Note: An organization should review the laws of its state of organization to determine allowable delegation in this regard, especially regarding delegation to nonboard members.) The organization does not have to describe in Schedule O delegations of authority that are limited in scope to particular areas or matters, such as delegations to an audit committee, investment committee, or compensation committee of the governing body.

(2) Line 2 (Family and Business Relationships). This question asks whether any officer, director, trustee, or key employee has a family relationship or a business relationship with any other officer, director, trustee, or key employee.

This question is designed to identify relationships (sometimes called "horizontal relationships") that could create a bias in the decision-making process. Answer "yes" if any of the listed persons had a family or business relationship with another listed person at any time during the organization's tax year. For each family and business relationship, the reporting organization must identify the persons and describe their relationship in Schedule O. It is sufficient for the organization to state "family relationship" or "business relationship" without greater detail.

The family of an individual includes only his or her spouse, ancestors, brothers and sisters (whether whole or half blood), children (whether natural or adopted), grandchildren, and spouses of brothers, sisters, children, and grandchildren. Business relationships between two persons include any of these relationships:

1. One person is employed by the other in a sole proprietorship or by an organization with which the other is associated as a trustee, director, officer, key employee, or greater-than-35-percent owner.

2. One person is transacting business with the other (other than in the ordinary course of either party's business on the same terms as are generally offered to the public), directly or indirectly, in one or more contracts of sale, lease, license, loan, performance of services, or other transaction involving transfers of cash or property valued in excess of $10,000 in the aggregate during the tax year. Indirect transactions are transactions with an organization with which the one person is associated as a trustee, director, officer, key employee, or greater-than-35-percent owner.

3. The two persons are each a director, trustee, officer, or greater than 10-percent owner in the same business or investment entity.

Ownership is measured by stock ownership (either voting power or value) of a corporation, profits or capital interest in a partnership or limited liability company, membership interest in a nonprofit organization, or beneficial interest in a trust. Ownership includes indirect ownership (e.g., ownership in an entity that has ownership in the entity in question); there may be ownership through multiple tiers of entities.

The IRS, in the Form 990 instructions, provides an exception to the definition of a business relationship for three privileged relationships: attorney and client, medical professional (including psychologist) and patient, and priest/clergy and penitent/communicant. If the business relationship between two persons is solely based on a privileged relationship, the two individuals do not have a business relationship for purposes of line 2.

The final Form 990 instructions added five examples of a business relationship:

> **Example 1.** B is an officer of the organization, and C is a member of the organization's governing body. B is C's brother-in-law. The organization must report that B and C have a family relationship.

> **Example 2.** D and E are officers of the organization. D is also a partner in an accounting firm with 300 partners (with a 1/300th interest in the firm's profits and capital) but is not an officer, director, trustee, or key employee of the accounting firm. D's accounting firm provides services to E in the ordinary course of the accounting firm's business, on terms generally offered to the public, and receives $100,000 in fees during the year. The relationship between D and E is not a reportable business relationship, either because (1) it is in the ordinary course of business on terms generally offered to the public, or (2) D does not hold a greater-than-35-percent interest in the accounting firm's profits or capital.

> **Example 3.** F and G are trustees of the organization. F is the owner and CEO of an automobile dealership. G purchased a $45,000 car from the dealership during the organization's tax year in the ordinary course of the dealership's business, on terms generally offered to the public. The relationship between F and G is not a reportable business relationship, because the transaction was in the ordinary course of business on terms generally offered to the public.

> **Example 4.** H and J are members of the organization's board of directors. Both are CEOs of publicly traded corporations and serve on each other's boards. The relationship between H and J is a reportable business relationship, because each is a director or officer in the same business entity.

Example 5. K is a key employee of the organization, and L is on its board of directors. L is a greater-than-35-percent partner of a law firm that charged $60,000 during the organization's tax year for legal services provided to K that were worth $600,000 at the law firm's ordinary rates (thus, the ordinary course of business exception does not apply). However, the relationship between K and L is not a reportable business relationship, because of the privileged relationship of attorney and client.

The organization is not required to provide information about a family or business relationship between two officers, directors, trustees, or key employees if it is unable to secure the information after making a reasonable effort to obtain it. An example of a reasonable effort is for the organization to distribute a questionnaire annually to each such person that includes the name, title, date, and signature of each person reporting information and contains the pertinent instructions and definitions regarding line 2 reporting. This questionnaire can be part of the annual disclosure statement used to determine actual or potential conflicts of interest under an organization's conflicts-of interest policy. (See § 5.1(i)(1).)

(3) Line 3 (Delegation to a Management Company).   This question asks whether the organization delegated control over management duties customarily performed by or under the direct supervision of officers, directors or trustees, or key employees to a management company or other person. It is designed to determine the extent to which a tax-exempt organization has outsourced its management functions and the extent to which it may have ceded control of the organization to others (see discussion of private benefit at § 6.1(b)). Management duties include, but are not limited to, hiring, firing, and supervising personnel, planning or executing budgets or financial operations, or supervising exempt operations or unrelated trades or businesses of the organization. Management duties do not include administrative services, such as payroll processing, that do not involve significant managerial decision making. In addition, management duties do not include investment management unless the filing organization conducts investment management services for others.

(4) Line 4 (Significant Changes to Organizational Documents).   This question requests information on whether the organization made any significant changes to its organizational documents since the prior Form 990 was filed or that were not reported on a prior Form 990. See § 5.1(k) for examples of significant changes reportable on the Form 990. Tax-exempt organizations are instructed to describe its significant changes in Schedule O but not to attach a copy of the amendments or amended document (or recite the entire amended document verbatim), unless such amended documents reflect a change in the organization's name.

If the Form 990 is being filed on behalf of a group under a group exemption, the Form 990 instructions state that the group should report changes only to standardized organizational documents maintained by the central organization that subordinates are required to adopt.

(5) Line 5 (Material Diversion of Assets).   This question asks if the organization became aware during the year of a material diversion of the organization's assets. A *diversion of assets* includes any unauthorized conversion or use of the organization's assets other than for the organization's authorized purposes, which includes embezzlement or theft. An organization should report diversions by the organization's officers, directors, trustees, employees, volunteers, independent contractors, grantees (diverting grant funds), or any other person, even if not associated with the organization other than by the diversion. A diversion of assets does not include an authorized transfer of assets for fair market value consideration, such as to a joint venture or for-profit subsidiary in exchange for an interest in the joint venture or subsidiary. For this purpose, a diversion is considered material if the gross dollar amount (not taking into account restitution, insurance, or similar recoveries) exceeds the lesser of $250,000 or 5 percent of the lesser of organization's gross receipts for its tax year or total assets as of the end of its tax year. This threshold should be sufficiently high to exclude more minor infringements, such as smaller misappropriations and expense account abuse.

If the organization answers "yes" to line 5, the organization must explain the nature of the diversion, amounts or property involved, corrective actions taken to address the matter, and pertinent circumstances surrounding the diversion on Schedule O. The person or persons who diverted the assets should not be identified by name. According to the IRS, this question was added to the Form 990 to give organizations that became aware of a material diversion an opportunity to explain the circumstances regarding the diversion and any corrective actions taken to address the matter. A diversion of assets may constitute an excess benefit transaction reportable on Schedule L. See §18.1(a).

(6) Lines 6–7 (Members and Stockholders). Line 6 asks if the organization has members or stockholders. In answering the question, an organization does not have to indicate which it has (members or stockholders) but merely that it has one or the other. An organization should respond in the affirmative to line 6 if the organization is organized as a stock corporation, a joint-stock company, a partnership, a joint venture, or a limited liability company. An organization should also respond "yes" if the organization is organized as a nonstock, nonprofit, or not-for-profit corporation or association with members. *Member* means (without regard to what a person is called in the governing documents) any person who, pursuant to a provision of the organization's governing documents or applicable state law, has the right to participate in the organization's governance, or to receive distributions of income or assets from the organization. For example, an organization is a membership organization if it has members with the right to (1) elect the members of the governing body (but not if the persons on the governing body are the organization's only members) or their delegates, (2) approve significant decisions of the governing body, or (3) receive a share of the organization's profits, excess dues, or net assets upon the organization's dissolution. An organization should answer "no" if it is a trust for federal tax purposes. In Schedule O, the organization must describe the classes of its members or stockholders.

The first part of line 7 asks whether the organization has members, stockholders, or other persons who may elect one or more members of the governing body. An organization should answer line 7a "yes" if there are one or more persons (other than the organization's governing body itself, acting in such capacity) that have the right to elect or appoint one or more members of the organization's governing body, whether periodically, as vacancies arise, or otherwise. If line 7a is answered "yes," the organization should describe in Schedule O the class or classes of such persons and the nature of their rights. The second part of the question (line 7b) asks if any decisions of the governing body are subject to approval by members, stockholders, or other person. An organization should answer "yes" to line 7b if there are one or more persons (whether members, stockholders, or otherwise) who have the right to approve or ratify decisions of the governing body, such as approval of the governing body's election or removal of members of the governing body, or approval of the governing body's decision to dissolve the organization. If line 7b is answered "yes," the organization must describe in Schedule O the class or classes of such persons, the decisions that require their approval, and the nature of their voting rights.

(7) Line 8 (Documentation of Meetings). On this line, an organization is asked whether it contemporaneously documented by any means permitted by state law every meeting held or written action undertaken during the year by (a) the governing body, and (b) each committee with authority to act on behalf of the governing body. Documentation may include minutes, strings of e-mails, or similar writings that explain the action taken, when it was taken, and who made the decision. For this purpose, *contemporaneous* means by the later of (a) the next meeting of the governing body or committee, or (b) 60 days after the date of the meeting or written action. If the organization answers either line 8a or line 8b "no," it must explain in Schedule O the organization's practices or policies, if any, regarding documentation of these meetings and written actions.

If the Form 990 is being filed on behalf of a group under a group exemption, lines 8a and 8b should be answered "no" if the answer is "no" for any organization in the group.

(8) Line 9 (Local Chapters, Branches, and Affiliates). This question asks if an organization has local chapters, branches, or affiliates, and if so, whether the organization has written policies and procedures governing the activities of these chapters, branches, and affiliates to ensure their operations are consistent with the reporting organization. See § 5.1(h)(4) for a discussion of these policies and procedures. The organization is instructed to answer "yes" to line 9a if the organization had during its tax year any local chapters, branches, lodges, units, or similar affiliates, including organizations over which the organization has the legal authority to exercise supervision and control, such as subordinate organizations in a group exemption, as well as local units that are not separate legal entities under state law over which the organization has such authority. If the organization answers "no" to line 9b, the organization is instructed to explain in Schedule O how the organization ensures that the local unit's activities are consistent with its own. If the Form 990 is being filed as a group return, line 9b should be answered "no" if the answer is "no" for any subordinate entity in the group.

(9) Line 10 (Review of Final 990). On line 10, a filing organization is asked whether its Form 990 was provided to the organization's governing body before it was filed. Organizations may answer "yes" only if a copy of the organization's final Form 990 (including required schedules), as ultimately filed with the IRS, was provided to each voting member of the organization's governing body, whether in paper or electronic form, *prior to* its filing with the IRS. See § 5.2(a)(1) for a definition of *voting members*. Note that the question does not ask whether the Form 990 was *reviewed* by the governing body prior to filing but merely whether it was *provided* to each voting member of the governing body. A filing organization may respond "yes" even if no board member undertakes any review of the Form 990 either before or after filing, so long as each board member was provided with a copy of the final version before it was filed.

In responding to line 10, all organizations are required to describe, on Schedule O, the process, if any, the organization uses to review the Form 990 whether before or after it was filed with the IRS, including specifics regarding who conducted the review, when they conducted it, and the extent of any such review. If the organization does not have a process for reviewing its Form 990, a filing organization should state "No review was or will be conducted" on Schedule O. While there is no federal tax law requirement that the governing body receive or review the Form 990 before it is filed, a tax-exempt organization would be wise to have a procedure for the review of its Form 990 prior to its filing, such as a review by its executive committee or its audit committee.

(10) Line 11 (Addresses for Officers, Directors, Trustees, and Key Employees). This question asks if there is any officer, director or trustee, or key employee listed in Part VII, Section A, who cannot be reached at the reporting organization's mailing address. The IRS asks this question because filing organizations may use their official mailing addresses on the first page of the Form 990 as the mailing address of these individuals. Thus, if there is any individual listed who should be contacted at a different address, the filing organization must provide the names and addresses of these persons on Schedule O. Note: This information is available to the public.

(b)   Section B (Policies)

There is no federal tax law requirement that tax-exempt organizations adopt the policies mentioned in Part VI of the Form 990. Tax-exempt organizations should, however, consider adopting at least some of the policies mentioned in the new Form 990 as a matter of good governance and to demonstrate they are well governed, in the event of an audit or investigation.

Appendix F to the Form 990 instructions contains a specific rule for responding to Part VI's policy questions for exempt organizations with disregarded entities. In responding to the questions regarding policies, the answer given should be based on the filing organization's policies, but for each "yes" response, the organization must report on Schedule O whether the policy applies to all of the organization's disregarding entities.

(1) Line 12 (Conflicts-of-Interest Policy).   Line 12a asks whether the organization has a conflict-of-interest policy. If the organization has a conflict-of-interest policy, then the organization on line 12b is asked to indicate whether or not the officers, directors or trustees, and key employees are required to disclose at least annually interests that could give rise to conflicts. This is typically accomplished through an annual disclosure statement signed by the individuals. See § 5.1(i)(1) for a discussion of annual disclosure statements. The Form 990 instructions give as an example requiring a list of family members, substantial business or investment holdings, and other transactions or affiliations with businesses and other organizations. In answering line 12c, a filing organization must disclose whether it regularly and consistently monitors and enforces compliance with the policy. If the answer is "yes," the organization is instructed to disclose on Schedule O the manner in which this is done, with a significant level of detail. The Schedule O description should include an explanation of which persons are covered under the policy, the level at which determinations of whether a conflict exists are made, and the level at which actual conflicts are reviewed. A filing organization should also explain any restrictions imposed on persons with a conflict, such as prohibiting them from participating in the governing body's deliberations and decision regarding the transaction.

If the Form 990 is being filed as a group return, lines 12b and 12c should be answered "no" if the answer is "no" for any subordinate to which the line applies, and an explanation should be provided on Schedule O.

(2) Lines 13–14 (Whistleblower and Document Retention and Destruction Policies). Line 13 asks if the organization has a written whistleblower policy, and line 14 asks if the organization has a written document retention and destruction policy. See § 5.1(i)(2) for a description of these policies. An organization should answer "yes" to these questions if the organization implemented these policies on or before the last day of the organization's tax year. Following the enactment of the Sarbanes-Oxley Act, all organizations are advised to have a whistleblower policy and a document retention and destruction policy.

(3) Line 15 (Process for Determining Compensation). Line 15 solicits information on the method a tax-exempt organization uses in setting compensation. The question asks if the process for determining compensation of the following persons include a review and approval by independent persons, comparability data, and contemporaneous substantiation of the deliberation and decision of:

- The organization's chief executive officer, executive director, or top management officials
- Other officers or key employees of the organization

If "yes," then the organization is instructed to describe the process it uses to set compensation on Schedule O, identify the offices or positions for which the process was used to establish compensation of the persons who served in those offices or positions, and state the year in which this process was undertaken. Line 15 is effectively asking if the organization invokes the rebuttable presumption of reasonableness under the intermediate sanctions rules, which is applicable to public charities and social welfare organizations. For a discussion of this procedure, see § 6.1(b)(8). Line 15(b) may be answered "yes" if the process for determining compensation of one or more officers or key employees other than the top management official included all of the elements just listed.

(4) Line 16 (Participation in a Joint Venture). Line 16 asks if the organization invested in, contributed assets to, or participated in a joint venture or similar arrangement with a taxable entity during the year regardless of whether the venture or arrangement is taxed as a partnership or as an association taxable as a corporation. An organization, in responding to the question, should include all such arrangements, whether the purpose is to conduct an exempt activity, an investment activity, or an unrelated trade or business activity, and regardless of whether the organization controls the joint venture or arrangement. Joint ventures with only tax-exempt entities do not need to be disclosed on line 16. See § 5.1(i)(3) for a discussion of joint ventures.

An organization should answer "yes" to line 16b if the organization has both (1) adopted a written policy or procedure that requires the organization to negotiate into its transactions and arrangements with other members of the partnership such terms and safeguards adequate to ensure that the organization's tax-exempt status is protected, and (2) taken steps to safeguard the organization's tax-exempt status with respect to the venture or arrangement. See § 5.1(i)(3) for examples of safeguards from the Form 990 instructions.

(c)   Section C (Disclosure)

Section C requests information on a tax-exempt organization's disclosure practices. Questions in Section C relate to filing copies of an organization's Form 990 with state officials, disclosure of which documents an organization makes publicly available and by what method it makes them available, and disclosure regarding the organization's books and records.

(1) Line 17 (States with Which a Copy of Form 990 Is Filed).   Line 17 asks the organization to list the states in which a copy of this Form 990 is required to be filed. With the exception of private foundations, tax-exempt organizations are not required under federal income tax law to file a copy of the Form 990 with the states in which they conduct their activities. For other reasons, however, an exempt organization may be required to file a Form 990 with various states. For example, most states require a copy of the Form 990 as part of the charitable solicitation registration process.

(2) Lines 18–19 (Disclosure of Documents).   Line 18 asks the reporting organization to identify the method that it uses to make certain documents available to the public. These documents are its IRS Application (Form 1023 or 1024), Form 990, and, if a public charity, Form 990-T (for Forms 990-T filed after August 17, 2006). The documents referenced in line 18 are the documents that tax-exempt organizations are required to disclose under federal tax law. The Form 990 requests the disclosing organization to identify whether it makes these documents available by posting them on a public Web site maintained by the organization, posting them on another publicly available Web site, or providing them on request, checking all methods that apply. If the organization does not make any documents publicly available that are required to be disclosed by law, it must provide an explanation in Schedule O.

Line 19 instructs the reporting organization to describe on Schedule O whether (and if so, how), the organization makes its governing documents, conflicts-of-interest policy, and financial statements available to the public. There is no federal tax law requirement that these documents be made available to the public, other than the documents that are filed as part of the Form 1023 or Form 1024 application for recognition of exemption. However, the IRS and other interested organizations encourage organizations to make these documents publicly available as a matter of good governance practices.

(3) Line 20 (Books and Records of Organization). This question asks the reporting organization to state the name, physical address, and telephone number of the person who possesses the books and records of the organization. If the books and records are kept at more than one location, an organization is instructed to provide the name, business address, and telephone number of the person responsible for coordinating the maintenance of the books and records.

An organization is not required to provide the address or telephone number of a personal residence of an individual. If, however, it chooses to do so, the information will be available to the public. If an organization's books and records are located at an individual's personal residence, the organization should provide the name of the person who possesses the books and records and provide either the business address of the individual or the address of the filing organization. If the Form 990 is being filed as a group return, line 20 should be used to identify the person who possesses the books and records used to prepare the group return.

§ 5.3   NEW FORM 990 COMPLIANCE TASKS

All tax-exempt organizations should consider taking these 13 actions regarding governance of their organization:

1. **Policies.** Prior to year-end, consider adopting these policies, if applicable: whistleblower, document retention and destruction, and conflicts of interest policies; a policy regarding participation in joint venture arrangements and safeguarding tax-exempt status; and a policy regarding branches, chapters, and affiliates.

2. **Additional policies.** Although not mentioned in the Form 990, consider adopting an executive compensation policy, an investment policy, a fundraising policy, and code of ethics. (These policies are mentioned by the IRS in the IRS Life Cycle Governance Document.)

3. **Board size.** Evaluate the organization's board size, ascertain the number of independent members, and consider whether the organization would benefit from having a larger or smaller board and additional independent board members.

4. **Amendments to organizational documents.** Determine if the organization made any amendments to its organizational documents and policies during the current year that were not reported to the IRS on a prior Form 990 that need to be reported.

5. **Annual questionnaire.** Annually distribute a questionnaire to the board of directors, officers, trustees, and key employees requesting information on potential conflicts of interest, the independence of the board member, direct or indirect transactions with the organization, and family and business relationships with any other officers, directors, trustees, or key employees. Ensure that the questionnaire contains pertinent instructions and definitions of the relevant terms sufficient to enable the individuals to complete the questionnaire accurately.

6. **Minutes.** Contemporaneously document all meetings of the organization's governing body and all committees with authority to act on behalf of the

governing body by preparing minutes no later than the later of the next meeting of the governing body or committee or 60 days after the date of the meeting or written action.

7. **Review of Form 990.** Develop and implement a process for a review of the Form 990 by the board or an appropriate independent committee prior to its filing.

8. **Copy of final 990 to entire board before filing.** Distribute a copy of the Form 990 in final form (in paper copy or electronically) to each voting member of the organization's governing body prior to its filing with the IRS.

9. **Board review of compensation.** Cause the governing body of the filing organization to regularly review the compensation of the organization's top executives and consider invoking the rebuttable presumption of reasonableness by having the board of directors (if all are independent) or a committee of independent persons review and approve the compensation, obtain comparability data regarding the compensation, and contemporaneously substantiate in writing the deliberation and decision regarding the compensation.

10. **State filings.** Monitor the states in which a copy of the Form 990 is required to be, and actually is, filed.

11. **Disclosure of IRS application and returns.** Ensure the organization is complying with the disclosure requirements for its Form 1023 and 1024, its Forms 990, and (for public charities) its Forms 990-T by posting the documents on its Web site, making the documents available for public inspection, or otherwise.

12. **Additional disclosure.** Consider making the organization's governing documents, conflicts-of-interest policy, financial statements, and annual report available to the public.

13. **Annual report.** If the organization does not prepare an annual report, consider adopting this practice.

CHAPTER SIX

Part VII and Schedule J—Compensation

The IRS has always carefully scrutinized compensation arrangements between exempt organizations and insiders of the organization, including officers, directors, trustees, key employees, and, in some cases, independent contractors. This has particularly been the case for charities due to the private inurement, excess benefit, and private benefit proscriptions. The current core Form 990 requires disclosure of these compensation arrangements for all exempt organizations; additional information is required on the current Schedule A for charities. Part VII of the new core form, along with new Schedule J, significantly expands this disclosure. Part VII and the new Schedule J bring consistency and enhanced transparency to the reporting of compensation.

Basic compensation information is reported in Part VII including disclosure of average hours worked, reportable compensation from the filing organization and related organizations, and certain other income. More detailed compensation information is reported in Schedule J for certain individuals. For example, additional information must be reported in Schedule J for current directors or trustees, officers, key employees, and highly compensated employees if reportable compensation and other compensation is in excess of $150,000.

§6.1 LAW AND POLICY

Compensation is a focus of the IRS and Congress because of the potential for abuse. A recent example is an IRS initiative launched in 2004. Prompted by media reports of ostensible excess compensation paid by nonprofit organizations to insiders, the IRS engaged in an enforcement effort to "identify and halt" the practice. The agency initiated contact with approximately 2,000 charitable organizations to seek compensation information. The IRS termed this undertaking its Tax Exempt Compensation Enforcement Project. Compensation has also been a focus of the nonprofit community relative to good governance and corporate best practices. For example, the Panel on the Nonprofit Sector in its final report to Congress in 2005 suggested that board compensation should be discouraged. It emphasized that if board compensation is paid, it should be reasonable and should be disclosed. In the case of executive compensation, the Panel stated that it should be disclosed with more clarity and that additional penalties should be imposed for unreasonable compensation. Further, the rebuttable presumption of reasonableness procedure should be followed in establishing executive compensation and the compensation of others. Finally, the Panel suggested that clear and enforceable policies should be implemented for expense reimbursement. Its primary focus in this regard related to travel reimbursement policies stating that the policies should include the type of expenses that can be reimbursed, the documentation required to receive reimbursement, and charitable organizations should be required to disclose whether they have a travel policy in their Form 990. The Panel also emphasized that charitable organizations should not pay for, nor reimburse, travel expenditures for spouse, dependents, or others for accompanying an individual conducting business for the organization, unless the additional person is also conducting business for the organization.

Some of these Panel suggestions are contained in the new Form 990, Part VII, and Schedule J. The schedule covers travel reimbursement as well as a variety of other benefits including housing allowances, discretionary spending accounts, social and health club dues, and other benefits. Schedule J also focuses on deferred compensation and compensation that is not fixed in advance. Information is requested on a variety of different types of nonfixed compensation, including compensation contingent on revenues, compensation contingent on net earnings, equity-based compensation, and other nonfixed payments. Compensation can come not only from the filing organization but also from related organizations and joint ventures. Reportable compensation is provided in Part VII from the filing organization and all related organizations. More detailed information on all forms of compensation from the filing organization and all related organizations is reported in Schedule J.

There are a number of legal doctrines that police exempt organizations relative to the payment of excessive compensation. They include the private inurement and private benefit prohibitions and the excess benefit transaction rules.

(a) Private Inurement

The doctrine of private inurement, which is the essential principle of law distinguishing nonprofit and for-profit organizations, is applicable to nearly all types of tax-exempt organizations. It is most pronounced and developed, however, for charitable organizations.

The federal law of tax exemption for charitable organizations requires that each such entity be organized and operated so that "no part of . . . [its] net earnings . . . inures to the benefit of any private shareholder or individual." Literally, this means that the profits of a charitable organization (and any other type of entity subject to the doctrine) may not be passed along to individuals or other persons in their private capacity, in the way that dividends are paid to shareholders. In actual fact, the private inurement rule, as expanded and amplified by the IRS and the courts, means much more.

The contemporary concept of private inurement is broad and wide-ranging. Lawyers for the IRS advised that inurement is "likely to arise where the beneficial benefit represents a transfer of the organization's financial resources to an individual solely by virtue of the individual's relationship with the organization, and without regard to accomplishing exempt purposes." That description is essentially correct for today's private inurement doctrine but it is a substantial embellishment of the original (and antiquated) statutory rule.

The essence of the private inurement concept is to ensure that a charitable organization is serving public, not private, interests. To be exempt, an organization must establish that it is not organized and operated for the benefit of private interests—designated individuals, the creator of the entity or his or her family, shareholders of the organization, persons controlled (directly or indirectly) by private interests, or any persons having a personal and private interest in the activities of the organization.

(1) Insiders. The federal securities laws that govern for-profit business corporations target the notion of the *insider*—someone who has a special and close relationship with a corporation, frequently because he or she is a director, officer, and/or significant shareholder. Thus, for example, the securities laws prohibit insider trading. The private inurement rules, using the odd phrase *private shareholder or individual*, mirror the concept of the insider.

An insider for private inurement purposes includes an organization's directors, trustees, and officers. It also encompasses key employees, particularly where they have duties or responsibilities normally vested in officers and can include independent contractors, such as management companies, which are delegated such duties. Further, the family members of insiders and entities controlled by insiders (such as corporations, partnerships, trusts, and estates) are covered. Indeed, the contemporary version of the term *insider* in the exempt organizations context is that it is any person who is in a position to exercise control over a significant portion of the affairs of an organization. It is not necessary that this control in fact be exercised.

The inurement doctrine prohibits a transaction between a tax-exempt organization subject to the rule and a person who is an insider, where the latter is able to cause the organization's net earnings to be turned to private purposes as the result of his, her, or its control or influence. The IRS once observed that, as a general rule, an organization's "trustees, officers, members, founders, or contributors may not, by reason of their position, acquire any of its funds." Stating its view another way, the IRS has rather starkly said that the "prohibition of inurement, in its simplest terms, means that a private shareholder or individual cannot pocket the organization's funds."

The instructions provide these definitions of persons who are, in most cases, insiders, and compensation paid by the organization to these persons is reported in Part VII.

A *director or trustee* is a member of the organization's governing body, but only if the member has any voting rights. Members of advisory boards that do not exercise any governance authority over the organization are not considered directors or trustees.

An *officer* is a person elected or appointed to manage the organization's daily operations, such as a president, vice-president, secretary, or treasurer. An officer who served at any time during the organization's tax year is deemed a current officer. The officers of an organization may be determined by reference to its organizing document, bylaws, resolutions of its governing body, but in all cases include those officers required by applicable state law. This definition encompasses "officers of the board" and "officers of the corporation." For purposes of Form 990 reporting, the following persons are also officers:

1. **Top management official.** The person who has ultimate responsibility for implementing the decisions of the governing body or for supervising the management, administration, or operation of the organization.

2. **Top financial official.** The person who has ultimate responsibility for managing the organization's finances.

A *key employee* is usually an insider for private inurement purposes. For purposes of Form 990 reporting, a current key employee is an employee of the organization (other than an officer, director, or trustee) who meets three tests:

1. **$150,000 Test.** Receives reportable compensation from the organization and all related organizations in excess of $150,000 for the calendar year ending with or within the organization's tax year.

2. **Responsibility Test.**

   • Has responsibilities, powers or influence over the organization as a whole that is similar to those of officers, directors, or trustees;

   • Manages a discrete segment or activity of the organization that represents 10 percent or more of the activities, assets, income, or expenses of the organization, as compared to the organization as a whole; or

   • Has or shares authority to control or determine 10 percent or more of the organization's capital expenditures, operating budget, or compensation for employees.

3. **Top 20 Test.** Is one of the 20 employees (who satisfy the $150,000 test and responsibility Test) with the highest reportable compensation from the organization and related organizations for the calendar year ending with or within the organization's tax year.

If the organization has more than 20 individuals who meet the Responsibility Test and $150,000 Test, report as key employees only the 20 individuals who have the highest reportable compensation from the organization and related organization(s). Note that any others, up to five, might be reportable as current highest-compensated employees over $100,000. Use the calendar year ending with or within the organization's tax year for determining the organization's current key employees.

An individual who is not an employee of the organization (or of a disregarded entity of the organization) is treated as a key employee if he or she serves as an officer or director of a disregarded entity of the organization and otherwise meets the standards of a key employee. Independent contractors should not be reported as key employees.

In the examples provided in the instructions as set forth below, assume that the individual involved is an employee of the organization who satisfies the $150,000 Test and Top 20 Test, and is not an officer, director, or trustee.

> **Example 1.** T is a large section 501(c)(3) university. L is the dean of the law school of T, which generates more than 10% of the revenue of T, including contributions from alumni and foundations. Although L does not have ultimate responsibility for managing the university as a whole, L meets the Responsibility Test and is thus reportable as a key employee of T.

Example 2. S chairs a small academic department in the College of Arts and Sciences of the same university T described above. As department chair, S supervises faculty in the department, approves the course curriculum, and oversees the operating budget for the department. The department represents less than 10% of the university's activities, assets, income, expenses, capital expenditures, operating budget, and employee compensation. Under these facts and circumstances, S does not meet the Responsibility Test and thus is not a key employee of T.

Example 3. U is a large acute-care section 501(c)(3) hospital. U employs X as a radiologist. X gives instructions to staff with respect to the radiology work X conducts, but X does not supervise other U employees, manage the radiology department, or have or share authority to control or determine 10% or more of U's capital expenditures, operating budget, or employee compensation. Under these facts and circumstances, X does not meet the Responsibility Test and thus is not a key employee of U.

Example 4. W is a cardiologist and head of the cardiology department of the same hospital U described above. The cardiology department is a major source of patients admitted to U and consequently represents more than 10% of U's income, as compared to U as a whole. As department head, W manages the cardiology department. Under these facts and circumstances, W meets the Responsibility Test and thus is a key employee of U.

Note that the instructions, including the examples, use 10 percent as the threshold level for determining whether an activity conducted by an employee is substantial. This threshold dictates whether a person is found to be a key employee for purposes of Part VII disclosure. The key employee reference is similar to the disqualified person examples under the excess benefit transaction rules (see § 6.2(b)).

In addition to officers, directors, trustees, and key employees, the organization is required to report in Part VII the highest-compensated employees whose reportable compensation combined from the organization and related organizations is greater than $100,000 for the year and who are not also an officer, director, trustee, or listed key employee of the organization. The organization is not required to list more than the top five such persons, ranked by amount of reportable compensation. The list may contain persons who meet some but not all of the tests for key employee status. In some cases highly compensated individuals will be insiders; in some cases they will not be insiders. In any event, the IRS requires information on highly compensated individuals. The calendar-year compensation ending with or within the organization's tax year is used for determining the organization's current five highest-compensated employees.

Example. X is an employee of Y University and is not an officer, director, or trustee. X's reportable compensation for the calendar year exceeds $150,000, and X meets the Responsibility Test. X would qualify as a key employee of Y, except that 20 employees had higher reportable compensation and otherwise qualify as key employees; therefore, those 20 are listed as the organization's key employees. X has the highest reportable compensation from the organization and related organizations of all employees other than the 20 key employees. X must be listed as one of the organization's five highest-compensated employees.

Disregarded entities (such as a limited liability company that is wholly owned by the organization and not treated as a separate entity for federal tax purposes) are treated as part of the organization rather than as related organizations for purposes of Form 990, Part VII, and Schedule J. A person is not considered an officer or director of the filing organization by virtue of being an officer or director of a disregarded entity, but he or she may qualify as a highest compensated employee of the organization, or as a key employee. An officer, director, or employee of a disregarded entity is a key employee of the organization if he or she meets the $150,000 and Top 20 tests for the filing organization as a whole and if, with respect to the Responsibility Test, the person has responsibilities, powers, or influence over a discrete segment or activity of the disregarded entity that represents at least 10 percent of the activities, assets, income, or expenses of the filing organization as a whole, or has or shares authority to control or determine the disregarded entity's capital expenditures, operating budget, or compensation for employees that constitutes at least 10 percent of the filing organization's respective items as a whole. If an officer or director of a disregarded entity also serves as an officer, director, trustee, or key employee of the organization, report this individual as an officer, director, trustee, or key employee, as applicable, of the organization, and add the compensation, if any, paid by the disregarded entity to this individual to the compensation, if any, paid directly by the organization to this individual. The total aggregate amount is reported in Part VII, Column (D).

A central or parent organization (as described in General Instruction I) that files a group Form 990 return must generally file a separate Form 990 for itself (unless it is excepted from filing Form 990) in addition to the group return. With respect to Form 990, Part VII, and Schedule J, Part II, however, the central organization has these two choices: (1) File separately a Form 990, Part VII, and Schedule J, Part II for itself with its return, and a Form 990, Part VII, and Schedule J, Part II with the group return for each subordinate included in the group return, or (2) file a single consolidated Form 990, Part VII, and Schedule J, Part II for itself and all included subordinates with the group return. The central organization must state in Schedule O whether it has adopted the first or second method of reporting and may not change it without IRS consent. If an organization reports by the consolidated method, it must report the five highest-compensated employees and independent contractors above $100,000 for each subordinate, not the five highest for the whole group. If an organization reports by the consolidated method and one or more officers, directors, trustees, key employees, or highest compensated employees receive compensation from more than one organization in the group, the person's compensation from the several organizations must be reported once, but not more than once. Regardless of the method used, indicate which organization(s) paid the compensation.

(2) Standard of Reasonableness. Persons can receive private benefits in many ways; private inurement can take many forms. Still, a charitable organization may incur ordinary and necessary operating expenditures without losing its tax-exempt status. It may pay compensation, rent, interest, and maintenance costs without penalty, because these expenses, even if paid to insiders, further the organization's exempt purposes. The costs, however, must be justifiable and be for reasonable amounts.

The matter of *reasonableness* is one of *fact*, not *law*. The exercise in determining what is reasonable is closely akin to *valuation*. In complex instances, the services of an independent, competent consultant may be warranted. The law that is developing in the excess benefit transaction setting (see § 6.1(b)) is helping to define the parameters of the term *reasonable*.

(3) Compensation. Excessive compensation is the most common form of private inurement. Compensation can come not only from the reporting organizations but also from related organizations, both exempt and for-profit. Thus, reasonableness must be measured based on aggregate compensation, not just compensation from the filing organizations. The new Form 990 requires the aggregation of compensation from all related sources. This aggregate number is reported on Part VII and on Schedule J in some cases. The related party relationships are also reported on Schedule R (see Chapter 21). When a charitable organization pays an employee a salary, it is paying a portion of its earnings to an individual in his or her private capacity. Payment of reasonable compensation is not private inurement, but payment of excessive compensation is private inurement when it is paid to an insider (see § 6.1(a)(1)). In this context, *compensation* is not confined to payment of a salary or wage; it includes bonuses, commissions, royalties, expense accounts, insurance coverages, deferred compensation, and participation in retirement plans. Reporting of these various forms of compensation is significantly expanded in Schedule J.

Whether compensation paid by an exempt organization is reasonable is, as noted, a question of fact, to be decided in the context of each case. Generally, allowable compensation is ascertained by comparing the compensation paid to individuals who have similar responsibilities and expertise, serving organizations of comparable type and size, in the same or similar communities. Where similar entities are operating in the for-profit sector, compensation paid by them can be included in the evaluation. Other factors are the need of the organization for a particular individual's services, the amount of time devoted to the job, whether an independent or captive board approved the compensation, the complexity of the organization's corporate structure, and other factors.

Thus, individuals (and other persons) serving charitable (and other) tax-exempt organizations are allowed fair compensation for their efforts. A court observed that the "law places no duty on individuals operating charitable organizations to donate their services; they are entitled to reasonable compensation for their services." Likewise, a congressional committee report contained the observation that "an individual need not necessarily accept reduced compensation merely because he or she renders services to a tax-exempt, as opposed to a taxable, organization."

Three aspects of compensation can make it unreasonable. One is the sheer amount of the compensation, in absolute terms. A federal court, in finding private inurement because of excessive compensation, characterized the salaries as being "substantial" amounts. Other courts, however, tolerate substantial amounts of compensation where the employees' services and skills warrant the level of payment.

The second aspect is extraordinary jumps—or spikes—in the level of compensation. A spike can sometimes be supported if the organization is able to document that the spike is due to underpayment for prior services or for current extraordinary services. Generally, however, a sudden significant increase in pay will be suspect. A case in point: Two individuals who for years received annual compensation of $20,000 were each awarded a $700,000 bonus; the IRS and two courts found that level of compensation to be unreasonable. Another telling factor is whether the spike in compensation level causes the recipient to enjoy far more compensation than anyone else on the payroll.

The third aspect of compensation that can lead to private inurement is the manner in which the amount is calculated. Some compensation arrangements are not fixed payments based on a salary, wage, or bonus but are based, in whole or in part, on a percentage of a tax-exempt organization's gross revenue or net revenue. This type of arrangement can be categorized as revenue-sharing, percentage-based compensation, commission-based compensation, or revenue distributed pursuant to a joint venture. These nonfixed income arrangements are a focus of the IRS in the Schedule J reporting.

(4) Nonfixed Income Including Revenue Sharing. The case law on revenue sharing and other nonfixed compensation is unclear and inconsistent. In one case, a court held that a percentage compensation arrangement involving a charity organization amounted to private inurement, because there was no upper limit, or cap, as to total allowable compensation. This court subsequently restricted the import of this decision, however, when it held that private inurement did not occur when an exempt organization paid its president a commission determined by a percentage of the contributions obtained by him. The court in the second of these cases held that the standard is whether the compensation is reasonable rather than the manner in which the compensation is ascertained. The issue often rises in the fundraising context. Fundraising commissions that are "directly contingent on success in procuring funds" were held by one court to be an "incentive well suited to the budget of a fledgling [charitable] organization." In reaching this conclusion—and saying nothing about caps on levels of compensation—the court reviewed states' charitable solicitation acts governing payments to professional solicitors, which the court characterized as "[s]anctioning such commissions and in many cases endors[ing] percentage commissions higher than" the percentage commission paid by the organization involved in the case.

Another court subsequently introduced more confusion in this area when it ruled that "there is nothing insidious or evil about a commission-based compensation system" and thus that an arrangement, by which those who successfully secured contributions for a charitable organization were paid a percentage of the gift amounts, is "reasonable," despite the absence of any limit as to an absolute amount of compensation (and despite the fact that the law requires compensation to be reasonable, not the percentage by which it is determined).

The issue also arises in the hospital setting. Physician compensation is sometimes tied to the performance of one or more hospital departments. In some rulings the IRS found that compensation payments determined in part on a percentage of the excess revenue over budgeted amounts did not give rise to private inurement where the plans were not devices to distribute profits to principles, were the result of arm's-length bargaining, and did not result in unreasonable compensation. Employing similar reasoning, the IRS approved guaranteed minimum annual salary contracts pursuant to which physicians' compensation was subsidized so as to induce them to commence employment at a hospital. In addition, the IRS approved a compensation plan where a radiologist received a percentage of the gross billings attributed to the physician's department. A showing that the overall salary is reasonable and that the employee's performance has a direct impact on the revenue stream are persuasive in the analysis. The IRS has not approved revenue-sharing arrangements in all settings; the IRS found private inurement resulted in the case of a joint venture between a hospital and a physician involving a sharing of the net stream of the hospital's income. The IRS found private inurement per se, regardless of whether the revenue stream was reasonable in amount.

Compensation contingent in part on the gross or net revenue of a department should be distinguished from compensation contingent on the net earnings of the organization as a whole. The rulings just discussed are of the variety where compensation is based in part on gross or net revenues of a department tied to the performance of the insider. Compensation based on net earnings of the organization as a whole will result in a finding of private inurement in most cases.

In 2002, the IRS issued an information letter addressing physician incentive compensation and the factors to which the IRS will look in determining whether compensation paid by a hospital results in private inurement or impermissible private benefit. Among the factors set forth in the information letter are (a) having compensation determined by an independent board of directors or compensation committee; (b) whether the compensation results in total overall reasonable compensation to the physician; (c) whether the compensation arrangement contains a ceiling or reasonable maximum on the amount of compensation paid; (d) if a compensation arrangement is based on net revenues, then it should accomplish a charitable purpose, such as keeping expenses within budgeted amounts where expenses determine the amounts the organization charges for charitable services; and (e) the arrangement should not effectively be a joint venture between the parties.

In a private letter ruling, the IRS held that a charity's revenue-sharing arrangement pursuant to which it shared revenue with inventors and others who contributed to development of the intellectual property did not jeopardize the organization's tax-exempt status. The charity in this instance was engaged in biotechnology efforts for economic development and job creation. The charity's federal research agreements required the charity to share, with the inventors, royalties derived from patents, and the charity allowed the inventors of a particular patent, copyright, process or formula to share in one-third of sharable revenue from an invention.

In addition, this public charity had a method of sharing revenue with employees who make significant contributions to certain intellectual property. If royalties or other value was received by the public charity from the licensing or other transfer of intellectual property that had been donated to the charity, then employees who made "unique, significant and nonroutine contributions to evaluating and assessing the donation" received a 15 percent share of the sharable revenue allocated to the particular item. In addition, the charity was adopting a new bonus policy, under which managers and senior scientists would receive a bonus determined by an employee's overall performance and which would be computed based on a percentage of compensation, up to a maximum of 20 percent.

The IRS ruled that the shared-income policy and contingent compensation bonus policy were reasonable compensation plans that did not adversely affect the charity's tax-exempt status. In making this determination, the IRS noted several features of the shareholder income policy:

- The sharable income policy was established by its board of trustees in an arm's-length relationship with its employees.
- Payments under the sharable income policy serve a real and discernible business purpose in line with the normal practices of similar businesses.
- The amount of payments is dependent on the employee's contributions to the purposes and objectives of the charity.
- The policy contains a maximum percentage (capped at 20 percent of compensation) and specific factors to be considered in determining compensation.

What is puzzling about the conclusion in the ruling is the language that the policy contains a maximum amount of compensation an employee could receive. In the recitation of facts, there is no mention that the charity imposed a maximum limit on the income an employee could receive under the sharable income policy. Only the bonus policy was stated as having a maximum. Even so, in support of its conclusion that the sharable income policy would not adversely affect the charity's exempt status, the IRS stated the policy contained a maximum amount an employee could receive, in addition to stating the policy was established by the board of trustees in an arm's-length relationship with its employees and serves a real and discernible business purpose, and that payments under the policy were dependent on an employee's contributions to the charity.

(5) Transactions with Insiders and Organization's Owned by Insiders. Other transactions (in addition to compensation) between the filing organization and insiders scrutinized under the private inurement doctrine include business transactions of all types, both direct and indirect. An example of a direct transaction would be if an officer or director of the filing organization sold an asset or provided services for a fee that were not reported in Part VII as compensation. An example of an indirect transaction would be if that same officer or director owned more than a 35-percent interest in a business organization that entered into a business transaction for goods or services with the filing organization. Like the compensation analysis, the goods or services purchased by the filing organization, directly or indirectly, from the insider must be for no more than fair market value. Following proper procedures like the rebuttable presumption of reasonableness is important for these types of transactions as well. Some of these transactions are reported in Schedule L. In some cases, the transactions may also have to be reported in Schedule R if related organizations are involved. An example would be if the filing organization entered into a transaction with an organization owned more than 50 percent by one or more insiders.

(6) Loans. A charitable organization generally may make loans. The private inurement doctrine, however, requires that—where the lender or borrower is an insider—the arrangement must be beneficial for the organization, and the terms must be reasonable. Disclosure of loan arrangements are made in Schedule L (see Chapter 18). Loan disclosure may also be required in Schedule R if a loan is made to an organization controlled more than 50 percent by one or more insiders.

The terms of any loan involving a charitable organization should be financially advantageous to the organization and in line with its exempt purposes. Where a charity is the borrower and an insider is the lender, the interest charges, amount of security, repayment period, terms of repayment, and other aspects of the loan must be reasonable. The scrutiny will heighten where an insider is borrowing from the charity (assuming state law and organization documents permit the transaction). If a loan from a charity is not timely repaid, questions of private inurement may be raised. A federal court observed that the "very existence of a private source of loan credit from [a charitable] organization's earnings may itself amount to inurement of benefit."

Some charitable organizations are called on to guarantee the debt of another entity, such as a related nonprofit or even a for-profit organization. The terms of such an arrangement should be carefully reviewed, particularly where an insider is involved. If the loan guarantee does not advance exempt purposes or cannot be characterized as part of a reasonable investment, private inurement may be occurring.

(7) Joint Ventures. Charitable organizations are increasingly involved in partnerships with individuals and/or for-profit entities. Reporting of joint ventures is required in Schedule R, if the entity is a "related" organization (see Chapter 21). The development of a joint venture policy is encouraged in Part VI as part of good governance and corporate best practices (see Chapter 5). Disclosure is also required on Schedule R for unrelated partnerships if the filing organization conducts more than 5 percent of its activities through the partnership. In a general partnership, all of the partners are subject to liability for the acts committed in the name of the partnership. In a limited partnership, which will have at least one general partner, the limited partners are essentially investors; their liability is confined to the extent of their investment. The general partner(s) in a limited partnership has the responsibility to operate the partnership in a successful manner; this includes efforts to enable the limited partners to achieve an economic return that is worth the commitment of their capital.

In this structure and set of expectations, there is the potential for private inurement. The most direct form would be if insiders were involved and they paid less for their partnership interests than the charity or if the charity assumed more risk in the arrangement than the insider partners. More of an indirect benefit occurs if a partnership with a charitable organization as the general partner at the helm is construed as the running of a business for the benefit of private interests (the limited partners), particularly where the limited partners involved are insiders. This has rarely been the case in the nonprofit organizations context. A partnership (general or limited) basically is an entity formed to attract financing—it is a means to an end. In this fashion, a charitable organization is able to secure the funds of others for a legitimate purpose. As long as involvement in the partnership does not deter the charity from advancing its exempt ends and as long as the limited partners' return on their investment is reasonable, there will not be private inurement—notwithstanding the participation of any insiders.

The IRS is having some success in situations where a tax-exempt charitable organization is involved in a joint venture (usually where the venture vehicle is a limited liability company) to the extent that the entirety of the entity is in the venture. If the charitable organization loses control of its resources to (or, as one court put it, "cedes its authority" to) one or more for-profit companies, the charity will lose its tax-exempt status. This may, however, entail application of the private benefit doctrine (see § 6.1(c)) rather than the private inurement doctrine.

(8) Loss of Exempt Status. The sanction for violation of the private inurement doctrine is loss or denial of the organization's tax-exempt status. There is no sanction imposed on the insider who received the unwarranted benefit, and there is no other penalty under the private inurement rules. Fortunately, however, loss of exempt status should occur only in egregious circumstances. The IRS normally will impose the excess benefit taxes on the persons who benefit instead of revoking the exempt status of the organization (see § 6.1(b)(16)). Nonetheless, it is certainly possible for the IRS to simultaneously apply both bodies of law, thus penalizing both the insider or insiders who obtained the excess benefit and the tax-exempt organization that provided it.

(b) Excess Benefit Transactions and Intermediate Sanctions

The intermediate sanctions rules impose a series of excise taxes on persons who engaged in impermissible private transactions with certain types of tax-exempt organizations and on certain managers of the organization who participated in the transaction knowing that it was improper. These taxes are applied to the amount of the excess benefit derived from the transaction. The taxes consist of an "initial" tax and an "additional" tax.

(1) Organizations Subject to Intermediate Sanctions. The law as to excess benefit transactions applies with respect to public charities and social welfare organizations. These entities are collectively termed, for this purpose, *applicable tax-exempt organizations*. Organizations of this nature include any organization described in either of these two categories of exempt organizations at any time during the five-year period ending on the date of the transaction.

(2) Disqualified Persons. A person who has a close relationship with an applicable tax-exempt organization is a *disqualified person*. A disqualified person generally is a person who has, or is in a position to have, some type or degree of control over the operations of the applicable tax-exempt organization involved. The term "disqualified person" is defined under the intermediate sanctions rules as (1) any person who was, at any time during the five-year period ending on the date of the transaction involved, in a position to exercise substantial influence over the affairs of the organization (whether by virtue of being an organization manager or otherwise), (2) a member of the family of an individual described in the preceding category, and (3) an entity in which individuals described in the preceding two categories own more than a 35 percent interest. Persons who are disqualified persons for excess benefit transaction purposes are usually insiders for private inurement purposes (see § 6.1(a)(1)).

Certain individuals are deemed to be persons having substantial influence over the affairs of a tax-exempt organization and thus a disqualified person with respect to the organization. These individuals include voting members of the governing body (i.e., the directors and trustees); an individual who serves as president, chief executive officer, or chief operating officer of an organization; and an individual who has ultimate responsibility for managing the finances of an applicable tax-exempt organization is a disqualified person. An individual who serves as treasurer or chief financial officer of an organization generally has this ultimate responsibility (unless the individual demonstrates otherwise). In addition, an individual who has ultimate responsibility for implementing the decisions of the governing body of an applicable tax-exempt organization or for supervising the management, administration, or operation of the organization is a disqualified person with respect to the organization, regardless of whether the person is designated as president, chief operating officer, or otherwise.

In other situations, whether or not a person is a disqualified person depends on the relevant facts and circumstances. Facts and circumstances that tend to show that a person has substantial influence include the fact that a person's compensation is based primarily on revenues derived from activities of the organization or of a particular department or function of the organization that the person controls. In addition, if the person manages a discrete segment or activity of the organization that represents a substantial portion of the activities, assets, income or expenses of the organization as compared to the organization as a whole, this factor will indicate that the person has substantial influence over the organization. Note that for purposes of defining key employees, 10% is *substantial*.

(3) Excess Benefit Transaction. The intermediate sanctions apply if there has been an *excess benefit transaction*. Excess benefit transactions are reported in Schedule L (see Chapter 18). In general, an excess benefit transaction is a transaction in which an economic benefit is provided by an applicable tax-exempt organization, directly or indirectly, to or for the use of a disqualified person, and the value of the economic benefit provided by the organization exceeds the value of the consideration (including the performance of services) received for providing the benefit. The difference between the value provided by the exempt organization and the consideration (if any) it received from the disqualified person is an *excess benefit*.

An excess benefit transaction includes a payment of unreasonable (excessive) compensation by an applicable tax-exempt organization to a disqualified person with respect to it. The value of services, in the intermediate sanctions setting, is the amount that ordinarily would be paid for like services by like organizations under like circumstances. Compensation in this context includes all economic benefits (other than certain disregarded benefits) provided by an applicable tax-exempt organization to or for the use of a person, in exchange for the performance of services, including all forms of cash and noncash compensation.

(4) Amount of the Excise Taxes. The intermediate sanctions rules entail an initial tax, which is 25 percent of the excess benefit, payable by the disqualified person or persons involved. The transaction must be undone, by placing the parties in the same economic position they were in before the transaction was entered into; this is "correction" of the transaction. If the initial tax is not timely paid and the transaction is not timely and properly corrected, an additional tax may have to be paid; this tax is 200 percent of the excess benefit.

In addition to the tax imposed on disqualified persons, an excise tax is imposed on organization managers who knowingly participated in the excess benefit transaction, unless such participation was not willful and was due to reasonable cause. Any organization manager who so participated in the excess benefit transaction must pay the tax. In general, an organization manager is, with respect to any applicable tax-exempt organization, any officer, director, or trustee of such organization or any individual having powers or responsibilities similar to officers, directors, or trustees of the organization regardless of title. The tax paid is equal to 10 percent of the excess benefit.

(5) Excessive Compensation as Excess Benefit Transaction. Compensation paid by an applicable tax-exempt organization to a disqualified person is not an excess benefit transaction unless it is unreasonable. Reasonable compensation is the amount that would ordinarily be paid for like services by like enterprises (whether taxable or not) under like circumstances. Other than certain excludable benefits, compensation for purposes of determining reasonableness includes all economic benefits provided by the tax-exempt organization in exchange for the performance of services. An economic benefit is not treated as consideration for the performance of services unless the organization providing the benefit clearly indicates its intent to treat the benefit as compensation when the benefit is paid. Other than for nontaxable benefits, a tax-exempt organization is treated as clearly indicating its intent to provide an economic benefit as compensation for services only if the organization provides written contemporaneous substantiation of the benefit. If an organization fails to provide this contemporaneous substantiation, any services provided by the disqualified person will not be treated as provided in consideration for the economic benefit for purposes of determining reasonableness.

(6) Revenue-Sharing Impact on Compensation. The intermediate sanctions statute states that, to the extent provided by the IRS in regulations, the term *excess benefit transaction* includes any transaction in which the amount of any economic benefit provided to or for the use of a disqualified person is determined in whole or in part by the revenues of one or more activities of the organization, but only if the transaction results in impermissible private inurement. In the event of an excess benefit revenue-sharing transaction, the excess benefit is the amount of inurement not permitted.

When the IRS issued the temporary regulations under the intermediate sanctions, the agency deleted the regulations governing revenue-sharing transactions and reserved the section for the promulgation of regulations at a future date. As a result, the general rule under the intermediate sanctions regime, which is that an excess benefit transaction will be found if the economic benefit provided to the disqualified person exceeds the value of the services or other consideration provided by the disqualified person to the tax-exempt organization, applies to revenue-sharing transactions. While there is no clear direction under the intermediate sanctions rules as to when a revenue-sharing transaction will be treated as an excess benefit transaction, the standard of "reasonableness" provides guidance as to whether a revenue-sharing transaction would be an excess benefit transaction. As discussed in § 6.1(a)(4), the IRS is not bound by the reasonableness standard in the private inurement setting.

The IRS has directed its agents to scrutinize these arrangements under the general intermediate sanctions rules until regulations are issued to deal specifically with revenue sharing. A finding of an excess benefit transaction under the general rules depends on all relevant facts and circumstances; the transaction will be subject to intermediate sanctions excise tax liability only to the extent that the value of the economic benefits provided to the disqualified person under the revenue-sharing arrangement exceeds the value of the services (or other consideration) received in turn.

(7) Other Excess Benefit Transactions with Disqualified Persons. In addition to compensation arrangements with disqualified persons, other transactions directly with disqualified persons or indirectly through an entity owned more than 35 percent by the disqualified person are scrutinized under the excess benefit transaction rules. Such transactions can include the purchase or sale of goods or services between the disqualified persons and applicable tax-exempt organization. Like compensation arrangements, if the exempt organization pays more than fair value for goods or services to the disqualified person or the entity controlled by a disqualified person, an excess benefit transaction will result. The transactions are reported on Schedule L (see Chapter 18). The transactions could also be reported on Schedule R if the organization involved in the transaction is commonly controlled or otherwise meets the related party criteria (see § 21.1).

(8) Rebuttable Presumption of Reasonableness. The intermediate sanctions regulations set forth a procedure, called the *rebuttable presumption of reasonableness*, under which payments of compensation are presumed to be reasonable. If the procedure is followed, the burden of proof is shifted to the IRS to prove that the transfer was not reasonable. Accordingly, if at all possible, charitable organizations will want to invoke the rebuttable presumption of reasonableness.

The three requirements of the rebuttable presumption follow.

1. **Approval by an independent body.** The compensation must be approved by an independent, authorized body, which may include a committee. No one approving the compensation can have a conflict of interest with respect to the transaction.

2. **Appropriate data as to comparability.** The approving board or committee, in determining the appropriateness of the compensation, takes into account appropriate data as to comparability. Relevant data include, but are not limited to, compensation levels paid by similarly situated organizations, both taxable and tax-exempt, for functionally comparable positions, the availability of similar services in the geographic area of the applicable tax-exempt organization, current compensation surveys compiled by independent firms, and actual written offers from similar institutions competing for the services of the compensated individual. For transfers of property, relevant information includes, but is not limited to, current independent appraisals of the value of all property to be transferred and offers received as part of an open and competitive bidding process.

3. **Documentation.** The decision by the board or compensation committee on the amount of compensation paid to an individual should be documented adequately and contemporaneously in written form. The records of the committee or board should note (a) the terms of the transaction that was approved and the date it was approved, (b) the members of the authorized body present during debate on the transaction and those who voted on it, (c) the comparability data obtained and relied on by the authorized body and how that data was obtained, and (d) any actions taken with respect to consideration of the transaction by anyone who is otherwise a member of the authorized body but who had a conflict of interest with respect to the transaction. For a decision to be

documented concurrently, records must be prepared before the later of the next meeting of the authorized body or 60 days after the final action of the authorized body are taken. Records must be reviewed and approved by the authorized body as reasonable, accurate, and complete within a reasonable period thereafter.

If an organization can meet these three requirements with respect to a transaction, the IRS may rebut the presumption that arises only if it develops sufficient contrary evidence to rebut the probative value of the comparability data relied on by the authorized body.

(9) Correction of an Excess Benefit Transaction. To avoid additional excise taxes on an excess benefit transaction, the transaction must be "corrected," which involves undoing the excess benefit, to the extent possible, and taking any additional measures necessary to place the tax-exempt organization in a financial position not worse that that in which it would be if the disqualified person were dealing under the highest fiduciary standards.

(10) Forms of Correction. The form of correction of an excess benefit transaction generally must be in cash or cash equivalents. Unless otherwise provided, a disqualified person corrects an excess benefit only by making a payment in cash or cash equivalents, excluding the payment of a promissory note, to the tax-exempt organization equal to the "correction amount." If the excess benefit transaction results, in whole or in part, from the vesting of benefits provided under a nonqualified deferred compensation plan, then, to the extent that such benefits have not yet been distributed to the disqualified person, the disqualified person may correct the portion of the excess benefit resulting from the undistributed deferred compensation by relinquishing any right to receive the excess portion of the undistributed deferred compensation (including any earnings thereon). In addition, a disqualified person may correct an excess benefit transaction involving the transfer of property by returning, with the agreement of the tax-exempt organization, specific property previously transferred in the excess benefit transaction. In this instance, the disqualified person is treated as making a payment equal to the lesser of:

- The fair market value of the property determined on the date the property is returned to the organization; or
- The fair market value of the property on the date the excess benefit transaction occurred.

Thus, if the property's value is less than the correction amount, the disqualified person will need to make a cash payment to the organization equal to the difference. If, however, the property's value is more than the correction amount, the organization may make a cash payment to the disqualified person equal to the difference.

(11) Correction When Tax-Exempt Organization Is No Longer in Existence or No Longer Tax-Exempt. Correction of an excess benefit transaction is required even if the charity or social welfare organization with which the transaction occurred is no longer in existence or is no longer tax-exempt. In the case of an excess benefit with a charity, the disqualified person must pay the correction amount to another tax-exempt charitable organization in accordance with the dissolution clause of constitutive documents of the entity, provided three conditions are met:

1. The organization receiving the correction amount is a public charity and has been in existence and so described for a continuous period of at least 60 calendar months ending on the date of correction.

2. The disqualified person is not also a disqualified person with respect to the organization receiving the correction amount.

3. The organization receiving the correction amount does not allow the disqualified person (or family members or controlled entities of the disqualified persons) to make or recommend any grants or other distributions by the organization.

If correction is to be made with respect to an excess benefit transaction involving a social welfare organization, the disqualified person must pay the correction amount to a successor social welfare organization or, if there is no tax-exempt successor, to any tax-exempt charitable or social welfare organization, provided the three conditions just listed are satisfied (aside from the requirement that the entity be a public charity).

(12) Correction Amount.   The "correction amount" with respect to an excess benefit transaction is the sum of the excess benefit and interest on the excess benefit. The interest rate used for this purpose is the applicable federal rate, compounded annually, for the month in which the transaction occurred.

(13) Reimbursement of the Excise Tax.   Any reimbursement by the applicable tax-exempt organization of excise tax liability is treated as an excess benefit transaction itself, unless it is included in the disqualified person's compensation for the year in which the reimbursement is made. Further, the compensation package, including the amount of the reimbursement, would have to be analyzed under the reasonableness test. If the package taken as a whole, including the reimbursement, is not reasonable, an excess benefit transaction would occur with regard to the compensation. If the payment by an applicable tax-exempt organization of premiums for an insurance policy providing liability insurance to the disqualified person for the excess benefit tax may be an excess benefit transaction itself, unless the amounts of the premium are treated as part of the compensation paid to a disqualified person and the total compensation, including the premiums is reasonable.

(14) Initial Contract Exception.   The intermediate sanctions do not apply to any fixed payment made to a person pursuant to an initial contract. This is known as the *initial contract exception*. A *fixed payment* is an amount of money where the property specified in the contract, or determined by a fixed formula specified in the contract, which is to be paid or transferred in exchange for the provision of specified services or property. An *initial contract* is a written contract between an organization or a person who is not a disqualified person immediately prior to entering into the contract. The compensation package can be partially sheltered by this initial contract exception; for example, an individual can have a base salary that is fixed payment pursuant to the initial contract and also have an annual performance based bonus that is subject to the excess benefit transaction analysis.

(15) Automatic Excess Benefit Transaction (Supporting Organizations). If a supporting organization makes a grant, loan, payment of compensation, or similar payment (such as an expense reimbursement) to a substantial contributor or related person of the supporting organization, the substantial contributor is regarded, for purposes of the intermediate sanction rules, as a disqualified person. This type of payment is treated as an *automatic excess benefit transaction*. As such, the entire amount of the payment is treated as an excess benefit. If this were to occur, a substantial contributor would be subject to the initial intermediate sanctions excise tax on the amount of the payment. Further, the organization manager who knowingly participated in the making of the payment is also subject to the excise tax. The second-tier taxes under the other intermediate sanctions rules are also applicable to these payments. Loans by a supporting organization to a disqualified person with respect to the supporting organization are treated as excess benefit transactions. The entire amount of this loan is regarded as an excess benefit and is reported in Schedule L.

(16) Loss of Exempt Status in Egregious Circumstances. The intermediate sanctions rules, albeit with sanctions different from those under the private inurement doctrine, in many ways parallel the private inurement doctrine. That is, an excise benefit transaction and a private inurement transaction are essentially the same. The legislative history of the intermediate sanctions law makes it clear, however, that the body of law to generally apply is that pertaining to intermediate sanctions. That is, the private inurement doctrine is to apply only in connection with facts and circumstances that are egregious. More particularly, the intermediate sanctions are to be the sole penalty imposed in cases in which the excess benefit does not rise to such a level as to call into question whether, on the whole, the organization functions as an exempt charitable organization.

The IRS imposes a facts-and-circumstances test to determine whether exempt status should be revoked. The test includes these five factors:

1. The size and scope of the organization's regular and ongoing activities that further exempt purposes before and after one or more excess benefit transactions occurred

2. The size and scope of one or more excess benefit transactions in relation to the size and scope of the organization's regular and ongoing exempt functions

3. Whether the organization has been involved in multiple excess benefit transactions

4. Whether the organization has implemented safeguards that are reasonably calculated to prevent future violations

5. Whether the excess benefit transaction has been corrected or the organization has made good-faith efforts to seek correction from the disqualified person or persons who benefited from the excess benefit transaction

The fourth and fifth of these factors "weigh more strongly" in favor of continuing exemption where the organization has discovered the excess benefit transaction and has taken corrective action before the IRS learns of the matter. Retaining the services of a lawyer to attempt to recover excess payments made in a private inurement transaction is an effort to pursue correction of the violation that mitigates in favor of retention of the exempt status of the organization.

(c) Private Benefit

(1) Generally. The usual IRS focus when investigating unreasonable compensation is the private inurement and excess benefit transaction rules (see § 6.1(a) and (b)). The sale of goods and services between a charity and its insiders, or entities owned more than 35 percent by insiders, are also scrutinized under the private inurement and excess benefit transaction rules. If an unfair transaction is entered into by the insider and disqualified person, respectively, the organization's exempt status can be lost and/or the intermediate sanctions can be imposed on the individuals involved.

The private benefit doctrine can also impact the compensation analysis. Whether an organization's activities serve private interests more than incidentally in violation of the private benefit proscription is a factual determination that generally involves an analysis of the relationship between the charity and one or more for-profit entities as a whole, not just a single transaction. Private benefit can come in many forms. As with private inurement and excess benefit transactions, the most direct form is excessive payments for goods or services. But private benefit also can exist when the flow of funds is not excessive and even when there is no direct flow of funds between the charity and a for-profit entity. One court, in its explanation of the many forms private benefit can take, explained that private benefit can be "an advantage, fruit, privilege, gain or interest." One commentator suggested that even "imprudent contracts, lax oversight by a board, irresponsible management, or even the continuation of the organization when it would have been more prudent to dissolve it . . . " may fit within the private benefit doctrine. Examples include secondary benefits realized by a political party relating to a charity's education of students and benefits conferred on restaurant owners relating to a charity's improvement of the area of a city surrounding the restaurants. Further, excessive private benefit has been found when the activity benefits one individual or entity, a select few such as the residents of one city block, or a larger number such as members of a political party. It can also apply to benefits conferred on other exempt organizations such as social welfare organizations and associations/business leagues.

In the context of reporting on the Form 990, many transactions in addition to compensation are scrutinized under the private benefit doctrine. For example, transactions reported in Schedule L (see Chapter 18) would be scrutinized under private benefit as well as the private inurement and excess benefit transaction rules. One of the transactions reported in Schedule L, for example, is the direct business transactions between the filing organization and a current or former officer, director, trustee, or key employee (other than as an officer, director, trustee, or employee) and/or family members of these individuals. Indirect business relationships between the filing organization and entities owned more than a 35-percent interest by current or former officers, directors, trustees, or key employees (individually or collectively) are also reported in Schedule L. Finally, if such individuals also serve as an officer, director, trustee, key employee, partner, or member of an entity (or a shareholder of a professional corporation) doing business with the filing organization, the relationship and transactions must be reported in Schedule L.

Transactions listed in Schedule R, in the context of related organizations, will also be scrutinized under the private benefit doctrine. The classic case is when a for-profit entity, such as a management company, is controlled by the same directors who control the charity or other exempt organization (see § 21.1(e)).

(2) Qualitatively and Quantitatively Incidental. To avoid a finding of more than incidental benefit, the private benefit must be both qualitatively and quantitatively incidental. *Qualitatively incidental* means that the private benefit is merely a by-product of the public benefit. It must be a necessary concomitant of the exempt activity in that the exempt objectives cannot be achieved without necessarily benefiting certain individuals privately. In one example, an organization was formed to preserve and enhance a lake as a public recreation facility by treating the water. The lake bordered on several municipalities, and the public used it extensively for recreation. The organization was financed through contributions from lakefront property owners as well as members of the adjacent community and municipalities. The ruling held that private benefits derived by the lakefront property owners did not lessen the public benefits, and, in fact, it would be impossible for the organization to accomplish its purposes without providing benefits to the lakefront owners.

Quantitatively incidental means that the amount in question must be insubstantial. The private benefit must be compared to the public benefit of the specific activity in question, not the public benefit provided by all the organization's activities. The more precisely the private benefit can be quantified, the more likely the private benefit will be considered more than incidental. In one case, the residents of a city block formed an organization to preserve and beautify the block, to improve all public facilities within the block, and to prevent physical deterioration of the block. These activities consisted of paying the city government to plant trees on public property within the block, organizing residents to pick up litter and refuse in the public streets and on public sidewalks within the block, and encouraging residents to take an active part in beautifying the block by placing shrubbery in public areas within the block. Membership in the organization was restricted to residents in the block and those owning property or operating businesses there. The organization's support was derived from receipts from block parties and volunteer contributions from the members. The IRS found that, by enhancing the value of the roadway sections abutted by property of its members, the organization was enhancing the value of its members' property rights. The restrictive nature of the membership and the limited area in which its improvements are made indicate that the organization is organized and operated to serve the private interests of its members.

(3) Related Party's Control of the Charity's Activities. Because the application of the private benefit is difficult under the qualitatively and quantitatively incidental standard, it is instructive to review the factors that have contributed to a finding of private benefit. Perhaps the most critical element of the analysis is determining who "controls" the charity and how the control impacts whether private interests are furthered by the charity's activities. The most common situation for a finding of private benefit is when control of the charity is transferred to a substantial degree to a private party with which the charity has a financial relationship directly or indirectly. This can occur in situations where the transaction is with an insider and/or an entity in which the insider holds an ownership interest of more than 35 percent. These transactions are reported on Schedule L.

Control is sometimes determinative of whether private benefit exists even if the arrangement clearly furthers exempt purposes. The series of joint venture cases and rulings issued over the past several years illustrate the importance of control in the analysis. The IRS, in its annual continuing professional education textbook for fiscal year 2001 (*2001 CPE Text*), also emphasizes control in its examples of private benefit. If an organization is closely controlled, either by a board of directors comprised of related persons or a for-profit management company that operates with a great amount of autonomy, a finding of private benefit is more likely. Close control will not always result in private benefit, but additional scrutiny will be imposed to ensure that the organization serves public rather than private purposes.

The most direct form of control is if the for-profit entity controls the charity's board of directors through common board members, placing its officers or employees on the charity's board or through other mechanisms. In this case when there is more than 50 percent common control, information on the related organization is reported in Schedule R. In the joint venture rulings, the initial focus was whether the charity could name a majority of the directors of the joint venture. Again, in this case, the filing organization would report the partnership or limited liability company as a related organization in Schedule R. If less than 50 percent is held in the joint venture but the joint venture is conducting an activity and the filing organization's share of that activity is more than 5 percent of the filing organization's total exempt activities, it would be reported in Schedule R, and the IRS would be aware of the charity's participation in a joint venture with a lack of control. In later cases, equal tax-exempt and for-profit control was sufficient to ensure that control was not ceded to a for-profit provided certain safeguards were placed in the governing documents (For more discussion of joint ventures, see § 21.1(f). Control also can be affected through agreements outside the joint venture context. The most common example of a transfer of control involves a management contract that covers all of the charity's operations. Other examples are fundraising or financial services agreements. Finally, advertising, public relations, or other arrangements can result in the transfer of control over significant segments of the charity's activities. If a for-profit organization itself forms the charity and becomes an exclusive or almost exclusive provider of services, a finding of private benefit is increased substantially even if the for-profit organization does not actually control the charity's board of directors. Where control is obtained by contract, the reporting is not as clear. Management contracts are reported in Part VI, question 3 if the management company assumes some of the duties of the filing organization's officers or directors (see Chapter 5). If the management company is owned more than 35 percent by insiders, it will also be reported in Schedule L (see Chapter 18).

In the Situation 1 example of the 2001 CPE Text, the IRS found private benefit where the for-profit management company had control over the school because the owners of the management company comprised two of the three school directors. The for-profit management company also formed the charity. Direct control over the charity by the private parties who benefited from the charity's operations was also present in a number of cases.

The IRS also found private benefit in Situation 2 of the 2001 CPE Text article even though the management company did not have technical control of the board of directors. In Situation 2, the for-profit management company did not control the directors of the tax-exempt school but the exempt school entered into a five-year agreement with the management company. The management company also entered into an equipment lease with the exempt school and a revolving loan and security agreement. Under the terms of the agreement, the school had no ability to make decisions independently of the management company. The IRS found that the motivation for forming the exempt school was simply to economically benefit the management company. The IRS asserted that the educational activities of the school could be undertaken without conferring the benefit on the management company. While the management company was not technically in control of the exempt school, control was ceded through a "web of related contracts." Factors the IRS looked to included:

- Contract between school and management company was entered into prior to formation of school.

- Management agreement and other agreements were automatically renewable.

- All decisions concerning the school must be agreed to by management company.

- Management company employed all faculty and staff at exempt school.

In another example, effective control was created through multiple agreements and financial integration of a charity with for-profit organizations. Private benefit was found in this case involving tax-exempt seminar organizations formed to provide educational programs. The exempt organizations formed by alumni contracted with three for-profit entities to conduct their activities under a franchise arrangement. The charities entered into exclusive contracts with these for-profit entities for various training and development services. While board control of the charity was not ceded to the for-profit entities, the integration of the charity's delivery of services with the for-profit entities occurred through an exclusive franchise arrangement. The success of these for-profit entities was dependent on the success of the charity's programs through the integration of the delivery of services and the charity's exclusive use of these for-profit entities for services.

(4) Motivation for Formation of Charity. Even when control is not transferred directly or effectively, private benefit may be found on the basis of the motivation for forming the charity and the integration of the charity's activities with the business of private individuals or entities. The IRS concludes that discerning the "true purposes" for the formation of the charity is critical to the analysis. The best guide to making the determination is the actual result or operation of an organization's activities.

If all of an organization's business dealings are with a single entity, promoter, or developer, private benefit is more likely to be found. While a formal competitive bidding is not always necessary, the failure to consider alternative sources or compare prices is another indicator of private benefit. The qualitatively incidental requirement is often invoked in the analysis when the arrangement involves the charity's exclusive use of a vendor or management company. This is the result because the charity's exclusive use of the for-profit management company or vendor is not a necessary by-product of the exempt activity.

A number of cases and rulings focus on this factor. In the two school examples of the 2001 CPE Text, the IRS emphasized the motivation for formation of the schools. In one court case, the court found that formation of an academy by the Republican National Committee was motivated by its desire to train Republican Party members. The three restaurant owners in another case wanted to improve the area surrounding their restaurants to improve business. In other cases charities were created by the residents of residential block and property owners along a waterway who wanted to improve property values, the trade association that wanted to improve the business of its members by creating standardized engineering codes and specifications, and the radio station that wanted to keep its listeners by providing classical music. While the public benefited to different degrees by the formation and operation of the charities in these cases, it was the motive behind the formation that was persuasive in the finding that there was a substantial private interest furthered by the operations. Had the charity been formed to deliver the exempt services independent of the for-profit entities in question, the likelihood of a finding of private benefit would be substantially less.

(5) Integration.   In addition to the motivation for the formation of the charity and the control of the charity after its formation, the financial integration of the charity to for-profit enterprises is important in the analysis. The franchise arrangement in one case involved an integrated delivery of services provided by both charities and for-profit entities. The services of the for-profit entity could not be separated from the exempt organizations. The Situation 3 and Situation 4 examples of the 2001 CPE Text also illustrate financial integration. In these examples, it was the need of a charity for tax-exempt bond financing and the tax credits, respectively, that necessitated the involvement of a charity.

In Situation 4, a for-profit developer asked the charity to form a partnership to acquire and renovate the properties for low-income housing. The developer acknowledged that a nonprofit joint venture partner was needed to secure key funding sources and to facilitate lender and governmental agency approval of the transfers. The developer's management company served as property manager for the properties. It was to be paid a fee for its services. The charity granted to the developer, for a period of two years, the right of first refusal to be a joint venture partner with the charity if the charity should acquire and develop properties not identified by the developer. In the IRS's analysis of this fact pattern, the IRS acknowledges that the charity was closely in line with the developer with respect to the property acquisition and development. The IRS acknowledged that the transaction was commercial in nature and that the charity was involved "only to secure to the tax credits." Low-income tax credits are allocated by various state agencies established for that purpose. States are required to allocate at least 10 percent of such credits to organizations that have charitable or social welfare status. Many states give priority to applicants holding exempt status.

Situation 3 of the 2001 CPE Text involved the formation of the charity by a developer and manager of nursing home facilities. The proposed facility would be financed with tax-exempt bond proceeds and developed by a partnership in which the founder was a partner. The IRS concluded that the operation of the charity benefited founder and his controlled entities to expand and extend their commercial activities, and one substantial purpose of the charity is to further that benefit. The activities of the charitable organization were viewed as benefiting both the charitable class of persons and the founder's business entities, but the IRS concluded that the private interests were more than incidental, even though the transactions between the founder and founder's entities are at or below fair market value.

In other examples, the integration of a church, which conducted its ministry through the mail with an advertising entity to provide printing and mailing services, was found to substantially benefit the advertising agency, and a charity's certification services provided as an integral part of the structural steel fabrication industry to ensure quality was also private benefit.

(6) Number of Persons Benefiting. The fewer the number of persons that benefit from the charity's activities, the more likely private benefit is found. Benefits conferred on a single management company or consultant will more likely constitute private benefit than if a larger number benefits from the activity. However, benefits realized by multiple residents of a city block or navigable waterway can also constitute private benefit, and benefits realized by an entire industry or political party can result in private benefit. However, recreation benefits realized by lakefront residents and other residents in a community from a charity's preservation activity was a large enough class to avoid private benefit.

The number of entities privately benefiting from the charitable activity was also important in an IRS ruling. In this ruling, an organization conducted an educational program for bank employees. It furnished classrooms and employed university professors and others to teach courses on various banking subjects. It had insubstantial social activities. Only members could take courses, but membership was open to employees of all banks in the area, not just the employees of one bank. If training was available only for employees of one bank, the organization may not have qualified for exemption. Compare this result to a case where only one partisan group benefited from the education activity. Had the training been provided on a nonpartisan basis, the result might have been different.

§6.2 PREPARATION OF NEW FORM 990, PART VII AND SCHEDULE J

All organizations are required to complete Part VII and, when applicable, Schedule J. Part VII is divided into two parts. Section A provides a detailed table for disclosures of compensation paid to certain individuals, and Section B asks for disclosure of independent contractor compensation. Use the Schedule J-2, Continuation Sheet for compensation, if more space is needed to list additional persons.

(a) Section A (Compensation Information)

In Section A, compensation information is reported for certain persons from the reporting organization and all related organizations. See § 6.1(a)(1) for a discussion of key employees, officers, highly compensated individuals, and other information necessary to complete Part VII and Schedule J.

(1) Line 1a (Compensation Reporting—Definitions). On line 1a, the organization must disclose "reportable" compensation and an estimate of "other" compensation for the following individuals (see § 6.1(a)(1) for definitions):

- Current officers, directors, and trustees (whether individuals or organizations), regardless of the amount of compensation

- Current key employees with reportable compensation of more than $150,000

- Five current highest-compensated employees (other than officers, directors, trustees, and key employees), who have reportable compensation in excess of $100,000 from the reporting organization and any related organizations

- Former officers, key employees, or highly compensated employees who receive more than $100,000 from the organization and all related organizations

- Former directors or trustees who received, in the capacity as a former director or trustee of the organizations, more than $10,000 of reportable compensations from the organizations and all related organizations

> *Caution:* The form indicates that all current key employees must be listed "regardless of amount of compensation." The instructions, however, provide that, by definition, a person should not be listed as a key employee unless his or her reportable compensation from the organization and related organizations exceeds $150,000.

The instructions indicate that reportable compensation consists of:

- For officers and other employees: amounts reported in Box 5 of Form W-2.

- For directors and individual trustees: amounts reported in Box 7 of Form 1099-MISC (plus Box 5 of Form W-2 if also compensated as an officer or employee).

- For institutional trustees: fees for services paid pursuant to a contractual agreement or statutory entitlement. An institutional trustee is an organization rather than an individual or natural person (e.g., a bank or trust company). While the compensation of institutional trustees must be reported in Form 990, Part VII, it need not be reported in Schedule J.

If the organization does not file a Form W-2 or 1099-MISC because the amounts paid were below the threshold reporting requirement, then include and report the amount actually paid.

Corporate officers are considered employees for purposes of Form W-2 reporting, unless they perform no services as officers, or perform only minor services and neither receive nor are entitled to receive, directly or indirectly, any compensation. Corporate directors are considered independent contractors, not employees, and director compensation, if any, generally is required to be reported on Form 1099-MISC. For certain kinds of employees, such as certain members of the clergy and religious workers who are not subject to Social Security and Medicare taxes as employees, Box 5 of Form W-2 may be zero or blank. In such case, the amount required to be reported in Box 1 of Form W-2 must be reported as reportable compensation.

To determine whether an individual received more than $100,000 (or $150,000) in reportable compensation in the aggregate from the organization and related organizations, add these amounts:

- Amounts reported in Box 5 of Form W-2 and/or Box 7 of Form 1099-MISC issued to the individual by the organization and all related organizations.

- Amounts reported in Box 5 of Form W-2 and/or Box 7 of Form 1099-MISC issued to the individual by each related organization. Disregard payments from a related organization if below $10,000.

To determine whether an individual received solely in the capacity as a former trustee or director of the organization more than $10,000 in reportable compensation for the calendar year with or within the organization's tax year, in the aggregate, from the organization and all related organizations (and thus must be reported in Form 990, Part VII, and Schedule J, Part II), add the amounts reported in Box 7 of all Forms 1099-MISC and, if relevant, Box 5 of all Forms W-2 issued to the individual by the organization and all related organizations for the calendar year with or within the organization's tax year. Report the amounts only to the extent that such amounts relate to the individual's past services as a trustee or director of the organization (and do not disregard payments from a related organization below $10,000 for this purpose).

(2) Line 1a, Column (A) (Name and Title). In Column (A), report the person's name in the top of each row and the person's title or position in the bottom of the row. List all titles or positions if more than one. List persons in this order: individual trustees or directors; institutional trustees; officers; key employees; highest-compensated employees; and former such persons. If additional space is needed for additional title or persons, use Schedule J-2.

(3) Line 1a, Columns (B) and (C) (Average Hours Worked and Position). In Column (B), report average hours worked per week for each person. The average hours per week should be reported for the organization and all related organizations for which compensation is reported during the calendar year ending with or within the organization's tax year. The entry of a specific number is required for a complete answer. The instructions indicate that statements such as "as needed," "as required," or "40-plus" are not acceptable. If the average is less than one hour per week, then the organization may report a decimal rounded to the nearest tenth (e.g., 0.2 hours per week). The hours devoted to related organizations may be reported in Schedule O.

In Column (C), report the position of the individual. The instructions provide guidance as to the designation of both current and former positions. A "current" officer, director, or trustee is a person who was an officer, director, or trustee at any time during the organization's tax year. A "current" key employee or highest-compensated employee is a person who was a key employee or highest-compensated employee for the calendar year ending with or within the organization's tax year.

If the organization files Form 990 based on a fiscal year, use the fiscal year to determine the organization's "current" officers, directors, and trustees. Whether or not the organization files Form 990 based on a fiscal year, use the calendar year ending with or within the organization's tax year to determine the organization's "current" key employees and five highest-compensated employees.

Do not check the "Former" box if the person was a current officer, director, or trustee at any time during the organization's tax year, or a current key employee or among the five highest-compensated employees for the calendar year ending with or within the organization's tax year. A current employee (other than a current officer, director, trustee, key employee, or highest-compensated employee) may be reported in Part VII and Schedule J, Part II as (1) a former director or trustee because he or she formerly served as a director or trustee and received more than $10,000 reportable compensation in the capacity as a former director or trustee, or (2) a former officer or key employee (but not as a former highest-compensated employee) because he or she qualified as an officer or key employee within the last five years and received more than $100,000 of reportable compensation. In such case, indicate the individual's former position in his or her titles (e.g., "former president").

Check the "Former" box with respect to former officers, directors, trustees, and key employees only if both of these conditions apply:

1. The organization reported (or should have reported, applying the instructions in effect for such years) an individual on any of the organization's Forms 990, 990-EZ, or 990-PF for one or more of the five prior years in one or more of these capacities: officer, director, trustee, or key employee; and

2. The individual received reportable compensation in the calendar year ending with or within the organization's current tax year in excess of the threshold amount ($100,000 for former officers and key employees, $10,000 for services in the capacity as a director or trustee).

If a person was reported (or should have been reported) as an officer, director, trustee, or key employee on any of the organization's prior five Forms 990, 990-EZ, or 990-PF, and the person was still employed at any time during the organization's tax year either (1) by the organization in a capacity other than as an officer, director, trustee, key employee, or highest-compensated employee, or (2) by a related organization in any capacity, check only the "Former" box.

Whether or not the organization files Form 990 based on a fiscal year, use the calendar year ending within the organization's tax year to determine all "former" officers, directors, trustees, key employees, and five highest-compensated employees (because their status depends on their reportable compensation, which is reported for the calendar year).

Check the "Former" box with respect to former five highest-compensated employees only if all three of these conditions apply. "Former" highest-compensated employees are reported by charities only in 2008. For years after 2008, all exempt organizations will have to report information on former highly compensated employees.

1. The individual was not an employee of the organization at any time during the calendar year ending with or within the organization's tax year;

2. The individual's reportable compensation exceeded $100,000 for the calendar year ending with or within the organization's tax year; and

3. The amount of the individual's reportable compensation for such year would place him or her among the organization's current five highest-compensated employees if the individual were an employee during the calendar year ending with or within the organization's tax year.

Example 1. X was reported as one of Y Charity's five highest-compensated employees over $50,000 in Y's 2006 Form 990. For 2008, X is not a current officer, director, trustee, key employee, or highest-compensated employee of Y. X is not an employee of Y during the 2008 calendar year ending with or within Y's tax year. X receives reportable compensation in excess of $100,000 from Y for past services and would be among Y's five highest-compensated employees if X were a current employee. Y must report X as a former highest-compensated employee in Y's 2008 Form 990, Part VII, Section A.

Example 2. T was reported as one of Y Charity's five highest-compensated employees over $50,000 in Y's 2007 Form 990. For 2008, T is not a current officer, director, trustee, key employee, or highest-compensated employee of Y, although T is still an employee of Y during the 2008 calendar year ending with or within Y's tax year. T receives reportable compensation in excess of $100,000 from Y and related organizations for such calendar year. T is not reportable as a former highest-compensated employee in Y's 2008 Form 990, Part VII, Section A, because T was an employee of Y during the calendar year ending with or within Y's tax year.

Example 3. Z was reported as one of Y Charity's key employees in Y's 2006 Form 990. For 2008, Z is not a current officer, director, trustee, key employee, or highest-compensated employee of Y. For 2008, Z receives reportable compensation of $90,000 from Y as an employee (and no reportable compensation from related organizations). Because Z receives less than $100,000 reportable compensation in 2008 from Y and its related organizations, Y is not required to report Z as a former key employee in Y's 2008 Form 990, Part VII, Section A.

An employee is a person who performs services for an employer, if the employer has the right to control and direct the results of the work and the way in which it is done. Management companies and similar entities that are independent contractors should not be reported as employees.

(4) Line 1a, Column (D) (Reportable Compensation from Filing Organization). In Column (D), indicate the reportable compensation from the filing organization for the calendar year ending with or within the filing organization's tax year.

(5) Line 1a, Column (E) (Reportable Compensation from Related Organizations). In Column (E), indicate reportable compensation from related organizations (as defined in Schedule R; see Chapter 21). For organizations with fiscal years, compensation is reported for the calendar ending with or within the fiscal year. The instructions indicate that amounts paid by a common paymaster for services performed for the organization should be reported as if paid directly by the organization. Likewise, treat amounts paid by a common paymaster for services performed for related organization as if paid directly by the related organization. For purposes of Column (E), the organization need not include payments from a single related organization of less than $10,000 for the calendar year ending with or within the tax year, except to the extent paid to a former director or a former trustee of the organization for services as a director or trustee of the organization. For example, if an officer of an organization receives compensation of $6,000, $15,000, and $50,000 from three separate related organizations for services provided to those organizations, the organization needs to report only $65,000 in Column (E) for the officer.

Volunteer Exception. The organization need not report in Column (E) or (F) compensation from a related organization paid to a volunteer officer, director, or trustee of the organization if the related organization is a for-profit organization, is not owned or controlled directly or indirectly by the organization or one or more related tax-exempt organizations, and does not provide management services for a fee to the organization.

Bank or Financial Institution Trustee Exception. If the organization is a trust with a bank or financial institution trustee that is also a trustee of another trust, it need not report in Column (E) or (F) compensation from the other trust or services provided as the trustee to the other trust.

Reasonable Effort. The organization is not required to report compensation from a related organization to a person listed in Part VII, Section A if the organization is unable to secure the information on compensation paid by the related organization after making a reasonable effort to obtain it. In such case, the organization shall report the efforts undertaken in Schedule O. An example of a reasonable effort is for the organization to distribute a questionnaire annually to each such listed person that includes the name, title, date, and signature of each person reporting information and contains the pertinent instructions and definitions for Part VII, Section A, Columns (E) and (F).

(6) Line 1a, Column (F) (Other Compensation). In Column (F), an estimate of "other compensation" should be reported from the organization and related organizations. The instructions direct the organization to use Schedule J-2 if additional space is needed. The instructions indicate that other compensation includes compensation other than reportable compensation including deferred compensation not currently reported on Form W-2, Box 5, or Form 1099-MISC, Box 7, and certain nontaxable benefits, as discussed in detail in Schedule J. See the table in Appendix B for a detailed list of compensation types and where to report in Schedule J and in Part VII.

The instructions provided that these items of compensation must be reported as "other compensation" in all cases, regardless of the amount (unless the $10,000 exception for compensation from a related organization applies):

- Tax-deferred contributions by the employer and employee to a qualified defined-contribution retirement plan.

- The annual increase in actuarial value of a qualified defined-benefit plan whether or not funded or vested.

- The value of health benefits provided by the employer, whether or not qualified, that are not included in reportable compensation. For this purpose, health benefits provided by the employer include payments of health benefit plan premiums, medical reimbursement and flexible spending programs, and the value of health coverage (rather than actual benefits paid) provided by an employer's self-insured or self-funded arrangement. Health benefits include dental, optical, drug, and medical equipment benefits. They do not include disability or long-term care insurance premiums or benefits for this purpose.

- Tax-deferred contributions by the employer and employee to a nonqualified defined contribution plan, whether or not funded, vested, or subject to a substantial risk of forfeiture.

- The annual increase in actuarial value of a nonqualified defined benefit plan, whether or not funded, vested, or subject to a substantial risk of forfeiture.

Neither the organization nor a related organization is required to report in Part VII, Section A any other item of other compensation if its value is less than $10,000 for the calendar year ending with or within the organization's tax year.

Amounts excluded under the two separate $10,000 exceptions (the $10,000 per related organization and $10,000 per item exceptions) are to be excluded from compensation in determining whether an individual's total reportable and other compensation exceeds the thresholds set forth in Form 990, Part VII, Section A, line 4. If the total exceeds the relevant threshold, then the amounts excluded under the $10,000 exceptions are not included in the individual's compensation reported in Schedule J. Thus, the total amount of compensation reported in Schedule J may be higher than the amount reported in Part VII. The $10,000 exceptions apply separately with respect to each item of other compensation from the organization and from each related organization.

EXAMPLE: ORGANIZATION X PROVIDES THIS COMPENSATION TO ITS CURRENT OFFICER:	
$110,000	Reportable compensation (including $5,000 pretax employee contribution to qualified defined-contribution retirement plan)
5,000	Tax-deferred employer contribution to qualified defined-contribution retirement plan
5,000	Nontaxable employer contribution to health benefit plan
4,000	Nontaxable dependent care assistance
500	Nontaxable group life insurance premium
8,000	Moving expense (nontaxable as qualified under Section 132)

Organization Y, a related organization, also provides this compensation to the officer:

$21,000	Reportable compensation (including $1,000 pre-tax employee contribution to qualified defined contribution retirement plan)
1,000	Tax-deferred employer contribution to qualified defined-contribution retirement plan
5,000	Nontaxable tuition assistance

The officer receives no compensation in the capacity as a former director or trustee of X, and no unrelated organization pays the officer for services provided

to X. The organization may disregard as other compensation (a) the $4,500 (depen-
dent care and group life) payments from the organization under the $10,000 per item
exception; (b) the $8,000 moving expense from the organization because such amount
is excluded from reportable and other compensation under Section 132 (in both Part
VII and Schedule J, Part II; and (c) the $5,000 tuition from the related organization
under $10,000 per item exception in determining whether the officer's total reportable
and other compensation from the organization and related organizations exceeds
$150,000. In this case, total reportable compensation is $131,000, and total other compensation (excluding the excludible items below $10,000) is $11,000. Under these circumstances, the officer's dependent care, group life, moving expenses, and tuition
items need not be reported as other compensation in Part VII, Column (F) and the
officers total reportable and other compensation (142,000 is not reported in schedule
J). If instead the officer's reportable compensation from Y were $30,000 rather than
$21,000, then the officer's total reportable and other compensation ($151,000) would
be reportable in Schedule J, including the dependent care, group life, and tuition
items even though these items would not have to be reported as other compensation
in Part VII.

(7) Line 2 (Total Number with Greater than $100,000 of Compensation). On line 2,
report the total number of individuals who receive reportable compensation of more
than $100,000 from the organization and related organizations. Report a reasonable
estimate if the actual numbers are not readily available.

(8) Lines 3 and 4 (Reporting Required on Schedule J). On line 3, indicate "yes" or
"no" as to whether any of the former officers, directors or trustees, key employees, or
highest-compensated employees leave in listed in Section A. On Line 4, indicate
"yes" or "no" as to whether any individual listed in Section A had reportable compensation in excess of $150,000 from the organization and related organizations. To
determine whether any listed individual received or accrued more than $150,000 of
reportable and other compensation, add all compensation included in Columns (D),
(E), and (F) of Section A. The instructions in the next table provide assistance in determining filing requirements for Schedule J.

POSITION	CURRENT OR FORMER	LIST IN FORM 990, PART VII, SECTION A:	LIST IN SCHEDULE J, PART II:
Directors and trustees	current	All	if reportable and other compensation > $150,000 in the aggregate from organization and related organizations (do not report institutional trustees)

(Continued)

Position	Current or Former	List in Form 990, Part VII, Section A:	List in Schedule J, Part II:
	former	if reportable compensation in capacity as former director or trustee > $10,000 in the aggregate from organization and related organizations	if listed in Form 990, Part VII, Section A (do not report institutional trustees)
Officers	current	All	if reportable and other compensation > $150,000 in the aggregate from organization and related organizations
	former	if reportable compensation > $100,000 in the aggregate from organization and related organizations	if listed in Form 990, Part VII, Section A
Key employees (meeting the three tests)	current	All	All
	former	if reportable compensation > $100,000 in the aggregate from organization and related organizations	if listed in Form 990, Part VII, Section A
Other five highest-compensated employees	current	if reportable compensation > $100,000 in the aggregate from organization and related organizations	if reportable and other compensation > $150,000 in the aggregate from organization and related organizations
	former	if reportable compensation > $100,000 in the aggregate from organization and related organizations	if listed in Form 990, Part VII, Section A

(9) Line 5 (Reporting Compensation from Certain Unrelated Organizations). On line 5, indicate "yes" or "no" if the person receives or accrues compensation from an unrelated organization for services rendered to the filing organization in the person's capacity as an officer, director, trustee, or employee of the filing organization. Also, specify in Part III of Schedule J the name of the unrelated organization, the type and amount of compensation it paid or accrued, and the person receiving or accruing such compensation. The organization must report as compensation amounts received or accrued by the person from the unrelated organization for services rendered to the organization, whether the unrelated organization treats the amounts as compensation, grants, or otherwise. The organization is required to report compensation from an unrelated organization only if it has knowledge of the compensation arrangement. The compensation from the unrelated organization for services provided to the filing organization must be reported as compensation from the filing organization both in Part VII, and in Schedule J. The amounts from the unrelated organization must be taken into account in determining whether the dollar thresholds are met for reporting such persons in Part VII and Schedule J.

For purposes of Line 5, disregard: (1) payments from a deferred compensation trust or plan established, sponsored, or maintained by the organization (or a related organization), and deferred compensation held by such trust or plan; (2) payments from a common paymaster for services provided to the organization (or to a related organization); and (3) payments from an unrelated taxable organization that employs the individual and continues to pay the individual's regular compensation while the individual provides services without charge to the organization, but only if the unrelated organization does not treat the payments as a charitable contribution or distribution to the organization.

> **Example 1.** A is the CEO (and thus the top management official) of the organization. In addition to compensation paid by the organization to A, A receives payments from B, an unrelated corporation (using the definition of relatedness in Schedule R), for services provided by A to the organization. B also makes rent payments for A's personal residence. The organization is aware of the compensation arrangement between A and B, and does not treat the payments as paid by the organization for Form W-2 reporting purposes. A, as the top management official of the organization, must be listed as an officer of the organization in Part VII. However, the amounts paid by B to A require that the organization answer "yes" to line 5 and complete Schedule J with respect to A.

> **Example 2.** C is an attorney employed by a law firm that is not a related organization with respect to the organization. The organization and the law firm enter into an arrangement where C serves the organization, a 501(c)(3) legal aid society pro bono, on a full-time basis as its vice-president and as a board member while continuing to receive her regular compensation from the law firm. The organization does not provide any compensation to C for the services provided by C to the organization and does not report C's compensation on Form W-2 or Form 1099-MISC. The law firm does not treat any part of C's compensation as a charitable contribution to the legal aid society. Under these circumstances, the amounts paid by the law firm to C do not require that the organization answer "yes" to Line 5 with respect to C. Also, nothing in these facts would prevent C from qualifying as an

independent member of the organization's governing body for purposes of Part VI, line 1b.

Example 3. D, a volunteer director of the organization, is also the sole owner and CEO of M management company (an unrelated organization), which provides management services to the organization. The organization pays M an annual fee of $150,000 for the management services. Under the circumstances, the amounts paid by M to D (in the capacity as owner and CEO of M) do not require that the organization answer "yes" to line 5 with respect to D. The organization must report in Schedule L, Part IV, however, the transaction with M, including the relationship between D and M. Also, D does not qualify as an independent member of the organization's governing body because D receives indirect financial benefits through M.

(b) Section B (Independent Contractors)

In Section B, report information regarding independent contractor compensation.

(1) Line 1 (Five Highest-Compensated Independent Contractors). On line 1, report the five highest-compensated independent contractors who received more than $100,000 of compensation from the organization. Independent contractors include individuals and organizations. Examples include law firms, accounting firms, and management companies. The name and business address is listed in Column (A), a description of services is listed in Column (B), and the compensation amount is listed in Column (C). Enter the amount the organization paid, whether reported on Form 1099-MISC, Box 7, or paid pursuant to the parties' agreement or applicable state law, for the calendar year ending with or within the organization's tax year. Compensation includes fees and similar payments to independent contractors but not reimbursement of expenses. For this purpose, however, the organization may report the gross payment to the independent contractor that includes expenses and fees if the expenses are not separately reported to the organization. The instructions suggest that the Form 1099-MISC is not always required to be issued for payments to an independent contractor.

(2) Line 2 (Total Number in Excess of $100,000 in Compensation of Independent Contractors). On line 2, report the total number of independent contractors, including those listed in line 1, who received more than $100,000 in compensation from the organization.

(c) Schedule J (Additional Compensation Information)

Schedule J requires detailed information regarding every component of compensation. The various forms include employee fringe benefits, deferred compensation, revenue sharing, equity-based compensation, and other forms. Part I asks for compensation practices of only the filing organization unless specifically asked otherwise. Lines 5 through 8 of Part I must be answered only by charities and social welfare organizations. Part II requires more detailed information from organizations answering "yes" to line 23, Part IV. Part III is used to provide explanations to answers as required in Parts I and II. The Panel on the Nonprofit Sector reported to Congress its belief that fringe benefits, including travel reimbursement, should be carefully monitored. Further, policies for reimbursement should be established and enforced. The Panel suggested that charitable organizations should not pay for nor reimburse travel expenditures for a spouse, dependents, or others who are accompanying an individual conducting business for the organization unless the additional person is also conducting business for the organization.

(1) Part I, Line 1a (Fringe Benefits).   On line 1a, report fringe benefits of all types by checking the appropriate box. There are eight boxes including first-class or charter travel, travel for companions, tax indemnification and gross-up payments, discretionary spending account, housing allowance, a residence for personal use, payments for business use of personal residence, health or social club dues or initiation fees and personal services (e.g., maid, chauffeur, chef). Boxes are checked regardless of whether the benefit was included in compensation on Form W-2, Box 5, or Form 1099-MISC, Box 7. In asking whether these various benefits are available, the IRS implicitly is scrutinizing the appropriateness of the benefits. In some cases the benefits may be appropriate, but in other cases they may not. In any event, the IRS wants full disclosure to make that determination. After the initial draft of the new Form 990 was released, there was much confusion about the definitions of various fringe benefits. Therefore, the revised instructions provide a number of different definitions of fringe benefits. The definitions are provided in the next paragraphs.

First-class travel refers to any travel on a passenger airplane, train, or boat with first-class seat or accommodations, for which a listed person or his or her companion is availed the first-class accommodations and any portion of the cost above the lower-class fare is paid by the organization. First-class travel does not include intermediate classes between first class and coach, such as business class on commercial airlines. Bump-ups to first class free of charge or as a result of using frequent flyer benefits, or similar arrangements that are at no additional cost to the organization, may be disregarded.

Charter travel refers to travel on an airplane, train, or boat under a charter or rental arrangement. Charter travel also includes any travel on an airplane or boat that is owned or leased by the organization.

Travel for companions refers to any travel of a listed person's guest that is not traveling primarily for bona fide business purposes of the organization. It also refers to any travel of a listed person's *family members*, whether or not for bona fide business purposes.

Tax indemnification and *gross-up payments* refer to the organization's payment or reimbursement of any tax obligations of a listed person.

Discretionary spending account refers to an account or sum of money under the control of a listed person with respect to which he or she is not accountable to the organization under an accountable plan, whether or not actually used for any personal expenses. Accountable plans are discussed in the instructions for Part II.

Housing allowance or residence for personal use refers to any payment for, or provision of, housing by the organization for personal use by a listed person.

Payments for business use of personal residence refer to any payment by the organization for the use of all or part of a listed person's residence for any purpose of the organization.

Health or social club dues or initiation fees refer to any payment of dues by the organization for the membership of a listed person in a health or fitness club or a social or recreational club, whether or not such clubs are tax-exempt. It does not include membership fees for an organization described in sections 501(c)(3) or 501(c)(6) unless such organization provides health, fitness, or recreational facilities available for the regular use of a listed person. "Health club dues" do not include provision by the organization of an on-premises athletic facility described in section 132(j)(4), or provision by a school of an athletic facility available for general use by its students, faculty, and employees. "Dues" include the entrance fee, periodic fees, and amounts paid for use of such facilities.

Personal services are any services for the personal benefit of a listed person or the family or friends of a listed person, whether provided regularly (on a full-time or part-time basis) or as needed, whether provided by an employee of the organization or independent contractor (and whether the independent contractor is an individual or an organization). They include, but are not limited to, services of a babysitter, bodyguard, butler, chauffeur, chef, concierge or other person who regularly runs nonincidental personal errands, escort, financial planner, handyman, landscaper, lawyer, maid, masseur/masseuse, nanny, personal trainer, personal advisor or counselor, pet sitter, physician or other medical specialist, tax preparer, and tutor for nonbusiness purposes. Personal services do not include services provided to all employees on a nondiscriminatory basis under a qualified employee benefit plan.

(2) Part I, Line 1b (Written Policies). On line 1b, indicate "yes" or "no" as to whether there is a written policy for the payment or reimbursement of expenses for any box items checked on Line 1. If no policy exists, the organization is asked to explain in Part III why there is not a policy. This opportunity to explain was added to the schedule in the final version of the form. The instructions clarify that the explanation on why no written policy exists should indicate who in the organization determined that the organization would provide such benefits and the decision-making process. As part of the report to Congress provided by the Panel on the Nonprofit Sector, written policies for travel reimbursement are considered important for good governance and corporate best practices. Thus, if there is no such policy, the IRS may assume that the travel reimbursement practices of the organization may not be appropriate.

(3) Part I, Line 2 (Substantiation). On line 2, indicate "yes" or "no" as to whether the organization required substantiation of all expenses or benefits prior to reimbursing or allowing expenses incurred by all the officers, directors, and trustees, including the CEO/Executive Director or other top management official regarding the fringe benefit items checked in line 1a. The instructions specify that an organization may answer "yes" if it checked the "discretionary spending account" box on line 1 and it required substantiation of expenses under the rules for accountable plans for all listed benefits in line 1 other than for discretionary spending accounts.

The issue is whether the reimbursement followed the rules for accountable plans. Expense reimbursements and allowances provided to employees under an accountable plan are working condition fringe. An accountable plan is a reimbursement or other expense allowance arrangement that meets these rules:

- The expenses covered under the plan must be reasonable employee business expenses that are deductible under Section 162 or other provisions of the Code.

- The employee must adequately account to the employer for the expenses within a reasonable period of time.

- The employee must return any excess allowance or reimbursement within a reasonable period of time.

The method by which benefits under an accountable plan are provided (whether reimbursement, cash advance with follow-up accounting, or charged by the employee on company credit card) is not material. Payments that do not qualify under the accountable plan rules, such as payments for which the employee did not adequately account to the organization, or allowances that were more than the payee spent on serving the organization, constitute reportable compensation.

Directors and trustees are treated as employees for purposes of the working condition fringe provisions of Section 132. Therefore, treat cash payments to directors or trustees made under circumstances substantially identical to the accountable plan provisions as a Section 132 working condition fringe.

(4) Part I, Line 3 (Compensation Methods).   On line 3, indicate "yes" or "no" as to whether any of the compensation sources listed were used by the organization to establish the compensation of the organization's top management official. Boxes should be checked only with respect to the filing organization, not related organizations. The purpose of this line is to determine whether the organization used compensation comparability data and proper procedures and agreements in setting the compensation of the top management official. Comparability data helps document reasonable compensation and helps satisfy the rebuttable presumption of reasonableness in setting the compensation (see § 6.1(b)). The question asks the organization to check the applicable boxes. The list of boxes includes:

- Compensation committee

- Independent compensation consultant

- Form 990 of other organizations

- Written employment contract

- Compensation survey or study

- Approval by the board or compensation committee

The instructions ask that an explanation be provided in Part III if the organization shared the top management official's services with a related organization that used one of the methods listed. The instructions include the definitions in the next paragraphs in this regard.

Compensation committee refers to a committee of the organization's governing body responsible for determining the top management official's compensation package, whether or not the committee has been delegated the authority to make an employment agreement with the top management official on behalf of the organization. The compensation committee may also have other duties.

Compensation consultant refers to a person outside the organization that advises the organization regarding the top management official's compensation package, holds himself or herself out to the public as a compensation consultant, or performs valuations of nonprofit executive compensation on a regular basis and is qualified to make valuations of the type of services provided. The consultant is independent if he or she does not have a family or business relationship with the top management official, and if a majority of his or her appraisals made during his or her taxable year are performed for persons other than the organization, even if the consultant's firm also provides tax and audit, and other professional services to the organization.

Form 990 of other organizations refers to compensation information reported in Forms 990, 990-EZ, or 990-PF of similarly situated organizations.

Written employment agreement refers to one or more recent or current written employment agreements to which the top management official and another organization are or were parties, written employment agreements involving similarly situated top management officials with similarly situated organizations, or written employment offers to the top management official from other organizations dealing at arm's length.

Compensation survey or study refers to a study of top management official compensation or functionally comparable positions in similarly situated organizations.

Approval by the board or compensation committee refers to the ultimate decision by the governing body or compensation committee on behalf of the organization as to (1) whether to enter into an employment agreement with the top management official, and (2) the terms of such agreement.

(5) Part I, Line 4 (Severance, Change of Control, Supplemental Retirement and Equity-Based Compensation). On lines 4a through 4c, indicate "yes" or "no" as to whether any person listed in Part VII, Section A, during the reporting year:

- 4a—received a severance payment or change of control payment

- 4b—participated in, or received payment from, a supplemental nonqualified retirement plan

- 4c—participated in, or received payment from, an equity-based compensation arrangement

If "yes" is the answer to any of lines 4a–4c, the person should be listed and the applicable amounts for each item should be included in Part III. The instructions indicate that the explanation should include the terms and conditions of any arrangement in which one or more listed persons participated during the year. The instructions provide definitions of each of these items:

- **Line 4a. Severance or change-of-control payments.** Answer "yes" if a listed person received a severance or change-of-control payment from the organization or a related organization. A severance payment is a payment made if the right to the payment is contingent solely upon the person's severance from service in specified circumstances, such as upon an involuntary separation from service. Payments under a change-of-control arrangement are made in connection with a termination or change in the terms of employment resulting from a change in control of the organization. Treat as a severance payment any payment to a listed person in satisfaction or settlement of a claim for wrongful termination or demotion.

- **Line 4b. Supplemental nonqualified retirement plan.** Answer "yes" if a listed person participated in or received payment from any supplemental nonqualified retirement plan established, sponsored, or maintained by or for the organization or a related organization. A supplemental nonqualified retirement plan is a nonqualified retirement plan that is not generally available to all employees but is available only to a certain class or classes of management or highly compensated employees. For this purpose, include as a supplemental nonqualified retirement plan, a plan described in Section 457(f), but do not include a plan described in Section 457(b).

- **Line 4c. Equity-based compensation.** Answer "yes" if a listed person participated in or received payment from the organization or a related organization of any equity-based compensation (such as stock, stock options, stock appreciation rights, restricted stock, or phantom or shadow stock), or participated in any equity compensation plan or arrangement sponsored by the organization or a related organization, whether the compensation is determined by reference to equity in a partnership, limited liability company, or corporation. Equity-based compensation does not include compensation contingent on the revenues or net earnings of the organization, which are addressed by lines 5 and 6 below.

> **Example.** A, a listed person, is an employee of the organization (B). B owns an interest in a for-profit subsidiary (C) that is a stock corporation. As part of A's compensation package, B provides stock options to A that permit A to obtain C stock for a price other than the fair market value of the C stock at the time of the acquisition of the stock by A. This is an equity-based compensation arrangement for purposes of line 4c. The same would be true if C were a partnership, limited liability company, or publicly traded corporation and B provided A profits, interest, capital interest, or stock in C under similar terms.

Equity-based compensation as well as all other nonfixed compensation has been a hot button of the IRS for many years. These forms of nonfixed compensation are a focus of Schedule J. While nonfixed income including equity-based compensation has been carefully scrutinized by the IRS, some variations have been allowed. The filing organization should carefully consider whether the compensation arrangement in question could cause a private inurement challenge. At a minimum, the equity-based portion of compensation must be considered in the total compensation package to determine if the total compensation is reasonable. The placing of caps on the equity-based portion of the compensation is often suggested by the IRS in its rulings and by the courts to ensure reasonableness. (For complete discussion of nonfixed compensation, see § 6.1(a)(4).)

(6) Part I, Line 5 (Compensation Contingent on Revenues). On line 5, indicate "yes" or "no" as to whether the organization paid or accrued compensation for any of the persons listed in Part VII, Section A, which was contingent in whole, or in part, on the revenues (gross or net) of one or more activities of the filing organization or any related organization or on the revenues of the organization or related organization as a whole. If the answer to the question is "yes," a description should be provided in Part III. The instructions clarify that, for this purpose, net revenues means gross revenues less certain expenses but does not mean net income or net earnings. An example is provided in the instructions:

> **Example.** A, a listed person, is a physician employed by the organization (B). As part of A's compensation package, A is to be paid a bonus equal to x% of B's net revenues from a particular department operated by B for a specified period of time. This arrangement is a payment contingent on revenues of the organization, and must be reported for Line 5 purposes, regardless of whether the payment is conditioned on achieving a certain revenue target. However, if instead the bonus payment is a specific dollar amount (for instance, $5,000) to be paid only if a gross revenue or net revenue target of the department is achieved, the payment is not contingent on revenues of the organization for this purpose.

The distinction between compensation contingent on revenues reported in Part I, line 5 and compensation contingent on net earnings reported below in Part I, line 6 is that compensation contingent on gross or net revenues of a particular activity (department) of an organization is different from compensation based on the net earnings of the organization as a whole. Further, compensation based on gross revenues of the organization as a whole is different from compensation based on net income or net earnings of the organization as a whole. Compensation contingent on net earnings is the essence of the private inurement doctrine and will result in a finding of private inurement in most cases.

All forms of nonfixed compensation, including revenue-based compensation are carefully scrutinized by the IRS. In general, compensation based on net earnings should be avoided. For example, management contracts based on net earnings are prohibited under the private business use rules (see § 17.1(a)). (For a complete discussion of nonfixed income including revenue sharing, see § 6.1(a)(4).)

(7) Part I, Line 6 (Compensation Contingent on Net Earnings). On line 6, indicate ''yes'' or ''no'' as to whether the organization paid or accrued any compensation determined in whole or in part by the net earnings of one or more activities of the filing organization or any related organization or by the net earnings of the filing organization or related organization as a whole. Like line 5, if the answer to line 6 is ''yes,'' an explanation should be provided in Part III. The instructions provide this example:

> **Example.** A, a listed person, is an employee of the organization B. As part of A's compensation package, A is to be paid a bonus equal to x% of B's net earnings for a specified period of time. This arrangement is a payment contingent on net earnings of the organization for line 6 purposes, regardless of whether the payment is conditioned on achieving a certain net earnings target. However, if instead the bonus payment is a specific dollar amount to be paid only if a net earnings target is achieved, the payment is not contingent on the net earnings of the organization for this purpose.

This is an example of prohibited private inurement as a percentage of net earnings of the organization paid to an insider. See discussion in §§ 6.2(c)(5) and (c)(6).

(8) Part I, Line 7 (Other Nonfixed Compensation). On line 7, indicate ''yes'' or ''no'' as to whether the organization provides any nonfixed payments not described in lines 5 and 6. If such nonfixed payments were made, an explanation should be provided in Part III. The instructions indicate that a fixed amount, as opposed to a nonfixed amount, is an amount of cash or other property specified in the contract, or determined by a fixed formula specified in the contract, which is to be paid or trans-ferred in exchange for the provision of specified services or property. A fixed formula may incorporate an amount that depends on future specified events or contingencies, provided that no person exercises discretion when calculating the amount of a pay-ment or deciding whether to make a payment (such as a bonus). If payment arrange-ments are not made pursuant to these guidelines, they would be considered nonfixed payments. The instructions clarify that an example is a person who receives reim-bursement where discretion is exercised by persons with respect to the amount of expenses incurred or reimbursed. In this event, it is not a nonfixed payment. The in-structions also clarify that one exception to this rule would be amounts payable pur-suant to a qualified pension, profit-sharing, or stock bonus plan under Section 401(a) of the Code or pursuant to an employee benefit program that is subject to and satisfies coverage and nondiscrimination rules under the Code (e.g., Sections 127 and 137) other than nondiscrimination rules under Section 9802, are treated as fixed payments regardless of the organization's discretion. The fact that a person contracting with the organization is expressly granted the choice whether to accept or reject any economic benefit is disregarded in determining whether the benefit constitutes a fixed payment for purposes of line 7.

(9) Part I, Line 8 (Initial Contract Exception).   On line 8, indicate "yes" or "no" as to whether amounts paid to persons reported in Part VII, Section A were paid or ac-crued pursuant to a contract that was subject to the initial contract exception de-scribed in the excess benefit transaction regulations. If yes, this arrangement must be disclosed in Part III. The instructions indicate that an initial contract is a binding writ-ten contract between the organization and a person who is not a disqualified person with respect to the organization immediately prior to entering into the contract. The instructions also direct that payments made under a contract approved using the re-buttable presumption of reasonableness should be disregarded (see § 6.1(b)(8)). This initial contract exception is an important exception in the context of a compensation arrangement between a charity or social welfare organization and an individual who is not a disqualified person or insider at the time the contract is entered into. Thus, when an officer or key employee is originally hired by a charity, careful consideration should be given to structuring the contract to fit within the initial contract exception. If the contract fits within the exception, the intermediate sanctions will not be applied to the arrangement even if it is found to be a transaction that is unfair and would otherwise constitute an excess benefit transaction. The term of the contract, for exam-ple, should be carefully considered in this regard (see § 6.1(b)(14)).

(10) Part II, Column (A) (Names).   In Part II of Schedule J, additional information must be reported for all individuals who answered "yes" to lines 3, 4 and 5 in Section A, Part VII. The names of these individuals will also appear in Section A, Part VII, Column (A).

(11) Part II, Column (B) (Reportable Compensation).   Reportable compensation listed in Part VII is also reported in Column (B) of Part II, Schedule J. For each person listed, a separate row is provided to report compensation of the organization and its related organizations. The reported compensation is divided into three categories: (1) base compensation; (2) bonus and incentive compensation; and (3) other compensation. The sum of Column (B) (1) through (3) should equal the applicable Column (D) or Column (E) in Part VII. The instructions provide these definitions:

1. **Base compensation.** Report the listed person's base compensation that is included in Box 5 (or Box 1, if no compensation is reported in Box 5) of Form W-2, or Box 7 of Form 1099-MISC, issued to the person. Base compensation means nondiscretionary payments to a person agreed upon in advance, contingent only on the payee's performance of agreed-upon services (such as salary or fees).

2. **Bonus and incentive compensation.** Report the listed person's bonus and incentive compensation that is included in Box 5 (or Box 1, if no compensation is reported in Box 5) of Form W-2, or Box 7 of Form 1099-MISC, issued to the person. Examples include payments based on satisfaction of a performance target (other than mere longevity of service) and payments at the beginning of a contract before services are rendered (i.e., signing bonus).

3. **Other reportable compensation.** Report all other payments to the listed person included in Box 5 (or Box 1, if no compensation is reported in Box 5) of Form W-2 or Box 7 of Form 1099-MISC issued to the person but not reflected in Columns (B)(i) or (ii). Examples may include, but are not limited to, current-year payments of amounts earned in a prior year, payments under a severance plan, payments under an arrangement providing for payments upon the change in ownership or control of the organization or similar transaction, and awards based on longevity of service.

(12) Part II, Column (C) (Deferred Compensation). In Column (C), report all current-year deferrals of compensation under any retirement or other deferred compensation plan, whether qualified or nonqualified, that is established, sponsored, or maintained by or for the organization or related organization. Also include the annual increase in actuarial value, if any, of a defined benefit plan, but do not report earnings accrued on deferred amounts in a defined benefit plan. Do not report in Column (C) amounts included in Box 5 (or in Box 1, if no compensation is reported in Box 5) of Form W-2 or Box 7 of Form 1099-MISC issued to the person for the calendar year ending with or within the organization's tax year. The instructions indicate that if a definitive amount of deferred compensation cannot be determined, a reasonable estimate should be provided. For purposes of reporting in Column (C), deferred compensation is compensation that is earned or accrued in, or is attributed to, one year and deferred to a future year for any reason, whether or not funded, vested or subject to a substantial risk of forfeiture. Do not report deferred compensation in Column (C) (before it is earned). Deferred compensation is treated as earned in the year that the services are rendered except when entitlement to payment is contingent on satisfaction of specified performance criteria (other than mere longevity of service) under the deferred compensation plan. If the payment of an amount of deferred compensation requires the employee to perform services for a period of time, the amount is treated as accrued and earned ratably over the course of the service period, even though the amount is not funded and may be subject to a substantial risk of forfeiture until the service period is completed.

Report deferred compensation for each listed person in Schedule J regardless of whether such compensation is deferred as part of a deferred compensation plan that is administered by a separate trust, as long as the plan is established, sponsored, or maintained by or for the organization or a related organization for the benefit of the listed person. The instructions provide these examples:

> **Example 1.** Executive participates in Organization A's nonqualified deferred compensation plan. Under the terms of the plan beginning January 1 of the calendar year 1, she earns for each year of service an amount equal to 2% of her base salary of $100,000 for that year. These additional amounts are deferred and they are not vested until Executive has completed three years of service with Organization A. In year 4, the deferred amounts for years 1 through 3 are paid to Executive. For each of the years 1 through 3, Organization A reports $2,000 of deferred compensation for Executive in Column (C). For year 4, Organization A reports $6,000 in Column (B)(iii) and $6,000 in Column (F).

> **Example 2.** Under the terms of his employment contract with Organization B beginning July 1 of calendar year 1, Executive is entitled to receive $50,000 of additional compensation after he has completed five years of service with the organization. The compensation is contingent only on the longevity of service. The $50,000 is treated as accrued and earned ratably over the course of the five years of service, even though it is not funded or vested until Executive has completed the five years. Organization B makes payment of $50,000 to Executive in calendar year 6. Organization B reports $5000 of deferred compensation in Column (C) for calendar year 1 and $10,000 for each of calendar years 2–5. For calendar year 6 Organization B reports $50,000 in Column (B)(iii) and $45,000 in Column (F).

> **Example 3.** Executive participates in Organization C's incentive compensation plan. The plan covers calendar years 1 through 5. Under the terms of the plan, Executive is entitled to earn 1% of Organization C's total productivity savings for each year during which Organization C's total productivity savings exceed $100,000. Earnings under the incentive compensation plan will be payable in year 6, to the extent funds are available in a certain "incentive compensation pool." For the years 1 and 2, Organization C's total productivity savings are $95,000. For each of the years 3, 4 and 5, Organization C's total productivity savings are $120,000. Accordingly, Executive earns $1200 of incentive compensation in each of years 3, 4 and 5. She does not earn anything under the incentive compensation plan in years 1 and 2 because the relevant performance criteria were not met in those years. Although the amounts earned under the plan for years 3, 4 and 5 are dependent upon there being a sufficient incentive compensation pool from which to make the payment, Organization C reports $1200 of deferred compensation in Column (C) in years 3, 4 and 5. In year 6 Organization C pays $3,600 attributable to years 3, 4, and 5 and reports $3,600 in Column(B)(ii) and $3600 in Column (F).

(13) Part II, Column (D) (Nontaxable Benefits).   In Column (D), report nontaxable benefits specifically excluded from taxation. The instructions clarify that the value of all nontaxable benefits provide to or for the benefit of the listed person other than the benefits disregarded for purposes of the excess benefit regulations.

Examples of nontaxable and disregarded benefits under the excess benefit regulations are listed in the instructions. The instructions specify that the next list is not exclusive:

- Value of housing provided by the employer
- Education assistance
- Health insurance
- Medical reimbursement programs
- Life insurance
- Disability benefits
- Long-term care insurance
- Dependent care assistance
- Adoption assistance
- Payment or reimbursement by the organization of (or payment of liability insurance premiums for) any penalty, tax, or expense or correction owed under Chapter 42 of the Code, any expense not reasonably incurred by the person in connection with a civil judicial or civil administrative proceeding arising out of the person's performance of services on behalf of the organization, or any expense resulting from an act or failure to act with respect to which the person has acted willfully and without reasonable cause

The disregarded benefits referred to in the excess benefit regulations that need not be recorded in Column (D) include:

- No additional cost services
- Qualified employee discount
- Working condition fringe
- De minimis fringe
- Qualified transportation fringe
- Qualified moving expense reimbursement
- Qualified retirement plan services and
- Qualified military base realignment enclosure fringe

A de minimis fringe is a property or service the value of which, after taking into account the frequency with which similar fringes are provided by the employer to the employees, is so small as to make accounting for it unreasonable or administratively impractical.

A working condition fringe is any property or service provided to an employee to the extent that, if the employee paid for the property or service, the payment would be deductible by the employee under Section 162 (ordinary and necessary business expense) or Section 167 (depreciation). In some cases, property provided to employees may be used partly for business and partly for personal purposes, such as automobiles. In that case, the value of the personal use of such property is taxable compensation, and the value of the use for business purposes a working condition fringe benefit.

(14) Part II, Column (F) (Compensation Reported in Prior Form 990). In Column (F), the organization reports any payment reported in Column (B) to the extent such payment was already reported as compensation of the listed person in a prior Form 990, Form 990 EZ, or Form 990 PF. The instructions specify that the amount must have been reported as compensation specifically for the listed person on the prior form. Inclusion of the amount in the organization's compensation expense reported in its statement of functional expenses in Part IX is not sufficient. For example, do not include in Column (F) amounts reported in a prior Form 990 but that were forfeited or repaid by the listed person or otherwise received by the organization during this tax year and which are not reported in Column (B) for this year.

(15) Part III (Supplemental Information). Use Part III to provide narrative information, explanations, or descriptions required for Part I, lines 1a, 1b, 3, 4a, 4b, 4c, 5a, 5b, 6a, 6b, 7, and 8. Also use Part III to provide other narrative explanations and descriptions, as applicable.

§6.3 PART VII AND SCHEDULE J COMPLIANCE TASKS

For purposes of preparing Part VII and Schedule J, consider these 15 compliance tasks.

1. **Compile officer and director compensation.** Compile compensation information for all officers and directors, including compensation from the filing organization and all related organizations (see Chapter 21 for definition of *related organizations*).

2. **Compile employee compensation.** Review reportable compensation paid to all employees, and prepare a list of employees who receive more than $100,000 of reportable compensation.

3. **Identify key employees.** From the list in item 2, identify all employees who receive $150,000 or more of compensation from the filing organization and related organizations and who supervise an activity of the organization representing at least 10 percent of the organization's total activities.

4. **Identify former officers, key employees or highly compensated employees.** Identify whether any compensation is paid in the reporting year by the filing organization or any related organization to any former officers, key employees, or other highly compensated employees. The key employees and highly compensated employees would be those persons who were reported on prior Form 990s. If so, were any of these persons paid reportable compensation of more than $100,000?

5. **Identify former directors or trustees.** Identify whether compensation is paid to any former directors or trustees in excess of $10,000 from the organization or any related organization.

6. **Prepare schedule of additional compensation.** For persons identified in numbers 1 to 5, prepare list of all compensation paid to such individuals, including all fringe benefits, travel reimbursement, nonfixed compensation, accountable plans, tax gross-ups, discretionary spending, housing allowances,

club dues, personal services, business use of personal residence, and other benefits.

7. **Identify compensation paid by unrelated organizations.** Identify whether compensation is paid to any of the organization's employees by unrelated organizations.

8. **Identify independent contractors.** Prepare a list of all independent contractors paid more than $100,000. The list should include name and business address, description of services, and the amount paid.

9. **Identify accountable plans.** Identify whether the organization is involved in any accountable plans. If so, confirm compliance procedures.

10. **Prepare expense reimbursement policy.** Prepare or update any expense reimbursement policy to cover items listed in Schedule J.

11. **Identify nonfixed income arrangements.** Review all arrangements that could constitute nonfixed income.

12. **Review deferred compensation plans.** Review deferred compensation plans for reporting in Part VII and Schedule J.

13. **Consider use of initial contract exception.** Consider use of exception for all contracts with new officers and key employees.

14. **Confirm rebuttable presumption compliance.** As discussed in Chapter 5, ensure that a rebuttable presumption of reasonableness policy is followed for all compensation arrangements.

15. **Identify revenue-sharing arrangements.** To the extent any nonfixed income plans are equity-based or contingent on revenues, review cases and rulings to determine compliance.

CHAPTER SEVEN

Parts VIII to XI—Revenue, Expenses, and Balance Sheet

Parts VIII to XI of the core form contain the Statements of Revenue and Functional Expenses, the Balance Sheet, and questions about financial reporting, including whether the financials are complied, reviewed, or audited by an independent accountant and whether the organization has a committee that oversees the audit process. The Statements of Revenue and Functional Expenses and the Balance Sheet (Parts VIII–X) are substantially similar to their counterparts in the current 990. Part XI is new.

§ 7.1 LAW AND POLICY

The financial statements raise a number of issues of law and policy, many of which are addressed in other chapters. These areas are summarized in § 7.1(a). The two substantive bodies of law and policy that affect Form 990 financial statement preparation are (1) the unrelated business income rules (discussed in § 7.1(b)) and (2) Sarbanes-Oxley and its nonprofit progeny that address the concepts of financial accountability, transparency, and integrity (discussed in § 7.1(c)).

(a) Introduction to Issues Addressed Elsewhere in Book

Preparation of the Form 990 financial statements requires an understanding of a wide breadth of law and policy issues. Many of these are discussed in detail in other parts of the book, including:

- Fundraising and gaming: §§ 3.1(r), (s), and (t); Chapter 14
- Contributions and public charity status: § 3.1(b); Chapter 8
- Related organizations: § 3.1(oo); Chapter 21
- Noncash gifts: §§ 3.1(jj) and (kk); Chapter 19
- Grants to U.S. and foreign entities and individuals: §§ 3.1(n)–(q) and (v)–(w); Chapters 13 and 16
- Director and officer compensation and expense reimbursement: § 3.1(x); Chapter 6

- Loans to disqualified persons: § 3.1(ee); Chapter 18
- Lobbying: §§ 3.1(c) and (d); Chapters 9 and 10
- Management companies: Chapter 15

(b) Unrelated Business Income

This section summarizes the federal tax law concerning the conduct of unrelated businesses by tax-exempt organizations. This field is one of the major components of the law of tax-exempt organizations. Inasmuch as nearly every undertaking of a nonprofit organization is a business, as that term is defined for tax purposes, it is critical for these organizations to know if their activities are related or unrelated businesses. Specifically, this section:

- Analyzes the rules for determining whether an activity is a business
- Reviews the rules for ascertaining whether a business is regularly carried on
- Explores the difference between related and unrelated businesses
- Enumerates the various exceptions to the unrelated business rules
- Identifies the exceptions to these exceptions
- Looks at special rules relating to qualified sponsorship payments and Internet activities
- Discusses the relation of the doctrine of commerciality with the unrelated business rules

(1) Statutory Framework. For over 50 years, the federal tax law has categorized the activities of tax-exempt organizations as those that are related to the performance of exempt functions and those that are not. The revenue occasioned by the latter type of activities, *unrelated activities*, is subject to tax. This has a certain intuitive appeal: If exempt activities form the basis for tax exemption, then activities unrelated to exempt activities should not be exempt from tax. The objective of the unrelated business income tax is to prevent unfair competition between tax-exempt organizations and for-profit, commercial enterprises. The rules are intended to place the unrelated business activities of an exempt organization on the same tax basis as those of a nonexempt business with which it competes.

To be tax-exempt, a nonprofit organization must be organized and operated *primarily* for exempt purposes (see § 1.6(c)). The federal tax law allows a tax-exempt organization to engage in a certain amount of income-producing activity that is unrelated to its exempt purposes. Where the organization derives net income from one or more unrelated business activities, known as *unrelated business taxable income*, a tax is imposed on that income. A nonprofit organization's tax exemption will be denied or revoked if too much of its activities are unrelated to its exempt purposes. If the organization's primary purpose is carrying on a business for profit, it is denied exempt status, usually on the ground that it is a *feeder organization*.

(2) Affected Tax-Exempt Organizations. Nearly all types of tax-exempt organizations are subject to the unrelated business rules. They include religious organizations (including churches), educational organizations (including universities, colleges, and schools), healthcare organizations (including hospitals), scientific organizations (including major research institutions), and similar organizations. Beyond the realm of charitable entities, the rules are applicable to social welfare organizations (including advocacy groups), labor organizations (including unions), trade and professional associations, fraternal organizations, employee benefit funds, and veterans' organizations.

Special rules tax all income not related to exempt functions (including investment income) of social clubs, homeowners' associations, and political organizations.

Some exempt organizations are not generally subject to the unrelated income rules, simply because they are not allowed to engage in any active business endeavors. The best example of this is private foundations, where the operation of an active unrelated business (internally or externally) would trigger application of the excess business holdings restrictions. Generally, an exempt title-holding company cannot have unrelated business taxable income. An exception permits such income in an amount up to 10 percent of its gross income for the tax year, where the income is incidentally derived from the holding of real property.

Instrumentalities of the United States, like governmental agencies generally, are exempt from the unrelated business rules. This exception, however, is not applicable to colleges and universities that are agencies or instrumentalities of a government, or to corporations owned by such institutions of higher education, all of which are subject to the unrelated business rules.

(3) Unrelated Business Activities and Income. An organization engages in an unrelated business activity that generates taxable income if the organization: (a) conducts a trade or business, (b) that is regularly carried on, (c) that is unrelated to the organization's exempt purpose, and (d) which does not qualify for an exception. The next sections discuss each of these elements in more detail.

(A) CONDUCT OF BUSINESS

For purposes of the federal tax rules, the term *trade or business* includes any activity that is carried on for the production of income from the sale of goods or the performance of services. Most activities that would constitute a trade or business under basic tax law principles are considered a trade or business for the purpose of the unrelated business rules.

This definition of the term *trade or business*—often referred to simply as *business*—embraces nearly every activity of a tax-exempt organization; only passive investment activities and the provision of administrative services among related organizations generally escape this classification. In this sense, a nonprofit organization is viewed as a bundle of activities, each of which is a business. (It must be emphasized that this term has nothing to do with whether a particular business is related or unrelated; there are related businesses and unrelated businesses, as discussed in § 7.1(b)(3)(C.)

The IRS is empowered to examine each of a nonprofit organization's activities in search of unrelated business. Each activity can be examined as if it existed wholly independently of the others; an unrelated activity cannot, as a matter of law, be hidden from scrutiny by tucking it in among a host of related activities. As Congress chose to state the precept, an "activity does not lose identity as a trade or business merely because it is carried on within a larger aggregate of similar activities or within a larger complex of other endeavors which may, or may not, be related to the exempt purposes of the organization." This is known as the *fragmentation rule*, by which—as a matter of legal fiction—a nonprofit organization's disparate activities may be fragmented and each discrete fragment reviewed in isolation. For example, the activity of advertising in a nonprofit organization's exempt publication is severed from the publication activity and regarded as an unrelated activity, even though otherwise the publication activity is a related business.

The federal law also provides that, where an activity "carried on for profit constitutes an unrelated trade or business, no part of such trade or business shall be excluded from such classification merely because it does not result in profit." In other words, just because an activity results in a loss in a particular year, that is insufficient basis for failing to treat the activity as an unrelated one. Conversely, the mere fact that an activity generates a profit is not alone supposed to lead to the conclusion that the activity is unrelated (although on occasion that is the conclusion).

An activity that consistently results in annual losses likely will not be regarded as a *business*. If that is the only unrelated activity, then it cannot be an *unrelated business*. Some nonprofit organizations, however, have more than one unrelated business. They can offset the losses generated by one business against the gains enjoyed by another business in calculating unrelated business taxable income. But if the loss activity is not a business, its losses cannot be credited against unrelated gain.

It is common for a tax-exempt organization to provide management or other administrative services to another exempt organization. These services, where they are not inherently exempt functions, are known as *corporate services*. The general rule is that the provision of these types of services, even where the exempt organizations involved have the same exempt status, is a business. (Indeed, the providing of corporate services is generally considered by the IRS to be an unrelated business.) Nonetheless, where the relationship between the exempt organizations is that of parent and subsidiary, or is analogous to that of parent and subsidiary, the financial dealings will be regarded as a *matter of accounting*, which means they will be disregarded for federal income tax purposes.

Just as the element of *profits* is not built into the statutory definition of the term *trade or business*, so too is the factor of *unfair competition* missing from the definition. Yet unfair competition was the force that animated enactment of the unrelated business rules. Thus, the IRS and the courts sometimes take the matter of competition into consideration in assessing whether an activity is a *trade or business* and/or whether it is related or unrelated to exempt purposes.

Similarly, another term absent from the definition of *trade or business* is *commerciality*. Nothing in that definition authorizes the IRS and the courts to conclude that an activity is trade or business, let alone an unrelated one, solely because it is conducted in a commercial manner, which basically means it is undertaken the way a comparable activity is carried on by for-profit businesses (see § 7.1(b)(7)). Yet they engage in the practice anyway.

(B) REGULARLY CARRIED ON BUSINESS

To be considered an unrelated business activity, a business activity must be *regularly carried on* by a nonprofit organization. That is, income from an activity is considered taxable only when (assuming the other criteria are satisfied) the activity is conducted more often than sporadically or infrequently. The factors that determine whether an activity is regularly carried on are the frequency and continuity of the activities, and the manner in which the activities are pursued.

These factors are to be evaluated in light of the purpose of the unrelated business rules, which is to place nonprofit organizations' business activities on the same tax law basis (what some are wont to call a level playing field) as those of their non-exempt competitors. Specific business activities of a tax-exempt organization will generally be deemed to be regularly carried on if they are, as noted, frequent and continuous, and pursued in a manner that is generally similar to comparable commercial activities of for-profit organizations.

Where a nonprofit organization duplicates income-producing activities performed by commercial organizations year-round, but conducts these activities for a period of only a few weeks a year, they do not constitute the regular carrying on of a business. Similarly, occasional or annual income-producing activities, such as fundraising events, do not amount to a business that is regularly carried on. The conduct of year-round business activities, such as the operation of a parking lot one day every week, however, constitutes the regular carrying on of a business. Where commercial entities normally undertake income-producing activities on a seasonal basis, the conduct of the activities by an exempt organization during a significant portion of the season is deemed the regular conduct of the activity. For this purpose, a season may be a portion of the year (such as the summer) or a holiday period.

Generally, the law, in ascertaining regularity, looks only at the time consumed in the actual conduct of the activity. The IRS, however, is of the view that time expended preparing for the event (*preparatory time*) should also be taken into account. This can convert what appears to be an isolated activity into one regularly carried on.

(C) Related or Unrelated

The term *unrelated trade or business* is defined to mean "any trade or business the conduct of which [by a tax-exempt organization] is not substantially related (aside from the need of such organization for income or funds or the use it makes of the profits derived) to the exercise or performance by such organization of its charitable, educational, or other purpose or function constituting the basis for its exemption." The parenthetical clause means that an activity is not related, for these purposes, simply because the organization uses the net revenue from the activity in furtherance of exempt purposes.

The revenue from a regularly conducted trade or business is subject to tax, unless the activity is substantially related to the accomplishment of the organization's exempt purposes. The key to taxation or nontaxation in this area is the meaning of the words *substantially related*. Yet the law provides merely that, to be substantially related, the activity must have a *substantial causal relationship* to the accomplishment of an exempt purpose.

The fact that an asset is essential to the conduct of an organization's exempt activities does not shield from taxation the unrelated income produced by that asset. The income-producing activities must still meet the causal relationship test if the income is not to be subject to tax. This issue arises when a tax-exempt organization owns a facility or other assets that are put to a dual use. For example, the operation of an auditorium as a motion picture theater for public entertainment in the evenings is regarded as an unrelated activity even though the theater is used exclusively for exempt functions during the daytime hours. The fragmentation rule (see § 7.1(b)(3)(A)) allows this type of use of a single asset or facility to be split into two businesses.

Activities should not be conducted on a scale larger than is reasonably necessary for the performance of exempt functions. Activities in excess of what is needed for the achievement of exempt purposes may be seen as unrelated businesses.

A host of court opinions and IRS rulings provide illustrations of related and unrelated activities. Colleges and universities operate dormitories and bookstores as related businesses but can be taxed on travel tours and the conduct of sports camps. Hospitals may operate gift shops, snack bars, and parking lots as related businesses but may be taxable on sales of pharmaceuticals to the general public and on performance of routine laboratory tests for physicians. Museums may, without taxation, sell items reflective of their collections but are taxable on the sale of souvenirs and furniture. Trade associations may find themselves taxable on sales of items (such as uniforms, tools, and manuals) and particular services to members, but dues and subscription revenue are nontaxable. Fundraising events may be characterized as unrelated activities, particularly where the activity is regularly carries on or compensation is paid.

(4) Exceptions. The foregoing general rules notwithstanding, there are certain exceptions to the unrelated business rules. This section addresses (a) certain types of activities that are exceptions, (b) certain types of income that are exceptions, and (c) certain exceptions to the exceptions.

(A) EXEMPT ACTIVITIES

Certain businesses and activities conducted by tax-exempt organizations are exempted from unrelated business income taxation.

(i) VOLUNTEER EXCEPTION

One of the frequently used exemptions from this taxation is for a business in which substantially all the work is performed for the organization without compensation. Thus, if an exempt organization conducts an unrelated business using services provided substantially by volunteers, the net revenue from that business is spared taxation. This exemption protects from taxation many ongoing fundraising activities for charitable organizations. Caution must be exercised, however, because *compensation* is not confined to a salary, wage, or fee; the slightest amount of remuneration (such as gratuities) can nullify an individual's status as a *volunteer*.

(ii) CONVENIENCE EXCEPTION

Also exempted is a business carried on by the organization primarily for the convenience of its members, students, patients, officers, or employees. This exception is available, however, only to organizations that are charitable, educational, and the like, or are governmental colleges and universities. Hospital gift shops and cafeterias and college and university bookstores often avail themselves of the convenience exception.

(iii) DONATION EXCEPTION

Exemption is accorded a business that consists of the selling of merchandise, substantially all of which has been received by the exempt organization as contributions. This exemption shelters the revenue of thrift stores from unrelated income taxation. Its use, though, is not confined to thrift shops. For example, it can protect revenue from the ubiquitous silent auction from taxation—even if auctions are regularly carried on. Likewise, this exemption applies in the case of used vehicle donation programs; the charity involved is not taxed as though it is in the used car business.

(iv) QUALIFIED PUBLIC ENTERTAINMENT ACTIVITIES

Unrelated trade or business does not include qualified public entertainment activities. A *public entertainment activity* is any entertainment or recreational activity traditionally conducted at fairs or expositions promoting agricultural and educational purposes. Typically, these activities attract the public to fairs or expositions or promote the breeding of animals or the development of products or equipment.

To be *qualified*, a public entertainment activity must be conducted (1) in conjunction with an international, national, regional, state, or local fair or exposition; (2) in accordance with the provisions of state law which permit the activity to be operated or conducted solely by a qualifying organization or by a governmental agency; or (3) in accordance with the provisions of state law which permit a qualifying organization to be granted a license to conduct no more than 20 days of the activity, on payment to the state of a lower percentage of the revenue from the licensed activity than the state requires from nonqualifying organizations.

To warrant application of the public entertainment activities exception, a *qualifying organization* must be a tax-exempt charitable, social welfare, or labor organization that regularly conducts, as one of its substantial exempt purposes, an agricultural or educational fair or exposition.

(v) QUALIFIED CONVENTION AND TRADE SHOW ACTIVITIES

The term *unrelated trade or business* also does not include *qualified convention and trade show activities*. Activities of this nature, traditionally conducted at conventions, annual meetings, or trade shows, are designed to attract attention from persons in an industry. There is no requirement for these persons to be members of the sponsoring organization. The purposes of these shows are to display industry products; to stimulate interest in, and demand for, industry products or services; or to educate persons within the industry in the development of new products and services or new rules and regulations affecting industry practices.

To be *qualified*, a convention and trade show activity must be carried out by a qualifying organization in conjunction with an international, national, regional, state, or local convention, annual meeting, or show that the organization is conducting. One of the purposes of the organization in sponsoring the activity must be the promotion and stimulation of interest in, and demand for, the products and services of that industry in general or the education of attendees regarding new developments or products and services related to the exempt activities of the organization. The show must be designed to achieve its purpose through the character of the exhibits and the extent of the industry products displayed. A *qualifying organization* is a charitable, social welfare, or labor organization, or a trade association that regularly conducts such a show as one of its substantial exempt purposes.

(vi) Cooperative Hospital Service Organizations

The concept of unrelated business does not include situations where cooperative hospital service organizations furnish services to one or more tax-exempt hospitals. The services, however, (1) must be furnished solely to hospitals that have facilities for no more than 100 inpatients; (2) if performed on its own behalf by the recipient hospital, must constitute exempt activities of that institution; and (3) must be provided for a fee or cost that does not exceed the actual cost of providing the services. The cost must include straight-line depreciation and a reasonable amount for return on capital goods used to provide the services.

(vii) Bingo Games

Unrelated business also does not include bingo games conducted by tax-exempt organizations. The game must be (1) of a type in which usually the wagers are placed, the winners are determined, and the prizes or other property are distributed in the presence of all persons placing wagers in the game; (2) not an activity ordinarily carried out on a commercial basis; and (3) not in violation of any state or local law.

(viii) Low-Cost Articles

For a charitable, veterans', or other organization, as to which contributions are deductible, the term *unrelated business* does not include activities relating to a distribution of low-cost articles that is incidental to the solicitation of charitable contributions. A *low-cost article* is an item that has a maximum cost of $5.00 (indexed for inflation) to the organization that distributes the article (directly or indirectly). A *distribution* qualifies under this rule if it is not made at the request of the recipients, if it is made without their express consent, and if the articles that are distributed are accompanied by a request for a charitable contribution to the organization and a statement that the recipients may retain the article whether or not a contribution is made.

(ix) Exchange of Donor and Member Lists

For a charitable, veterans', or other organization to which deductible contributions may be made, the term *business* does not include exchanging with another like organization the names and addresses of donors to or members of the organization, or the renting of these lists to another like organization.

(x) Other Exceptions

Still other exceptions apply with respect to certain local organizations of employees, the conduct of certain games of chance, and the rental of poles by mutual or cooperative telephone or electric companies.

(B) Exempted Income

Certain types of passive and other income (principally research revenue) are exempt from the unrelated business income tax.

(i) PASSIVE INCOME

Because the unrelated income tax applies to businesses *actively* conducted by tax-exempt organizations, most types of *passive* income are exempt from taxation. This exemption generally embraces dividends, interest, securities lending income, annuities, royalties, rent, capital gains, and gains on the lapse or termination of options written by exempt organizations. Income in the form of rent, royalties, and the like from an active business undertaking is taxable; that is, merely labeling an item of income as rent, royalties, and so forth does not make it tax-free.

For the most part, the tax law is clear regarding what constitutes *dividends*, *interest*, an *annuity*, *rent*, and *capital gain*. There can be, however, considerable controversy concerning what constitutes a *royalty*. The term, not defined by statute or regulation, is being defined by the courts.

Generally, a *royalty* is a payment for the use of one or more valuable intangible property rights. In the tax-exempt organizations setting, this is likely to mean payment for the use of an organization's name and logo. The core issue usually is the extent to which the exempt organization receiving the (ostensible) royalty can provide services in an attempt to increase the amount of royalty income paid to it. This issue was the subject of extensive litigation spanning many years, principally involving revenue from the rental of mailing lists and revenue derived from affinity credit card programs. The resulting rule is that these services are permissible as long as they are insubstantial. Beyond that, the IRS may contend that the exempt organization is in a *joint venture* (see § 11.1(f)), which is an active business undertaking that defeats the exclusion.

Rents are also subject to some special rules. Generally, rent from real estate is excluded, but rent from personal property is taxable. Rent from personal property can be excluded when leased with real property and when the rent attributable to the personal property does not exceed 10 percent of the total rent. Rent from real estate is generally excluded if: (1) the determination of the rent is not based on the income or profits derived by any person from the rental property other than an amount based on a fixed percentage of gross receipts or sales; (2) the lease does not include personal services other than customary ones such as trash removal and cleaning of public areas; (3) any portion attributable to personal property is 10 percent or less of the total rent; and (4) the real property is not debt financed (see § 7.1(b)(4)(C)(i)).

(ii) RESEARCH INCOME

These exemptions apply to the conduct of research: income derived by an exempt organization from research performed for (1) the United States, or any of its agencies or instrumentalities, or any state or political subdivision of a state; (2) a college, university, or hospital; or (3) an organization operated primarily for purposes of carrying on fundamental research (as opposed to applied research), the results of which are freely available to the general public.

Some organizations do not engage in *research*; rather, they merely test products for public use just prior to marketing or undertake certification tasks. The IRS considers income from mere testing to be taxable unrelated business income. Other organizations, principally universities and scientific research institutions, are engaging in research, but their discoveries are licensed or otherwise transferred to for-profit organizations for exploitation in the public marketplace. This closeness between businesses and nonprofit organizations—known as *technology transfer*—can raise questions as to how much commercial activity is being sheltered from tax by the research exception.

(C) EXCEPTIONS TO EXCEPTIONS

There are two exceptions to the foregoing exceptions, one involving unrelated debt-financed income, the other concerning income from subsidiaries.

(i) DEBT-FINANCED INCOME

A tax-exempt organization may own *debt-financed property*; the use of the property may be unrelated to the organization's exempt purposes. In a situation where both facts are present, when the exempt organization computes its unrelated business taxable income, income from the debt-financed property must be included as gross income derived from an unrelated business. The income is subject to tax in the same proportion that the property is financed by debt. The debt involved must be what the federal tax law terms *acquisition indebtedness*. This body of law applies even where the income is paid to an exempt organization in one of the otherwise exempted forms, such as interest or rent.

(ii) INCOME FROM SUBSIDIARIES

Some tax-exempt organizations elect to spin off their unrelated activities to taxable subsidiaries. The tax on the net income of the unrelated business is then not borne directly by the exempt organization. The managers of an exempt organization may be averse to reporting any unrelated business income, or the unrelated activity may be too large in relation to related activity.

If funds are transferred from a taxable subsidiary to an exempt parent, that income will be taxable as unrelated business income to the parent, if (1) it is interest, rent, royalties, or capital gains, and (2) the parent has, directly or indirectly, more than 50 percent control of the subsidiary. As an exception to an exception to an exception, if the subsidiary pays dividends to the tax-exempt parent, the dividends are not taxable to the parent because they are not deductible by the subsidiary.

(5) Qualified Sponsorship Payments. A subject of some controversy surrounds the provision of substantial financial support by a for-profit corporation to a tax-exempt (almost always charitable) entity, as sponsorship of a program, event, or other function of the entity. The business corporation receives considerable favorable publicity in exchange for its largesse. The law struggles to differentiate between treatment of the payment as a gift, with the publicity merely an acknowledgment of the contribution, and treatment of it as a payment for advertising services, in which case it would likely be unrelated business income. Unique statutory rules address the tax law aspects of *corporate sponsorships*.

In general, the receipt of a qualified sponsorship payment by a tax-exempt organization is not the receipt of income that is considered unrelated business income. These rules hinge, in considerable part, on two concepts: the qualified sponsorship payment and the substantial return benefit.

(A) QUALIFIED SPONSORSHIP PAYMENT

A *qualified sponsorship payment* is any payment of money, transfer of property, or performance of services by a person engaged in a trade or business to an exempt organization, with respect to which there is no arrangement or expectation that the person will receive any substantial return benefit. For this purpose, it is irrelevant whether the sponsored activity is related or unrelated to the recipient organization's exempt purposes. It is also irrelevant whether the sponsored activity or other function is temporary or permanent.

(B) SUBSTANTIAL RETURN BENEFIT

A *substantial return benefit* is any benefit other than: (1) certain uses and acknowledgments, and (2) goods, services, or other benefits of insubstantial value that are disregarded.

(i) CERTAIN USES AND ACKNOWLEDGMENTS

A substantial return benefit includes advertising; the provision of facilities, services, or other privileges to the payor or persons designated by the payor (collectively, the payor) (subject to certain exceptions discussed in § 7.1(b)(5)(B)(ii)); and granting the payor an exclusive or nonexclusive right to use an intangible asset (such as a trademark, patent, logo, or designation) of the exempt organization.

A *substantial return benefit* does not include the use or acknowledgment of the name or logo (or product lines) of the payor's trade or business in connection with the activities of the exempt organization. *Use or acknowledgment* does not include advertising but may include logos and slogans that do not contain qualitative or comparative descriptions of, or inducements to purchase, the payer's products, services, facilities, or company; a list of the payor's locations, telephone numbers, or Internet address; value-neutral descriptions, including displays or visual depictions, of the payor's product line or services; and the payor's brand or trade names and product or service listings.

Logos or slogans that are an established part of a payor's identity are not considered to contain qualitative or comparative descriptions. Mere display or distribution, whether without charge or for remuneration, of a payor's product by the payor or the exempt organization to the general public at the sponsored activity is not considered an inducement to purchase, sell, or use the payor's product and thus will not affect the determination of whether a payment is a qualified sponsorship payment.

An arrangement that acknowledges the payor as the exclusive sponsor of an exempt organization's activity, or the exclusive sponsor representing a particular trade, business, or industry, generally does not, alone, result in a substantial return benefit. For example, if, in exchange for a payment, an organization announces that its event is sponsored exclusively by the payor (and does not provide any advertising or other substantial return benefit to the payor), the payor has not received a substantial return benefit.

By contrast, an arrangement that limits the sale, distribution, availability, or use of competing products, services, or facilities in connection with an exempt organization's activity generally results in a substantial return benefit. For example, if, in exchange for a payment, an exempt organization agrees to allow only the payor's products to be sold in connection with an activity, the payor has received a substantial return benefit. Thus, the tax law distinguishes between an *exclusive sponsor* and an *exclusive provider*.

For these purposes, the term *advertising* means a message or other programming material that is broadcast or otherwise transmitted, published, displayed, or distributed, and that promotes or markets any trade or business, or any service, facility, or product. Advertising includes messages containing qualitative or comparative language, price information or other indications of savings or value, an endorsement, or an inducement to purchase, sell, or use any company, service, facility, or product. A single message that contains both advertising and an acknowledgment is nonetheless considered advertising.

(ii) DISREGARDED GOODS AND SERVICES

Goods, services, or other benefits are disregarded as substantial return benefits under two sets of circumstances. One is where the benefits provided to the payor have an aggregate fair market value that is not more than 2 percent of the amount of the payment or $75 (adjusted for inflation), whichever is less.

The other situation where benefits are disregarded is where the only benefits provided to the payor are token items (such as bookmarks, calendars, key chains, mugs, posters, and T-shirts) bearing the exempt organization's name or logo that have an aggregate cost within the limit established for *low-cost articles*. Token items provided to employees of a payor, or to partners of a partnership that is the payor, are disregarded if the combined total cost of the token items provided to each employee or partner does not exceed the low-cost article limit.

(C) OFFSETTING QUALIFIED SPONSORSHIP PAYMENTS WITH SUBSTANTIAL RETURN BENEFIT

If the fair market value of the benefits (or, in the case of token items, the cost) exceed the above amount or limit, then (unless they constitute a use or acknowledgment) the entire fair market value of the benefits, not merely the excess amount over the limit, is a substantial return benefit.

If there is an arrangement or expectation that the payor will receive a substantial return benefit with respect to a payment, then only the portion of the payment (if any) that exceeds the fair market value of the substantial return benefit is a qualified sponsorship payment. The fair market value is determined on the date on which the sponsorship arrangement was created. If, however, the exempt organization does not establish that the payment exceeds the fair market value of any substantial return benefit, then no portion of the payment constitutes a qualified sponsorship payment.

(D) TREATMENT AS UBI

The unrelated business income (UBI) tax treatment of any payment (or portion of one) that is not a qualified sponsorship payment is determined by application of the general unrelated business rules. For example, payments related to the exempt organization's provision of facilities, services, or other privileges to the payor, advertising, exclusive provider arrangements, a license to use intangible assets of the exempt organization, or other substantial return benefits are evaluated separately in determining whether the exempt organization realizes unrelated business income.

To the extent necessary to prevent avoidance of this allocation rule, where the exempt organization fails to make a reasonable and good-faith valuation of any substantial return benefit, the IRS is empowered to determine the portion of a payment allocable to the substantial return benefit. The IRS can treat two or more related payments as a single payment.

(E) QUALIFIED SPONSORSHIP PAYMENTS AS PUBLIC SUPPORT

Qualified sponsorship payments in the form of money or property (but not services) are treated as contributions received by the exempt organization for purposes of determining public support. This is the case irrespective of whether the *donative organization* or the *service provider organization* rules are applicable (see Chapter 8).

(F) DEDUCTION OF QUALIFIED SPONSORSHIP PAYMENT BY PAYOR

The fact that a payment is a qualified sponsorship payment that is treated as a contribution to the payee organization is not determinative of whether the payment is a business expense or a charitable contribution from the standpoint of the payor.

(G) WRITTEN SPONSORSHIP AGREEMENTS

The existence of a written corporate sponsorship agreement does not, in itself, cause a payment to fail to be a qualified sponsorship payment. The terms of the agreement—not the fact its existence or degree of detail—are relevant to the determination of whether a payment is a qualified sponsorship payment. Likewise, the terms of the agreement and not the title or responsibilities of the individuals negotiating the agreement determine whether a payment (or a portion of one) made pursuant to the agreement is a qualified sponsorship payment.

(H) CONTINGENT AND VARIABLE SPONSORSHIP PAYMENTS

The term *qualified sponsorship payment* does not include any payment the amount of which is contingent, by contract or otherwise, on the level of attendance at one or more events, broadcast ratings, or other factors indicating the degree of public exposure to the sponsored activity. The fact that a payment is contingent on sponsored events or activities actually being conducted does not, alone, cause the payment to fail to be a qualified sponsorship payment.

(I) QUALIFIED CONVENTION AND TRADE SHOWS AND PERIODICAL ADVERTISING

These rules do not apply with respect to payments made in connection with qualified convention and trade show activities (§ 7.1(b)(4)(A)(v)). These rules also do not apply to income derived from the sale of advertising or acknowledgments in exempt organization periodicals. For this purpose, the term *periodical* means regularly scheduled and printed material published by, or on behalf of, the exempt organization. A periodical is not related to, or primarily distributed in connection with, a specific event conducted by the exempt organization.

(6) Internet Activities.   The IRS observed that the "use of the Internet [by tax-exempt organizations] to accomplish a particular task does not change the way the tax laws apply to that task. Advertising is still advertising and fundraising is still fundraising." In general, unrelated business is still unrelated business.

Regarding marketing, merchandising, advertising, and the like via the Internet, the IRS has yet to provide much guidance as to application of the unrelated business rules. The agency has stated that it is "reasonable to assume that as the Service position develops it will remain consistent with our position with respect to advertising and merchandising and publishing in the off-line world."

The IRS has gingerly broached the subject of charity Web site hyperlinks to related or recommended sites. Link exchanges may be treated as mailing list exchanges. Compensation for a linkage may be unrelated business income. The purpose of the link will be determinative: Is its purpose furtherance of exempt purposes (such as referral of the site visitor to additional educational information), or is it part of an unrelated activity (such as advertising)?

Also involved are corporate sponsorships, inasmuch as exempt organizations sometimes seek corporate support to underwrite the production of all or a portion of the organization's Web site. Such corporate support for Web sites may qualify as a qualified sponsorship payment exempt from UBI (see § 7.1(b)(5)). These relationships may be short term or long term. The financial support may be acknowledged by means of display of a corporate logo, notation of the sponsor's Web address and/or 800 number, a *moving banner* (a graphic advertisement, usually a moving image, measured in pixels), or a link. The issue is whether the support is a *qualified sponsorship payment*, in which case the revenue is not taxable, or advertising income, in which case the revenue is generally taxable as unrelated business income.

A tax-exempt organization may provide a link to a corporate sponsor and still preserve treatment of the revenue as a nontaxable corporate sponsorship. Even with a link, the organization's public statement of appreciation for the payment can retain its character as a mere acknowledgment. That is, without more, the presence of a link is not considered a substantial return benefit. A statement on a sponsor's Web site, whereby an exempt organization endorses the sponsor's products or services, by contrast, will be attributed to the exempt organization, considered a substantial return benefit, and the safe harbor protection for qualified corporate sponsorships will be forfeited.

Other issues involving use of the Internet by tax-exempt organizations for unrelated purposes include application of special rules by which an online publication may be considered a *periodical*, tax treatment of *virtual trade shows*, online storefronts, online auctions, and affiliate and other coventure programs with merchants.

(7) Commerciality Doctrine. The courts are fashioning a body of jurisprudence known as the *commerciality doctrine*. This doctrine is rested on the presumption that, if an activity is conducted in the for-profit sector, it ought not to be undertaken in the nonprofit sector. That is, charitable organizations should not, pursuant to this view, be operating in a *commercial* manner. The commerciality doctrine is usually applied in determining eligibility for tax-exempt status, although the IRS occasionally uses it to detect unrelated business.

Courts employ a variety of criteria when inquiring as to commerciality. The principal elements are competition with for-profit entities, the extent and degree of low-cost services provided, pricing policies, and the reasonableness of financial services. Other factors include, as one court stated, "commercial promotional methods," namely, advertising; a court was disturbed that an organization had a "jingle." Other facts that can lead to a finding of commercial behavior are the use of employees rather than volunteers, training of employees, and the lack of charitable contributions.

The commerciality doctrine appears only briefly in the Internal Revenue Code, where Congress has legislated as to prohibitions on charitable and social welfare organizations' issuance of *commercial-type insurance*. Congress is beginning, however, to review other situations involving alleged commerciality (and competition). A primary area is that of hospitals, where comparisons with the operations of for-profit hospitals are causing some to call for more charity care by nonprofit health care institutions (see Chapter 15). Another area is nonprofit credit unions, with the commercial banking community demanding an end to credit unions' tax exemption. Still another field engendering this type of controversy is the insurance activities of exempt fraternal beneficiary societies in relation to those of taxable commercial insurers.

(c)   Sarbanes-Oxley and Its Progeny

(1) Sarbanes-Oxley Act.   Historic federal accounting reform and for-profit corporate responsibility legislation—the Sarbanes-Oxley Act—was signed into law in 2002. This measure is focused on publicly traded companies and public accounting firms. The emergence of this law, however, raises a number of questions for tax-exempt organizations as to the applicability of the act's principles to them. Many nonprofit industry groups, regulators, and overseers have suggested that nonprofits adopt a number of the Sarbanes-Oxley provisions and other best practices regarding financial accountability and corporate governance. Thus, a basic understanding of Sarbanes-Oxley is critical to proper financial oversight and preparation of the financial statements in Parts VIII to XI of the Form 990.

(A)   TERMINOLOGY

There are certain terms that are essential to understand for appreciation of the scope of this body of law as it relates to tax-exempt organizations.

An *audit committee* is a committee established "by and amongst" the board of directors of an organization for the purpose of overseeing the accounting and financial reporting processes of the organization and audits of the financial statements of the organization.

An *audit report* is a document prepared following an audit, and in which a public accounting firm either states the opinion of the firm regarding a financial statement, report, or other document, or asserts that such an opinion cannot be expressed.

A *code of ethics* means standards that are reasonably necessary to promote honest and ethical conduct, including the handling of conflicts of interest; full, fair, accurate, timely, and understandable disclosure in reports of an organization; and compliance with applicable governmental rules and regulations.

A *financial expert* is an individual who has an understanding of generally accepted accounting principles and financial statements, and experience in the preparation or auditing of financial statements, the application of these principles, experience with internal accounting controls, and an understanding of audit committee functions.

An *issuer* is a for-profit corporation, the stock of which is registered pursuant to the federal securities laws, and that is otherwise required to comply with those laws, including the filing of reports (also known as a *public company*).

Nonaudit services means any professional services provided to an audit client by a public accounting firm, other than those provided to an audit client in connection with an audit or review of the financial statements of an issuer.

A *public accounting firm* is a legal entity (such as a corporation or partnership) that is engaged in the practice of public accounting or preparing or issuing audit reports.

(B) Principal Features of Act

The statute establishes a number of requirements to ensure the integrity of an organization's financial statements and internal financial controls.

- **Nonaudit services.** The law amended the securities laws to generally prohibit a public accounting firm from providing any nonaudit service to an audit client. The board under certain circumstances has the authority to grant exemptions. These nonaudit services include bookkeeping services, financial information systems design and implementation, appraisal and valuation services, fairness opinions, actuarial services, internal audit outsourcing services, investment adviser services, and legal services.

- **Audit partner rotation.** The statute amended the securities laws to make it unlawful for a registered public accounting firm to provide audit services to an issuer if the lead (or coordinating) audit partner, or the audit partner responsible for reviewing the audit, has performed audit services for that issuer in each of the five previous fiscal years of the issuer. The statute provides for a study of mandatory rotation of registered public accounting firms.

- **Audit committees.** The law in essence mandated the creation and functioning of audit committees of issuers. This is done, in part, by requiring the Securities and Exchange Commission (SEC) to in turn direct the national securities exchanges and associations to prohibit the listing of the securities of issuers that fail to establish and use these committees. The audit committee of an issuer must be directly responsible for the appointment, compensation, and oversight of the work of a registered public accounting firm employed by the issuer for the purpose of preparing or issuing an audit report or related work. Each such registered public accounting firm must report directly to the audit committee. Each member of an audit committee must be a member of the board of directors of the issuer involved. He or she may not accept any consulting, advisory, or other compensation from the issuer. The SEC issued rules to require each issuer to disclose whether or not, and if not why not, the audit committee of the issuer is comprised of at least one member who is a financial expert.

- **Certifications.** The law requires the principal executive officer and principal financial officer of an issuer to certify each annual or quarterly report filed by the issuer in compliance with the securities laws. This includes certification that the report does not contain any untrue statement of a material fact or failure to state a material fact necessary in order to make the statements made not misleading. Executive officers must also certify that they have assessed the adequacy of the issuer's internal controls.

- **Disgorgement of bonuses.** If an issuer is required to prepare an accounting restatement due to the material noncompliance of the issuer, as a result of misconduct, with a financial reporting requirement under the securities laws, the chief executive officer and chief financial officer of the issuer must reimburse the issuer for any bonus or other incentive-based or equity-based compensation received by that individual from the issuer during a prior 12-month period. This disgorgement rule can also encompass profits realized from the sale of stock of the issuer. If the SEC obtains a disgorgement order against a person for violation of the securities laws, and that includes a civil penalty, the penalty is to be added to and become part of a disgorgement fund for the benefit of the victims of the violation.

- **Prohibition on loans to directors and officers.** It is generally unlawful for an issuer to extend or maintain credit in the form of a personal loan to or for any director or executive officer of that issuer. This includes the use of a subsidiary for this purpose.

- **Code of ethics.** The SEC issued rules requiring each issuer to disclose whether or not, and if not why not, the issuer has adopted a code of ethics for senior financial officers.

- **Lawyers.** The SEC, in accordance with this statute, issued rules setting forth minimum standards of professional conduct for lawyers practicing before the SEC. These rules require a lawyer to report evidence of a major violation of securities law or breach of fiduciary duty or similar violation by the company to the chief legal counsel or the chief executive officer of the company. If there is not an appropriate response to the evidence presented, including remedial measures, the lawyer is to report the evidence to the audit committee of the issuer or another committee of the board.

- **Document destruction.** The act prohibits any individual from the knowing destruction or falsification of corporate records with intent to impede or influence a federal investigation. Like the *whistleblower protection* provisions of the act (see next item), this is one of the two provisions of the act that applies to individuals employed by nonprofit organizations.

- **Whistleblower protection.** The act prohibits the knowing retaliation against individuals who provide to a law enforcement officer truthful information regarding the commission or possible commission of any Federal offense. Like the *Document Destruction* provisions (see preceding item), this is one of the two provisions of the act that applies to individuals employed by nonprofit organizations.

(C) Import of Act for Tax-Exempt Organizations

This body of law generally does not, as noted, apply to tax-exempt organizations (other than protection of whistleblowers and the provision regarding destruction of documents). Again, it applies to, and with respect to, issuers and public accounting firms. Nonetheless, Sarbanes-Oxley standards as to corporate governance and financial accountability parallel in many ways the fiduciary principles applicable to exempt organizations; developments with respect to the act will inevitably help shape corporate governance standards for exempt organizations.

Those who manage tax-exempt organizations, and perhaps those who make contributions to them, may want to give consideration to some or all of these points: whether:

- The accounting firm retained by an exempt organization should be a registered public accounting firm

- An exempt organization should have an audit committee or similar body
- An exempt organization should develop a code of ethics for its senior officers (this would go beyond a conflict-of-interest policy)
- An exempt organization should require certification of its financial statements and/or annual information returns by its executive
- An exempt organization should have a policy of prohibiting loans to its senior executives
- In an instance of a need for an accounting restatement by an exempt organization, due to some form of misconduct, any bonuses and/or the like to executive personnel should be reimbursed
- An exempt organization should follow the rules as to audit partner rotation
- An exempt organization should separate audit and nonaudit service providers
- Whether an exempt organization's lawyers should be required to report breaches of fiduciary responsibility to its executive
- Given the increasing focus on compensation matters, an exempt organization may want to consider establishment of a compensation committee

(2) Implementation of Sarbanes-Oxley in Nonprofit Context. A number of organizations have issued pronouncements and white papers on how nonprofits can implement Sarbanes-Oxley-type policies and procedures. A number of these are summarized in the text boxes that follow.

Fitch Ratings: Sarbanes-Oxley and Not-for-Profit Hospitals: Increased Transparency and Improved Accountability

In June 2005, Fitch Ratings, an independent firm that provides creditworthiness ratings to issuers of bonds, released this special report. Fitch states that nonprofit hospitals that borrow bond proceeds and are seeking credit rating will be evaluated based on whether nine sections of Sarbanes-Oxley have been adopted and implemented. These could be considered best practices for all nonprofits:

1. **Section 201:** Prohibition of Certain Nonaudit Services by Auditors. The audit committee must approve the provision of any nonaudit services by the auditor. Certain nonaudit services cannot be performed by the auditor (even if approved by the audit committee). These include bookkeeping, financial system design, appraisals and valuations, and investment banking.

2. **Section 203:** Audit Partner Rotation Every Five Years. The lead and reviewing audit partner should be rotated every five years.

3. **Section 204:** Independent Communications between Audit Committee and Auditor. All communications regarding critical accounting practices and policies, alternative treatments, and any other material audit communication should be made directly to the audit committee and not management.

4. **Section 301:** Adoption of Audit Committee Standards. The audit committee should be responsible for hiring the auditor. The committee should be composed only of independent members. The committee should establish procedures for receipt of and response to allegations of financial wrongdoing. The committee should be responsible for hiring, compensating, and overseeing the auditor.

5. **Section 302:** CEO and CFO Certifications. CEOs and CFOs should certify that the financial statements accurately reflect the financial condition of the organization in all material respects. CEOs and CFOs should certify that they have evaluated the effectiveness of the company's internal controls.

6. **Section 304:** Forfeiture of Executive Bonuses if Financials Are Restated. If the organization's financial statements have to be materially restated, the CEO and CFO should forfeit (or be required to repay) any bonus or incentive compensation earned in the period being restated.

7. **Section 404:** Implementation of Plan of Internal Financial Controls to Minimize Fraud. Management should assess the effectiveness of the organization's internal controls and the auditor should attest to management's assessment.

8. **Section 406:** Adoption of Code of Ethics. Adopt a code of ethics that promotes honest and ethical conduct; full, fair, accurate, timely, and understandable financial disclosures; and compliance with applicable government rules and regulations.

9. **Section 407:** Requirement of "Financial Expert" Serving on Audit Committee. At least one person on the audit committee should have an understanding of generally accepted accounting principles; the preparation or auditing of financial statements and the accounting for estimates, accruals, and reserves; experience in internal accounting controls; and an understanding of audit committee functions.

Moody's: Governance of Not-for-Profit Healthcare Organizations

In June 2005, Moody's released the above special report. Like Fitch Ratings, Moody's rates the creditworthiness of borrowers of bond proceeds and takes the position that implementation of certain financial and accounting safeguards will affect a borrower's rating. Rather than specifying provisions of Sarbanes-Oxley that nonprofits need to adopt, like Fitch, Moody's takes a more generalized approach and recommends a number of governance policies and procedures that will be reviewed in a bond-rating process. While aimed at nonprofit hospitals borrowing tax-exempt bond proceeds, these points can be considered best practices, whether or not a nonprofit hospital and whether or not a borrower of bond proceeds.

- **Development of borrower's mission:** Moody's will look at such issues as whether the borrower has developed performance metrics for determining the extent to which the borrower is meeting its charitable purpose and how the borrower balances mission against margin (e.g., how does the borrower balance the need to provide charity care with the need to operate in the black?). Moody's will also look to see if key governance and board-level policies have been adopted (e.g., operational policies and policies addressing investments, debt, and conflicts of interest.)

- **Selection and evaluation of senior management:** Moody's will determine whether the board has established written performance objectives and measures for the CEO and senior management team. Such objectives and measures would normally include, at a minimum, achieving financial budgets and industry benchmarks, limiting clinical errors, and maintaining patient and employee satisfaction. The CEO and senior management team should be evaluated annually through a formal process.

- **Board composition and performance:** Moody's will evaluate board members' backgrounds, selection processes for new board members, committee structure and processes, the size of the board, membership tenure and board limits, and the development and education of board members.

- **Board's understanding and interpretation of financial reporting:** Moody's will look at such factors as the existence and function of various committees (e.g., finance, investment, and audit), the audit process, maintenance of a system of internal controls over the financial reporting process, and how the board understands, monitors, and evaluates the financial performance of the borrower.

- **Use of performance metrics:** Moody's will evaluate whether the board has implemented a system of performance metrics to measure the success of the borrower's operations. Such metrics could include a "report card" on management performance and benchmarking against industry standards.

- **Maintaining and building the borrower's financial resources:** Moody's expects the boards of nonprofit borrowers to pay due regard to all sources of income and expense. While categories such as investment income and charitable donations merit attention, the board should focus careful attention on income and expense from operations. Operating income, especially in the case of hospitals, should fund operating expenses, debt service, and deprecation/capital reserves. The balance of operating income, if any, plus investment income and donations can be used to fund strategic capital and clinical initiatives.

- **Avoidance of conflicts of interest:** Moody's, like everyone else, will look closely at executive compensation and insider deals in assessing creditworthiness. Moody's will expect all borrowers to have comprehensive conflicts of interest policies in place.

American Bar Association: Guide to Nonprofit Governance in the Wake of Sarbanes-Oxley
Written by the ABA Coordinating Committee on Nonprofit Governance, this guide sets forth 10 principles that should guide nonprofit governance: Principle 1. Establish the role of board in governance and financial integrity. Principle 2. The board should be controlled by independent directors.

Principle 3. Establish an audit committee.

Principle 4. Establish a governance and nominating committee.

Principle 5. Establish a compensation committee.

Principle 6. Establish protocols for the disclosure and integrity of corporation information.

Principle 7. Adopt ethics and business codes of conduct.

Principle 8. Establish policies regarding executive and director compensation.

Principle 9. Monitor compliance with laws, investigate complaints, and take appropriate corrective action when wrongdoing is discovered.

Principle 10. Implement a document destruction and retention policy.

Board Source and Independent Sector: The Sarbanes-Oxley Act and Implications for Nonprofit Organizations

This joint publication authored by two of the most respected members of the nonprofit community suggests practical ways that nonprofits can implement certain provisions of Sarbanes-Oxley. Independent Sector provides this executive summary of the publication on its Web site, which also contains a link to the publication: http://www .independentsector.org/PDFs/sarbanesoxley.pdf.

1. Insider Transactions and Conflicts of Interest

    • Understand and fully comply with all laws regarding compensation and benefits provided to directors and executives (including "intermediate sanctions" and "self-dealing" laws).

    • Do not provide personal loans to directors and executives.

    • In cases in which the board feels it is necessary to provide a loan, however, all terms should be disclosed and formally approved by the board, the process should be documented, and the terms and the value of the loan should be publicly disclosed.

    • Establish a conflict-of-interest policy and a regular and rigorous means of enforcing it.

2. Independent and Competent Audit Committee

    • Conduct an annual external financial audit (the boards of very small organizations, for whom the cost of an external audit may be too burdensome, should at least evaluate carefully whether an audit would be valuable).

    • Establish a separate audit committee of the board.

    • Board members on the audit committee should be free from conflicts of interest and should not receive any compensation for their service on the committee.

    • Include at least one "financial expert" on the audit committee.

- The audit committee should select and oversee the auditing company and review the audit.
- Require full board to approve audit results.
- Provide financial literacy training to all board members.

3. Responsibilities of Auditors

- Rotate auditor or lead partner at least every five years.
- Avoid any conflict of interest in staff exchange between audit firm and organization.
- Do not use auditing firm for non-auditing services except tax form preparation with pre-approval from audit committee.
- Require disclosure to audit committee of critical accounting policies and practices.
- Use audit committee to oversee and enforce conflict-of-interest policy.

4. Certified Financial Statements

- CEO and CFO should sign off on all financial statements (either formally or in practice), including Form 990 tax returns, to ensure they are accurate, complete, and filed on time.
- The board should review and approve financial statements and Form 990 tax returns for completeness and accuracy.

5. Disclosure

- Disclose Form 990 and 990-PF in a current and easily accessible way (also required of all nonprofit organizations by IRS law).
- File 990 and 990-PF Forms in a timely manner, without use of extensions unless required by unusual circumstances.
- Disclose audited financial statements.
- Move to electronic filing of Form 990 and 990-PF.

6. Whistle-Blower Protection

- Develop, adopt, and disclose a formal process to deal with complaints and prevent retaliation.
- Investigate employee complaints and correct any problems or explain why corrections are not necessary.

7. Document Destruction

- Have a written, mandatory document retention and periodic destruction policy, which includes guidelines for electronic files and voicemail.
- If an official investigation is underway or even suspected, stop any document purging in order to avoid criminal obstruction.

Panel on the Nonprofit Sector: Strengthening Transparency, Governance and Accountability of Charitable Organizations: A Final Report to Congress and the Nonprofit Sector

The Panel was convened at the urging of the Senate Finance Committee to make recommendations to the Committee and the industry about legal reforms and best practices. The Final Report (issued in June 2005) is the result of the Panel's work and is available at www.nonprofitpanel.org. A summary of the Panel's 15 recommendations follows.

1. **Federal tax law enforcement:** Congress should increase oversight of the charitable sector and increase resources allocated to the IRS for tax enforcement.

2. **Form 990 reporting:** The Form 990 should be reviewed by the organization's board or appropriate committee. The organization's highest-ranking officer should sign and certify the 990.

3. **Governance self-review:** Exempt organization boards should undertake a thorough and comprehensive review of their governing documents at least once every five years.

4. **Financial audits and reviews:** Prepare financial statements in accordance with generally accepted accounting principles. Organizations with $1 million or more in annual revenue should have their financial statements audited by an independent public accountant. Organizations with annual revenues between $250,000 and $1 million should have their financial statements reviewed by an independent public accountant.

5. **Disclosure of performance data:** Every organization should provide detailed information about its operations, including methods it uses to evaluate the outcomes of its programs, to the public through its Web site, annual report, and other means.

6. **Donor-advised funds:** The Panel recommends a number of legislative changes, many of which were included in the Pension Protection Act of 2006. The Panel recommends that charities that sponsor donor-advised funds disclose certain information about them. These recommendations were largely adopted by the IRS in designing the Revised Form 990. (See Chapter 11 regarding Schedule D.)

7. **Type III supporting organizations:** The Panel recommends a number of legislative changes, many of which were included in the Pension Protection Act of 2006. The Panel recommends that supporting organizations be required to disclose certain information about their operations and their supported organizations. These recommendations were largely adopted by the IRS in designing the Revised Form 990. (See Chapter 8 regarding Schedule A.)

8. **Abusive tax shelters:** The Panel warns that nonprofits, like for-profits, should be prohibited from engaging in abusive "listed" and other "reportable" tax shelter transactions. (See § 4.1(i) for a discussion of prohibited tax shelters.)

9. **Noncash contributions:** The Panel makes a number of recommendations regarding contributions of appreciated property, conservation and facade easements, and clothing and household items, many of which were incorporated by the IRS into the Revised Form 990. (See Chapter 19 on Schedule M.)

10. **Board compensation:** Board compensation should be discouraged but to the extent that directors are compensated, the amount and reason for the compensation should be disclosed, as well as the method used to determine the reasonableness of the compensation. (See Chapter 6 on Part VII and Schedule J.)

11. **Executive compensation:** The Panel recommends increased disclosure of executive compensation on the Form 990. Many of the recommendations were incorporated by the IRS in the Revised Form 990. (See Chapter 6 on Part VII and Schedule J.) The Panel recommends that exempt organization boards review CEO compensation annually and review the full staff compensation program periodically.

12. **Travel expenses:** Organizations should adopt and enforce clear policies regarding the types of expenses that can be reimbursed and the documentation needed to receive reimbursement. Payment of spouse or companion travel should be discouraged. (See Chapter 6 on Part VII and Schedule J.)

13. **Structure, size, and composition of governing board:** Boards should have at least three members. At least one-third of the board should be independent. *Independence* is defined as someone who does not receive compensation from the organization (directly or indirectly), whose compensation is not determined by other board or staff members, and who is not related to someone who receives compensation from the organization. Individuals barred from serving on boards of publicly traded corporations or who have been convicted of crimes regarding breaches of fiduciary duties should not be allowed to serve on a nonprofit board. Nonprofit boards should review board size periodically to determine appropriate size to ensure effective governance. Nonprofit boards should establish mechanisms to ensure the board carries out its oversight function and that board members are aware of their legal and ethical responsibilities. (See Chapter 5 on Part VI.)

14. **Audit committees:** Some members of the board should have financial literacy. If the organization has its financial statements independently audited, it should consider establishing a separate audit committee. If the board does not have sufficient financial literacy, and if state law permits, the organization should establish an advisory committee of nonboard, nonstaff members to help it with its financial oversight.

15. **Conflicts of interest and misconduct:** Nonprofit organizations should adopt and enforce a conflicts of interest policy. They should also adopt codes of ethics and whistleblower policies that encourage individuals within the organization to report wrongdoing and protect such reporters from retaliation.

Panel on the Nonprofit Sector: A Supplemental Report to Congress and the Nonprofit Sector

In April 2006, the Panel released a supplemental report (to supplement the final report issued in June 2005). The supplemental report is available at www.nonprofitpanel.org. A summary of the Panel's eight recommendations follows.

1. **International grantmaking:** Charities should adhere to certain principles in carrying out their international charity work. (See Chapter 13 on Schedule F.)

2. **Charitable solicitation:** Charities should adhere to certain best practices when engaging in fundraising. (See Chapter 14 on Schedules B and G.)

3. **Compensation of trustees of charitable trusts:** The Panel sets forth guidelines for compensating individual and corporate trustees of charitable trusts. (See Chapter 6 on Part VII and Schedule J.)

4. **Prudent investor standard:** Both nonprofit corporations and charitable trusts should adhere to uniform investment standards such as the Uniform Prudent Investor Act and the Uniform Management of Institutional Funds Act. (See Chapter 11 on Schedule D.)

5. **Nonprofit conversion transactions:** Nonprofit boards should use great care and diligence when engaging in transactions that will result in all, or substantially all, of the nonprofit's assets being transferred to a for-profit entity. At a minimum, boards should ensure that they are receiving fair market value for the transferred assets and that the nonprofit's mission will be able to continue through appropriate use of the sale proceeds. (See Chapter 20 on Schedule N.)

6. **Sales of donated property:** The Panel recommends increased scrutiny of non-cash contributions to charities and subsequent resale by the charity (e.g., vehicle donation programs). (See Chapter 19 on Schedule M.)

7. **Consumer credit counseling organizations:** The Panel recommends increased scrutiny of consumer credit counseling organizations. Many of the recommendations were incorporated by Congress into Section 501(q) of the Internal Revenue Code. (See Chapter 11 on Schedule D.)

8. **Disclosure of unrelated business activities:** The Panel urges increased disclosure of unrelated business activities by nonprofits, much of which has been incorporated into the Revised Form 990.

Panel on the Nonprofit Sector: Principles for Good Governance and Ethical Practice: A Guide for Charities and Foundations

After issuing its final and supplemental reports to Congress on charitable transparency and accountability, in October 2007 the Panel released the 33 principles of good governance. Organized under four categories, the principles are predicated on the need for a "careful balance between the two essential forms of regulation—that is, between prudent legal mandates to ensure that organizations do not abuse the privilege of their exempt status, and, for all other aspects of sound operations, well-informed self-governance and mutual awareness among nonprofit organizations." The principles are available in full on the Panel's Web site at www.nonprofitpanel.org.

1. Legal Compliance and Public Disclosure
   - An organization must *comply with applicable federal, state, and local laws.* If the organization conducts programs outside the United States, it must abide by

applicable international laws and conventions that are legally binding on the United States.

- An organization should have a formally adopted, *written code of ethics* with which all of its directors, staff, and volunteers are familiar and to which they adhere.

- An organization should implement policies and procedures to ensure that all *conflicts of interest*, or appearance of them, within the organization and its board are appropriately managed though disclosure, recusal, or other means.

- An organization should implement policies and procedures that enable individuals to come forward with information on illegal practices or violations of organizational policies. This *whistleblower policy* should specify that the organization will not retaliate against, and will protect the confidentiality of, individuals who make good-faith reports.

- An organization should implement policies and procedures to *preserve the organization's important documents and business records*.

- An organization's board should ensure that the organization has adequate plans to *protect its assets*—its property, financial and human resources, programmatic content and material, and integrity and reputation—against damage or loss. The board should regularly review the organization's need for general liability and directors' and officers' liability insurance as well as take other actions to mitigate risk.

- An organization should *publicly disseminate information* about its operations, including its governance, finances, programs, and other activities. Charitable organizations should also consider making information available on the methods they use to evaluate the outcomes of their work and sharing the results of the evaluations.

2. Effective Governance

- An organization should establish the *role of the governing body* in the areas of mission and strategic direction, annual budget, and key financial transactions, compensation practices, and fiscal and governance policies.

- The board of an organization should *meet regularly to conduct business* and fulfill its duties.

- The board of an organization should *establish and periodically review board size and structure*. The board should have enough members to allow for full deliberation and diversity of thinking on organizational matters. Except for very small organizations, this generally means there should be at least five members.

- The board of an organization should *include members with diverse backgrounds* (including ethnic, racial, and gender perspectives), experience, and organizational and financial skills necessary to advance the organization's mission.

- The organization should establish an *independent board*, which generally means that a substantial majority of the board (usually at least two-thirds) should be independent. Independent members should not: be compensated by the organization; have their compensation determined by individuals who are compensated by the organization; receive material financial benefits from the organization except as a member of a charitable class served by the organization; or be related to or reside with any person described above.

- The board should *hire, oversee, and annually evaluate the performance of the chief executive* of the organization, and should conduct such an evaluation prior to any change in that individual's compensation, unless a multiyear contract is in force or the change consists solely of routine adjustments for inflation or cost of living.

- The board of an organization that has paid staff should ensure that *separate individuals hold the positions of chief staff officer, board chair, and board treasurer*. Organizations without paid staff should ensure that the position of board chair and treasurer are separately held.

- The board should establish an effective, systematic process for educating and communicating with board members to ensure that they are aware of their *legal and ethical responsibilities*, are knowledgeable about the programs and other activities of the organization, and can effectively carry out their oversight functions.

- Board members should conduct a *self-assessment* to evaluate their performance as a group and as individuals no less than every three years, and should have clear procedures for removing board members who are unable to fulfill their responsibilities.

- The board should establish clear policies and procedures to *establish the length of terms and the number of consecutive terms a board member may serve*.

- The board should *review the organization's governing instruments* at least every five years.

- The board should regularly *review the organization's mission and goals*, and evaluate at least every five years the organization's goals, programs, and other activities to be sure they advance its mission and make prudent use of its resources.

- *Board compensation* should generally be avoided, other than reimbursement for expenses incurred to fulfill board duties. An organization that provides compensation to its board members should use appropriate comparability data to determine the amount to be paid, document the decision, and provide full disclosure to anyone, on request, of the amount and rationale for the compensation.

3. Strong Financial Oversight

- An organization must keep *complete, current, and accurate financial records*. Its board should review timely reports of the organization's financial activities and have a *qualified, independent financial expert audit or review these statements annually* in a manner appropriate to the organization's size and scale of operations.

- The board of an organization must institute policies and procedures (and, if applicable, its subsidiaries) *responsible management and investment of funds*, in accordance with requirements of law. The full board should *approve the annual budget and monitor performance* against the budget.

- An organization should *avoid loans to directors and officers* (or the equivalent, such as loan guarantees, purchasing or transferring ownership of a residence or office, or relieving a debt or lease obligations).

- An organization should *spend a significant portion of its annual budget on programs that pursue its mission*. The budget should provide sufficient resources for effective administration of the organization and, if it solicits contributions for appropriate fundraising activities.

- An organization should establish clear, *written policies regarding payment or reimbursement travel and entertainment expenses* incurred by anyone conducting business or traveling on behalf of the organization, including the types of expenses that can be paid or reimbursed and the documentation required. These policies should require that travel on behalf of the organization be undertaken in a cost-effective manner.

- An organization should neither pay for nor reimburse *spousal or companion travel* expenditures for those who are accompanying someone conducting business for the organization unless they are also conducting the business.

4. Responsible Fundraising

- *Solicitation materials* and other communications addressed to prospective donors and the public must clearly identify the organization, and be accurate and truthful.

- Contributions must be used for purposes consistent with the *donor's intent*, whether as described in the solicitation materials or as directed by the donor.

- An organization must provide donors with *acknowledgments of charitable contributions*, in accordance with federal tax law requirements, including information to facilitate the donor's compliance with tax law requirements.

- An organization should adopt a *gift acceptance policy* to determine whether acceptance of a gift would compromise its ethics, financial circumstances, program focus, or other interests.

- An organization should provide *appropriate training and supervision of the people soliciting funds* on its behalf to ensure that they understand their responsibilities and applicable law, and do not employ techniques that are coercive, intimidating, or intended to harass potential donors.

- An organization should establish a policy on *compensation of internal or external fundraisers* that prohibits compensation on the basis of a commission or percentage of the amount raised.

- An organization should respect the privacy of individual donors and, except where disclosure is required by law, should not sell or otherwise make available the names and contact information of its donors without providing them an opportunity to at least annually opt out of use of their names.

Independent Sector: Checklist for Accountability

The Checklist for Accountability combines recommendations made by the Independent Sector and the Panel on the Nonprofit Sector. It was developed with the additional input of the Ethics and Accountability Committee and Communications and Marketing Advisory Task Force. The checklist is available on the Independent Sector Web site at: www.independentsector.org/issues/accountability/Checklist/index.html. The Web site also contains commentary and links to additional resources to help nonprofits with drafting and implementation of corporate governance policies and standards. The Checklist recommends that nonprofit organizations:

1. Develop a culture of accountability and transparency.
2. Adopt a statement of values and code of ethics.
3. Adopt a conflict-of-interest policy.
4. Ensure that the board of directors understand and can fulfill its financial responsibilities.
5. Conduct independent financial reviews and audits.
6. Ensure the accuracy of and make public the 990.
7. Be transparent.
8. Adopt a whistleblower protection policy.
9. Remain current with the law.

BBB Wise Giving Alliance Standards for Charity Accountability

The Wise Giving standards were developed to assist donors in making sound giving decisions and to foster public confidence in charitable organizations. The Alliance is the result of a merger of the National Charities Information Bureau and the Council of Better Business Bureaus' Foundation and its Philanthropic Advisory Service. The standards can be viewed on the Alliance Web site at www.give.org/standards/newcbbbstds.asp. The 20 standards are divided into four broad categories.

GOVERNANCE AND OVERSIGHT

The governing board has the ultimate oversight authority for any charitable organization. The standards seek to ensure that the volunteer board is active, independent. and free of self-dealing.

1. A board of directors should provide *adequate oversight* of the charity's operations and its staff.
2. A board of directors should have a *minimum of five voting members*.
3. A board of director should have a minimum of *three evenly spaced meetings per year* of the full governing body with a majority in attendance, with face-to-face participation.
4. A board of directors should not have more than one or 10 percent (whichever is greater) directly or indirectly *compensated person(s) serving as voting*

member(s) of the board. Compensated members shall not serve as the board's chair or treasurer.

5. A board of directors should not engage in any transaction(s) in which any board or staff members have *material conflicting interests* with the charity resulting from any relationship or business affiliation.

MEASURING EFFECTIVENESS

An organization should regularly assess its effectiveness in achieving its mission. The standards seek to ensure that an organization has defined, measurable goals and objectives in place and a defined process in place to evaluate the success and impact of its program(s) in fulfilling the goals and objectives of the organization and that also identifies ways to address any deficiencies.

1. No less than every two years, the board should *assess the organization's performance and effectiveness* and of determining future actions required to achieve its mission.

2. Executive staff should submit to the board, for its approval, a written report that outlines the results of the aforementioned performance and effectiveness assessment and *recommendations for future actions*.

FINANCES

The standards seek to ensure that the charity spends its funds honestly, prudently, and in accordance with statements made in fundraising appeals.

1. The ratio of total program service expenses to total expenses should be at least 65 percent.

2. The ratio of total fundraising expenses to total related contributions should not exceed 35 percent.

3. The organization should *avoid accumulating funds that could be used for current program activities*. To meet this standard, the charity's unrestricted net assets available for use should not be more than three times the size of the past year's expenses or three times the size of the current year's budget, whichever is higher.

4. The organization should *disclose* to all, on request, complete *annual financial statements* prepared in accordance with generally accepted accounting principles.

5. The organization should include in the financial statements a *breakdown of expenses* (e.g., salaries, travel, postage, etc.) that shows what portion of these expenses was allocated to *program, fundraising, and administrative activities*.

6. An organization should *accurately report the charity's expenses*, including any joint cost allocations, in its financial statements.

7. The organization should have a *board-approved annual budget* for its current fiscal year, outlining projected expenses for major program activities, fund raising, and administration.

FUNDRAISING AND INFORMATIONAL MATERIALS

A fundraising appeal is often the only contact a donor has with a charity and may be the sole impetus for giving. The standards seek to ensure that a charity's representations to the public are accurate, complete, and respectful.

1. The organization should have *solicitations and informational materials* that are accurate, truthful, and not misleading, both in whole and in part.

2. The organization should have an *annual report*, available to all upon request, that includes: the organization's mission statement; a summary of the past year's program service accomplishments; a roster of the officers and members of the board of directors; financial information that includes total income in the past fiscal year, expenses in the same program, fundraising and administrative categories as in the financial statements, and ending net assets.

3. The organization should include on any charity *Web sites* that solicit contributions the same information that is recommended for annual reports, as well as the mailing address of the charity and electronic access to its most recent IRS Form 990.

4. The organization should *address privacy concerns of donors* by

   a. Providing in written appeals, at least annually, a means (e.g., such as a check box) for both new and continuing donors to inform the charity if they do not want their name and address shared outside the organization, and

   b. Providing a clear, prominent, and easily accessible privacy policy on any of its Web sites that tells visitors
      i. what information, if any, is being collected about them by the charity and how this information will be used;
      ii. how to contact the charity to review personal information collected and request corrections;
      iii. how to inform the charity (e.g., a check box) that the visitor does not wish personal information to be shared outside the organization; and
      iv. what security measures the charity has in place to protect personal information.

5. The organization should clearly disclose how the charity benefits from the sale of products or services, known as *cause-related marketing*, that state or imply that a charity will benefit from a consumer sale or transaction. Such promotions should disclose, at the point of solicitation:

   a. The actual or anticipated portion of the purchase price that will benefit the charity (e.g., 5 cents will be contributed to abc charity for every xyz company product sold)

   b. The duration of the campaign (e.g., the month of October)

   c. Any maximum or guaranteed minimum contribution amount (e.g., up to a maximum of $200,000)

6. The organization should respond promptly to and act on complaints brought to its attention by the BBB Wise Giving Alliance and/or local Better Business Bureaus about fundraising practices, privacy policy violations, and/or other issues.

American Red Cross Modernization Act of 2007

In 2007, Congress passed an act to amend the congressional charter of the American Red Cross in order to modernize its structure and enhance the ability of the board of governors to support the mission of the Red Cross. The main functions of the act were to reduce the board size of the Red Cross, cause the board to have staggered terms, impose term limits on board members, authorize an executive committee, establish an advisory committee, and disallow proxy voting by directors. In addition, the act outlines the board's responsibilities, as follows, which can serve as a checklist for all nonprofit boards:

- Reviewing and *approving the mission statement* for the American National Red Cross
- Approving and *overseeing the corporation's strategic plan* and maintaining strategic oversight of operational matters
- Selecting, evaluating, and *determining the level of compensation* of the corporation's chief executive officer
- Evaluating the performance and establishing the compensation of the senior leadership team and *providing for management succession*
- *Overseeing financial matters*, including reporting and audit process, internal controls, and legal compliance
- *Holding management accountable* for performance
- Providing *oversight of the financial stability* of the corporation
- Ensuring the *inclusiveness and diversity* of the corporation
- Ensuring the chapters of the Red Cross are *geographically and regionally diverse*
- Providing *oversight of the projection of the brand* of the corporation
- *Assisting with fundraising* on behalf of the corporation

Treasury Department's Voluntary Best Practices

The Treasury Anti-Terrorist Financing Guidelines establish a number of governance and financial accounting best practices that nonprofits can consider adopting.

Governing Instruments. An organization's governing instruments should:

- Delineate the organization's basic *goals and purposes*.

- Define the *structure of the organization*, including the composition of the board, how the board is selected and replaced, and the authority and responsibilities of the board.

- Set forth requirements concerning *financial reporting*, accountability, and practices for the solicitation and distribution of funds.

- State that the charity shall *comply with all applicable laws*, including federal, state, and local law.

Board of Directors. The board of directors is responsible for the organization's compliance with relevant laws, and should:

- Be an active governing body.

- Oversee implementation of the governance practices to be followed by the organization.

- Exercise effective and independent oversight of the organization's operations.

- Establish a conflict-of-interest policy for board members and employees.

- Establish procedures to be followed if a board member or employee has a conflict, or perceived conflict, of interest.

- Maintain records of all decisions made, with these records available for inspection by the appropriate regulatory and law enforcement authorities.

Financial Practices. The organization should have:

- An *annual budget* approved and overseen by the board.

- A *board-appointed financial/accounting officer* who is responsible for day-to-day management of the charity's assets.

- An *audit of the finances* of the organization, when annual gross income is in excess of $250,000, by an independent certified public accounting firm, with the audited financial statement available for public inspection.

- Accounting for all funds received and disbursed in accordance with *generally accepted accounting principles*, including the name of each recipient of funds, the amount disbursed, and the date of the disbursement.

- *Prompt deposit of all funds* into an account maintained by the charity at a financial institution.

- The *making of disbursements by check or wire transfer*, rather than in currency, whenever that is reasonably feasible.

Maintenance of Records Regarding Board Members. Organizations should:

- Maintain and make publicly available a current *list of their board members* and the salaries they are paid.

- Maintain records (while fully respecting individual privacy rights) containing additional *identifying information about their board members*, such as home addresses, Social Security numbers, and citizenship.

- Maintain records (while respecting individual privacy rights) *identifying information about the board members of any subsidiaries or affiliates* receiving funds from them.

Maintenance of Records Regarding Key Employees. Organizations should:

- Maintain and make publicly available a current *list of their five highest-paid or most influential employees* and the salaries and/or other direct or indirect benefits they are provided.

- Maintain records (while respecting privacy rights) containing *identifying information about their key, non-U.S. employees* working abroad.

- Maintain records (while respecting individual privacy rights) *identifying information about the key employees of any subsidiaries or affiliates* receiving funds from them.

Disclosures. Organizations should make publicly available:

- A current *list of any branches, subsidiaries, and/or affiliates* that receive resources and services from them.

- An *annual report*, which describes the organization's purposes, programs, activities, tax-exempt status, structure and responsibility of the governing body, and financial information.

- Complete *annual financial statements*, including a summary of the results of the most recent audit, which present the overall financial condition of the organization and its financial activities in accordance with generally accepted accounting principles and reporting practices.

Senate Finance Committee Draft Staff Paper

The Senate Committee on Finance, in 2004, held a hearing on a range of subjects pertaining to tax-exempt organizations. In connection with that hearing, the staff of the committee prepared a paper containing a variety of proposals as a discussion draft. A number of these proposals address issues of financial accountability and governance.

Board Responsibilities. The proposals recommend that the board of a tax-exempt organization should:

- Establish basic *organizational and management policies* and procedures for the organization, and review any proposed deviations.

- Establish, review, and approve *program objectives and performance measures*.

- Review and approve *significant transactions*.

- Review and approve the *auditing and accounting principles and practices* used in preparing the organization's financial statements, and retain and replace the organization's independent auditor.

- Review and approve the organization's *budget and financial objectives*, as well as significant investments, joint ventures, and business transactions.

- *Oversee the conduct of the organization's activities*, and evaluate whether the activities are being properly managed.

- Approve *compensation* for management positions in advance.

- Establish a *conflict-of-interest policy* and prepare a summary of conflicts determinations made during each year.

- Establish and oversee a *compliance program* to address regulatory and liability concerns.

- Establish procedures to address complaints and prevent retaliation against *whistleblowers*.

Board Structure and Composition. The proposals recommend that:

- *Only one board member can be compensated* by the organization.

- At least *one-fifth of the board should be independent*.

- Any individual who is not permitted to serve on the board of a publicly traded company, because of a law violation, should not serve on the board of a tax-exempt organization.

- The *IRS be granted authority to remove any director, officer or employee* who violates self-dealing rules, conflict-of-interest standards, excess benefit transaction rules, private inurement rules, or charitable solicitation laws.

- The U.S. Tax Court be invested with *equity powers to remedy any detriment to a charitable organization* resulting from a violation of the substantive rules, including the power to rescind transactions, surcharge trustees and directors, order accountings, and substitute trustees or directors.

Committee for Purchase Proposed Best Practices

The Committee for Purchase from People Who Are Blind or Severely Disabled administers the Javits-Wagner-O'Day Act. In an effort to ensure that participants in the JWOD program meet the highest standards of governance and accountability, the committee proposed a number of financial and governance best practices. The committee believes its best practices are "widely considered as benchmarks of good nonprofit agency governance practices."

BOARD STRUCTURE

- A nonprofit organization's board of directors should be composed of individuals who are *personally committed to the mission* of the organization and possess the specific skills needed to accomplish the mission.

- Where an employee of the organization is a voting member of the board, the circumstances must ensure that the *employee will not be in a position to exercise undue influence*.
- The board should have *at least five unrelated directors*.
- The *chair of the board* should not simultaneously be serving as the entity's CEO/president.
- There should be *term limits* for board members.
- *Board membership should reflect the diversity* of the communities served by the organization.
- Board members should *serve without compensation*.

EXECUTIVE COMPENSATION

- The board or a designated committee of it should *hire the CEO/president/executive director*, set the executive's compensation, and evaluate the executive's performance at least annually.
- The board of directors should *monitor compensation* paid to all other highly compensated individuals.
- The board should approve all compensation packages for all highly compensated employees through a *rebuttable presumption process* to determine reasonableness.
- The board should periodically *review the appropriateness of the overall compensation structure* of the entire organization.

FINANCIAL OVERSIGHT

- The board should have at least one *financial expert* among its membership.
- The board should subject the accuracy of the organization's financial reports to *audit* by a certified public accountant.
- The board should *approve the findings of the organization's annual audit* and management letter.
- The board should approve a plan to *implement the recommendations of the management letter*.
- The board should adopt a *conflict-of-interest policy* that identifies the types of conflict or transactions that raise conflict-of-interest concerns, sets forth procedures for disclosure of actual or potential conflicts, and provides for review of individual transactions by the disinterested members of the board.
- The board should periodically conduct an *internal review of the organization's compliance* with existing statutory, regulatory, and financial reporting requirements.
- The board should *disclose annually to the public* information about the organization's mission, program activities, and audit and other financial data.

§7.2 PREPARATION OF NEW FORM 990, PARTS VIII–XI

(a) Part VIII (Statement of Revenue)

The Statement of Revenue in the Form 990 is a combination of the Statement of Revenue in the prior form (2007, Part I) and the Analysis of Income Producing Activities in the prior form (2007, Part VII). These two parts were combined to eliminate redundancy and increase accuracy. The combined form eliminates (1) use of the exclusion codes for revenue exempt from tax under Sections 512, 513, or 514; and (2) Schedules for Other Investment Income, Sales of Inventory, and Sales of Assets Other Than Inventory. The instructions to the Form 990 are comprehensive and thorough and provide guidance not found in the current instructions. What follows is a summary of those instructions and, where appropriate, additional commentary on the instructions.

Reporting of revenue is broken down into three categories: (1) contributions, gifts and grants; (2) program service revenue; and (3) other revenue (mostly passive investment income). All revenue must be further classified as:

- **Total Revenue (Column (A)).** All organizations must report their gross receipts or all sources of revenue in Column A. All organizations except 527 political organizations must complete Columns (B) through (D).

- **Related or Exempt Function Revenue (Column (B)).** In this column report all revenue from all activities related to the organization's exempt purpose. This includes any revenue exempt from tax except for gross income excluded from tax under Sections 512, 513, or 514 (which is reported in Column (D)).

- **Unrelated Business Revenue (Column (C)).** In this column report any unrelated business revenue received from an unrelated trade or business. (See § 7.1(b) for a discuss of unrelated business income.)

- **Unrelated Business Revenue Excluded From Tax (Under Sections 512, 513, or 514) (Column (D)).** Report any revenue excluded from tax under Sections 512, 513, or 514 (such as interest, dividends, rents, royalties, cooperative hospital service revenue, qualified bingo revenues, etc.).

(1) Line 1 (Contributions, Gifts, Grants, and Other Similar Amounts). Report cash and noncash voluntary contributions, gifts, grants, or other similar amounts from the general public, governmental units, foundations, and other exempt organizations. The *general public* includes individuals, corporations, trusts, estates, and other entities. *Voluntary contributions* are payments, or the part of any payment, for which the donor does not receive something of equivalent value in return. If the donor receives something of value in return, then the contribution portion is reported in line 1 and the portion representing the payment for value is reported in line 8 (income from fundraising). See the example for line 1c discussed in § 7.2(a)(1). Some additional rules for reporting line 1 revenue include:

- Report gross amounts of contributions collected in the organization's name by professional fundraisers. Fees paid to professional fundraisers are reported as an expense in Part IX, line 11(e), Column (D). Internal costs of fundraising (e.g., staff salaries and the pro rata portion of occupancy and office expense) are reported in Part IX, Column (D) on the appropriate line (e.g., staff salaries on line 7, office expenses on line 13, and occupancy on line 16).

- Report noncash contributions at the fair market value on the date of contribution.

- Contributions do not include (1) fees paid by governmental units for a service, facility, or product that primarily benefits the payer (this gets reported as program service revenue on line 2); the portion of any fundraising revenue that represents payments for goods or services (this gets reported as fundraising revenue on line 8); or donations of services or use of material, equipment, or facilities (this does not get reported anywhere); unreimbursed expenses of officers, employees, or volunteers (this does not get reported anywhere); and payments received from employers for welfare benefits under plans described in Code sections 501(c)(9), (17), and (18) (this gets reported on line 2, program service revenue).

- Contributions are reported on line 1 regardless of whether they are deductible by the contributor. The noncash portion of contributions on lines 1a through 1f is also reported on line 1g.

Breakdown contributions, gifts, grants and other similar amounts into the following categories:

- **Federated Campaigns (line 1a).** Report any amounts received indirectly from the public through campaigns conducted by organizations such as the United Way that solicit funds from the public and allocate net proceeds to participating organizations. Note: Federated fundraising agencies such as the United Way, like all other filers, must identify the sources of contributions made to them on lines 1a through 1g of their respective Forms 990, likely on line 1f, but the directions do not specify. See the example for Part VIII, line 1f, in § 7.2(a)(1).

- **Membership Dues (line 1b).** Report membership dues and assessments that represent contributions from the public rather than payments for benefits received. Membership dues representing payment for goods or services are reported on line 2. The instructions provide the example of members of the symphony whose membership fees entitle them to attend rehearsals and buy tickets at regular price before they go on sale to the public. Because the members are not receiving goods or services, this is reported as a contribution. Contrast this with the example in line 2, where membership fees entitle the member to subscriptions to publications or newsletters of a commercial quality, free or reduced-rate admissions, use of facilities, and discounts on goods. Because these represents goods or services received in exchange for payment, they are reported as program service revenue on line 2. If membership payments represent both contributions and payment for goods and services, the payment will have to be allocated between line 1b and line 2.

- **Fundraising Events (line 1c).** Report contributions received for gaming events, dinners, auctions and other events whose sole or primary purpose is to raise funds. Also report on this line sales or gifts of goods of nominal value; income from sweepstakes, lotteries or raffles; and solicitation campaigns that generate only contributions. (Note: If the combined amount on line 1c and line 8a is more than $15,000, answer "yes" to Part IV, line 18 and complete Part II of Schedule G—see Chapter 14.) If there is both a contribution element and a payment for which something of value is received (other than something of nominal value), the payment must be allocated between line 1c and line 8 (fundraising events). For example, the instructions say, if the organization holds a gala dinner and charges $400—with $160 representing the cost of the dinner and $240 representing a contributions)— the organization would report a $240 contribution on line 1c and in the parenthetical on line 8a, and the organization would report the $160 in the right-hand column on line 8a. Revenue Ruling 67-246 and Publication 526 (Charitable Contributions) explain this principle in detail.

- **Related Organizations (line 1d).** Report any contributions from a related organization (as defined in the glossary to the IRS instructions) when there is nothing of value given to the donor. If the donor receives goods or services in return for the payment, report as program service revenue on line 2. Do not report any amount reportable on line 1a.

- **Government Grants (line 1e).** Report any payments from government entities when the beneficiary of the payment is the public in general and not the government entity. If the government entity, rather than the public in general, is the beneficiary, report as program service revenue on line 2. For example, this information would be reported on line 1e: (1) payments from a government entity for construction of a library open to the public; (2) payments from a government entity to a nursing home to provide care to the nursing home's residents; and (3) payments from a government entity under a government program to serve children in the community. The instructions to line 2 provide additional examples. Government payments to a medical clinic to provide vaccinations to the general public would be reported on line 1e, but government payments to provide vaccinations to government employees would be reported on line 2. Payments from a government entity to provide job training and placement for disabled individuals would be reported on line 1e, but payments by the government entity to an organization for its disabled beneficiaries to operate the government entity's internal mail room would be program service revenue reported on line 2.

Note: Distinguishing government payments that are contributions (line 1e) versus program service payments (line 2) is a critical distinction when it comes to satisfying the public support calculations on Schedule A (see Chapter 8). For 509(a)(1) organizations (referred to in Chapter 8 as donative publicly supported charities), the full amount of line 1e contributions can go to the public support test without being subject to the 2% limitation (see § 8.1(d)(2)). If the amount is reported as line 2 program service revenue, 509(a)(1) organizations cannot treat it as public support (see § 8.1(d)(3)). For 509(a)(2) organizations (referred to in Chapter 8 as service provider publicly supported organizations), the full amount of line 1e contributions can go to the public support test but line 2 program service can only be included to the extent it does not exceed the greater of $5,000 or 1 percent of the organization's revenues (see § 8.1(e)(3)).

- **All Other Contributions, Gifts and Similar Amounts (line 1f).** Report in line 1f any other amount, meeting the definition of a contribution given earlier, that does not meet one of the above categories. This would include contributions from donor-advised funds and the value of noncash gifts valued at their date of donation. Contributions received by federated fundraising agencies, such as the United Way, should be reported on Part VIII, line 1 (likely line 1f— although the instructions do not specify), even if the donation is designated for a particular agency. Such organizations should report grants to member agencies on Part IX, line 1. Quotas, dues, or support payments to state or national affiliates are reported on Part IX, line 21. For example, if a local United Way agency receives a contribution for $x that is designated for Organization Y, then the United Way agency reports $x of income on Part VIII, line 1f; reports the payment of $x to Organization Y on Part IX, line 1; and reports any dues or payments made to the national United Way on Part IX, line 21.

- **Noncash Contributions (line 1g).** Report noncash contributions included in lines 1a through 1f. (Note: In other words, noncash contributions will always be reported twice, once in line 1a through 1f and again in line 1g. There will be no double counting because line 1g is not included in the totals calculate in 1h.) Value noncash contributions at their value on the date of donation. If line 1g exceeds, $25,000, answer "yes" to Part IV, line 29 and complete and attach Schedule M (see Chapter 19). Note: Museums and other organizations that elect not to capitalize their collections (in accordance with SFAS 116) should not report an amount on line 1g for works of art and other collection items donated to them.

- **Total (line 1h)** Report the total of lines 1a through 1f. In order to avoid double counting do not include line 1g because anything reported in line 1g must also be reported on the appropriate line 1a through 1f.

> *Tip:* For all program service revenue reported on lines 2a through 2e, also enter a business code from *Codes for Unrelated Business Activity* from the instructions for Form 990-T. If none of the codes accurately describes the activity, enter 900099. Use of these codes does not imply that the business activity is unrelated to the organization's exempt purpose.

(2) Line 2 (Program Service Revenue). On lines 2a through 2e, report the organization's five largest sources of program service revenue. On line 2f enter the amount received from all other program service areas not reported on lines 2a through 2e. Program services are those that serve the basis of the organization's exemption. They can include provision of services to a government entity, payments received by a hospital for provision of medical services (including payments from individuals, insurance companies, or government programs such as Medicare and Medicaid), tuition received by a school, revenue from admissions to a performing arts concert or museum, royalties received as an author of an educational publication, interest income on loans a credit union makes to members, payments received by a 501(c)(9) organization for provision of health and welfare benefits, insurance premiums received by a fraternal benefit society, and registration fees in connection with a meeting or convention. These types of revenue are also reported on line 2 as program service revenue:

- Program service revenue can also include income from *program-related investments*. These are investments made primarily to accomplish exempt purposes rather than produce income. Examples include scholarship/student loans and low-interest loans to charities, indigents, and victims of disaster.

- *Rents* can also be a program-related investment if, for example, the organization rents space at below-market rates to a tenant to help the tenant achieve its exempt purpose. Similarly, rent received from providing low-income housing to persons with low income would be report as program service revenue. Arguably, rent that constitutes program service revenue should be reported in Column (B) rather than in Column (D). All rent from an affiliated organization is reported as program service revenue on line 2. Rental income that constitute investment income should be reported on line 6 (see § 7.2(a)(3)). With respect to reporting rent payments made by the organization, see Part IX, line 16 (§ 7.2(b)(14)). With respect to reporting expenses associated with rental property held for investment, see Part VIII, line 6 (§ 7.2(a)(3)).

- *Unrelated business income* (see § 7.1(b)) is reported as program service revenue. This, presumably, is the case despite the definition in the instructions of program service revenue as revenue from activities that form the basis of the organization's exemption. Unrelated business income, since it is by definition not related to the organization's exempt purposes, cannot form the basis of its exemption. Nevertheless, the instructions indicate that unrelated business income should be reported in line 2 as program service revenue. Presumably, 100 percent of this amount would be reported in Column (C).

- *Sales of inventory items by hospitals colleges and universities* can be reported on line 2 as program service revenue. Generally, this should be reported on Column (B). If this election is made, the cost of goods sold is reported as a program service expense on Column (B) of Part IX, presumably on line 24, although the instructions do not say. No other organization is allowed to report sales of inventory on line 2; instead they must report such revenue on line 10a.

- *Government payments* in return for goods or services that primarily benefit the government payer are reported on line 2, generally in Column (B). Government payments that primarily benefit the public in general are reported on line 1e. See the examples in the discussion of line 1e.

- *Membership dues and assessments* received that compare reasonably with the membership benefits provided are reported on line 2, generally in Column (B). Examples of such membership benefits include subscriptions to publications and newsletters of commercial quality, free or reduced-rate admissions to organization events, use of the organization's facilities, and discounts on goods or services. See the examples in the discussion of line 1b for additional examples and discussion regarding the distinction of membership dues and assessments reported on line 1b versus line 2. Organizations described in 501(c)(5), (6), or (7) generally provide the types of benefits to their members that would require membership dues to be reported on line 2 rather than line 1b.

(3) Lines 3–11 (Other Revenue). Break down other revenue into these categories:

- **Investment Income (line 3).** Report interest and dividend income from savings, temporary cash investments, equity and debt securities, amounts received from payments on securities loans (as defined in 512(a)(5)) and interest from notes and loans receivable. Generally, line 3 income will be reported in Column (D). Do not report any interest reported on line 2 as a program-related investment (e.g., interest on student loans or loans to other charities to help them carry out their exempt purposes). Do not report realized or unrealized gains.

- **Income from Tax-Exempt Bond Proceeds (line 4).** Report on line 4 all investment income actually or constructively received from investing the proceeds of a tax-exempt bond. Generally, line 4 income will be reported in Column (D). Only report income that is under the control of the organization. Do not report any income received from investing proceeds, which are technically under the control of the government issuer. For example, proceeds deposited into a defeasance escrow that is irrevocably pledged to pay principal and interest (debt service) on a bond issue is not under the control of the organization.

- **Royalties (line 5).** Report royalties received by the organization from licensing ongoing use of its property to others. Royalties can include revenue from patents and trademarks as well as from natural resources such as oil, natural gas, and minerals. Generally, line 5 income will be reported in Column (D).

- **Rents (lines 6a–6d).** Report gross rental income on line 6a. Do not include income if the rental activity is a program service related to the organization's exempt function. For example, rental income from a low-income housing project would be reported as program service revenue on line 2. Generally, rental income from an unrelated organization (exempt or nonexempt) would be reported here. However, if below-market rent is provided to another charity to help it achieve its exempt purpose, that would be reported on line 2 as program service revenue. See the discussion of rents in line 2 for more guidance. Any rental income from a related organization is to be reported as program service revenue on line 2. Rental expenses such as interest and depreciation, if ordinarily carried on the organization's books, is reported on line 6b. (Note: If such interest and depreciation expenses are related to rent from a program-related service whose revenue is reported on line 2, do not report such expenses on line 6b; rather, report them on Part IX, Column (B), presumably on lines 20 (interest) and 22 (depreciation).) Also see §§ 7.2(a)(2) and 7.2(b)(14) for additional guidance on reporting rental income and expense. On line 7d, report the combined amounts from line 7c, Columns (i) and (ii). Generally, report this amount in Column (D).

- **Gains (or Losses) from Sales of Assets Other than Inventory (lines 7a–7d).** Use Column (i) to report sales of securities and use Column (ii) to report all other types of investments (e.g., real estate, royalty interests, or partnership interests) and all other noninventory assets (such as program-related investments and fixed assets used for related and unrelated activities). Enter the total gross sales price on line 7a and the total cost or other basis (less depreciation) and selling expenses on line 7b. On line 7c report the gain or loss. Include on line 7c capital gains dividends (e.g., received on mutual fund investments), and the organization's share of capital gains and losses from a partnership and capital gains distributions from trusts. Report on 7d the sum of 7c Columns (i) and (ii). Generally, report this amount in Column (D), although sometimes capital gains can be unrelated business income reportable in Column (C) if, for example, the gain results from the sale of inventory or property to customers in the ordinary course of business (e.g., the frequent purchase and sale of real estate akin to a real estate developer).

- **Gross Income from Fundraising Events (lines 8a–8c).** If the combined amount reported on line 1c and line 8a exceeds $15,000, the organization should answer "yes" on Part IV, line 18 and complete Part II of Schedule G (see Chapter 14). Fundraising events include dinners, dances, door-to-door sales of merchandise, concerts, carnivals, sports event, and auctions. Fundraising does *not* include gifts of goods of nominal value (e.g., giving a key chain with the organization's logo to every donor); lotteries or raffles that have prizes with only nominal value; and solicitation campaigns that generate only contributions. This revenue should be reported as contributions on line 1c (and, to the extent there are associated costs or expenses, such as the cost of the key chain in the above example, these should be reported in Part IX, Column (D), on line 12 or 24). Fundraising events do *not* include events or activities that further the organization's exempt purpose (e.g., a folk music festival conducted by an organization whose exempt purpose is to foster folk music). Fundraising that involves both contributions and income, such as when an individual pays more than retail value for goods or services furnished, requires an allocation of income between line 1c contribution income and line 8a fundraising income. See the discussion of fundraising in line 1c for examples. Report *direct* fundraising expenses on line 8b but report indirect fundraising expenses on the appropriate line of Part IX, Column (D). For example, in the gala dinner example discussed in line 1c, the cost of the dinner would be reported on line 8b while indirect costs of advertising the dinner would be reported on Part IX, Column (D), line 12. Report the net income (loss) on line 8c by subtracting line 8b from line 8a. Generally, report line 8 amounts in Column (D), although sometimes fundraising activities can generate unrelated business income reportable in Column (C) if, for example, bingo exceptions or qualified trade or convention show exceptions or other exceptions to unrelated business rules are not met.

- **Gross Income from Gaming Activities (lines 9a–9c).** Report gross income from gaming on line 9a. Gaming includes bingo, instant bingo, pull-tabs, raffles, scratch-offs, all other gaming tickets and cards, Las Vegas or casino nights, and coin-operated gambling devices such as slot machines and video games such as poker, blackjack, keno, and bingo. Most games of chance generate unrelated business income, except qualified bingo games (see § 7.1(b)(4)). To the extent they constitute unrelated business income, the revenue is reported in Column (C), and to the extent they meet the qualified bingo exception, the revenue is reported in Column (D). Report *direct* expenses on line 9b. These include cash prizes, noncash prizes, compensation to bingo callers and workers, rental of gaming equipment, and cost of bingo supplies such as pull-tabs and the like. Indirect costs are reported on the appropriate lines in Part IX, Column D; for example, advertising on line 12 or use of the organization's hall on line 16. Report on line 9c the difference between line 9a and line 9b.

- **Gross Sales of Inventory, Less Returns and Allowances (lines 10a through 10c).** Report sales of items the organization makes to sell to others or buys for resale. For example, this could include sales from a museum gift shop or from an organization's thrift shop. Sales of inventory do *not* include the sales of goods related to a fundraising event (which are reported on line 8a), sales of assets for which the organization expects to profit because of appreciation (which are reported on line 7a), or sales of inventory by hospitals, colleges and universities (which are reported on line 2). Sales are reported regardless of whether the constitute an exempt function or an unrelated trade or business and would be reported in Column (B) or (C), respectively. Thus, even if selling secondhand clothes to low-income persons is part of the exempt purpose, the sales still are reported on line 10a. Report the usual items included in cost of goods sold on line 10b. These include direct and indirect labor, materials, supplies consumed, freight-in, and a portion of overhead expense. Marketing and distribution costs are not included on line 10b but are reported on the appropriate line in Part IX, Column (B). Report the difference between line 10a and 10b on line 10c.

- **Other Revenue (line 11).** List the three largest sources of revenue (not otherwise reported on lines 1 through 10) on lines 11a through 11c. List all other revenue not reported on lines 1 through 11c on 11d. For each amount reported on lines 11a through 11c, enter the corresponding business code from *Codes for Unrelated Business Activity* from the instructions for the Form 990-T. If none of the codes accurately describes the activity, enter 900099. Use of these codes does not imply that the business activity is unrelated to the organization's exempt purpose.

(b) Part IX (Statement of Functional Expenses)

The Statement of Functional Expenses in the Form 990 is substantially similar to the Statement of Functional Expenses in the prior form (2007, Part II). The form has been revised to reflect the most frequently incurred expenses to reduce the amount of expenses reported in line 24 "Other Expenses." The revised form eliminates the schedules previously required for Benefits Paid to Members, Payments to Affiliates, and Depreciation including Form 4562. The instructions to the Form 990 are comprehensive and thorough and provide guidance not found in the current instructions. What follows is a summary of those instructions and, where appropriate, additional commentary on the instructions.

These general rules apply in preparing the Statement of Functional Expenses: (1) the organization should use its normal accounting method (e.g., cash or accrual) in preparing the statement; (2) if the organization's system does not allocate expenses, the organization should use a reasonable method of allocation; (3) the organization should maintain documentation supporting its method of allocation; (4) the organization should not report expenses associated with generating rental income (which should be reported in Part VIII, line 6b), cost or other basis, and sales expense of disposed assets (which should be reported in Part VIII, line 7b), direct expenses associated with fundraising events (which should be reported in Part VIII, line 8b), direct expenses associated with gaming activities (which should be reported in Part VIII, line 9b), or costs of goods sold (which should be reported in Part VIII, line 10b).

In addition, expenses must be categorized in these ways:

- **Total Expenses (Column (A)).** All organizations must report total expenses in Column (A). Organizations described in 501(c)(3) or 501(c)(4) and nonexempt charitable trusts described in 4947(a)(1) must (and all other organizations may) complete Columns (B) through (D).

- **Program Service Expense (Column (B)).** Report in this column the portion of any expense related to activities that further the organization's exempt purposes. This can include lobbying expenses if the lobbying is related to the exempt purpose (e.g., if an exempt entity organized to improve healthcare for seniors lobbies its state legislature to improving funding for senior care). Include in this column expenses for an unrelated trade or business. Also include costs incurred by the organization to secure a private or government grant or contribution to conduct research, produce an item or perform a service, whether the activities meet the grantor's specific needs (program service revenue reported in Part VIII, line 2) or benefit the public generally (grant revenue reported in Part VIII, line 1). Even though these expenses of conducting the work are paid by a grant, do not report them in Column (D) as fundraising expenses. However, count the expense of soliciting the grant (e.g., the grant request and associated work) as a fundraising expense in Column (D).

- **Management and General Expense (Column (C)).** Report in this column expenses related to overall management and operations that do not relate to fundraising and program services. In general, report the following in this column: (a) salaries of the CEO/executive director and his or her staff (unless part of the time is devoted to directly supervising program or fundraising activities in which case part of the salaries must be allocated to Columns (B) or (D), respectively); (b) expenses incurred to manage investments; (c) lobbying expenses not related to the organization's purposes (if related they are reported in Column (B)); (c) costs of meetings for the board, committees, or staff (unless such meetings relate to program or fundraising activities in which case the expense must be allocated to Columns (B) or (D), respectively); (d) general legal services; (e) accounting (including patient accounting and billing); (f) general liability insurance; (g) office management; (h) auditing, human resources, and other centralized services (e.g., information technology); (i) preparation, publication, and distribution of an annual report.

Do not report (a) expenses related to generating program-related income (which should be reported in Column (B)); (b) expenses associated with generating rental income (which should be reported in Part VIII, line 6b) (however, do report rent that the organization pays for its office space or facilities on line 16); (c) cost or other basis and sales expense of disposed assets (which should be reported in Part VIII, line 7b); (d) direct expenses associated with fundraising events (which should be reported in Part VIII, line 8b); (e) direct expenses associated with gaming activities (which should be reported in Part VIII, line 9b); or (f) costs of goods sold (which should be reported in Part VIII, line 10b).

- **Fundraising Expenses (Column (D)).** Report any expenses incurred in soliciting contributions, gifts, and grants. This would include publicizing and conducting fundraising campaigns, participating in federated fundraising campaigns, preparing and distribution fundraising materials, and *indirect* costs (such as advertising and promotions) of conducting fundraising events for which revenue is reported on Part VIII, lines 1c or 8a. (Note: *Direct* costs of fundraising events is reported in Part VIII, line 8b.) It would also include soliciting bequests and grants from foundations or other organizations, or government grants reportable in Part VIII, line 1 (but presumably do not report costs associated with soliciting government payment for program services which would be reported in Column (B)). Also, if grants are solicited to conduct program services, the costs associated with conducting those services would be reported in Column (B); i.e., only the cost associated with soliciting the grant is reported in Column (D) but the cost of carrying out the grant-funded program is reported in Column (D). Report both direct and a pro rata share of indirect costs. Direct costs are those associated specifically with a fundraising activity (e.g., gift tracking software) while indirect costs cannot be associated specifically with fundraising (e.g., word processing software). The instructions contain detailed directions on reporting of indirect cost centers.

(1) Lines 1–3 (Grants).   Grants paid by the organization get reported on lines 1 to 3. Grants include allocations, stipends, scholarships, and other types of payments to organizations or individuals for exempt purposes. (Note: Expenses incurred in selecting recipients and monitoring grant compliance should be reported on the appropriate line 5 to 24 not as a grant expense on lines 1 to3). Break down grants into these categories:

- **Grants to Governments and Organizations in the United States (line 1).** Report voluntary payments to governments and organizations in the United States. Do not report taxes paid as grants to a government entity—these would be reported on line 16 (if real estate taxes related to occupancy) or another appropriate line. If line 1 exceeds $5,000, complete Parts I and II of Schedule I (see Chapter 16). United Way and similar federated fundraising organizations should report grants to member agencies on line 1. Quotas, dues, or support payments to state or national affiliates are reported on line 21. Contributions received should be reported on Part VIII, line 1 (likely line 1f), even if the donation is designated for a particular agency. For example, if a local United Way agency receives a contribution for $x that is designated for Organization Y, then the United Way agency reports $x of income on Part VIII, line 1 (likely on line 1f); reports the payment of $x to Organization Y on Part IX, line 1; and reports any dues or payments made to the national United Way on Part IX, line 21.

- **Grants and Other Assistance to Individuals in the United States (line 2).** Report the amount paid to individuals for scholarships, stipends, research grants, and other similar payments. This would presumably include cash and in-kind contributions given directly to indigent persons and victims of disaster. Also report grants or other assistance to third parties for the benefit of specified individuals. For example, a grant to a hospital to provide care to the general public is reported on line 1, but a grant to a hospital to cover the care of a specific person is reported on line 2. If line 2 exceeds $5,000, complete Parts I and III of Schedule I (see Chapter 16).

- **Grants and Other Assistance to Governments, Organizations, and Individuals Outside the United States (line 3).** Report any grant or other assistance to foreign governments, foreign organizations, and foreign individuals outside the United States. Grants to U.S. government agencies (even if used abroad) should not be reported on line 3 but rather on line 1. Similarly, any grant to a U.S. citizen, even if used abroad (e.g., for study, research, or travel), should not be reported on line 3 but rather on line 2. If line 3 exceeds $5,000, complete parts II (if a grant to an organization) and/or III (if a grant to an individual) of Schedule F (see Chapter 13).

(2) Line 4 (Benefits Paid to or for Members). Report costs of providing benefits to members such as expenses of providing insurance to members of 501(c)(8), (9), or (17) organizations. Do not report costs of insurance for employees of the organization (which should be reported on lines 8 and 9).

(3) Line 5 (Compensation of Current Officers, Directors, and Key Employees). Report compensation based on the organization's accounting method (cash or accrual) and reporting period (calendar or fiscal). This means these compensation figures will not track with the figures reported in Part VII and Schedule J, which are reported on a calendar-year cash basis and are tied to W-2s and 1099s (see Chapter 6).

Compensation includes all forms of income and other benefits earned or received for services rendered, including pension plan contributions and other employee benefits. Compensation does not include noncompensatory expense reimbursements or allowances (but the organization should report them on other appropriate lines, such as line 17 "Travel"). To the extent pension, fringe, and other benefits are reported in line 5 for directors, officers, and key employees, do not include again on lines 8 and 9.

Allocate all salaries among Columns (B) through (D) as appropriate and as described in § 7.2(b). Report all amounts paid to the director, officer, or key employee even if paid for services performed in a capacity other than director, officer, or key employee. For example, if a director serves without compensation but also receives payment as a part-time fundraiser, report in line 5, Column (D).

(4) Line 6 (Compensation to Disqualified Persons Not Included in Line 5). Section 501(c)(3) and (c)(4) organizations need to report compensation to disqualified persons not otherwise reported on line 5. For the definition of compensation, see the discussion for line 5 in § 7.2(b)(3). For the definition of disqualified person see § 6.1(b)(2). Because the definition of a director, officer, and key employee contained in the glossary to the instructions is so closely tied to the definition of disqualified person, it is not clear exactly who will be reported in line 6. In other words, disqualified persons will probably also be directors, officers, or key employees and therefore reported in line 5 rather than line 6. The only common exception would be disqualified persons making less than $150,000 per year because such persons are excluded from the definition of key employee.

(5) Line 7 (Other Salaries and Wages). Report all cash compensation not reported in lines 5 and 6 including salaries, wages, fees, bonuses, severance payments, and similar amounts. Do not include pension, fringe, or other benefits—these are reported on lines 8 and 9.

(6) Line 8 (Pension Plan Contributions). Report the amount of pension plan contributions to both qualified and nonqualified plans. Do not include any amounts included in lines 5 and 6.

(7) Line 9 (Other Employee Benefits). Report the amount of contributions to employee benefit plans such as insurance, health and welfare benefit plans, and other employee benefits. Do not include anything reported on lines 5, 6, or 8. Also report expenses for activities such as holiday parties and employee picnics.

(8) Line 10 (Other Employee Benefits). Report any taxes that are imposed on the organization as employer such as employer's share of Social Security and Medicare and the federal unemployment tax (FUTA) and any state and local payroll taxes. Do not include any taxes withheld from the employees' paychecks and remitted to various government agencies. These are reported on compensation on lines 5, 6 or 7.

(9) Line 11 (Fees for Services Paid to Nonemployees (Independent Contractors)). Report amounts required in lines 11a through 11g regardless of whether a Form 1099 was required. Do not report any amounts paid to employees that should be reported on lines 5, 6 or 7. Break down payments in these ways:

- **Management Fees (line 11a).** Report total fees paid for management services provided by outside individuals or companies.

- **Legal Fees (line 11b).** Report total fees paid to outside firms and individuals. Do not include penalties, fines, settlements, or judgments imposed by reason of legal proceedings—these should be reported on line 24 "Other Expenses."

- **Accounting Fees (line 11c).** Report total fees paid to outside firms and individuals for accounting and auditing services.

- **Lobbying Fees (line 11d).** Report total fees paid to outside firms and individuals for lobbying and legislative liaison services. This includes any amounts paid for activities intended to influence foreign, national, state, or local legislation, including direct lobbying and grassroots lobbying. Do not include activities to influence actions by executive, judicial, or administrative officials or bodies, or other advocacy services (report all these amounts on line 11g).

- **Professional Fundraising Fees (line 11e).** Report total fees paid to outside firms and individuals for professional fundraising services, including solicitation campaigns and advise or consulting for in-house fundraising. If the organization is able to distinguish between fees paid for professional fundraising services and amounts paid for fundraising expenses such as printing, paper, envelopes, postage, mailing list rentals, and equipment rental, then fees paid for professional fundraising services should be reported on line 11e and the other amounts paid for fundraising expenses should be reported on line 24 "Other Expenses." Note, however, that the instructions for line 12 (see below) indicate that at least some of these fundraising expenses could be reported on line 12 "Advertising and Promotion." Organizations should be able to use any reasonable basis for determining whether to report on line 12 versus line 24. See the examples for line 24 in § 7.2(b)(22) for more information.

- **Investment Management Fees (line 11f).** Report total fees paid to outside firms and individuals who are not employees for investment counseling and portfolio management. Monthly account fees are included, but transaction costs pursuant to a purchase or sale such as brokerage fees and commissions are reported on Part VIII, line 7b.

- **Other Fees for Services (line 11g).** Report total fees paid to other nonemployees not reported in lines 11a through 11f. For example, hospitals would include payments to nonemployee healthcare professionals.

(10) Line 12 (Advertising and Promotion). Report amounts for print and electronic media advertising, Internet site link costs, signage, and advertising costs for in-house fundraising campaigns. Note that the instructions for line 11e indicate that fundraising expenses such as printing, paper, envelopes, postage, mailing list rentals, and equipment rental should be reported as "Other Expense" on line 24, but the instructions for line 12 indicate that at least the advertising costs associated with such activities can be reported here as "Advertising and Promotion." Do not report fees paid to professional fundraisers or fundraising consultants—these are reported on line 11e. See the examples for line 24 in § 7.2(b)(22) for more information.

(11) Line 13 (Office Expense). Report amounts for supplies (office, classroom, medical, or other supplies); telephone and facsimile (including cell phones and landlines);

postage and mailing expense (including overnight delivery, parcel delivery, trucking, and other delivery expenses); shipping materials; equipment rental (phone, fax, copier); bank fees and other similar costs. General printing costs should be included, but printing costs for a specific purpose should be reported on another appropriate line. For example, printing for fundraising could be reported on line 12 (Advertising and Promotion) and printing for a meeting or convention could be reported on line 19 (Conferences, Conventions and Meetings).

(12) Line 14 (Information Technology). Report expenses associated with hardware, software, support services (such as maintenance and help desks), and other technical support. The instructions say that organizations should include Web site costs (Web site design and operations, virus protection and other security programs and services to keep the organization's Web site operational and secure); however, these arguably could be included in line 12 (Advertising and Promotion).

(13) Line 15 (Royalties). Report amounts paid that allow the organization to use intellectual property such as copyrights and trademarks. Do not report software license costs that would be included in line 14.

(14) Line 16 (Occupancy). Report utility costs such as gas and electricity, rent, property insurance (as opposed to reporting on line 23), real estate taxes, and mortgage interest (as opposed to reporting on line 20). Do not report items that would be reported in line 13 (Office Expenses), such as telephone expense. Do not net any rental income received from renting or subletting rented space against the expenses reported in line 16. If the rental activity is related to the organization's exempt purposes, the rental income is reported in Part VIII, line 2 as program-related income, and the expenses are reported on this line 16, Column (B). If the rental activity is not related to the organization's exempt purposes, then rental income is reported on Part VIII, line 6a and expenses on Part VIII, line 6b. See §§ 7.2(a)(2) and (3) for additional discussions on reporting rental income and expense.

(15) Line 17 (Travel). Report transportation costs (fares, mileage allowances, automobile expenses, car rentals), meals and lodging, and per-diem payments. Include expenses of purchase, leasing, operating, and repairing vehicles owned or leased by the organization and used for its activities. If vehicles are provided to employees as part of their compensation, report on lines 5 through 7.

(16) Line 18 (Payment of Travel Expenses for Public Officials). Report total amounts for travel and entertainment expenses (including reimbursement) for federal, state, or local public officials (as defined in Section 4946(c)) and their family members (as determined in Section 4946(d)). Report amounts for a particular public official only if aggregate expenditures for the year relating to such official (including family members of such official) exceed $1,000. Amounts that fall below these thresholds may be reported on line 18 or on line 24 (Other Expenses).

(17) Line 19 (Conferences, Conventions, and Meetings). Report all expenses for conferences, conventions, and meetings related to the organization's activities. For such meetings the organization conducts (e.g., board meetings, membership meetings, annual conventions and trade shows), include facility rental, speakers' fees and expenses, and printed materials. For meetings that organization directors, officers, and employees attend that are conducted by other organizations, include registration costs on line 19. For all meetings attended by directors, officers, and employees (whether conducted by the organization or by another organization), report travel costs of attending such meetings on line 17.

(18) Line 20 (Interest).   Report all interest paid except interest attributable to rental property (which is reported on Part VIII, line 6b) and mortgage interest (which is reported as an occupancy expense on line 16).

(19) Line 21 (Payments to Affiliates).   Report payments to organizations affiliated with or closely related to the filing organization pursuant to these rules:

- Report dues paid by a local organization to a state or national affiliate. Dues are fixed or predetermined amounts. Voluntary grants or awards should be reported on line 1 or 3.

- Do not report goods or services purchased from a state or national affiliate— these should be reported on other appropriate lines. For example, if the organization buys specialized software from a national affiliate, report this on line 14.

- Report expenses incurred on behalf of a state or national affiliate only if the expenses do not relate to the filing organization's program services or connected with the filing organization's management or fundraising. For example, if a local organization incurs costs in production of a solicitation film to be used by the national affiliate, this would be reported on line 21. Or, if a local organization provides its mailing list to the national affiliate, the cost of making the copy would be reported on line 21, but the cost of maintaining the list (which benefits the filing organization) would be reported on line 12.

- Federated fundraising agencies (such as United Way) report the full amount of contributions they receive on Part VIII, line 1 (even if such contributions are designated for another agency). When the payments are distributed to such agencies, they are reported on Part IX, line 1. Quotas, dues, or support payments to state or national affiliates are reported on line 21. For example, if a local United Way agency receives a contribution for $x that is designated for Organization Y, then the United Way agency reports $x of income on Part VIII, line 1 (likely on line 1f); reports the payment of $x to Organization Y on Part IX, line 1; and reports any dues or payments made to the national United Way on Part IX, line 21.

- Membership dues paid to another organization are not reported on line 21 but rather on line 24 (Other Expenses). For example, if a nonprofit hospital pays dues to a state or national hospital association, that is not reported on line 21 but rather line 24.

(20) Line 22 (Depreciation, Depletion and Amortization).   Report any depreciation, depletion, and amortization on line 22, including such costs associated with leasehold improvements and intangible property. IRS Publication 946 provides guidance on computing these expenses. If such expenses are incurred with respect to property that generates rental income and the renting of the property is not related to the organization's exempt purposes, such expenses should be reported on Part VIII, line 6b (see the discussion of rents under § 7.2(a)(3) for further information).

(21) Line 23 (Insurance). Report total insurance expenses on line 23 except as follows. Do not include insurance expenses with respect to property that generates rental income and the renting of the property is not related to the organization's exempt purposes. Such expenses should be reported on Part VIII, line 6b (see the discussion of rents under § 7.2(a)(3) for further information). Do not report the cost of providing insurance to members if the organization is described in 501(c)(8), (9), or (17). Such expenses are reported on line 4 (Benefits Paid to or for Members). Do not report the cost of purchasing health insurance benefits for employees. These should be reported on line 8 or 9. Do not report property insurance for the organization's offices and facilities, as this is reported as an occupancy-related expense on line 16.

(22) Line 24 (Other Expenses). Report other expenses not included in lines 1 through 23. Enter the five largest dollar amounts on lines 24a through 24e and the total of all remaining expenses on line 24f; however, the organization must report separately the amount of unrelated business income tax paid on line 24, even if not one of the five largest amounts. If lines 24a through 24e contain an item labeled "miscellaneous expense" or "other expense" or some other similar term, the amount reported cannot exceed 5 percent of the total expenses reported on line 25.

Include payments by the organization for fundraising expenses such as printing, paper, envelopes, postage, mailing list rental, and equipment rental on line 24. (Note, however, that to the extent any of these expenses relate to advertising costs of fundraising, they should probably be reported on line 12.) Further, to the extent the organization is able to distinguish payments to a professional fundraiser from such fundraising expenses, then the payments for the services of the professional fundraiser should be reported on line 11e and the costs associated with the other fundraising expenses should be reported on line 24 (and line 12 to the extent they are advertising costs associated with fundraising). If such an allocation cannot reasonably be made, the entire payment to a professional fundraiser should be reported on line 11e.

Some examples should prove helpful:

- The organization pays a professional fundraiser $w for a fundraising campaign. The professional fundraiser breaks down the $w fee in this way: $x is for the consulting services of the fundraiser, $y is for advertising, and $z is for other costs incurred by the fundraiser such as printing, postage, and mailing list rentals. The organization should report $x on line 11e, $y on line 12, and $z on line 24.

- The organization pays a professional fundraiser $w for a fundraising campaign. The fee includes professional consulting, advertising, and the costs of printing, postage and mailing list rental, but neither the organization nor the professional fundraiser is able to reasonably allocate the $w fee among the different goods and services. The organization would report $w on line 11e.

(23) Line 25 (Total Functional Expenses).   Organizations described in 501(c)(3) and (c)(4) and nonexempt charitable trusts described in Section 4947(a)(1) should total lines 1 through 24f for each separate Column (A) through (D). Enter these amounts in Columns (A) through (D) on line 25. All other organizations only need to total lines 1 through 24f for Column (A) and enter the amount on line 25, Column (A).

(24) Line 26 (Joint Costs).   To the extent that the organization included in Column (B) (lines 1–24f) any joint expenses from a combined educational campaign and fundraising solicitation, the organization should check the box on line 26. Any costs reported here are not to be deducted from the other lines in Part IX on which they are reported. Rather, the total joint expenses should be reported on line 26, Column (A), the portion allocable to the educational campaign reported on line 26, Column (B), and the portion allocable to the fundraising solicitation on line 26, Column (D). An organization conducts a combined educational campaign and fundraising solicitation when it solicits contributions (by mail, telephone, broadcast media, or other means) and includes with the solicitation educational material about the organization or other information that furthers a bona fide nonfundraising exempt purpose of the organization. Information about the organization itself, its use of past contributions or planned use of future contributions is a fundraising expense and must be reported in Column (D), not Column (B). AICPA Statement of Position 98-2 provides guidance on this allocation.

(c) Part X (Balance Sheet)

The Balance Sheet in the Revised Form 990 is substantially similar to the Balance Sheet in the current form (2007, Part IV). The revised Balance Sheet has these three changes: (1) It eliminates the schedules for Other Notes and Loans Receivable and Other Mortgages and Notes Payable; (2) it adds Schedule L (see Chapter 18) to report loans, grants, and other transactions between the organization and officers, directors, trustees, key employees, and other disqualified persons; and (3) it adds Schedule D (see Chapter 11) to consolidate schedules previously requested for other line items (e.g., securities, land, buildings, other assets, and other liabilities). The instructions to the Revised Form 990 are comprehensive and thorough and provide guidance not found in the current instructions. What follows is a summary of those instructions and, where appropriate, additional commentary on the instructions.

These general rules apply in preparing the Balance Sheet:

- All organizations must complete Part X—attaching a substitute balance sheet is not acceptable.

- In Column (A) (Beginning of Year), report what was reported on the prior year's 990 for Column (B) (End of Year). If no 990 was filed the prior year, report what would have been reported. The IRS does not address what to do for new line items that have no corresponding line item in the prior return. For example, line 13 (Investments—Program Related) is a new line item. In the 2007 Form 990, this would have been included with other assets on line 58 of Part IV. An organization should report the amount for the 2007 Part IV, line 58, Column (B) that was attributable to program-related investments. For new organizations, enter "0" in Column (A) for lines 16, 26, 33, and 34.

- In Column (B) (End of Year), report end-of-year amounts for each line item. If reporting an item on Schedule D, report end-of-year amounts, not beginning-of-year amounts. If this is the final return, report "0" in Column (B) for lines 16, 26, 33, and 34.

(1) Line 1 (Cash (Non–Interest-Bearing)). Report total funds held in cash, including petty cash and amounts held in non–interest-bearing accounts. Do not include cash balances held in an investment account with a financial institution reported on line 11 through 13.

Note: With respect to lines 1 and 2, the instructions are clear that cash balances held in an investment account with a financial institution reported on lines 11 through 13 should not also be reported on lines 1 or 2. However, based on the instructions for lines 11 through 13, it is not clear that such accounts should properly be reported there either. For example, many organizations maintain investment accounts at financial institutions where endowments and other funds are invested. While such accounts frequently hold stocks, bonds, mutual funds and other investments (which would properly be reported on lines 11–13), they usually hold cash-type accounts (e.g., money market funds, interest-bearing cash management accounts, and certificates of deposit). Such cash investments do not appear to meet the definition of publicly traded securities for line 11 or other securities for line 12. They could arguably meet the definition for line 13 of a program-related investment if held or devoted for a specific program-related investment. The most logical place to report such cash-type accounts is in line 1 if they are non–interest bearing and in line 2 if they are interest bearing. The key is not to double count if, for some supportable reason, the accounts are otherwise reported on lines 11 through 13.

---

(2) Line 2 (Savings and Temporary Cash Investments). Report amounts in interest-bearing checking and savings accounts, deposits in transit, temporary cash investments (money market funds, commercial paper, and certificates of deposit), U.S. Treasury bills, or other governmental obligations that mature in less than one year. Do not include cash balances held in an investment account with a financial institution reported on line 11 through 13. Do not report advances to employees or officers— the instructions for line 4 clarify that these should be reported on line 5 for officers and line 7 for employees. Do not report refundable deposits paid to vendors or suppliers—the instructions for line 4 clarify that these should be reported on line 4 if insignificant or on line 15 (Other Assets) if more than insignificant. The instructions do not provide a dollar threshold for determining significance.

(3) Line 3 (Pledges and Grants Receivable, Net). Report pledges receivable less any amounts estimated to be uncollectible. Include pledges made by officers, directors, trustees, or other related parties. Also report grants receivable (generally, with no allowance for doubtful uncollectible grants). Organizations following Statement of Financial Accounting Standards 116 may report the present value of grants receivable.

(4) Line 4 (Accounts Receivable, Net).   Report the total accounts receivable (less any allowance for doubtful accounts) for the sale of goods and the performance of services (whether or not related to the organization's exempt purpose). Report refundable deposits paid to vendors and suppliers, if not significant in amount. (Note: The instructions do not provide a dollar threshold for determining significance.) Otherwise report on line 15 (Other Assets). Do not report loans and advances to officers, directors, trustees, or key employees (these should be reported on line 5), loans and advances to other disqualified persons (these should be reported on line 6), or loans and advances to employees (these should be reported on line 7).

(5) Line 5 (Receivables from Current and Former Officers, Directors, Trustees, Key Employees).   Report all receivables due from current or former officers, directors, trustees, key employees, highest-compensated employees, and other related parties. Receivables include secured and unsecured loans and advances. For credit unions, only report loans to such persons that are not made on the same terms and conditions as made to other members. According to the instructions for Part VII, "current" means someone who holds the position at any time during the tax year being reported and "former" means someone who would have been reported as "current" on any one of the organization's five prior Forms 990. If any amount is reported on line 5, the organization may need to answer "yes" to Part IV, line 26 and complete Part II of Schedule L (see Chapter 18).

(6) Line 6 (Receivables from Other Disqualified Persons).   Organizations described in Section 501(c)(3) and (c)(4) must report receivables (as described above for line 5 in § 7.2(c)(5)) from disqualified persons (see § 6.1(b)(2)). Do not report any receivable reported in line 5. Because the definition of key employee is so closely tied to that of disqualified person, many disqualified persons will already be reported on line 5. Key employees do not include anyone with reportable compensation of $150,000 or below (see § 6.1(a)(1)). So, the practical result is that generally the only persons being reported on line 6 are disqualified persons receiving reportable compensation of $150,000 or less because those receiving more than $150,000 in reportable compensation will generally be key employees reported on line 5. (See § 6.2(a)(1) for the definition of "reportable compensation.") If an amount is entered on line 6, the organization should answer "yes" to Part IV, line 26 and complete Part II of Schedule L (see Chapter 18).

(7) Line 7 (Notes and Loans Receivable, Net).   Report receivables (as described above for line 5 in § 7.2(c)(5)) not listed on lines 5 or 6 including all receivables from employees not listed on lines 5 or 6 and receivables from unrelated third parties including independent contractors. Do not report: (1) accounts receivable from the sale of goods and services (which should be reported on line 4); (2) program-related investments (which should be reported on line 13); and (3) notes receivable acquired as investments (which should be reported on line 12).

(8) Line 8 (Inventories for Sale or Use).   Report the amount of materials and goods and supplies held for future sale or use whether purchased or manufactured by the organization or donated by third parties. Thus, for hospitals, this would include all inventory (gauze, syringes, etc.) purchased from third parties and used in patient care; for a secondhand thrift shop, it would include all clothes donated by the public. Report all items held for resale regardless of whether the resale activity is related or unrelated to the organization's exempt purpose and whether or not such sales will generate unrelated business income.

(9) Line 9 (Prepaid Expenses and Deferred Charges). Report short-term and long-term prepayments of expenses attributable to one or more future accounting periods, such as prepayments of rent, insurance, pension expenses, and expenses incurred for a solicitation campaign to be conducted in a future accounting period.

(10) Line 10 (Land, Buildings, and Equipment). On line 10a, report the cost or other basis of all land, buildings, and equipment held at the end of the year (using end-of-year basis amounts). Include both property held for investment purposes and property used for the organization's exempt functions. If an amount is reported on line 10a, answer "yes" to Part IV, line 11 and complete Part VI of Schedule D (see Chapter 11). The amount reported on line 10a must equal the total of the amounts on Schedule D, Part VI, Columns (a) and (b).

On line 10b, report accumulated depreciation with respect to the assets reported on line 10a (using end-of-year accumulated depreciation amounts). This amount must equal the total of the amounts reported on Schedule D, Part VI, Column (c).

On line 10c, Column (A) (Beginning of Year), report the cost or other basis of land, buildings, and equipment, less any accumulated depreciation, as of the beginning of the year.

On line 10c, Column (B) (End of Year), report the sum of line 10a minus line 10b. The amount reported must equal the total of Schedule D, Part VI, Column (d).

(11) Line 11 (Investments: Publicly Traded Securities). Report the total value of publicly traded securities held by the organization as investments such as common and preferred stock, bonds, and publicly traded mutual funds or funds that are traded over the counter or on an established exchange and for which market quotations are published or are otherwise readily available (e.g., some hedge funds would meet this criteria). Do not report any publicly traded stock for which the organization holds 5 percent or more of the outstanding shares of the same class. These should be reported on line 12 and require additional disclosure on Schedule D, Part VII (Chapter 11).

(12) Line 12 (Investments—Other Securities). Report any ownership interest in corporations, partnerships, funds, joint ventures, or other entities that are not publicly traded. Also report ownership of publicly traded stock for which the organization owns 5 percent or more of the outstanding shares of the same class. Do not include program-related investments—these are reported on line 13. If an amount is reported on line 12 that is 5 percent or more of the amount reported on Part X, line 16, answer "yes" to Part IV, line 11 and complete Part VII of Schedule D (Chapter 11). The amount reported in line 12, Column (B) must equal the total of the amounts on Schedule D, Part VII, Column (b).

(13) Line 13 (Program-Related Investments). Report the total value of all investments made primarily to achieve exempt purposes rather than produce income.

Examples include student loans and notes receivable from other exempt organizations that obtained funds to pursue the filing organization's exempt purposes. Investments in subsidiaries or joint ventures that achieve the organization exempt purposes arguable would be reported here rather than line 12. For example, a hospital that invests in a rehabilitation hospital joint venture, a school that invests in a distance learning subsidiary, or a housing organization that is a partner in low-income housing development could all arguably report those investments in line 13 rather than line 12. If the amount reported on line 13 is 5 percent or more of the amount reported on Part X, line 16, answer "yes" to Part IV, line 11 and complete Part VIII of Schedule D (Chapter 11). The amount reported in line 13, Column (B) must equal the total of the amounts reported on Schedule D, Part VIII, Column (b).

(14) Line 14 (Intangible Assets).   Report nonmonetary, nonphysical assets, such as copyrights, patents, trademarks, mailing lists, and goodwill.

(15) Line 15 (Other Assets).   Report any other asset not reported on lines 1 to 14. If an amount is reported on line 15 that is 5 percent or more of the amount reported on Part X, line 16, answer "yes" to Part VI, line 11 and complete Part IX of Schedule D (Chapter 11). The amount reported on line 15, Column (B) must equal the total of the amounts reported on Schedule D, Part IX, Column (b).

(16) Line 16 (Total Assets).   For both Columns (A) and (B), total the amounts on lines 1 through 15 and report on line 16. Either "0" or an amount must be reported on line 16 for both Columns. Line 16 must equal line 34.

(17) Line 17 (Accounts Payable and Accrued Expense).   Report accounts payable to suppliers, service providers, property managers, and other independent contractors. Report accrued expenses such as salaries payable, accrued payroll taxes, and interest payable.

(18) Line 18 (Grants Payable).   Report the unpaid portion of grants and other awards that the organization has committed to pay other organizations or individuals, regardless of whether the commitments have been communicated to grantees.

(19) Line 19 (Deferred Revenue).   Report revenue the organization has received but not yet earned as of the balance sheet date under its method of accounting.

(20) Line 20 (Tax-Exempt Bond Liabilities).   Report the amount of tax-exempt bonds for which the organization has a direct or indirect liability. This includes bonds issued either by the organization on behalf of a state or local governmental unit, or by a state or local governmental unit on behalf of the organization. Tax-exempt bonds include state and local bonds and any obligations, including direct borrowing from a lender, or certificates of participation, the interest on which is excluded from the gross income of the recipient under Code Section 103. If an amount is reported here, see Part IV, line 24 and Schedule K (Chapter 17).

(21) Line 21 (Escrow Account Liability).   Report the amount of funds or assets held in an escrow or custodial account for other individuals or organizations, but only to the extent that assets related to these liabilities are reported in lines 1 through 15. If an amount is reported in this line, answer "yes" to Part IV, line 9 and complete Part IV of Schedule D (Chapter 11). If the organization has signature authority over, or another interest in, an escrow or custodial account for which it does not report assets or liabilities, it must still answer "yes" to Part IV, line 9 and complete Part IV of Schedule D (Chapter 11). For example, if a credit counseling organization collects cash from debtors to remit to creditors and reports this cash temporarily in its possession on line 1, it must then report the liability (the amount due to creditors) on line 21.

(22) Line 22 (Payables to Current and Former Officers, Directors, Trustees, Key Employees, Highest-Compensated Employees, and Disqualified Persons). Report unpaid balances of any loans payable to such persons. See the discussion in § 7.2(c)(5) regarding the meaning of "current" and "former." An organization that reports an amount on line 22 may need to answer "yes" to Part IV, line 26 and complete Part II of Schedule L (Chapter 18).

(23) Line 23 (Secured Mortgages and Notes Payable to Unrelated Third Parties). Report the total amount of mortgages and other notes payable to financial institutions and other third parties that are secured by investment or other real property as of the end of the tax year. Do not report any amount that was reported on line 22. Do not report secured debt payable to a related organization—this should be reported on line 25 (Other Liabilities).

(24) Line 24 (Unsecured Notes and Loans Payable). Report the total amount of notes and loans payable that are owed to financial institutions and other unrelated third parties but are not secured by the organization's assets. Do not report any amount that was reported on lines 22 or 23. Do not report secured debt payable to a related organization—this should be reported on line 25 (Other Liabilities).

(25) Line 25 (Other Liabilities). Report the amount of all other liabilities of the organization not properly reportable on lines 17 through 24. Include federal income taxes payable and secured and unsecured payables to related organizations. If any amount is entered on this line, answer "yes" to Part IV, line 11 and complete Schedule D, Part X (Chapter 11). The amount reported on line 25, Column (B) must equal the total of the amounts reported on Schedule D, Part X, Column (b).

(26) Line 26 (Total Liabilities). Report the totals for Columns (A) and (B), lines 17 through 25. All organizations must enter either a dollar amount or a zero on line 26.

Note: Lines 27 through 29 apply only to organizations that prepare their financial statements in accordance with Statement of Financial Accounting Standards 117 (*Financial Statements of Not-for-Profit Organizations*). SFAS 117 does not apply to credit unions, voluntary employees' beneficiary associations, supplemental unemployment benefit trusts, Section 501(c)(12) cooperatives, and other member benefit or mutual benefit organizations. The IRS does not require preparation of the 990 in accordance with SFAS 117, but it is acceptable to the IRS. If the organization follows SFAS 117, check the box above line 27 and complete lines 27 through 29. Also complete lines 33 and 34.

> *CAUTION:* At the time this book and the IRS instructions went to print, the Financial Accounting Standards Board was considering adopting FASB Staff Position 117-a, effective for reporting years ending after December 15, 2008. FASB Staff Position 117-a addresses reporting of endowments as permanently restricted or temporarily restricted funds. Further, a number of states have enacted or are considering enacting the Uniform Prudent Management of Institutional Funds Act (UPMIFA). If the organization is subject to UPMIFA or FASB Staff Position 117-a, the amounts reported on lines 27 through 29 may be affected.

(27) Line 27 (Unrestricted Net Assets). Report the balance of unrestricted net assets. Unrestricted assets are those assets without donor-imposed restrictions as to purpose, time, income, or otherwise. If the board of the organization voluntarily imposes such restrictions (sometimes referred to as board-designated funds or quasi-endowments), these are reported as unrestricted net assets. Do not report any restricted assets on line 27—these are reported on lines 28 and 29.

(28) Line 28 (Temporarily Restricted Net Assets). Report the balance of temporarily restricted net assets. Include assets with donor-imposed restrictions as to time (to be used after a certain date or upon the occurrence of a specified event) or purpose (to be used only for specified purposes). If the board of the organization voluntarily imposes such restrictions (sometimes referred to as board-designated funds or quasi-endowments), these are reported as unrestricted net assets on line 27.

(29) Line 29 (Permanently Restricted Net Assets). Report the balance of permanently restricted net assets. Include assets where the donor has prohibited the expenditure of principal or corpus or permitted expenditures only with respect to income or appreciation. Also include land or works of art that are donated with the stipulation that they not be sold and that they be used for a specific purpose (e.g., display or exhibition in the case of art, or conservation in the case of land). If the board of the organization voluntarily imposes such restrictions (sometimes referred to as board-designated funds or quasi-endowments), these are reported as unrestricted net assets on line 27.

> *Note:* Lines 30 through 32 apply only to organizations that do not follow SFAS 117. If the organization does not follow SFAS 117, check the box above line 30 and complete lines 30 through 32. Also complete lines 33 and 34.

(30) Line 30 (Capital Stock, Trust Principal, or Current Funds). For corporations, enter the balance of capital stock accounts. Show par or stated value (or for stock with no par or no stated value, total amount received on issuance) of all classes of stock issued and not yet cancelled. For trusts, report trust principal or corpus. For organizations using fund accounting, report fund balances for current restricted and unrestricted accounts.

(31) Line 31 (Paid-In or Capital Surplus, or Land, Building, and Equipment Fund). For corporations, report paid-in capital in excess of par or stated value for all stock issued and not yet cancelled. If stockholders or others made donations that the organization records as paid-in capital, report them here. For fund accounting, report the fund balance for land, building, and equipment.

(32) Line 32 (Retained Earnings or Accumulated Income, Endowment, or Other Funds). For corporations, report the balance of retained earnings minus the cost of any treasury stock. For trusts, report the amount of accumulated income or other similar amount. For fund accounting, report the total fund balances for the permanent and term endowment funds, as well as any other funds not reported on lines 31 and 32.

Note: Regardless of whether an organization follows SFAS 117, all organizations should complete lines 33 and 34.

---

(33) Line 33 (Total Net Assets or Fund Balances). For organizations that follow SFAS 117, report the total of lines 27 through 29. For organizations that do not follow SFAS 117, report the total of lines 30 through 32. The organization must report either a dollar amount or a zero on this line.

(34) Line 34 (Total Liabilities and Net Assets/Fund Balances). Report the total of line 26 and line 33. This amount must equal the amount on line 16. The organization must report either a dollar amount or a zero on this line.

(d) Part XI—Financial Statements and Reporting

(1) Line 1 (Accounting Method). Indicate which accounting method the organization used to prepare the 990 (cash, accrual, or other). Answer only with respect to the organization; do not answer with respect to any joint venture in which the organization is an owner. (For example, if the organization maintains its books on the accrual method but is an owner in a joint venture that keeps its books pursuant to the cash method, the organization should check the "accrual" box.) Generally, the organization should use the same accounting method for the 990 that it uses to maintain its books. Provide an explanation in Schedule O if (1) the organization changed its accounting method from a prior year, or (2) the organization's accounting method if the organization checked the "other" box for accounting method.

(2) Line 2 (Financial Statements and Independent Accountant). In line 2a, answer whether the organization's financial statements have been compiled or reviewed by an independent accountant. A *compilation* is merely a presentation of the finances without the more thorough analysis that is part of a review or audit. A *review* is an examination by the accountant of the organization's financial statements with the objective of assessing whether they are plausible, without the extensive testing and external validation procedures required by an audit.

In line 2b, answer whether the organization's financial statements have been audited by an independent accountant. An audit is the formal explanation of the organization's financial statements with the objective of assessing their accuracy and reliability.

If the organization answers "yes" to either lines 2a or 2b, the organization is to answer in line 2c whether it has an audit committee that is responsible for the oversight of the compilation, review, or audit and the selection of the independent accountant. Answer "yes" to line 2c only if there is a committee with board-delegated authority or authority under governing documents to *both* (1) oversee the compilation, review or audit, *and* (2) select the independent accountant that performs the compilation, review or audit. (Note: The definition of *audit committee* contained in the glossary to the instructions imposes four additional duties on audit committees: (1) oversight of the organization's financial reporting processes; (2) monitoring the choice of accounting policies and principles; (3) monitoring internal control processes; and (4) overseeing the performance (as well as the selection) of the external auditor.)

For lines 2a through 2c, an accountant is *independent* if he or she meets the standards of independence set forth by the American Institute of Certified Public Accountants, the Public Company Accounting Oversight Board, or other similar body that oversees or sets standards for the accounting or auditing professions.

For group returns, answer "no" on lines 2a and 2b if the organization's financial statements were compiled, reviewed, or audited as part of a consolidated financial statement only. The organization may explain in Schedule O that its financial statements were compiled, reviewed, or audited on a consolidated basis. If the organization's financials were compiled, reviewed, or audited separate from the rest of the group and the organization files a separate return, it can answer "yes" on lines 2a and 2b. Just because a joint venture in which the organization is an owner fails to obtain a compilation, review, or audit, this does not preclude the organization from answering "yes" to line 2a or 2b if the organization itself obtained a compilation, review, or audit.

(3) Line 3 (Single Audit Act and OMB Circular A-133). The Single Audit Act of 1984, as amended in 1996, and Office of Management and Budget Circular A-133 require organizations to undergo audits if they expend $500,000 or more of federal awards in a year. If the organization is required to undergo an audit because of the act and the circular, answer accordingly on line 3a. If the organization in fact obtained an audit in accordance with the act and circular, answer accordingly on line 3b. If the answer is "no," explain in Schedule O why the organization has not undergone the required audit and what steps are being taken to undergo such an audit. Do not answer with respect to any joint venture in which the organization is an owner. For example, if a joint venture in which the organization is an owner is required by the act and circular to get an audit, but the organization itself is not so required, answer line 3a "no."

§ 7.3   NEW FORM 990 COMPLIANCE TASKS

A nonprofit organization should take these five steps in order to prepare for the reporting requirements of Parts VIII to XI.

1. **Determine accounting policies.** The organization should determine whether (1) it prepares its financials on a cash or accrual basis; (2) it is a calendar- or fiscal-year taxpayer; and (3) whether it follows *Statement of Financial Accountings Standards* 116 and 117. The 990 should be prepared accordingly.

2. **Determine role of board in overseeing financial accounting.** There are a number of steps the board should undertake in overseeing the financial accounting of the organization, including:
   - Barring individuals who are prohibited from serving on publicly traded boards (e.g., those individuals convicted of crimes having to do with theft and embezzlement) from serving on the organization's board and audit committee
   - Establishing and empowering an audit committee
   - Approving annual budgets and monitoring actual performance compared to budget
   - Expending a significant portion of the budget on programs that achieve the organization's exempt purpose
   - Prohibiting loans to directors and officers
   - Disclosing financial information to the public through the Web site or upon request
   - Determining executive compensation and benefits pursuant to the rebuttable presumption of reasonableness (see § 6.1(b)(8))
   - Assisting in fundraising and assuring fundraising integrity and privacy of donors
   - Adequately documenting the decisions of the board and audit committee through minutes and record keeping
   - Approving all significant transactions of the organization
   - Reviewing and approving the audit and implementing the recommendations of the auditor's management letter
   - Overseeing compliance with all federal, state and local laws

3. **Determine role of the audit committee.** The audit committee should:
   - Consist solely of independent board members, at least one of whom is a financial expert
   - Oversee the financial reporting process
   - Monitor the choice of accounting policies and principles
   - Monitor the internal control processes
   - Hire, fire, compensate, and oversee the performance of the auditor
   - Ensure that all auditor communications flow to the audit committee and not management
   - Ensure that a review or audit is conducted annually (compilations generally should be avoided except for the smallest organizations and audits should

generally be required whenever annual budgets are in the range of $250,000 to $500,000 or above)

- Institute a procedure whereby financial wrongdoing can be reported to the audit committee and responded to and/or corrected by the audit committee

4. **Determine role of auditor.** The audit committee should establish clear expectations and roles for the auditor, including:

- Prohibiting the auditor from performing nonaudit services for the organization
- Ensuring that the lead audit partner, or partner responsible for reviewing the audit, is rotated every five years
- Requiring the auditor to certify that there are no conflicts of interest between the auditor's employees and senior management of the organization
- Requiring the auditor to disclose all critical accounting policies and practices to the audit committee
- Requiring all the auditors to communicate directly with the audit committee rather than management or staff

5. **Adopt critical accounting policies and procedures.** The board and/or audit committee should adopt these policies and procedures:

- CEO/CFO certification of financials and assessment of internal controls
- Bonus forfeitures for senior management if financials are restated
- Implementation of effective internal control processes
- Code of ethics
- Conflict-of-interest policy
- Whistleblower policy
- Document retention and destruction policy
- Travel and entertainment expense reimbursement policy (that is consistent with the IRS accountable plan rules)

CHAPTER EIGHT

Schedule A—Public Charity Status

By definition, a charitable organization filing the new Form 990 is a public charity, inasmuch as private foundations file Form 990-PF. The new Form 990 is accompanied by a Schedule A, which is used by the filing organization to identify its public charity status and, in the case of a publicly supported organization, calculate public support. (A public charity may instead file Form 990-EZ (see § 1.9); a nonexempt charitable split-interest trust may file Form 990 or 990-EZ. In either instance, the Schedule A is required.) An organization that answered "yes" to the new Form 990, Part IV, line 1, must complete and attach this schedule to the return.

§ 8.1 LAW AND POLICY

In approaching preparation of Schedule A, it is necessary to know the distinctions between public charities and private foundations, and the various ways in which a charitable organization can be a public charity.

(a) *Private Foundation* Defined

A *private foundation* is a form of tax-exempt charitable organization. In this context, the term *charitable* includes program undertakings that are classified as *educational*, *scientific*, and *religious* (see § 2.1(e)). Generically, however, a private foundation typically has four other characteristics:

1. A private foundation is usually funded from a single source, often an individual, a family, or a corporation.

2. This funding is usually a one-time occasion, by means of a sizable charitable contribution. While a private foundation may receive an ongoing flow of gifts, that is a rarity.

3. The year-by-year revenue derived by a private foundation is almost always in the form of investment income earned on their assets (also known as *principal* or *corpus*).

4. The typical private foundation makes grants for charitable purposes to other persons (individuals and/or organizations) rather than conduct its own programs.

The *private* aspect of the concept of a private foundation, then, principally reflects the nature of its financial support, particularly its initial funding. The *private* nature of a foundation, however, is often reflected in its governing board structure.

Because private foundations are generally exempt from federal income tax, the term *private foundation* appears in the Internal Revenue Code. This technical tax law definition, however, does not match the generic definition. Congress could have crafted a definition of private foundation in accord with the four unique attributes of foundations, but it elected another approach. The reason for this distinction is rooted in the history of private foundation law, which came into being in 1969.

When most of the law as to private foundations was created in that year, Congress was in a horrific anti-foundation mood. The antipathy toward foundations at that time was substantial, largely because members of Congress were being regaled with tales of foundation abuse (mostly apocryphal) and many were in a populist mind-set, with foundations seen as playthings (and pocketbooks) of the wealthy. Consequently, when fashioning a definition of the term *private foundation*, Congress was careful to write it in such a way as to minimize the likelihood that crafty tax lawyers would find ways around the foundation laws.

Thus, the technical definition of *private foundation* has two key characteristics.

1. Despite the fact that the Internal Revenue Code purports to define the term, it does not. Instead, the Code defines what a private foundation is not. (A private foundation is a tax-exempt charitable organization that is not a public charity.)

2. A unique feature in the law causes every tax-exempt charity in the United States to be *presumed* to be a private foundation. Among other outcomes, this forces nearly all charities that are not private foundations to convince the IRS of that fact and be officially classified as public entities. Put another way, a charitable organization that cannot, or subsequently fails to, qualify as a public charity is, by operation of law, a private foundation.

(b) Concept of *Public Charity*

The dichotomy thus established in the Internal Revenue Code forces every U.S. charity to be classified as a public charity or a private foundation. This is by no means an equal division, in that, while there are millions of public charities, there are about 80,000 private foundations. (This disparity as to numbers, however, is not reflected in any balancing of the volume of federal tax law concerning charitable organizations; there are many pages of rules in the Internal Revenue Code that are applicable only to private foundations.)

As noted, a private foundation is a tax-exempt charitable organization that is not a public charity. The Code "definition" of *private foundation* focuses on the meaning of the term *public charity*. There are many categories of public charities. From a big-picture standpoint, however, there are four types of public charities: *institutions*, *publicly supported charities, supporting organizations,* and (of minor import) *public safety testing organizations.*

As will be seen, public charities tend to be organizations with inherently *public* activity, entities that are financially supported by the public or entities that have a close operating relationship with one or more other public charities. The term *public* can, however, be misleading; it is not used in the sense of a governmental entity (department, agency, etc.). The confusion is emblematic in the notion that a private school is a public charity. (Governmental entities are public charities.)

Most private foundations confine their grantmaking to public charities. Therefore, it is essential (to avoid tax penalties) that foundations having that approach understand the various ways in which a tax-exempt charitable organization can also be a public charity.

(c)   Institutions

A category of public charity is loosely defined as *institutions*. These are entities that have inherently public activity. Embraced by the ambit of the institutions are churches, certain other religious organizations, schools, colleges, universities, hospitals, medical research organizations, and governmental units.

(1) Churches.   A *church* (including a synagogue and a mosque) is a public charity. The federal tax law is imprecise in defining this term, largely due to constitutional law (First Amendment) constraints. Although the term is not defined in the Internal Revenue Code, the IRS formulated criteria, generally accepted by the courts, that it uses to ascertain whether a religious organization constitutes a *church*. Originally, these criteria (unveiled in 1977) were in a list of 14 elements, not all of which needed to be satisfied. These elements include a distinct legal existence, a recognized creed and form of worship, an ecclesiastical government, a formal code of doctrine and discipline, a distinct religious history, a literature of its own, established places of worship, regular congregations, regular religious services, and schools for the religious instruction of youth and preparation of its ministers.

Over the ensuing years, however, the IRS has added criteria and become more rigid (and inconsistent) in its interpretation of the term *church*. It is currently the position of this agency that, to be a church, an organization must—in addition to being *religious*—have a defined congregation of worshippers, an established place of worship, and regular religious services. Some of the criteria in the original 14-element list have been downgraded in importance, as being common to tax-exempt organizations in general.

(2) Associations and Conventions of Churches.   Some religious entities are public charities because all of their members are churches. An *association of churches* is a church-membership entity where the membership is confined to churches in a state. A *convention of churches* is a church-membership entity where the membership embraces a multistate region of the United States or perhaps the entire nation.

(3) Educational Institutions.   An *educational institution* is a public charity. The concept of what is *educational* is much broader than *educational institution*, so it is insufficient for these purposes that an organization is merely educational in nature. To be an educational institution, an organization must normally maintain a regular faculty and curriculum and normally have a regularly enrolled body of pupils or students in attendance at the place where its educational activities are regularly carried on. This type of institution is generically a *school*; consequently, it must have as its primary function the presentation of formal instruction. (See Chapter 12.)

Educational institutions that qualify for public charity status include primary, secondary, preparatory, and high schools, and colleges and universities. (Public schools are public charities by virtue of being units of government (see § 8.1(c)(8)).) An organization cannot achieve public charity status as an operating educational institution where it is engaged in educational (institution-type) and educational (non–institution-type) activities, unless the latter activities are merely incidental to the former. For example, an organization cannot qualify as this type of public charity if its primary function is the operation of a museum rather than the presentation of formal instruction.

A *university* generally is an institution of higher learning with teaching and research facilities, comprising an undergraduate school that awards bachelor's degrees and a graduate school and professional schools that award master's or doctor's degrees. A *college* is generally referred to as a school of higher learning that grants bachelor's degrees in liberal arts or sciences; the term is also frequently used to describe undergraduate divisions or schools of a university that offer courses and grant degrees in a particular field. The term *school* is defined as a division of a university offering courses of instruction in a particular profession; the term is also applicable to institutions of learning at the primary and secondary levels of education.

An organization may be regarded as presenting formal instruction even though it lacks a formal course program or formal classroom instruction. For example, an organization that conducted a survival course was classified as a public charity, even though its course periods were only 26 days and it used outdoor facilities more than classrooms; it had a regular curriculum, faculty, and student body. By contrast, an organization, the primary activity of which was providing specialized instruction by correspondence and a 5- to 10-day seminar program of personal instruction for students who completed the correspondence course, did not qualify as an operating educational institution.

Even if an organization qualifies as a school or other type of formal educational institution, it will not be able to achieve public charity (or tax-exempt) status if it maintains racially discriminatory admissions policies or if it benefits private interests to more than an insubstantial extent. As an illustration of the latter, an otherwise qualifying school, which trained individuals for careers as political campaign professionals, was denied exempt status because of the private benefit accruing to a national political party and its candidates, inasmuch as nearly all of the school's graduates became employed by or consultants to the party's candidates. (See Chapter 10.)

(4) Hospitals. A tax-exempt organization, the principal purpose or functions of which are the provision of medical or hospital care, medical education, or medical research, if the organization is a hospital, is a public charity. The term *hospital* includes exempt federal government hospitals; state, county, and municipal hospitals that are instrumentalities of governmental units; rehabilitation institutions; outpatient clinics; extended care facilities; community mental health or drug treatment centers; and cooperative hospital service organizations. This term does not include convalescent homes, homes for children or the elderly, or institutions the principal purpose or function of which is to train disabled individuals to pursue a vocation, nor does it include free clinics for animals. The term *medical care* includes the treatment of any physical or mental disability or condition, whether on an inpatient or outpatient basis, as long as the cost of the treatment is deductible by the individual treated. (See Chapter 15.)

(5) Cooperative Hospital Service Organizations. A *cooperative hospital service organization* is an entity that is organized and operated solely for the benefit of two or more tax-exempt member hospitals, and is organized and operated on a cooperative basis. These organizations must perform certain specified services on a centralized basis for their members, namely, data processing, purchasing, warehousing, billing and collection, food, clinical, industrial engineering, laboratory, printing, communications, records center, and personnel services. To qualify, these services must constitute exempt activities if performed on its behalf by a participating hospital. These organizations must otherwise satisfy the criteria for exempt charitable organizations.

(6) Medical Research Organizations. A *medical research organization* directly engaged in the continuous active conduct of medical research in conjunction with a public charity hospital can qualify as a public charity. The term *medical research* means the conduct of investigations, experiments, and studies to discover, develop, or verify knowledge relating to the causes, diagnosis, treatment, prevention, or control of physical or mental diseases and impairments of human beings. To qualify, an organization must have the appropriate equipment and professional personnel necessary to carry out its principal function. *Medical research* encompasses the associated disciplines spanning the biological, social, and behavioral sciences; the term means investigations, studies, and experiments performed to discover, develop, or verify knowledge relating to physical or mental diseases and impairments, and their causes, diagnosis, prevention, treatment, or control.

An organization, to be a public charity under these rules, must have the conduct of medical research as its principal purpose or function and be primarily engaged in the continuous active conduct of medical research in conjunction with a qualified hospital. The organization need not be formally affiliated with an exempt hospital to be considered primarily engaged in the active conduct of medical research in conjunction with the hospital. There must, however, be a joint effort on the part of the research organization and the hospital to maintain close cooperation in the active conduct of the medical research. An organization is not considered to be primarily engaged directly in the continuous active conduct of medical research unless it, during a computation period, devotes more than one-half of its assets to the continuous active conduct of medical research or it expends funds equaling at least 3.5 percent of the fair market value of its endowment for the continuous active conduct of medical research.

If an organization's primary purpose is to disburse funds to other organizations for the conduct of research by them or to extend research grants or scholarships to others, it is not considered directly engaged in the active conduct of medical research.

(7) Government College Support Foundations. Public charity status is accorded to certain organizations providing support for public (governmental) colleges and universities. This type of organization must normally receive a substantial part of its support (exclusive of income received in the performance of its tax-exempt activities) from the United States and/or direct or indirect contributions from the public. It must be organized and operated exclusively to receive, hold, invest, and administer property and to make expenditures to or for the benefit of a college or university that is a public charity and that is an agency or instrumentality of a state or political subdivision of a state, or that is owned or operated by a state or political subdivision or by an agency or instrumentality of one or more states or political subdivisions.

These expenditures include those made for any one or more of the regular functions of these colleges and universities, such as the acquisition and maintenance of real property comprising part of the campus; the construction of college or university buildings; the acquisition and maintenance of equipment and furnishings used for or in conjunction with regular functions of these colleges and universities; or expenditures for scholarships, libraries, and student loans.

(8) Governmental Units.   The United States, possessions of the United States, the District of Columbia, states, and their political subdivisions are classified as *governmental units*, which are public charities. This type of a unit qualifies as a public charity without regard to its sources of support, partly because it is responsive to all citizens. The concept of a governmental unit also embraces government instrumentalities, agencies, and entities referenced by similar terms.

(9) Other Institutions.   One of the many anomalies of the federal tax law is that some of the charitable institutions in U.S. society, which are not generically private foundations, are not accorded a public charity classification, unlike churches, schools, hospitals, and the like. Organizations in this position include museums, libraries, and organizations that operate orchestras and operas. To be public charities, these entities must be publicly supported or (much less likely) be structured as supporting organizations (see § 8.1(h)). Some of these types of organizations are private operating foundations or exempt operating foundations and thus do not file Form 990.

(d)   Donative Publicly Supported Organizations

A way for a tax-exempt charitable organization to be a public charity is to receive its financial support from a suitable number of sources. A publicly supported charity is the antithesis of a private foundation, in that a foundation customarily derives its funding from one source, whereas a publicly supported charitable organization is (by definition) primarily or wholly supported by the public. One type of publicly supported charity—the *donative* type—is an organization the revenues of which are in the form of a range of contributions and grants.

(1) General Rules.   An organization is a donative publicly supported entity if it is a tax-exempt charitable organization that normally receives a substantial part (defined later in this section) of its support (other than income from the performance of one or more exempt functions) from a governmental unit or from direct or indirect contributions from the public. It is this focus on support in the form of gifts and grants that causes this type of organization to be considered a *donative* one.

Organizations that qualify as donative publicly supported entities generally are organizations such as museums of history, art, or science; libraries; community centers to promote the arts; organizations providing facilities for the support of an opera, symphony orchestra, ballet, or repertory drama group; organizations providing some other direct service to the public; and organizations such as the American National Red Cross or that conduct federated fundraising campaigns, such as those operating for the benefit of United Way agencies.

The principal way for an organization to be a publicly supported charity under these rules is for it to derive normally at least one-third of its financial support from qualifying contributions and grants. (This one-third threshold is the definition of the phrase *substantial part* in this context.) Thus, an organization classified as this type of publicly supported charity must maintain a *support fraction*, the denominator of which is total gift and grant support received during the computation period (see § 8.1(d)(2)) and the numerator of which is the amount of support qualifying in connection with the one-third standard from eligible public and/or governmental sources for the period. The cash basis method of accounting is used in making these calculations.

(2) Two-Percent Rule. A 2-percent ceiling is generally imposed on contributions and grants in determining public support. Only this threshold amount of a particular gift or grant is counted as public support, under this rule, irrespective of whether the contributor or grantor is an individual, corporation, trust, private foundation, or other type of entity (taking into account amounts given by related parties). In computing public support in this manner, the IRS has traditionally used a four-year measuring period, consisting of the organization's most recent four years. Beginning with the 2008 tax year, however, the measuring period is the organization's most recent five years.

An illustration will undoubtedly be helpful. Consider a charitable organization that received total gift and grant support in the amount of $1 million during the measuring period. In that instance, all contributions and grants up to $20,000 each are counted as public support (the total of them being the numerator of the support fraction). The amount of all gifts and grants during the period comprise the denominator of that fraction. If a person gave, for example, $80,000 during the measuring period, only $20,000 is public support from that source for that period. This organization thus must receive, during the period, at least $333,334 in contributions or grants of $20,000 or less each. It could receive $666,666 from one source and $10,000 each from 34 sources, or $20,000 each from 17 sources, for example.

A meaningful exception to this rule is available. Support received by a donative publicly supported charity from governmental units and/or other donative publicly supported charities is considered to be a form of *indirect* contributions from the public (in that these grantors are regarded as conduits of direct public support). This type of support is public support in its entirety. That is, this form of funding is not limited by the 2-percent rule. The same is true with respect to support from charitable organizations that satisfy the donative publicly supported organization definition even though they are classified as some other form of public charity (such as a church).

For these purposes, the legal nature of the donors and/or grantors is not relevant. That is, in addition to individuals, charities, and governments, public support can be derived from for-profit entities (such as corporations and partnerships) and nonprofit entities (including various forms of charitable and noncharitable tax-exempt organizations). In another example of the English language failing in this regard, private foundations can be sources of public support. Generally, the fact that contributions or grants are restricted or earmarked does not detract from their qualification as public support.

Nonetheless, the 2-percent limitation applies with respect to support received from a donative publicly supported charitable organization or governmental unit if the support represents an amount that was expressly or impliedly earmarked by a donor or grantor to the publicly supported organization or unit of government as being for or for the benefit of the organization asserting status as a publicly supported charitable organization.

(3) Support Test. A matter that can be of considerable significance in determining whether a charitable organization can qualify as a donative publicly supported entity is the meaning of the term *support*. For this purpose, *support* means amounts received in the form of, as noted, contributions (including corporate sponsorships) and grants, along with net income from unrelated business activities (see § 7.1(b)), gross investment income, tax revenues levied for the benefit of the organization and paid to or expended on behalf of the organization, and the value of services or facilities (exclusive of services or facilities generally furnished to the public without charge) furnished by a governmental unit to the organization without charge. All of these items comprise the denominator of the support fraction. (The larger the denominator, the greater the amount of public support that is allowed by the 2-percent threshold.) *Support* does not include gain from the disposition of property that is gain from the sale or exchange of a capital asset; the value of exemption from any federal, state, or local tax or any similar benefit; or funding in the form of a loan.

As to tax revenues levied for the organization's benefit, these are to be reported whether or not the organization has included these amounts as revenue on its financial statements. As to the value of services or facilities furnished by a governmental unit, the organization should not include the value of services or facilities generally furnished to the public without charge. For example, an organization would include the fair rental value of office space furnished by a governmental unit without charge but would not do so if the governmental unit generally furnished similar office space to the public without charge.

In constructing the support fraction, an organization must exclude from the numerator and the denominator any amounts received from the exercise or performance of its exempt purpose or function and contributions of services for which a charitable contribution deduction is not allowable. An organization will not be treated as meeting this support test, however, if it receives *almost all* of its support in the form of gross receipts from related activities and an insignificant amount of its support from governmental units and/or the public. Moreover, the organization can exclude from the numerator and the denominator of the support fraction an amount equal to one or more unusual grants (see below).

(4) Concept of *Normally*. In computing the support fraction, the organization's support that is *normally* received must be reviewed. This means that the organization must meet the one-third support test for a period encompassing the five tax years immediately preceding the year involved, on an aggregate basis. (Prior to 2008, this measuring period was four years.) When this is accomplished, the organization is considered as meeting the one-third support test for its current tax year and for the tax year immediately succeeding its current tax year. For example, if an organization's current tax year is calendar year 2009, the computation period for measuring public support pursuant to these rules is calendar years 2004 to 2008; if the support fraction requirement is satisfied on the basis of the support received over this five-year period, the organization satisfies this support test for 2009 and 2010. (A five-year period for meeting this support test is available for organizations during the initial five years of their existence.)

(5) Unusual Contributions or Grants.   Under the *unusual grant* rule, a contribution or grant may be excluded from the public support fraction. A gift or grant is *unusual* if it is an unexpected and substantial amount attracted by the public nature of the organization and received from a disinterested party. (Thus, this term is somewhat of a misnomer. The exception is not confined to grants and the operative word should be *unexpected*, not *unusual*.)

A number of factors are taken into account in this regard; no single factor is determinative. The positive factors follow, with their opposites (negative factors) in parentheses:

- The contribution or grant is from a person with no connection to the charitable organization. (The contribution or grant is received from a person who created the organization, is a substantial contributor to it, is a board member, an officer, or is related to one of these persons.)

- The gift or grant is in the form of cash, marketable securities, or property that furthers the organization's exempt purposes. An example of the latter is a gift of a painting to a museum. (The property is illiquid, difficult to dispose of, and/or not suitable in relation to the organization's functions.)

- No material restrictions or conditions are placed on the transfer.

- The organization attracts a significant amount of support to pay its operating expenses on a regular basis, and the gift or grant adds to an endowment or pays for capital items. (The gift or grant is used for operating expenses for several years; nothing is added to an endowment.)

- The gift is a bequest. (The gift is an *inter vivos* (lifetime) transfer.)

- An active fundraising program attracts significant public support. (Gift and grant solicitation programs are limited or unsuccessful.)

- A representative and broad-based governing body controls the organization. (Related parties are in control.)

- Prior to the receipts of the unusual grant, the organization qualified as a publicly supported entity. (The unusual grant exclusion was relied on in the past to satisfy the test.)

(6) Facts-and-Circumstances Test.   One of the defects of the donative organization support rules is that organizations that are not private foundations in a generic sense, because they have many of the attributes of a public organization, may nonetheless be classified as private foundations because they cannot meet the somewhat mechanical one-third support test. Charitable organizations with this dilemma can include entities such as museums and libraries that heavily rely on their endowments for financial support and thus have little or no need for contributions and grants. Although the statutory law is silent on the point, the tax regulations somewhat ameliorate this rigidity of the general rule by means of a *facts-and-circumstances test*.

The history of an organization's programmatic and fundraising efforts, and other factors, can be considered as an alternative to the rather strict mechanical formula for qualifying as a public charity under the general donative publicly support charitable organization rules. These factors must be present for this test to be met:

- Public support (computed pursuant to the general rule) must be at least 10 percent of the total support, and the higher the better.

- The organization must have an active "continuous and bona fide" fundraising program designed to attract new and additional public and governmental support. Consideration will be given to the fact that, in its early years of existence, the charitable organization may limit the scope of its gift and grant solicitations to those persons deemed most likely to provide seed money in an amount sufficient to enable it to commence its charitable activities and expand its solicitation program.

- Other favorable factors must be present, such as:
  - The composition of the organization's governing board is representative of broad public interests.
  - Support is derived from governmental and other sources representative of the public.
  - Facilities and programs are made available to the public.
  - The organization's programs appeal to a broad range of the public.

As to the governing board factor, the organization's public charity status will be enhanced where it has a governing body that represents the interests of the public rather than the personal or private interests of a limited number of donors. This can be accomplished by the election of board members by a broad-based membership or by having the board composed of public officials, individuals having particular expertise in the field or discipline involved, community leaders, and the like.

As noted, one of the important elements of this facts-and-circumstances test is the availability of facilities or services to the public. Examples of entities meeting this standard are a museum that holds its building open to the public, a symphony orchestra that gives public performances, a conservation organization that provides services to the public through the distribution of educational materials, and a home for the elderly that provides domiciliary or nursing services for members of the public.

(7) Issues. Nine issues can arise in computing the public support component (the numerator) of the support fraction for donative publicly supported organizations. They are:

1. Proper calculation of the denominator of the support fraction.
2. Whether a payment constitutes a contribution or a grant.
3. Whether a membership fee can be treated as a contribution rather than a payment for services. The IRS's instructions state that a membership fee can be treated as a contribution to the extent it is a payment to "provide support for the organization rather than to purchase admissions, merchandise, services, or the use of facilities."
4. Whether a payment pursuant to a contract is a grant rather than revenue from a related activity (exempt function revenue).

5. Whether a grant is from another donative publicly supported charity (or a charity *described in* the rules).

6. Whether a grant from a publicly supported charity or governmental unit is a pass-through transfer from another grantor.

7. Whether a grant constitutes an unusual grant.

8. Whether an organization is primarily dependent on gross receipts from related activities.

9. Whether the organization needs to rely on the facts-and-circumstances test.

The fourth item warrants additional mention. When the term *contract* is used in this context, it usually connotes a payment for services rendered or goods provided, which means that the funds involved are exempt function revenue and thus must be excluded from the support fraction. Confusion can arise because a grant is often the subject of a contract, although in that setting the term used usually is *agreement*. Although sometimes it is difficult to differentiate between the two, a *grant* is a payment made to a charitable organization to enable it to operate one or more programs, while a payment pursuant to a contract is for the acquisition of a good or service.

The principal point with these issues is that the resolution of them can materially affect the construct of the support fraction and thus the public support percentage. Sometimes an organization will want to exclude a large amount from the fraction (such as a payment made in accordance with a contract) so as to increase the support percentage. It is not uncommon for a support fraction to be improperly computed, so that the resulting public support percentage is below the one-third threshold. It can be a great joy for a tax lawyer to review a draft of an anemic public support fraction calculation and discover, for example, that a grant that was limited by the 2-percent threshold can in fact be counted in full as public support (issue 5) or that a large grant can in fact be excluded from the fraction as an unusual grant (issue 7), thereby enabling the charitable organization to report a public support ratio that is considerably in excess of the one-third minimum.

(8) Community Foundations. In the world of charities, the term *foundation* is often used in conjunction with an organization that is not a *private foundation*. An illustration of this word interplay is the *community foundation*, which usually is a donative publicly supported charity. These foundations almost always attract, receive, and depend on financial support from members of the public on a regular, recurring basis. Community foundations are designed to attract large contributions of a capital or endowment nature, with the gifts often received and maintained in separate trusts or funds. These entities are generally identified with a particular community and are controlled by a representative group of persons in that area.

For classification as a public charity, however, a community foundation wants to be regarded as a single entity rather than an aggregation of funds. To be treated as a component part of a community foundation, a trust or fund must be created by gift or similar transfer and may not be subjected by the transferor to any material restriction. A community foundation must, to be considered a single entity, be appropriately named, be so structured as to subject its funds to a common governing instrument, have a common governing body, and prepare periodic financial reports that treat all funds held by the foundation as its assets. The board of a community foundation must have the power to modify any restriction on the distribution of funds where it is inconsistent with the charitable needs of the community, must commit itself to the exercise of its powers in the best interests of the foundation, and must commit itself to seeing that the funds are invested in accordance with standards of fiduciary conduct.

A private foundation may make a grant to a designated fund within a community foundation (often a donor-advised fund (see § 11.1(a)). The private foundation can receive a payout credit for this type of grant, even though it acquires the ability to make recommendations as to distributions to other charitable organizations from the fund, as long as there are no prohibited material restrictions. Grants of this nature are regarded as made to the community foundation as an entity and not to a discrete fund.

(e) Service Provider Publicly Supported Organizations

Another way that a tax-exempt charitable organization can be a publicly supported entity is to be a *service provider* organization. As is the case with the donative organization rules, qualification for public charity status focuses on sources of revenue, although there are considerable differences between the two ways to compute public support. Public support in this context includes gifts and grants, but also includes forms of exempt function revenue. Thus, this type of publicly supported charity usually has a major portion of its support in the form of fees and like charges derived from the conduct of its programs, such as exempt dues-based entities, theaters, arts organizations, educational publishers, day care centers, and animal shelters.

A two-part support test must be met for an organization to qualify as this type of publicly supported charity:

- Investment income cannot exceed one-third of total support. *Total support* basically is all of the organization's gross revenue normally received (see § 8.1(e)(5)), other than capital gains and the value of exemptions from local, state, and federal taxes.

- More than one-third of total support must be a combination of:

  ○ Contributions, grants, and membership dues from sources other than disqualified persons (see § 8.2)

  ○ Admission fees to exempt function facilities or activities, such as payments for theater tickets, access to a museum or historical site, seminars, lectures, and athletic events

  ○ Fees for performance of services, such as day care fees, counseling fees, testing fees, laboratory fees, library fines, animal neutering charges, and athletic activity fees

  ○ Sales of merchandise related to the organization's exempt purpose, including books and other educational literature, pharmaceuticals and medical devices, handicrafts, reproductions and copies of original works of art, byproducts of a blood bank, and goods produced by disabled workers

Exempt function revenue from one source may not be treated as public support to the extent it is in excess of $5,000 or 1 percent of the total support of the organization, whichever is higher.

(1) Permitted Sources.   Generally, to be public support under these rules, the support must be derived from *permitted sources*. Consequently, a charitable organization seeking to qualify as a publicly supported entity under these rules must construct a support fraction, with the amount of support from permitted sources constituting the numerator of the fraction and the total amount of support being the fraction's denominator.

Permitted sources are certain public and publicly supported charitable organizations, governmental units, and persons other than disqualified persons with respect to the organization. Thus, in general, support (other than from disqualified persons) from another service provider publicly supported organization, a supporting organization (see § 8.1(h)), any other tax-exempt organization (other than the institutions and donative publicly supported organizations (see § 8.1(c), (d)), a for-profit organization, or an individual constitutes public support for this type of organization, albeit limited in some instances (see § 8.1(e)(3)). The cash basis method of accounting is used in making these determinations.

(2) Support.   The term *support* means (in addition to the categories of public support, which may include corporate sponsorships) (1) net income from any unrelated business (see § 7.1(b)), (2) gross investment income, (3) tax revenues levied for the benefit of the organization and either paid to or expended on behalf of the organization, and (4) the value of services or facilities (other than services or facilities generally furnished to the public without charge) furnished by a governmental unit. These items of support are combined to constitute the denominator of the support fraction.

The concept of support does not include (1) any gain from the disposition of a capital asset; (2) the value of local, state, and/or federal tax exemptions or similar benefits; and (3) the proceeds of a loan.

(3) Limitations on Support.   The support taken into account in determining the numerator of the support test under these rules must come from permitted sources. Thus, transfers from disqualified persons cannot qualify as public support under the service provider publicly supported organizations rules. The fact that a contribution or grant is restricted or earmarked does not detract from its qualification as public support.

In determining the amount of support in the form of gross receipts that is allowable in calculating the numerator of this support fraction, gross receipts from related activities (other than membership fees) from any person or from any bureau or similar agency of a governmental unit are includible in any tax year only to the extent that these receipts do not exceed the greater of $5,000 or 1 percent of the organization's total support for that year.

The phrase *bureau or similar agency* of a government means a specialized operating (rather than a policymaking or administrative) unit of the executive, judicial, or legislative branch of a government, usually a subdivision of a department of a government. Therefore, an organization receiving gross receipts (a grant) from both a policymaking or administrative unit of a government (e.g., the Agency for International Development) and an operational unit of a government's department (e.g., the Bureau for Latin America, an operating unit within AID) is treated as receiving gross receipts from two sources, with the amount from each agency separately subject to the $5,000/1-percent limitation.

A somewhat similar *permitted sources* limitation excludes support from a disqualified person, including a substantial contributor. In general, a *substantial contributor* is a person who contributes, grants, or bequeaths an aggregate amount of more than $5,000 to a charitable organization, where that amount is more than 2 percent of the total contributions, grants, and bequests received by the organization before the close of its tax year in which the contribution or the like from the person is received. As noted, however, grants from governmental units and certain public charities are not subject to this limitation.

The federal tax law defines and distinguishes the various forms of support referenced in the service provided publicly supported organizations rules: *contributions* or *gross receipts, grant* or *gross receipts, membership fees, gross receipts* or *gross investment income*, and *grant* or *indirect contribution*. For example, the term *gross receipts* means amounts received from the conduct of an activity related to an exempt function where a specific service, facility, or product is provided to serve the direct and immediate needs of the payor; a *grant* is an amount paid to confer a direct benefit for the public. A payment of money or transfer of property without adequate consideration generally is a *contribution* or a *grant*. The furnishing of facilities for a rental fee or the making of loans in furtherance of an exempt purpose will likely give rise to *gross receipts* rather than *gross investment income*. The fact that a membership organization provides services, facilities, and the like to its members as part of its overall activities will not result in the fees received from members being treated as *gross receipts* rather than *membership fees*.

(4) Investment Income Test. An organization, to be classified as a service provider publicly supported charity, must normally receive no more than one-third of its support from (1) gross investment income, including interest, dividends, royalties, rent, and payments with respect to securities loans; and (2) any excess of the amount of unrelated business taxable income over the amount of tax on that income. To qualify under this test, an organization must construct a *gross investment income fraction*, with the amount of gross investment income and any unrelated income (net of the tax paid on it) constituting the numerator of the fraction and the total amount of support being the denominator. On occasion, there may be an issue as to whether a revenue item is a *gross receipt* from the performance of an exempt function or is *gross investment income*.

(5) Concept of *Normally*. These public support and investment income tests are computed on the basis of the nature of the organization's *normal* sources of support. An organization is considered as *normally* receiving at least one-third of its support from permitted sources and no more than one-third of its support from gross investment income for its current tax year and immediately succeeding tax year if, for the *measuring period*, the aggregate amount of support received over the period from permitted sources is more than one-third of its total support and the aggregate amount of support over the period from gross investment income is not more than one-third of its total support.

In computing support under these rules, the IRS has traditionally used a four-year measuring period, involving the organization's most recent years. Beginning with the 2008 tax year, however, the measuring period is the organization's most recent five years. For example, if an organization's current tax year is calendar year 2009, the computation period for measuring support pursuant to these rules is calendar years 2004 to 2008; if the support fraction is satisfied on the basis of the support received over this five-year period, the organization satisfies this support test for 2009 and 2010. (A five-year period for meeting these support tests has long been available for organizations during the initial five years of their existence.)

(6) Issues. The issues that arise in connection with calculation of public support under the service provider publicly supported organization rules are somewhat the same as those that can emerge in the donative publicly supported organization context (see § 8.1(d)). Of the 9 issues in that setting, numbers 1 to 4 and 7 apply equally here. (A facts-and-circumstances test is not available for service provider entities.) There are 5 other potential issues (and thus a total of 10 issues) for service provider publicly supported organizations:

1. Accurate identification of the organization's disqualified persons.

2. Correct computation of exempt function revenue.

3. Correct application of the 1-percent rule.

4. Whether a grant is from another service provider publicly supported organization (or a charity described in the rules).

5. Correct ascertainment of gross investment income.

(f) Comparative Analysis of Publicly Supported Charities

The two principal types of publicly supported charities can simultaneously meet both public support tests if they have a broad base of financial support in the form of contributions and grants. Indeed, many charities can easily satisfy either test at any time.

A significant deviation arises, however, concerning the matter of *exempt function revenue.* In the case of donative publicly supported charities, exempt function revenue is omitted from the fraction and too much of it can prevent or cause loss of public charity status. By contrast, some or all of exempt function revenue can be public support for service provider publicly supported charities. This distinction is one of the principal determinants for a charitable organization in deciding which category of publicly supported charity is appropriate. A dues-based charitable organization, for example, would almost always select the service provider publicly supported charity classification.

There are other considerations. The donative publicly supported charity calculates its public support using a rather mechanical formula, while the service provider publicly supported charity must go through the machinations of determining whether any of its financial support has bee derived from disqualified persons. The donative publicly supported charity status has a preferred aura, if only because the service provider publicly supported charity (usually being fee-based) can appear too commercial in nature. Most service provider publicly supported charities are not permitted to maintain a pooled income fund, although today this is not much of a distinction because these funds are out of favor.

(g) New Publicly Supported Charities

The IRS's rules as to classification of new tax-exempt organizations as public charities have changed, in conjunction with the development of the new Form 990.

(1) Prior Rules. Under the prior system, an organization applying for recognition of tax exemption as a charitable entity and requesting public charity status as a publicly supported charity (either type), which had completed less than one tax year consisting of at least eight full months, was required to request an *advance ruling* as to its public charity status. Other organizations seeking recognition of exemption as a charitable entity and a publicly supported charity, and that had not completed five years of existence, could also request an advance ruling. An organization to which the IRS issued an advance ruling was treated as a public charity during a five-year advance ruling period. At the end of this five-year period, the organization was expected to file Form 8734 to establish that it was publicly supported during the five-year period.

(2) New Rules. The IRS is no longer issuing advance rulings to organizations applying for recognition of exemption as charitable entities. Instead, an organization applying for exemption recognition as a charitable entity and requesting publicly supported charity status will receive a determination letter that it is a public charity (assuming it qualifies for exemption), if the IRS determines that the organization can reasonably be expected to be publicly supported. The organization has five tax years to establish that it is publicly supported (similar to the prior advance ruling period). At the end of this five-year period, the organization will not have to file Form 4734. Beginning with its sixth tax year, if the organization files Form 990 (or 990-EZ), it will have to establish on Schedule A that it is not a private foundation (essentially using prior-law tests).

Under the prior rules, a charitable organization used a four-year computation period to determine whether it met the donative publicly supported charity or service provider publicly supported charity test, using the four years immediately preceding the current year. Under the new rules, a charitable organization will use a five-year computation period, consisting of the current year and the immediately preceding four tax years.

(h) Supporting Organizations

A category of tax-exempt charitable organization that is a public charity is the *supporting organization*. Charitable supporting organizations usually are entities that do not qualify as *institutions* or *publicly supported charities* (see § 8.1(c)–(e)) but are sufficiently related to one or more charitable organizations that are institutions or are publicly supported organizations so that the requisite degree of public control and involvement is considered present. Certain types of noncharitable tax-exempt organizations also may be supported organizations (see § 8.1(h)(8)).

A supporting organization must be organized, and at all times operated, exclusively for the benefit of, to perform the functions of, or to carry out the purposes of one or more eligible supported organizations. Also, a supporting organization must be operated, supervised, or controlled by one or more qualified supported organizations, supervised or controlled in connection with one or more such organizations, or operated in connection with one or more such organizations. A parsing of this rule has led to a quadruple classification of supporting organizations:

- Parents and subsidiaries (also known as Type I supporting organizations)
- Commonly controlled organizations (Type II)

- Functionally integrated organizations (Type III)
- Nonfunctionally integrated organizations (also Type III)

A third fundamental requirement is that a supporting organization must not be controlled, directly or indirectly, by one or more disqualified persons (other than foundation managers or eligible supported organizations).

A supporting organization may be created by one or more donors or by an organization that becomes the supported organization. To qualify as a supporting organization, a charitable entity must meet an organizational test and an operational test.

(1) Organizational Test. A supporting organization must be organized exclusively to support or benefit one or more specified public institutions, publicly supported charitable organizations, or certain noncharitable organizations. Its articles of organization must limit its purposes to one or more of the purposes that are permissible for a supporting organization, may not expressly empower the organization to engage in activities that are not in furtherance of these purposes, must state the specified entity or entities on behalf of which it is to be operated, and may not expressly empower the organization to operate to support or benefit any other organization.

To qualify as a supporting organization, an organization's stated purposes may be as broad as, or more specific than, the purposes that are permissible for a supporting organization. Thus, an organization that is formed "for the benefit of" one or more eligible supported organizations will meet this organizational test, assuming the other requirements are satisfied. An organization that is *operated, supervised, or controlled by* (a Type I entity) or *supervised or controlled in connection with* (Type II) one or more qualified supported organizations to carry out their purposes will satisfy these requirements if the purposes stated in the articles of organization are similar to, but no broader than, the purposes stated in the articles of the supported organization or organizations.

An organization will not meet this organizational test if its articles of organization expressly permit it to operate to support or benefit any organization other than its specified supported organization or organizations. The fact that the actual operations of the organization have been exclusively for the benefit of one or more specified eligible supported organizations is not sufficient to permit it to satisfy this organizational test.

(2) Operational Test. A supporting organization must be operated exclusively to support or benefit one or more specified qualified supported organizations. Unlike the definition of the term *exclusively*, as applied in the context of charitable organizations generally, which has been held by the courts to mean *primarily* (see §§ 1.6(e), 2.1(a)), the term *exclusively* in the supporting organization context means *solely*.

A supporting organization must engage solely in activities that support or benefit one or more eligible supported organizations. One way to do this, although it is not mandated but will be in certain instances (see § 8.1(h)(10)), is for the supporting organization to make grants to the supported organization; this is often done, for example, where the supporting organization houses an endowment for the benefit of a supported organization. Another form of support or benefit occurs where a supporting organization carries on a discrete program or activity on behalf of a supported organization. In one instance, a tax-exempt hospital wanted a facility near the hospital in which patients about to undergo serious surgery, and their families and friends, could stay in immediate advance of the surgical procedure; the hospital created a supporting organization, which purchased a nearby motel and converted it into the facility the hospital needed. In another case, a supporting organization, supportive of the academic endeavors of the medical school at an exempt university, was used to operate a faculty practice plan in furtherance of the teaching, research, and service programs of the school. A supporting organization may engage in fundraising activities, such as solicitation of contributions and grants, special events, and unrelated business, to raise funds for one or more supported organizations or other permissible beneficiaries.

The allowable activities of a supporting organization may include making payments to or for the use of, or providing services or facilities for, members of the charitable class benefited by the charitable supported organization. A supporting organization may make a payment indirectly through an unrelated organization to a member of a charitable class benefited by a supported charitable organization, but only where the payment constitutes a grant to an individual rather than a grant to the organization.

A supporting organization has many characteristics of a private foundation, such as a grantmaking function and the absence of any requirement that it be publicly supported. Thus, like a private foundation, a supporting organization can be funded entirely by investment income. It can satisfy this organizational test by engaging solely in investment activity, assuming charitable ends are being served.

(3) *Specification* **Requirement.**   As noted, a supporting organization must be organized and operated to support or benefit to support or benefit one or more *specified* supported organizations. This specification must be in the supporting organization's articles of organization, although the manner of the specification depends on which of the types of relationships with one or more eligible supported organizations is involved.

Generally, it is expected that the articles of organization of the supporting organization will designate (i.e., *specify*) each of the supported organizations by name. If the relationship is one of *operated, supervised, or controlled by* (Type I) or *supervised or controlled in connection with* (Type II), however, designation by name is not required as long as the articles of organization of the supporting organization require that it be operated to support or benefit one or more beneficiary organizations that are designated by class or purpose and that include one or more supported organizations, as to which there is one of these two relationships, or organizations that are closely related in purpose or function to supported organizations as to which there is one of the two relationships (in either instance, where there is no designation of the organization(s) by name). If the relationship is one *operated in connection with* (Type III), the supporting organization must designate the supported organization or organizations by name.

A supporting organization is deemed to meet the specification requirement, even though its articles of organization do not designate each supported organization by name—irrespective of the nature of the relationship—if there has been a historical and continuing relationship between the supporting organization and the supported organizations, and, by reason of that relationship, there has developed a substantial identity of interests between the organizations.

Nonetheless, in practice, it is common to specify the supported organization or organization in the supporting organization's articles of organization, irrespective of the type of supporting organization involved.

(4) Required Relationships. As noted, to meet these requirements, an organization must be operated, supervised, or controlled by or in connection with one or more eligible supported organizations. Thus, if an organization does not stand in at least one of the required relationships with respect to one or more eligible supported organizations, it cannot qualify as a supporting organization. Regardless of the applicable relationship (Type I, II, or either of the IIIs), it must be ensured that the supporting organization will be *responsive* to the needs or demands of one or more eligible supported organizations and that the supporting organization will constitute an *integral part* of or maintain a *significant involvement* in the operations of one or more qualified supported organizations.

(5) Operated, Supervised, or Controlled By. The distinguishing feature of the relationship between a supporting organization and one or more eligible supported organizations encompassed by the phrase *operated, supervised, or controlled by* is the presence of a substantial degree of direction by one or more supported organizations in regard to the policies, programs, and activities of the supporting organization. This is a relationship comparable to that of a parent and subsidiary (Type I).

(6) Supervised or Controlled in Connection With. The distinguishing feature of the relationship between a supporting organization and one or more eligible supported organizations encompassed by the phrase *supervised or controlled in connection with* is the presence of common supervision or control by the persons supervising or controlling the supporting organizations and the supported organization(s) to ensure that the supporting organization will be responsive to the needs and requirements of the supported organization(s). Therefore, in order to meet this requirement, the control or management of the supporting organization must be vested in the same individuals who control or manage the supported organization(s) (Type II).

(7) Operation in Connection With. Qualification as a supporting organization by reason of the *operated in connection with* relationship entails the least intimate of the relationships between a supporting organization and one or more supported organizations. This relationship usually is more of a programmatic one than a governance one. This type of relationship (Type III), prevalent for example in the health care field, is often structured so as to avoid legal liability, from the standpoint of a supported organization, for something done by the supporting organization.

The distinguishing feature of the relationship between a supporting organization and one or more supported organizations encompassed by this phrase is that the supporting organization must be responsive to and significantly involved in the operations of the supported organization or organizations. Generally, to satisfy the criteria of this relationship, a supporting organization must meet a *responsiveness test* and an *integral part test*.

(8) Noncharitable Supported Organizations. Certain tax-exempt organizations that are not charitable entities qualify as supported organizations; this means that a charitable organization that is supportive of one or more of these noncharitable entities constitutes a supporting organization. These eligible supported organizations are exempt social welfare organizations; labor, agricultural, and horticultural organizations; and business leagues, such as trade associations. The principal requirement is that these organizations have to satisfy the one-third support test applicable to service provider publicly supported organizations. These organizations frequently meet this support requirement because they have a membership that pays dues.

This rule is principally designed to facilitate public charity status for related foundations and other funds (such as scholarship, award, and research funds) operated by the specified noncharitable organizations. This type of supporting organization can be in an awkward position: It must be charitable in function to be tax-exempt yet be supportive of a noncharitable entity to be a public charity.

(9) Substitutions. The federal tax law is vague as to how a supported organization with respect to a supporting organization can be changed (substituted) without loss of the supporting organization's public charity status. In what may be the only example of this type of substitution to date, the IRS ruled that a tax-exempt entity could retain its status as a supporting organization, notwithstanding a transaction in which a supported organization was substituted. An exempt university caused a related supporting organization to become affiliated with another entity that also functioned to support and benefit the university. This ruling is of limited utility in understanding the bounds of supported organization substitution, however, because, under the facts of the ruling, the functions of the supporting organization remained essentially the same and it continued to indirectly support the university.

An organization that is *operated in connection with* one or more eligible supported organizations can satisfy the specification requirement (see § 8.1(h)(3)) even if its articles of organization permit an eligible supported organization that is designated by class or purpose to be substituted for the supported organizations designated by name in its articles but only if the substitution is conditioned on the occurrence of an event that is beyond the control of the supporting organization. This type of event includes, as to a supported organization, loss of tax exemption, substantial failure or abandonment of operations, or dissolution of the entity.

(10) Recent Law. Recent years have not been kind to supporting organizations in terms of law development. Abuses (or the potential for abuses) have caused Congress to crack down hard on supporting organizations, enacting legislation that has substantially increased the regulation of these organizations and, in too many instances, is crippling their use. Even more burdensome and harmful regulation is in the works, in the form of Treasury Department and IRS regulations and rules. As a consequence, supporting organizations are not the attractive alternative to private foundations they once were.

Congress, in 2006, passed new law, much of it rather intricate, in connection with supporting organizations. Some of this law involved application of some of the private foundation rules to supporting organizations. Other law brought in specific application of the intermediate sanctions rules. The most stringent provisions of new law are directed at Type III supporting organizations, particularly those that are not functionally integrated with a supported organization.

A grantmaking private foundation (as contrasted with a private operating foundation) may not treat as a qualifying distribution an amount paid to a Type III supporting organization that is not a functionally integrated Type III supporting organization or to any other type of supporting organization if a disqualified person with respect to the foundation directly or indirectly controls the supporting organization or a supported organization of the supporting organization. An amount that does not count as a qualifying distribution under this rule is regarded as a taxable expenditure.

An organization is not considered to be operated, supervised, or controlled by a qualified supported organization (the general criterion for a Type I organization) or operated in connection with a supported organization (the general criterion for Type IIIs) if the organization accepts a contribution from a person (other than a qualified supported organization) who, directly or indirectly, controls, either alone or with family members and/or certain controlled entities, the governing board of a supported organization. A supporting organization is considered to not be operated in connection with a supported organization unless the supporting organization is only operated in connection with one or more supported organizations that are organized in the United States.

The private foundation excess business holdings rules are applicable to Type III supporting organizations, other than functionally integrated Type III supporting organizations. Until more specific guidance is issued, a *functionally integrated Type III supporting organization* is a Type III supporting organization that is not required by the tax regulations to make payments to supported organizations. Solely for purposes of certain due diligence requirements (see § 8.1(h)(11)), an entity is a functionally integrated Type III supporting organization if it is engaged in activities for or on behalf of a supported organization that are activities to perform the functions of, or to carry out the purposes of, a supported organization and, but for the involvement of the supporting organization, would normally be engaged in by the supported organization (the *but for* test).

These excess business holdings rules also apply to a Type II supporting organization if the organization accepts a contribution from a person (other than a public charity that is not a supporting organization) who controls, either alone or with family members and/or certain controlled entities, the governing body of a supported organization of the supporting organization. Nonetheless, the IRS has the authority to not impose the excess business holdings rules on a supporting organization if the organization establishes that the holdings are consistent with the organization's tax-exempt status.

A supporting organization is required to file annual information returns with the IRS, irrespective of the amount of the organization's gross receipts. (Generally, small organizations, other than private foundations, do not have to file these returns.) A supporting organization must report its type on its annual information returns. The supported organization(s) must be identified on the returns. A Type III supporting organization must apprise each organization that it supports of information regarding the supporting organization in order to help ensure the responsiveness by the supporting organization to the needs or demands of the supported organization(s). A Type III supporting organization that is organized as a trust must establish to the satisfaction of the IRS that it has a sufficiently close and continuous relationship with the supported organization so that the trust is responsive to the needs or demands of the supported organization.

An excise tax is imposed on disqualified persons if they engage in one or more excess benefit transactions with public charities and/or social welfare organizations. (This rule is part of the *intermediate sanctions* regime, which is somewhat akin to the private foundation self-dealing rules.) A grant, loan, compensation, or other similar payment (such as an expense reimbursement) by any type of supporting organization to a substantial contributor or a person related to a substantial contributor, as well as a loan provided by a supporting organization to certain disqualified persons with respect to the supporting organization, is automatically an excess benefit transaction. Thus, the entire amount paid to the substantial contributor, disqualified persons, and related parties is an excess benefit.

To demonstrate the complexity of this new body of law (as if the foregoing is not sufficient), one of the ways that a charitable organization can qualify as a Type III supporting organization is to satisfy a *responsiveness test* and an *integral part test*. Before these law changes, there were two ways in which the responsiveness test could be met. One way to meet this test was to be a charitable trust, with the supported organization(s) specified in the trust instrument and the supported organization(s) accorded the power to enforce the trust and compel and accounting. That approach to satisfaction of the test was eliminated by statute. Consequently, trusts previously classified as Type III supporting organizations may be classified as private foundations. (A trust can continue to qualify as a supporting organization if it meets the other way to satisfy the responsiveness test and thus remain a Type III entity, or if it meets the requirements of a Type I or II supporting organization.) The IRS provided some transitional relief in this regard by stating that charitable trusts that became private foundations by reason of this law change could file the standard annual information return (Form 990) for tax years beginning before January 1, 2008, and begin filing the private foundation annual information return (Form 990-PF) for subsequent years.

A supporting organization must annually demonstrate that one or more of its disqualified persons (other than its managers and supported organization(s)) do not, directly or indirectly, control it. This is done by means of a certification on its annual information return.

Another law change enacted in 2006 provided certain individuals the opportunity to distribute, from their individual retirement arrangements, funds to public charities without the amounts includible in the gross income of the contributors. (This income exclusion rule was in effect for only two years and has expired; the rule may be resuscitated.) Under this law, however, distributions to any type of supporting organization did not qualify for the exclusion.

The Department of the Treasury, at the direction of Congress, is undertaking a study on the organization and operation of supporting organizations, considering whether (1) the deductions allowed for income, estate, or gift taxes for charitable contributions to supporting organizations are appropriate in consideration of the use of contributed assets or the use of the assets of these organizations for the benefit of the person making the charitable contribution, and (2) these issues are also issues with respect to other forms of charitable organizations or charitable contributions.

(11) Private Foundations' Due Diligence Requirements. The IRS, at the end of 2006, issued guidance regarding certain elements of the law, enacted earlier that year, that affect supporting organizations, donor-advised funds, and private foundations that make grants to supporting organizations.

The federal tax law imposes, as noted, certain burdens where a private foundation makes a grant to (1) a Type III supporting organization that is not functionally integrated with one or more supported organizations or (2) any other type of supporting organization if one or more disqualified persons with respect to the private foundation directly or indirectly controls the supporting organization or one of its supported organizations. In one of these instances, the grant fails to constitute a qualifying distribution and is a taxable expenditure unless the private foundation exercises expenditure responsibility with respect to the grant. Similar rules apply (with treatment of the payment as a taxable distribution) in connection with distributions from donor-advised funds (see § 11.1(a)).

Pursuant to this guidance, a grantor, acting in good faith, may, in determining whether the grantee is a public charity, rely on information from the IRS Business Master File or the grantee's current IRS determination letter recognizing the grantee's tax exemption and indicating the grantee's public charity status. In addition, a grantor, acting in good faith, may rely on a written representation from a grantee and certain specified documents (see the next bullet points) in determining the grantee's supporting organization type. In any event, the grantor must verify that the grantee is listed in the IRS's Publication 78 or obtain a copy of the grantee's determination letter.

To establish that a grantee is a Type I or II supporting organization, a grantor, acting in good faith, may rely on a written representation signed by a trustee, director, or officer of the grantee that the grantee is a Type I or II supporting organization, provided that:

- The representation describes how the grantee's trustees, directors, and/or officers are selected, and references any provision in the governing documents that establish a Type I or II relationship between the grantee and its supported organization(s), and

- The grantor collects and reviews copies of the governing documents of the grantee and, if relevant, of the supported organization(s).

To establish that a grantee is a functionally integrated Type III supporting organization, a grantor, acting in good faith, may rely on a written representation signed by a trustee, director, or officer of the grantee that the grantee is a functionally integrated Type III supporting organization, provided that:

- The grantee's representation identifies the one or more supported organizations with which the grantee is functionally integrated,

- The grantor collects and reviews copies of governing documents of the grantee (and, if relevant, of the supported organization(s)) and any other documents that set forth the relationship of the grantee to its supported organization(s), if the relationship is not reflected in the governing documents, and

- The grantor reviews a written representation signed by a trustee, director, or officer of each of the supported organizations with which the grantee represents that it is functionally integrated, describing the activities of the grantee and confirming that, but for the involvement of the grantee engaging in activities to perform the functions of, or to carry out the purposes of, the supported organization, the supported organization would normally be engaged in those activities itself.

- As an alternative to the foregoing, a grantor may rely on a reasoned written opinion of counsel of either the grantor or the grantee concluding that the grantee is a Type I, Type II, or Type III functionally integrated supporting organization.

A private foundation considering a grant to a Type I, Type II, or Type III functionally integrated supporting organization may need to obtain a list of the grantee's supported organizations from the grantee to determine whether any of the supported organizations is controlled (see § 8.1(h)(12)) by disqualified persons with respect to the foundation. Likewise, a sponsoring organization considering a grant from a donor-advised fund to one of these types of supporting organizations may need to obtain such a list to determine whether any of the supported organizations is controlled by the fund's donor or donor advisor (and any related parties).

Until regulations are issued, in determining whether a disqualified person with respect to a private foundation controls a supporting organization or one of its supported organizations, the standards as to control established in the mandatory payout regulations apply. Under these standards, an organization is controlled by one or more disqualified persons with respect to a foundation if any of these persons may, by aggregating their votes or positions of authority, require the supporting or supported organization to make an expenditure or prevent the supporting or supported organization from making an expenditure, regardless of the method by which the control is exercised or exercisable.

Similarly, a supported organization is controlled by one or more donors or donor advisors (and any related parties) of a donor-advised fund if any of these persons may, by aggregating their votes or positions of authority, require a supported organization to make an expenditure or prevent a supported organization from making an expenditure, irrespective of the method by which the control is exercised or exercisable.

Because of this guidance, coupled with the statutory law changes that preceded it, one wonders whether private foundation grants to supporting organizations are doomed. Foundations are unlikely to take the time and make the effort to go through the collection and review processes, and secure the requisite written representations to determine a supporting organization's type. These developments may give rise to a general antipathy on the part of private foundations toward grants to all supporting organizations.

(12) Limitation on Control. As noted, one or more disqualified persons with respect to a supporting organization, other than its officers and the like (technically termed *foundation managers*), cannot (without jeopardizing its public charity status), directly or indirectly, control the organization. An individual who is a disqualified person with respect to a supporting organization does not lose that status because a beneficiary-supported organization appoints or designates him or her to be a foundation manager of the supporting organization, to serve as a representative of the supported organization

A supporting organization is considered *controlled* if the disqualified persons, by aggregating their votes or positions of authority, may require the organization to perform an act that significantly affects its operations or may prevent the supporting organization from performing this type of an act. Generally, control exists if the voting power of these persons is 50 percent or more of the total voting power of the organization's governing body or if one or more disqualified persons have the right to exercise veto power over the actions of the organization. All pertinent facts and circumstances, including the nature, diversity, and income yield of an organization's holdings, the length of time particular securities or other assets are retained, and the manner of exercising its voting rights with respect to securities in which members of its governing body also have an interest, are taken into consideration in determining whether a disqualified person does in fact indirectly control an organization.

Caution needs to be exercised in this context. The IRS can find indirect control of a supporting organization by disqualified persons by going beyond the foregoing rules. One such instance involved a charitable organization that made distributions to a tax-exempt university. The organization's board of directors was composed of a substantial contributor to the organization, two employees of a business corporation of which more than 35 percent of the voting power was owned by the disqualified person, and an individual selected by the university. None of the directors had veto power over the organization's actions. Conceding that disqualified persons did not directly control the organization, the IRS said that "one circumstance to be considered is whether a disqualified person is in a position to influence the decisions of members of the organization's governing body who are not themselves disqualified persons." Thus, the IRS concluded that the two directors who were employees of the disqualified person corporation should be considered the equivalent of disqualified persons for purposes of applying the 50-percent control rule. This position led to the conclusion that the organization was indirectly controlled by disqualified persons and, therefore, could not be a public charity by virtue of being a qualified supporting organization.

(i) Public Safety Testing Organizations

Another category of organization that is deemed to be a public charity is an organization that is organized and operated exclusively for testing for public safety. Although these entities are considered public charities, they are not eligible to receive tax-deductible charitable contributions.

(j) Import of Public–Private Dichotomy

As a general proposition—and this is from a law standpoint—public charity status is preferable to private foundation status. That is, again, purely from the perspective of the law, there is no advantage to a charitable organization in being a private foundation. (There is nothing inherently wrong in being a private foundation, of course, and, as noted, about 80,000 of them function quite nicely in that capacity.)

The biggest disadvantage of classification as a private foundation is that a charitable organization is subject to and expected to comply with the private foundation rules concerning mandatory payouts, self-dealing, excess business holdings, jeopardizing investments, and prohibited expenditures. Public charities are generally not caught up in this barrage of restrictions and requirements.

Having said that, however, some of the private foundation rules are being applied in the public charity setting. The excess business holdings rules are applicable to certain supporting organizations. At this time, Congress and the IRS are working on mandatory payout requirements for some supporting organizations. Although the self-dealing rules do not apply to public charities, rules as to excess benefit transactions apply in connection with public charities; in several instances, the requirements are the same. Certain basic principles of the law, such as the private inurement and private benefit doctrines (see §§ 6.1, 6.3), are applicable to both categories of charitable organizations.

Another disadvantage to private foundation status is that the charitable giving rules (see Chapter 19) considerably favor public charities. This problem (if there is one) usually is presented at the time a private foundation is initially funded, either because percentage limitations restrict the extent of a charitable contribution deduction or because a deduction for a gift of property is confined to the donor's basis in the property.

(k) Nonexempt Charitable Trusts

Nonexempt charitable trusts are trusts that are not tax-exempt but are treated as private foundations for federal tax law purposes. These trusts are funded and operated in nearly identical fashion as exempt private foundations. This type of trust has exclusively charitable interests; donors to these trusts are allowed to claim a tax deduction for charitable contributions. Unlike private foundations, nonexempt charitable trusts are required to pay an annual tax on income that is not distributed for charitable purposes.

(l) Disqualified Persons

A basic concept of the federal tax laws pertaining to public charities and private foundations is that of the *disqualified person*. Essentially, a disqualified person is a person (including an individual, corporation, partnership, trust, estate, or other private foundation) standing in one or more close relationships with respect to a tax-exempt charitable organization, its trustees, and/or its founders.

(1) Foundation Managers. The most obvious category of disqualified person is the *foundation manager*, defined to encompass trustees, directors, and officers of charitable organizations, or individuals having powers or responsibilities similar to those holding one of these three positions. An individual is considered an *officer* of a charitable organization if he or she (1) is specifically designated as an officer in the governing instruments of the foundation (usually the bylaws) or (2) regularly exercises general authority to make administrative or policy decisions on behalf of the foundation. A person who has authority merely to make recommendations pertaining to administrative or policy decisions, but lacks the authority to implement them without approval of someone in a superior position, is not a foundation manager. Independent contractors, such as lawyers, accountants, and investment mangers and advisors, acting in that capacity also are not officers or other managers.

An individual with sufficient authority may be what the IRS terms a *key employee*, which is a person having responsibilities or powers similar to those who are formally denominated trustees, directors, or officers. Pursuant to this concept, the chief management and administrative officials of an organization (such as executive directors and chancellors) are key employees, while the heads of separate departments or smaller units within an organization are not. A chief financial officer and the officer in charge of administration or program operations are key employees if they have the authority to control the organization's activities and/or its finances.

Even if an individual lacks the authority to be classified as a foundation manager on an overall basis, he or she can be regarded as a foundation manager with respect to a particular act (or failure to act) over which he or she has the requisite authority.

(2) Substantial Contributors. A category of disqualified person with respect to a private foundation is a person who is a substantial contributor to the foundation. The term *substantial contributor* means any person who contributed (including a transfer by bequest) to a private foundation an aggregate amount that is more than the higher of (1) 2 percent of the total contributions received by the foundation before the close of its tax year in which the contribution is received by the foundation from that person or (2) $5,000. In computing this 2-percent/$5,000 threshold, all contributions to the foundation since its creation are taken into account.

In determining whether a contributor is a substantial contributor, the totals of the amounts from the contributor and the aggregate total contributions received by the organization must be accumulated as of the last day of each tax year. This determination as to aggregate gifts does not mean that a foundation must keep records dating back to ancient history; generally, all contributions made before October 9, 1969, are deemed to have been made on that date. An individual is treated as making all contributions made by his or her spouse. Each contribution of property is valued at its fair market value on the date received. Thus, a charitable organization should maintain a running tally of contributions, recording amounts, dates, and sources. An unusual grant exclusion rule is not available in calculating aggregate contributions for purposes of identifying substantial contributors.

A donor becomes a substantial contributor as of the first date on which the organization received from him, her, or it an amount that is in excess of the 2-percent/$5,000 threshold. But the *final* (and controlling) determination as to substantial contributor status is not made until the last day of the tax year, so that contributions made subsequent to the gift(s) of the contributor in question but within the same tax year may operate to keep him, her, or it out of substantial contributor status even though that status was *temporarily* (as it turned out) obtained at an earlier point during the year.

In the case of a trust, the term *substantial contributor* also means the creator of the trust. The term *person*, in this context, usually includes tax-exempt organizations but does not include governmental units. Generally, however, the term *substantial contributor* does not include most charitable organizations that are not private foundations or organizations that are wholly owned by a public charity. This term includes a decedent, even at the point in time preceding the transfer of any property from the estate to the organization.

To be a substantial contributor, the person involved must first be a *contributor*. Consequently, where the transfer of money or property to a private foundation is not in the form of a gift or grant, the substantial contributor rules are not applicable. Also, although this discussion of these rules is framed in terms of contributions to private foundations, the rules are also applicable in connection with service provider publicly supported charities and supporting organizations.

(3) 20-Percent-Plus Owners. An owner of more than 20 percent of the total combined voting power of a corporation, the profits interest of a partnership, or the beneficial interest of a trust or unincorporated enterprise, any of which is (during the period of ownership) a substantial contributor to an organization, is a disqualified person.

The phrase *combined voting power* includes voting power represented by holdings of voting stock, actual or constructive, but does not include voting rights held only in the capacity as a director or trustee. Thus, for example, an employee stock ownership trust that held 30 percent of the stock of a corporation that was a substantial contributor to a private foundation, on behalf of the corporation's participating employees who direct the manner in which the trust votes the shares, was held by the IRS to have merely the voting power of a trustee and not the ownership of the stock, and thus to not be a disqualified person with respect to the foundation.

The term *voting power* includes outstanding voting power but does not include voting power obtainable but not obtained, such as voting power obtainable by converting securities or nonvoting stock into voting stock, by exercising warrants or options to obtain voting stock, or voting power that will vest in preferred stockholders only if and when the corporation has failed to pay preferred dividends for a specified period of time or has otherwise failed to meet specified requirements.

For the purpose of determining combined voting power, profits interest, or beneficial interest of an individual, attribution rules must be applied. In respect to combined voting power, stock (or profits or beneficial interests) owned directly or indirectly by or for a corporation, partnership, estate, or trust is considered as being owned proportionately by or for its shareholders, partners, or beneficiaries. Moreover, an individual is considered as owning the stock owned by members of his or her family (see § 8.2(d)). Stockholders that have been counted once (whether by reason of actual or constructive ownership) in application of these rules are not counted a second time.

The *profits interest* of a partner is that amount equal to his or her distributive share of the income of the partnership as determined in accordance with special federal tax rules. The term *profits interest* includes an interest that is outstanding but not an interest that is obtainable but has not been obtained.

The *beneficial interest* in an unincorporated enterprise (other than a trust or estate) includes any right to receive a distribution of profits of the enterprise or, in the absence of a profit-sharing agreement, any right to receive the assets of the enterprise on its liquidation, except as a creditor or employee. A *right to receive a distribution of profits* includes a right to receive any amount from the profits, other than as a creditor or employee, whether as a sum certain or as a portion of profits realized by the enterprise. In the absence of an agreement fixing the rights of the participants in an enterprise, the fraction of the respective interests of each participant in the enterprise is determined by dividing (1) the amount of all investments or contributions to the capital of the enterprise made or obligated to be made by the participant by (2) the amount of investments or contributions to capital made or obligated to be made by all of them.

A person's beneficial interest in a trust is determined in proportion to the actuarial interest of the person in the trust. The term *beneficial interest* includes an interest that is outstanding but not an interest that is obtainable but has not been obtained.

(4) Members of Family. The reach of the disqualified person rules is considerably enhanced by inclusion of the family members of disqualified persons in the definition. Thus, a category of disqualified person with respect to an organization is a member of the family of an individual who is a foundation manager, a substantial contributor to the foundation, or is a 20-percent-plus owner of a substantial contributor entity (see § 8.2(b), (c)). The phrase *member of the family* means an individual's spouse, ancestors, children, grandchildren, great-grandchildren, and the spouses of children, grandchildren, and great-grandchildren. Consequently, simply by being a member of a particular family, an individual can be a disqualified person with respect to a charitable organization.

A legally adopted child of an individual is treated, for purposes of the disqualified persons rules, the same as a child of an individual by blood. A brother or sister of an individual is not, however, for these purposes considered a member of the family.

The determination as to who is a member of a family, for purposes of ascertaining whether he or she is a disqualified person in relation to a private foundation, can be a tricky proposition, particularly if the foundation has been in existence for a long period of time and/or the foundation has a large governing board. Individuals are constantly being born and die, children are adopted, and individuals marry and get divorced. The mix of who is in and who is out of a family can entail a swirl of activities that are difficult to make static at a point in time.

(5) Corporations. A corporation is a disqualified person with respect to a private foundation if more than 35 percent of the total combined voting power in the corporation (see § 8.2(c)) is owned by foundation managers, substantial contributors to the foundation, 20-percent-plus owners, or members of the family of any of these individuals.

(6) Partnerships. A partnership is a disqualified person with respect to a private foundation if more than 35 percent of the profits interest in the partnership (see § 8.2(c)) is owned by foundation managers, substantial contributors to the foundation, 20-percent-plus owners, or members of the family of any of these individuals.

(7) Trusts or Estates. A trust or estate is a disqualified person with respect to a private foundation if more than 35 percent of the beneficial interest in the trust or estate (see § 8.2(c)) is owned by foundation managers, substantial contributors to the foundation, 20-percent-plus owners, or members of the family of any of these individuals.

§8.2 PREPARATION OF NEW FORM 990 SCHEDULE A

Schedule A of the new Form 990 consists of four parts.

(a) Part I (Reason for Public Charity Status)

Part I of Schedule A of the new Form 990 principally consists of an inventory of the various ways a tax-exempt charitable organization can be a public charity. Thus, this part must be prepared and filed by all organizations that file a Form 990. Only one of the 11 boxes should be checked.

Organizations should exercise some caution when preparing this Part I. Some charitable organizations report a public charity status that is different from the one reflected on its determination letter or ruling. For example, an organization that is a supporting foundation with respect to a school operated by a governmental unit received a determination letter with the IRS classifying it as a donative publicly supported charity (see § 8.1(d)) is reporting on its annual information return that it is a support foundation with respect to a public (governmental) college (see § 8.1(c)(7)).

An organization that believes the reason it is a public charity is different from the reason stated in its determination letter or ruling should check the box corresponding to the reason it believes it is a public charity and explain the difference in Part IV. If an organization believes it qualifies for public charity status for more than one reason, the organization should check only one of these boxes and may explain the other reasons it qualifies in Part IV.

The 14 choices as to public charity status are:

1. Church (see § 8.1(c)(1))—check box 1.

2. Convention of churches (see § 8.1(c)(2))—check box 1.

3. Association of churches (see § 8.1(c)(2))—check box 1.

4. School (see § 8.1(c)(3))—check box 2. An organization that checks this box must complete Schedule E. (See Chapter 12.)

5. Hospital (see § 8.1(c)(4))—check box 3. An organization that checks this box must complete Schedule H. (See Chapter 15.)

6. Cooperative hospital service organization (see § 8.1(c)(5))—check box 3. An organization that checks this box must complete Schedule H. (See Chapter 15.)

7. Medical research organization (see § 8.1(c)(6)—check box 4 and enter the affiliated hospital(s)' name, city, and state.

8. An organization supporting a college or university owned or operated by a governmental unit (see § 8.1(c)(7))—check box 5 and complete the support schedule in Schedule A, Part II.

9. A federal, state, or local government or governmental unit (see § 8.1(c)(8))—check box 6.

10. A donative publicly supported charity (see § 8.1(d))—check box 7 and complete the support schedule in Schedule A, Part II.

11. A community trust (foundation) (see § 8.1(d)(8))—check box 8 and complete the support schedule in Schedule A, Part II.

12. A service provider publicly supported charity (see § 8.1(e))—check box 9 and complete the support schedule in Schedule A, Part II.

13. A public safety testing organization (see § 8.1(h))—check box 10. An organization should check this box only if it has a determination letter or ruling from the IRS that it is organized and operated primarily to test for public safety.

14. A supporting organization (see § 8.1(g))—check box 11.

Because of recent law changes concerning supporting organizations (see, e.g., § 8.1(g)(10)), much more information is required in Schedule A, Part I. It should be noted that the reference to supporting organizations in connection with box 11 refers only to supporting organizations that provide benefit to public charities. A supporting organization may, in fact, provide support and benefit to certain other types of tax-exempt organizations (see § 8.1(g)(8)).

A supporting organization must check one of four boxes that describe the type of supporting organization that it is (see § 8.1(1), (5)–(7)): box ''a'' for Type I, box ''b'' for Type II, box ''c'' for functionally integrated Type III, and box ''d'' for nonfunctionally integrated Type III. A check in the box in line 11e is required for a certification that the supporting organization is not controlled, directly or indirectly, by one or more disqualified persons (see § 8.2), other than managers and supported organizations. Again, this certification does not reflect the fact that a supporting organization may provide support and benefit to certain other types of tax-exempt organizations (see § 8.1(g)(8)); a statement should be attached to the schedule to incorporate that fact when necessary.

If the organization has received a determination letter or ruling from the IRS as to its type, it will check the box in line 11f. In reflection of the new law (see § 8.1(g)(10)), there are three questions in 11g, each of which must be answered ''yes'' or ''no'' by checking a box. The questions are, since August 17, 2006, has the organization received a contribution from any of these persons:

1. A person who directly or indirectly controls, either alone or together with persons described in 2 or 3 following, the governing board of the supported organization (box 11g(i)).

2. A family member of a person described in 1 above (box 11g(ii)).

3. A 35 percent controlled entity of a person described in 1 or 2 above (box 11g(iii)).

There is no requirement for a statement if any of these three questions are answered ''yes.''

In response to Schedule A, Part I, line 11h, the filing supporting organization must provide this information about its supported organization or organizations:

- The name or names of these entities (column 11h(i)).

- The employer identification number of each supported entity (column 11h(ii)).

- The type of the organization if a public charity or the appropriate section of the Internal Revenue Code in the case of another type of supported organization (column 11h(iii)).

- Whether the supported organization is listed (specified) in the filing organization's governing document (see § 8.1(g)(3)) (column 11h(iv)).

- Whether the filing organization has notified the supported organization(s) of its support (see § 8.1(g)(10)) (column 11h(v)).

- Whether the supported organization(s) is/are organized in the United States (see § 8.1(g)(10)) (column 11h(vi)).

- The amount of support provided to the supported organization(s) (column 11h(vii)). This question is problematic because a supporting organization need not provide financial support to a supported organization; it can provide support in other ways (see § 8.1(g)(2)). Thus, it may be difficult or impossible to quantify an *amount* of support provided by a supporting organization to a supported organization.

(b)   Part II (Support Schedule for Donative Type Entities)

Part II of Schedule A is the support schedule used by donative publicly supported charities (see § 8.1(d)), community foundations (see § 8.1(d)(8)), and supporting foundations for colleges and universities owned or operated by governmental units (see § 8.1(c)(7)). These computations are based on the most recent five years of the organization (see § 8.1(d)(3)); thus, an organization reporting in 2009 using the calendar year will have a public support measuring period of 2004 to 2008.

In preparing this Part II, the organization takes these steps:

- It calculates and reports its public support for the measuring period (lines 1–6).

- It calculates and reports its other forms of financial support (such as investment and net unrelated business income), other than capital gain, for the measuring period (lines 7–11).

- It calculates and reports its gross receipts from related activities (line 12).

- If this Form 990 is for any year in the organization's five-year advance ruling period, the box accompanying line 13 is checked and the organization does not prepare any other subsequent portions of Schedule A.

- It calculates and reports its public support percentage for 2008 (public support (line 6, column (f)) divided by total support (line 11, column (f)) (line 14).

- It reports its public support percentage for 2007 (from its 2007 Schedule A, Part IV-A, line 26f) (line 15).

- If the filing organization is beyond its advance ruling period (line 13) and its public support percentage for 2008 is at least $33\frac{1}{3}$, the organization checks the box accompanying line 16a and does not prepare any more of the Schedule A. It has qualified as a publicly supported charity.

- If the filing organization is beyond its advance ruling period, did not check the box accompanying line 16a, and has a public support percentage for 2007 of at least $33\frac{1}{3}$, the organization checks the box accompanying line 16b and does not prepare any more of the Schedule A. It has qualified as a publicly supported charity.

- Line 17a pertains to qualification under the facts-and-circumstances test (see § 8.1(d)(6)) as of 2008. If three elements are satisfied, the organization has qualified as a publicly supported charity, checks the box accompanying line 17a, and does not prepare any more of the Schedule A:

  1. The organization did not check a box accompanying lines 13, 16a, or 16b.

  2. The public support percentage for 2008 (line 14) is at least 10 percent.

  3. The organization adequately explains in Part IV of Schedule A how it is meeting the test.

- Line 17 b pertains to qualification under the facts-and-circumstances test as of 2007. If three elements are satisfied, the organization has qualified as a publicly supported charity, checks the box accompanying line 17b, and does not prepare any more of the Schedule A:

  1. The organization did not check a box accompanying lines 13, 16a, 16b, or 17a.

  2. The public support percentage for 2007 (line 15) is at least 10 percent.

  3. The organization adequately explains in Part IV of Schedule A how it is meeting the test.

- If the organization did not check a box in connection with lines 13, 16a, 16b, 17a, or 17b, then it will be a private foundation unless it otherwise qualifies as a public charity (line 18).

A donative publicly supported charity is required to prepare a list for its files showing the name of and amount contributed by each donor or grantor (other than another donative publicly supported charity, a charity described in these rules, or a governmental unit), the total gifts and grants from which during the years reported exceed the 2-percent threshold. This list should not be filed with the Form 990 (or 990-EZ).

(c) Part III (Support Schedule for Service Provider-Type Entities)

Part III of Schedule A is the support schedule used by service provider publicly supported charities (see § 8.1(e)). These computations are based on the most recent five years of the organization; thus, an organization reporting in 2009 using the calendar year will have a public support measuring period of 2004 to 2008.

In preparing this Part III, the organization takes these steps:

- It calculates and reports its public support for the measuring period (lines 1–8).

- It calculates and reports its other forms of financial support, other than capital gain, for the measuring period (lines 9–13).

- If this Form 990 is for any year in the organization's five-year advance ruling period, it checks the box accompanying line 12 and does not prepare any other subsequent portions of Schedule A.

- It calculates and reports its public support percentage for 2008 (public support (line 8, column (f)) divided by total support (line 13, column (f)) (line 15).

- It reports its public support percentage for 2007 (from its 2007 Schedule A, Part IV-A, line 27g) (line 16).

- It calculates and reports its investment income percentage for 2008 (public support (line 10c, column (f)) divided by total support (line 13, column (f)) (line 17).

- It reports its investment income percentage for 2007 (from its 2007 Schedule A, Part IV-A, line 27g) (line 18).

- As line 19a, concerning the two percentage tests for 2008, indicates, if three elements are satisfied, the organization has qualified as a publicly supported charity, checks the box accompanying line 19a, and does not prepare any more of the Schedule A:

1. The organization did not check a box accompanying line 14 (advance ruling period).

2. The public support percentage for 2008 (line 15) is at least $33\frac{1}{3}$ percent.

3. The investment income percentage for 2008 (line 17) is no more than $33\frac{1}{3}$ percent.

- As line 19a, concerning the two percentage tests for 2007, indicates, if three elements are satisfied, the organization has qualified as a publicly supported charity, checks the box accompanying line 19a, and does not prepare any more of the Schedule A:

    1. The organization did not check a box accompanying line 14 or 19a.

    2. The public support percentage for 2007 (line 16) is at least $33\frac{1}{3}$ percent.

    3. The investment income percentage for 2007 (line 18) is no more than $33\frac{1}{3}$ percent.

- If the organization did not check a box in connection with lines 13, 16a, 16b, 17a, or 17b, then it may be a private foundation unless it otherwise qualifies as a public charity (line 18).

- If the organization did not check a box in connection with lines 14, 19a, or 19b, then it will be a private foundation unless it otherwise qualifies as a public charity (line 18).

A service provider publicly supported charity is required to prepare a list for its files showing the name of and amount provided in each year by one or more disqualified persons. A similar list is required for any amounts received from government agencies in excess of the 1-percent/$5,000 threshold. These lists should not be filed with the Form 990 (or 990-EZ).

(d) Part IV (Supplemental Information)

This part of Schedule A is used to provide the information required to demonstrate compliance with the facts-and-circumstances test (see § 8.1(d)) in 2008 or 2009 (Part II, line 17a or 17b).

§ 8.3 NEW FORM 990 COMPLIANCE TASKS

A tax-exempt charitable organization that is claiming public charity status should be attending to these 12 tasks:

1. **Public status.** It should be certain that it understands why it is a public charity (an entity that is one of the 11 categories).

2. **Reporting.** It should ascertain that it is reporting its correct public charity status.

3. **Percentage tests.** If the organization is claiming status as a publicly supported organization, it should be certain that the applicable percentage test(s) are being satisfied correctly.

4. **Facts-and-circumstances test.** If the organization is relying on the facts-and-circumstances test, it should be certain that it has a sufficient explanation of its compliance with the rules.

5. **Type of supporting organizations.** If the filing organization is a supporting organization, it should know its type.

6. **Control.** If the organization is a supporting organization, it should be certain that disqualified persons do not control it (so it can make the requisite certification).

7. **Certain contributions.** If the organization is a supporting organization, it should know if it has received a contribution from person(s) who control the governing body of a supported organization.

8. **Status of supported organization(s).** If the organization is a supporting organization, it should be certain that it knows the public charity or other tax status of its supported organization(s).

9. **Specifications.** If the organization is a supporting organization, it should be certain that the specification requirement has been satisfied.

10. **Notification.** If the organization is a supporting organization, it should be certain that it has properly notified its supported organization(s) of its support.

11. **Private foundation due diligence.** If the organization is a supporting organization, it should be considering practices and procedures to minimize the loss of support from one or more private foundations.

12. **Amount of support.** If the organization is a supporting organization, it should be cautious as to how and on what basis it reports the *amount* of its support.

CHAPTER NINE

Schedule C—Legislative Activities

Charitable organizations may engage in only limited lobbying activity and no political campaign activity. Many other exempt organizations may engage in almost unlimited lobbying activity and some political activity. The focus of the IRS in this regard is on social welfare organizations, labor and agricultural organizations, and associations/business leagues. The current Form 990 requires disclosure of a charitable organization's legislative activity on Schedule A. It also asks questions about deductibility of dues for social welfare organizations, labor and agricultural organizations, and trade associations/business leagues and whether any taxes are paid by charities for excessive lobbying expenditures.

The new Schedule C consolidates the reporting of legislative and political activities. From a legislative activity point of view, it expands the required information from social welfare organizations, labor and agricultural organizations, and associations/business leagues. The information relates to the deductibility of dues by the organization's members. This chapter addresses the reporting of legislative activity. Chapter 10 addresses the reporting of political campaign activity.

§9.1 LAW AND POLICY

No substantial part of a charity's activities can be to influence legislation. There is no such restriction applicable to other exempt organizations including social welfare organizations, labor and agricultural organizations, and associations/business leagues. Dues paid to such organizations, however, are not deductible to the extent the organization engages in lobbying activity.

(a) Types of Lobbying Activity

Lobby activities can take many forms. Some activities constitute *direct* lobbying, and other activities constitute *grassroots* lobbying. Direct lobbying occurs when one or more representatives of an organization make contact with a legislator and/or his or her staff and/or the staff of a legislative committee. Direct lobbying includes office visits, presentation of testimony at hearings, correspondence, publication and dissemination of material, e-mail, and other Internet communications.

The instructions state that direct lobbying is any attempt to influence any legislation through communication with:

- A member or employee of a legislative or similar body

- A government official or employee (other than a member or employee of a legislative body) who may participate in the formulation of the legislation, but only if the principal purpose of the communication is to influence legislation

- The public in a referendum, initiative, constitutional amendment, or similar procedure

A communication with a legislator or government official will be treated as a direct lobbying communication, if, but only if, the communication:

- Refers to specific legislation, and

- Reflects a view on such legislation.

Specific legislation includes (1) legislation that has already been introduced in a legislative body and (2) specific legislative proposals that an organization either supports or opposes.

Direct lobbying also includes attempts to influence legislation through communication with the public in a referendum, initiative, constitutional amendment, or similar procedure.

Grassroots (indirect) lobbying is another form of lobbying. This type of lobbying occurs when the organization urges the public, or a segment of the public, to contact members of a legislative body or their staffs for the purpose of proposing, supporting, or opposing legislation. To be grassroots lobbying, the communications call recipients to action in addition to referring to specific legislation.

The instructions indicate that a communication encourages a recipient to take action when it:

1. States that the recipient should contact legislators

2. States a legislator's address, phone number, etc.

3. Provides a petition, tear-off postcard, or similar material for the recipient to send to a legislator

4. Specifically identifies one or more legislators who:
   - Will vote on legislation
   - Opposes the communication's view on the legislation
   - Is undecided about the legislation
   - Is the recipient's representative in the legislature
   - Is a member of the legislative committee that will consider the legislation

A communication described in number 4 generally is grassroots lobbying only if, in addition to referring to and reflecting a view on specific legislation, it is a communication that cannot meet the full and fair exposition test as nonpartisan analysis, study, or research.

Generally, the rules concerning lobbying and political campaign activities (see Chapter 10) are separate, discrete bodies of law. If, however, an exempt organization engages in lobbying, particularly grassroots lobbying, doing so in the context of a political campaign, so that the advocacy of the issue(s) involved can be tied to the political fortunes of a candidate (such as an incumbent legislator pursuing reelection), the lobbying activity can also be regarded as political campaign activity. Undertakings of this nature are known as public policy advocacy communications; they are said to have a dual character.

The substantial part test discussed in § 9.1(d) does not differentiate between direct and indirect lobbying, nor does it distinguish between lobbying that is related to an organization's exempt purposes and lobbying that is not. The function remains lobbying; the various types of it are subject to the proscription. There is a distinction between the types of lobbying for purposes of the expenditure test discussed in § 9.1(e).

(b) Exceptions to Treatment as Lobbying

There are certain exceptions to treatment as lobbying. For example, a charitable organization that does not initiate any action with respect to pending legislation but merely responds to a request from a legislative committee to testify is not, solely because of that activity, considered an action organization. Also, a charitable organization can engage in nonpartisan analysis, study, and research, and publish the results. Even where some of the plans and policies formulated can be carried out only through legislative enactments, as long as the organization does not advocate the adoption of legislation or legislative action to implement its findings, it escapes classification as an action organization.

There can be a fine line between nonpartisan analysis, study, or research, and lobbying. A charitable organization may evaluate proposed or pending legislation and present an objective analysis of it to the public, as long as it does not participate in the presentation of suggested bills to a legislature and does not engage in any campaign to secure passage of the legislation. If the organization's primary objective can be attained only by legislative action, however, it is an action organization, and it is conducting lobbying activity.

(c) What Is *Legislation*?

The term *legislation* refers principally to action by the U.S. Congress, a state legislative body, a local council, or similar governing body. A referendum, initiative, constitutional amendment, or similar procedure can also be legislative activity. The general public acts as the law makers in these actions.

Legislation generally does not include action by an executive branch of a government, such as the promulgation of rules and regulations, nor does it include action by independent regulatory agencies. Litigation activities, including the filing of amicus curiae briefs, does not constitute legislative action.

(d) Substantial Part Test

Under the substantial part test for allowable lobbying activity, the most important concept is the meaning of the word *substantial*. In determining what is substantial, the instructions clarify that activities of flow-through entities owned by the charity must be included in the reporting of lobbying activities. The law offers no general formula for computing *substantial* or *insubstantial* legislative undertakings.

There are at least three ways to measure *substantiality* in this context:

1. Determine what percentage of an organization's annual *expenditures* are devoted to efforts to influence legislation.

2. Apply a percentage to legislative *activities*, in relation to total activities.

3. Ascertain whether an organization had a substantial *impact* on or *influence* over a legislative process simply by virtue of its prestige or because of significant information provided during consideration of legislation.

The true measure of substantiality in the lobbying setting remains elusive. In reports accompanying tax legislation over the years, the Senate Finance Committee characterized this state of affairs well. In 1969, the Committee wrote that the "standards as to the permissible level of [legislative] activities under the present law are so vague as to encourage subjective application of the sanction." In 1976, the Committee portrayed the dilemma this way: "[M]any believe that the standards as to the permissible level of [legislative] activities under present law are too vague and thereby tend to encourage subjective and selective enforcement."

(e) Expenditure Test

The *expenditure test* is an alternative to the subjective substantial part test. The purpose of this test is to offer charitable entities some reasonable certainty concerning how much lobbying they can undertake without endangering their tax-exempt status. The expenditure test election can be done on a year-to-year basis. Charitable organizations that choose not to make the election are governed by the substantial part test. The election is made by filing a form with the IRS.

The expenditure test rules provide definitions of terms such as *legislation*, *influencing legislation*, *direct* lobbying, and *grassroots* lobbying. These terms are essentially the same as those used in connection with the substantial part test discussed in § 9.1(d). In an attempt to define when the legislative process commences (and, therefore, when a lobbying process begins), however, the expenditure test offers a definition of legislative *action*: the "introduction, amendment, enactment, defeat, or repeal of Acts, bills, resolutions, or similar items."

In general, exempt purposes expenditures are paid or incurred by an electing charity to accomplish exempt purposes, including:

- The total amount paid or incurred for religious, charitable, scientific, literary, or educational purposes, or for the prevention of cruelty to children or animals, or to sponsor a national or international amateur sports competition (not including providing athletic facilities or equipment, other than by qualifying amateur sports organizations described in Section 101(j)(2)

- The allocation portion of administrative expenses paid or incurred for the just-listed purposes

- Amounts paid or incurred to try to influence legislation, whether for the purposes described in the first bullet point or not

- Allowances for depreciation or amortization

- Fundraising expenditures, except that exempt purpose expenditures do not include amounts paid to or incurred for either the organization's separate fundraising unit or other organizations, the amounts are primarily for fundraising

The expenditure test measures permissible and impermissible legislative activities of charitable organizations in terms of sets of declining percentages of total exempt purpose expenditures. These expenditures do not include fundraising expenses. The basic permitted level of expenditures for legislative efforts (termed the *lobbying nontaxable amount*) is 20 percent of the first $500,000 of an organization's expenditures for an exempt purpose (including legislative activities), plus 15 percent of the next $500,000, 10 percent of the next $500,000, and 5 percent of any remaining expenditures. The total amount spent for legislative activities in any year by an electing charitable organization may not exceed $1 million. A separate limitation— amounting to 25 percent of the foregoing amounts—is imposed on grassroots lobbying expenditures.

A charitable organization that has elected these limitations and has lobbying expenditures that exceed either the general lobbying ceiling amount or the grassroots lobbying ceiling amount becomes subject to an excise tax of 25 percent of the excess lobbying expenditure. The tax is applied to the greater of the two excesses. Further, if an electing organization's lobbying expenditures normally (an average over a four-year period) exceed 150 percent of either limitation, it will forfeit its tax-exempt status as a charitable organization.

The expenditure test rules contains specific exceptions for five categories of activities. Consequently, the term *influencing legislation* does not include:

1. Making available the results of nonpartisan analysis, study, or research.

2. Providing technical advice or assistance in response to a written request by a governmental body.

3. Appearances before, or communications to, any legislative body in connection with a possible decision of that body that might affect the existence of the organization, its powers and duties, its tax-exempt status, or the deductibility of contributions to it.

4. Communications between the organization and its bona fide members regarding legislation or proposed legislation that is of direct interest to them, unless the communications directly encourage the members to influence legislation or to urge nonmembers to influence legislation.

5. Routine communications with government officials or employees.

The third of these exceptions is known as the *self-defense exception*. Sheltered by this exception is all lobbying by a public charity, as long as it can be reasonably rationalized as coming within one or more of the allowable forms of lobbying.

The fourth exception treats certain communications between an organization and its members more leniently than communications to nonmembers. Expenditures for a communication that refers to, and reflects a view on, specific legislation are not lobbying expenditures if the communication satisfies these requirements:

1. The communication is directed only to members of the organization

2. The specific legislation the communication refers to, and reflects a view on, is of direct interest to the organization and its members

3. The communication does not directly encourage the member to engage in direct lobbying (whether individually or through the organization)

4. The communication does not directly encourage the member to engage in grassroots lobbying (whether individually or through the organization)

Expenditures for a communication directed only to members that refers to, and reflects a view on, specific legislation and that satisfies the requirements of numbers 1, 2, and 4 but does not satisfy the requirements of number 3 are treated as expenditures for direct lobbying. Expenditures for a communication directed only to members that refers to, and reflects a view on specific legislation and satisfies the requirements of numbers 1 and 2, but does not satisfy the requirements of number 4, are treated as grassroots expenditures, whether or not the communication satisfies the requirements of number 3.

There are special rules regarding certain paid mass media advertisements about highly publicized legislation; allocation of mixed purpose expenditures; certain transfers treated as lobbying expenditures; and special rules regarding lobbying on referenda, ballot initiatives, and similar procedures.

Members of an affiliated group are treated as a single organization to measure lobbying expenditures and permitted lobbying expenditures under the expenditure test. Two organizations are affiliated if one is bound by the other organization's decisions on legislative issues (control) or if enough representatives of one belong to the other organization's governing board to cause or prevent action on legislative issues (interlocking directorate). If the organization is not sure whether its group is affiliated, it may ask the IRS for a letter ruling.

Members of an affiliated group measure both lobbying expenditures and permitted lobbying expenditures on the basis of the affiliated group's tax year. If all members of the affiliated group have the same tax year, that year is the tax year of the affiliated group. However, if the affiliated group's members have different tax years, the tax year of the affiliated group is the calendar year, unless all of the members of the group elect otherwise.

In some cases, two organizations have a control relationship that is limited only to lobbying activity because their governing instruments provide that the decisions of one will control the other only as applied to national lobbying efforts. This is known as a *limited control* arrangement. In this event, the instructions provide that the two organizations are subject to these provisions:

- Charge the controlling organization with its own lobbying expenditures and the national legislation expenditures of the affiliated organizations.
- Do not charge the controlling organization with other lobbying expenditures (or other exempt-purpose expenditures) of the affiliated organizations.
- Treat each local organization as though it were not a member of an affiliated group. For example, the local organization should account for its own expenditures only and not any of the national legislation expenditures deemed as incurred by the controlling organization.

In making the determination as to the merits of an election, a number of factors should be considered. Some of the factors include:

1. The certainty of the expenditure test as compared to the subjectivity of the substantial part test
2. The separate and more severe grassroots lobbying limitation of the expenditure test

3. The possibility that the IRS may enforce the substantial part test using one or more standards other than the volume of legislative activity

4. The fact that the time expended by volunteers for lobbying is taken into account for the substantial part test but not for the expenditure test

5. For purposes of determining whether status is lost, lobbying activity is assessed annually under the substantial part test but a four-year averaging rule is applied with the expenditure test

6. The additional record-keeping and reporting responsibilities imposed by the expenditure test

7. The fact that a public charity that has elected the expenditure test may report lobbying expenses to congress by using the tax law definition of lobbying expenses

8. The special exceptions that are available under the expenditure test (such as the self-defense exception)

9. The difficulty of staying below the overall $1 million limitation under the expenditure test in the case of large charities

(f)   Lobbying Taxes

To strengthen the general restriction on a charity's lobbying activity under the substantial part test, a system of excise taxes are imposed. If a charitable organization loses its tax exemption because of attempts to influence legislation, a tax of 5 percent of the *lobbying expenditures* is imposed on the organization. This tax, however, does not apply to an organization that is under the expenditure test or that is ineligible to make this election.

A separate 5-percent tax is applicable to each of the organization's managers (directors, officers, key employees) who agreed to the lobbying expenditures, knowing they were likely to result in revocation of exemption, unless the agreement was not willful and was due to reasonable cause. The burden of proof as to whether a manager knowingly participated in the lobbying expenditure is on the IRS. The IRS has, in every instance involving a charitable organization's excessive lobbying, the discretion as to whether to revoke tax-exempt status, impose these taxes, or do both.

(g)   Lobbying by Other Exempt Organizations

The federal tax law does not restrict lobbying activities of exempt organizations other than charitable ones. The only constraint is that the organization must pursue its exempt functions as its primary purpose and that any lobbying it may do (other than an insubstantial amount) must further that principal requirement. Thus, entities such as social welfare organizations, labor and agricultural organizations, associations/ business leagues, and certain other organizations may engage in substantial lobbying. Special rules can cause members' dues to not be fully deductible in an instance of lobbying by associations/business leagues, labor and agricultural organizations, and social welfare organizations. Legislative activities are not normally exempt functions for political organizations. (See Chapter 10.)

(h) Deductibility of Dues

(1) Nondeductibility of Lobbying Expenditures. There is no business expense deduction for: amounts paid or incurred in connection with lobbying activities (whether by direct or grassroots lobbying); any attempt to influence the general public, or segments of it, with respect to legislative matters or referendums; or any direct communication with a covered executive branch official in an attempt to influence the official action or positions of the official. This deduction disallowance rule, however, does not apply to local legislation. In this context, influencing legislation means (1) any attempt to influence legislation through a lobbying communication and (2) all activities, such as research, preparation, planning, and coordination, including deciding whether to make any lobbying communication, engaged in for a purpose of making or supporting a lobbying communication, even if not made.

A de minimis exception applies in connection with certain in-house expenditures if the organization's total amount of these expenditures for a tax year does not exceed $2,000 (computed without taking into account general overhead costs otherwise allocable to most forms of lobbying). The term *in-house expenditures* means expenditures for lobbying (such as labor and material costs). In-house expenditures do not include payments to a professional lobbyist to conduct lobbying for the organization and dues paid to another organization or other similar payments that are allocable to lobbying (such as association dues).

An organization may use any reasonable method for allocating labor costs and administrative costs to lobbying activities, including a ratio method, a gross-up method, or tax rules concerning allocation of service costs. An organization may disregard time spent by an individual on lobbying activities if less than 5 percent of his or her time was so spent, although this de minimis test is not applicable with respect to direct contact lobbying, which is a meeting, a telephone conversation, letter, or other similar means of communication with the federal or state legislator or covered executive branch official that otherwise qualifies as a lobbying activity.

(2) Annual Notice. Trade, business, and professional associations, and similar organizations, generally are required to provide annual information disclosure to their members, estimating the portion of their dues allocable to lobbying and political expenditures and thus not deductible. Disclosure of this information is made on new Schedule C, Part III-A. The organization is generally required to provide notice to each person paying dues (or similar payments), at the time of assessment or payment of the dues, of the portion of dues that the organization reasonably estimates will be allocable to the organization's lobbying and political expenditures during the year and that is, therefore, not deductible by the member. This estimate must be reasonably calculated to provide organization members with adequate notice of the nondeductible amount. The notice must be provided in a conspicuous and easily recognizable format. These requirements of annual disclosure and notice to members are applicable to all exempt organizations other than charitable entities.

(3) Proxy Tax. If an organization's actual lobbying and political expenditures for a tax year exceed the estimated allocable amount of the expenditures (either because of higher-than-anticipated expenses or lower-than-projected dues receipts), the organization must pay a *proxy tax* on the excess amount or seek permission from the IRS to adjust the following year's notice of estimated expenditures. The proxy tax rate is equal to the highest corporate tax rate in effect for the taxable year. If an organization does not provide its members with reasonable notice of anticipated lobbying and political expenditures allocable to dues, the organization is subject to the proxy tax on its aggregate lobbying and political expenditures for the year.

If an organization elects to pay the proxy tax rather than provide the requisite information disclosure to its members, no portion of any dues or of any payments made by the members of the organization is rendered nondeductible because of the organization's lobbying and political activities. That is, if the organization pays the tax, the dues payments are fully deductible by the members as business expenses (assuming they otherwise qualify). This disclosure notice element is not required, however, in the case of an organization that (1) incurs only de minimis amounts of in-house expenditures, (2) elects to pay the proxy tax on its lobbying expenditures incurred during the tax year, or (3) establishes, pursuant to an IRS regulation or procedures, that substantially all of its dues monies are paid by members who are not entitled to deduct the dues in computing their taxable income.

The concept of de minimis in-house expenditures in this setting is the same as that in the disallowance rules (including the $2,000 maximum). Amounts paid to outside lobbyists or as dues to another organization that lobbies do not qualify for this exception. Regarding this third component, if an organization establishes, to the satisfaction of the IRS, that substantially all of the dues monies that it receives are paid by members who are not entitled to deduct their dues in any event, and obtains a waiver from the IRS, the organization is not subject to a disclosure and notice requirements (or the proxy tax). In this context the term *substantially all* means at least 90 percent. Examples of organizations of this nature are (1) an organization that receives at least 90 percent of its dues monies from members that are tax-exempt charitable organizations and (2) an organization that receives at least 90 percent of its dues monies from members who are individuals not entitled to deduct the dues payments because the payments are not ordinary and necessary business expenses. The IRS provides a complete exemption from the reporting and notice requirements (and proxy tax) for all tax-exempt organizations, other than social welfare organizations that are not veterans' organizations; agricultural organizations; horticultural organizations; trade, business, and professional associations; other business leagues; chambers of commerce; and boards of trade.

If the amount of lobbying expenditures exceeds the amount of dues or other similar payments for the taxable year, the proxy tax is imposed on an amount equal to the dues and similar payments; any excess lobbying expenditures are carried forward to the next taxable year.

§ 9.2 PREPARATION OF SCHEDULE C

Lobbying activity is reported on Schedule C (see Chapter 10 for political activity). In addition, information regarding nondeductibility of dues for certain organizations is reported on Schedule C.

(a) Organizations Required to Report on Schedule C

Organizations that answer "yes" to lines 3, 4, or 5 of Part IV of the Core Form must complete Schedule C. The bullet headings at the top of page 1 of Schedule C also indicate what portions of Schedule C must be completed. As to lobbying activities, charities must report lobbying activities in Part II-A and Part II-B, depending on whether the organization elected to be subject to the expenditure test (see § 9.1(e)).

If the expenditure test election was made with a filing of Form 5768, the organization reports on Part II-A. If no election is made, the lobbying activity is reported on Part II-B under the substantial part test (see § 9.1(d)). The other organizations required to report lobbying activities on Schedule C are social welfare organizations, labor and agricultural organizations, and associations/business leagues. These organizations report in Part III-A and Part III-B.

(b) Part II-A—Expenditure Test

Charities electing to be subject to the expenditure test report their expenditures in Part II-A. The lobbying activity reporting for the expenditure test is more detailed than for the substantial part test. The organization reports its expenditure information in Column (a), and if it is a member of an affiliated group, the group reports in Column (b).

(1) Boxes A and B (Affiliated Groups). Boxes A and B indicate whether the organization is a member of an affiliated group and, if so, whether the "limited control" provision applies. The instructions direct the organization to provide a list of affiliated group members in Part IV of Schedule C including name, address, employer identification number (EIN), and respective lobbying expenses. The list should indicate which organizations made the election, and each member's share of excess lobbying expenditure should be included. Limited control is defined in the instructions as two organizations that are affiliated because their governing instruments and provide that the decisions of one will control the other only on national legislation. Such organizations are subject to certain rules relative to the allocation and reporting of expenditures (see § 9.1(e)).

(2) Lines 1a–1c (Grassroots and Direct Lobbying). In general, lobbying expenditures are expenditures (including allocable overhead and administrative costs) paid or incurred for the purpose of attempting to influence legislation. Through communication with any member or employee of a legislative or similar body, or with any government official or employee who may participate in the formulation of the legislation, and by attempting to affect the opinions of the general public.

To determine if an organization has spent excessive amounts on lobbying, the organization must know which expenditures are lobbying expenditures and which are not lobbying expenditures. An electing public charity's lobbying expenditures for a year are the sum of its expenditures during that year for (1) direct lobbying communications (direct lobbying expenditures) plus (2) grassroots lobbying communications (grassroots expenditures).

Because of the separate limitations on grassroots and direct lobbying (see § 9.1(e)), the respective expenditures are delineated on lines 1a and 1b. The grassroots and direct expenditures are aggregated on line 1c. Report in Column (a) for the organization and Column (b) for the affiliated group.

(3) Line 1d (Other Exempt Purpose Expenditures). On line 1d, report exempt purpose expenses. This expense represents all other expenses of the organization (excluding lobbying expenditures).

(4) Line 1e (Total Exempt Purpose Expenditures). On line 1e, report the total of lobbying expenses and other exempt expenses.

(5) Line 1f (Nontaxable Lobbying Limit). On line 1f, report the expenditure limit based on the sliding scale of allocable expenses under the expenditure test (see § 9.1(e)). The sliding percentage is computed using the organization's total expenditures reported on line 1e.

> **Example.** If an organization has $700,000 of exempt purpose expenditures and $100,000 of lobbying expenditures comprised of $30,000 of grassroots lobbying and $70,000 of direct lobbying expenditures, then $30,000 is reported on line 1a, $70,000 on line 1b, $100,000 on line 1c (total of $30,000 and $70,000). On line 1d, $700,000 is reported. On line 1e, total organization expenses of $800,000 are reported. The general lobbying limitation is $145,000 reported on line 1f. This amount is based on $800,000 of total expenditures with 20% of the first $500,000 or $100,000 (20% × $500,000) plus 15% of $300,000 (the excess over $500,000 ($800,000 − $500,000)) or $45,000 for a total of $145,000 ($100,000 + $45,000).

(6) Line 1g (Nontaxable Grass Roots Lobbying). On line 1g, report the nontaxable grassroots lobbying amount. The grassroots lobbying limitation is 25 percent of the aggregate lobbying limitation reported on line 1f. In the last example, the amount reported on line 1f would be $36,250 (25% × $145,000).

(7) Line 1h (Taxable Grassroots Lobbying). On line 1h, report the amount of excess grassroots lobbying by comparing the limitation of line 1g with the actual grassroots expenditures reported on line 1a. If 1a is less than 1g, insert "0" on line 1h. If the amount on 1a is greater than the line 1g limitation amount, the excess is reported on line 1h. In the last example, insert "0" on line 1h because the grassroots lobbying of $30,000 is less than the $36,250 grassroots lobbying limit. If the grassroots lobbying was $40,000 of the $100,000 expenditures and the total expenditures remained the same, $5,000 would be inserted on line 1h.

(8) Line 1i (Taxable Total Lobbying Expenditures). On line 1i, report the amount of excess total lobbying expenditures by comparing the limitation of line 1f with the total lobbying expenditures reported on line 1c. As with grassroots lobbying, if total expenditures are less than the total limit reported on line 1f, insert "0" on line 1i. If the amount on line 1c exceeds the amount on line 1f, then report the excess on line 1i. In the last example, the amount entered would be zero because total lobbying expenditures are $100,000 with a limit of $145,000. If the total lobbying expenditures were

$150,000 in the example instead of $140,000 and the total expenditures remained at $800,000, $5,000 would be inserted on line 1h ($150,000 − $145,000).

(9) Line 1j (Filing of Return and Payment of Tax). If an amount greater than zero is reported on line 1h or 1i, then indicate "yes" or "no" on line 1i as to whether a Form 4720 is being filed to report the Section 4911 tax for the excess lobbying expenditures (see § 9.1(e).) If the organization reports with an affiliated group, the organization's proportionate share is reported on line 1h and 1i. The instructions also ask the organization to attach an Affiliated Group List showing the amount allocated.

(10) Lines 2a–2f (Four-Year Averaging Under 501(h)). Four-Year Averaging information is reported in lines 2a to 2f to determine if excessive lobbying occurs over a four-year period. If it does, exempt status may be revoked (see § 9.1(e)). The instructions indicate that lines 2a to 2f must be completed for all organizations reporting in Part II-A except in these situations:

- An organization first treated as a Section 501(c)(3) organization in its tax year beginning in 2008 does not have to complete any part of lines 2a through 2f.

- An organization does not have to complete lines 2a through 2f for any period before it is first treated as a Section 501(c)(3) organization.

- If 2008 is the first year for which an organization's first Section 501(h) election is effective, that organization must complete line 2a, Columns (a) and (e). The organization must then complete all of Column (e) to determine whether the amount on line 2c, Column (e), is equal to or less than the lobbying ceiling amount calculated on line 2b and whether the amount on line 2f is equal to or less than the grassroots ceiling amount calculated on line 2e. The organization does not satisfy both tests if either its total lobbying expenditures or grassroots lobbying expenditures exceed the applicable ceiling amounts. When this occurs, all five columns must be completed and a recomputation made unless an exception in bullets 1 or 2 above applies.

- If 2008 is the second or third tax year for which the organization's first Section 501(h) election is in effect, that organization is required to complete only the columns for the years in which the election has been in effect, entering the totals for those years in Column (e). The organization must determine, for those two or three years, whether the amount entered in Column (e), line 2c, is equal to or less than the lobbying ceiling amount reported on line 2b and whether the amount entered in Column (e), line 2f, is equal to or less than the grassroots ceiling amount calculated on line 2e. The organization does not satisfy both tests if either its total lobbying expenditures or grassroots lobbying expenditures exceed applicable ceiling amounts. When that occurs, all five columns must be completed and a recomputation made, unless an exception in the first or second bullet points applies. If the organization is not required to complete all five columns, provide a statement explaining why in Part IV. In the statement, show the ending date of the tax year in which the organization made its first Section 501(h) election and state whether or not that first election was revoked before the start of the organization's tax year that began in 2008.

If the organization belongs to an affiliated group, enter the appropriate affiliated group totals from Column (b), lines 1a through 1i, when completing lines 2a, 2c, 2d, and 2f.

(11) Line 2a (Lobbying Nontaxable Amount). On line 2a, Columns (a) through (e), report the lobbying expenditure limit (nontaxable amount) for the reporting year and prior three years. For years reported on new Schedule C, this is line 1f. For years prior to 2008, the amount reported is line 41 of Schedule A, Part VI-A.

(12) Line 2b (Lobbying Ceiling Amount). On line 2b, Column (e), report the lobbying ceiling amount equal to 150 percent of line 2a, Column (e). For example, if the lobbying nontaxable amount in Column 2a is $100,000, the lobbying ceiling amount reported on line 2b would be $150,000 (150 percent of $100,000). Columns (a) through (d) are not completed for line 2b.

(13) Line 2c (Total Lobbying Expenditures). On line 2c, Columns (a) through (e), report total lobbying expenditures for reporting year and prior three years. For years prior to 2008, enter the amount from line 38 of Schedule A, Part VI-A filed for each year. For 2008 and later years, enter the amount from line 1c of Schedule C, Part II-A filed for each year.

(14) Line 2d (Grassroots Nontaxable Amount). On line 2, Columns (a) through (e), report the grassroots nontaxable amount for reporting years and prior three years. For years prior to 2008, enter the amount from line 42 of Schedule A, Part VI-A filed for each year. For 2008 and later years, enter the amount from line 1g of Schedule C, Part II-A filed for each year.

(15) Line 2e (Grassroots Ceiling Amount). On line 2e, Column (a), report the grassroots ceiling amount equal to 150 percent of line 2d Column (e).

(16) Line 2f (Grassroots Lobbying Expenditures). On line 2f, Columns (a) through (e), report grassroots lobbying expenditures for reporting year and prior three years. For years prior to 2008, enter the amount from line 36 of Schedule A, Part VI-A filed for each year. For 2008 and later years, enter the amount from line 1a of Schedule C, Part II-A filed for each year.

(c) Part II-B—Substantial Part Test

Organizations that did not elect to be subject to the expenditure test, or have revoked a previous election, are subject to the substantial part test and report lobbying activity in Part II-B (see § 9.1(d)).

(1) Line 1a (Reporting of Volunteers). On line 1a, indicate "yes" or "no" as to whether the organization used volunteers to engage in lobbying activity. If volunteers were used to engage in lobbying activity, the "yes" box is checked in Column (a). Column (b) is not completed for line 1a.

(2) Line 1b (Paid Staff or Management). On line 1b, Column (a) indicate "yes" or "no" as to whether the organization paid staff or management to conduct lobbying activity. In Column (b), report the actual dollar amount. In the case of paid staff or management, the allocable portion of the individual's salary should be reported in Column (b). Any reasonable method can be used. For example, one common method used to allocate an employee's salary to lobbying activities would be to divide the employee's lobbying hours by total hours to determine a percentage of total compensation.

(3) Line 1c (Media Advertisements). On line 1c, indicate "yes" or "no" in Column (a) as to whether the organization engaged in media advertisements. The dollar amount incurred for the media advertisements should be reported in Column (b).

(4) Line 1d (Mailings). On line 1d, Column (a), indicate "yes" or "no" as to whether the mailings were made to members, legislators, or the public in a lobbying activity. In Column (b), report the dollar amount incurred for the mailings. The actual cost to mail the items should be added to the cost of allocable staff time and overhead to determine the total dollar amount.

(5) Line 1e (Publication and Broadcasts). On line 1e, Column (a), indicate "yes" or "no" as to whether the organization published materials or made broadcasts to influence legislation. In Column (b), report the cost of the activity.

(6) Line 1f (Grants to Other Organizations). On line 1f, Column (a), indicate "yes" or "no" as to whether grants were made to other organizations specifically for lobbying purposes. In Column (b), report the amount of the grants.

(7) Line 1g (Direct Contact with the Legislators and Their Staffs). On line 1g, Column (a), indicate "yes" or "no" as to whether the organization contacted legislators, their staffs, governmental officials, or a legislative body in an effort to influence legislation. In Column (b), report the cost associated with the contact including personnel time.

(8) Line 1h (Rallies, Demonstrations, and Seminars). On line 1h, Column (a), indicate "yes" or "no" as to whether the organization engaged in rallies, demonstrations, seminars, conventions, speeches, lectures, or any other means to influence legislations. In Column (b), report the dollar amount allocable to such activities.

(9) Line 1i (Other Activities). On line 1i, indicate "yes" or "no" as to whether other lobbying activities where conducted by the organization. The instructions indicate that the detailed description of the other activities should be described in Part IV. This description should include all lobby activities, whether expenses were incurred or not. For example, even lobbying activities carried out by unreimbursed volunteers should be reported.

(10) Line 1j (Total). On line 1j, report the totals for lines (c) through (i).

(11) Line 2a (More than Insubstantial Lobbying?). On line 2a, indicate "yes" or "no" as to whether the activities listed in lines 1a through 1j resulted in loss of the organization's Section 501(c)(3) status because the organization engaged in more than insubstantial lobbying.

(12) Line 2b (Taxable Lobbying). On line 2b, indicate the tax resulting from the excess lobbying activity. The organization must pay a 5-percent tax on the amount of lobbying expenditures. Column (a) is not applicable to line 2b (see § 9.1(f)).

(13) Line 2c (Organization Manager Tax). On line 2c, insert the amount of tax applicable to the organization manager for the excess lobbying expenditures. The tax is 5 percent of the lobbying expenditures. Column (a) is not applicable to line 2c (see § 9.1(f)).

(14) Line 2d (Form 4720 Filing). On line 2d, indicate "yes" or "no" as to whether the organization filed Form 4720 for the year. This is the form used to report and pay the taxes listed in lines 2b and 2c. Column (b) is not applicable.

(d) Part III-A—Deductibility of Dues

This part is completed by Section 501(c)(4) organizations (social welfare organizations), Section 501(c)(5) labor organizations (but not agricultural or horticulture organizations), and Section 501(c)(6) organizations (associations/business leagues). The issue is what portion of the dues paid by members to the respective organizations are partially nondeductible because of the organization's lobbying and political activity.

(1) Lines 1 (Nondeductible Dues). On line 1, indicate "yes" or "no" as to whether substantially all (90 percent or more) of the dues are nondeductible by members due to the level of lobbying and political activity conducted by the organization. The instructions indicate that "yes" should be answered if any of these exceptions apply:

- Local associations of employees and veterans' organizations described in Section 501(c)(4) but not Section 501(c)(4) social welfare organizations
- Labor unions and other labor organizations described in Section 501(c)(5) but not Section 501(c)(5) agricultural and horticultural organizations
- Section 501(c)(4), (5), and (6) organizations that receive more than 90 percent of their dues from
  - Organizations exempt from tax under Section 501(a), other than Section 501(c)(4), (5), and (6) organizations
  - State or local governments
  - Entities whose income is exempt from tax under Section 115
  - Organizations described in the first two bullets above.
- Section 501(c)(4) and (5) organizations that receive more than 90 percent of their annual dues from:
  - Persons
  - Families
  - Entities

who each paid annual dues of an amount equal to or less than a minimum amount adjusted annually for inflation each year and reported in the annual revenue procedures

- Any organization that receives a Private Letter Ruling from the IRS stating that the organization satisfies the Section 6033(a)(3) exception

- Any organization that keeps records to substantiate the 90 percent or more of its members cannot deduct their dues (or similar amounts) as business expenses whether or not any part of their dues are used for lobbying purposes

- Any organization that is not a membership organization

Note: The instructions caution that special rules treat affiliated social welfare organizations, agricultural and horticultural organizations, and business leagues as part of a single organization for purposes of meeting the nondeductible dues exception.

---

(2) Line 2 (In-House Lobbying). On line 2, indicate "yes" or "no" as to whether the organization satisfies these criteria for the $2,000 in-house lobbying exception. Answer "yes" if the organization meets both requirements:

- Did not make any political or foreign lobbying expenditures during the 2008 reporting year

- Made lobbying expenditures during the 2008 reporting year consisting only of in-house direct lobbying expenditures totaling $2,000 or less but excluding:

  ○ Any allocable overhead expenditures

  ○ All direct lobbying expenses of a local counsel regarding legislation of direct interest to the organization or its members.

If the organization's in-house direct lobbying expenditures during the 2008 reporting year were $2,000 or less, but the organization also paid or incurred other lobbying or political expenditures during the 2008 reporting year, it should answer "no" to question 2. If the organization is required to complete Part III-B, the $2,000 or less of in-house direct lobbying expenditures should not be included in the total on line 2a.

(3) Line 3 (Lobbying and Political Expenses Carryover). On line 3, indicate "yes" or "no" as to whether the organization on its prior year report agreed to carryover an amount to be included in the current year's reasonable estimate of lobbying and political expenses.

(e) Part III-B—Dues Notice, Reporting Requirements, and Proxy Tax

This section is completed by social welfare organizations, labor and agriculture organizations, and associations/business leagues if the questions on lines 1 and 2 in Part III-A are answered "no" or the question on line Part III-A is answered "yes." An organization that is required to complete Part III-B must send dues notices to its members at the time of assessment or payment of dues, unless the organization chooses to pay the proxy tax instead of informing its members of the nondeductible portion of its dues. These dues notices must reasonably estimate the dues allocable to the nondeductible lobbying and political expenditures reported in Part III-B, line 2a. An organization that checked "yes" for Part III-A, line 3, must send dues notices to its members at the time of assessment or payment of dues and include the amount it agreed to carry over in its reasonable estimate of the dues allocable to the nondeductible lobbying and political expenditures reported on Part III-B, line 2a.

The tables that follow are provided in the instructions for assistance in determining whether Part III-B must be completed and whether a proxy tax must be paid.

IF . . .	THEN . . .
The organization's lobbying and political expenses are more than its membership dues for the year,	The organization must: (a) Allocate all membership dues to its lobbying and political activities, and (b) Carry forward any excess lobbying and political expenses to the next tax year.
The organization: (a) Had only de minimis in-house expenses ($2,000 or less) and no other nondeductible lobbying or political expenses (including any amount it agreed to carry-over); or (b) Paid a proxy tax, instead of notifying its members on the allocation of dues to lobbying and political expenses; or (c) Established that substantially all of its membership dues, etc., are not deductible by members.	The organization need not disclose to its membership the allocation of dues, etc., to its lobbying and political activities.

Proxy Tax

IF . . .	THEN . . .
The organization's actual lobbying and political expenses are more than it estimated in its dues notices,	The organization is liable for a proxy tax on the excess.
The organization: (a) Elects to pay the proxy tax, and (b) Chooses not to give its members a notice allocating dues to lobbying and political campaign activities,	All the members' dues remain eligible for a section 162 trade or business expense deduction.
The organization: (a) Makes a reasonable estimate of dues allocable to nondeductible lobbying and political activities, and (b) Agrees to adjust its estimate in the following year.*	The IRS may permit a waiver of the proxy tax.

*A facts-and-circumstances test determines whether a reasonable estimate was made in good faith or not.

(1) Line 1 (Dues, Assessments and Similar Amounts). On line 1, report the dues, assessments, and similar amounts the organization collected from its members. Dues are the amounts the organization requires a member to pay in order to be recognized as a member. Payments that are similar to dues include: (1) member's voluntary payments, (2) assessments to cover basic operating costs, and (3) special assessment to conduct lobbying and political activities.

(2) Line 2 (Lobbying and Political Expenditures). On line 2a, report the total amount of expenses incurred in the 2008 reporting year in connection with (1) influencing legislation, (2) participating or entering any political campaign on behalf of (or in opposition to) any candidate for public office, (3) attempting to influence any segment of the general public with respect to elections, legislative matters or referendums, or (4) communicating directly with the covered executive branch official in an attempt to influence the official's actions or positions of such official. Do not include on line 2a: (1) any direct lobbying of any local council or any similar governing body with respect to legislation of direct interest to the organization or its members, (2) in-house direct lobbying expenditures if the total of such expenditures is $2,000 or less (excluding allocable overhead), or (3) political expenditures for which the Section 527(f) tax is being paid (on Form 1120-POL)

Reduce the current year's lobbying expenditures, but not below zero, by cost previously allocated in a prior year to lobbying activities that were canceled after a return reporting those costs were filed. Carry forward any amounts not used as a reduction to subsequent years.

Include on line 2b: (1) lobbying and political expenditures carried over from the preceding tax year, and (2) an amount equal to the taxable lobbying and political expenditures reported on line 85f for the preceding tax year, if the organization received a waiver from the proxy tax imposed on that amount. (See Appendix B for allocation methods provided in the instructions.)

(3) Line 3 (Aggregate Nondeductible Dues). On line 3, report the total amount of nondeductible dues, assessments, and similar amounts received allocable to the reporting year and included in the member notice (Section 6033(a)(1)(A)). The instructions provide this example:

> **Example.** If membership dues were $100,000 for the reporting year, and the organization timely provides notices to members that 25 percent of the member dues are nondeductible, the line 3 entry should be $25,000.

(4) Line 4 (Carryover Lobbying and Political Expenditures). On line 4, report the amount by which line 2c exceeds the amount on line 3. If notices were sent at the time of assessment or payment of dues, include the amount on line 4 that the organization agrees to carry over to the reasonable estimate of nondeductible lobbying and political expenditures next year and include the amount on Part III-B, line 2b (carryover lobbying and political expenditures) or the equivalent, on the next year's Form 990, Schedule C. If the organization did not send notices to its members, enter "0" on line 4.

(5) Line 5 (Taxable Lobbying and Political Expenditures—Proxy Tax). On line 5, report the taxable amount of dues, assessments, and similar amounts received: (1) allocable to the reporting year, and (2) attributable to lobbying and political expenditures that the organization did not timely notify its members were non-deductible. Report this tax on Form 990-T. The instructions provide these guidelines:

- If the amount on line 1 (dues, etc.) *is greater* than the amount of line 2c (lobbying and political expenditures), then:

    Line 2c (lobbying and political expenditures), *less* line 3 (dues shown in notices), *less* line 4 (carryover) *equals* line 5 (taxable lobbying and political expenditures).

- If the amount on line 1 (dues, etc.) *is less* than the amount of line 2c (lobbying and political expenditures), then:

    Line 1 (dues, etc.), *less* line 3 (dues shown in notices), *less* line 4 (carryover) *equals* line 5 (taxable lobbying and political expenditures), *and*

    Line 2c (lobbying and political expenditures), *less* line 1 (dues, etc.) *equals* the excess amount to be carried over to the following tax year reported in Part III-B, line 2b (carryover lobbying and political expenses), or its equivalent, on the next year's Form 990 along with the amounts the organization agreed to carry over in line 4

An organization is subject to the proxy tax of 2008 reporting year for underreported lobbying and political expenses only to the extent that these expenses (if actually reported) would have resulted in a proxy tax liability for that year. A waiver of proxy tax for the tax year applies only to reported expenditures.

An organization that underreports its lobbying and political expenses is also subject to the Section 6652(c) daily penalty for filing an incomplete or inaccurate return (see Form 990 general instruction H).

See Appendix B for examples provided in the instructions.

(f) Part IV—Supplemental Information

This part is provided so that descriptions required for Part I-A, line 1, Part I-B, line 4, Part I-C, line 5, Part II-A, line 1, Part II-A, line 2a, and Part II-B, line 1. The instructions also indicate that this part should be used for any additional information the organization desires to disclose. Include the specific part and line number that the response supports, in the order in which they appear in Schedule C.

§9.3 SCHEDULE C COMPLIANCE TASKS

For purposes of preparing Schedule C as it applies to lobbying activities, the organization should consider these 13 compliance tasks.

1. **Identify lobbying activities.** Review all activities to determine if the activity constitutes lobbying.

2. **Identify direct lobbying.** Ascertain whether the activities are direct lobbying. Direct lobbying includes communications with legislators and their staffs and the general public relative to a public referendum, initiative, constitutional amendment, or similar procedure.

3. **Identify grassroots lobbying.** Ascertain whether the activities relate to communication with the general public. Educational activities that include a "call

to action" may constitute lobbying activities. In this event, even the expenditures incurred in the educational portion of the activity may be viewed as expenditures for the lobbying activity.

4. **Track expenses.** All expenses incurred in the identified lobbying activities should be documented, including travel reimbursement, printing, mailing costs, speaker fees, and research materials. The grassroots expenditures should be separated from the direct expenditures.

5. **Track staff time.** The time spent by staff members in lobbying activity should be tracked. Each employee should keep their time records attributable to the lobbying activity with direct activity separated from grassroots activity.

6. **Track volunteer time.** Volunteer time should be included in addition to tracking staff time. Time sheets or time cards should be completed and submitted for volunteers.

7. **Consider 501(h) election.** Review advantages and disadvantages of Section 501(h) election. For example, does the organization have volunteers? Is the self-defense exception important? Is the organization's budget substantial? (See § 9.1(e).)

8. **Make dues calculation.** Gather dues information and prepare procedures to track lobbying and political expenditures of the filing organization. Consider various allocation options listed in Appendix B.

9. **Mail nondeductible dues notice.** Does the organization provide adequate notice of the nondeductible dues to its members. This is applicable to the following organizations: social welfare organizations, labor agricultural organizations, and associations/business leagues.

10. **Review exceptions to notice.** Review exceptions to nondeductible dues notice provisions listed in § 9.2(d)(1) and (2).

11. **Identify affiliated group.** If the organization is affiliated with other organizations and it elects the expenditure test, the lobbying expenditures of all members must be gathered using the same methods as discussed above.

12. **Compile data for four-year averaging.** Compile data for years 2005 through 2007 using prior year Form 990s if the expenditure test is elected.

13. **Review prior-year reporting.** Review prior-year Form 990s and dues calculations to determine if any carryovers exist. In some cases, certain items will carry over into the next filing year.

CHAPTER TEN

Schedule C—Political Activities

Charitable organizations are prohibited from engaging in political campaign activity, but other exempt organizations are allowed to engage in some political campaign activity. Organizations that engage in permissible political activity must pay a tax on the lesser of their political campaign expenditures and their net investment income. For many years, Congress and the IRS have believed that there is significant noncompliance in this area. In both 2004 and 2006, the IRS conducted audit programs to ascertain the level of noncompliance. The results of the program indicate that a high percentage of charities engaged in prohibited political campaign activity. There is very little disclosure of political campaign activities in the current Form 990. Schedule C of the new Form 990 significantly expands the disclosure of political campaign activity.

§ 10.1 LAW AND POLICY

Charitable organizations may not "participate in, or intervene in (including the publishing or distributing of statements), any political campaign on behalf of or in opposition to any candidate for public office." Other exempt organizations may engage in political campaign activities, provided this activity does not become the organization's primary purpose.

(a) Charitable Organizations

Charitable organizations may not engage in political campaign activity. Most of the law amplifying the political campaign proscription is found in IRS rulings. For many years the rulings consistently held that nearly any activity relating to a political process would prevent the charitable organization from retaining exempt status. In recent years, however, the IRS has relented somewhat, with the agency ruling that voter education activities are permissible for charitable organizations. The instructions to Form 990 cite Revenue Ruling 2007-41 as a source for examples of both prohibited political campaign activity and permissible activity. As an illustration, a charitable organization can prepare and disseminate a compilation of the voting records of legislators on a variety of subjects, as long as there is no editorial comment and no approval or disapproval of the voting records is implied. A charitable organization may also conduct public forums where there is a fair and impartial treatment of political candidates.

(1) Definition of Participation or Intervention in a Political Campaign. Participation or intervention in a political campaign includes any activity that would, directly or indirectly, support or oppose a particular candidate for public office. Such activities need not involve an explicit endorsement of (or statement in opposition to) a candidate. Implicit endorsements can also constitute prohibited activity, such as an advertisement applauding a candidate for a particular position without specifically asking voters to vote for that candidate. Making contributions to organizations that engage primarily or exclusively in political activity is considered political activity. Contributions are also a violation of federal election law. Political activity can involve relatively covert attempts to influence the general public with respect to any particular election. For example, developing or distributing advertising that has the effect of encouraging the public to support a particular candidate or party is political activity.

The touchstone for distinguishing prohibited electioneering from permissible election-related activities is that the latter must be strictly nonpartisan in both form and substance. In determining whether an activity meets this standard, the IRS will consider evidence as to a partisan motive in conducting the activity and whether the organization should have reasonably foreseen that the activity would benefit a particular candidate or party.

While there are many election-related activities a charity can support, no single fact will prevent an activity from being partisan for federal tax purposes. For example, a nonpartisan motive alone is not sufficient if the activity is, in fact, biased in favor of one candidate. Similarly, avoiding explicit endorsements of candidates is necessary but not sufficient; for example, a mailing asking voters to "Remember who will protect unborn children on Election Day" would almost certainly be a violation of federal tax law if it were clear to recipients which candidate they were encouraged to support, even though the advertisement does not name a candidate. An advertisement applauding a candidate for a particular position, without specifically asking voters to vote for that candidate, is also prohibited.

Any activity conducted in coordination with a candidate, a candidate's campaign, or a political party, such as cooperating in the timing of an event or release of a report, is clearly prohibited. Such activities are generally barred both by federal tax law and by applicable federal or state election law.

(2) Definition of Candidate. A person is a candidate for public office (i.e., elected office at the federal, state, or local level) if *any* of these events have occurred:

- Public announcement of candidacy.
- Official filing as a candidate.
- Formation of a committee for fundraising or exploratory purposes
- Formation of a coordinated "Draft X for Y Position" effort, such as the "Draft Wesley Clark for President" effort, even if the person publicly states he is not running for Y position; media speculation that the person may run for public office is *not* the formation of a coordinated draft effort, however.
- The walk-like-a-duck rule: taking actions that effectively make the person a candidate even without a formal declaration or committee. An example of this situation would be a "listening tour" of a state by a person who is widely

considered a likely candidate for the upcoming election for U.S. Senate election. If it walks like a candidate and talks like a candidate, it is probably a candidate.

(3) Election-Related Activities that Are Not Political Activities. Revenue Procedure 2007-41 provides a number of examples of both permissible and impermissible activities.

(i) NONPARTISAN VOTER REGISTRATION AND GET-OUT-THE-VOTE (GOTV)

Charities may engage in, and fund, voter registration and get-out-the-vote (GOTV) activities if these activities are strictly nonpartisan. A charitable organization is also permitted to focus its voter registration and GOTV activities on a particular demographic group if that group has historically been discriminated against. Such groups include, for example, most ethnic minority groups.

A charity may not, however, target its election-related activities based on party affiliation or positions on candidates. For example, a GOTV effort may not screen the people it will take to the polls by first asking them what party they belong to, or whether they support or oppose a particular candidate.

A charity engaged in voter registration and GOTV activities must not express support for or opposition to any candidate or political party in any way. For example, the driver of the GOTV van should not be handing out candidate flyers or wearing a political party button. Further, if a caller asks questions about candidate preferences, any suggestion of support or opposition to a candidate must be avoided. Some examples include:

- "We are a nonpartisan organization and therefore do not support or oppose any particular candidate."

- "You should learn about the candidates and their positions and then decide who to vote for based on what is important to you."

Example. B, a charity that promotes community involvement, sets up a booth at the state fair where citizens can register to vote. The signs and banners in and around the booth give only the name of the organization, the date of the next upcoming statewide election, and notice of the opportunity to register. No reference to any candidate or political party is made by the volunteers staffing the booth or in the materials available at the booth, other than the official voter registration forms, which allow registrants to select a party affiliation. B is not engaged in political campaign intervention when it operates this voter registration booth.

(ii) NONPARTISAN VOTER EDUCATION

Charities are permitted to engage in voter education activities, as long as such activities are conducted in a strictly nonpartisan manner. Such activities can include educating voters on issues, candidate questionnaires, legislative scorecards, and candidate forums.

Issue Education. The key to permitted voter education is a focus on issues as opposed to candidates. Thus, it is appropriate to remind voters about the important issues to be decided by the politicians elected to office, as long as no mention is made of any particular candidate or political party. The one exception is if an issue has become one of the key distinctions between candidates.

Example. C is a charity that educates the public on environmental issues. Candidate G is running for the state legislature, and an important element of her platform is challenging the environmental policies of the incumbent. Shortly before the election, C sets up a telephone bank to call registered voters in the district in which Candidate G is seeking election. In the phone conversations, C's representative tells the voter about the importance of environmental issues and asks questions about the voter's views on these issues. If the voter appears to agree with the incumbent's position, C's representative thanks the voter and ends the call. If the voter appears to agree with candidate G's position, C's representative reminds the voter about the upcoming election, stresses the importance of voting in the election, and offers to provide transportation to the polls. C is engaged in political campaign intervention when it conducts this get-out-the-vote drive.

(iii) CANDIDATE QUESTIONNAIRES

Candidate questionnaires will be nonpartisan only if they carefully avoid any suggestion of support for or opposition to any candidates. In general, this means that questionnaires must have these characteristics:

- They are sent to all candidates.

- The organization publishes all responses.

- The questions and list of issues do not indicate a bias toward the organization's preferred answer.

- The organization does not compare the responses to its preferred answers, or otherwise grade or rate the answers.

- The questions are selected on the basis of their interest to the public at large and cover a wide range of issues relevant to the elected public office at issue.

- The organization does not edit the candidates' responses (except to cut off a response to conform to a length limit, if needed).

(iv) LEGISLATIVE SCORECARDS

Legislative scorecards will be nonpartisan only if they are not disguised attempts to support or oppose particular candidates. In general, this means that scorecards must have these characteristics:

- They are published on a regular basis (i.e., in both election and nonelection years).

- They are published on a timetable unrelated to the election cycle (e.g., for the organization's annual meeting or after each legislative session).

- They include the voting records of all members of the legislative body representing the region in which the publication is distributed.

- They do not identify individual legislators as candidates.

- They do not refer to an upcoming election.

- They report on votes on a broad range of issues.

- They do not express the organization's agreement or disagreement with particular votes (e.g., by pluses or minuses) unless the distribution is very circumscribed (e.g., only to the organization's membership) and the publication acknowledges the "inherent difficulty of evaluating legislators on simply a few selected votes."

(v)   CANDIDATE FORUMS

A charity can support or sponsor a candidate forum, but only if the forum is completely nonpartisan. In general, that means the forum must have these characteristics:

- All legally qualified candidates are invited. (There is some leeway to exclude candidates with only de minimis support based on independent polls.)
- At least two candidates attend for each position.
- The questions are prepared and presented by an independent nonpartisan panel, or, for a forum has been widely advertised to the public, questions from the audience.
- The topics discussed cover a broad range of issues of interest to the public.
- Each candidate has an equal opportunity to present his or her views on the issues discussed.
- The moderator does not comment on the questions or otherwise make comments that imply approval or disapproval of any of the candidates or their positions.

(vi)   CANDIDATE APPEARANCES

The IRS has also stated that a charity can invite all of the candidates to speak at a meeting or other event, as long as each candidate is given an equivalent speaking opportunity. The IRS has provided this example of what is permitted:

> **Example.** Minister E is the minister of Church N. In the month prior to the election, Minister E invited the three congressional candidates for the district in which Church N is located to address the congregation, one each on three successive Sundays, as part of regular worship services. Each candidate was given an equal opportunity to address and field questions on a wide variety of topics from the congregation. Minister E's introduction of each candidate included no comments on their qualifications or any indication of a preference for any candidate.

(4) Other Permitted Activities

(i)   PARTICIPATION BY CANDIDATES IN EVENTS FOR NONCANDIDACY REASONS

A charity may support an event involving a candidate if the candidate is involved for reasons other than his or her candidacy and certain conditions are met. For example, the candidate may be a current public official. The conditions that must be met are:

- The individual is invited based on his or her current position or expertise and not on candidacy.
- There is no mention of the public official's candidacy in any of the literature relating to the event or during the event itself (this includes asking the speaker not to mention his or her candidacy during the event).

- No campaign activity (such as fundraising) occurs during or in connection with the event.

The IRS has provided these examples of permitted activities:

Example 1. Chairman H is the chairman of the board of Hospital Q, a charity. Hospital Q is building a new wing. Chairman H invites Congressman Z, the representative for the district containing Hospital Q, to attend the groundbreaking ceremony for the new wing. Congressman Z is running for reelection at the time. Chairman H makes no reference in her introduction to Congressman Z's candidacy or the election. Congressman Z also makes no reference to his candidacy or the election and does not do any fundraising while at Hospital Q. Hospital Q has not intervened in a political campaign.

Example 2. University X is a charity. X publishes an alumni newsletter on a regular basis. Individual alumni are invited to send in updates about themselves which are printed in each edition of the newsletter. After receiving an update letter from Alumnus Q, X prints the following: "Alumnus Q, class of 'XX is running for mayor of Metropolis." The newsletter does not contain any reference to this election or to Alumnus Q's candidacy other than this statement of fact. University X has not intervened in a political campaign.

Example 3. Mayor G attends a concert performed by Symphony S, a charity in City Park. The concert is free and open to the public. Mayor G is a candidate for reelection, and the concert takes place after the primary and before the general election. During the concert, the chairman of S's board addresses the crowd and says, "I am pleased to see Mayor G here tonight. Without his support, these free concerts in City Park would not be possible. We will need his help if we want these concerts to continue next year so please support Mayor G in November as he has supported us." As a result of these remarks, Symphony S has engaged in political campaign intervention.

Example 4. Church P is located in the state capital. Minister G customarily acknowledges the presence of any public officials present during services. During the state gubernatorial race, Lieutenant Governor Y, a candidate, attended a Wednesday evening prayer service in the church. Minister G acknowledged the Lieutenant Governor's presence in his customary manner, saying "We are happy to have worshiping with us this evening Lieutenant Governor Y." Minister G made no reference in his welcome to the Lieutenant Governor's candidacy or the election.

Example 5. Minister H is the minister of Church Q. Church Q is building a community center. Minister H invites Congressman Z, the representative for the district containing Church Q, to attend the groundbreaking ceremony for the community center. Congressman Z is running for reelection at the time. Minister H makes no reference in her introduction to Congressman Z's candidacy or the election. Congressman Z also makes no reference to his candidacy or the election and does not do any fundraising while at Church Q.

(ii) FUNDRAISING BY CANDIDATES FOR A CHARITY

Candidates and current federal government officials are allowed to raise funds for tax-exempt organizations, without limitation, if either (1) the organization does not make expenditures for activities in connection with federal election, or (2) the organization's principal purpose is not to conduct such activities and the solicitation is not to obtain funds for such activities. To comply with these conditions, a candidate or officeholder may rely on a certification from the Section 501(c) organization that its principal purpose is not to engage in activities in connection with any federal election. If these conditions are not met, however, such an individual can still solicit contributions for a charity for voter identification or get-out-the-vote activity as long as the solicitation is made only to individuals and the amount solicited from any particular individual does not exceed $20,000 per calendar year. There are no restrictions, as of yet, on state and local candidates and officeholders raising funds for tax-exempt charitable organizations.

One recent ruling found that the fundraising activity did not entail participation in political campaigns because the letters were not mailed to the jurisdictions represented by the two candidates, nothing in the letters suggested that contributions be made to the campaigns, and the results of the survey contained in the letters were not made available to the candidates. The IRS stated that, in determining whether the communication constitutes an intervention in a political campaign, the determination does not hinge on whether the communication constitutes express advocacy for federal election purposes; rather, for purposes of exempt status as a charity, one looks to the effect of the communication as a whole, including whether support for or opposition to a candidate for public office is expressed or implied.

National committees of a political party are prohibited from soliciting or making donations to charities, including charities that make expenditures in connection with an election for federal office. In order not to be covered by this provision, a charity must provide a certification that it has not made and does not intend to make any such expenditures during the current election cycle. A similar prohibition applies to state, district, and local committees of a political party.

(iii) ADVERTISEMENTS

An IRS ruling states that all facts and circumstances must be considered to determine whether issue advertisements are political activities but then provides two lists of specific factors: one list of six factors that tend to show that an issue advertisement is political activity ("political factors") and one list of five factors that tend to show it is not ("nonpolitical factors"). The political factors are, verbatim:

1. The communication identifies a candidate for public office.
2. The timing of the communication coincides with an electoral campaign.
3. The communication targets voters in a particular election.
4. The communication identifies the candidate's position on the public policy issue that is the subject of the communication.
5. The position of the candidate on the public policy issue has been raised as distinguishing the candidate from others in the campaign, either in the communication itself or in other public communications.
6. The communication is not part of an ongoing series of substantially similar advocacy communications by the organization on the same issue.

The nonpolitical factors are, verbatim:

1. The absence of any one or more of the [political factors].

2. The communication identifies specific legislation, or a specific event outside the control of the organization, that the organization hopes to influence.

3. The timing of the communication coincides with a specific event outside the control of the organization that the organization hopes to influence, such as a legislative vote or other major legislative action (for example, a hearing before a legislative committee on the issue that is the subject of the communication).

4. The communication identifies the candidate solely as a government official who is in a position to act on the public policy issue in connection with the specific event (such as a legislator who is eligible to vote on the legislation).

5. The communication identifies the candidate solely in the list of key or principal sponsors of the legislation that is the subject of the communication.

The ruling then applies these factors to six factual situations. Two of the situations provide particularly useful illustrations of the application of these factors:

Situation 2. O, a trade association, advocates for increased international trade. Senator C represents State V in the United States Senate. O prepares and finances a full-page newspaper ad that is published in several large circulation newspapers in State V shortly before an election in which Senator C is a candidate for nomination in a party primary. The ad states that increased international trade is important to a major industry in State V. The ad states that S. 24, a pending bill in the United States Senate, would provide manufacturing subsidies to certain industries to encourage export of their products. The ad also states that several manufacturers in State V would benefit from the subsidies, but Senator C has opposed similar measures supporting increased international trade in the past. The ad ends with the statement "Call or write Senator C to tell him to vote for S. 24." International trade concerns have not been raised as an issue distinguishing Senator C from any opponent. S. 24 is scheduled for a vote in the United States Senate before the election, soon after the date that the ad is published in the newspapers. The IRS concluded that this ad is *not* political activity.

Situation 3. P, a social welfare organization, advocates for better health care. Senator D represents State W in the United States Senate. P prepares and finances a full-page newspaper ad that is published repeatedly in several large circulation newspapers in State W beginning shortly before an election in which Senator D is a candidate for re-election. The ad is not part of an ongoing series of substantially similar advocacy communications by P on the same issue. The ad states that a public hospital is needed in a major city in State W but that the public hospital cannot be built without federal assistance. The ad further states that Senator D has voted in the past year for two bills that would have provided the federal funding necessary for the hospital. The ad then ends with the statement "Let Senator D know you agree about the need for federal funding for hospitals." Federal funding for hospitals has not been raised as an issue distinguishing Senator D from any opponent. At the time the ad is published, a bill providing federal funding for hospitals has been introduced in the United States Senate, but no legislative vote or other major legislative activity on that bill is scheduled in the Senate. The IRS concluded that this ad *is* political activity.

An example of when a communication does not become political activity follows.

> **Example.** University O, a charity prepares and finances a full-page newspaper advertisement that is published in several large-circulation newspapers in State V shortly before an election in which Senator C is a candidate for nomination in a party primary. Senator C represents State V in the United States Senate. The advertisement states that S. 24, a pending bill in the United States Senate, would provide additional opportunities for State V residents to attend college, but Senator C has opposed similar measures in the past. The advertisement ends with the statement "Call or write Senator C to tell him to vote for S. 24." Educational issues have not been raised as an issue distinguishing Senator C from any opponent. S. 24 is scheduled for a vote in the United States Senate before the election, soon after the date that the advertisement is published in the newspapers. Even though the advertisement appears shortly before the election and identifies Senator C's position on the issue as contrary to O's position, University O has not violated the political campaign intervention prohibition because the advertisement does not mention the election or the candidacy of Senator C, education issues have not been raised as distinguishing Senator C from any opponent, and the timing of the advertisement and the identification of Senator C are directly related to the specifically identified legislation University O is supporting and appears immediately before the United States Senate is scheduled to vote on that particular legislation. The candidate identified, Senator C, is an officeholder who is in a position to vote on the legislation.

(iv) PERSONAL ACTIVITIES OF STAFF

When a charity employee speaks on behalf of the organization or uses the organization resources, he or she is not permitted to support or oppose candidates. For example, when a pastor speaks from the pulpit, he or she is speaking on behalf of the church even if the pastor states he or she is expressing only personal views. This is particularly true since the church paid for the sound system, the pulpit, and the sanctuary, so it is paying for the pastor's speech. This is also true for statements made in a church newsletter or other official church publications.

A charity employee can, however, support or oppose candidates if he or she is not speaking on behalf of the organization. For example, a pastor can endorse a candidate personally and even have the church listed with his or her name as long as it is made clear that the church is listed for identification purposes only. The IRS has provided this example of when this is permitted:

> **Example.** Minister A is the minister of Church J and is well known in the community. With their permission, Candidate T publishes a full-page ad in the local newspaper listing five prominent ministers who have personally endorsed Candidate T, including Minister A. Minister A is identified in the ad as the minister of Church J. The ad states, "Titles and affiliations of each individual are provided for identification purposes only." The ad is paid for by Candidate T's campaign committee. Since the ad was not paid for by Church J, the ad is not otherwise in an official publication of Church J, and the endorsement is made by Minister A in a personal capacity, the ad does not constitute campaign intervention by Church J.

(b) Political Activity Taxes Paid by Charities

In addition to the potential loss of exempt status, a tax is imposed on a charity's political expenditures. A political expenditure can trigger an initial tax, payable by the organization, of 10 percent of the amount of the expenditure. An initial tax of 2.5 percent of the expenditure can also be imposed on each of the organization's managers (such as directors and officers), where these individuals knew it was a political expenditure, unless the agreement to make the expenditure was not willful and was due to reasonable cause. The IRS has the authority to abate these initial taxes where the organization is able to establish that the violation was due to reasonable cause and not to willful neglect, and timely corrects the violation.

An additional tax can be levied on a charitable organization, at a rate of 100 percent of the political expenditure, where the initial tax was imposed and the expenditure was not timely corrected. Such a tax can also be levied on an organization's manager, at a rate of 50 percent of the expenditure, where the additional tax was imposed on the organization and the manager refused to agree to part or all of the expenditure. The IRS has the discretion as to whether to revoke tax-exempt status, impose these taxes, or do both.

Under certain circumstances, the IRS is empowered to commence an action in federal district court to enjoin a charitable organization from making further political expenditures and for other relief to ensure that the assets of the organization are preserved for charitable purposes. If the IRS finds that a charitable organization has flagrantly violated the prohibition against political expenditures, the IRS is required to immediately determine and assess any income and/or excise tax(es) due, by terminating the organization's tax year.

(c) Political Activity by Other Exempt Organizations

Other exempt organizations (other than charities), such as social welfare organizations, labor and agricultural organizations, and associations, may engage in political campaign activities provided the activities do not become the primary purpose of the organization. For example, a social welfare organization is an entity that is primarily operated for the promotion of social welfare. It must be engaged in promoting, in some way, the common good and general welfare of the people of a community. An organization is an exempt social welfare organization if it is operated primarily for the purpose of bringing about civic betterments and social improvement. Thus, tax exemption for this type of organization fundamentally hinges on satisfaction of a primary purpose test.

The tax regulations also state that the promotion of social welfare does not include direct or indirect participation or intervention in political campaigns on behalf of or in opposition to a candidate for public office. Thus, an exempt social welfare organization can engage in politics, without jeopardizing its exemption, but the political activity cannot be its primary purpose.

Whether an organization is participating or intervening, directly or indirectly, in any political campaign activity on behalf of or in opposition to a candidate for public office depends on all of the facts and circumstances of each case.

IRS rulings in this area have concerned organizations that have political campaign activity as their primary function, namely, candidate-rating or direct candidate support. On one of the infrequent occasions where the IRS has qualified this type of permissible activity, the agency said that there is no "complete ban" on political activities by exempt social welfare organizations; a social welfare organization may engage in them as long as it is primarily engaged in activities that promote social welfare.

It may be noted that *dual-character activities* of exempt social welfare organizations may be political activities (for IRC Section 527 purposes). A dual-character activity is an activity that, on its face, appears to be an attempt to influence legislation but also is, in the context of the particular circumstances, a political activity. An example is support of a bill bearing a legislator's name at a time when the legislator is in the midst of a reelection campaign.

Certain expenditures that are related to political activities are not viewed as political activities, both for federal election law purposes and for tax purposes. Such expenses relate to the formation and administration of a political action committee known as a *separate segregated fund*. Under both federal election law and tax law, expenses incurred in connection with the administration of such entities do not constitute a *contribution* to the separate segregated fund for purposes of the prohibition on corporate contributions under federal election law. Further, such qualifying expenditures will not be considered political expenditures for purposes of the primary purpose rule and the tax paid on political expenditures discussed in the next section (see § 10.1(d)).

(d) Political Taxes Paid by Other Exempt Organizations

Exempt organizations other than charities or political organizations pay a tax equal to the lesser of its political expenditures or its net investment income. The lesser of these two amounts times the highest corporate rate is the tax imposed on the exempt organization. Net investment income, for this purpose, is the excess of:

1. The gross amount of interest, dividends, rents, and royalties, plus the excess, of gains from the sale or exchange of assets over the losses from the sale or exchange of assets, over

2. The deductions directly connected with the production of this income.

Political expenditures are *exempt function* expenditures. Political expenditures do not include certain expenses incurred by a sponsor of a separate segregated fund.

§ 10.2 PREPARATION OF SCHEDULE C

Charities and all other exempt organizations must report on Schedule C if the question on Line 3, Part IV is answered "yes." Charities complete Part I-A and Part I-B but not I-C. Other exempt organizations (other than Section 527 political organizations) complete Part I-A and Part I-C but not I-B. Section 527 political organizations complete Part I-A only.

(a) Part I-A (Reporting of Political Campaign Activity)

All organizations report their political campaign activities on Part I-A, lines 1 to 3. Because political campaign activities are prohibited, it should be a rare case that a charity will be reporting activities in Part I-A as the result may be the revocation of the charity's exempt status and/or the imposition of taxes (see § 10.1(b)).

(1) Line 1 (Description of Activities). On line 1, report the organization's direct and indirect political campaign activities. The description should be provided in Part IV of Schedule C. The instructions specify that Section 527 organizations should also describe their exempt function expenditures in Part IV. The description would include all prohibited activities discussed in § 10.1. For example, education activities that are partisan activities would be reported as political campaign activities. Exempt organizations other than charities may establish political action committees, known as separate segregated funds, to engage in political activity. Separate segregated funds are subject to certain requirements. If the exempt organization collects political contributions and member dues earmarked for a separate segregated fund and promptly and directly transfers them to the fund as required under IRS rules, the transfer should not be reported on line 1 of Part I-A; rather, such amount should be reported in Part I-C, line 5e.

(2) Line 2 (Political Expenditures). On line 2, report the amount of political expenditures incurred by the organization. The political expenditures would include both direct and indirect expenditures. These expenditures would be costs of goods and services, any contributions, and the allocable share of salaries of the organization's employees engaged in the activity. Any reasonable method of allocation of such salaries should be used. For example, daily time cards could be used to record the political campaign activity time of employees. The hours devoted to political campaign activity divided by the total hours spent on all organization's activities would be the percentage used to allocate the employee's total compensation to the political campaign activity.

(3) Line 3 (Volunteer Hours). On line 3, report volunteer hours engaged in political activity. Any reasonable method can be used to estimate the volunteer time allocable to political activities. For example, if the organization's educational activity favors a particular candidate, that activity becomes a political activity and the volunteer hours engaged in that activity are reported on line 3.

(b) Part I-B

Part I-B is completed only by charities. Political excise taxes are reported in this part.

(1) Lines 1 and 2 (Political Activity Excise Taxes). On line 1, report the tax due on political expenditures of charitable organizations (see § 10.1(b)). The tax due is 10 percent of the political expenditures reported on line 2 of Part I-A. Like many other excise tax provisions applicable to exempt organizations, an excise tax is also imposed on organization managers who knowingly approved the expenditure in addition to the tax imposed on the organization itself. The tax imposed on organization managers in this case is 2.5 percent of the expenditure. Political expenditures of other exempt organizations are reported in Part I-C.

(2) Lines 3 and 4 (Filing Form 4720).   On line 3, indicate "yes" or "no" as to whether Form 4720 was filed to report and pay the political excise taxes. On line 4, indicate "yes" or "no" as to whether a correction was made to avoid the second-tier excise tax equal to 100 percent of the political expenditure. If a correction was made, the form directs the organization to explain the correction in Part IV (see § 10.1(b)). The explanation should include a description of the organization's steps taken to correct the activity. Correction of a political expenditure means recovering the expenditure to the extent possible and establishing safeguards to prevent future political expenditures. Recovery of the expenditure means recovering part or all of the expenditure to the extent possible, and, where full recovery cannot be accomplished by any additional corrective action that is necessary. The organization that made the political expenditure is not under any obligation to attempt to recover the expenditure with legal action if the action would in all probability not result in an execution of the judgment.

(c)   Part I-C (Political Expenditure Subject to Tax)

Part I-C is completed by exempt organizations other than charities and Section 527 political organizations. The purpose of this part is to identify the magnitude of the permissible political campaign activity conducted by these organizations and to report the expenditures also reported on Form 1120-POL. This form is used to compute the Section 527 tax on political campaign activity of exempt organizations other than charities.

(1) Lines 1 and 2 (Exempt Function Expenditures).   On line 1, report political expenditures other than contributions. Exempt organizations that collect political contributions or member dues earmarked for a separate segregated fund, and promptly and directly transfer them to the fund as prescribed by IRS rules, should not report them on lines 1 or 2. Such amounts should be reported on line 5(e). On line 2, report contributions to political action committees (PACs) (and other political organizations).

(2) Lines 3 and 4 (Filing of Form 1120-POL).   On line 3, report the total of lines 1 and 2. The organization is directed to also report the total on Form 1120 POL, line 17b. On line 4, indicate "yes" or "no" as to whether Form 1120 POL is filed. These questions obviously are designed to encourage filing of Form 1120 POL. If the "yes" box is not checked, the IRS may send a letter to the filing organization asking why the form was not filed.

(3) Line 5 (Reporting of Recipients of Contributions).   On line 5, complete the table asking for the name, address, employer identification number (EIN), amount paid, and amount transferred to a separate segregated fund or political action committee. Enter the amount paid and indicate if the amount was paid from (1) the filing organization's own internal funds, or (2) were political contributions received and promptly and directly delivered to a separate political organization, such as a separate segregated fund or political action committee. If additional space is needed, provide the information in Part IV of this schedule.

§10.3 SCHEDULE C COMPLIANCE TASKS

For purposes of preparing Schedule C as it relates to political campaign activities, consider these 12 compliance tasks.

1. **Identify political activities.** Depending on the type of exempt organization in question, every activity that may be a political campaign activity should be reviewed. The most common example would be an educational activity of a charity or social welfare organization that includes an express or implied preference for a candidate.

2. **Track political expenditures.** To the extent a political activity is engaged in, the organization should develop procedures to track expenditures. The expenditures would include all costs of the political activity, including mailings, travel expenses, costs of materials, costs of speakers, advertisements, publications, and contributions.

3. **Track staff time.** Time cards or time sheets should be considered for the tracking of staff time engaged in political campaign activity.

4. **Track volunteer time.** The organization should develop policies to track the time spent on the political activity by volunteers requiring volunteer time cards or time sheets and descriptions of activities.

5. **Payment of charity tax.** To the extent a charity is engaged in political campaign activity, the amount of the activity should be documented for purposes of the tax.

6. **File Form 4720.** If the charity has conducted political campaign activity and the tax is due, Form 4720 should be timely filed and the tax submitted.

7. **Consider abatement of tax.** If reasonable cause for the expenditure can be established, it should be contemporaneously documented, so a request can be filed.

8. **Correct political expenditures.** If the tax is due and paid by a charity, correction of the expenditures should be made and documented.

9. **Document PAC contributions.** PAC contributions should be contemporaneously documented and a schedule maintained. This would include contributions to outside PACs as well as the collection of funds and transfer to the organization's separate segregated fund.

10. **Calculate Section 527 tax.** For exempt organizations other than charities, the timing of contributions and expenses should be coordinated to minimize the organization's net investment income where possible, as the Section 527 tax is imposed on the lesser of net investment income and political expenditures.

11. **File Form 1120-POL.** Compile information for the Form 1120-POL. It should be the same information as reported on Schedule C.

12. **Consider forming a separate segregated fund.** Exempt organizations other than charities should consider the formation of a separate segregated fund to reduce the Section 527 tax and to avoid election law violations.

Schedule D—Supplemental Financial Statements

§ 11.1 LAW AND POLICY

(a) Donor-Advised Funds

(1) Background. For donors that want to retain some control over their donated assets, an alternative to a private foundation or a supporting organization is the donor-advised fund. Although this term is not formally defined in the law, in this circumstance, a donor makes a gift to a public charity where the donee, instead of placing the gift property in its general treasury, deposits the gift item in a discrete fund (segregated account) within the charity (with the fund usually bearing the name of the donor). By contract, the donor is provided the opportunity to thereafter advise the charity as to dispositions from the fund, such as grants to other charitable organizations. The charitable deduction is likely to be defeated, however, where the arrangement amounts to a *donor-directed fund*, which provides a donor with the contractual right to direct (rather than merely advise as to) the subsequent distributions of the gifted money or property.

Donor-advised funds are controversial. Some contend that the maintenance of these funds is not a charitable activity. An extension of this assertion is that an organization that has maintenance of these funds as its primary or sole activity cannot qualify for tax exemption as a charitable organization. Critics argue that the process is akin to establishing and maintaining a commercial bank account holding deposits for the private benefit of a customer. (This is not the case; with a bank account, the customer can withdraw the deposited funds, while a transfer to a donor-advised fund is an irrevocable gift.) The courts are rejecting these arguments.

Another contention is that these transfers are not *gifts* in the first instance (and thus are not payments giving rise to a charitable deduction). The ostensible reason: The *donor* has not, by reason of the agreement with the charity, parted with all of his, her, or its right, title, and interest in and to the gifted money or property. To assess this, the IRS applies a set of *material restrictions* rules that were promulgated in the private foundation setting to test whether a private foundation has properly terminated its status when granting its assets to one or more public charities.

Still another issue is whether charitable organizations that maintain donor-advised funds are publicly supported charities (see § 8.1). The gifts (assuming that is what they are) to the charity (assuming that is what it is) are forms of public support for purposes of both the donative publicly supported charity (see § 8.1(d)) and the service provider public charity (see § 8.1(e)). Almost always, however, these entities are the donative type. Then, when a grant is made from an account within a public charity to another charity, it can be public support for the grantee. Some in the IRS and elsewhere are uncomfortable with the view that a gift (or a portion of it) can constitute public support for two charities. That is, nonetheless, the case.

The ultimate criticism of donor-advised funds is that they constitute a way to avoid the private foundation restrictions. That is, as a matter of literal fact, true. They are, however, a *lawful* way to sidestep the private foundation rules. Because of all these criticisms, Congress passed the Pension Protection Act of 2006 to increase oversight and regulation of donor advised funds.

(2) Pension Protection Act of 2006. Legislation that generally took effect for tax years beginning after August 17, 2006, brought a statutory definition of the term *donor-advised fund*. Essentially, it is a fund or account that is (1) separately identified by reference to contributions of one or more donors, (2) that is owned and controlled by a sponsoring organization, and (3) as to which a donor or a donor advisor has, or reasonably expects to have, advisory privileges with respect to the distribution or investment of amounts held in the fund or account by reason of the donor's status as a donor. A *sponsoring organization* is a public charity that maintains one or more donor-advised funds. A donor-advised fund does not include funds that make distributions only to a single identified organization or governmental entity, or certain funds where a donor or donor advisor provides advice as to which individuals receive grants for travel, study, or other similar purposes.

A distribution from a donor-advised fund is taxable if it is to (1) a natural person or (2) any other person if (a) it is for a noncharitable purpose or (b) if the organization does not exercise expenditure responsibility with respect to the distribution. Expenditure responsibility requires the sponsoring organization to take additional oversight steps to ensure that the distribution is used for charitable purposes. A tax equal to 20 percent of the distribution is imposed on the sponsoring organization. Another tax of 5 percent is imposed on any fund manager who agreed to the making of a taxable distribution, where the manager knew that the distribution was a taxable one. A fund manager is any director, officer, trustee, or executive employee of the sponsoring organization. The tax on fund managers is subject to a joint and several liability requirement. This tax does not apply to a distribution from a donor-advised fund to most public charities, the fund's sponsoring organization, or another donor-advised fund.

If a donor, donor advisor, or a person related to a donor or donor advisor with respect to a donor-advised fund provides advice as to a distribution that results in any of those persons receiving, directly or indirectly, a benefit that is more than incidental, an excise tax equal to 125 percent of the amount of the benefit is imposed on the person who advised as to the distribution and on the recipient of the benefit. Also, if a manager of the sponsoring organization agreed to the making of the distribution, knowing that the distribution would confer more than an incidental benefit on a donor, donor advisor, or related person, the manager is subject to an excise tax equal to 10 percent of the amount of the benefit. These taxes are subject to a joint and several liability requirement.

The private foundation excess business holdings rules apply to donor-advised funds. The excess business holdings rules prevent a private foundation (and in this case a donor advised fund) from generally owning more than 20 percent of a trade or business. In calculating the 20-percent threshold, the donor advised fund must also count the ownership of any disqualified person. For this purpose, the term *disqualified person* means, with respect to a donor-advised fund, a donor, donor advisor, member of the family of either, or a 35-percent controlled entity of any such person.

Contributions to a sponsoring organization for maintenance of a donor-advised fund are not eligible for a charitable deduction for federal income tax purposes if the sponsoring organization is a fraternal society, a cemetery company, or a veterans' organization. Contributions to a sponsoring organization for such maintenance are not eligible for a charitable deduction for federal estate or gift tax purposes if the sponsoring organization is a fraternal society or a veterans' organization. Contributions to a sponsoring organization for such maintenance are not eligible for a charitable deduction for income, estate, or gift tax purposes if the sponsoring organization is a Type III supporting organization (other than a functionally integrated Type III supporting organization) (see § 8.1(h)). A donor must obtain, with respect to each charitable contribution to a sponsoring organization to be maintained in a donor-advised fund, a contemporaneous written acknowledgment from the sponsoring organization that the organization has exclusive legal control over the funds or assets contributed.

The Pension Protection Act of 2006 instructed the Department of the Treasury to undertake a study on the organization and operation of donor-advised funds, to consider whether (1) the deductions allowed for income, estate, or gift taxes for charitable contributions to sponsoring organizations of donor-advised funds are appropriate in consideration of the use of contributed assets or the use of the assets of such organizations for the benefit of the person making the charitable contribution, (2) donor-advised funds should be required to distribute for charitable purposes a specified amount in order to ensure that the sponsoring organization with respect to the donor-advised fund is operating in a manner consistent with its tax exemption or public charity status, (3) the retention by donors to donor-advised funds of "rights or privileges" with respect to amounts transferred to such organizations (including advisory rights or privileges with respect to the making of grants or the investment of assets) is consistent with the treatment of these transfers as completed gifts, and (4) these issues are also issues with respect to other forms of charitable organizations or charitable contributions.

(3) Automatic Excess Benefit Transactions and Donor-Advised Funds. The Pension Protection Act of 2006 amended certain provisions of the intermediate sanctions law (see § 6.1(b)) to provide that certain transactions by a donor-advised fund would be considered automatic excess benefit transactions (see § 6.1(b)(15)). A grant, loan, compensation, or other similar payment from a donor-advised fund to a person that, with respect to the fund, is a donor, donor advisor, or a person related to a donor or donor advisor automatically is treated as an excess benefit transaction for intermediate sanctions law purposes. Again, this means that the entire amount paid to any of these persons is an excess benefit and subject to the intermediate sanctions excise taxes/fines (see § 6.1(b)(15)).

Donors and donor advisors with respect to a donor-advised fund, and related persons, are disqualified persons for intermediate sanctions law purposes with respect to transactions with the donor-advised fund (although not necessarily with respect to transactions with the sponsoring organization generally).

(b) Conservation Easements

Special federal tax rules pertain to contributions to charity of real property for conservation purposes. These rules are an exception to the general rule that there is no charitable contribution deduction for contributions of partial interests in property.

These rules are in the context of the income tax charitable contribution deduction for qualified conservation contributions. A *qualified conservation contribution* has three fundamental characteristics: It is (1) a contribution of a qualified real property interest, (2) to a qualified organization, (3) exclusively for conservation purposes.

The amount allowed as a charitable contribution deduction for a qualified conservation easement is the difference between the fair market value of the burdened property before the gift and the value of it following the gift.

(1) Qualified Real Property Interests. A *qualified real property interest* is one of the following interests in real property: (1) the donor's entire interest in the property other than a qualified mineral interest, (2) a remainder interest, or (3) a restriction (granted in perpetuity) on the use that may be made of the real property. A *qualified mineral interest* is the donor's interest in subsurface oil, gas, or other minerals, and the right to access to these minerals.

A real property interest is not treated as an entire interest in the property (other than a qualified mineral interest) if the property in which the donor's interest exists was divided prior to the contribution to enable the donor to retain control of more than a qualified mineral interest or to reduce the real property interest donated. Minor interests, which will not interfere with the conservation purposes of the gift, such as rights-of-way, may, however, be transferred prior to the conservation contribution without adversely affecting the treatment of a property interest as a qualified real property interest. An entire interest in real property may consist of an undivided interest in the property.

(2) Qualified Organizations. A *qualified organization* is a unit of government, a publicly supported charitable organization, or a supporting organization that is controlled by one or more of the foregoing two types of entities. In addition, an organization must have a commitment to protect the conservation purposes of the donation and have the resources to enforce the restrictions. A qualified organization is not required to set aside funds to enforce the restrictions that are the subject of the contribution.

A deduction is allowed for a contribution under these rules only if, in the instrument of conveyance, the donor prohibits the donee from subsequently transferring the easement (or, in the case of a remainder interest or the reservation of a qualified mineral interest, the property), whether or not for consideration, unless the donee, as a condition of the subsequent transfer, requires that the conservation purposes which the contribution was originally intended to advance be carried out. Moreover, subsequent transfers must be restricted to organizations qualifying, at the time of the subsequent transfer, as qualified organizations. Nonetheless, when a later unexpected change in the conditions surrounding the property that is the subject of a donation makes impossible or impractical the continued use of the property for conservation purposes, these requirements will be met if the property is sold or exchanged and any proceeds are used by the donee organization in a manner consistent with the conservation purposes of the original contribution.

(3) Conservation Purpose. The term *conservation purpose* means (1) preservation of land areas for outdoor recreation by, or for the education of, the general public; (2) protection of a relatively natural habitat of fish, wildlife, or plants, or similar ecosystem; (3) preservation of open space (including farmland and forest land), when the preservation is for the scenic enjoyment of the general public, is pursuant to a clearly delineated federal, state, or local governmental policy, and/or will yield a significant public benefit; or (4) preservation of an historically important land area or a certified historic structure.

To satisfy these rules, a contribution must be *exclusively* for conservation purposes. A conservation deduction will not be denied, however, when an incidental benefit inures to the donor merely as a result of conservation restrictions limiting the uses to which the donor's property may be put. In general, a conservation deduction will not be allowed if the contribution would accomplish one of the enumerated conservation purposes but would also permit destruction of other significant conservation interests. Nonetheless, a use that is destructive of conservation interests will be permitted if the use is necessary for protection of the conservation interests that are subject of the contribution.

A contribution cannot be treated as being exclusively for conservation purposes unless the conservation purpose is protected in perpetuity. Thus, any interest in the property retained by the donor (and the donor's successors in interest) must be subject to legally enforceable restrictions that will prevent uses of the retained interest that are inconsistent with the conservation purposes of the donation. A deduction is not permitted for a contribution of an interest in property that is subject to a mortgage, unless the mortgagee subordinates its rights in the property to the right of the charitable organization to enforce the conservation purposes of the gift in perpetuity. A conservation deduction will not be disallowed, however, merely because the interest that passes to, or is vested in, the donee charitable organization may be defeated by the performance of some act or the happening of some event, if on the date of the gift it appears that the possibility that the act or event will occur is so remote as to be negligible.

(4) Valuation. The amount of the charitable contribution deduction, in the case of a contribution of a donor's entire interest in conservation property (other than a qualified mineral interest), is the fair market value of the surface rights in the property contributed. The value for the deduction is computed without regard to the mineral rights. In the case of a contribution of a remainder interest in real property, depreciation and depletion of the property must be taken into account in determining the value of the interest. The value of a charitable contribution of a perpetual conservation restriction is the fair market value of the restriction at the time of the contribution. In the case of a contribution of a qualified real property interest for conservation purposes, the basis of the property retained by the donor must be adjusted by the elimination of that part of the total basis of the property that is properly allocable to the qualified real property interest granted.

(5) Substantiation. If a donor makes a qualified conservation contribution and claims a charitable contribution deduction for it, the donor must maintain written records of the fair market value of the underlying property before and after the contribution, and the conservation purpose furthered by the donation. This information may have to be part of the donor's income tax return.

(c) Art, Historical Treasures, and Other Similar Assets

Contributions of works of art may, of course, be made to charitable organizations. Works of art may also be loaned to these organizations.

(1) Gifts. In general, the federal income tax charitable contribution deduction for a gift of a work of art is an amount equal to the fair market value of the property. There are, however, exceptions to this general rule:

1. The charitable deduction for a year may be limited by certain percentage limitations contained in Section 170 of the Code.

2. The work of art that is contributed may be the creation of the donor, in which case the deduction is confined to the donor's basis in the property.

3. The work of art may be put to an unrelated use by the charitable recipient, in which case the deduction is confined to the donor's basis in the property.

Of these elements, the third situation is the most likely to occur. A work of art, being an item of tangible personal property, is subject to a special rule: When a gift of tangible personal property is made to a charitable organization and the donee's use of it is unrelated to its tax-exempt purposes, the amount of the charitable deduction that would otherwise be determined must be reduced by the amount of gain that would have been long-term capital gain if the property contributed had been sold by the donor at its fair market value, ascertained at the time of the contribution.

The greatest controversy surrounding the charitable deduction of a work of art is likely to be the value of the item. Not infrequently, there is a dispute between the IRS and a donor as to the fair market value of a work of art. Usually these disputes are settled; sometimes they are resolved in court. The appropriate value of an item of property is a question of fact, not law; thus, the testimony of one or more expert witnesses can be significant. A trial court's valuation of an item of property will be set aside on appeal only if the finding of value is clearly erroneous.

(2) Loans. Rather than contribute a work of art to a charitable organization, a person may decide to loan the artwork to a charity. This type of transfer does not give rise to a federal income tax charitable contribution deduction. The transaction is nonetheless a gift. The transaction is disregarded as a transfer for gift tax purposes, however, when (1) the recipient organization is a charitable entity, (2) the use of the artwork by the charitable donee is related to the purpose or function constituting the basis for its tax exemption, and (3) the artwork involved is an archaeological, historic, or creative item of tangible personal property.

(3) Future Interests in Tangible Personal Property. A charitable contribution consisting of a transfer of a future interest in tangible personal property such as art is treated as made (and therefore deductible) only when all intervening interests in, and rights to the actual possession or enjoyment of, the property have expired or are held by persons other than the donor or those related to the donor.

The term *future interest* includes:

- Reversions, remainders, and other interests or estates, whether vested or contingent, and whether or not supported by a particular interest or estate, which are limited to commence in use, possession, or enjoyment at some future date or time, and

- Situations in which a donor purports to give tangible personal property to a charitable organization but has an understanding, arrangement, agreement, or the like, whether written or oral, with the charitable organization which has the effect of reserving to, or retaining in, the donor a right to the use, possession, or enjoyment of the property.

These rules do not apply with respect to a transfer or an undivided present interest in property. For example, a contribution of an undivided one-quarter interest in a painting with respect to which the charitable donee is entitled to possession during three months of each year is treated as made on receipt by the donee of a formally executed and acknowledged deed of gift. The period of initial possession by the donee may not, however, be deferred for more than one year.

(d)   Trust, Escrow, and Custodial Arrangements

Part IV of Schedule D asks organizations to disclose information about certain trust, escrow, and custodial arrangements. While this includes more common trust arrangements (e.g., the organization serves as the trustee of a charitable remainder trust) and custodial arrangements (e.g., a national association holds assets in custody for local chapters), the IRS is primarily focused on credit counseling organizations and down payment assistance programs. The IRS views these two types of organizations with great scrutiny and special rules apply to them.

(1) Credit Counseling Organizations. As to tax years beginning after August 17, 2006, the Pension Protection Act of 2006 imposes criteria for tax-exempt credit counseling organizations. For entities that were exempt credit counseling organizations on that date, the statutory law applies with respect to tax years beginning after August 17, 2007.

Credit counseling organizations are those organizations that provide credit counseling services. The phrase *credit counseling services* is defined as (1) provision of educational information to the public on budgeting, personal finance, financial literacy, saving and spending practices, and the sound use of consumer credit; (2) assisting individuals and families with financial problems by providing them with counseling; and/or (3) a combination of these activities.

An organization that has provision of credit counseling services as its substantial purpose may not be tax-exempt under the general requirements above unless it also (1) provides credit counseling services tailored to the specific needs and circumstances of consumers; (2) does not make loans to debtors (other than loans without fees or interest) and does not negotiate the making of loans on behalf of debtors; (3) provides services for the purpose of improving a consumer's credit record, credit history, or credit rating only to the extent that these services are incidental to provision of credit counseling services; and (4) does not charge a separately stated fee for services for the purpose of improving a consumer's credit record, credit history, or credit rating.

The organization may not refuse to provide credit counseling services to a consumer due to the inability of the consumer to pay for, the ineligibility of the consumer for enrollment in, or the unwillingness of the consumer to enroll in, a debt management plan ("DMP"). The phrase *debt management plan* means services related to the repayment, consolidation, or restructuring of a consumer's debt, and includes the negotiation with creditors of lower interest rates, the waiver or reduction of fees, and the marketing and processing of DMPs.

The organization must establish and implement a fee policy that requires that any fees charged to a consumer for services are reasonable, allows for the waiver of fees if the consumer is unable to pay, and, except to the extent allowed by state law, prohibits charging any fee based in whole or in part on a percentage of the consumer's debt, the consumer's payments to be made pursuant to a DMP, or the projected or actual savings to the consumer resulting from enrollment in a DMP.

Moreover, the organization may not own more than 35 percent of the voting power of a corporation, the profits interest of a partnership, or the beneficial interest of a trust or estate that is in the business of lending money, repairing credit, or providing DMP services, payment processing, or similar services. Finally, this type of organization may not receive any amount for providing referrals for DMP services and may not pay for referrals of consumers.

Tax-exempt credit counseling organizations must have a governing body (1) that is controlled by persons who represent the broad interests of the public, such as public officials acting in their capacities as such, persons having special knowledge or expertise in credit or financial education, and community leaders; (2) not more than 20 percent of the voting power of which is vested in individuals who are employed by the organization or who will benefit financially, directly or indirectly, from the organization's activities (other than through the receipt of reasonable directors' fees or the repayment of consumer debt to creditors other than the credit counseling organization or its affiliates); and not more than 49 percent of the voting power of which is vested in individuals who are employed by the organization or who will benefit financially, directly or indirectly, from the organization's activities (other than though the receipt of reasonable directors' fees).

In addition, if a credit counseling organization is to qualify as a tax-exempt charitable entity, it may not solicit contributions from consumers during the initial counseling process or while the consumer is receiving services from the organization. Also, the aggregate revenues of the organization derived from payments of creditors of consumers of the organization and that are attributable to DMPs generally may not exceed 50 percent of its total revenues. In addition, if a credit counseling organization is to qualify as a tax-exempt social welfare entity under 501(c)(4), it must apply for recognition of exempt status by filing a Form 1024 with the IRS. (Note that generally (c)(4) organizations are not required to file a Form 1024 with the IRS.)

(2) Down Payment Assistance Organizations.   Qualification of a down payment assistance provider organization as a tax-exempt charitable (or educational) entity is a subject of considerable and ongoing controversy. Generically, a down payment assistance program is conducted by a nonprofit organization, either as its entire or primary focus or as one of several discrete programs, pursuant to which grants (in this context, sometimes termed *gifts*) are made to individuals to enable them to purchase a home. Down payment assistance programs offer prospective homebuyers the opportunity to qualify for mortgages when they have sufficient earnings to make the monthly loan payments but cannot afford the down payment. A down payment assistance program provides this type of assistance to low-income individuals and others who may be distressed. Some assistance may be provided to moderate-income individuals.

Programs administered by the Department of Housing and Urban Development include programs that are designed to increase home ownership. One of these programs, the Federal Housing Administration's home loan mortgage program, assists certain potential home owners in obtaining mortgages to purchase homes. This program requires a minimum down payment; the source of down payment money can be a gift, from a permissible source, to the borrower. One of these permissible sources is a charitable organization. Note that Department of Housing and Urban Development Handbook 4155, Chapter 2, § 3 requires that the donor may not be a person with an interest in the sale of the property, such as the seller, real estate agent or broker, or builder.

The issues in this context are whether a down payment assistance provider can be tax-exempt as a charitable (or educational) organization, whether unwarranted private benefit (see § 6.1(c)) is provided to a home seller and/or real estate professional, whether the organization is being operated in a commercial manner, and whether fees paid by home sellers to down payment assistance organizations are gifts.

The IRS has ruled that certain types of down payment assistance organizations qualify as tax-exempt charitable entities. One category of down payment assistance provider that is exempt makes the assistance available to low-income individuals and families. This type of entity also offers financial counseling seminars and conducts other educational activities to help prepare potential low-income buyers for the responsibility of home ownership. These organizations require a home inspection report for the property that the applicant intends to purchase to ensure that the house will be habitable. The staff of these entities does not know the identity of the person selling the home to the grant applicant or the identities of any other parties, such as real estate agents or developers, who may receive a financial benefit from the sale. These organizations conduct a broad-based fundraising program that attracts contributions and grants from foundations, businesses, and the public. Contributions that are contingent on the sale of a particular property or properties are not accepted.

The IRS ruled that organizations of this nature qualify for tax exemption as charitable entities because they relieve the poor, distressed, and underprivileged by enabling low-income individuals and families to obtain decent, safe, and sanitary homes. The low-income beneficiaries of this type of down payment assistance provider constitute a charitable class. Any benefit to other parties, such as home sellers, real estate agents, or developers, who participate in the transaction "does not detract" from the achievement of charitable purposes (and thus is, presumably, incidental).

Organizations that combat community deterioration in an economically depressed area comprise the other category of down payment assistance providers that are exempt as charitable entities. These organizations cooperate with government entities and community groups to develop an overall plan to attract new businesses to the area and to provide stable sources of decent, safe, and sanitary housing for the area's residents. As part of these renewal projects, these organizations receive funds from government agencies to build affordable housing units for sale to low- and moderate-income families. In addition to the provision of down payment assistance, these organizations provide (as is the case with the first category of these exempt organizations) counseling and other educational activities, and have a broad-based fundraising program.

As to the category of down payment assistance providers that cannot, according to the IRS, qualify for exemption, their staff, when considering an application for assistance, knows the identity of the person selling the home to the grant applicant and may also know the identities of others in the transaction. In substantially all of the cases in which down payment assistance is provided, the organizations receive a payment from the home seller. There is a "direct correlation" between the amount of the assistance to the buyer and the amount of the home sellers' payments to the organization. These organizations do not have broad-based fundraising; most of their support comes from home sellers and real estate–related businesses that may benefit from the sales of the homes. The IRS stated that the organizations' reliance on home sellers' payments for most of their funding "indicate that the benefit to the home seller is a critical aspect" of their operations, leading the agency to conclude that the "business purpose" of the organizations is their "primary goal."

(e) Endowment Funds

(1) Uniform Management of Institutional Funds Act. Most states have adopted some form of the Uniform Management of Institutional Funds Act (UMIFA), which gives the board of an exempt organization broad authority to manage, and expend funds from, its endowment. The board of a charitable organization may, pursuant to UMIFA, appropriate for expenditure for the purposes for which an endowment fund is established so much of the net appreciation, realized and unrealized, in the fair value of the assets of the fund over the historic dollar value of the fund as is prudent. This rule does not apply if the gift instrument involved indicates the donor's intention that net appreciation shall not be expended. For example, net appreciation cannot be spent if the donative interest says that principal must be preserved and only interest and dividends can be expended. However, if the donative interest merely says that principal must be preserved (without limiting expenditures to principal and interest), then any realized or unrealized appreciation over the historic dollar value can be expended. The historic dollar value is the aggregate amount of all donations to the fund valued as of the date of donation and not increased or decreased due to accounting income (interest and dividends) or realized or unrealized appreciation.

The board may invest and reinvest an endowment fund in any real or personal property deemed advisable by it, whether or not it produces a current return, including mortgages, stocks, bonds, and debentures. It may retain property contributed by a donor to an endowment fund for as long as it deems advisable. The board may include all or any part of an endowment fund in a pooled or common fund maintained by the institution.

Unless the law or the gift document provides otherwise, the board may delegate to its committees, officers, or employees of the institution or the fund, or agents, the authority to act in place of the board in investment and reinvestment of the organization's funds. It may contract with independent investment advisors, investment counsel or managers, banks, or trust companies for this purpose. It is authorized to pay compensation for investment advisory or management services.

In the administration of its powers in this regard, the members of the board are required to exercise ordinary business care and prudence under the facts and circumstances prevailing at the time of the action or decision. In so doing, they are to consider long- and short-term needs of the organization in carrying out its charitable purposes, its present and anticipated financial requirements, expected total return on its investments, price level trends, and general economic conditions.

(2) Uniform Prudent Investor Act. Most states have adopted some form of the Uniform Prudent Investor Act (UPIA). Where UMIFA governs how a nonprofit corporation invests, manages, and expends its assets, UPIA governs how a nonprofit trust invests, manages and expends its assets. The two acts are similar in that they are both based on modern portfolio theory, that is, they allow the organization to expend realized and unrealized gains as well as interest and dividends. The two acts also both have a prudent investor requirement.

Under UPIA, a trustee must manage trust assets as a prudent investor would, exercising reasonable skill, prudence, and caution. Trustees should make investment decisions based on the risk and return of the portfolio as a whole rather than an independent evaluation on an asset-by-asset basis. No type of asset is per se prohibited. For example, while certain types of investments may be considered risky, and investing 100 percent of the portfolio in such assets would not be prudent, investing a small portion of the overall portfolio in such investments may in fact be prudent.

(3) Securities Laws Affecting Endowments. At the federal level, the principal securities laws are the Securities Act of 1933, the Securities Exchange Act of 1934, and the Investment Company Act of 1940. These laws are administered and enforced by the Securities Exchange Commission (SEC). Generally, this body of law is designed to preserve a free market in the trading of securities, provide full and fair disclosure of the character of securities sold in interstate commerce and through the mails, and prevent fraud and other abuse in the marketing and sale of securities. State securities laws have the same goal.

The federal securities law broadly defines the term *security* as including not only stocks and bonds but notes, debentures, evidences of indebtedness, certificates of participation in a profit-sharing agreement, investment contracts, and certificates of deposit for securities. It is rare for a charitable organization to offer a financial benefit or package to the general public where that benefit or package is considered a security, but some nonprofit organizations offer *memberships*, which, technically, constitute securities. There are, however, exceptions from the federal securities laws for these types of securities.

Nonetheless, a charitable organization may find itself at least within the potential applicability of the securities laws if it maintains one or more *charitable income funds*. The federal securities laws include rules that are designed to shield charities against the allegation that these funds are investment companies subject to the registration and other requirements of the Investment Company Act. This legislation, introduced by the Philanthropy Protection Act of 1995, provides exemptions under the federal securities laws for charitable organizations that maintain these funds.

A charitable income fund is a fund maintained by a charitable organization exclusively for the collective investment and reinvestment of one or more assets of a charitable remainder trust or similar trust, a pooled income fund, an arrangement involving a contribution in exchange for the issuance of a charitable gift annuity, a charitable lead trust, the general endowment fund or other funds of one or more charitable organizations, or certain other trusts the remainder interests of which are revocably dedicated to or for the benefit of one or more charitable organizations. The SEC has the authority to expand the scope of these exemption provisions to embrace funds that may include assets not expressly defined.

A fund that is excluded from the definition of an investment company must provide, to each donor to a charity by means of the fund, at the time of the contribution written information describing the material terms of operation of the fund. This disclosure requirement, however, is not a condition of exemption from the Investment Company Act. Thus, a charitable income fund that fails to provide the requisite information to donors is not subject to the securities laws, although the fund may be subject to an enforcement or other action by the SEC.

This exemption is also engrafted onto the Securities Act and the Securities Exchange Act. Thus, for example, the exemption in the securities act (from registration and other requirements) is available for "any security issued by a person organized and operated exclusively for religious, educational, benevolent, fraternal, charitable, or reformatory purposes and not for pecuniary profit, and no part of the net earnings of which inures to the benefit of any person, private stockholder, or individual."

The Securities Exchange Act provides that a charitable organization is not subject to the Act's broker-dealer regulation rules solely because the organization trades in securities on its behalf, or on behalf of a charitable income fund, or the settlors, potential settlors, or beneficiaries of either. This protection is also extended to trustees, directors, officers, employees, or volunteers of a charitable organization, acting within the scope of their employment or duties with the organization.

Exemptions from the reach of the Investment Advisors Act (similar to those available in the broker-dealer setting) are provided for charitable organizations and certain persons associated with them, in connection with the provision of advice, analyses, or reports.

Interests in charitable income funds excluded from the definition of an investment company, and any offer or sale of these interests, are generally exempt from state laws that require registration or qualification of securities. A charitable organization or trustee, director, officer, employee, or volunteer of a charity (acting within the scope of his or her employment or duties) is not generally subject to regulation as a dealer, broker, agent, or investment advisor under most state securities law because the organization or person trades in securities on behalf of a charity, charitable income fund, or the settlors, potential settlors, or beneficiaries of either.

(f) Investments—Subsidiaries and Joint Ventures

This section addresses the principal ways in which tax-exempt organizations can bring more structure, protection, and sophistication to their operations through investment in subsidiaries and joint ventures. Certainly for the larger exempt organizations, one entity often is insufficient. Tax-exempt entities today are finding creative and productive uses of subsidiaries, partnerships, limited liability companies, and other joint ventures. Specifically, this section:

- Summarizes the fundamentals of bifurcation.
- Reviews the rules concerning tax-exempt and taxable subsidiaries.
- Summarizes the law pertaining to public charities in partnerships.
- Focuses on the use by exempt organizations of limited liability companies.
- Addresses the legal consequences of exempt organizations' involvement in other joint ventures.
- Summarizes the rules concerning the tax treatment of revenue from controlled entities.
- Reviews the rules as to liquidation of for-profit subsidiaries.

(1) Fundamentals of Bifurcation. The word *bifurcation* essentially means the separation of something into two parts. Many tax-exempt organizations find that their operations are enhanced (although not necessarily simplified) by the use of two organizations instead of one. Indeed, this phenomenon is not confined to a division of functions but may extend to utilization of three or four, or perhaps tens, of organizations. As to the former, there may be an association with a related foundation and political action committee. The latter is illustrated by a health care or university system.

From a law standpoint, the creation and maintenance of a fruitful parent–subsidiary relationship requires a variety of elements. One is that the new entities must have real and substantial business functions. This means that there must be some substance as to their operations. Also, success of a venture necessitates a certain degree of separation of the entities, in terms of both governance and operational structure, and form. Overall, from the federal tax law viewpoint, it is essential that the substance and independence of the entities are respected. This outcome is critical when the parent is a nonprofit, tax-exempt entity and the subsidiary is a for-profit, taxable one. It is usually desirable when the subsidiary is also a tax-exempt organization, particularly where the exemptions of the two entities are based on different tax law provisions.

If the extent of control and management is inordinate, in that the parent organization's control of the affairs of the subsidiary is so pervasive that the latter is merely an extension of the former, the subsidiary may be disregarded—by the IRS or a court—as a separate entity. In extreme situations, the parent-subsidiary relationship is regarded as a sham and consequently ignored for tax purposes. With this outcome, the tax consequences (undesirable from a planning standpoint) are that the two "entities" are deemed to be one.

All of this pivots on the element of *day-to-day management*: If the parent organization is involved in the day-to-day management of the subsidiary organization, the two are likely to be treated as one entity. The factors that determine these conclusions are the identity and overlap of officers and employees, location(s) of operations, office sharing, and coinvesting. Also important is record keeping (as to expenses and time allocations) and contracts between the organizations (such as for cost reimbursement and/or rental arrangements). Nonetheless, IRS rulings illustrate the fact that close and intertwined operations do not necessarily defeat tax planning in connection with a parent-subsidiary structure.

In one instance, a tax-exempt organization established a for-profit subsidiary to serve as the sole general partner in a limited partnership (see § 11.1(f)(3)(A)(i)), to limit legal liability for claims to the assets of the two organizations, and to isolate exempt functions from unrelated business activities (see § 7.1(b)). The exempt organization elected all of the directors of the subsidiary. No more than three of the seven members of the subsidiary's board of directors were also members of the board of the exempt organization. The subsidiary rented office space and purchased professional services from the parent; the two organizations shared employees. The two entities shared investment leads and made joint investments, and the subsidiary generally had, in the words of the IRS, a "close working relationship" with the parent organization. Both organizations maintained separate accounting and corporate records. The IRS ruled that this subsidiary had a "separate corporate existence and business purpose" and that the tax-exempt parent did not "actively participate" in the day-to-day management of the subsidiary, so that the subsidiary was not regarded as a mere instrumentality of the parent and the "corporate existence" of the subsidiary would not be disregarded for federal tax purposes.

This ruling takes the two organizations to the edge of permissibility in this context. To reiterate: (1) the two organizations share office space, (2) the subsidiary purchases administrative and professional services from the parent, (3) the subsidiary reimburses the parent for the services of some of the parent's employees, (4) the two organizations share "investment leads" and coinvest, and (5) the parent and subsidiary "maintain a close working relationship. " This ruling reflects a most munificent view of the facts by the IRS and illustrates how closely a tax-exempt organizations and its subsidiary (in this instance, a for-profit one) can operate in tandem without crossing the line into attribution and causing the exempt entity to become entangled in what the IRS termed the "daily operations" of the subsidiary.

The tax consequences of a finding that a parent-subsidiary relationship will not be respected for federal tax purposes can be enormous. A large unrelated business in the subsidiary could cause the parent to lose its tax-exempt status if the subsidiary is treated as a mere instrumentality of the parent (i.e., the relationship is regarded as a sham). The same adverse outcome could result if the parent is a charitable entity and lobbying activities (see § 9.1) in the subsidiary are attributed to it. By contrast, if both the parent and the subsidiary are charitable organizations, the collapsing of operations presumably would not trigger any adverse tax consequences—and thus there is little likelihood that attribution would be imposed.

(2) Subsidiaries

(A) Definition of *Subsidiary*

A *subsidiary organization* is an entity that is controlled by another organization, with that other entity often termed the *parent organization*. Thus, the element of *control* is built into the definition of the term: The subsidiary organization is subordinate or supplementary to the parent entity. By contrast, organizations can be *related* or *affiliated* without the presence of a control relationship.

The control relationship can be manifested in several ways. There are, however, essentially three choices:

1. **Interlocking directorate.** One way for an organization to control another one is by means of the origin and composition of the subsidiary's governing board. That is, an organization can be the parent of another organization by having the power to determine who constitutes at least a majority of the other organization's board of directors or trustees. There are many mechanisms for achieving this. The common ones are:

   - The board of the parent organization appoints at least a majority of the board of the subsidiary organization.

   - Individuals holding certain positions with the parent organization (such as officers) are members of the board of the subsidiary organization by virtue of those positions (termed *ex officio* positions), with those positions representing at least a majority of the subsidiary's board.

   - There may be a blend of the foregoing options.

   - The members of the board of the parent organization are also members of the board of the subsidiary organization (complete overlap).

2. **Membership.** The subsidiary organization can be organized as a membership organization, with the parent entity serving as the sole member of the subsidiary. The parent/member is responsible for selecting the board of the subsidiary.

3. **Stock.** The subsidiary organization can be organized as a stock-based corporation, with the parent organization owning a majority or all of the stock of the subsidiary entity. The stockholder is responsible for selecting the board of the subsidiary.

The federal tax law generally is silent on this subject. Tax-exempt organizations are generally free to structure parent-subsidiary relationships as they wish, subject to the particulars of state law. For example, it is rare for a state to allow the formation of a nonprofit organization as a stock-based corporation, although some states do in fact allow this. At the federal level, one of the few pronouncements of the law on this point is that disqualified persons may not control supporting organizations.

(B) Determining Need for Subsidiary

Conceptually, the principal reasons a tax-exempt organization may desire to utilize one or more subsidiaries is that a facet of the law and/or a management consideration suggests or requires it.

A nontax law reason (although one with legal overtones) for using a subsidiary is to avoid or minimize legal liability on the part of the parent organization. That is, the parent-subsidiary relationship will (or is intended to) insulate assets in the two entities from liability that may be incurred by the parent.

The chief tax law reasons for a subsidiary is to house an activity, in which the parent organization may not or should not engage, in the subsidiary organization, or to enhance the parent's operations by use of a subsidiary. Thus, for example, deployment of a subsidiary may be used to preserve the tax-exempt status of the parent. The types of activities that are commonly spun off to or incubated in a subsidiary (particularly by a charitable organization) are unrelated business, attempts to influence legislation, and political campaign efforts.

Another tax law use for a subsidiary is its function as a partner in a limited partnership or limited liability company (see § 11.1(f)(3)(A)). A for-profit entity may be used to attract capital and/or create assets (stock).

Management considerations (as contrasted with legal ones) often lead to a decision to place the fundraising function of a tax-exempt organization and/or one or more program activities of an exempt organization in a subsidiary organization. The latter approach may lead to deductibility of contributions and/or access to grant funding that would not otherwise be available.

Where the parent tax-exempt organization is not a charitable entity (e.g., is described in 501(c)(4), (6), (7), etc.), placement of the fundraising function in a separate foundation is nearly essential. In this fashion, contributions and grants can be attracted to support the charitable programs within the charitable subsidiary. Without the separate charitable subsidiary, this type of gift support would not be available because of the absence of eligibility for the charitable contribution deduction for contributions to the parent. Once the two entities are operational, one of two models (or, perhaps, a blend of the two) can be selected. Pursuant to one approach, all of the charitable activities are placed in the charitable organization and the fundraising supports these activities. Under the other approach, the charitable activities remain in the parent organization. The fundraising entity makes restricted grants to the parent organization in support of these programs.

Bifurcation involving fundraising, where both entities are tax-exempt charitable organizations, is a classic example of the use of a subsidiary primarily for nonlaw reasons. (Where the two organizations are charitable, contributions to either of them are deductible.) This type of bifurcation is predicated on two factors: Fundraising activities usually are not considered program activities, and the fundraising function often is best separated from the overall governance function. With a related fundraising foundation, there can be a board of directors (or trustees) that has fundraising as it sole concern and function. Board members of the parent organization may be averse to fundraising; others relish the opportunity. By means of bifurcation, the fundraising function is placed in an entity where those who direct it know that fundraising (not the organization's governance) is their responsibility.

Allocation of programs between two exempt charitable programs may be appropriate, depending on the facts and circumstances of the particular case. Generalizations as to which of these types of bifurcation is suitable are not possible; much depends on the personalities and politics involved.

A subsidiary may be essential to maximizing an income flow or creating a more favorable (from a tax law standpoint) type of income. Thus, for example, a tax-exempt educational organization was ruled to be able to, without adversely affecting its exempt status, create and wholly own (and receive tax-free licensing income from) a for-profit subsidiary formed to maximize for membership and business purposes what would otherwise be the organization's Web site. Likewise, a medical research organization formed a supporting organization that in turn created a for-profit subsidiary to facilitate the transfer of technology incubated in the research organization. Following commercialization of the technology, the for-profit subsidiary will provide tax-free royalty income to the research organization.

The spin-off approach as opposed to the incubation approach may not be appropriate. For example, this election is not available in the case of an association that must utilize a political action committee to avoid tax (see § 10.1(a)). In other situations, an activity can begin as a function of the exempt organization and be transferred to a subsidiary when and if the activity expands to the point where the spin-off is desirable or necessary. Thus, the lobbying activity of a public charity may be appropriately transferred to a controlled social welfare organization if that activity increases beyond the bounds of insubstantiality (see § 9.1(d)). Similarly, an unrelated business of a tax-exempt may have to be moved to a subsidiary if it becomes too extensive to be conducted within the exempt organization.

(C) Legal Form of Subsidiary

Once the decision is made to create and use a subsidiary, the question as to its form may arise. If the subsidiary entity is to be a tax-exempt organization, the choices as to form generally are nonprofit corporation, trust, or unincorporated association. (Note, however, that more recently the IRS has recognized certain LLCs, if properly structured, as also qualifying for exemption.) If the subsidiary organization is to be a taxable entity, the choices as to form generally are a regular (C) corporation, small business (S) corporation, or a limited liability company.

The factors that dictate the nature of the subsidiary include:

- The value of or need for tax exemption for the subsidiary.

- The motives of those involved in the enterprise (such as a profit motive).

- The desirability of creating an asset (such as stock that may appreciate in value and/or serve as the means for transfer of ownership) for equity owners of the enterprise.

- The compensation arrangements contemplated for employees (including deferred and retirement compensation).

(D) Tax-Exempt Subsidiaries

It is common, in a parent-subsidiary relationship, for the parent entity and the subsidiary entity to both be tax-exempt organizations. An illustration of this type of in-tandem arrangement is the supporting organization (see § 8.1(h)).

(i) Choice of Form

The form of the tax-exempt subsidiary is essentially the same as that selected by its parent: nonprofit corporation, trust, or unincorporated association. For the most part, the form of both organizations is likely to be a nonprofit corporation.

(ii) Bifurcation Revisited

The elements as to successful bifurcation (see § 11.1(f)(1)) usually apply when both organizations are tax-exempt. For example, the exempt charitable organization does not want the activities of its exempt lobbying subsidiary to be attributed to it for tax purposes, nor does the exempt business league want the functions of its exempt political action committee attributed to it. Where both organizations are exempt charitable entities, the adverse tax consequences of attribution are minimized, although in most instances attribution should be avoided (if only for management purposes).

(iii) COMMON RELATIONSHIPS

The most common forms of these relationships when an exempt charitable organization is the parent include:

- A charitable organization with an exempt social welfare organization as the (or a) subsidiary. The function of this subsidiary probably is lobbying (see § 9.1(g)).

- A charitable organization with an exempt business league as its subsidiary. The function of the subsidiary may be a certification program.

The most common forms of these relationships when an exempt charitable organization is the subsidiary include:

- An exempt business league with a charitable foundation. This subsidiary, which is likely to be a supporting organization, conducts charitable, educational, and/or scientific programs; may engage in fundraising activities and/ or maintain an endowment; and/or own real property.

- An exempt social welfare organization with a charitable foundation. This entity is structured and functions much like the charitable foundation associated with a business league.

- Another type of noncharitable tax-exempt organization with a charitable foundation. These exempt parent organizations include labor organizations, agricultural organizations, social clubs, fraternal organizations, and veterans' organizations. Again, the functions of this type of subsidiary are likely to be the same as above. The subsidiary is likely to be, in cases involving labor and agricultural organizations, a supporting organization.

- A foreign charitable organization with an exempt U.S.-based charitable entity. This subsidiary, usually a fundraising organization (to facilitate deductibility of contributions), is also likely to be a supporting organization.

- An exempt charitable organization (parent) with an exempt charitable organization (subsidiary). The function of this type of charitable organization subsidiary will probably be fundraising, holding and growing one or more endowment funds, and/or operating one or more programs. As before, this type of subsidiary is likely to be a supporting organization.

As to supporting organizations, it is important to reiterate that there are different types of these entities (creatively called Type I, II, and III supporting organizations—see § 8.1(h)). Only one of these types (Type I) is the parent-subsidiary model. The brother-sister model (Type II) can, however, look much like the parent-subsidiary structure. With the Type III model, a supporting organization can function without being formally controlled by one or more supported organizations.

These tax-exempt organizations are subsidiary organizations, with the parent exempt organization potentially one of a wide variety of tax-exempt organizations:

- Political organizations

- Title-holding companies
- Employee benefit funds

(E) FOR-PROFIT SUBSIDIARIES

Nearly all types of tax-exempt organizations may utilize a for-profit, taxable sub-sidiary. This is, however, less common than use of a tax-exempt subsidiary (see § 11.1(f)(2)(D) with the issues in play nonetheless often more complex.

(i) CHOICE OF FORM

The taxable subsidiary of a tax-exempt organization is likely to be a corporation. Here, some of the interests of the exempt parent organization and those of the sub-sidiary may diverge. The exempt organization presumably would want the subsidi-ary to be a regular (C) corporation, so that the resulting income would be in the form of tax-free dividends. Those involved with the subsidiary may want it to be a small business (S) corporation or a limited liability company so as to avoid double taxation. The exempt organization (here, only a charitable one), however, should avoid use of an S corporation, if only because all resulting income and gain are automatically considered unrelated business income, and should be cautious when contemplating use of a limited liability company or partnership, because the exempt organization's share of LLC or partnership income may be unrelated business in-come if the LLC's activities are not related to the exempt purposes of the exempt parent organization.

Another choice is the taxable nonprofit corporation. These entities are taxed the same as the for-profit corporation, yet it may prove advantageous for the parent exempt entity to have its subsidiary cast as a nonprofit organization.

In nearly all instances, the function of this type of subsidiary is to house one or more businesses that are, in relation to the exempt organization involved, unrelated businesses.

(ii) CAPITALIZATION

Although there is no specific law on the point, a tax-exempt organization should give serious consideration to the amount of capital contributed to a taxable subsidiary. This is particularly the case where the parent is a charitable entity and charitable dol-lars are thus being applied for noncharitable purposes (albeit it in a controlled organi-zation). The best guiding standard in this regard is that of the prudent investor—primarily, is the investment reasonable and at fair market value.

(iii) ACCUMULATIONS

A nonprofit organization may find that its subsidiary has accumulated a substantial amount of assets, due to successful business activity and/or investment performance. At some point, the IRS may contend that these accumulations are evidence of a sub-stantial nonexempt purpose.

It is the view of the agency that, in situations involving tax-exempt organiza-tions, the entities "bear a very heavy burden" to demonstrate, by "contemporaneous and clear evidence," that they have plans for the use of substantial assets for exempt purposes. "This growth [of assets in a subsidiary] presents a continuing obligation," the IRS has said, on the organization to "translate this valuable asset into funds, and use these funds for the expansion" of its exempt activities. The IRS suggests that some of the subsidiary's assets be sold or a portion of the subsidiary's stock be sold, with the proceeds used to fund programs. The "highest priority" should be given to repayment by the subsidiary of any loans made by the exempt organization. These funds too can be devoted to exempt ends. The IRS's lawyers said that the organization "cannot be allowed to focus its energies on expanding its subsidiary's commercial business and assets, and neglect to translate that financial success into specific, definite and feasible plans for the expansion" of the charitable parent's exempt activities.

An IRS pronouncement concluded that the "fact that the assets are being accumulated in a for-profit company under the formal legal control of [a tax-exempt organization] does not excuse [the exempt organization] from using such assets" for exempt purposes. This analysis ended with this sweeping pronouncement: "Excess accumulations maintained in a subsidiary entity under legal control of the exempt organization, but under the de facto control of the founder, are deemed to be for the founder's personal purposes if no exempt purpose is documented or implemented."

(iv) BIFURCATION REVISITED

The elements as to successful bifurcation (see § 11.1(f)(1)) certainly apply when the parent organization is tax-exempt and the subsidiary is a taxable entity. In this setting, it is almost always critical that the activities of the subsidiary are not attributed to the parent. Even in the best of circumstances, treatment of this type of subsidiary as an instrumentality of the parent is likely to result in unrelated business income to the parent, or in the worst circumstances loss of exempt status for the parent.

Thus, the properly managed tax-exempt organization is cautious when organizing and operating a taxable subsidiary, so as not to be placed in a position where it is cast (or perceived) as being involved in the day-to-day management of the subsidiary, so that the subsidiary is disregarded for tax purposes. The principal elements to be taken into account in assessing these situations include:

- Overlap of board directors (although this element is of lesser concern because control is assumed, at the same time, control is manifested by means of stock, so there is no need to have a complete or majority interlock of directors).

- Overlap of officers.

- Overlap of employees.

- Sharing of office space, furniture, and/or equipment.

- Coinvestment arrangements.

- Other circumstances that indicate undue involvement by the parent in the daily operations of the subsidiary.

(v) LIQUIDATIONS

If a taxable subsidiary liquidates and distributes its assets to its tax-exempt parent, the general rule is that the distribution is treated for tax purposes as though the assets are being sold to the parent organization. This means that, to the extent these assets are capital assets, there is potential for exposure to the tax on capital gains.

There are other noteworthy elements of these rules:

- If a capital asset transferred in this fashion is used by the parent in an unrelated business, capital gains taxation is not triggered (as long as the asset is used in that manner).

- The rules as to liquidation are basically the same, irrespective of whether the liquidating entity is a subsidiary of the transferee or not.

- These rules generally apply when a taxable entity *converts* (assuming that is permissible under state law) to a tax-exempt organization.

- In a situation where the transferee is *not* the parent of the liquidating entity, there are exceptions that may need to be considered. Where these exceptions are applicable, the IRS is requiring the recipient organization to file an application for recognition of tax-exempt status, even though the tax regulations generally would not require filing of an exemption application in these situations.

(vi) Tax Treatment of Revenue from a Taxable Subsidiary

Most tax-exempt organizations develop an unrelated business with the anticipation that it will serve as a source of revenue. If the unrelated business is conducted in and by means of a subsidiary, presumably a revenue flow to the parent is likewise desired.

Generally, passive income received by tax-exempt organizations is not taxable as unrelated business income (see § 7.1(b)(4)(B)(i)). A major exception to this rule pertains to the receipt of certain income by an exempt parent organization from a controlled subsidiary. That is, interest, rent, annuity, or royalty payments made by a controlled entity to an exempt organization are includable in the exempt organization's unrelated business income (other than in the rare instance where the revenue is from an exempt function) and are subject to the unrelated business income tax to the extent the payment reduces the net unrelated income (or increases any net unrelated loss) of the controlled entity (determined as if the entity were tax-exempt). (See § 7.1(b)(4)(C)(ii)) for a discussion of the unrelated business income rules as they apply to controlled entities.)

A *controlled entity* is subsidiary that is at least 50 percent controlled by the parent tax-exempt organization. In the case of a stock-based subsidiary, *control* means ownership by vote or value of 50 percent or more of the stock. In the case of a partnership or other entity, *control* means ownership of 50 percent or more of the profits, capital, or beneficial interests. Moreover, there are constructive ownership rules by which a parent exempt organization is deemed to control an entity indirectly, such as in the case of a second-tier subsidiary.

(3) Partnerships and Joint Ventures

(A) Partnership and Joint Venture Basics

A *partnership* is a form of business entity, recognized in the law as a separate legal organization, as is a corporation or trust. It is usually evidenced by a document (partnership agreement). The term *joint venture* is broader than, and subsumes, the concept of a partnership. There can be a joint venture without establishment of an entity and without a document signifying it. Indeed, the joint venture form can be imposed on parties in particular factual circumstances, even contrary to their intent and wish. A joint venture can, however, be a formal legal entity other than a partnership. The best example of this is the *limited liability company* (see § 11.1(f)(3)(A)(iii)).

The parties to a partnership are *partners*. Parties to another type of joint venture, including a limited liability company, are *members*.

(i) PARTNERSHIPS

Partnerships basically are of two types. This delineation largely turns on the nature of the partners, who can be *general* or *limited*. Generally, liability for the consequences of a partnership's operations rests with the general partner(s), while the exposure to liability (if any) for the functions of the partnership for the limited partners is confined to the amount of the limited partner's or partners' contribution(s) to the partnership.

The partnership that has only general partners is the *general partnership*. In this type of partnership, the interests of the general partners may or may not be equal. These partners are generally equally liable for satisfaction of the obligations of the partnership and can be called on to make additional capital contributions to the entity.

Capital in a partnership can be derived from investors, namely, limited partners. A limited partner is in the venture not to control and administer the underlying business but to obtain a return on investment and perhaps to procure some income tax advantages. A partnership with both general and limited partners is termed a *limited partnership*.

A tax-exempt organization may be a general partner or limited partner in a partnership. Nearly all of the federal tax law on this point pertains to public charities functioning as a (or the) general partner in a limited partnership.

(ii) JOINT VENTURES

A *joint venture* is an association of two or more persons with intent to carry out a business enterprise for joint profit, for which purpose they combine their efforts, property, money, skill, and knowledge. Often, as noted, this arrangement is something less than a formal legal entity such as a partnership.

The three types of joint ventures are:

1. One or more of the venturers places itself, in its entirety, in the venture.

2. One or more of the venturers places a primary portion of its operations in the venture.

3. One or more of the venturers places a small portion of its operations in the venture.

From the standpoint of the law of tax-exempt organizations, the first type of these joint ventures is the *whole-entity joint venture* (see § 11.1(f)(3)(E)). This arrangement started in the health care context and is thus known in that setting as the *whole-hospital joint venture*. The second and third of these joint ventures is the *ancillary joint venture* (see § 11.1(f)(3)(F)). Thus, a tax-exempt organization can be a participant in a joint venture.

(iii) LIMITED LIABILITY COMPANIES

A limited liability company is a legal entity that has some of the attributes of a corporation (e.g., limitations as to legal liability for persons other than the entity) and (as the consequence of an election) some of the characteristics of a partnership (princi-pally, taxation as a partnership).

A limited liability company may have two or more members. If state law permits, a limited liability company may have only one member. A single-member liability company generally is disregarded for federal income tax purposes. A tax-exempt organization may be a member of either type of limited liability company.

(B) Flow-Through Entities

Partnerships and other joint venture entities are, for federal income tax purposes, *flow-through entities*. This means that these entities are not taxpaying organiza-tions—rather, they are conduits of net revenue (and perhaps other items) to the partners or members, who bear the responsibility for the payment of tax on their net income.

For tax-exempt organizations, the receipt of income from a joint venture raises issues as to unrelated business income taxation and, in some instances, ongoing eligi-bility for exempt status. In resolving these issues, a *look-through rule* is used. Pursuant to that rule, if a business regularly carried on by a partnership or other joint venture, of which an exempt organization is a member, is an unrelated business with respect to the exempt organization, in computing its unrelated business income the exempt organization must include its share of the gross income of the venture. Likewise, if the business in the joint venture is related to the exempt organization's exempt pur-pose, the resulting income is treated as exempt function revenue. Thus, in application of the look-through rule, the business conducted by the joint venture is evaluated to determine what the outcome would be if the exempt organization directly conducted the business.

The IRS and the courts apply an *aggregate approach rule* in this context. This means that, when the eligibility for tax-exempt status of the nonprofit organization is being evaluated (anew or on an ongoing basis) because of its involvement in a joint venture, the activities of the organization *and* the activities of the venture in which the organi-zation is a partner or member are taken into consideration.

(C) Public Charities as General Partners

The concern of the IRS with the matter of public charities as general partners in limited partnerships (or, for that matter, public charities in a joint venture with for-profit entities, whether the form is limited partnerships, general partnerships, or lim-ited liability companies) has been and continues to be that the resources of a charita-ble organization are being used to provide substantial benefits to the for-profit participants in the partnership (usually the limited partners). The issue then is eligi-bility for tax-exempt status when a public charity is engaged in this endeavor.

A three-step analysis is used in this context. Where they are satisfied, exemption is allowed or is preserved:

1. Does the public charity's involvement in the joint venture further a charitable purpose?

2. Does the joint venture agreement reflect an arrangement that permits the exempt organization to act primarily in furtherance of its exempt (charitable) purposes? That is, does the organization's participation preclude or deter it from advancing its exempt ends?

3. Does the arrangement cause the exempt organization to provide an impermissible private benefit (see § 6.1(c)) to the for-profit coventurers?

With respect to the first criterion, participation in the joint venture by a public charity is in furtherance of charitable ends if such participation results in the raising of needed capital, the creation of new programs, the sharing of a risk inherent in a new exempt activity, and/or the pooling of diverse areas of expertise.

The second criterion looks to means by which the exempt organization may, under the particular facts and circumstances, be insulated from the day-to-day responsibilities as general partner. For example, will the exempt organization, as a participant in the joint venture, be required to pursue the profit motive of the joint venture at the expense of pursuing the exempt organization's exempt purposes?

The third criterion is met where the economic benefits to the for-profit parties are reasonable. Elements to avoid in this regard include disproportionate allocation of profits and/or losses in favor of the for-profit parties, commercially unreasonable loans by the exempt organization to the joint venture, insufficient capital contributions by the for-profit parties, and guarantees by the exempt organization to the for-profit parties (such as in connection with return on investment or projected tax credits).

(D) SUBSIDIARIES IN PARTNERSHIPS

One use of a subsidiary by a tax-exempt organization is its participation as a partner in a partnership, in lieu of participation in the partnership by the parent exempt organization. One reason to do this is to avoid endangering the exempt status of the parent entity. (A single-member limited liability company may also be used for this purpose.)

This can be an effective stratagem as long as all of the requirements of the law as to the bona fides of the subsidiary are satisfied, including the requirement that the subsidiary organization be an authentic business entity. As discussed, however, if the tax-exempt organization parent is intimately involved in the day-to-day management of the subsidiary, the IRS or a court may impute the activities of the subsidiary to the parent, thereby possibly jeopardizing the exempt status of the parent by treating it as if it were directly involved as a partner in the partnership.

(E) WHOLE-ENTITY JOINT VENTURES

As noted, an exempt organization is a participant in a whole-entity joint venture when it places itself, in its entirety, in the venture. The law to date concerns only public charities in this type of arrangement. The participation in the venture becomes the charitable organization's sole activity. A for-profit entity usually is the other venturer. The joint venture vehicle is likely to be a limited liability company.

The key issue in this context is the element of *control*. That is, the IRS and the courts will look to see whether the charity, by involving itself in this type of venture, lost control of its resources to the for-profit coventurer. The phraseology often used is determination as to whether the exempt organization "ceded its authority" over its operations to the other venturer. Elements to be considered are the composition of the board of the limited liability company and whether the arrangement is managed by a for-profit management company that is affiliated with the for-profit coventurer. Tax-exempt status is forgone where this control is forfeited by the charitable organization.

As noted, the law on this subject has unfolded to date in the health care setting. In one case where tax exemption was lost, the court termed the public charity's involvement "passive participation in a for-profit health-service enterprise." The for-profit participant was portrayed as having an "independent economic interest in the same activity," that is, the activity previously conducted solely by the charitable health care organization. Further, the venture itself had "no obligation to put charitable purposes ahead of profit-making objectives." Exemption was lost because the exempt organization conferred "significant private benefits" on the for-profit party (see § 6.1(c)).

Consequently, a public charity contemplating involvement in a whole-entity joint venture should, to retain tax-exempt status, strive not to lose control over program activities. The composition of the board of the venture and the nature of any management company are, as noted, critical elements. Another factor is documentation: The agreements and other documents involved should stress the powers and functions of the nonprofit organization. Contracts should be negotiated at arm's length. Contracts for services performed by a for-profit coventurer or any of its affiliates should not have unduly long terms. The joint venture documentation should be clear that, should the venturers' interests clash, the charitable purposes of the exempt party will trump commercial the profit-making motives of the for-profit party.

(F) ANCILLARY JOINT VENTURES

It is the view of the IRS that the principles involved in the jurisprudence concerning whole-entity joint ventures (see § 11.1(f)(3)(E)) apply fully when an exempt organization is involved in an ancillary joint venture. Thus, the element of control and application of the private benefit doctrine is seen by the agency as likewise applicable in this context. A difference, however, is that, in the instance of an ancillary joint venture, the adverse outcome may be limited to unrelated business income taxation rather than loss of exempt status.

In one instance, a tax-exempt university entered into a joint venture (a limited liability company) with a for-profit company that specialized in the conduct of interactive video training programs. The sole purpose of the venture was to offer teacher-training seminars at locations off the university's campus using interactive video technology. The university and the for-profit company each held a 50 percent interest in the venture, which was proportionate to the value of their respective capital contributions. All returns of capital, allocations, and distributions were to be made in proportion to the members' respective ownership interests. The company was managed by a governing board composed of three directors selected by the university and three selected by the company. The university retained the exclusive right to approve the curriculum, training materials, and instructors and to determine the standards for successful completion of the seminars. The company had the exclusive right to select the locations where participants could receive a video link to the seminars and to approve other personnel (such as camera operators).

Under these facts, the IRS concluded that the university retained control over the venture. This guidance leaves certain issues unresolved because the agency concluded that (1) the business of the venture was related to the exercise of the university's exempt functions and (2) the activities the university conducted through the limited liability company are merely an insubstantial part of its total activities.

It is not clear, therefore, what the outcome is in a situation such as this, where the business of the venture is unrelated to the public charity's exempt purposes and/or its involvement is more than insubstantial. The IRS seemed to indicate that, if the public charity loses control over its resources in an ancillary joint venture, the business of the venture would be transformed from a related one to an unrelated one—a novel theory. Also, even if the activities in the ancillary venture are related, if the public charity cedes authority over the resources to the for-profit venturer and the exempt organization's participation in the venture is more than incidental, it would seem that the organization's tax exemption would be jeopardized, by application of the private inurement or private benefit doctrine (see §§ 6.1(a) and (c)).

(G) Limited Liability Companies

As noted, limited liability companies are of two varieties: the multi-member company and the single-member company. The former is emerging as the joint venture vehicle of choice in the tax-exempt organizations context.

(i) Multi-Member LLC

A limited liability company can have two or more members. One or more of the members may be tax-exempt organizations. There may be for-profit members as well. For that matter, all of the members of a limited liability company may be exempt organizations.

In assessing whether the participation by a charitable organization as a member of a multi-member limited liability company, also consisting of one or more nonexempt persons, will have an adverse impact of the charitable organization's tax-exempt status, the criteria summarized earlier must be applied (see §§ 11.1(f)(3)(C)–(F)). To reiterate, the tax law outcome will turn on the element of control.

Examples of tax-exempt organizations' involvement in a multi-member limited liability company involving for-profit entities include:

- An exempt health care system and a group of physicians formed a limited liability company for the purpose of owning and operating an ambulatory surgery center.

- An exempt hospital owned and operated six cardiac catheterization laboratories. These facilities were in the hospital's building. The hospital wanted to develop a seventh cardiac catheterization laboratory as an outpatient facility and wanted to involve the physicians who had staff privileges at the institution. The hospital created a limited liability company, consisting of its supporting organization and the physicians, for this purpose.

Examples of tax-exempt organizations' involvement in multi-member limited liability companies involving only exempt entities include:

- An exempt institution of higher education operated two neonatal intensive care units in its capacity as a component of an academic medical center. An exempt hospital also operated a neonatal intensive care unit. The two organizations formed a limited liability company for the purpose of administering the hospital's existing facility and a new and expanded neonatal intensive care unit.

- Private colleges and universities can maintain their own qualified prepaid tuition plans. A single plan was established, structured for use by these colleges and universities throughout the nation. This program was stitched together by means of a consortium agreement. The vehicle for this plan is a limited liability company, with the colleges and universities its members.

- Three trade associations having comparable exempt purposes and members with congruent interests for years operated their own trade shows. To reduce the administrative costs of the shows, the associations created a limited liability company for the purpose of conducting a single trade show.

(ii) Single-Member LLC

A limited liability company may be formed with only one member (assuming state law permits). The member may be a tax-exempt organization. This type of entity is disregarded for federal tax purposes. This means that, while the company has the feature as to limitation on liability afforded pursuant to state law, the federal tax law regards the economic activity in the exempt organization and in the limited liability company as conducted in one entity (the exempt organization). Consequently, the exempt organization in this circumstance must report on its Form 990 the economic activity, assets, and/or liabilities of the single member LLC as if they were conducted directly by the exempt organization.

A disregarded limited liability company is treated as a branch or division of its member owner. Thus, although the single-member limited liability company is a separate legal entity for nontax purposes, it is regarded as a component of its owner for federal income tax purposes. The IRS observed that, when the sole member of a limited liability company is a tax-exempt organization, the function of the company is seen as an "activity" of the exempt organization.

Tax-exempt organizations are making creative use of the single-member limited liability company. Examples include:

- A public charity was working with a city government to transform the older, downtown sections of the city into a center of industry, commerce, housing, transportation, government services, and cultural and educational opportunities. These sections lacked adequate parking due to the completion of several major development projects. The charity organized a single-member limited liability company to address the need for affordable downtown parking. It acquired a parking garage and two parking lots by means of a bond issue. The IRS held that the LLC was a disregarded entity for tax purposes and that the LLC's operations would not jeopardize the charity's exempt status because the charity, by means of the LLC, was lessening the burdens of the city government.

- A charitable organization may accept a gift of property that carries with it exposure of the donee to legal liability (such as environmental or premises tort liability). Before the advent of the single-member limited liability company, a charitable organization could attempt to shield its other assets from liability by placing the gift property in a separate exempt entity, such as a supporting organization (see § 8.1(h)) or a title-holding company. Among the difficulties with this approach is the need or desire to file an application for recognition of tax exemption for the new entity and/or file Forms 990 on its behalf. As an alternative, however, a charitable organization can utilize a single-member limited liability company as the vehicle to receive and hold a contribution of this nature. Each of these contributed properties can be placed in a separate single-member limited liability company, thereby offering protection in relation to each of the other gift properties and providing the charity overall liability protection.

- A public charity, with the objective of constructing, owning, and leasing student housing for the benefit of a tax-exempt college, developed and operated the project through a single-member limited liability company. In this fashion it issued taxable and tax-exempt bonds, and provided temporary construction jobs and permanent employment opportunities in the community.

- A private operating foundation took over the operation of a school within a tax-exempt university. The school was suffering financial difficulties. The foundation assumed management and financing of the school. It did so via a single-member limited liability company. (It is not an everyday occurrence for a private foundation to control and actively manage a program component of a public charity.)

§ 11.2 PREPARATION OF NEW FORM 990 SCHEDULE D

Schedule D asks for supplemental financial reporting regarding certain types of assets and liabilities, including donor-advised funds, conservation easements, art and museum collections, escrow accounts and custodial arrangements, and endowment funds.

(a) Part I (Donor-Advised Funds)

Organizations must complete Part I if they answer "yes" to Form 990, Part IV, line 6. Organizations answer "yes" to this question if they maintain any donor-advised funds or other accounts where donors have the right to provide advice on the distribution or investment of amounts in such funds or accounts. Understanding Part I and donor-advised funds requires understanding certain key terms: *sponsoring organization*, *donor-advised fund*, and *donor advisor*.

- A *sponsoring organization* is any organization that: (1) is described in Section 170(c), except for governmental entities or organizations described in Section 170(c)(1) or 170(c)(2)(A); (2) is not a private foundation as defined in Section 509(a); and (3) maintains one or more donor-advised funds. (Note: Section 170(c)(1) describes states, possessions of the United States and any political subdivision or either states or possessions (e.g., cites, counties, townships, etc.).)

- A *donor-advised fund* is a fund or account: (1) that is separately identified by reference to contributions of a donor or donors; (2) that is owned and controlled by a sponsoring organization; and (3) for which the donor or donor advisor has or reasonably expects to have advisory privileges in the distribution or investment of amounts held in the donor-advised funds or accounts because of the donor's status as a donor. However, a donor-advised fund does not include any fund or account:

- That the Secretary of the Treasury exempts from being treated as a donor advised fund because either such fund or account is advised by a committee not directly or indirectly controlled by the donor or donor advisor or such fund benefits a single identified charitable purpose. For example, see Notice 2006-109, 2006-51 I.R.B. 1121;

- That makes distributions only to a single identified organization or governmental entity; or

- In which a donor or donor advisor gives advice about which individuals receive grants for travel, study, or other similar purposes, if:

  - the donor or donor advisor's advisory privileges are performed exclusively by such person in his or her capacity as a committee member in which all of the committee members are appointed by the sponsoring organization;

  - no combination of donors or donor advisors (and related persons of donors and donor advisors) directly or indirectly control the committee; and

  - all grants from the fund or account are awarded on an objective and non-discriminatory basis following a procedure approved in advance by the board of directors of the sponsoring organization. The procedure must be designed to ensure that all grants meet the requirements of Sections 4945(g)(1), (2), or (3).

- A *related person* is any family member (as defined in Section 4958(f) of the Code) of the donor or donor advisor and any 35-percent controlled entity (as defined in Section 4958(f) of the Code) of the donor or donor advisor.

  - A *family member* includes the donor's or donor advisor's spouse, ancestors, children, grandchildren, and great-grandchildren; the spouses of children, grandchildren, and great-grandchildren; and the brothers and sisters (whether by the whole or half blood) of the individual and their spouses.

  - A *35-percent controlled entity* includes: a corporation in which the donor, donor advisor, or their family members own more than 35 percent of the total combined voting power; a partnership in which such persons own more than 35 percent of the profits interest; and a trust or estate in which such persons own more than 35 percent of the beneficial interest. For purposes of determining stock and partnership ownership, the constructive ownership rules of Section 267(c) apply.

- A *donor advisor* is any person appointed or designated by a donor to advise a sponsoring organization on the distribution or investment of amounts held in the donor's fund or account.

In the table on Schedule D, Part I, lines 1 through 4, Columns (a) and (b), the organization is supposed to report certain information about any fund or account where donors have the right to provide advice on distributions from such fund or account. All funds or accounts that meet the definition of a donor-advised fund (as defined earlier), and that are held at any time during the tax year by the organization as a sponsoring organization, are aggregated into Column (a). Any other fund held by the organization at any time during the tax year for which donors, or persons appointed by the donors, can advise on distributions or investments but which do not meet the definition of a donor-advised fund (as defined earlier) are aggregated into Column (b). Examples of funds to be reported in Column (b) include, but are not limited to, funds or accounts that meet the exceptions described earlier in this section or that are otherwise prescribed by statute as excepted from the meaning of a donor-advised fund.

For each Column, on lines 1 through 4, the organization should report:

Line 1. Report in Column (a) the total number of donor-advised funds and in Column (b) the total number of other similar funds or accounts held by the organization at the end of the year.

Line 2. Report in Column (a) the aggregate amount of contributions during the year to all donor-advised funds and in Column (b) the aggregate amount of contributions during the year to all other similar funds or accounts held by the organization.

Line 3. Report in Column (a) the aggregate amount of grants made during the year from all donor-advised funds and in Column (b) the aggregate amount of grants made during the year from all other similar funds or accounts held by the organization.

Line 4. Report in Column (a) the aggregate value at the end of the year of all donor-advised funds and in Column (b) the aggregate value at the end of the year of all other similar funds or accounts held by the organization. Although the instructions do not say whether to report book value or fair market value, a reasonable approach would be to report the value at which the funds are reported in Form 990, Part X, Balance Sheet, Column (B). Also, the instructions do not say whether to report beginning-of-year or end-of-year values, but Part I, line 4 of Schedule D clearly states end-of-year values.

Line 5. Answer this line "yes" if the organization informs all donors and donor advisors in writing that funds held in donor-advised funds are the property of the organization and subject to the organization's exclusive legal control. Otherwise answer "no."

Line 6. Answer this line "yes" if the organization advises all grantees, donors, and donor advisors that grant funds cannot be used for the benefit of the donor or donor advisor or their families. Otherwise answer "no."

> *TIP:* With respect to lines 5 and 6, if the organization is filing a group return for a group of subordinate members under a group exemption, answer "no" if the answer is "no" for any subordinate member included in the group return. Explain the answer in Schedule O (e.g., "3 subordinate members can answer 'yes' but 1 subordinate member answers 'no'").

(b)   Part II (Conservation Easements)

Organizations that answer "yes" to Form 990, Part IV, line 7 must prepare Part II. Organizations answer "yes" to that question if they receive or hold a *conservation easement*, including easements to preserve open space, the environment, historic land areas, or historic structures.

> *TIP:* Report any conservation held by a joint venture formed for the purpose of holding such conservation easements.

Part II and the glossary to the instructions distinguish a *conservation easement* from a *qualified conservation contribution*. For all practical purposes, the difference between the two is that a qualified conservation contribution is a contribution of a conservation easement that is a qualified real property interest. Thus, every qualified conservation contribution is a conservation easement, but every conservation easement is not necessarily a qualified conservation contribution (unless it is also a qualified real property interest). Some lines in Part II apply to all conservation easements, and some apply only to qualified conservation contributions. For the definition of a qualified conservation contribution (including the definition of a qualified real property interest, which is the key distinguisher of a qualified conservation contribution from a conservation easement), see § 11.1(b). A conservation easement is defined as:

> A restriction on the use that may be made of, or changes made to, real property that is granted in perpetuity to a qualified organization exclusively for conservation purposes. Conservation purposes include protection of natural habitat, the preservation of open space, or the preservation of property for historic, educational, or recreational purposes. Qualified organizations include governmental units and certain tax-exempt organizations described in Section 501(c)(3) of the Internal Revenue Code that have a commitment to protect the conservation purposes of the easement and the resources to enforce the restrictions. A conservation easement also includes other real property interests in real property that under state law have attributes similar to an easement (e.g., a restrictive covenant or equitable servitude).

> *TIP:* In short, the primary difference between a qualified conservation contribution and a conservation easement is that the former can include fee interests and remainder interests in real property as well as easements and restrictions on real property, but the latter only includes easements and restrictions on real property.

(1) Line 1.   Answer line 1 with respect to all conservation easements held by the organization during the tax year and check all boxes that apply.

(2) Line 2.   Answer lines 2a to d if the organization held a qualified conservation contribution in the form of a conservation easement on the last day of the tax year.

> **Line 2a.**   Enter the number of conservation easements held by the organization at the end of the year. This should not be an estimate or a rounded off number.

Line 2b. Enter the total acreage restricted by conservation easements held by the organization at the end of the tax year. Complete the total acreage by adding together all the acres of land subject to all the easements held as of the end of the year. Do not include conservation easements on certified historic structures (since the acreage occupied by a building would be de minimis and hard to calculate—conservation easements on certified historic structures are expressed in terms of a number of easements, not acreage, and are reported in line 2c). Acreage may be expressed in decimal points for properties subject to easements where the acreage consists of less than whole numbers. For example, two and one-half acres may be expressed as 2.5 acres.

Line 2c. Enter the number of conservation easements on certified historic structures held by the organization at the end of the tax year. A certified historic structure is any building or structure listed in the National Register as well as any building certified as being of historic significance to a registered historic district.

Line 2d. Enter the number of conservation easements included in the answer to line 2c that the organization acquired after August 17, 2006. August 17, 2006, is the effective date of the Pension Protection Act of 2006, which contained special rules for conservation easements on a certified historic structure. See line 8 for additional questions about easements on certified historic structures obtained after August 17, 2006. Note: Section 170(h)(4)(B) of the Code contains special rules that apply to contributions made after August 17, 2006.

(3) Line 3. Generally, a grant of a conservation easement to a qualified organization is required to be made in perpetuity. Enter the total number of conservation easements held by the organization that were modified, transferred, released, extinguished, and/or terminated during the tax year. For example, if two easements were modified and one easement was terminated during the tax year, enter the number 3. For each easement that was modified, transferred, released, extinguished, or terminated, explain the changes in Part XIV of this schedule. An easement is modified when the terms of easement are amended. For example, if the deed of easement is amended to increase or decrease the amount of land subject to the easement and/or to add or remove restrictions regarding the use of the property subject to the easement, the easement is modified. An easement is transferred when the organization assigns the deed of easement whether with or without consideration. An easement is released or terminated when it is condemned, extinguished by court order, transferred to the landowner, or in any way rendered void and unenforceable.

> *Note:* Before any easement is modified, transferred, released, or terminated, the organization should consult legal counsel to determine if there are any adverse consequences. For example, a modification, transfer, release, or termination that benefits the donor or another private party and for which the organization is not adequately compensation could result in private inurement, private benefit, or an excess benefit transaction. (See § 6.1(a)–(c).) In Part XIV, the organization should articulate why such modification, transfer, release, or termination did not constitute private inurement, private benefit, or an excess benefit transaction.

(4) Line 4. Enter as a total number the number of states where property is located that is subject to a conservation easement or easements held by the organization during the tax year.

(5) Line 5. Report whether the organization has a written policy or policies regarding how the organization will monitor, inspect, respond to violations, and enforce conservation easements. If "yes," briefly summarize such policy or policies in Part XIV of Schedule D. Indicate whether such policy or policies are reflected in the organization's easement documents. *Monitoring* means that the organization investigates the use or condition of the real property restricted by the easement to determine if the property owner is adhering to the restrictions imposed by the terms of the easement to ensure that the conservation purpose of the easement is being achieved. *Inspection* means an on-site visit to observe the property to carry out a monitoring purpose. *Enforcement of an easement* means action taken by the organization after it discovers a violation to compel a property owner to adhere to the terms of the conservation easement. Such activities may include communications with the property owner explaining his or her obligations with respect to the easement, arbitration, or litigation.

> *TIP:* With respect to line 5, if the organization is filing a group return for a group of subordinate members under a group exemption, answer "no" if the answer is "no" for any subordinate member included in the group return. Explain the answer in Schedule O (e.g., "3 subordinate members can answer 'yes' but 1 subordinate member answers 'no'").

(6) Line 6. Enter the total number of hours devoted by the organization during the year to monitoring, inspecting, and enforcing easements, as those terms are defined for line 5. Include the hours devoted to this purpose by any paid staff, by any unpaid volunteers, and by any agents or contractors.

(7) Line 7. Enter the total amount of expenses incurred by the organization during the year to monitor, inspect, and enforce the easements it held during the year as those terms are defined for line 5.

(8) Line 8. Answer "yes" if each conservation easement on a certified historic structure (sometimes referred to as a façade easement) acquired after August 17, 2006, satisfies the requirements of both Section 170(c)(4)(B)(i) and (ii) of the Code. Section 170(c)(4)(B)(i) requires each façade easement donated after August 17, 2006, to include a restriction that preserves the entire exterior of the building, including the front, sides, rear, and height of the building, and to prohibit any change in the exterior of the building that is inconsistent with the historical character of such exterior. Section 170(c)(4)(B)(ii) requires the donor and donee to enter into a written agreement certifying, among other things, that the donee organization has the resources to manage the historic preservation property and a commitment to do so.

> *TIP:* With respect to line 8, if the organization is filing a group return for a group of subordinate members under a group exemption, answer "no" if the answer is "no" for any subordinate member included in the group return. Explain the answer in Schedule O (e.g., "3 subordinate members can answer 'yes' but 1 subordinate member answers 'no'").

> *Note with respect to lines 4 to 8:* A qualified organization must have a commitment to protect the conservation purposes of the easement and have the resources to enforce the restrictions. If an organization reports too many easements in too many states, it could raise a question for the IRS whether the organization has sufficient resources to enforce the restrictions. Although the organization gets to report both hours and expenses devoted to enforcing restrictions (see lines 6 and 7), if a large number of easements or numerous states are reported, the organization can consider supplemental reporting in Part XIV to makes its case that it is taking reasonable steps and devoting reasonable resources to protecting its interests and enforcing the restrictions.

(9) Line 9. Enter on Part XIV of this schedule a description of how the organization reports conservation easements (1) in its revenue and expense statements, and (2) on its balance sheets. Include in Part XIV, if applicable, the text of the footnote to the organization's financial statements that describes the organization's accounting for conservation easements and the basis for its reporting position (e.g., FASB EITF 02-7, Example 1). (Note: FASB Emerging Issues Task Force Statement 02-7, Example 1, deals with reporting of easements on financial statements.)

(c) Part III (Collections of Art, Historical Treasures, and Other Similar Assets)

The organization should complete Part III if it answers "yes" to Form 990, Part IV, line 8. The organization answers "yes" to line 8 if it maintains collections of art, historical treasures, or other similar assets.

Organizations that receive contributions of works of art, historical treasures, and similar assets that do not maintain collections as described in SFAS 116 are not required to complete Part III.

The preparation and completion of Part III is governed by SFAS 116. Pursuant to paragraph 11 of SFAS 116, an organization does not have to recognize as income (nor carry as an asset on its balance sheet) contributions of works of art, historical treasures, and other similar assets if the donated items are added to existing collections that meet all three of the following conditions:

1. The collections are held for public exhibition, education, or research in furtherance of public service rather than financial gain.

2. The collections are protected, kept unencumbered, cared for, and preserved.

3. The collections are subject to an organizational policy that requires the proceeds from sales of collection items to be used to acquire other items for the collection.

An organization that meets these criteria and opts not to recognize and capitalize its collections for financial statement purposes (i.e., opts not to report on the statement of revenue and balance sheet) will report its collections on the face of its statement of activities, separately from revenues, expenses, gains, losses, and assets. An organization that does not meet these criteria (e.g., because the collections are held for financial gain) will recognize and capitalize its collections for financial statement purposes and will report its collections as assets and revenues based on its fair value measurement.

Line 1 pertains to collection items held by the organization in furtherance of public service, with line 1a for those organizations that do not recognize and capitalize their collections and line 1b for those organizations that do recognize and capitalize their collections. Line 2 pertains to collection items held by the organization for financial gain, as those terms are described in SFAS 116. Such collection items must be recognized and capitalized.

(1) Line 1. If an organization has elected not to recognize and capitalize its collections, then provide in Part XIV of Schedule D the footnote(s) to the organization's financial statements that describe these collection items.

If an organization has elected to recognize and capitalize its collections, then (1) provide on line 1(b)(i) the revenues reported as to these collection items from the total revenues reported on Form 990, Part VIII, line 1; and (2) provide on line 1(b)(ii) the asset value assigned to these collection items from the total assets reported on Form 990, Part X.

(2) Line 2. If an organization has received or held collections for financial gain, then (1) provide on line 2(a) the revenues reported as to these collection items from the total revenues included on Form 990, Part VIII, line 1; and (2) provide on line 2(b) the asset value assigned to these collection items from the total assets reported on Form 990, Part X.

(3) Line 3. Based on the organization's acquisition, accession, and other records, check all boxes that best describe how the organization utilizes its collections, including the collection's most significant use.

(4) Line 4. On Part XIV of Schedule D, provide a description of the organization's collections and explain how these collections further the organization's exempt purposes. More specifically, the organization should explain how the collection is made available for public viewing, assists in scholarly research, assists in education, how the collection is preserved for future generations, and whether the organization makes the collection available for loan or exchange programs.

(5) Line 5. Answer "yes" to line 5 if during the year the organization solicited or received donations of art, historical treasures, or other similar assets to be sold in order to raise funds rather than to be maintained as part of the organization's collection. The answer to this question may have some bearing on the amount of deduction the donor can take for the contribution (see § 19.1(d)).

(d) Part IV (Trust, Escrow, and Custodial Arrangements)

Organizations must complete Part IV if they answer "yes" to Form 990, Part IV, line 9, regarding escrow or custodial accounts or arrangements. An organization answers "yes" to line 9 if (1) the organization provides credit counseling, debt management, credit repair, or debt negotiation services; (2) reports an escrow liability on Form 990, Part X, line 21; or (3) serves as a trustee or custodian for amounts not listed on Form 990, Part X. Although the IRS seems primarily concerned with credit counseling and down payment assistance organizations, completion of Part IV can also be required of organizations that serve as trustees or that are custodian for another organization's assets. For example, an organization may serve as a trustee of a charitable remainder trust, an endowment may hold funds as custodian for other organizations, or a national association may hold funds as custodian for regional chapters.

(1) Line 1. If the organization acts as an escrow agent, trustee, custodian, or other intermediary for funds payable to other organizations or individuals and has not reported those amounts on Form 990, Part X, as an asset or liability, answer "yes" and provide an explanation in Part XIV. In addition, the organization must complete lines 1c through 1f with respect to increases or decreases in such funds. On line 1c, report the beginning balance of such funds; on line 1d, the additions during the year; on line 1e, distributions of such funds; and on line 1f, the ending balance.

Examples:

- A credit counseling organization that collects amounts from debtors to remit to creditors may hold funds in an escrow or custodial account. If the organization acts as a go-between and does not report these funds as its assets or liabilities on Form 990, Part X, it must report the fund balances on lines 1c through 1f.

- An organization providing down payment assistance that collects amounts from donors to be used toward the purchase of qualifying housing may hold funds in an escrow or custodial account. If the organization acts as a go-between and does not report these funds as its assets or liabilities on Form 990, Part X, it must report the fund balances on lines 1c through 1f.

(2) Line 2. If the organization reports any amounts in Form 990, Part X, line 21 (Escrow Account Liability), then answer "yes" for line 2a, and explain in Part XIV the arrangement under which the amounts reported in line 21 are held, including any obligations the organization has to other persons under such arrangements. (See § 7.2(c)(21) for a discussion of Form 990, Part X, line 21.)

(e) Part V (Endowment Funds)

Complete Part V if the organization answered "yes" to Form 990, Part IV, line 10. Answer "yes" to line 10 if the organization holds assets in term, permanent, or quasi-endowment (sometimes called a board-designated endowment). For this Part V, the definitions of endowments and types of endowments are governed by SFAS 117, paragraphs 14 through 17. Information reported in Part V should pertain to the aggregate of the organization's endowments.

TIP: While the Form 990 refers to term endowments, permanent endowments, and quasi-endowments, SFAS 117 refers to, respectively, temporarily restricted net assets, permanently restricted net assets, and unrestricted net assets.

- *Term endowments* (referred to in SFAS 117 as *temporarily restricted net assets*) are endowment funds that are maintained to provide a source of income for either a specified period of time or until a specific event occurs.

- *Permanent (true) endowments* (referred to in SFAS 117 as *permanently restricted net assets*) are endowment funds that are maintained to provide a permanent source of income, with the stipulation that principal must be invested and kept intact in perpetuity, while only the income generated can be used by the organization.

- *Board designated* or *quasi-endowments* (referred to in SFAS 117 as *unrestricted net assets*) are funds functioning as an endowment that are established by the organization itself, from either donor or institutional funds.

Note: For 2008, Columns (b) through (e) may be left blank. In future years, prior-year information will be required to be reported, but the record keeping required to complete Part V for prior years will be applied only on a prospective basis.

(1) Line 1.

Line 1a. Enter the beginning year balance of the organization's endowment funds. The amount entered should agree with the organization's total of permanent (true), term, and quasi-endowment funds at the beginning of the year.

Line 1b. Enter the amount of current-year contributions to the organization's endowment funds. This amount includes all donor gifts, grants, and contributions received as well as additional funds that have been established by the organization's governing board to function like an endowment (a quasi-endowment or board-designated endowment) but that may be expended at any time at the discretion of the board.

Line 1c. Enter the current-year net amount of investment earnings, gains, and losses, including both realized or unrealized amounts. For earnings reported net of transaction costs, enter the net amount in line 1c. For earnings reported on a gross basis, enter the gross earnings on line 1c, and enter the transaction costs in line 1f.

Line 1d. Enter the current-year amounts distributed for grants or scholarships. Because scholarships represent direct aid to individuals, they are distinguished from general programmatic aid referenced in line 1e.

Line 1e. Enter the current-year amounts distributed for facilities and programs. Amounts on this line should include withdrawn amounts and amounts disinvested from an organization's quasi-endowments.

Line 1f. Enter the amount of current year administrative expenses charged to the endowment fund. These expenses can arise from either internal or third-party sources. For example, if internal administrative costs are allocated to, or charged against, the endowment fund, include these amounts in line 1f as well as investment fees paid to a third-party investment advisor.

Line 1g. Enter the year-end balance of the endowments. To determine the year-end balance, add lines 1a, 1b, and investment earnings of line 1c, and subtract line 1c investment losses and the amounts on lines 1d through 1f.

Note (with respect to line 1): How the organization is supposed to calculate grants and scholarships (line 1d), other facility and program expenditures (line 1e), and administrative expenses (line 1f) is not entirely clear. For example, if there is a permanent endowment restricted to Program A, and during the year the organization spends $x on Program A out of its operating budget (without drawing down the permanent endowment), does the organization record $x on line 1e even though it came out of operating income rather than drawing down the endowment? A good rule of thumb here would be to follow SFAS 117 for purposes of reporting in Part V. Thus, in the above example, if SFAS 117 would permit the reclassification of $x from permanently restricted net assets to unrestricted net assets, it would be reasonable to report $x on line 1e.

Moreover, it is not clear whether valuation should occur on a book or fair market value basis, or if such amount should tie back to the Form 990, Part X, Balance Sheet. Because there is no requirement to tie back to the Part X, Balance Sheet, it is reasonable to prepare the table in line 1 based on market value of endowments.

Caution (with respect to line 2): At the time this book and the IRS instructions went to print, the Financial Accounting Standards Board was considering adopting FASB Staff Position 117-a, effective for reporting years ending after December 15, 2008. FASB Staff Position 117-a addresses reporting of endowments as permanently restricted or temporarily restricted funds. Further, a number of states have enacted or are considering enacting the Uniform Prudent Management of Institutional Funds Act (UPMIFA). If the organization is subject to UPMIFA or FASB Staff Position 117-a, it may affect the amounts reported on lines 2a through 2c.

---

(2) Line 2. On lines 2a through 2c, enter the estimated percentage of the organization's total endowment funds at year end held in (a) board-designated or quasi-endowment funds (referred to as unrestricted assets in SFAS 117), (b) permanent endowments funds (referred to as permanently restricted net assets in SFAS 117), or (c) term endowment funds (referred to as temporarily restricted net assets in SFAS 117). The total of these three percentages should equal 100 percent.

(3) Line 3. Answer "yes" on line 3a(i) if any of the organization's endowment funds are in the possession of and administered by unrelated organizations. This could be the case if, for example, the organization's endowment is held by a community foundation or the organization is a local chapter and its endowment is pooled with the national association and other local chapters. (Note that the relationship between national associations and local chapters often will not meet the control requirement necessary for them to be related organizations.)

Answer "yes" on line 3a(ii) if any of the organization's endowment funds are in the possession of and administered by related organizations (as defined in the glossary to the IRS instructions). This is commonly the case when an organization creates a subsidiary foundation or endowment corporation to hold its endowment assets, or when the organization and such endowment are under the common control of a parent organization.

All related organizations are required to be reported on Schedule R. Answer "yes" on line 3b if the organization answered "yes" to line 3a(ii) and the organization listed all of the related organizations referred to in line 3a(ii) in Schedule R. (See Chapter 21 for a discussion of Schedule R.)

(4) Line 4. Describe in Part XIV of Schedule D the intended uses of the organization's endowment funds. For example, for permanent (true) and term endowments (referred to in SFAS 117, respectively, as permanently restricted and temporarily restricted net assets), describe the restrictions that apply to the endowments (e.g., scholarships, charity care, education, etc.). For board-designated or quasi-endowments (referred to in SFAS 117 as unrestricted net assets), describe the board restrictions placed on the endowments. For unrestricted net assets that have no board restriction, state the intended use (e.g., maintaining cash reserves for bond ratings, operating reserves, set-asides for future capital projects, etc.). It is important to communicate that the assets are actually being held for a charitable purpose and that the organization is not amassing wealth without any apparent intention to use the wealth to achieve its mission.

(f) Part VI (Investments—Land, Buildings, and Equipment)

The organization must prepare Part VI if it answers "yes" on Form 990, Part IV, line 11 by virtue of reporting any amount on Form 990, Part X, Balance Sheet, lines 10a, 10b, or 10c, Column (B). Line 10 of the balance sheet pertains to land, buildings, and equipment. Reporting in Part VI of Schedule D is required if any amount other than zero is reported on lines 10a to c of the Form 990, Part X, Balance Sheet (which differs from Parts VII, VIII, and IX where assets are only reported if they exceed 5 percent of total assets).

Note: If the organization answers "yes" to Form 990, Part IV, line 11 by virtue of reporting any amount on Form 990, Part X, Balance Sheet, lines 12, 13, 15, or 25, then see the instructions for Schedule D, Parts VII, VIII, IX, and X, respectively.

Real property and improvements must be categorized as land (reported on line 1a), buildings (reported on line 1b), leasehold improvements (reported on line 1c), and equipment (reported on line 1d). Information for each category of asset should be reported in this way:

Column (a). Enter the cost or other basis of all land, buildings, leasehold improvements, equipment, and other fixed assets held for investment purposes (such as rental properties). Assets held for other than investment purposes (such as charitable operations) should be reported in Column (b).

Column (b). Enter the cost or other basis of all other land, buildings, leasehold improvements, equipment, and other fixed assets held for other than investment purposes, including any land, buildings, and equipment owned and used by the organization in conducting its exempt activities. The total amounts reported in Columns (a) and (b) must equal the amount reported on Form 990, Part X, Balance Sheet, line 10a.

Column (c). Enter the accumulated depreciation recorded with respect to the assets listed in Columns (a) and (b). Do not enter an amount in Column (c) for line 1a ("Land") because land cannot be depreciated. The total of Column (c) must equal the amount reported on Form 990, Part X, line10b.

Column (d). Enter the sum of Column (a) and Column (b) minus Column (c). The total of Column (d) must equal the amount reported on Form 990, Part X, line 10c, Column (B), which would require reporting in Column (d) the sum of Column (a) and (b) minus Column (c).

TIP: Although the instructions do not say so, all values reported on Part VI should be end-of-year values because Part VI must tie back to the Form 990, Part X, Balance Sheet, lines 10a through 10c, Column (B), all of which use end-of-year values.

(g) Part VII (Investments—Other Securities)

Complete Part VII if the organization answers "yes" to Form 990, Part IV, line 11, by virtue of reporting an amount in Form 990, Part X, Balance Sheet, line 12. Line 12 of the balance sheet is used to report non–publicly traded securities and publicly traded securities for which the organization owns 5 percent or more of the outstanding shares of a single class. Only prepare Part VII if the amount on Form 990, Part X, line 12 is 5 percent or more of the total assets reported on Part X, line 16.

Note: If the organization answers "yes" to Form 990, Part IV, line 11 by virtue of reporting any amount on Form 990, Part X, Balance Sheet, lines 10, 13, 15, or 25, then see the instructions for Schedule D, Parts VI, VIII, IX and X, respectively.

Include in Part VII:

- Stock in a closely held company whose stock is not available for sale to the general public or which is not widely traded.

- Publicly traded stock for which the organization holds 5 percent or more of the outstanding shares of the same class. List each separate class of publicly traded stock held by the organization that meets the 5 percent ownership test.

Do not include program-related investments as these are reported in Part VIII.

Column (a). Describe the type of investment (e.g., partnership interest, limited liability corporation interest, closely held stock, etc.). For each class of publicly traded stock for which the organization holds 5 percent or more of the outstanding shares, list stock by name and class (Class A Common, Preferred, etc.) and include the number of shares held (e.g., 1,000,000 shares of Class B Preferred of XYZ Corporation).

Column (b). Enter the book value for each investment. The total of Column (b) must equal the amount reported on Form 990, Part X, Balance Sheet, line 12, Column (B).

Column (c). Indicate whether the investment is listed at cost or end-of-year market value. When reporting securities at fair market value, use commonly accepted valuation methods.

> *TIP:* Although the instructions do not say so, all values reported on Part VII should be end-of-year values because Part VII must tie back to the Form 990, Part X, Balance Sheet, line 12, Column (B), which uses end-of-year values.

(h) Part VIII (Investments—Program Related)

Complete Part VIII if the organization answers "yes" in Form 990, Part IV, line 11 by virtue of reporting an amount in Form 990, Part X, Balance Sheet, line 13. Line 13 is used to report program-related investments. Only prepare Part VIII if the amount on Form 990, Part X, line 13 is 5 percent or more of the total assets reported on Part X, line 16.

> *Note:* If the organization answers "yes" to Form 990, Part IV, line 11 by virtue of reporting any amount on Form 990, Part X, Balance Sheet, lines 10, 12, 15, or 25, then see the instructions for Schedule D, Parts VI, VII, IX and X, respectively.

Program-related investments are investments made primarily to accomplish the organization's exempt purposes rather than to produce income. Examples of program-related investments include student loans and notes receivable from other exempt organizations that obtained the funds to pursue the filing organization's exempt function, such as to make loans to students to pursue higher education. Arguably, investments in subsidiaries or joint ventures that achieve the organization's exempt purposes could be reported here rather than in Part VII. Examples of such joint ventures could include a hospital that invests in a rehabilitation hospital joint venture, a school that invests in a distance learning subsidiary, or a housing organization that is a partner in low-income housing development. In any event, such subsidiaries and joint ventures should be reported in Part VIII (rather than Part VII) only to the extent they are reported on Form 990, Part X, Balance Sheet, line 13 (Program-Related Investments) rather than line 12 (Other Securities) because Part VIII must tie to line 13 of the Part X, Balance Sheet. In other words, whether such assets are reported on line 12 or 13 of the Part X, Balance Sheet will determine whether they are reported on Schedule D, Part VII or VIII. (See §§ 7.2(c)(12) and (13) for a discussion of lines 12 and 13 to the Part X, Balance Sheet.)

With respect to reporting in Part VIII:

Column (a). List each type of program related investment.

Column (b). Enter the book value of each program related investment. The total of the amounts reported in this Column must equal the amount in Form 990, Part X, Balance Sheet, line 13, Column (B).

Column (c). Indicate whether the investment is listed at cost or end-of-year market value.

> *TIP:* Although the instructions do not say so, all values reported on Part VIII should be end-of-year values because Part VIII must tie back to the Form 990, Part X, Balance Sheet, line 13, Column (B), which uses end-of-year values.

(i) Part IX (Other Assets)

Complete Part IX if the organization answers "yes" to Form 990, Part IV, line 11 by virtue of reporting an amount in Form 990, Part X, Balance Sheet, line 15. Line 15 of the Balance Sheet pertains to other assets not otherwise reported in lines 1 through 14 of the Balance Sheet. Only prepare Part IX if the amount on the Form 990, Part X, Balance Sheet, line 15 is 5 percent or more of the total assets reported on Part X, Balance Sheet, line 16.

> *Note:* If the organization answers "yes" to Form 990, Part IV, line 11 by virtue of reporting any amount on Form 990, Part X, Balance Sheet, lines 10, 12, 13, or 25, then see the instructions for Schedule D, Parts VI, VII, VIII, and X, respectively.

With respect to reporting in Part IX:

Column (a). Enter a description of assets reported on Form 990, Part X, line 15. The organization may use any reasonable basis to classify these assets. For example, an organization might list a category of "intellectual property" instead of listing every trademark, copyright, and patent separately.

Column (b). Enter the total book value of these assets. The instructions say that the total of Column (b) must equal the amount reported on Form 990, Part X, line 16, Column (B). The authors believe this is a typographical error and that Column (b) should tie to line 15 (Other Assets) of the Part X, Balance Sheet and not line 16 (Total Assets).

> *TIP:* Although the instructions do not say so, all values reported on Part IX should be end-of-year values because Part IX must tie back to the Form 990, Part X, Balance Sheet, line 15, Column (B), which uses end-of-year values.

(j)   Part X (Other Liabilities)

Complete Part X of Schedule D if the organization answers "yes" to Form 990, Part IV, line 11 by virtue of reporting an amount in Form 990, Part X, Balance Sheet, line 25. Line 25 of the Part X, Balance Sheet is used to report liabilities not otherwise reported on lines 17 through 24 of the Part X, Balance Sheet. Unlike Parts VII, VIII and IX of Schedule D, which require reporting only if the applicable 5 percent thresholds are exceeded, Part X of Schedule D must be prepared if any amount is reported on line 25 of the Part X, Balance Sheet.

> *Note:* If the organization answers "yes" to Form 990, Part IV, line 11 by virtue of reporting any amount on Form 990, Part X, Balance Sheet, lines 10, 12, 13, or 15, then see the instructions for Schedule D, Parts VI, VII, VIII, and IX, respectively.

With respect to reporting in Part X:

Column (a). List each type of liability not reported on lines 17 through 24 of Form 990, Part X, Balance Sheet. The organization may use any reasonable basis to classify these liabilities; provided, however, that these two liabilities must be reported separately and cannot be combined into other categories:

1. Federal income taxes must be reported separately on the line provided.

2. Amounts payable to related organizations must also be separately reported (related organizations are defined in the glossary to the instructions).

Column (b). Enter the book value of each liability. The total of the amounts reported in Column (b) should equal the amount reported on the Form 990, Part X, Balance Sheet, line 25, Column (B).

> *TIP:* Although the instructions do not say so, all values reported on Part X should be end-of-year values because Part X must tie back to the Form 990, Part X, Balance Sheet, line 25, Column (B), which uses end-of-year values.

Every organization required to complete Part X must provide the text of the footnote to its financial statements, if applicable, regarding the organization's liability for uncertain tax positions under FIN 48.

FIN 48 refers to Financial Accounting Standards Board (FASB) interpretation no. 48, *Accounting for Uncertainty in Income Taxes—An Interpretation of FASB Statement No. 109* (FIN 48). FIN 48 clarifies the accounting for uncertain tax positions taken on tax returns and requires recognition of these positions on an organization's financial statements in accordance with FASB Statement No. 109, *Accounting for Income Taxes* (SFAS 109). FIN 48 is effective for fiscal years beginning after December 15, 2006.

While an uncertain position taken on a tax return may be well grounded and based on good faith, the tax law is complex and the organization may not ultimately prevail. With respect to uncertain tax positions taken or expected to be taken on a tax return, FIN 48 requires recognition and measurement of the financial statement effects. For nonprofit organizations, this includes, for example, the description of a liability for unrelated business income tax or tax that may be assessed as a result of the revocation of exempt status. Any portion of the FIN 48 footnote that addresses only the filing organization's liability must be provided verbatim. The filing organization may summarize that portion, if any, of the footnote that applies to the liability of multiple organizations including the organization (e.g., as a member of a group with consolidated financial statements), to describe the filing organization's share of the liability.

(k) Parts XI, XII, and XIII (Reconciliation of Changes in Net Assets, Revenues, and Expenses from Form 990 to Audited Financial Statements)

Complete Part XI, Part XII, and Part XIII if the organization answers "yes" to Form 990, Part IV, line 12. An organization answers "yes" to line 12 if it receives an audited financials prepared in accordance with generally accepted accounting principles. If an organization just receives a compilation or review, it does not complete Parts XI through XIII.

If the organization did not receive an audited financial statement for the reporting year for which it is completing the Form 990, it is not required to complete Parts XI, XII, or XIII even if it prepared the Form 990 in accordance with SFAS 117.

Use the reconciliation statements of Parts XII and XIII to reconcile the differences between the revenue and expenses reported on the organization's audited financial statement prepared in accordance with SFAS 117 and the revenue and expenses reported on the organization's Form 990.

On line 4a of Parts XII and XIII, include only those investment expenses netted against investment income in the revenue portion of the organization's audited financial statement. Do not include program-related investment expenses or other expenses reported as program service expenses in the audited statement of activities.

> ▪ *TIP:* Parts XI, XII, and XIII do not have to be completed for group returns.

(l) Part XIV (Supplemental Information)

Use Part XIV to provide narrative information required in:

- Part II, line 9 (financial statement reporting of conservation easements)
- Part III, lines 1a and 4 (footnotes regarding collections of art, historical treasures, or other similar assets, and description of how such collections further the organization's exempt purposes)
- Part IV, lines 1b and 2b (explanation of trust, escrow, and custodial arrangements, and explanation of escrow liabilities reported on balance sheet)
- Part V, line 4 (intended uses of endowment funds)
- Part X (FIN 48 footnote text)
- Part XI, line 8 (reconciliation of change in net assets)

- Part XII, lines 2d and 4b (reconciliation of revenue)
- Part XIII, lines 2d and 4b (reconciliation of expenses)

The sections of the book that discuss these parts and lines (generally §§ 11.2(b) through (k)) contain additional information on what needs to be disclosed in Part XIV.

In addition, while the instructions to Part XIV do not require it, the instructions for these parts require supplemental Part XIV disclosure:

- Part II, line 3 (modification, transfer, release or termination of conservation easements)
- Part II, line 5 (summary of policy regarding periodic monitoring, inspection, and enforcement of conservation easements)

See the instructions for Part II, lines 3 and 5 for additional information on what needs to be disclosed on Part XIV.

Also use Part XIV to provide additional narrative explanations and descriptions. Identify the specific part and line number that the response supports, in the order that it appears on Schedule D.

§ 11.3 NEW FORM 990 COMPLIANCE TASKS

In order to complete Schedule D, organizations should take these steps:

1. **Donor-advised funds.** If the organization maintains donor-advised funds or accounts, it should:

   ○ Develop a policy regarding minimum distribution of funds from donor-advised funds and accounts. If the organization never reports distributions from donor-advised funds and accounts, this could raise concerns with the IRS that the organization is not using such funds to achieve its exempt purposes.

   ○ Advise donors and donor advisors in writing that funds held in donor-advised funds are the property of the organization and subject to the organization's exclusive legal control.

   ○ Advise all grantees, donors, and donor advisors in writing that grant funds cannot be used for the benefit of the donor or donor advisor or their families.

2. **Conservation easements.** If the organization accepts donations of conservation easements, it should:

   ○ Adopt a conservation easement policy if the organization owns conservation easements. The policy should address the monitoring, inspection, and enforcement of conservation easements.

   ○ For each conservation easement on a certified historic structure (sometimes referred to as a façade easement) acquired after August 17, 2006, make sure to (1) include a restriction that preserves the entire exterior of the building, including the front, sides, rear, and height of the building, and to prohibit any change in the exterior of the building that is inconsistent with the historical character of such exterior; and (2) enter into a written agreement certifying, among other things, that the donee organization has the resources to manage the historic preservation property and a commitment to do so. These steps are required to comply with Code Section 170(c)(4)(B)(ii).

- Before a conservation easement is modified, transferred, released, or terminated, consider any possible adverse consequences such as private inurement, private benefit, or excess benefit transaction, especially if the transaction includes the donor and lacks consideration.

3. **Collections of art and historical treasures.** If the organization maintains collections of art and historical treasures, it should determine whether it will elect under SFAS 116 not to report contributions of such items in its revenue statement and balance sheet.

4. **Endowment funds.** If the organization maintains an endowment fund, it should develop a policy regarding minimum distribution of endowment funds. If the organization never reports distributions from endowment funds, this could raise concerns with the IRS that the organization is not using such funds to achieve its exempt purposes.

CHAPTER TWELVE

Schedule E—Tax-Exempt Schools

A tax-exempt school can also qualify as a public charity if it meets certain criteria. If an organization claims status as such, additional information must be provided. The reporting of the additional information is made in Schedule A of the current Form 990, along with other information applicable to charities. The questions asked in the current Schedule A focus primarily on whether the organization has adopted a racially nondiscriminatory policy and follows the policy in the operation of the school. There is no reporting on the other criteria necessary for qualification as a school. The new Form 990 reporting is essentially the same as the current Form 990, but the reporting now is required in a separate Schedule E.

§ 12.1 LAW AND POLICY

To qualify for public charity status as a school, the organization must maintain a regular faculty and curriculum and normally have a regularly enrolled body of pupils or students in attendance at the place where its educational activities are regularly carried on. It also must adopt and implement a racially nondiscriminatory policy. The Schedule E reporting relates exclusively to the nondiscrimination policy requirement. The rules as to the adequacy of the nondiscriminatory policy and its procedures are found in an IRS revenue procedure. The relevant portions of the revenue procedure are found in the instructions to Schedule E and are reproduced in §§ 12.1(b) to 12.1(1).

(a) Public Charity Requirements

An organization will be treated as a school for purposes of qualifying as a public charity if the organization normally maintains a regular faculty and curriculum and normally has a regularly enrolled body of pupils or students in attendance at the place where its educational activities are regularly carried on. The organization's primary function must be the presentation of formal instruction in order for the organization to qualify as a formal educational organization. An organization that provides formal classroom instruction for students as merely an incidental activity will not meet the requirements. Thus, the IRS denied exemption where the organization's primary activity was the operation of a museum, not the presentation of formal instruction. The formal instruction need not take place in a formal classroom setting. For example, an organization that conducted a survival course was granted exempt status as a school even though the course periods were for only 26 days in an outdoor setting.

The *curriculum* requirement does not mandate that an organization present courses in traditional academic subjects, such as English or mathematics. The IRS has ruled that an organization operating a training school and presenting classes on development skills useful for a particular type of industry qualifies as a curriculum. To be a *regular* curriculum, however, the organization's courses must be offered recurrently, such as on a quarterly or semester basis. As to the *regular faculty* requirement, the classes or other means of instruction must be conducted by teachers, instructors, or other qualified persons who perform their duties on a recurrent basis. Similarly, a *regularly enrolled body of pupils* requires students who are enrolled in a regular, recurring program of instruction. Finally, the school's own facilities, or facilities in another school, must be used to meet the facility requirement.

(b)   Organizational Requirements (4.01)

A school must include a statement in its charter, bylaws, or other governing instrument, or in a resolution of its governing body, that it has a racially nondiscriminatory policy as to students and therefore does not discriminate against applicants and students on the basis of race, color, and national or ethnic origin.

(c)   Statement of Policy (4.02)

Every school must include a statement of its racially nondiscriminatory policy as to students in all its brochures and catalogs dealing with student admissions, programs, and scholarships. A statement substantially similar to the notice described in Paragraph (a) of subsection 1 of Section 4.03 (§ 12.1(d), will be acceptable for this purpose. Further, every school must include a reference to its racially nondiscriminatory policy in other written advertising that it uses as a means of informing prospective students of its programs. The following references will be acceptable: The (name) school admits students of any race, color, and national or ethnic origin.

(d)   Publicity (4.03)

The school must make its racially nondiscriminatory policy known to all segments of the general community served by the school.

(1) Requirements.   The school must use one of the following two methods to satisfy this requirement:

1.   The school may publish a notice of its racially nondiscriminatory policy in a newspaper of general circulation that serves all racial segments of the community. This publication must be repeated at least once annually during the period of the school's solicitation for students or, in the absence of a solicitation program, during the school's registration period. Where more than one community is served by a school, the school may publish its notice in those newspapers that are reasonably likely to be read by all racial segments of the communities that it serves. The notice must appear in a section of the newspaper likely to be read by prospective students and their families, and it must occupy at least three column inches. It must be captioned in at least 12-point boldface type as a notice of nondiscriminatory policy as to students, and its

text must be printed in at least 8-point type. The following notice will be acceptable:

Notice of Nondiscriminatory Policy as to Students
The (name) school admits students of any race, color, national and ethnic origin to all the rights, privileges, programs, and activities generally accorded or made available to students at the school. It does not discriminate on the basis of race, color, national and ethnic origin in administration of its educational policies, admissions policies, scholarship and loan programs, and athletic and other school-administered programs.

2. The school may use the broadcast media to publicize its racially nondiscriminatory policy if this use makes such nondiscriminatory policy known to all segments of the general community the school serves. If this method is chosen, the school must provide documentation that the means by which this policy was communicated to all segments of the general community was reasonably expected to be effective. In this case, appropriate documentation would include copies of the tapes or script used and records showing that there was an adequate number of announcements, that they were made during hours when the announcements were likely to be communicated to all segments of the general community, that they were of sufficient duration to convey the message clearly, and that they were broadcast on radio or television stations likely to be listened to by substantial numbers of members of all racial segments of the general community. Announcements must be made during the period of the school's solicitation for students or, in the absence of a solicitation program, during the school's registration period.

Communication of a racially nondiscriminatory policy as to students by a school to leaders of racial groups as the sole means of publicity generally will not be considered effective to make the policy known to all segments of the community.

(2) Exceptions. The requirements of subsection (1) of this section will not apply when one of the following paragraphs applies:

1. If for the preceding three years the enrollment of a parochial or other church-related school consists of students at least 75 percent of whom are members of the sponsoring religious denomination or unit, the school may make known its racially nondiscriminatory policy in whatever newspapers or circulars the religious denomination or unit utilizes in the communities from which the students are drawn. These newspapers and circulars may be those distributed by a particular religious denomination or unit or by an association that represents a number of religious organizations of the same denomination. If, however, the school advertises in newspapers of general circulation in the community or communities from which its students are drawn and Paragraphs (ii) and (iii) of this subsection are not applicable to it, then it must comply with Paragraph (i) of subsection (1) of this section.

2. If a school customarily draws a substantial percentage of its students nationwide or worldwide or from a large geographic section or sections of the United States and follows a racially nondiscriminatory policy as to students, the

publicity requirement may be satisfied by complying with Section 4.02 (§ 12.1(c)). Such a school may demonstrate that it follows a racially non-discriminatory policy within the meaning of the preceding sentence either by showing that it currently enrolls students of racial minority groups in meaningful numbers or, when minority students are not enrolled in meaningful numbers, that its promotional activities and recruiting efforts in each geographic area were reasonably designed to inform students of all racial segments in the general communities within the area of the availability of the school. The question whether a school satisfies the preceding sentence will be determined on the basis of the facts and circumstances of each case.

3. If a school customarily draws its students from local communities and follows a racially nondiscriminatory policy as to students, the publicity requirement may be satisfied by complying with Section 4.02 (§ 12.1(c)). Such a school may demonstrate that it follows a racially nondiscriminatory policy within the meaning of the preceding sentence by showing that it currently enrolls students of racial minority groups in meaningful numbers. The question whether a school satisfies the preceding sentence will be determined on the basis of the facts and circumstances of each case. One of the facts and circumstances that the Service will consider is whether the school's promotional activities and recruiting efforts in each area were reasonably designed to inform students of all racial segments in the general communities within the area of the availability of the school. The Service recognizes that the failure by a school drawing its students from local communities to enroll racial minority group students may not necessarily indicate the absence of a racially nondiscriminatory policy as to students when there are relatively few or no such students in these communities. Actual enrollment is, however, a meaningful indication of a racially nondiscriminatory policy in a community in which a public school or schools became subject to a desegregation order of a federal court or otherwise expressly became obligated to implement a desegregation plan under the terms of any written contract or other commitment to which any federal agency was a party.

The Service encourages schools to satisfy the publicity requirement by the methods described in subsection 1 of this section, regardless of whether a school considers itself within subsection 2, because it believes these methods to be the most effective to make known a school's racially nondiscriminatory policy. In this regard it is each school's responsibility to determine whether Paragraphs (a), (b), or (c) of subsection 2 applies to it. On audit, a school must be prepared to demonstrate that the failure to publish its racially nondiscriminatory policy in accordance with subsection 1 of this section was justified by the application to it of Paragraphs (a), (b), or (c) of subsection 2. Further, a school must be prepared to demonstrate that it has publicly disavowed or repudiated any statements purported to have been made on its behalf (after November 6, 1975) that are contrary to its publicity of a racially nondiscriminatory policy as to students, to the extent that the school or its principal official were aware of such statements.

(e) Facilities and Programs (4.04)

A school must be able to show that all of its programs and facilities are operated in a racially nondiscriminatory manner.

(f) Scholarship and Loan Programs (4.05)

As a general rule, all scholarship or other comparable benefits procurable for use at any given school must be offered on a racially nondiscriminatory basis. Their availability on this basis must be known throughout the general community being served by the school and should be referred to in the publicity required by this section in order for that school to be considered racially nondiscriminatory as to students. . . . [S]cholarships and loans that are made pursuant to financial assistance programs favoring members of one or more racial minority groups that are designed to promote a school's racially nondiscriminatory policy will not adversely affect the school's exempt status.

Financial assistance programs favoring members of one or more racial groups that do not significantly derogate from the school's racially nondiscriminatory policy similarly will not adversely affect the school's exempt status.

(g) Certification (4.06)

An individual authorized to take official action on behalf of a school that claims to be racially nondiscriminatory as to students is required to certify annually, under penalties of perjury, that to the best of his or her knowledge and belief the school has satisfied the applicable requirements of Sections 4.01 through 4.05 of the Revenue Procedure. *This certification is line 7 of Schedule E.*

(h) Faculty and Staff (4.07)

The existence of a racially discriminatory policy with respect to employment of faculty and administrative staff is indicative of a racially discriminatory policy as to students. Conversely, the absence of racial discrimination in employment of faculty and administrative staff is indicative of a racially nondiscriminatory policy as to students.

(i) Specific Records (7.01)

Except as provided in Section 7.03, each exempt private school must maintain for a minimum period of three years, beginning with the year after the year of compilation or acquisition, the following records for the use of the Service on proper request:

1. Records indicating the racial composition of the student body, faculty, and administrative staff for each academic year.

2. Records sufficient to document that scholarship and other financial assistance is awarded on a racially nondiscriminatory basis.

3. Copies of all brochures, catalogs, and advertising dealing with student admissions, programs, and scholarships. Schools advertising nationally or in a large geographic segment or segments of the United States need only maintain a record sufficient to indicate when and in what publications their advertisements were placed.

4. Copies of all materials used by or on behalf of the school to solicit contributions.

(j) Limitation (7.02)

1. For purposes of Section 7.01, the racial composition of the student body, faculty, and administrative staff may be an estimate based on the best information readily available to the school, without requiring student applicants, students, faculty, or administrative staff to submit information to the school that the school otherwise does not require. For each academic year, however, a record of the method by which racial composition is determined must be maintained. . . .

2. The IRS does not require that a school release personally identifiable records or personal information contained therein except in accordance with the requirements of the "Family Educational Rights and Privacy Act of 1974," 20 U.S.C. Section 1232g (1974). Similarly, the Service does not require a school to keep records the maintenance of which is prohibited under state or federal law.

(k) Exceptions (7.03)

The records described in Section 7.01 need not be independently maintained for Internal Revenue Service use if:

1. Substantially the same information that each of these records would provide has been included in a report or reports filed in accordance with law with an agency or agencies of federal, state, or local government, and this information is current within one year.

2. The school maintains copies of these reports from which this information is readily obtainable. Records described in Section 7.01 providing information not included in reports filed with an agency or agencies must be maintained by the school for Service use.

(l) Failure to Maintain Records (7.04)

Failure to maintain or to produce upon the proper request the required records and information will create a presumption that the organization has failed to comply with these guidelines.

§12.2 PREPARATION OF SCHEDULE E

The questions asked in Schedule E all relate to the adequacy of the racially nondiscriminatory policy and implementation of the policy.

(a) Public Charity and Nondiscriminatory Policy.

If "yes" is answered to Part IV, line 13 , of the Core Form and if the box on line 2 of Schedule A is checked, Schedule E must be filed.

(1) Line 1 (Racially Nondiscriminatory Policy). On line 1, indicate "yes" or "no" as to whether the organization has a racially nondiscriminatory policy. The policy guidelines and the sample policy are provided in Section 4.03 of the Revenue Procedure (see § 12.1(d)). The sample policy is stated in this way:

Notice of Nondiscriminatory Policy as to Students
The (name) school admits students of any race, color, national and ethnic origin to all the rights, privileges, programs, and activities generally accorded or made available to students at the school. It does not discriminate on the basis of race, color, national and ethnic origin in administration of its educational policies, admissions policies, scholarship and loan programs, and athletic and other school-administered programs.

(2) Line 2 (Inclusion of Policy in Brochures, Catalogs, and Other Written Communications). On line 2, indicate "yes" or "no" as to whether the organization includes a statement of its racially nondiscriminatory policy toward students in all of its brochures, catalogs, and other written communications with the public dealing with student admissions, programs and scholarships. This requirement is found in Section 4.02 of the Revenue Procedure (see § 12.1(c)). Section 4.02 indicates that the statement can be substantially similar to the notice in Section 4.03 as stated in § 12.2(a)(1). Further, every school must include a reference to its racially nondiscriminatory policy in other written advertising that it uses as a means of informing prospective students of its programs. This line will be acceptable: "The (name) school admits students of any race, color, and national or ethnic origin."

(3) Line 3 (Publication Requirement). On line 3, indicate "yes" or "no" as to whether the organization publicized its racially nondiscriminatory policy through newspaper or broadcast media during the period of solicitation for students, or during the registration period but has no solicitation program, in a way that makes the policy known to all parts of the general community it serves. If "yes" is answered, then the question asks the organization to describe. If "no" is answered, an explanation is also requested in the space provided.

Section 4.03 of the Revenue Procedure provides two alternative methods to satisfy the requirement (see § 12.1(d)). The publication alternative is repeated below. The alternative broadcast requirement can be found in § 12.1(d)(1).

The school may publish a notice of its racially nondiscriminatory policy in a newspaper of general circulation that serves all racial segments of the community. This publication must be repeated at least once annually during the period of the school's solicitation for students or, in the absence of a solicitation program, during the school's registration. Where more than one community is served by the school, the school may publish its notice in those newspapers that are reasonably likely to be read by all racial segments of the communities that it serves. The notice must appear in a section of the newspaper likely to be read by prospective students and their families and must occupy at least three column inches. It must be captioned in at least 12-point boldface type as a notice of nondiscriminatory policy as to students, and its text must be printed in at least 8-point type. An example of the notice is provided in § 12.2(a)(1).

(4) Line 4 (Records). On lines 4a through 4d, indicate "yes" or "no" as to whether records are kept for each of the following:

- Line 4a. Records indicating the racial composition of the student body, faculty, and administrative staff.

- Line 4b. Records documenting that scholarships and other financial assistance are awarded to a racially nondiscriminatory basis.

- Line 4c. Copies of all catalogs, brochures, announcements, and other written communications to the public dealing with student admissions, programs, and scholarships.

- Line 4d. Copies of all material used by the organization or on its behalf to solicit contributions.

If "no" is answered to any of these bullets, an explanation should be provided in line 4. If more space is needed, a separate statement should be attached to the schedule.

(5) Line 5 (Discrimination Questions). On line 5, indicate "yes" or "no" as to whether the organization discriminates by race in any way with respect to:

- Students rights or privileges

- Admissions policies

- Employment of faculty or administrative staff

- Scholarships or other financial assistance

- Educational policies

- Use of facilities

- Athletic programs

- Other extracurricular activities

If "yes" is answered to any of these questions, an explanation should be provided in the space at the bottom of line 5. If additional space is needed, a separate statement should be attached to the schedule.

As a general rule, all scholarships or other comparable benefits procurable for use at any given school must be offered on a racially nondiscriminatory basis. Their availability on this basis must be known throughout the general community being served by the school and should be referred to in the publicity required by this section in order for that school to be considered racially nondiscriminatory as to students. Scholarships and loans that are made pursuant to financial assistance programs favoring members of one or more racial minority groups that are designed to promote a school's racially nondiscriminatory policy will not adversely affect the school's exempt status. Financial assistance programs favoring members of one or more racial groups that do not significantly derogate from the school's racially nondiscriminatory policy similarly will not adversely affect the school's exempt status (see § 12.1(f)).

(6) Line 6 (Government Funding). On line 6a, report "yes" or "no" as to whether the organization receives government funding. On line 6b, indicate "yes" or "no" as to whether such funding has been ever revoked or suspended. The organization is asked to explain in an attached statement if the answer to either 6a or 6b is "yes."

(7) Line 7 (Certification). On line 7, the organization must indicate "yes" or "no" as to whether it certifies that it meets the nondiscriminatory requirements of Sections 4.01 through 4.05 of the Revenue procedure. The certification is made by an individual authorized to take official action on behalf of the school, under penalties of perjury, that to the best of his or her knowledge and belief, the school has satisfied the applicable requirements of Sections 4.01 through 4.05 of the Revenue Procedure (see § 12.1(g)).

§12.3 SCHEDULE E COMPLIANCE TASKS

For purposes of preparing Schedule E, consider the next six compliance tasks.

1. **Review nondiscrimination policy.** Review nondiscrimination policy to ensure compliance.

2. **Make annual publication.** Make required annual publication or broadcasts of policy.

3. **Review other materials.** Review brochures, advertisements, program materials to ensure policy is adequately stated.

4. **Review scholarship criteria.** Review scholarship criteria and materials to ensure compliance.

5. **Review programs and facilities.** Review programs and facilities to ensure compliance.

6. **Review public charity status.** Review regular curriculum, faculty, student body, and facility criteria to ensure compliance.

CHAPTER THIRTEEN

Schedule F—Foreign Activities

Following the attacks on September 11, 2001, the United States government has been more closely monitoring the foreign activities of tax-exempt organizations. Congress passed many new laws enacting counterterrorism regulations and enforcement programs designed to fight terrorism both in the United States and abroad. There is concern that charities and other exempt organizations located in the United States may be engaging in or supporting terrorist activities, or may be fundraising to finance terrorist activities, whether they are aware of this or not.

The Department of Treasury and the IRS have taken actions to more closely examine the foreign activities of U.S. tax-exempt organizations. These actions include increasing the reporting requirements of foreign activities and grantmaking on both the Form 1023, Application for Recognition of Exemption, and on the redesigned Form 990. Prior to the new Form 990, reporting on foreign activities on the Form 990 was limited to a few questions regarding foreign bank accounts, foreign grants, and offices located outside the country.

Schedule F is to be completed by tax-exempt organizations that conduct fundraising, grantmaking, business, or exempt activities outside the United States or have accounts, offices, or employees outside the country. In response to comments received by the IRS regarding the public availability of the Form 990, Schedule F limits the detail of information requested in an effort to protect the safety of foreign workers and grantees.

§13.1 LAW AND POLICY

U.S. charities and other tax-exempt organizations may conduct activities abroad so long as its activities are consistent with their exempt purposes and organizational documents. In addition, exempt organizations may lawfully make grants to foreign organizations and individuals in furtherance of their exempt purposes. There are no geographic restrictions on foreign activities and grantmaking. Although private foundations are subject to strict requirements for investigating, documenting, and monitoring their foreign grants, public charities and other exempt organizations generally are not subject to these same rules. Even so, these organizations may wish to voluntarily follow the private foundation expenditure responsibility rules (see § 16.(1)(b)) to ensure their funds are being used for exempt purposes.

(a) Foreign Activities of an Exempt Organization

There is no limit on the amount of activities an exempt organization may conduct abroad, provided the activities are in furtherance of its exempt purposes and consistent with its governing documents. Many U.S. tax-exempt organizations, especially international humanitarian organizations, conduct most of their activities abroad.

Schedule F requests information on the activities of a tax-exempt organization conducted outside the United States. In the first draft of the revised Form 990, the IRS requested reporting of an organization's foreign activities by country rather than by region. Based on comments received that disclosure of this information by country could negatively impact the personal safety of workers, volunteers, and others involved in an organization's work in certain unsafe foreign areas, the IRS revised Form 990 to require this reporting only by region. See § 13.2(a)(2)(i) for a listing of the regions and the countries composing the regions.

For purposes of the new Form 990, *activities conducted outside the United States* includes grantmaking, fundraising activities, an unrelated trade or business, program services, or maintaining officers, employees, or agents for the purpose of conducting any such activities. It includes passive investments other than financial accounts that are reported on Form 990, Part V, lines 4a and b, which are generally bank accounts, securities accounts, or other financial accounts. *United States* includes the 50 states and the District of Columbia, the Commonwealth of Puerto Rico, the Commonwealth of the Northern Mariana Islands, Guam, American Samoa, and the United States Virgin Islands). A *foreign country* is any sovereignty that is not the United States.

Maintaining offices, employees or agents includes principal, regional, district or branch offices, offices maintained by agents, and persons situated at those offices paid wages for services performed. For a listing of the regions outside the United States, and the countries comprising each region, see § 13.2(a)(2)(i). *Grantmaking* includes awards, prizes, cash allocations, stipends, scholarships, fellowships, research grants, and similar payments and distributions made by the organization at any time during the tax year to foreign organizations, foreign governments, or foreign individuals. It does not include salaries or other compensation to employees. *Fundraising* includes soliciting contributions, gifts, grants, or conducting special events specifically to generate gifts or contributions outside the United States. *Program services* are activities that form the basis of the organization's exemption from federal income tax conducted by the organization outside the United States. An example of a program services activity is providing assistance to foreign individuals, such as providing food, shelter, clothing, medical assistance, or supplies. The operation of an orphanage, church, or hospital would also be a program service activity. For a discussion of an unrelated business activity, see § 4.2(b).

Organizations must report foreign activities that are conducted by the organization directly or indirectly through a disregarded entity or through a joint venture taxed as a partnership. The Form 990 instructions do not provide a de minimis exception to this reporting requirement. Thus, even if an exempt organization is a 1-percent partner in a partnership, it must report its proportionate share of the foreign activities on Schedule F. As instructed in the appendix to the Form 990 instructions, reporting is made to the extent of the filing organization's profits or capital interest in a joint venture or partnership, whichever is greater.

(b) Grants to Foreign Organizations

A tax-exempt organization may make grants to foreign organizations as part of its exempt activities. *Grantmaking*, for purposes of reporting foreign activities, includes awards, prizes, cash allocations, stipends, scholarships, fellowships, research grants, and similar payments and distributions made by the organization during the tax year to foreign organizations, foreign governments, or foreign individuals. A *foreign organization* is a foreign estate or trust, nonprofit or other nongovernmental organization (often referred to as an *NGO*), partnership, corporation, or other business entity that is not created or organized in the United States or under the laws of the United States or of any state or U.S. territory or possession. A *foreign organization* includes an affiliate that is organized as a legal entity separate from the filing organization but does not include any branch office, account, or employee of the filing organization located outside the United States. *Foreign governments* include political subdivisions thereof. *Foreign governments* do not include a United States government agency regardless of where it is located or operated.

With respect to cross-border grantmaking, a tax-exempt organization may make grants to either foreign organizations or foreign governments, provided the grants further the grantor organization's exempt purposes and are consistent with its organizational documents. For example, a U.S. charity can make a grant to a foreign governmental unit, such as a foreign public university, provided the grant is for charitable, not governmental, purposes.

United States organizations that fundraise to make grants to foreign organizations should not act as mere conduits that transfer earmarked funds to foreign grantees. If a U.S. organization solicits contributions that are to, or for the use of, a foreign organization, the contribution will likely be treated as having been made directly to the foreign organization. Rather than fundraising on behalf of a foreign entity, an exempt organization should raise funds over which it has discretion and control, and should limit its foreign grants to specific projects that are in furtherance of its exempt purposes. This is especially important for public charities, where acting as a conduit may prevent a charity's donors from receiving charitable deductions for their contributions. If a public charity is acting as a conduit, a contribution to the charity earmarked for a foreign grantee is not treated as a donation to a U.S. charity. It is instead treated as a donation to the foreign organization and generally will be nondeductible for U.S. income tax purposes. If, however, the charity retains control over the donations it receives, has discretion as to the use of the funds, and maintains records establishing that its funds were used for charitable purposes, contributions to the charity are deductible even if they are ultimately granted to a foreign organization.

Whether a U.S. charity has maintained sufficient discretion and control over the funds it receives is a facts-and-circumstances determination. The IRS states that the test in each case is whether the organization has "full control of the donated funds, and discretion as to their use, so as to insure that they will be used to carry out its functions and purposes." To establish the necessary discretion and control, many U.S. charities either voluntarily apply the private foundation expenditure responsibility rules (see § 16.1(b)) or adopt a modified version of these rules.

U.S. charities that make grants to foreign organizations are often formed as *friends* organizations, which are U.S. charities formed to solicit and receive contributions in the United States but that expend funds to or on behalf of a charitable organization in another country for specific projects of the foreign organization. Provided such an organization is not acting as a conduit, a contribution to a *friends* organization is typically deductible by a donor as a charitable contribution.

(c) Foreign Grants from Donor-Advised Funds

Donor-advised funds have become an increasingly popular charitable giving vehicle. Donor-advised funds are created and maintained within a public charity and are funds over which the donor has advisory privileges. For a discussion of donor-advised funds, see § 11.1(a).

Donor-advised funds are restricted as to the nature of permissible grants that may be made from the funds. Donor-advised funds cannot be used to make distributions to natural persons. As a result, grants to individuals, foreign or otherwise, cannot be made from donor-advised funds (see § 16.1(a)(3)). In addition, grants to organizations can be made from donor-advised funds only if the sponsoring organization of the donor-advised fund exercises *expenditure responsibility* over the grant. See § 16.1(b) for an explanation of expenditure responsibility. There is an exception from the expenditure responsibility requirement for grants to a public charity (other than a disqualified supporting organization), to the sponsoring organization of the donor-advised fund, or to another donor-advised fund. If a grant is made from a donor-advised fund to one of these organizations or funds, there is no expenditure responsibility requirement. As a result, if a grant is made from a donor-advised fund to a foreign organization that is a public charity, no expenditure responsibility must be exercised over the grant. Donor-advised funds may use the equivalency determination process (see § 13.1(d)) to determine if a foreign grantee is the equivalent of a U.S. public charity.

(d) U.S. Recognition of Foreign Charities and Equivalency Determinations

Schedule F requests a filing organization to indicate how many of its foreign grantees are recognized as a charitable organization by the Internal Revenue Service, recognized as a charity by a foreign country, or for which the grantmaking entity has made a good-faith determination, based on an affidavit from the grantee or the opinion of counsel, that the grantee is the equivalent of a public charity. Foreign charities or other foreign tax-exempt organizations may take it upon themselves to seek a determination letter or ruling from the IRS that the organization is recognized as a public charity or other tax-exempt entity for U.S. income tax purposes. A foreign organization may seek an IRS determination letter or ruling because it is operating or investing in the United States and wants recognition of tax exemption for U.S. income tax purposes, or (more likely) to assist with seeking grant funding from U.S. private foundations and other grantmaking organizations. If a U.S. exempt organization makes a grant to a foreign charity that has been recognized by the IRS as a U.S. charity, the level of diligence the grantmaking entity needs to exercise over the grant is reduced.

Foreign organizations may be recognized as tax exempt in the United States without seeking an IRS determination or ruling by virtue of an income tax treaty between the United States and a foreign jurisdiction. For example, the U.S. tax treaties with both Canada and Mexico provide for automatic reciprocal recognition of the charitable status of organizations recognized as charitable entities in the other country. Grantmaking entities that need to ensure public charity, not merely charitable, status of a foreign organization will need to determine whether the IRS provides reciprocal public charity status recognition of the other country's public charities. If public charity recognition is not reciprocal, the grant maker may want to make an equivalency determination (see next paragraph) that the foreign organization is the equivalent of a U.S. charity.

Equivalency determinations (sometimes referred to as *equivalency letters*) are used with great frequency by private foundations with respect to their foreign grantmaking activities when a foreign grantee does not have a determination letter or ruling from the IRS recognizing it as a U.S. charity. Other types of tax-exempt organizations may also utilize the equivalency determination process to establish that its grants are being used in furtherance of exempt purposes.

Private foundation grants to foreign charities or foreign private operating foundations are treated as qualifying distributions for purposes of the required annual minimum private foundation distribution and do not cause the private foundation to be subject to excise taxes if made to a charity or the equivalent of a U.S. charity. If a foreign grantee does not have a ruling or determination letter from the IRS, a private foundation's distribution to a foreign grantee is treated as made to the *equivalent* of a U.S. charity or private operating foundation only if the distributing foundation has made a *good-faith determination* that the grantee is a public charity or private operating foundation.

A good-faith determination is ordinarily considered as made where the determination is based on an equivalency determination regarding the foreign grantee. Although a private foundation is not required to make an equivalency determination regarding a foreign grantee and may instead choose to exercise expenditure responsibility over the grant (see § 16.1(b)), an equivalency determination can eliminate continuous oversight over the use of a grant and may be more efficient in the case of long-term support to a foreign charity.

The equivalency determination process involves obtaining a currently qualified affidavit from the foreign grantee organization or an opinion of the grantee's or grantor organization's counsel that the grantee qualifies as a public charity or private operating foundation for U.S. federal income tax purposes. This is sometimes referred to as an *equivalency letter*. The affidavit must be written in English, be attested to by a principal officer of the grantee organization, and include the substantive information required to determine that the organization is the equivalent of a U.S. charity or private operating foundation. An affidavit is considered currently qualified as long as the facts in it are up to date, either because they reflect the grantee's latest accounting year or, in the case of public charities or private operating foundations whose status is not dependent on public support, if the affidavit is updated at the request of the prospective grantor to reflect the grantee's current data.

Generally, public charities and other tax-exempt organizations that are not private foundations are not required to obtain equivalency letters from potential grantees prior to making a distribution to a foreign organization. If, however, the granting organization obtains an equivalency letter, it receives some level of assurance that its grant will be used in furtherance of charitable purposes and should reduce the amount of diligence that the organization needs to perform to establish that its grants were used in furtherance of exempt purposes. In determining whether to obtain an equivalency letter, an organization must weigh the cost and burden of the equivalency determination process with the reduction in oversight and monitoring that can be gained by obtaining an equivalency letter.

(e)   Grants to Foreign Individuals

Tax-exempt organizations may make grants to foreign individuals in furtherance of their exempt purposes. A *foreign individual* is a person who lives or resides outside the United States at the time the grant is paid or distributed, including a U.S. citizen or resident.

As with grants made to individuals in the United States, tax-exempt organizations should take certain actions regarding their grants to foreign individuals. First, the grantmaking organization must ensure that the individual receiving the grant is part of the class of individuals intended to be benefited. For example, if the granting organization is an international relief organization, it must determine that foreign recipients are in need of the type of relief the organization provides. A grantmaking organization should consider having a written policy and using a written application process or other documentation to demonstrate that the foreign individual is part of the class intended to be benefited.

Second, the grantmaking entity should ensure that its selection of recipients is on an *objective and nondiscriminatory basis*. Although the rules regarding selection of recipients on this basis is specifically applicable to private foundations, all organizations can effectively employ these rules in the individual grantmaking context. For a discussion of awarding grants on an objective and nondiscriminatory basis, see § 18.1(c)(3).

Third, the grantmaker should exercise some degree of diligence in determining the grant or the assistance was used for the proper purposes. For grants to individuals, monitoring the use of the grant funds can be performed by obtaining reports from the grantees on the manner in which the grant funds were spent and the progress made toward achieving the purpose of the grant. Often it may be impossible or impractical, especially for international relief organizations, to obtain reports in this regard, in which case supplying noncash assistance may be the preferred method for providing assistance. If a grantmaking organization receives information that leads it to believe grant funds may have been misspent or misdirected, it should investigate the grant, withhold future grant payments until it is satisfied the grant conditions are being fulfilled, and seek recovery of any funds that were diverted from their intended use.

Last, the grantmaking entity should keep records and case histories regarding the grant or assistance, including the names and addresses of the grant recipients, the amount distributed to each recipient (the amount of cash and the value of any noncash assistance), the purpose for which the grant was made, the manner in which the individual was selected, and the relationship, if any, between the recipient and the grant maker's officers, directors, trustees, key employees, and substantial contributors.

(f)   USA PATRIOT Act and Other Federal Acts Regarding Financing Terrorist Activities

Following the attacks of September 11, 2001, the U.S. government took a number of steps to ensure that charitable funds were not diverted to terrorists, both within and outside the United States. Just 45 days after the September 11 attacks, Congress passed the USA PATRIOT Act (the PATRIOT Act), which served to greatly strengthen the federal government's ability to prevent the support of terrorism. The acronym stands for "Uniting and Strengthening America by Providing Appropriate

Tools Required to Intercept and Obstruct Terrorism." The Patriot Act eases the restrictions on the government's ability to investigate suspected terrorists, encourages and mandates information sharing among federal law enforcement agencies and private industry, requires financial institutions to take affirmative steps to identify money laundering, and strengthens existing laws that prohibit the provision of material or financial support to terrorists and terrorist organizations. It is this last part—strengthening existing laws that prohibit the provision of support to terrorists and terrorist organizations—that has the greatest impact on tax-exempt organizations conducting foreign activities.

Under the Patriot Act, law enforcement officials have increased power to designate a group as a terrorist organization and then seize its property and freeze its assets while investigating the organization. This includes the designation of tax-exempt organizations as terrorist organizations. In addition, exempt organizations are subject to criminal penalties under the Patriot Act for providing material support or resources knowing or intending that such material support or resources will be used in terrorist acts. *Material support* is a broad term, and is defined as "currency or monetary instruments or financial securities, financial services, lodging, training, expert advise or assistance, safehouses, false documentation or identification, communications equipment, facilities, weapons, lethal substances, explosives, personnel, transportation, and other physical assets." It does not include medicine or religious materials. Civil penalties may also be imposed on organizations that provide material support for terrorism.

In response to the attacks of September 11, 2001, President Bush issued Executive Order 13224, which prohibits transactions with individuals and organizations deemed by the federal government to be associated with terrorism, and allows the government to freeze assets controlled by or in the possession of these organizations, and those who support them. Executive Order 13224 prohibits the provision of financial support, in-kind support, and technical assistance to terrorists. Humanitarian assistance is also prohibited, if provided to persons associated with terrorists or acts of terrorism. If a tax-exempt organization violates the executive order, its assets can be blocked and its exempt status revoked.

In 2005, Congress passed the USA PATRIOT Improvement and Reauthorization Act of 2005 (the Reauthorization Act), which served to make permanent many of the provision of the original Patriot Act that were due to expire on December 31, 2005. The Reauthorization Act also enhanced certain criminal penalties of the Patriot Act, expanded the reach of asset seizures, and increased the penalties associated with certain presidential orders, such as the executive order.

(g)   Treasury Anti-Terrorist Financing Guidelines

The United States Department of Treasury issued "Anti-Terrorist Financing Guidelines: Voluntary Best Practices for U.S.-Based Charities." The Treasury Department originally issued the guidelines in 2002, released a revised version in 2005 for public comment, and issued a third version in 2006. As the title suggests, the guidelines are voluntary and do not create any new legal requirements for tax-exempt organizations. The guidelines state that they "are designed to assist charities that attempt in good faith to protect themselves from terrorist abuse" and acknowledge that certain aspects will not be applicable to every charity, charitable activity, or circumstance.

The guidelines apply to all monetary grants, both foreign and domestic, and apply to grants involving services, in-kind contributions, and other goods. The guidelines include criteria as to governance accountability and transparency (focusing on the contents of governing instruments and independent oversight of their operations), financial accountability and transparency (including fundraising and funds disbursement), various aspects of programmatic verification (such as the supplying of charitable resources and services), and anti-terrorist financing best practices.

According to the guidelines, when supplying charitable *resources* (monetary and in-kind contributions), the fiscal responsibility on the part of a charity should include:

1. The determination that the potential recipient of monetary or in-kind contributions has the ability to accomplish the charitable purpose of the grant and protect the resources from diversion to noncharitable purposes, including any activity that supports terrorism

2. The reduction of the terms of the grant to a written agreement signed by the charity and the recipient

3. Ongoing monitoring of the grantee and the activities funded pursuant to the grant for the term of the grant

4. The correction of any misuse of resources by the grantee and termination of the relationship should misuse continue

When supplying charitable *services*, the fiscal responsibility on the part of a charity should include:

1. Appropriate measures to reduce the risk that its assets would be used for noncharitable purposes, including any activity that supports terrorism

2. Sufficient auditing or accounting controls to trace services or commodities between delivery by the charity and/or service provider and use by the grantee

Charitable organizations should, according to these guidelines, consider taking certain steps before distributing any charitable funds or in-kind items, including collecting this information about recipients:

1. The recipient's name in English, in the language of origin, and any acronym or other name(s) used to identify the recipient

2. The jurisdiction(s) in which a recipient maintains a physical presence

3. Any reasonably available historical information about the recipient that assures the charity of the recipient's identity and integrity

4. The address and telephone number of each place of business of a recipient

5. A statement of the principal purpose of the recipient, including a detailed report of the recipient's projects and goals

6. The names and addresses of individuals, entities, or organizations to which the recipient currently provides or proposes to provide funding, services, or material support

7. The names and addresses of any subcontracting organizations utilized by the recipient

8. Copies of any public filings or releases made by the recipient, including the most recent official registry documents, annual reports, and annual filings with the pertinent government

9. The recipient's sources of revenue, such as "official grants, private endowments, and commercial activities"

These guidelines suggest that a charitable organization should conduct "basic vetting" of recipients in this manner:

1. The charity should conduct a reasonable search of public information, including information available by means of the Internet, to determine whether the recipient is suspected of activity relating to terrorism, including terrorist financing or other support.

2. The charity should be assured that recipients do not appear on the list of the Office of Foreign Assets Control (OFAC) of Specially Designated Nationals and Blocked Persons.

3. With respect to key employees, board members, or other senior management at a recipient's principal place of business, and for key employees at the recipient's other business locations, the charity should obtain the full name in English, in the language of origin, and any acronym or other name(s) used, nationality, citizenship, current country of residence, and place and date of birth.

4. With respect to the foregoing individuals, the charity should consider consulting publicly available information to ensure that they are not suspected of activity relating to terrorism.

5. The charity should require recipients to certify that they do not employ, transact with, provide services to, or otherwise deal with any individuals, entities, or groups that are sanctioned by OFAC, or with any persons known to the recipient to support terrorism.

The charity should conduct basic vetting of its key employees by (1) consulting publicly available information to determine whether any of its key employees is suspected of activity relating to terrorism and (2) assuring itself that none of its key employees is sanctioned by OFAC.

Pursuant to these guidelines, a charitable organization should review the financial and programmatic operations of each recipient by (1) requiring periodic reports from recipients on their operational activities and their use of the disbursed funds; (2) requiring recipients to take reasonable steps to ensure that funds provided by the charity are not distributed to terrorists or their support networks; and (3) performing routine, on-site audits of recipients to the extent possible, consistent with the size of the disbursement, the cost of the audit, and the risks of diversion or abuse of charitable resources, to ensure that the recipient has taken adequate measures to protect its charitable resources from diversion to or abuse by terrorists or their support networks.

(h) Suspension of Tax-Exempt Status for Designation as a Terrorist Organization

Beginning November 11, 2003, the IRS is allowed to suspend the tax-exempt status and/or the eligibility to apply for exempt status of an organization designated as a terrorist organization. In addition, no deductions for charitable contributions to such organizations are allowed during any period that the organization is designated as a terrorist organization.

An organization is subject to these rules if it is designated or otherwise individually identified:

- Under certain provisions of the Immigration and Nationality Act as a terrorist organization or foreign terrorist organization

- In or pursuant to an executive order that is related to terrorism and issued under the authority of the International Emergency Economic Powers Act or section 5 of the United Nations Participation Act of 1945 for the purpose of imposed on such organization an economic or other sanction

- In or pursuant to an executive order issued under the authority of any federal law, if the organization is designated or otherwise individually identified in or pursuant to the executive order as supporting or engaging in terrorist activity and the executive order refers to the IRS authority to suspend the tax-exempt status or eligibility to apply for exempt status of an organization designated as a terrorist organization

Suspension of an organization's tax-exempt status begins on the date of the first publication of a designation or identification with respect to the organization, or November 11, 2003, whichever is later. The suspension continues until all designations and identifications of the organization are rescinded under the law or executive order under which the designation or identification was made.

§13.2 PREPARATION OF NEW FORM 990 SCHEDULE F

Schedule F must be completed if a reporting organization answered "yes" to Part IV, lines 14b, 15, or 16, as an organization reporting aggregate revenue or expenses of more than $10,000 from grantmaking, fundraising, business, and program service activities outside the United States; reporting more than $5,000 of grants or assistance to any organization or entity located outside the United States; or reporting more than $5,000 of aggregate grants or assistance to individuals located outside the United States. Schedule F requests details on these foreign activities and grantmaking. The information requested on Schedule F must be reported in U.S. dollars. The instructions to Schedule F do not provide information on how foreign currency should be converted to U.S. dollars, but presumably the conversion should be made as of the date the revenue was received, the grant was made, or the assistance was given.

(a) Part I (General Information on Activities Outside the United States)

Part I requests general information on an organization's activities outside the United States. It must be completed if an organization had aggregate revenue or expenses of more than $10,000 from grantmaking, fundraising, unrelated trade or business activities, and program service activities outside the United States during the filing year.

(1) Lines 1 and 2 (Records and Monitoring). Lines 1 and 2 are specific questions for grant makers. Line 1 asks if an organization maintains records to substantiate the amount of the grants or assistance, the grantees' eligibility for the grants or assistance, and the selection criteria used to award the grants or assistance. To respond to line 2, an organization describes in Part IV its procedures for monitoring the use of grant funds outside the United States. Unlike private foundations, public charities and other tax-exempt organizations are not subject to specific monitoring procedures for their foreign grants. However, guidance on methods of monitoring grants can be taken from the expenditure responsibility rules (see § 16.1(b)). In addition, the U.S. Department of Treasury "Anti-Terrorist Financing Guidelines: Voluntary Best Practices for U.S.-Based Charities" (§ 13.1(e)) offer recommendations for monitoring foreign grants. Examples of grant monitoring include periodic reports from foreign grantees, on-site audits of foreign grantees, or field investigations.

(2) Line 3 (Activities per Region).   Line 3 requests organizations to describe their activities per region by filling in a six-column table.

(i) COLUMN (A) (REGION)

In Column (a), an organization specifies the region in which its activities took place during the year, using a separate line for each region. There are nine regions for Form 990 reporting purposes:

- Central America and the Caribbean
- East Asia and the Pacific
- Europe (including Iceland and Greenland)
- Middle East and North Africa
- North America (which includes Canada and Mexico, but not the United States)
- Russia and the Newly Independent States
- South America
- South Asia
- Sub-Saharan Africa

The countries composing the nine regions are:

Central America and the Caribbean

Includes these countries:

Antigua and Barbuda, Aruba, Bahamas, Barbados, Belize, Cayman Islands, Costa Rica, Cuba, Dominica, Dominican Republic, El Salvador, Grenada, Guadeloupe, Guatemala, Haiti, Honduras, Jamaica, Martinique, Nicaragua, Panama, St. Kitts and Nevis, St. Lucia, St. Vincent and the Grenadines, Trinidad and Tobago, Turks and Caicos Islands, and Virgin Islands

East Asia and the Pacific

Includes these countries:

Australia, Brunei, Burma, Cambodia, China (including Hong Kong) East Timor, Fiji, Indonesia, Japan, Kiribati, Korea, Laos, Malaysia, Marshall Islands, Micronesia, Mongolia, Nauru, New Zealand, North Korea, Palau, Papua

New Guinea, Philippines, Samoa, Singapore, Solomon Islands, South Korea, Taiwan, Thailand, Timor Leste, Tonga, Tuvalu, Vanuatu, and Vietnam

Europe (including Iceland and Greenland)

Includes these countries:

Albania, Andorra, Austria, Belgium, Bosnia and Herzegovina, Bulgaria, Croatia, Czech Republic, Denmark, Estonia, Finland, France, FYR Macedonia, Germany, Greece, Greenland, Holy See, Hungary, Iceland, Italy, Ireland, Kosovo, Latvia, Liechtenstein, Lithuania, Luxembourg, Macedonia, Monaco, Montenegro, the Netherlands, Norway, Poland, Portugal, Romania, San Marino, Serbia, Slovakia, Slovenia, Spain, Switzerland, Turkey, and the United Kingdom (England, Northern Ireland, Scotland and Wales)

Middle East and North Africa

Includes these countries:

Algeria, Bahrain, Djibouti, Egypt, Iran, Iraq, Israel, Jordan, Kuwait, Lebanon, Libya, Malta, Morocco, Oman, Qatar, Saudi Arabia, Syria, Tunisia, United Arab Emirates, West Bank and Gaza, and Yemen

North America

Includes Canada and Mexico, but not the United States.

Russia and the Newly Independent States

Includes these countries:

Armenia, Azerbaijan, Belarus, Georgia, Kazakhstan, Kyrgyzstan, Moldova, Russia, Tajikistan, Turkmenistan, Ukraine, and Uzbekistan

South America

Includes these countries:

Argentina, Bolivia, Brazil, Chile, Colombia, Ecuador, French Guiana, Guyana, Paraguay, Peru, Suriname, Uruguay, and Venezuela

South Asia

Includes these countries:

Afghanistan, Bangladesh, Bhutan, India, Maldives, Nepal, Pakistan, and Sri Lanka

Sub-Saharan Africa

Includes these countries:

Angola, Benin, Botswana, Burkina Faso, Burundi, Cameroon, Cape Verde, Central African Republic, Chad, Comoros, Congo, Democratic Republic (DRC), Congo Rep, Cote d'lvoire, Equatorial Guinea, Eritrea, Ethiopia, Gabon, Gambia, Ghana, Guinea, Guinea Bissau, Kenya, Lesotho, Liberia, Madagascar, Malawi, Mali, Mauritania, Mauritius, Mozambique, Namibia, Nigeria, Rwanda, Sao Tome and Principe, Senegal, Seychelles, Sierra Leone, Somalia, South Africa, Sudan, Swaziland, Tanzania, Togo, Uganda, Zambia, and Zimbabwe.

(ii) Column (b) (Number of Offices)

In Column (b), the organization states the number of offices it maintains in the region. An organization is instructed to include principal, regional, district, or branch offices, and such offices maintained by agents, and persons situated in those offices that are paid wages for services performed. An *agent* is defined under traditional agency principles. Volunteers are not treated as agents.

(iii) Column (c) (Employees)

An organization, in Column (c), lists the number of employees or agents it maintained outside the United States that are working in the region during the year. An organization should not include any of its employees or agents whose only presence in the region is to conduct on-site visits, or persons who serve as volunteers.

(iv) Column (d) (Activity Conducted)

Column (d) requests an organization to list the type of activity conducted in the region. This may include grantmaking, fundraising, unrelated trade or business activities, or program services, such as the provision of food, shelter and clothing, in the region. See § 13.1(a) for the definition of these activities. If multiple activities are conducted in each region, list each type of activity on a separate line and repeat regions in Column (a) as necessary.

(v) Column (e) (Program Services)

If the activity conducted in the region is a program service activity, the organization must describe the specific type of service in the region in Column (e), such as operating an orphanage, school, or church, conducting disaster relief efforts, or providing indigent relief.

(vi) Column (f) (Total Expenditures)

In Column (f), an organization lists its total expenditures for activities conducted in the region. This may include salaries, wages, and other employment-related costs paid to or for the benefit of employees located in the region, rent and other costs relating to offices located in the region, grants to recipients located in the region, and payments to agents located in the region. Organizations are instructed to report expenditures based on the method used to account for them on the organization's financial statements, and to describe this method in Part IV.

(b) Part II (Grants and Other Assistance to Organizations and Entities Outside the United States)

Part II consists of a table that an organization must complete if the organization reports more than $5,000 in grants or other assistance to foreign governments, organizations, and individuals on Part IX, line 3 of the Form 990, for any organization or entity outside the United States who received more than $5,000 in total support during the filing year. If no one recipient received more than $5,000, the reporting entity should merely check the box at the top of page 2 and not complete the schedule. If the recipient is an interested person (§ 18.1(c)(1)) or a related organization (See Chapter 21), the organization needs to determine if the grant or assistance must also be reported on

Schedule L (Transactions with Interested Persons) and/or Schedule R (Related Organizations and Unrelated Partnerships).

(1) Columns (a) and (b) (Name, IRS Code Section, and EIN of Organization). Although Columns (a) and (b) in the schedule request the name, IRS code section, and employer identification number of the organization, the IRS has stated that due to safety concerns, it will not require these disclosures. Organizations are instructed to complete the rest of the schedule as if Columns (a) and (b) were completed. Information needs to be entered only for organizations receiving more than $5,000 in total as grants or other assistance from the organization.

(2) Column (c) (Region). In Column (c), a filing organization lists the region where the principal office of the recipient organization or entity is located. Organizations should use the same nine regions listed for Part I of Schedule F (see § 13.2(a)(2)(i)). The IRS stated that it expects to list the countries comprising each region in the Form 990 final instructions.

(3) Column (d) (Purpose of Grant). Column (d) requires the organization to list the purpose or ultimate use of the grant funds, using specific terms such as general support, hospital construction, payments for the purchase of medical supplies or equipment, or the provision of clothing. In the case of disaster relief, the description should include a description of the disaster, such as tsunami or earthquake relief.

(4) Columns (e) and (f) (Amount of Cash Grant and Manner of Disbursement). In Column (e), an organization should list the total dollar amount of cash grants to each foreign government or entity for the tax year. Cash grants include amounts paid by cash, check, money order, wire transfer, or other charges against funds on deposit at a financial institution. In Column (f), an organization discloses the manner of disbursement of its grants, such as by cash payment, money order, electronic fund or wire transfer, check, other charges against funds on deposit at a financial institution, or otherwise.

(5) Columns (g) through (i) (Noncash Assistance). In Column (g), the filing organization lists the fair market value of any noncash assistance provided in the region, in U.S. dollars. The organization, in Column (h), provides a description of the noncash property or assistance provided to the foreign organization. Examples of noncash assistance include medical supplies or equipment, pharmaceuticals, blankets, books, or educational supplies. An organization should list all that apply. In Column (i), an organization must provide a description of the method used for valuing the noncash assistance provided to the foreign entity. Property with a readily determinable market value must be reported at fair market value, while other property may be reported using an appraisal or an estimated value.

(6) Lines 2 and 3 (U.S.-Recognized Charities, Equivalency Letters, and Other Organizations). On line 2 of Part II, the reporting organization enters the total number of organizations that are recognized as charities by a foreign country, or for which the grantee or counsel has provided an equivalency letter (§ 13.1(d)). Line 2 does not specifically state that the organization is to include the number of organizations recognized by the IRS as charities (it only references charities recognized by a foreign country), but the Form 990 instructions state a filing organization is to include IRS-recognized charities in its line 2 reporting. In addition, the final Form 990 instructions clarify that a recipient foreign organization may be reported on line 2 if the grantmaking organization has made a good-faith determination, based on an affidavit from the grantee or an opinion of counsel, that the grantee is the equivalent of a public charity.

On line 3, a reporting entity should enter the total number of *other* foreign recipient organizations or entities on line 3, meaning the organizations and entities to which grants were made and reported in response to line 1, but for which the grantees are not recognized as charities by the IRS or a foreign county or for which the grantee or counsel has not provided an equivalency letter or for which the grantmaking organization has not made a good-faith determination, based on an affidavit from the grantee or an opinion of counsel, that the grantee is the equivalent of a public charity. Making grants only to grantees that are recognized public charities or that are the equivalent of a United States public charity is not a requirement for foreign grantmaking (other than for private foundations), but an organization can demonstrate that it has exercised responsible foreign grantmaking by restricting its grants in this manner.

(c) Part III (Grants and Other Assistance to Individuals Outside the United States)

Part III of Schedule F requests information for each type of grant or assistance reported on Form 990, Part IX, line 3, which is the organization's grants and other assistance to governments, organizations, and individuals outside the United States, if the aggregate amount of all grants and assistance made to individuals located outside the United States during the year exceeded $5,000.

Part III is a table, and should be completed for grants or assistance made directly to or for the benefit of foreign individuals, but not for grants or assistance provided to individuals through another organization or entity. For example, a grant made to a hospital to cover the medical expenses of a foreign individual to a hospital located outside the United States is reported in Part III, while a contribution to a hospital located outside the United States for services to the public or for unspecified charity patients is reported in Part II, because it is a grant to the hospital, not to an individual. Part III reporting includes grants made not only to foreigners, but also to U.S. citizens or residents who are living or residing outside the United States. Each type of assistance to individuals should be listed on a separate line of Part III. If there are more types of assistance than there is space available, report the additional transactions in Part III of Schedule F-1. If an individual receiving a grant or assistance is also an interested person (§ 18.1(c)), the organization will need to disclose the grant or assistance on Schedule L (Transactions with Interested Persons).

(1) Column (a) (Type of Grant or Assistance). In Column (a), an organization lists the type of grant or assistance, listing all that apply for the region. The organization should use specific terms to describe the type of grant or assistance, such as scholarships, food, clothing, shelter for indigents or disaster victims, direct cash assistance to indigents, medical supplies or equipment, or books or other education supplies.

(2) Column (b) (Region). In Column (b), an organization should list each region in which grants or other assistance was provided for foreign individual grantees. Organizations should use the same nine regions listed for Part I of Schedule F (see § 13.2(a)(2)(i)).

(3) Column (c) (Number of Recipients). For each type of assistance provided in each region listed, an organization reports, in Column (c), the number of recipients receiving that type of assistance in that region. Filing organizations may estimate this number, but must provide in Part IV of Schedule F how the number was estimated.

(4) Columns (d) and (e) (Cash Grants). In Column (d), an organization reports the amount of cash grants provided to recipients in each region for each type of assistance. Cash grants include only grants by cash, check, money orders, electronic fund or wire transfers, and other charges against funds on deposit at a financial institution. Cash grants should be reported in U.S. dollars. In Column (e), the organization states the manner of cash disbursement, such as cash payment, money order, electronic fund or wire transfer, or other charges against funds on deposit at a financial institution, listing all that apply.

(5) Columns (f) through (h) (Noncash Assistance). In Column (f), an organization should list the fair market value of any noncash assistance provided in the region for each type of assistance listed in Column (a). This value should be listed in U.S. dollars. If multiple properties were transferred for the type of assistance, an organization must provide information for each property. In Column (g), an organization provides a description of the noncash assistance provided, giving a description for each type of property.

In Column (h), the filing organization reports the method of valuation for the noncash assistance. Property with a readily determinable market value should be reported at its fair market value. Organizations should use an appraised or estimated value for other property.

(d) Part IV (Supplemental Information)

Part IV of Schedule F is designed for a reporting organization to disclose its procedures for monitoring the use of grant funds outside of the United States (requested in Part I, line 2). It is also used to disclose any other information relating to Schedule F, such as the method used to account for total expenditures per region in Part I, and the method used to estimate the number of individual foreign recipients in Part III.

§ 13.3 NEW FORM 990 COMPLIANCE TASKS

Tax-exempt organizations should attend to these 11 compliance tasks if engaged in activities or grantmaking outside the United States.

1. **Foreign activities.** Determine which of the organization's activities and grantmaking efforts occur outside the United States and determine the level of

revenue generated from these activities and the amount of grants and assistance given outside the United States.

2. **Record keeping for foreign activities.** If an organization has more than $10,000 in aggregate revenue from its activities outside the United States, create a record-keeping system that records, per region, the number of offices the organization maintains, the number of its employees or agents, the activities conducted, a description of any program service activities, and the total expenditures allocable to activities in the region.

3. **Due diligence for foreign grants.** Establish procedures for evaluating and monitoring the use of foreign grants by looking to the private foundation expenditure responsibility rules and the U.S. Department of Treasury Anti-Terrorist Financing Guidelines: Voluntary Best Practices for U.S.-Based Charities for guidance.

4. **Review listings.** Prior to providing any foreign support, ensure the recipient is not on the OFAC's list of Specially Designated Nationals and Blocked Persons, and any similar lists maintained by U.S. State Department and the Department of Treasury.

5. **Investigate potential foreign grantees.** In addition to checking these lists, investigate foreign grantees, their employees, and their associates.

6. **Expenditure responsibility.** Implement procedures for foreign grantmaking that includes approval of the grant by the organization's board or a committee of the board, a written grant agreement, periodic reporting from the grantee, a mechanism for return of grant funds in the event of misuse, and proper records regarding the grants.

7. **Record keeping for grants to entities.** Keep detailed records regarding each foreign entity recipient that received more than $5,000 in grant funds, including the region, the purpose of the grant, the amount of cash distributed, the manner of cash disbursement, the amount and a description of noncash assistance, and the method used to value the noncash assistance (fair market value, appraisal, or estimate).

8. **Charitable status of grantees.** Keep track of foreign grantees that are recognized as charities by the IRS or a foreign country, for which the grantee or counsel has provided an equivalency letter, and for which the grantmaking organization has made a good-faith determination, based on an affidavit from the grantee or an opinion of counsel, that the organization is the equivalent of a public charity.

9. **Equivalency determination.** Consider using the equivalency determination procedure for grants to foreign charities by making a good-faith determination, based on an affidavit from the grantee or an opinion of counsel, that the grantee is the equivalent of a United States public charity.

10. **Record keeping for grants to individuals.** For any grantmaking to foreign individuals, keep records regarding the type of grant or assistance, the region in which the grant was made, the number of recipients receiving grants in a region, the aggregate amount of the cash grants made in the region for each type of assistance, the manner of disbursement of the cash grants, the

amount of noncash assistance, a description of noncash assistance, and the method of valuation of the noncash assistance (fair market value, appraisal, or estimate).

11. **Interested person grants.** Keep records and obtain the necessary information to determine if foreign recipients are either interested persons or related organizations, for purposes of reporting on Schedule L and Schedule R.

CHAPTER FOURTEEN

Schedule G—Fundraising and Gaming Activities

The redesigned Form 990 seeks considerable information about the fundraising and/or gaming activities of tax-exempt organizations. The fundraising aspects of the return are, of course, principally applicable to public charities. One of the oddities of this aspect of the law is that there is little correlation between the eligibility of an organization for tax-exempt status and the nature and extent of its fundraising activities. Most of the Form 990 questions concerning fundraising and gaming are in Schedule G.

§ 14.1 LAW AND POLICY

Federal and state laws regulate the process of fundraising for charitable (and sometimes other) purposes. State regulation of charitable gift solicitation is sweeping; its magnitude is often underestimated. Recent years have witnessed the entry of the federal government into this field of law enforcement. Overall, government regulation of charitable fundraising is pervasive. This aspect of regulation is likely to increase with the advent of the new Form 990.

(a) Federal Tax Law Concept of *Fundraising*

The IRS's instructions define the term *fundraising activities* to mean "activities undertaken to induce potential donors to contribute money, securities, services, materials, facilities, other assets, or time." Fundraising activities, according to these instructions, include publicizing and conducting fundraising campaigns; maintaining donor mailing lists; conducting fundraising events; preparing and distributing fundraising manuals, instructions, and other materials; and conducting other activities involved with the solicitation of contributions and grants from individuals, private foundations, governments, and others. Fundraising activities do not include gaming (see § 14.1(l)) (other than gaming that is incidental to a fundraising activity) or the conduct of an unrelated business that is regularly carried on (see §§ 7.1(b), 14.1(i)(4)).

(b) Methods of Fundraising

Fundraising for charitable (and other) purposes is undertaken by means of 12 methods. They are:

1. In-person solicitations, including meetings and door-to-door solicitations
2. Solicitation using the U.S. mail system, ranging from individual correspondence to direct mail campaigns
3. Solicitation using one or more telephones, ranging from personal calls to "boiler room" campaigns
4. Solicitation by means of a Web site
5. Solicitation by e-mail
6. Solicitation in the form of public advertising, such as theater playbills and charitable sales promotions
7. Solicitation of private foundation and other nongovernmental grants
8. Solicitation of government grants
9. Fundraising events (see § 16.1(c))
10. Gaming in the nature of sweepstakes, lotteries, or raffles
11. Door-to-door sales of merchandise
12. Conduct of unrelated business

Fundraising methods vary depending on the types of organizations or programs being funded. A college or university is not likely to utilize a massive direct mail campaign, yet charities that raise money to combat diseases, aid children, or provide disaster relief rely on direct mail almost exclusively. A church will send personalized letters to its congregation. Hospitals and museums make special fundraising events a staple of their fundraising efforts. Associations and societies include contribution requests with their annual dues notices.

Methods of fundraising can correlate with the purpose of the fundraising. For example, a charitable organization's effort to attract planned gifts, conduct a capital campaign, or build an endowment may be more focused on a constituency and thus will be based on in-person solicitations, mailing of brochures and letters, and incidental use of telephones and e-mail; direct mail is not likely to be deployed. A more public effort to attract endowment and capital funds will also include Web site solicitation, public advertising, fundraising events, and solicitation of private foundation grants. A program to solicit charitable bequests will concentrate on special mailings and personal visits.

Fundraising methods vary greatly as to their costs. Direct mail can be relatively low in cost if the mailings are to those who have given previously to the organization or the cause; it can be more costly if a purpose of the mailing is to acquire first-time donors. Charitable sales promotions are conducted at no cost to the beneficiary charities. There are no or little costs to charities where volunteers conduct the fundraising, such as in-person solicitations, door-to-door campaigns, and the use of personal correspondence and telephone calls. The most expensive type of fundraising tends to be the fundraising event (other than those conducted by volunteers).

(c) Fundraising Events

The IRS's instructions define *fundraising events* (or *special events*) to include "dinners/dances, door-to-door sales of merchandise, concerts, carnivals, sports events, auctions, and casino nights that are not regularly carried on." These events do not include "sales of gifts or goods or services of only nominal value, sweepstakes, lotteries or raffles where the names of contributors or other respondents are entered in a drawing for prizes, raffle[s] or lotteries where prizes have only nominal value[,] or solicitation campaigns that generate only contributions."

Special-event fundraising is somewhat unique, in that the purpose of the event often is not entirely fundraising. Community outreach or education usually also is a component of these events. (This dichotomy can sometimes be found in direct mail fundraising, where one of the reasons for the mailing is public education.) Some fundraising professionals consider special events to involve "friendraising."

(d) Concept of Professional Fundraiser

A fundraising professional is often termed, under state law, a *professional fundraiser* or a *fundraising counsel*, frequently defined as a person who, for compensation, "plans, manages, advises, consults, or prepares material for" the solicitation in the state of contributions for a charitable organization; this type of person does not "employ, procure, or engage" any compensated person to solicit contributions. A volunteer or salaried employee of a charitable organization is not a fundraising counsel, nor are lawyers, investment counselors, or bankers.

A *paid solicitor* is often defined as a person who, for compensation, performs for a charitable organization any service in connection with which contributions are or will be solicited in the state by that person or by any other compensated person the solicitor employs, procures, or engages, directly or indirectly, to solicit. There is often an exclusion from this definition for officers, employees, and volunteers of charitable organizations.

The IRS's instructions define the phrase *professional fundraising services* to include services "performed for the organization requiring the exercise of professional judgment or discretion consisting of planning, management, the preparation of materials (e.g., direct mail solicitation packages), and the provision of advice and consulting regarding solicitation of contributions, or the direct solicitation of contributions." This term does not, however, include "purely ministerial tasks, such as printing, mailing services, or receiving and depositing contributions to a charity, such as the services provided by a bank or caging service."

(e) State Regulation of Fundraising

Government regulation of fundraising for charitable objectives has traditionally been at the state level. Forty-six states have some form of a *charitable solicitation act*—a statute regulating the charitable fundraising process (see § 14.1(f)). Many counties, cities, and towns compound the regulatory requirements with comparable ordinances.

Fundraising charitable organizations must comply with the charitable solicitation act (if any) in effect in the state in which they are principally located. They are also expected to adhere to the law in *each state* in which they are soliciting funds. These laws also frequently mandate compliance by professional fundraisers, paid solicitors, commercial coventurers, and others who assist in fundraising endeavors. A charitable organization that is fundraising nationwide and its fundraising advisors thus should be in compliance with these 46 laws. Enforcers of county and city ordinances on fundraising often expect the national charities to comply with their rules as well.

Compliance in this setting various from state to state but essentially the term means that a charity must obtain permission from the appropriate regulatory authorities before a fundraising effort can begin. This permission is usually termed a *permit* or *license*, acquired as the result of filing a *registration statement*. Most states also require a filing fee, a bond, and/or the registration of professional fundraisers and others who will assist in the effort. The registration is usually updated by annually filing a report on the fundraising program, including financial information.

This process would be amply difficult if the registration and annual reporting requirements were uniform. The staff time and expense required to obtain, maintain, and disseminate the information throughout the states can be enormous. Historically, there has not been uniformity; recent years have brought limited progress toward use of a uniform registration form by several states (often accompanied nonetheless with schedules requiring varying information). Charities must constantly face differing registration and reporting forms, accounting methods, due dates, enforcement attitudes, and other substantial twists in the states' statutes, regulations, and forms.

(f) State Charitable Solicitation Acts

The summary of the state charitable solicitation acts that follows is based on the principal features of these acts as found in the majority of these statutes.

(1) Definitions. The typical state charitable solicitation act opens with a series of definitions. Terms often defined in these laws are *charitable organization* (see 14.1(f)(2); *solicit, solicitation, charitable purpose, contribution, professional fundraiser* (see § 14.1(f)(3)); *paid solicitor* (see § 14.1(f)(4)); and *commercial coventurer* and *charitable sales promotion* (see § 14.1(f)(5)).

(2) Regulation of Charitable Organizations. Generally, every charitable organization desiring to solicit contributions in the state must, in advance, file a registration statement with the appropriate state agency. This requirement applies whether the charity is to solicit on its own behalf or have funds solicited for it by another organization, or be the recipient of gifts generated through the services of a commercial coventurer or paid solicitor.

If the organization is in compliance, the state issues a certificate of registration, and the solicitation can then proceed. The statement must be filed in every year in which the charitable organization is soliciting in the state. A registration fee is levied.

A charitable organization usually is also required to file an annual financial report with the state. An organization with gross support and revenue not exceeding a certain amount (which will vary from state to state) is, however, often excused from filing an annual financial report. The financial information sometimes may be provided by submitting a copy of the annual information return (usually Form 990) filed with the IRS. Where the gross support and revenue of a charitable organization exceeds a certain amount (again, it will vary), the organization must submit audited financial statements.

Churches, other religious organizations, and charitable organizations closely affiliated with them usually are exempt from the registration requirements. Also often exempt are organizations that engage in small annual solicitations—that is, they do not receive gifts in excess of a certain amount or do not receive gifts from more than a few persons—but sometimes only if all of their functions (including fundraising) are carried on by persons who are not paid for their services. Other states provide limited exceptions for schools, hospitals, and membership organizations.

Under some of these laws, every charitable organization engaged in a solicitation in the state must disclose, at the point of solicitation, its name, address, telephone number, a "full and fair" description of the charitable program that is the subject of the fundraising campaign and the fact that a financial statement is available on request. Where the services of a paid solicitor are utilized, additional disclosures at the point of solicitation are required (see § 14.1(f)(4)).

(3) Regulation of Professional Fundraisers.   Many state charitable solicitation acts go beyond the regulation of fundraising charities and impose obligations on professional fundraisers. The definition of this term varies considerably—an additional source of confusion generated by these laws.

Conceptually, a professional fundraiser is a person (an individual consultant or a company) retained by a charity who does not solicit contributions but rather designs and oversees implementation of a fundraising program. (As noted, employees of charitable organizations are usually excluded from professional fundraiser status for purposes of these laws.) Normally, they do not take custody of charitable gifts. They are usually paid a fixed fee for their advice and services in structuring a fundraising program.

Thus, under this conceptualization, the actual asking for and receipt of charitable gifts is left to others. In the contemporary era, however, this distinction has collapsed and the functions overlap. Those who plan may also solicit. Thus, the confusion in the law mirrors reality.

The registration of professional fundraisers is annual, for a fee. The application contains such requests for information as the state deems appropriate. The bond requirement and amount varies from state to state. Within a stated period (such as 90 days) following the completion of a solicitation, and on the anniversary of the commencement of a fundraising campaign longer than one year, the professional fundraiser must account in writing to the charitable organization for all income received and expenses paid.

Often, every contract between a charitable organization and a professional fundraiser must be in writing. The professional fundraiser must file it with the state prior to performing any material services. From the contract, the state regulator must be able to identify the nature of the services the professional fundraiser is to provide. Many of these state laws detail the contents of these contracts.

(4) Regulation of Paid Solicitors.   Confusion as to the regulation of solicitors also reigns throughout the states. A paid solicitor is often required to register annually with the state prior to any activity—using an application containing the information the state may require—and to pay a fee. At that time, the solicitor almost certainly will have to post a bond.

A paid solicitor conceptually is an (perhaps the) active participant in the gift solicitation process. He or she literally asks for gifts. This can be done by any form of communication, most likely in person (as in door to door or on a street corner) or by telephone. Other modes are letters, other publication (such as a newsletter or journal), fax, or Internet (see § 14.1(j)). Again, however, this fine distinction is often obliterated in modern charitable fundraising.

In many instances, prior to a solicitation campaign, the paid solicitor must file with the state a copy of his, her, or its contract with the charitable organization. In addition, the paid solicitor will likely have to file a solicitation notice with the state. In a typical requirement, the notice must include a copy of the contract, the projected dates when soliciting will commence and terminate, the location and telephone number from where the solicitation will be conducted, the name and residence address of each person responsible for directing and supervising the conduct of the campaign, a statement as to whether the paid solicitor will at any time have custody of contributions, and a full and fair description of the charitable program for which the solicitation campaign is being carried out.

Often, every contract between a paid solicitor and a charitable organization must be in writing. More than one state patronizingly requires that this document "clearly state the respective obligations" of the parties. The contract may have to provide for a fixed percentage of the gross revenue (or a reasonable estimate of it) from the solicitation effort, which is the amount the charitable organization will (or is expected to) receive. The stated minimum percentage may not include the expenses of the solicitation paid by the charity.

Many of these laws impose a *point-of-solicitation* requirement, for which paid solicitors are responsible. Under versions of this rule, before a verbal request or within a written request for a contribution, the potential donor must be advised that the solicitor is a paid solicitor and that the charitable organization will receive a percentage of gross receipts as stipulated in the contract. The disclosure must be "clear" and "conspicuous." In an oral solicitation, a written receipt must be sent to the contributor within a short period (such as five days), and it must include a clear and conspicuous disclosure of the point-of-solicitation items.

Following completion of a solicitation campaign (such as within 90 days), and on the anniversary of the start of a solicitation campaign longer than one year, the paid solicitor may be required to file with the state a financial report for the fundraising campaign.

A paid solicitor may be required to maintain certain information during each solicitation campaign and for a significant period of time (such as three years) afterward. This information is likely to include the name and address of each contributor, the date and amount of each contribution, the name and residence address of each employee or other person involved in the solicitation, and all expenses incurred during the course of the solicitation campaign.

Monies collected by a paid solicitor may have to be deposited in a bank account in a timely manner; the account almost certainly will have to be in the name of the charitable organization involved. The charity may have to have sole control over withdrawals from the account.

Special rules may be applicable in situations where paid solicitors represent that tickets to an event will be donated for use by other persons. These rules include limitations on solicitations for donated tickets and record-keeping requirements.

(5) Regulation of Commercial Coventuring.   Under the laws of some states, every charitable sales promotion must be the subject of a written contract, when a charitable organization enters into an arrangement with a commercial coventurer. A copy of the contract must be filed with the state prior to the start of the promotion.

The law defines a *commercial coventurer* as a person who for profit is regularly and primarily engaged in trade or commerce (other than in connection with charitable fundraising) and who conducts a charitable sales promotion. A *charitable sales promotion* is an advertising or sales campaign, conducted by a commercial coventurer, where there is a representation that the purchase or use of goods or services offered by the commercial coventurer will benefit, in whole or in part, a charitable organization or purpose. Example: Fast-food company franchise A, located in city B, advertises (by television, radio, and newspapers) that, during weekend C, every time there is a purchase of sandwich D, 5 cents of the sales amount will be paid to charity E. The promotion is undertaken both to encourage sales and to benefit a charity—hence the term *coventure*. More recently, this practice has taken on another name: *embedded giving*.

The charitable sales promotion contract must include a statement of the goods or services to be offered to the public, the geographic area where the promotion will occur, the starting and ending dates of the promotion, the manner in which the name of the charitable organization will be used (including the representation to be made to the public as to the amount or percent per unit of goods and services purchased or used that will benefit the charitable organization), a provision for a final accounting on a per-unit basis by the commercial coventurer to the charitable organization, and the date by when and the manner in which the benefit will be conferred on the charitable organization.

The commercial coventurer is required to disclose in each advertisement for the charitable sales promotion the amount per unit of goods or services purchased or used that will benefit the charitable organization or purpose. This amount may be expressed as a dollar amount or percentage.

The final accounting will probably have to be retained by the commercial coventurer for a period of time (such as three years) and made available to the state authorities on request.

(6) Prohibited Acts.   Nearly all of the state charitable solicitation acts contain a list of one or more types of conduct—often termed *prohibited acts*—that may not be lawfully engaged in by a charitable organization (and perhaps not by a professional fundraiser, paid solicitor, and/or commercial coventurer).

For example, state law may provide that a person may not, for the purpose of soliciting charitable contributions, use the name of another person without consent. Or it may state that a person may not, for gift solicitation purposes, use a name, symbol, or statement so closely related to that used by a charitable organization or government agency that it would tend to confuse or mislead the public.

Other examples of a prohibited act is to lead the public to believe that registration with the state constitutes an endorsement of the fundraising organization by the state or to represent that a solicitation is for a charitable organization without proper authorization from the organization.

(7) Other Provisions.   These laws may provide that all documents required to be filed with the state (principally applications, registration statements, reports, and contracts) are matters of public record.

Records may have to be maintained by every charitable organization, fundraising counsel, professional fundraiser, paid solicitor, and/or commercial coventurer required to register. These records, which must be retained for a stated period (as noted, usually three years), must be available to state officials for inspection.

The law may authorize the state to enter into reciprocal agreements with other states or the federal government for the purpose of exchanging or receiving information filed by a charitable organization in another state, instead of requiring the organization to file under the particular state's law.

The state agency (probably the attorney general's or secretary of state's office) will undoubtedly be authorized to conduct investigations and enjoin solicitations. Under various circumstances, a registration can be revoked, canceled, or suspended. Civil penalties can be imposed for failure to adhere to the law. Willful violations of portions of these laws may even amount to criminal behavior, occasioning imprisonment.

(g) States' Police Power

The authority underlying the enactment and enforcement of these charitable solicitation acts lies in the *police power* inherently possessed by each of the states (and municipalities). Its police power enables a state to regulate—within the bounds of constitutional law principles (see § 14.1(h))—the conduct of its citizens and others to the end of protecting the safety, health, and welfare of its people. Consequently, in requiring a charitable organization planning on fundraising in the jurisdiction to register with the appropriate regulatory authority, to periodically render reports on the results of the solicitation, and to impose fees and bonding requirements, the state is exercising its police power.

The rationale is that charitable solicitations may be reasonably be regulated by the states in order to protect the public from deceit, fraud, unreasonable annoyance, or the unscrupulous obtaining of money or property under a pretense that the money or property is being collected for a charitable purpose. The laws that regulate charitable solicitations are thus by no means constitutionally deficient; they are, instead, manifestations of the states' police power. At the same time, these laws, like all legislation, must conform to certain basic constitutional law standards.

It is highly unlikely that a court will void a charitable solicitation act in its entirety because of constitutional law violations. Rather, when a court acts in this area, it does so with precision, striking out only the discrete provision or provisions that are overbroad (i.e., go beyond the ambit of narrowest-of-means regulation). For example, a state charitable solicitation act was found to be unconstitutional because of the burden imposed by the requirement that a professional fundraiser obtain a bond or post a letter of credit and because of too much "unbridled discretion" conferred on state officials.

The principal legal issue in this context has been the attempts over the years by many states to preclude charities from fundraising in their jurisdictions if their fundraising costs are "excessive," as computed as a percentage of gifts received (see § 14.1(h)). The Supreme Court has, to the dismay of state regulators, repeatedly struck down laws of this nature as being unconstitutional. Nonetheless, a group of states recently tried to convince the Court that high fundraising costs evidence per se fraud, so that certain charities and their fundraisers could be prosecuted. The Court sidestepped the issue, however, holding only that fraudulent charitable fundraising cannot be protected by free speech principles—which was the state of the law before the litigation (consuming nearly 12 years) was initiated.

(h)   Constitutional Law Considerations

Fundraising regulation of charitable organizations is more than the states' charitable solicitation acts (see § 14.1(e)) and the rules governing the deductibility of charitable gifts. This aspect of the law also involves fundamental principles of constitutional law.

The principal constitutional law precept is the doctrine of free speech, protected at the federal level by the First Amendment to the U.S. Constitution and at the state level by the Fourteenth Amendment. There are two forms of free speech: *pure* free speech, which may be regulated by the states by only the narrowest of means, and *commercial* free speech, which may be regulated by the states by means that are reasonable. Fundraising by charitable organizations is one of the highest forms of free speech—it is pure free speech.

The courts have held that, although government has legitimate interests in regulating this field—such as in exercise of the states' police power—it may not do so by broad and arbitrary classifications. As the Supreme Court has written, government can regulate charitable fundraising but "must do so by narrowly drawn regulations designed to serve those interests without unnecessarily interfering with First Amendment freedoms." The Court has also observed: "Broad prophylactic rules in the area of free expression are suspect. Precision of regulation must be the touchstone."

One of the most significant clashes between governmental police power to regulate for the protection of a citizenry and rights of free speech involves the application of percentage limitations on fundraising costs as a basis for determining whether a charity may lawfully solicit funds in a jurisdiction. Many aspects of this head-on conflict were resolved in 1980, when the Supreme Court held that a municipal ordinance was unconstitutionally overbroad and in violation of free speech. The ordinance had prohibited solicitation by charitable organizations that expend more than 25 percent of their receipts for fundraising and administrative expenses (known as an *absolute percentage limitation*). Subsequently, the Court addressed a law stating that fundraising expenses in excess of a certain percentage are presumed to be unreasonable, with charities given the opportunity to demonstrate that the expenses are in fact reasonable (the *rebuttable percentage limitation*); the Court found that this type of law also is contrary to charities' rights of free speech. Thereafter, these principles of free speech rights were extended to apply in situations where charities obtain outside fundraising assistance (such as that provided by paid solicitors (see § 14.1(f)(4))).

Both the absolute percentage limitation and the rebuttable percentage limitation can entail another constitutional law violation: denial of due process. Laws regulating the fundraising activities of charitable organizations must afford due process rights to persons subject to the laws, as prescribed in the Fifth and Fourteenth amendments.

A state charitable solicitation act must be in conformance with the guarantee of equal protection of the laws provided by the Fourteenth Amendment. This means that such an act may not discriminate in its classification of organizations. An equal protection argument can be raised because of exceptions from the coverage provided in a charitable fundraising regulation law (see § 14.1(e)). Indeed, some state laws exclude from compliance charitable organizations by name.

A cardinal doctrine of administrative law is that a governmental agency may issue rules and regulations. The agency must do so, however, in the context of a policy established by the legislative body involved that has fixed standards for the guidance of the agency in the performance of its functions. A charitable solicitation act may run afoul of this doctrine (born of the separation-of-powers principle) where the executive regulatory agency is granted such a wide range of discretionary authority that it is impermissibly exercising legislative power.

(i) Federal Regulation of Fundraising

Although the regulation of charitable fundraising was once the sole province of the states, it is now also being vigorously undertaken at the federal level, largely by application of the tax law. Agencies such as the U.S. Postal Service, the Federal Trade Commission, and the Federal Election Commission may also be involved.

(1) Fundraising Disclosure. Congress brought the IRS into the realm of fundraising regulation when it legislated three forms of fundraising disclosure rules. One package of these rules requires that most charitable gifts be *substantiated* in writing. Another set of rules mandates certain disclosures where there is a *quid pro quo contribution*. The third area of disclosure is that occasioned by the requirement that copies of a tax-exempt organization's application for recognition of tax exemption and annual information returns be made available to the public on request.

(2) Exemption Recognition Process. To be tax-exempt as charitable entities and to be charitable donees, organizations are required to secure a letter to that effect from the IRS. The application process requires the organization to reveal much information about itself. The application for recognition of tax exemption requires the submission of details on the applicant's fundraising program and on its fundraising expenditures (in the financial statements or the proposed budgets submitted with the application).

(3) Reporting Requirements. The annual information return (Form 990) requires charitable and certain other organizations to report contributions and grants, including contributions generated by fundraising events (see § 14.2).

(4) Unrelated Business Rules. One of the ways in which the IRS is regulating the charitable fundraising process is by means of the unrelated business rules. These rules may cause the receipts from fundraising activities to be characterized as unrelated business income.

Many fundraising practices possess all of the technical characteristics of an unrelated business: They are trades or businesses, are regularly carried on, and are not efforts that are substantially related to the performance of tax-exempt functions (even though the resulting income is used to support exempt functions). Applying the tests often used by the IRS and the courts, there is no question that some fundraising endeavors have a commercial counterpart and are being undertaken in competition with for-profit businesses, and with the objective of realizing a profit.

Some fundraising activities, however, are sheltered by law from consideration as taxable businesses. Four examples are an activity in which substantially all of the work is performed for the organization by volunteers; one that is carried on primarily for the convenience of the organization's members, students, patients, officers, or employees; one that consists of the sale of merchandise, substantially all of which has been received by the organization as gifts; and the conduct of bingo games.

As the functional accounting method's rules (see above) indicate, the law regards program activities and fundraising activities as separate types of undertakings. Even a simple fundraising activity such as a car wash or bake sale technically is an unrelated business. These businesses, nonetheless, are usually immune from taxation because they are not regularly carried on or are protected from taxation by an exception. Yet occasionally, when considering a special fundraising event, the IRS takes into account not only the time consumed by the event but also the time expended by the organization in preparing for it (known as *preparatory time*) in concluding that the fundraising event is a business that is regularly carried on—and thus is taxable.

(5) Lobbying Restrictions. Tax regulations define the term *fundraising costs* and spell out rules by which these costs are distinguished from (often allocated across) the categories of program and administration expenses. These regulations were crafted as part of the effort to state the rules governing elective lobbying restrictions for eligible public charities.

Under these lobbying rules, certain percentages are applied to the organization's outlays for program expenditures but not most fundraising expenditures. An organization endeavoring to comply with these rules must, therefore, differentiate between its fundraising expenses and its other costs. The amounts against which these percentages are applied are termed *exempt purpose expenditures*. These expenditures do not include amounts paid or incurred to or for (1) a separate fundraising unit of the organization or an affiliated organization's fundraising unit, or (2) one or more other organizations, if the amounts are paid or incurred primarily for fundraising.

To adhere to these rules, an electing public charity must determine its direct and indirect fundraising costs, utilizing the scope of the term *fundraising* in this context.

(6) Public Charity Classifications. A charitable organization is classified as either a *public charity* or a *private* one—the latter being a private foundation (see Chapter 8). One of the ways to avoid private foundation status is to be a publicly supported charitable organization; one of the ways to accomplish that is to qualify as a *donative type* publicly supported charity. An organization can achieve that classification by satisfying a *facts-and-circumstances test*, where the amount of public support normally received by the organization may be as low as 10 percent of its total support.

A variety of criteria may be used to demonstrate compliance with this test. One criterion is the extent to which the charitable organization is attracting public support. Thus, an element of this test is whether the organization is able to show that it has an active and ongoing fundraising program. The tax regulations state that an entity may satisfy this aspect of the test "if it maintains a continuous and bona fide program for solicitation of funds from the general public, community, or membership group involved, or if it carries on activities designed to attract support from governmental units or other [publicly supported] organizations."

(7) Substantiation Rules. Another way that the federal tax law regulates the charitable fundraising process is by means of the gift substantiation rules. Under this body of law, a donor who makes a separate charitable contribution of at least $250 in a year, for which a charitable contribution deduction is claimed, must obtain written substantiation of the contribution from the donee charitable organization. This document must contain certain information. If these rules are not followed, the donor is deprived of the charitable deduction.

(8) Quid Pro Quo Contribution Rules. The federal tax law likewise regulates in the field of charitable fundraising by means of the quid pro quo contribution rules. A *quid pro quo contribution* is a payment made partly as a charitable contribution and partly in consideration for goods or services provided to the payor by the donee organization. These rules require the charitable donee to provide the donor with certain information in writing. Penalties are imposed for failure to comply with these rules.

(9) Other Aspects of Federal Regulation. Federal tax law prohibits a private educational institution from qualifying as a tax-exempt entity if it has racially discriminatory policies. Under IRS guidelines, schools must follow an assortment of record-keeping requirements. Every private school must maintain, for at least three years, copies of all materials used by or on behalf of it to solicit charitable contributions. Failure to maintain or to produce the required reports and information creates a presumption that the school has failed to comply with the guidelines and thus has a racially discriminatory policy toward its students. Loss or denial of tax-exempt status could result.

Charitable and other organizations solicit gifts via the mail; consequently, the rules imposed by the U.S. Postal Service are a component of federal regulation of fundraising. Other federal agencies are involved in fundraising regulation, such as the Federal Trade Commission and its rules concerning telemarketing, and the Federal Election Commission and its rules pertaining to fundraising for political purposes.

(j) Fundraising by Means of the Internet

The Internet has greatly expanded the number of charitable organizations capable of carrying out, and actually engaged in the practice of, multistate gift solicitation activities. Essentially, to reach potential donors in all of the states, an organization needs nothing more than a computer and an account with an Internet service provider. Once established, the organization's charitable appeal can instantly be sent or made available to the entire Internet community. The large national and international charities with the resources necessary to assure compliance with the various state regulatory regimes are thus no longer the only ones affected by the state charitable solicitation laws. Instead, even the smallest organizations are beginning to tap the national contribution market. Thus, the new technology indeed is altering the nature of communication in the charitable solicitations context—it renders these communications inexpensive.

(1) Law in General. One of the most difficult of contemporary issues in the nonprofit law setting is whether fundraising by charitable organizations by means of the Internet constitutes fundraising in every state and locality. Current thinking is that, technically, it does (see below). If states asserting jurisdiction over Internet fundraising are justified in doing so, the result will be that even the smallest organizations—those too small to afford multistate solicitation efforts using any other medium—will be required to register and report under tens, maybe hundreds, of state and local charitable solicitation laws simply by virtue of utilizing the new communications technology to seek contributions. If they do not or cannot assure state-law compliance, they will be forced to decide between risking adverse legal action in several states or refrain from engaging in this form of speech altogether. The question thus is whether, under this unfolding mix of facts, state laws enforced in this fashion would impermissibly restrict speech protected by free speech principles (see § 14.1(h)).

There is another question that needs to be addressed. From a legal perspective, should Internet fundraising appeals be treated any differently simply because they take place via the Internet? (For federal tax purposes, the answer to this question from the IRS is no.) That is, should communication over this newest medium be treated as anything other than communication, for which there already is a rich regulatory regime?

To determine whether the various state charitable solicitation schemes unduly intrude on the protected speech interest in this type of solicitation, the existing regulatory framework must be applied to the new set of facts. The first step in this analysis is to ascertain whether the act of an organization in placing an appeal for funds in a document on a computer in one state subjects the organization to the jurisdiction of one or more other states. There is as yet no law directly on this subject. Nonetheless, while not directly on point, a court opinion sheds some light on the matter.

A federal court of appeals had the opportunity to discuss the legal status of computer-borne communications in the First Amendment context. Two individuals operated an adult-oriented bulletin board service from their home. This site was accessible to others around the nation via modems and telephone lines.

Working with a U.S. Attorney's office in another state, a postal inspector purchased a membership in this bulletin board service and succeeded in downloading allegedly obscene images from the bulletin board. The U.S. Attorney's office filed criminal charges against these individuals for, among other reasons, transmitting obscenity over interstate telephone lines from their computer. The images involved were found by a jury to constitute obscene materials; the couple was convicted.

On appeal, this federal appellate court affirmed the convictions, holding that the crime of "knowingly us[ing] a facility or means of interstate commerce for the purpose of distributing obscene materials" did not require proof that the defendants had specific knowledge of the destination of each transmittal at the time it occurred. Of interest in the Internet setting, in determining that the crime occurred in the second state, the court placed considerable weight on its finding that "substantial evidence introduced at trial demonstrated that the . . . [bulletin board service] was set up so members located in other jurisdictions could access and order [obscene] files which would then be instantaneously transmitted in interstate commerce."

If the reasoning of this appellate court is followed by state courts, it appears that communication via computer constitutes sufficient contact with foreign states to subject the communicator to local law requirements. Applied in the charitable solicitation regulation context, then, the import of this court decision is clear: Soliciting funds by means of the Internet, where users residing in foreign jurisdictions download Web pages, in all likelihood will constitute sufficient contact to subject the organization to the jurisdiction of the foreign state or states and therefore to the foreign charitable solicitation regulatory regime or regimes.

It must next be determined whether interstate communication of this nature constitutes *solicitation* encompassed by the fundraising regulation laws of the states. Although a definite answer cannot be divined from the language of any one statute, a brief survey of some state laws strongly indicates that Internet solicitation will be held in many jurisdictions to be subject to regulation.

For example, in one state, solicitation embraced by the charitable solicitation act is defined as the making of a fundraising request "through any medium," regardless of whether any contribution is actually received. In another state, the charitable solicitation law applies to all "request[s] of any kind for a contribution." In another state, the law encompasses "each request for a contribution." The statutory scheme in another state applies to "any request, plea, entreaty, demand or invitation, or attempt thereof, to give money or property, in connection with which . . . any appeal is made for charitable purposes." In still another state, the law applies to organizations "soliciting or collecting by agents or solicitors, upon ways or in any other public places within the [state] to which the public have a right of access."

Certainly it is difficult to see how Internet fundraising is not caught by any of these strikingly broad provisions. As currently written, then, the statutes of at least five states can easily be construed to reach Internet charitable fundraising.

Indeed, it is likely that most, if not all, of the state charitable fundraising regulation regimes may be so construed and that these statutes that fail as currently written can be appropriately amended without much trouble.

(2) Charleston Principles. If the assumption is that the solicitation of funds (and perhaps other property) by charitable and other nonprofit organizations by means of the Internet constitutes, as a matter of law, fundraising in every state (and municipality), then, as suggested, the charitable community is facing an enormous burden. Many in the regulatory sector realize that, if this technically is the law, some form of relief for charities that solicit gifts by means of the Internet is warranted.

To this end, the National Association of State Charity Officials (NASCO) developed guidelines to assist state regulators, charitable organizations that solicit contributions, and their fundraisers in deciding whether it is necessary to register fundraising efforts in one or more states when the solicitations are made by e-mail or on the organizations' Web sites. These guidelines are a product of discussion initiated at a NASCO conference in Charleston, South Carolina; hence the guidelines are termed the "Charleston Principles" (Principles). The Principles are not law but rather nonbinding guidance to NASCO members.

The Principles rest on this proposition: "Existing registration statutes generally, of their own terms, encompass and apply to Internet solicitations." An unstated assumption is that it is untenable to require registration and reporting of all charities soliciting gifts solely by means of the Internet, and their fundraisers, in all of the states with reporting requirements. Thus, the scope of potential registration must be narrowed or, as the Principles put it, state charity officials should "address the issue of who has to register where."

The Principles differentiate between entities that are domiciled in a state and those that are domiciled outside the state. (An entity is domiciled in a state if its principal place of business is in that state.)

An entity that is domiciled in a state and uses the Internet to conduct charitable solicitations in that state must, according to the Principles, register in that state. This position reflects the prevailing view that the Internet is a form of communication and the law does not make a distinction between that type of communication and another (such as use of regular mail). The rule applies "without regard to whether the Internet solicitation methods it uses are passive or interactive, maintained by itself or another entity with which it contracts, or whether it conducts solicitations in any other manner."

Matters become more complex in situations where an entity is fundraising, using the Internet, in a state in which it is not domiciled. Registration in the state is nonetheless required if:

- The organization's non-Internet activities alone are sufficient to require registration.
- It solicits contributions through an interactive Web site.
- The entity—
  ○ Specifically targets persons physically located in the state for solicitation, or
  ○ Receives contributions from donors in the state on a repeated and ongoing basis or a substantial basis through its Web site; or
  ○ Solicits contributions through a site that is not interactive but either specifically invites further off-line activity to complete a contribution or establishes other contacts with that state, such as sending e-mail messages or other communications that promote the Web site, and the entity engages in one of the foregoing two activities.

Often considerable line-drawing will be required in the application of these guidelines. The matter becomes more intricate when some definitions are factored in.

An *interactive Web site* is a site that "permits a contributor to make a contribution, or purchase a product in connection with a charitable solicitation, by electronically completing the transaction, such as by submitting credit card information or authorizing an electronic funds transfer." These sites include those through which a donor "may complete a transaction online through any online mechanism processing a financial transaction even if completion requires the use of linked or redirected sites." A Web site is considered *interactive* if it has this capacity, irrespective of whether donors actually use it.

The phrase specifically target persons physically located in the state for solicitation means to engage in one of two practices:

1. Include on the Web site an express or implied reference to soliciting contributions from persons in that state; or
2. Otherwise affirmatively appeal to residents of the state, such as by advertising or sending messages to persons located in the state (electronically or otherwise) when the entity knows, or reasonably should know, that the recipient is physically located in the state.

Charities operating on a "purely local basis" or within a "limited geographic area" do not target states outside their operating area if their Web site makes clear in context that their fundraising focus is limited to that area, even if they receive contributions from outside that area on less than a repeated and ongoing basis or on a substantial basis.

To receive contributions from a state on a *repeated and ongoing basis* or a *substantial basis* means "receiving contributions within the entity's fiscal year, or relevant portion of a fiscal year, that are of sufficient volume to establish the regular or significant (as opposed to rare, isolated, or insubstantial) nature of these contributions."

States are encouraged to set, and communicate to the regulated entities, "numerical [*sic*] levels at which it [*sic*] will regard this criterion as satisfied." These levels should, the Principles provide, define *repeated and ongoing* in terms of a number of contributions and *substantial* in terms of a total dollar amount of contributions or percentage of total contributions received by or on behalf of the charity. The meeting of one of these thresholds would give rise to a registration requirement but would not limit an enforcement action for deceptive solicitations.

Another Principle is that an entity that solicits via e-mail in a particular state is to be treated the same as one that solicits by means of telephone or direct mail, if the soliciting party knew or reasonably should have known that the recipient was a resident of or was physically located in that state.

The Principles address the circumstance as to whether a charity is required to register in a particular state when the operator of a Web site, through which contributions for that charity are solicited or received, is required to register but the charity does not independently satisfy the registration criteria. If the law of the state does not universally require the registration of all charities on whose behalf contributions are solicited or received through a commercial fundraiser, commercial coventurer, or fundraising counsel who is required to register, then the state should independently apply the criteria to each charity and only require registration by charities that independently meet the tests. If, however, the law of the state universally requires registration of all charities under these circumstances, the state should consider whether, as a matter of "prosecutorial discretion, public policy, and the prioritized use of limited resources," it would take action to enforce registration requirements as to charities that do not independently meet the criteria.

Still another Principle is that solicitations for the sale of a product or service that include a representation that some portion of the price shall be devoted to a charitable organization or charitable purpose (*commercial coventuring, charitable sales promotion,* or *cause-related marketing* (see § 14.1(f)(5)) shall be governed by the same standards as otherwise set out in the Principles governing charitable solicitations.

There are two "exclusions" from the registration requirements. One is that maintaining or operating a Web site that does not contain a solicitation of contributions but merely provides program services by means of the Internet does not, by itself, invoke a requirement to register. This is the case even if unsolicited contributions are received.

The other exclusion is for entities that solely provide administrative, supportive, or technical services to charities without providing substantive content or advice concerning substantive content; they are not required to register. These entities include Internet service providers and organizations that do no more than process online transactions for a separate firm that operates a Web site or provide similar services.

This exclusion does not encompass professional fundraisers, fundraising counsel, or commercial coventurers.

The Principles provide that state charity officials "recognize that the burden of compliance by charitable organizations and their agents, professional fundraisers, commercial co-venturers and/or professional fundraising counsel should be kept reasonable in relation to the benefits to the public achieved by registration." Projects to create "common forms," such as the unified registration statement, are "strongly encouraged."

State charity offices are also "strongly encouraged" to publish their registration and reporting forms, their laws and regulations, and other related information on the Internet to facilitate registration and reporting by charitable organizations and their agents.

The Principles encourage development of information technology infrastructure to facilitate electronic registration and reporting. Also encouraged is Internet posting by charitable organizations of their application for recognition of tax-exempt status, their IRS determination letter, their most recent annual information returns, and their state registration statement(s). (This posting practice is also encouraged by the federal tax law, which obviates the need to provide hard copies of these federal documents to requestors when they are made available on the Internet.)

(k) Fundraising Contracts

Many of the state charitable solicitation acts (see § 14.1(f)) require that the relationship between a charitable organization and a professional fundraiser and/or professional solicitor be evidenced by a written agreement. This contract will usually have to be filed with the state soon after the document is executed.

Several state charitable solicitation acts contain rules that mandate certain provisions in a contract between a charitable organization and a professional fundraiser and/or professional solicitor. The law may require that these contracts contain (1) a statement of the charitable organization's right to cancel; (2) a statement as to the period during which the contract may be canceled; (3) the address to which any notice of cancellation is to be sent; (4) the address of the secretary of state, to whom a copy of any notice of cancellation is to be sent; and (5) a statement of the financial arrangement between the parties.

The IRS will be particularly interested in one of these contractual arrangements where the individual involved is a trustee, director, officer, or key employee of the charitable organization that is also a party to the contract.

(l) Federal and State Regulation of Gaming

Federal tax law is generally silent on the matter of gaming by tax-exempt organizations; the little law there is consists of the IRS's instructions accompanying the new Form 990 and the exception from treatment as unrelated business for qualified bingo games (see § 14.1(f)(4)).

(1) Definitions. The IRS's instructions provide that *gaming* includes "bingo, pull tabs/instant bingo (including satellite and progressive bingo), Texas Hold-Em Poker and other card games, raffles, scratch-offs, [use of] charitable gaming tickets, break-opens, hard cards, banded tickets, jar tickets, pickle cards, Lucky Seven cards, Nevada Club tickets, casino nights, Las Vegas nights, and coin-operated gambling devices." *Coin-operated gambling devices* include "slot machines, electronic video slot or line games, video poker, video blackjack, video keno, video bingo, [and] video pull tab games."

These instructions define *bingo* in this way:

> [A] game of chance played with cards that are generally printed with five rows of five squares each. Participants place markers over randomly called numbers on the cards in an attempt to form a pre-selected pattern such as a horizontal, vertical, or diagonal line, or all four corners. The first participant to form the pre-selected pattern wins the game. To be a bingo game, the game must be of the type described in which wagers are placed, winners are determined, and prizes or other property are distributed in the presence of all persons placing wagers in that game.

The IRS observed that certain "consolation bingo games within a progressive bingo game" may qualify as bingo.

The instructions define *pull-tabs* in this way:

> [This term includes] games in which an individual places a wager by purchasing preprinted cards that are covered with pull-tabs. Winners are revealed when the individual pulls back the sealed tabs on the front of the card and compares the patterns under the tabs with the winning patterns preprinted on the back of the card. Included in the definition of pull-tabs are "instant bingo," "mini bingo," and other similar scratch-off cards. Satellite, internet and progressive bingo are games conducted in many different places simultaneously and the winners are not all present when the wagers are placed, the winners are determined and the prizes are distributed. Revenue and expenses associated with satellite, internet and progressive bingo should be included under this category.

The instructions defined the phrase *partnership formed to administer charitable gaming* to mean "two or more organizations that are authorized under state law to conduct bingo or other gaming at the same location joining together to account for and/or share revenues, authorized expenses, and inventory related to bingo and gaming operations." This definition, however, was deleted in the final instructions.

(2) Law in General. The principal focus of the IRS in this regard, principally in the contexts of examinations, is on bingo and pull-tab games. Bingo games are excluded from the definition of unrelated business. Generally, however, the regular operation by a tax-exempt organization of gambling activities (including instant bingo, pull-tab games, etc.) is the conduct of an unrelated business, particularly where the activities involve the public. A gaming activity conducted entirely by volunteers may be exempt from unrelated business taxation.

In some instances, gaming activities can be substantially related activities, such as when conducted by a tax-exempt organization for social or recreational purposes for its members and their bona fide guests. These exempt organizations include social clubs, fraternal beneficiary societies, domestic fraternal societies, and veterans' organizations. Gaming activities involving only members and their guests directly furthers exempt purposes in these instances.

A *nonmember*, in this context, was defined in the draft instructions as an "individual who is not a member of the organization but who participates in recreational activities sponsored by the organization or receives services or goods from the organization and pays for the services or goods received." These instructions continued: "Such an individual, even when accompanied by a member, is generally considered to be the principal in a business transaction with the organization. Gaming open to the general public may result in unrelated business income tax (UBIT) or adversely affect exempt status." This material was, however, deleted from the final instructions.

Many states have gaming laws that identify the types of organizations that are allowed to conduct gaming activities and the conditions pursuant to which the games may be conducted (such as a requirement that volunteers be utilized or a limit on the number of nights in a week a tax-exempt organization can conduct gaming activity). If there is an IRS examination of an exempt organization as to gaming, it should be expected that the examining agent(s) will be aware of the state's agency in charge of gaming activities enforcement, policy memoranda, and reporting requirements.

(3) IRS Examination Practices.   An IRS examiner will likely ask questions such as: (1) what types of gaming activities does the organization conduct, (2) who conducts the activities, (3) who owns the facility where the gaming is conducted, (4) how are the games advertised, (5) who supplied the gaming equipment and/or supplies, (6) how long has the gaming been conducted, (7) what is the size and extent of the gaming activity (on an income, expense, and time basis), and (8) has the manner in which the games have been conducted changed over time? The examiner will review board minutes and contracts and interview current and past employees. Among the issues on the examiner's mind will be private inurement and private benefit.

An IRS examiner of bingo activity will determine whether the operation has a system of internal controls to adequately safeguard the revenue generated from the games. He or she will monitor the bingo game while it is under way, probably as an unannounced visit. A bingo game gross receipts analysis will be conducted, looking for unreported revenue. An expense analysis will be undertaken, such as where a charitable organization raises funds from gaming activities and makes payments to other charitable organizations.

An examination of pull-tab activity will likely entail a review of the tax-exempt organization's inventory of pull-tab supplies, comparing the boxes of pull-tabs to supplier invoices (the absence of which may indicate diversion of the exempt organization's funds). The examiner will monitor the pull-tab sales and will undertake a pull-tap gross receipts and expense analysis.

Gaming activities may adversely affect a tax-exempt organization's exempt status, such as where a charitable organization engages in these activities for nonexempt purposes and the activities are substantial. If, however, an exempt charitable organization has a program of making grants to other charities from its gaming activities revenue, the commercial or business aspects of the gaming may be considered incidental to the charitable purposes. A gaming activity that is illegal may jeopardize the exempt organization's tax exemption on the ground that it is contrary to public policy. Gaming activities may endanger exemption if they violate the doctrines of private inurement or private benefit; these activities may transgress the intermediate sanctions rules.

The receipt of gaming income may have an adverse effect on a charitable organization's public charity status if it is a publicly supported charity. This determination turns, in large part, on whether the income is unrelated business income. In ascertaining whether a charitable organization qualifies as a donative-type publicly supported charity, gross receipts from activities that do not constitute unrelated business (including nontaxable bingo receipts) are excluded from the computation of public support. In determining whether a charitable organization is a service provider publicly supported charity, gross receipts, if not unrelated business income, are likely to qualify as public support.

An IRS examiner will attempt to identify related entities. That is, the gaming operation may have related management, real estate, supply, equipment, or concession companies. Agreements (including subleases) will be reviewed, with the examiner searching for excessive compensation, lengthy contract terms, penalties on the tax-exempt organization in case of termination of an agreement, and lack of open bidding in selection of the gaming operator. If related entities are found, the examiner will determine the nature of the relationship between the parties: agency, joint venture, sales, license, or other arrangement.

The examiner will review the books and records of the tax-exempt organization conducting the gaming operations, examine the exempt organization's returns (and correlate them with the returns filed by gaming operators (Forms 1040, 1120)), and issuance of a tax form of prize winners (Form W-2G), to determine if the organization is liable for federal excise taxes on wagering and in compliance with the rules as to employment taxes and tip income.

(m) Schedule B

Schedule B of the new Form 990 is used to provide information about contributions the filing organization reported in Part VIII, line 1. Every organization must file Schedule B, unless it certifies that it does not meet this filing requirement (by answering "no" on Form 990, Part IV, line 2). When preparing this schedule, the organization must use the same accounting method previously reported (Form 990, Part XI, line 1).

(1) Definitions. The term *contributor* includes individuals, fiduciaries, partnerships, corporations, associations, trusts, governmental units, and other tax-exempt organizations. The term *contribution* means contributions, grants, bequests, devises of money or property, whether or not for charitable purposes (such as political contributions). Contributions do not include fees received for the performance of services.

A *cash contribution* includes contributions paid by cash, credit card, check, money order, electronic fund or wire transfers, and other charges against funds on deposit at a financial institution. The phrase *charitable deduction property* means property other than money or certain publicly traded securities.

(2) Reporting Thresholds. Generally, an organization must list, in Part I of Schedule B, every contributor who, during the tax year, gave the organization, directly or indirectly, money or any other type of property aggregating $5,000 or more for the year. In determining this threshold, the organization totals all of the contributor's contributions only if they are $1,000 or more for the year.

If the filing organization is a donative type publicly supported charity (see § 8.1(d)), under the general rules (i.e., not just pursuant to the facts-and-circumstances test), it lists in Part I only those contributors whose contribution of $5,000 or more is greater than 2 percent of its total support during the public support measuring period (see Form 990, Part VIII, line 1h).

> **Example.** Charity X, a donative-type public charity, reported $700,000 in contributions, grants, and the like for its public support measuring period. Two percent of $700,000 is $14,000. Thus, a contributor who gave $11,000 to X during the year would not be reported on Schedule B of X's Form 990. This is the case even though this contributor's contribution(s) for the year were in excess of $5,000.

In the case of contributions to tax-exempt social clubs and fraternal beneficiary and domestic fraternal societies that were not for an exclusively charitable purpose, the organizations lists each contributor who, during the year, contributed $5,000 or more, as determined above. In the case of contributions to these organizations that were for exclusively religious purposes, the organization reports each contributor whose aggregate contributions were more than $1,000 during the year (taking into account contributions of all amounts).

These three types of tax-exempt organizations provide further information on these contributions of more than $1,000 during the year in Part III of Schedule B and show the total amount received in the case of contributions that were for $1,000 or less during the year. If one of these organizations did not receive a contribution of more than $1,000 during the year for exclusively charitable purposes, and thus was not required to complete Parts I–III of Schedule B, it need only check the correct *Special Rules* box applicable to that organization on the front of Schedule B and enter, in the space provided, the total contributions it received during the year for an exclusively charitable purposes.

(3) Group Returns. A central (parent) organization with a group ruling that files a group Form 990 must file a separate Form 990 for itself (unless it is exempt from filing Form 990 (see § 1.1(b)). With respect to Schedule B, however, a central organization has two choices: It may file:

- A Schedule B for itself with its Form 990 and a separate Schedule B with the group return, or
- A consolidated Schedule B for itself and all included subordinates with the group return.

The same information must be reported, whichever method of reporting is used; the information is just formatted differently and appears in different returns.

The central organization must indicate, in Schedule O, which method of reporting it has adopted. Once a method is used, it cannot be changed without the consent of the IRS.

(4) Disclosure Considerations. For organizations that file Form 990, the names and addresses of contributors are not open to public inspection. If an organization files a copy of its Form 990 with one or more states, it should not include its Schedule B in the filing, unless the state requires a schedule of contributors. States that do not require the information might inadvertently make the schedule available for public inspection.

§ 14.2 PREPARATION OF NEW FORM 990 SCHEDULE G

Form 990, Schedule G, concerns fundraising and/or gaming activities by tax-exempt organizations. This schedule is comprised of three parts: Part I pertaining to fundraising in general, Part II pertaining to special-event fundraising, and Part III pertaining to gaming.

A tax-exempt organization is required to complete some or all of Schedule G if the organization is answering "yes" to one or more of these questions:

- The organization reported payment of more than $15,000 in the form of professional fundraising fees (see Form 990, Part IV, line 17; Form 990, Part IX, line 11e).

- The organization reported receipt of more than $15,000 in revenue from fundraising events (see Form 990, Part IV, line 18; Form 990, Part VIII, line 8a).

- The organization reported receipt of more than $15,000 in revenue from gaming (see Form 990, Part IV, line 19; Form 990, Part VIII, line 9a).

(a) Part I (Professional Fundraising Expenses)

Part I of Schedule G must be completed by organizations that reported, for the year, payment of more than $15,000 in professional fundraising expenses. This requires an understanding of the IRS's definition of the term *professional fundraising services* (see § 14.1(d)). This definition, however, rests on the definition of the term *fundraising activities* accorded it by the IRS: "activities undertaken to induce potential donors to contribute money, securities, services, materials, facilities, other assets, or time."

This definition of *fundraising activities* is too broad. It is nonsensical to include the solicitation of *services* or *time* in the definition of *fundraising*. The fundraising community, long ago, differentiated among contributions of "time, treasure, and talent." Fundraising pertains to the solicitation of money and/or other property; it does not relate to solicitations of services or time. If a charitable organization's president asks an individual to serve on the charity's board of trustees, the president is not engaged in fundraising. If a charitable organization's executive director asks an individual to volunteer to assist with a particular project (even a fundraising event), the executive director is likewise not engaged in fundraising. The IRS has overlooked the fact that the concept of and the word *fundraising* not only contains the word *fund* but is predicated on it.

The organization must indicate (in response to question 1, by checking a box in front of each method of fundraising used) whether it raised funds by means of one or more of these seven fundraising methods:

1. Mail solicitations
2. E-mail solicitations
3. Telephone solicitations

4. In-person solicitations

5. Solicitation of nongovernment grants

6. Solicitation of government grants

7. Special fundraising events

As discussed, this list is not a complete inventory of the various methods pursuant to which fundraising by tax-exempt organizations takes place. For example, the IRS's list does not include solicitations posted on Web sites. It is not clear how gifts received as the result of a charitable sales promotion are reported.

The organization is asked whether it has a written or oral agreement with any individual (including trustees, directors, officers, or key employees (see Form 990, Part VII)) or entity in connection with professional fundraising activities (line 2a, ending in "yes" or "no" boxes). This question does not apply with respect to trustees, directors, officers, or key employees of the organization, such as a development officer.

If the answer to this question is "yes," the organization must list the 10 highest-paid individuals or entities where the fundraiser is to be compensated at least $5,000 in the year by the organization (question 2b). In this list, the organization must provide this information:

- The name of the individual or entity (fundraiser) (Column (i)).

- A summary of the type of fundraising activity with respect to which the fundraiser performed services (Column (ii)).

- Whether the fundraiser has custody or control of contributions (Column (iii), "yes" or "no" boxes); *custody or control* means possession of the funds or the ability to deposit, direct the use of, of use the funds; any such custody or control should be described in Schedule O.

- Gross receipts that the organization collected or the fundraiser collected on behalf of the organization or in connection with the fundraising activity of the organization during the tax year (Column (iv)).

- Amount of fees paid to or retained (the instructions use the word *withheld*) by the fundraiser for its services (Column (v)); if the arrangement also provides for the payment by the organization of fundraising expenses (such as printing, paper, envelopes, postage, mailing list rental, and equipment rental), the organization must report those amounts paid during the year in Schedule O and describe how the arrangement distinguishes payments for professional fundraising services from expense reimbursements; the organization must also describe in Schedule O whether it entered into any arrangements under which payments were made exclusively for such expenses and no payment was made for professional fundraising services.

- Amount paid to or retained by the organization (Column (vi)); this equals the amount in Column (v) less the amount in Column (iv).

The filing organization must list all states in which it is registered or licensed to solicit funds or has been notified that it is exempt from such registration or licensing (question 3). The IRS's instructions state that, if the filing organization is registered, licensed, or exempted from registration or licensing "in all 50 States, it may answer 'All 50 States.' " This outcome, however, is impossible inasmuch as not all states have registration, licensing, or exemption laws.

(b) Part II (Fundraising Events)

Part II of Schedule G must be completed by organizations that reported, for the year, receipt of more than $15,000 in revenue from fundraising events.

> *Note 1:* There is an anomaly here. The filing of Part II is required when total special fundraising event revenue is more than $15,000. Yet Part II requires the listing of events the gross receipts of which are greater than $5,000. What does an organization do if it had, for example, five fundraising events, each of which grossed $4,000? The $15,000 threshold is exceeded but not the $5,000 threshold.
>
> *Note 2:* There is an error on the Form 990 in this regard. Part IV, line 18, indicates that Schedule G, Part II, is required if the amount on Part VIII, lines 1c and/or 8a are in excess of $15,000. Part VIII, however, indicates that this schedule is required only if the amount on line 8a is over $15,000. This narrower requirement is also reflected in the opening instruction to this Part II.

The table in Part II is to be completed by listing the two largest fundraising events (#1 and #2), as measured by gross receipts, in Columns (a) and (b) by indicating the name (the instructions state *type*); in Column (c), the organization reports the total number of other events that occurred. The organization also reports, as to these two events and the summary of the others (if any), this information:

- Gross receipts from the event(s) (line 1). The organization enters the total amount the organization received from each of the two largest events during the year (without subtracting any costs or expenses or charitable contributions received in connection with the event) (Columns (a) and (b)). The total amount the organization received from all other events during the year (without any offsets) is also reported (Column (c)). The sum of line 1, Columns (a) to (c) is reported in Column (d).

- Charitable contributions received in connection with the event(s) (line 2). The total amount of contributions and similar amounts (including the total value of any noncash contributions (see Chapter 19) received by the organization for the two largest events during the year is separately reported (Columns (a) and (b)). The total amount of contributions and the like received by the organization from the other events during the year is also reported (Column (c)). The sum of line 2, Columns (a)–(c) is reported in Column (d). This amount is also entered in Form 990, Part VIII, line 1c.

- Gross revenue from the event (gross receipts minus contributions) (line 3). The total amount of gross revenue received by the organization from the two largest events during the year (without reduction for catering, entertainment, cost of goods sold, compensation, fees, or other expenses) is separately reported (Columns (a) and (b)). The total amount of gross revenue received by the organization from the other events during the year is also reported (Column (c)).

The sum of line 3, Columns (a)–(c) is reported in Column (d). This amount is also entered in Form 990, Part VIII, line 8a.

- The total amount of cash prizes paid out (line 4). The prize amounts for the two largest events are separately reported (Columns (a) and (b)). The prize amounts for the other events are also reported (Column (c)). The sum of line 4, Columns (a)–(c) is reported in Column (d).

- The total amount (fair market value) of noncash prizes paid out (line 5). The prize amounts for the two largest events are separately reported (Columns (a) and (b)). The prize amounts for the other events are also reported (Column (c)). The sum of line 5, Columns (a)–(c) is reported in Column (d).

- Total expenses paid or incurred for the rent of property and/or other facilities (line 6). The rent/facility costs for the two largest events are separately reported (Columns (a) and (b)). The rent/facility costs for the other events are also reported (Column (c)). The sum of line 6, Columns (a)–(c) is reported in Column (d).

- Total other direct expenses (line 7). This is the sum of other direct expense items not included on lines 4 to 6, including catering and entertainment expenses. The other direct expenses for the two largest events are separately reported (Columns (a) and (b)). The prize amounts for the other events are also reported (Column (c)). The sum of line 7, Columns (a)–(c) is reported in Column (d).

- A summary of direct expenses for all reported events (line 8). This is the sum of line 8, Columns (a)–(c), reported in Column (d). The organization should enter this amount in Form 990, Part VIII, line 8b.

- A net income summary for all reported events (gross revenue less direct expenses) (line 9). This amount (reported in line 9, Column (d)) is the difference between the amount on line 3, Column (d), and the amount on line 8, Column (d)). The organization should enter this amount in Form 990, Part VIII, line 8c.

(c) Part III (Gaming)

Part III of Schedule G must be completed by organizations that reported (Form 990, Part VIII, line 9a), for the year, receipt of more than $15,000 in revenue from gaming. This part differentiates among bingo (Column (a)), pull tabs/instant bingo/progressive bingo (Column (b)), and other forms of gaming (Column (c)). The IRS's instructions state that "certain consolation bingo games within a progressive bingo game should be included in Column (a)." There is no monetary threshold in connection with the reporting of discrete gaming operations.

For each gaming operation, the organization must report:

- Gross revenue (line 1). The amount of gross revenue from gaming activities for each type gaming conducted is reported (Columns (a)–(c)), with the total in Column (d)). This amount should not be reduced by any amount of cash or noncash prizes, cost of goods sold, compensation, fees, or other expenses.

- Total amount of cash prizes paid out (line 2). This must be reported for each of the types of gaming reported on line 2 (Columns (a)–(c)) and totaled (Column (d)).

- Total fair market value of noncash prizes provided (line 3). This must be reported for each of the types of gaming reported on line 3 (Columns (a)–(c)) and totaled (Column (d)).

- Expenses paid or incurred for the rent of property and/or other facilities (line 42). These expenses must be reported for each of the types of gaming reported on line 4 (Columns (a)–(c)) and totaled (Column (d)).

- Other direct expenses (line 5). The organization must report the amount of other direct expenses (expenses not included on lines 2–4). These expenses should include labor costs and wages (including the total amount of compensation paid to gaming workers or paid to independent contractors for labor costs), employment taxes (including the amount of federal, state, and local payroll taxes paid for the year associated with gaming workers but only those that are imposed on the organization as an employer), and excise taxes. The foregoing includes the employer's share of Social Security and Medicare taxes, the federal unemployment tax, state unemployment compensation taxes, and other state and local payroll taxes. These expenses must be reported for each of the types of gaming reported on line 5 (Columns (a)–(c)) and totaled (Column (d)).

  The organization should not include in line 5 taxes withheld from the employees' salaries and paid to various governmental units, such as federal and state income taxes, and the employees' share of social security and Medicare taxes.

  The IRS, in its draft instructions, requires the organization to retain in its records a schedule providing an itemized listing of all other direct expenses.

  Gaming activities may be subject to a wagering excise tax, imposed on the amount of the wager (see IRS Form 730, *Tax on Wagering*), and an occupational tax, imposed on the persons engaged in receiving wagers (see IRS Form 11C, *Tax and Registration Return for Wagering*).

- Use of any volunteer labor, by "yes" or "no" boxes (if there is such labor, the percentage of it must be reported) (line 6). If the organization uses volunteer labor, where substantially all of the work is performed without compensation, to conduct gaming, one or more of the appropriate "yes" boxes is to be checked and the percentage of total labor performed by volunteers for each type of gaming conducted is to be reported. This percentage is determined by comparing the number of individuals who receive direct compensation for their services provided in the conduct of the gaming activity with the total number of workers used by the organization, whether paid or unpaid. For this purpose, the word *compensation* includes tips and noncash benefits. These answers and percentages (if any) must be reported for each of the types of gaming reported on line 6 (Columns (a)–(c)); Column (d) is to be left blank.

- A summary of direct expenses for all gaming (line 7). This amount is the sum of the amounts on lines 2, Column (d), through 7, Column (d), and reported on line 7, Column (d).

- A summary of net gaming income for all gaming (line 8). This amount is the difference between the amount on line 1, Column (d), and on line 7, Column (d).

  For organizations filing the new Form 990, the amounts in Column (d) of line 1, Column (d) of line 7, and Column (d) of line 8 must equal the amounts reported on Form 990, Part VIII, lines 9a, 9b, and 9c, respectively.

The organization must identify the states in which it operated gaming activities during the tax year (question 9); if additional space is needed, the organization should utilize Schedule O. The organization is asked whether it is licensed to operate gaming activities in each of these states (question 9a, "yes" or "no" boxes); if the answer to this question is "no," the organization must provide a narrative statement of explanation, preferably using Schedule O (question 9b).

The organization is asked whether any of its gaming licenses were revoked, suspended, or terminated during the year (question 10a, "yes" or "no" boxes). If the answer to this question is "yes," the organization must provide a narrative statement of explanation for each state in which there was a revocation or the like during the tax year, preferably using Schedule O (question 10b). The organization is asked whether it operates gaming activities with nonmembers (question 11, "yes" or "no" boxes). The organization is asked if it is a grantor, beneficiary, or trustee of a trust, or a member of a partnership or other entity formed to administer charitable gaming (question 12, "yes" or "no" boxes).

Part III of Schedule G seeks additional information in connection with gaming activities:

- The percentage of gaming activity operated in the organization's facility and/or an outside facility (question 13).

- The name and address of the person who prepares the organization's gaming/special events books and records (question 14).

- Whether the organization has a contract with an entity from whom it receives gaming revenue (question 15a, "yes" or "no" boxes). If the answer to this question is "yes," the organization must report the amount of gaming revenue it received and the amount of gaming revenue retained by the entity (question 15b). Also, if the answer to this question is "yes," the organization must provide the entity's name and address (question 15c). Schedule O is available if additional space is needed, such as where there is more than one third-party operator.

- Gaming manager information, that is, information about the person who has overall supervision and management of the gaming operation (question 16). Generally, this person has responsibilities that may include record keeping, money counting, hiring and firing of workers, and making bank deposits for the gaming operation. The information to be reported is the manager's name, compensation, services provided, and whether the manager is, with respect to the organization, a director, officer, employee, and/or independent contractor.

If more than one person shares these responsibilities, Schedule O is available to report that information.

- Whether the organization is required under state law to make charitable distributions from the gaming proceeds in order to retain its state gaming license (question 17a, "yes" or "no" boxes).

- The amount of distributions required under state law to other tax-exempt organizations or spent in furtherance of the organization's exempt activities during the year (question 17b). A breakdown of required distributions, by each state, must be provided in Schedule O.

§ 14.3 PREPARATION OF OTHER PARTS OF NEW FORM 990

In addition to Schedule G, other parts of the new Form 990 pertain to fundraising reporting.

(a) Part I, Line 16a (Professional Fundraising Expenses)

On line 16a of Part I, the filing organization reports its professional fundraising expenses. This is the amount that also appears in Part IX, line 11e, Column (A) (see § 7.2(b)(20)).

(b) Part IV, Line 14b (Fundraising Outside U.S.)

On line 14b of Part IV, the filing organization reports whether it has aggregate revenues or expenses of more than $10,000 from fundraising activities outside the United States (see 3.2(o)).

(c) Part VIII, Lines 1c, 8a, and 9a (Fundraising Events)

On line 1c of Part VIII, the filing organization reports the amount of contributions received from fundraising events. On line 8a of Part VIII, the filing organizations reports the amount of revenue derived from fundraising events, other than contributions. On line 9a of Part VIII, the filing organization reports the amount of its gross income from gaming activities (see Part IV, lines 18 and 19). (See § 3.2(s), (t).)

(d) Part IX, Line 11e (Professional Fundraising Expenses)

On Part IX, line 11e, the filing organization reports the amount of its professional fundraising expenses (see Part IV, line 17). (See § 3.2(r).)

(e) Schedule B (Information about Contributions)

Schedule B, a schedule of contributors, that accompanies the new Form 990 (and Forms 990-EZ and 990-PF) is the same as the Schedule B that accompanied the prior Form 990. A *contributor* (or *grantor*) is any donating person, whether it is an individual, fiduciary, corporation, trust, partnership, or tax-exempt organization.

(1) Part I. Generally, an organization must list in Part I of Schedule B every contributor who, during the year, gave the organization, directly or indirectly, money, securities, or other type of property aggregating $5,000 or more. In determining the $5,000 threshold, the organization totals all of the contributor's gifts only if they are $1,000 or more for the year. For a donative type publicly supported charity (see § 8.1(d)), however, a contributor of $5,000 or more is listed in Schedule B only where the contribution is greater than 2 percent of the total amount of gifts and grants it has received as of the close of the reporting year. Special rules apply in the case of contributions or bequests for use exclusively for charitable purposes received by tax-exempt social clubs and fraternal organizations.

Three pages for Part I are provided. If needed, additional pages may be photocopied. Each page should be consecutively numbered.

In Part I of Schedule B, contributors are to be numbered consecutively (Column (a)). The contributor's name and address (Column (b)), aggregate contributions for the year (Column (c)), and the type of contribution (Column (d)) must be reported. If a cash contribution came directly from a contributor, the "person" box is to be checked. The "payroll" box is to be checked if an employer forwarded an employee's contributions. The "noncash" box is to be checked in an instance of a contribution of property other than cash. The checking of a "noncash" box triggers the requirement to file Part II of Schedule B.

(2) Part II. Two pages of Part II are provided. Additional pages may be photocopied. These pages should be consecutively numbered. In Column (a) of this Part II, the filing organization shows the number that corresponds to the contributor's number in Part I. Column (b) is used to describe the noncash contribution received by the organization.

The fair market value of the contributed property is reported in Column (c). If the organization immediately sells gifted securities, the contribution nonetheless must be reported as a gift of property (with the value being the net proceeds of the sale plus any broker's fees and other expenses). If contributed securities are not immediately sold, and they are marketable securities registered and listed on a recognized securities exchange, the market value is measured by the average of the highest and lowest quoted selling prices (or the average between the bona fide bid and asked prices) on the contribution date.

When fair market value of an item of contributed property cannot be readily determined, the filing organization is to use, according to the IRS's draft instructions, an "appraised or estimated" value. To determine the amount of a noncash contribution that is subject to debt, the organization subtracts the amount of the debt from the property's fair market value.

The date the property was received by the organization is reported in Column (d) (assuming the transaction is, in fact, a completed gift).

If the organization received a partially completed Form 8283 from a donor, the organization should complete it and return it to the donor to enable the donor to obtain a charitable contribution deduction. The organization should retain a copy of this form for its records. Original and successor donee organizations must file Form 8282 if they sell, exchange, consume, or otherwise dispose of charitable deduction property within three years after the date the original donee received the property. (See § 19.1(v).)

(3) Part III. Tax-exempt social welfare and fraternal organizations that received contributions for exclusively charitable purposes must complete Parts I to III of Schedule B for those persons whose contributions totaled more than $1,000 for the year. The filing organization must also show, in the heading of Part III, total gifts to these organizations that were $1,000 or less for the year and were for an exclusively charitable purpose. This latter item of information is to be completed only on the first Part III page.

If an amount is set aside for an exclusively charitable purpose, the filing organization must describe, in Column (d), how the amount is held. For example, a set-aside amount may be commingled with amounts held for other purposes. If the organization transferred the gift to another organization, the filing organization should report the name and address of the transferee organization, and explain the relationship between the two organizations, in Column (e).

§ 14.4 NEW FORM 990 COMPLIANCE TASKS

A tax-exempt organization that engaged in fundraising and/or gaming activities during the reporting year should be attending to these 15 tasks:

1. **Fundraising methods.** Inventory the methods the organization uses to solicit contributions and grants.

2. **Fundraising expenses.** Determine that the amount of fundraising expenses were properly calculated (see Form 990, Part IX, Column D).

3. **Fundraising fees.** Determine whether the organization has or will be paying more than $15,000 in the form of professional fundraising fees (see Form 990, Part IV, line 17; Form 990, Part IX, line 11e).

4. **Fundraising events.** Determine whether the organization has or will be receiving more than $15,000 in revenue from fundraising events (see Form 990, Part IV, line 18; Form 990, Part VIII, line 8a).

5. **State law.** Ascertain whether the organization is in compliance with the appropriate state charitable solicitation act(s).

6. **Service providers.** Determine if, under state law, the organization is using the services of a professional fundraiser, professional solicitor, and/or professional fundraising consultant.

7. **Contracts.** If the organization is using one or more of these services, determine if it has the appropriate contract(s) in relation to state law requirements.

8. **Insiders.** If one or more of these contracts is in place, determine if the organization has contracted with an insider.

9. **Compensation.** If one or more of these contracts is in place, determine whether one or more fundraisers is to be compensated by the organization in the amount of $5,000 or more.

10. **Federal regulation.** Ascertain whether the organization is in compliance with the various ways in which fundraising is regulated under the federal tax law.

11. **Gaming revenue.** Determine whether the organization has or will be receiving more than $15,000 in revenue from gaming (see Form 990, Part IV, line 19; Form 990, Part VIII, line 9a).

12. **Related/unrelated gaming.** If the organization is engaged in a gaming activity, determine if it is being properly treated as an unrelated or a related business.

13. **Gaming law compliance.** Determine, if the organization is engaged in gaming, whether it is in compliance with state (or local) law.

14. **Gaming examinations.** If the organization is engaged in gaming, become prepared to answer the eight questions summarized above that an IRS agent is likely to ask in the context of an examination.

15. **Schedule B.** Assemble the information necessary to properly prepare Schedule B.

CHAPTER FIFTEEN

Schedule H—Hospitals[*]

§15.1 LAW AND POLICY

(a) Charity Care and Community Benefit

Parts I through III of Schedule H require reporting hospitals to disclose a significant amount of information about charity care and community benefit practices, charity care and collection policies, and the way in which the hospital is responding to community health needs and promoting the health of the public. A summary of federal and state law in these areas will aid preparation of the Schedule H.

(1) Congress and the IRS. The fact that Schedule H asks so many questions about charity care and community benefit begs the question: What is required of a tax-exempt hospital? The answer is not well settled, has changed over the last 30 years, and is currently the subject of debate in Congress and at the IRS. In fact, Schedule H could be viewed as the beginning of a policy change at the IRS about what is required for a nonprofit hospital to acquire and maintain tax-exempt status. In addition, there is speculation that the information disclosed on the Schedule H could eventually be used by Congress (or other federal or state legislators or regulators) in creating policy about what is expected or required of nonprofit hospitals. A "brief history of time" of the community benefit universe is in order.

In 1956, the IRS issued Revenue Ruling 56-185, which required hospitals to treat patients not able to pay for their care to the extent of the hospital's financial ability. In 1959, the Department of the Treasury published final regulations under Section 501(c)(3), which indicated that while the term *charitable*, as applied to a nonprofit hospital, could include care of those not able to pay (e.g., "relief of the poor and distressed and underprivileged"), it also included broader activities (e.g., "advancement of education or science," "lessening the burdens of government," and "promotion of social welfare"). Thus, while the 1956 Revenue Ruling required charity care (care of those not able to pay), the 1959 regulations took a broader view.

---

[*] The line-by-line commentary for this chapter (§ 15.2) and some of the compliance tasks (§ 15.3) were prepared for the 990 Hospital Coalition (www.990forhospitals.org) by Doug Anning and Keith Hearle with Verite Consulting (Keith.Hearle@VeriteConsulting.com) with some of the material previously prepared by the Catholic Health Association (www.chausa.org).

In 1969, the IRS issued Revenue Ruling 69-545, a seminal ruling with respect to exempt hospitals. In addition to repealing the charity care requirement of the 1956 revenue ruling, the 1969 ruling established what has come to be known as the community benefit standard. In order to be tax exempt, nonprofit hospitals have to demonstrate the presence of one or more of these factors to show that they promote the health of the community:

- A board consisting of independent community members
- A medical staff open to all qualified candidates
- An emergency room that accepts all patients regardless of ability to pay
- Acceptance of Medicare and Medicaid patients
- Use of excess or surplus funds to improve quality of patient care, expand facilities, or advance education and training programs

This 1969 ruling was amplified by Revenue Ruling 83-157, which states that while charity care offered through the emergency room is strong evidence of community benefit, it is not required. Some specialty hospitals (such as cancer hospitals, eye hospitals, or children's hospitals) may not have emergency rooms but still, because of their specialized services, provide an important community service.

In 1992, the IRS issued hospital audit guidelines that instruct hospital auditors to take these steps to determine whether hospitals are meeting the community benefit standard, thus focusing on the importance of charity care in meeting the community benefit standard:

- Interview ambulance drivers to determine whether they are instructed to take indigent patients to other hospitals
- Interview social workers to determine whether the community is aware of the availability of emergency services at the hospital
- Ascertain when and how a determination is made that a patient qualifies for charity care
- Determine whether the hospital is involved in projects and programs that improve the health of the community

In 2001, the IRS issued a Field Service Memorandum advising hospitals of certain requirements if they were relying on charity care to establish community benefit and justify their exemption. In short, the hospital must demonstrate that (1) the policy is communicated to the public; (2) charity care is actually provided at reasonable rates; and (3) charity care patients are not routinely discriminated against. While not requiring charity care, the IRS said it would look at these factors to determine whether charity care practices satisfy the community benefit standard:

- Existence of a written charity care policy
- Circumstances where the hospital deviates from the policy
- Communication of policy terms to hospital staff and the public
- Existence of an emergency room open to all regardless of ability to pay

- Directions to ambulance services about diverting poor or indigent patients to other facilities

- Range of inpatient, outpatient, and diagnostic services provided free of charge or at reduced rates

- Circumstances under which charity care is denied

- Whether there is an expectation of full payment from all patients

- How and when the determination is made that a patient is eligible for free or reduced-cost services

- Terms of any documents patients are required to sign

- Contents of any policy regarding admission of poor or indigent persons

- Patterns of referral of indigent patients to other facilities

- Whether the hospital maintains records detailing the number of times and circumstances under which it provides charity care

- Whether the hospital maintains a separate account for charity care and whether bad debt is distinguished from charity care

In 2006, the IRS sent a questionnaire to a number of hospitals inquiring about their charity care and community benefit practices. At about the same time, the Senate Finance Committee sent letters to a handful of large hospitals asking similar questions. Finally, in 2007, staff members of the Senate Finance Committee issued a draft position paper advocating, among other things, a minimum required amount of charity care expenditures by every exempt hospital. To date, while the IRS and Congress have stopped short of mandating a specific amount of charity care or other community benefit, there is no doubt that each institution expects significant charity care and community benefit expenditures in order for nonprofit hospitals to justify their exemption.

(2) State and Local Law. In addition to the IRS and Congress, state and local legislators and regulators have focused on charity care and community benefit issues. A number of state legislators have passed community benefit laws. These generally fall into two categories: (1) laws that require a fixed amount of charity care and/or community benefit and (2) laws that require hospitals to conduct community needs assessments and implement programs to meet those needs. Some county property tax assessors have revoked or threatened to revoke property tax exemptions if they think hospitals are not providing enough charity care. Some state attorneys general have instituted civil actions or investigations regarding hospitals' charity care and billing and collection practices. In 2003 and 2004, there were a number of class action lawsuits brought by uninsured and indigent patients challenging hospitals' charity care and billing and collection practices (although many of them were dismissed). No matter where hospitals look, someone (or everyone) is wanting to know about their charity care practices: legislators and regulators, attorneys general, class action litigants, newspaper reporters, and consumer advocacy groups. In other words, because everyone else is focused on it, hospitals are well advised to look closely at their charity care and community benefit practices to ensure that their activities have integrity, will pass community muster, and will be sufficient to maintain exempt status.

(3) Industry Guidance. Although federal, state, and local lawmakers and regulators have focused on exempt hospital's charity care and community benefit expenditures, the industry itself has been taking steps to self-regulate. A number of hospital industry associations (including the American Hospital Association) have published guidelines to help hospitals create, implement, and communicate effective charity care and community benefit programs. These can easily be found through an Internet search. Schedule H asks a number of questions about charity care policies, community needs assessments, and community benefit reports. The next sections present a summary of some industry guidance in each of these areas that can assist hospitals in developing these documents.

(A) CHARITY CARE POLICIES

The Patient Friendly Billing Project is an excellent resource for developing charity care and billing and collection policies. Spearheaded by the Healthcare Financial Management Association in collaboration with the American Hospital Association and the Medical Group Management Association, the project provides a wealth of useful information. In general, charity care policies should address these issues:

- What persons qualify for financial assistance
- What services are discounted
- What types of discounts are provided
- How policies are communicated to patients who may need financial assistance
- How patient accounts are resolved
- What structures are in place to implement the policy
- What is the relevant legal and regulatory context

(See www.hfma.org/library/revenue/PatientFriendlyBilling/for more information.)

(B) COMMUNITY BENEFIT REPORTS

The Schedule H asks if the hospital prepares an annual community benefit report and if it is made available to the public. Community benefit reports are a means for hospitals to communicate what they do to promote the health of their communities. The community benefit report can be used for fundraising, communicating with donors, media and press relations, and communicating with lawmakers and regulators. Often the community benefit report is part of a larger annual report. The seminal resource for creating a CBR is "A Guide for Planning and Communicating Community Benefit," published by the Catholic Health Association. In addition, the CHA Web site has a wealth of useful information on community benefit reporting. (See www.chausa.org/Pub/MainNav/ourcommitments/Community Benefits/.)

(C) COMMUNITY NEEDS ASSESSMENT

The Schedule H asks how hospitals assesses the healthcare needs of the community it serves. Many, though not all, hospitals engage in a periodic community needs assessment process. This process identifies critical community health needs so mission-driven hospitals can create and implement programs that respond to such needs. Some hospitals rely on assessments prepared by others (e.g., public health departments and private foundations that support public health), and this is certainly an acceptable practice. Other hospitals conduct their own assessments. If a hospital does not have access to good needs assessments prepared by other organizations and desires to engage in its own assessment process, there are several quality resources available:

- Catholic Health Association's "Guide for Planning and Communicating Community Benefit" has a valuable chapter on assessing community needs and planning for responsive programs.

- The Community Toolbox (http://ctb.ku.edu/en/) has a mission of improving community health and offers on its Web site free resources for identifying community healthcare needs and developing promising approaches to meet those needs.

- The Association for Community Health Improvement offers a Community Health Assessment Toolkit. The Toolkit is designed to help hospitals identify and understand community needs in order to design programs to better meet those needs and improve the health of the community. Information about the toolkits is available at: www.communityhlth.org.

(b) Management Companies and Joint Ventures

Schedule H asks whether hospitals participate in joint ventures or contract with management companies in which directors, officers, trustees, key employees or physicians on the medical staff own 10 percent or more of the stock or ownership interests in the joint venture or management company. Such ownership by "insiders" can present private inurement, private benefit, and/or excess benefit transaction issues for the hospital and the insiders. (See § 6.1 for a general discussion of private inurement, private benefit, excess benefit transactions, and joint ventures.)

Although a nonprofit organization may utilize the services of a management company, this type of company—often a for-profit entity—does not supplant the need for directors and officers of the nonprofit organization, although it may substitute, in whole or in part, for the organization's employees.

Although there is nothing inherently inappropriate about a nonprofit organization's use of a management company, the IRS (when the organization is tax-exempt) tends to accord these arrangements particular scrutiny. For example, if members of the board of the management company also serve as members of the board of the nonprofit organization (and/or there are other business or family ties between the two entities), the IRS may be even more sensitive to the potential for private inurement, private benefit, and/or excess benefit transactions. Also of concern to the IRS is whether insiders of the nonprofit have an ownership interest in the management company (the precise question the IRS asks on Schedule H). This too can present private inurement, private benefit, and/or excess benefit transaction issues. In the hospital context, management companies often arise with joint ventures. For example, the hospital will co-own a facility (e.g., an ambulatory surgery center) with physicians and/or a for-profit company and the for-profit company will also provide management services.

Some management companies perform only "back office" or other wholly administrative functions (bookkeeping, human resources, information technology). Others are more involved, undertaking efforts such as fundraising or meetings planning. Some of these companies assist the organization in the operation of its programs. Of particular concern in the hospital context is the complete outsourcing of all hospital operations functions to the management company so that, in the eyes of the IRS anyway, the nonprofit has ceded operational control to a for-profit. The concern, of course, is that the for-profit manager will not be attentive to serving the exempt purposes of the nonprofit, such as charity care and community benefit and promoting the health of the community. The more the management company is entrenched in the nonprofit, tax-exempt organization's operations, the greater will be the suspicions of the IRS. Government authorities almost always view this circumstance as a siphoning off of charitable resources for private gain. For all these reasons, whenever a nonprofit outsources some or all of its functions to a for-profit management company, the nonprofit should be able to demonstrate that the management company is necessary and that its fees are reasonable. This is even more critical when there is board and/or officer overlap between the nonprofit or when the nonprofit's insiders have an ownership stake in the management company.

§ 15.2 PREPARATION OF NEW FORM 990 SCHEDULE H

(a) Who Must File

Schedule H is to be filed by nonprofit organizations that operate one or more hospitals. A *hospital* is defined by reference to state licensure law. In other words, a filing organization that operates one or more facilities that are licensed, registered, or similarly recognized as a hospital under state law will be required to file Schedule H. The definition does not include hospitals located outside the United States or hospitals operated by entities organized as separate legal entities and taxed as corporations, even if such entities are affiliated or related to the organization (e.g., an affiliated system of healthcare entities under common control), unless such entities are members of a group exemption included in a group return filed by the organization. (See § 15.2(c) for more information about what entities and facilities are and are not included in Schedule H.)

Note that the definition of *hospital* for Schedule A, Part I, Line 3, and the definition of *hospital* for Schedule H are not the same. Even if an organization checks Box 3 in Part I of Schedule A that it is a hospital for public charity purposes, it prepares Schedule H only if it operates a facility licensed or registered as a hospital by state law. The definition of *hospital* for Schedule A is tied to Code Section 170(b)(1)(A)(iii), which can include certain facilities that would not be considered hospitals under state law (the Schedule H definition), such as a skilled nursing facility or outpatient center.

If an organization does not operate one or more facilities that meet the definition of a hospital, it will not file Schedule H. If an organization is not otherwise required to file the 990 (e.g., certain government-owned hospitals), it will not be required to file a Schedule H even if it operates one or more facilities licensed as a hospital under state law.

(b) Transition Rules for 2008

A number of the sections of Schedule H are optional when filing for tax years that begin in 2008. In fact, only Part V on Facility Information (§ 15.2(h)) is required for tax years that begin in 2008. A hospital should consider several factors in deciding whether to provide optional information for its fiscal year 2008:

- If the hospital is the only hospital in the community providing the optional information, press and regulatory scrutiny may focus on it.

- If the hospital is the only hospital in the community that does not provide the optional information, it may create the appearance of lacking transparency by trying to withhold information.

Regardless, all hospitals should prepare Schedule H internally in 2008 as a "dry run" for 2009, when all the information will be required.

(c)   Aggregation Rules

Schedule H, like the rest of the 990, is filed on an EIN-by-EIN basis. Thus, similarly situated hospital systems might file differently based on their corporate structure. If a system operates multiple hospitals under a single employer identification number (EIN), that system will file a consolidated Schedule H. If a system operates multiple hospitals under multiple EINs, that system will file a separate 990 and Schedule H for each EIN. The only exception is for group exemptions. If a number of separate hospital corporations with separate EINs are members of a group exemption, the subordinate members of the group that operate hospitals will file a single Schedule H and aggregate data from all such hospitals (see Appendix E to the instructions).

The filing organization will aggregate onto a single Schedule H information from all these sources: (1) hospitals operated directly by the filing organization; (2) hospitals operated by disregarded entities for which the organization is the sole member (this is presumably the case even if the disregarded entity has a separate EIN for payroll purposes); (3) any charity care, community benefit, community-building activity or other Schedule H information provided by any entity described in (1) or (2), or any of their programs or facilities, even if provided by a facility that is not a hospital or if provided separate from the hospital's license (e.g., this would include care or services provided by outpatient facilities, surgery centers, urgent care clinics, rehabilitation facilities, etc.); (4) any hospitals or other facilities (outpatient facilities, surgery centers, etc.) operated by any joint ventures taxed as a partnership to the extent of the organization's pro rata share in the joint venture (as defined by reference to the ending capital account percentage listed on the partnership's K-1, Part II, Line J) and presumably to the extent any entity described in (1) or (2) is a member or partner in the joint venture (Note: In determining pro rata share, the organization should use the K-1 for the partnership's tax year ending during the organization's tax year that is being reported, and if not available, the most recently available K-1 or other available business records both adjusted as appropriate to reflect facts known to the organization.); (5) in the case of a group return filed by the organization, include hospitals operated directly by a member of the group exemption that are included in the group return, hospitals operated by a disregarded entity of which a member of the group is the sole member, hospitals operated by a joint venture taxed as a partnership to the extent of the group member's proportionate share (determined pursuant to subsection (4) of this paragraph), and other facilities and programs of a group member even if provided by a facility that is not a hospital or if provided separate from the hospital's license as described in subsection (3) of this paragraph).

The instructions give this example:

> The organization is the sole member of a disregarded entity. The disregarded entity owns 50% of a joint venture taxed as a partnership. The partnership in turn owns 50% of another joint venture taxed as a partnership that operates a hospital and a freestanding outpatient clinic that is not part of the hospital's license. (Assume the respective proportionate shares of the partnerships based on capital account percentages listed on the partnerships' K-1s, Part II, Line J are also 50%.) The organization would report 25% (50% of 50%) of the hospital's *and* outpatient clinic's aggregated Schedule H items (e.g., charity care and community benefit activities in Part I, community building activities in Part II, Medicare and bad debt in Part III, etc.).

Note that reporting the pro rata share of joint ventures taxed as partnerships, while required by the IRS instructions, is not consistent with generally accepted accounting principles (GAAP), so reporting here will not track with the hospital's audited financials or with Part VIII of the core Form 990 (Statement of Revenues). Hospitals may want to make a disclosure to that effect in Part VI of Schedule H so discrepancies between Schedule H, Part VIII of the core Form, and the audited financials are adequately disclosed.

Although a system operating multiple hospitals within a single corporation and a single EIN is required to aggregate that information on a single Schedule H, such a system may decide to voluntarily provide some or all of the charity care and community benefit on a facility-by-facility basis. For example, if the system operates hospitals in multiple states or communities, the system may choose to break down some information on a state-by-state or community-by-community basis. A system might do this because regulators and members of the public in a particular community may want information on just the hospital in their community but not be able to cull that information out if it is aggregated with hospitals in other communities. If the system decides to do this, the additional information can be reported on Part VI, line 7 or on Schedule O.

Similarly, while a system that operates multiple facilities through multiple corporations with multiple EINs is required to file a separate Schedule H for each hospital, such a system may decide to voluntarily provide some or all of the charity care and community benefit information on an aggregated basis. For example, if the system operates all of its hospitals in a single community, it may choose to aggregate the information from hospitals in the same community. A system might do this because state regulators or members of the community may want to know what the system is doing in the aggregate for the community and not have to go to multiple 990s and Schedules H to acquire the information. If the system decides to do this, the additional information can be reported on Part VI, line 7 or on Schedule O.

Note: For Parts I through III and Part V of the Schedule H, do not report or aggregate information from foreign hospitals located outside the United States. However, information from foreign joint ventures and partnerships must be reported in Part IV (see § 15.2(g)). Also, information about foreign hospitals and facilities may be described in Part VI (see § 15.2(i)(1)(G)). Such information could include information that would be otherwise reported in Parts I through III if reporting foreign hospitals were permissible

---

(e.g., charity care, subsidized health services, research and education, bad debt, and community-building activities provided by the foreign hospital).

Also note that the organization does not report or aggregate information from an entity that is organized as a separate legal entity from the organization and taxed as a corporation for federal income tax purposes (except for members of a group exemption included in a group return filed by the organization), even if such entity is affiliated with or otherwise related to the organization (e.g., is part of an affiliated healthcare system under common control).

Finally, note that although the organization is required to aggregate information provided by different hospitals, programs, and facilities as described in this section, the organization is required to report in Part V each of its facilities that is required to be licensed, registered, or similarly recognized as a healthcare provider under state law, whether operated directly by the organization or indirectly through a disregarded entity or joint venture taxed as a partnership. In addition, information about facilities that are not required to be licensed or registered under state law is required in Part VI. (See §§ 15.2(h) and (i)(1)(H) for additional information.)

(d) Part I (Charity Care and Certain Other Community Benefits at Cost)

Note for lines 1 to 6: In answering lines 1 to 6, the organization should probably disregard charity care policies used by any joint ventures. Although the instructions do not say this, if the Schedule H includes charity care from a joint venture entity in which the organization owns an interest (see the Aggregation Rules in § 15.2(c)), then lines 1 through 6 would be answered more easily, taking into account only the charity care policies of the organization's hospitals. This includes any hospital operated through a disregarded entity of which the organization is the sole member or any hospital operated by a member of the group exemption (or operated through a disregarded entity for which a member of the group exemption is the sole member).

Hospitals should take care not to appear to be an outlier with respect to its charity care practices and policies. Accordingly, it would be helpful for organizations to review charity care policies that are present in their communities in order to know how their policies "benchmark" against what might be viewed as a community standard.

(1) Line 1 (Charity Care Policy).   Each-tax exempt organization should have a written, board-approved charity care policy that complies with state and federal requirements. Charity care should be provided only pursuant to the adopted policy. If no policy is available, resources to create one are available from the Health Finance Management Association Patient Friendly Billing Project: www.hfma.org/library/revenue/PatientFriendlyBilling/uninsured.htm.

In addition, HFMA Principles & Practices Board Statement 15 provides guidelines regarding policy content: www.hfma.org/library/accounting/reporting/ppb_charity_bad_debt.htm.

(2) Line 2 (Application of Charity Care Policy to Multiple Hospitals). Through check boxes, line 2 asks how charity care policies are applied across multiple hospitals. If such policies are *not* applied uniformly across entities that are part of the organization, an explanation regarding why would be warranted in Part VI. Some organizations have hospital or entity-specific discount factors in their financial assistance policy, and they thus offer different discounts for patients with similar means. This reflects the fact that charge description masters (CDMs) vary across hospitals. If the policy states, for example, that hospitals are to discount charges to specified levels (e.g., cost or Medicaid or Medicare rates), then it could be deemed "uniform" across hospitals even though resultant discount percentages would vary.

Financial assistance policies can be uniform but also flexible when it comes to documentation requirements (e.g., if they incorporate medical credit scoring into determinations regarding who qualifies for assistance).

If policies differ across hospitals due to differences in state or local regulation (e.g., for hospital systems that cross state lines), an explanation to that effect in Part VI is warranted.

(3) Line 3 (Discounts and Free Care). Line 3 instructs filing organizations to answer lines 3a, b, and c based on the eligibility criteria that apply to the largest number of the organization's patients. For example, the instructions state that if the organization operates two hospitals under its EIN and aggregates both hospitals on a single Schedule H, the organization should answer lines 3a, b, and c based on the eligibility criteria used by the hospital that has the most patient contacts or encounters.

(A) LINE 3A (FREE CARE)

Regardless of what box is checked, the filing organization should explain its answer in Part VI. For example, while 200 percent of the Federal Poverty Guidelines (FPGs) has become an industry benchmark for the provision of free care, for some hospitals in rural or poor areas this is not realistic. Providing free care at such levels would put the hospital's financial viability at risk, making it unable to provide community benefit in the future. The filing organization should take the opportunity in Part VI to explain its community's economic demographics, the hospital's own financial situation, and how these affect the threshold implemented by the hospital.

Some hospitals use guidelines other than FPGs (such as the HUD Very-Low Income Guidelines) in their charity care eligibility criteria. If the organization does not use FPGs, answer "no" and explain the criteria used in line 3c and Part VI, line 1.

Hospitals should assume this question does not apply to discounts based solely on uninsured status but only to those qualifying for discounts based on the hospital's income criteria. If hospitals grant discounts to *all* uninsured patients, this should be mentioned in line 3c and Part VI, line 1.

(B) LINE 3B (DISCOUNTED CARE)

The way this question is structured, it implies that hospitals should not be providing discounts if household income is less that 200 percent of FPGs (i.e., that at this level the hospital should be providing free care, not just discounted care). However, some hospitals do only provide discounts (not free care) at levels under 200 percent of the FPGs. If this is the hospital's practice, then a discussion of why this is the case should be provided in Part VI, including a discussion of the demographics of the hospital's service area(s) and the hospital's financial situation. For example, in some poor areas, giving free care to every household below 200 percent of the FPGs would result in giving free care to a substantial portion of the population and bankrupt the hospital. If discounts, rather than free care, are provided for these reasons, this should be explained in Part VI.

Some hospitals and health systems provide discounts for patients in households over 400 percent of federal poverty guidelines. Others provide discounts to all uninsured patients. These and other similar features of the hospital's charity care benefits should be described in Part VI.

Hospitals should assume this question does not apply to discounts based solely on uninsured status but only to those qualifying for discounts based on the hospital's income criteria. If hospitals grant discounts to *all* uninsured patients, this should be mentioned in line 3c and Part VI, line 1.

(C) LINE 3C (OTHER THRESHOLDS AND DISCOUNTS)

In addition to providing free or discounted care based on FPGs or other income levels, many hospitals provide free or discounted care based on other criteria and/or provide certain accommodations to patients who have trouble paying their bills. A list of such practices follows. Hospitals can consider incorporating some or all of these into their financial assistance policies, and to the extent such practices are utilized, they should be explained in Part VI.

- Providing discounts based on income levels other than FPGs, such as the Housing and Urban Development Very-Low Income Guidelines
- Providing discounts based on uninsured status (regardless of income)
- Providing discounts if the amount of hospital charges exceed certain levels or exceed certain percentages of family income
- Providing discounts to residents of certain geographic locations
- Providing discounts if net family or household assets fall below certain levels (regardless of income)
- Prompt-pay discounts
- Allowing patients to spread payments over a period of time (e.g., 18 to 24 months) at low or no interest
- Capping annual payments of hospital bills to a percentage of family income (e.g., annual payments will not exceed 10 percent of annual household income)

(4) Line 4 (Discounts for Medically Indigent). If the hospital provides discounts or assistance to the medically indigent, the type of assistance should be explained in Part VI (perhaps in line 1, when providing the information requested by Part I, line 3c). According to the instructions, *medically indigent* means persons whom the organization has determined are unable to pay some or all of their medical bills because their medical bills exceed a certain percentage of their family income and/or assets (e.g., due to catastrophic costs or conditions), even though they have income or assets that otherwise exceed the generally applicable eligibility requirements for free or discounted care under the organization's charity care policy.

It can be difficult for hospitals to determine the amount of medical care costs that patients have incurred outside of the organization's own billing system (e.g., pharmacy, physician services, laboratory, diagnostic services, etc.). Measuring medical indigency based only on hospital costs is a reasonable approach. Alternatively, hospitals can ask patients to attest to the amount of nonhospital costs they have incurred during the relevant period.

Hospitals may want to add the medically indigent component to their financial assistance policies if it currently is not present.

(5) Line 5 (Charity Care Budgets). Answer "yes" to line 5a if the organization established or had in place at any time during the tax year an annual or periodic budget for free or discounted care.

Answer "yes" to line 5b if the free or discounted care provided by the organization for the year exceeded the budgeted amount of costs or charges for that year. (Note that although elsewhere in Schedule H information is reported at costs, not charges, that is not necessarily the case with line 5b if the organization establishes budgets based on charges.)

With respect to line 5c, some charity care that hospitals provide occurs through the emergency room and/or urgent care or outpatient clinics. Generally, hospitals continue to provide such care even if budget projections are exceeded. Hospitals generally do not cease providing charity care in November or December once budgets are exceeded at year-end. However, hospitals frequently do budget for certain high-cost procedures. For example, an academic medical center may budget for a certain number of free organ transplants or a children's hospital may budget for a fixed number of specialty cases. Such hospitals may in fact turn down patients once that number of procedures has been performed. If the hospital answers "yes" to line 5c for these reasons, a narrative explanation should be provided in Part VI.

These questions put a premium on accurate budgeting of charity care and also on considering whether the charity care budget should be aligned with charity care accounting required by Schedule H.

Schedule H includes some questions with greater risk than others. Line 5c, if answered "no," is one of those questions. Like all other questions, line 5c must be answered accurately. An individual patient might decide to raise concerns if he or she perceives him- or herself eligible for financial assistance or discounted care and did not receive such services, yet the hospital answered "no" to this question. Hospitals should remember that the Schedule H will be a public document. If the hospital denies financial assistance to a patient for budget reasons but answers this question to the contrary, the hospital could be at risk for a newspaper exposé, an attorney general investigation, or other adverse consequences.

(6) Line 6 (Community Benefit Reports). Hospitals should consider preparing and disseminating a community benefit report. The Schedule H pigeonholes charity care and community benefit information into yes/no, check-the-box and numerical answers. But this may not tell the entire story. A community benefit report is an opportunity to tell the entire story in a format and substance of the hospital's choosing. If the hospital prepares a community benefit report, it should be shared with all stakeholders as part of a coordinated and comprehensive communications/public relations plan (newspaper editorial boards; civic, business, and community leaders; government officials such as mayors and city councils, county commissioners, state legislators, local and state department of health officials, U.S. congressional delegations, etc; patient advocacy groups; and area healthcare foundations). Just as important, a community benefit report should be posted on the hospital's Web site and the URL reported in Part VI, so that those reviewing the Form 990 know they can access a more comprehensive report on the Web. Further, posting on the Web site will generally enable the hospital to answer "yes" to line 6b—that the hospital makes the community benefit report available to the public.

Many hospitals prepare an annual report, which includes charity care and community benefit information. If the hospital prepares such an annual report, but no separate community benefit report, the hospital should still be able to answer "yes" to line 6a.

The CHA Web site has useful information about communicating community benefit. Go to www.chausa.org/whatcounts and on the left-hand side click on "Resources" and then "Resource Index." CHA's "A Guide for Planning and Reporting Community Benefit" also has useful information on preparing a community benefit report. For instructions on obtaining the guide, go to: www.chausa.org/Pub/Main-Nav/ourcommitments/CommunityBenefits.

Organizations should take care that published community benefit reports are aligned with numbers reported in Schedule H (or if there are variances that those variances are well explained). For example, the organization may decide to combine community benefit activities and community-building activities (see § 15.2(e)) in its community benefit report, but (as discussed for Part I, line 7 and Part II) community benefit activities and community-building activities must be distinguished and reported separately on Schedule H. In this event, an explanation between what is reported in Schedule H and the published, public community benefit report is warranted. Such an explanation could be put in Part VI.

> *Note:* The instructions on the Schedule H between lines 6b and 7 apply to line 7. In other words, all organizations filing Schedule H must complete the table in line 7 (except for 2008), not just those organizations answering "yes" to line 6b.

(7) Line 7 (Charity Care and Certain Other Community Benefits at Cost). Hospitals should use care to follow the instructions when completing the worksheets and the table entitled Charity Care and Certain Other Community Benefits at Cost. What follows are some additional general guidelines.

As with other elements of Schedule H, hospitals should learn how their numbers in the table benchmark against peer organizations in the community and across the United States. The easiest way to do this is to review the Schedule H of peer organizations.

Although the IRS is requiring hospitals to quantify and report charity care and community benefit on the table at line 7, the IRS has been clear, at least verbally, that the reporting requirements of Schedule H are not, and should not be construed as, a change in the law. In other words, as the law still currently stands, there is no IRS requirement to provide charity care, let alone a minimum dollar amount. Nevertheless, Revenue Ruling 69-545 does require that a hospital meet the community benefit standard and charity care, and engaging in the other activities described in line 7, is one way to do this (see § 15.1(a)).

Charity care and community benefits are supposed to be reported in the table on line 7 at costs not charges. This means the hospital cannot report chargemaster rates or average third-party reimbursement rates in calculating the amount of free or discounted services provided or in calculating the amount of unreimbursed costs of Medicaid and other means-tested government programs. Rather, the hospital should use the most accurate way to estimate the actual cost of providing such services. This could be a cost accounting system or a cost-to-charge ratio, in either case taking into account indirect costs, such as general administration overhead. Filing organizations can use Worksheet 2 in the instructions to establish a cost-to-charge ratio.

On Part VI, line 1, the organization is required to provide an explanation of how it calculates costs for the purposes of reporting on Part I, line 7. Although the instructions to Part I, line 7 do not indicate this, the instructions to Part VI, line 1 do clearly require this. See the discussion for Part VI, line 1 (§ 15.2(i)(1)(B)) for a more detailed explanation of what to explain.

Care should be taken to avoid double counting, both across rows in line 7 (e.g., Medicaid losses in line 7b should not be reported again as a subsidized health service in line 7g) and across Parts I, II, and III (e.g., Medicare losses from subsidized health services in line 7g should not be reported as Medicare losses in Part III).

The IRS has determined that certain activities are in a "gray zone" that, while not being categorized as charity care or community benefit (and therefore not reportable on the table in line 7), may have a component that promotes health and therefore constitutes community benefit. In other sections of Schedule H, the IRS requires filing organizations to quantify these activities and explain how the activities promote health and why they constitute community benefits. These categories include community-building activities (quantified in Part II with the promotion of health/community benefit rationale provided in Part VI, line 5), bad debt expense (quantified in Part III, Section A with the promotion of health/community benefit rationale provided in Part VI, line 1), and Medicare shortfalls (quantified in Part III, Section B with the promotion of health/community benefit rationale provided in Part VI, line 1).

Hospitals should consider the comparative risk of underreporting certain community benefits compared to overreporting. Underreporting can occur if the hospital is providing community benefit activities or programs and has not yet completed a thorough inventory of such programs. Overreporting can occur if hospitals are not careful about their accounting methods or include programs that do not meet the definition of community benefit (e.g., programs that primarily have a marketing purpose). On balance, there is greater risk associated with overreporting than with underreporting. Hospitals are advised to be appropriately conservative in what they count as community benefit and to follow the accounting methods described in the instructions with care.

Within the worksheets and the Schedule H accounting framework, there are several areas that require judgment and/or more detailed calculations than are present in the worksheets themselves. These include:

- The amount of cost for "non–patient care activities" that should be removed from the numerator of the Ratio of Patient Care Cost to Charges in Worksheet 2

- The allocation of Medicaid Disproportionate Share (DSH) funding either to Charity Care (Worksheet 1) or Medicaid and other Means Tested Public Programs (Worksheet 3)

- Assuring that education costs are not included in Worksheet 3 because they are fully accounted for in Worksheet 5

- The tracking of bad debt, and Medicare revenues and expenses for Subsidized Health Services, so these amounts can be subtracted from values reported in Part III

- Eliminating Medicare-related Graduate Medical Education (GME) from Medicare revenue and allowable costs in Part III

The instructions provide overall principles that indicate what should be counted as community benefit and what should not be counted on Schedule H, both in line 7 and in Part II (Community Building). To help organizations make these decisions, a good resource is: www.chausa.org/whatcounts.

(A) COLUMNS (A) THROUGH (F)

(i) COLUMN (A) (NUMBER OF ACTIVITIES OR PROGRAMS)

Reporting the "number of activities or programs" is optional. To the extent the organization decides to report this information, it is not entirely clear, in each situation, how the number of programs is to be reported. For example, it would seem that charity care is a single program. However, if a teaching hospital has a general charity care program for families below threshold levels of the FPGs, and in addition has a program that accepts up to 10 free liver transplant patients per year, it is not clear whether this is one program or two. Similarly, if a hospital provides a teaching program for medical students, nurses, and allied health professions, it is not clear whether this is one program or three. Filing organizations should use good faith in reporting the number of programs.

(ii) COLUMN (B) (PERSONS SERVED)

Reporting "persons served" is optional. To the extent the organization decides to report this information, it is not entirely clear, in each situation, how the number of persons served is to be calculated. In general, filing organizations should use good faith in reporting the number of persons served. The hospital can consider these points:

- For charity care, Medicaid and other means-tested programs (lines 7a–7c), report the number of inpatient admissions (both ER and non-ER). For outpatients, report the duration of the illness as only one person served (e.g., if an outpatient gets eight chemotherapy treatments, that is only one person served).

- For community health improvement services (line 7e), consider reporting persons served if it is easy to quantify. Otherwise, consider giving some narrative description of persons served in Part VI.

- For health professions education (line 7f), consider breaking down in Part VI how many nursing students served, allied health students served, medical students served, residents and fellows served, scholarship and continuing medical education recipients (if other than hospital medical staff), and so on. Also, for residency and fellow programs, the hospital might want to consider describing the different residency specialties in which the hospital participates and that have been approved by the Accreditation Council for Graduate Medical Education.

- For subsidized health services (line 7g), hospitals can consider listing admissions and outpatient cases, as described for charity care and/or providing descriptions on a program-by-program basis in Part VI (e.g., the number of persons enrolled in a drug rehabilitation program).

- For research (line 7h), hospitals should consider describing the program in Part VI and making a good-faith attempt to describe the persons served (e.g., number of clinical trial participants or number of potential beneficiaries of a treatment or drug). Reporting "all of humanity" for the number of persons served by research activities would, except in those rare cases of a significant discovery or breakthrough, seem to lack some integrity.

- For cash and in-kind contributions (line 7i), hospitals can attempt to give good-faith answers in Part VI. For example, if free space is provided for weekly Alcoholics Anonymous meetings, describing this and the number of weekly attendees would make good sense.

- For community benefits provided by taxable joint ventures that are reported on line 7 based on the organization's proportionate interest in the venture(s), consider including the number of persons served by those joint ventures on line 7 on a proportionate basis. For example, if the organization has a 50 percent ownership interest in the joint venture and the joint venture serves 1,000 persons, consider reporting 500 persons served.

(iii) COLUMN (C) (TOTAL COMMUNITY BENEFIT EXPENSE)

Total community benefit expense means the total gross expense (not charges) of the activity for the year, calculated by using the pertinent worksheets for each line item. *Total community benefit expense* includes both "direct costs" and "indirect costs." *Direct costs* means salaries and benefits, supplies, and other expenses directly related to the actual conduct of each activity or program. *Indirect costs* means costs that are shared by multiple activities or programs, such as facilities and administration costs related to the organization's infrastructure (e.g., space, utilities, custodial services, security, information systems, administration, materials management, and others). The instructions for each worksheet and each category of activity on line 7 contain additional information about direct and indirect costs specific to each activity. For example, the instructions for Worksheet 5 contain a number of examples of direct and indirect costs to be included when reporting the community benefit expense of health professions education on line 7f, Column (c) (e.g., resident and fellow stipends, faculty salaries, etc.).

Total expense also should include the total expense of taxable joint ventures (based on the organization's proportionate interest in those joint ventures).

(iv) Column (d) (*Direct Offsetting Revenue*)

Direct offsetting revenue means revenue from the activity during the year that offsets the total community benefit expense of that activity, as calculated on the worksheets for each line item. *Direct offsetting revenue* includes any revenue generated by the activity or program. This would include Medicaid reimbursement (including Medicaid managed care plan reimbursement) on line 7b, tuition and direct GME reimbursement for health profession education on line 7f, and sliding fees charged to patients who receive subsidized health services on line 7g. Direct offsetting revenue does *not* include restricted or unrestricted grants or contributions that the organization uses to provide community benefit. For example, if a critical access hospital receives a grant to provide free services to low-income individuals, or if a research hospital receives a research grant from the National Institutes for Health, such grants (even thought restricted), would *not* be counted as direct offsetting revenue. This will allow hospitals that have significant programs funded by significant grants to report the programs costs but not offset the grants, and thereby report significant net community benefit expenditures.

Prior-year revenue (e.g., from a Medicaid cost report settlement) should be included in "direct offsetting revenue" pursuant to GAAP. If prior-year revenue is material, a description in Part VI is warranted.

More detailed instructions about direct offsetting revenue for each line item are contained in the instructions for each worksheet. For example, the instructions for Worksheet 5 contain a number of examples of revenue to be included when reporting the direct offsetting revenue of health professions education on line 7f, Column (d) (e.g., GME reimbursement, tuition, etc.).

(v) Column (e) (*Net Community Benefit Expense*)

"Net community benefit expense" for each line item equals "Total community benefit expense" (Column (c)) minus "Direct offsetting revenue" (Column (d)). *If the calculated amount is less than zero, report such amount as a negative number.* This means that organizations that make money on Medicaid services will report a negative number on line 7b, Column (e). This will decrease the totals in lines (j) and (k) and arguably understate the total community benefit provided by the organization. See the discussion for Part I, Line 7, Column (f) (§ 15.2(d)(7)(A)(vi)) regarding supplemental reporting in Part VI in this event.

If a negative number is present in line 7, column (e), and if that negative number results from the inclusion of prior-year revenue (e.g., from a Medicaid cost report settlement), then a discussion regarding the amount of prior-year revenue is warranted in Part VI.

(vi) Column (f) (*Percent of Total Expense*)

"Percent of total expense" for each line equals the product of "net community benefit expense" (Column (e)) divided by sum of (1) the amount in Part IX, line 25, column (A) of the core Form 990, and (2) the organization's proportionate share of total expenses of all joint ventures for which it reports expenses in the table in Part I to the extent such expenses are not already reported in the core Form 990, Part IX, line 25, column (A). Report the percentage to two decimal places (x.xx%). Any bad debt expense included in Part IX, line 25, Column (A) should be removed from the denominator and an explanation of the amount removed should be provided in Part VI (presumably in line 1 but the instructions do not say). The instructions to Part VI do not require this disclosure, but the instructions to Part I, line 7, Column (f) clearly do.

Organizations that report amounts of direct offsetting revenue also might wish to report "total community benefit expense" (Column (c)), that is, gross community benefit expense rather than net community benefit expense, as a percentage of total expenses. This percentage may not be reported in Column (f) but may be described and reported in Part VI of Schedule H. This sometimes gives a more accurate account of community benefit expenditures, especially if some community benefit activities generate a surplus (due to direct offsetting revenue) that offsets other community benefit activities and decreases total net community benefit expenses reported in lines 7j and k. See the discussion in Part I, line 7, Column (e) (§ 15.2(d)(7)(A)(v)) regarding how surplus community activities must be reported as negative numbers that offset other community benefit expenses.

(B) LINES 7A THROUGH 7K

(i) LINE 7A (CHARITY CARE AT COST)

Charity care is defined in the instructions to Part I, line 1. *Charity care* means free or discounted healthcare services provided to persons who meet the organization's criteria for financial assistance and are therefore deemed unable to pay for all or a portion of such services. Charity care does not include:

- Bad debt or uncollectible charges that the hospital recorded as revenue but wrote off due to failure to pay by patients who did not qualify for charity care, or the cost of such care. These are reported in Part III, Section A, line 2.

- The difference between (a) the cost of care provided under Medicaid or other means-tested programs or under Medicare and (b) the income derived therefrom. Medicaid shortfalls are reported on line 7b, shortfalls from other means-tested programs are reported on line 7b, and Medicare shortfalls are reported in Part III, Section B, line 7.

- Contractual adjustments with any third-party payors. These are not reported anywhere on Schedule H.

Charity care, like the other benefits that are quantified and reported in lines 7a through 7k, is to be reported at cost, not charges.

Charity care is frequently not reported on audited financials. Sometimes charity care appears in a footnote but generally at charges, not cost. These discrepancies should be explained in Part VI, lest someone reviewing both the audited financials and the Schedule H be confused that charity care reported on Schedule H has no corresponding number on audited financials (or does not correspond with amounts disclosed in footnotes).

Use Worksheet 1 from the instructions to calculate charity care.

(ii) LINE 7B (UNREIMBURSED MEDICAID)

Only report Medicaid services in this line, not Medicare. Use Worksheet 3 from the instructions to calculate this amount.

(iii) L<small>INE</small> 7<small>C</small> (U<small>NREIMBURSED</small> C<small>OSTS</small> <small>OF</small> O<small>THER</small> M<small>EANS-</small>T<small>ESTED</small> G<small>OVERNMENT</small> P<small>ROGRAMS</small>)

This line applies only to the unreimbursed costs (not charges) of *means-tested* government programs. The instructions state that a "means-tested government program" is a program for which eligibility depends on the recipient's income and/or asset level (e.g., SCHIP—the State Children's Health Insurance Program, or a county-operated health insurance program for low-income consumers). Medicare is not a means-tested program—everyone qualifies regardless of income or asset level. Medicare revenues and allowable costs are reported in Part III, Section B, net of any Medicare amounts reported in Part I.

Arguably, this line could include services provided under the Indian Health Service program. The program may not meet the literal definition of a means-tested program because eligibility is not based on assets or income. Rather, eligibility is based on meeting the requirements of Native American heritage. Nevertheless, this is a historically underserved and at-risk population, so hospitals that provide these services have an argument that they can be included here.

Use Worksheet 3 from the instructions to calculate the amount of unreimbursed costs of means-tested government programs.

(iv) L<small>INE</small> 7<small>E</small> (C<small>OMMUNITY</small> H<small>EALTH</small> I<small>MPROVEMENT</small> S<small>ERVICES</small> <small>AND</small> C<small>OMMUNITY</small>
B<small>ENEFIT</small> O<small>PERATIONS</small>)

The activities to be reported on this line are actually two different categories of activities: (1) community health improvement services and (2) community benefit operations.

Include both direct costs (such as hospital staff who perform or oversee needs assessments, grant writing, and fundraising, or administer the community health improvement service, and/or the costs of outside consultants or vendors who perform such services) and indirect costs (such as the pro rata share of hospital overhead or general and administrative expense allocable to such activities). See the instructions for Part I, line 7(a) to (k), Column (c) for general direction on what constitutes includable direct and indirect costs.

Community benefit operations mean activities associated with community health needs assessments as well as community benefit planning and administration. Community benefit operations also include the organization's activities associated with fund raising or grant-writing for community benefit programs.

Community health improvement services mean activities or programs carried out or supported for the express purpose of improving community health that are subsidized by the healthcare organization. Such services do not generate inpatient or outpatient bills, although there may be a nominal patient fee or sliding scale fee for these services.

Activities or programs may not be reported if they are provided primarily for marketing purposes and the program is more beneficial to the organization than to the community; for instance, if the activity or program is designed primarily to increase referrals of patients with third-party coverage, required for licensure or accreditation, or restricted to individuals affiliated with the organization.

The Catholic Health Association (CHA) recommends that organizations adopt a "prudent layperson" approach (more cynically called the "laugh test") in determining whether an activity benefits the community. Further, CHA advises that activities that do not promote health or the hospital's mission should not be reported. Care should be taken not to report activities of employees rendered on their own time (rather than as part of their employment or on the hospital's time). Finally, do not report activities that represent a cost of doing business or activities that are consistent with current standards of care, for example, in-service training, licensure requirements, and Joint Commission or other accreditation. (For more information, see CHA's publication *A Guide to Planning and Reporting Community Benefit*.)

To be reported, community need for the activity or program must be established. Community need may be demonstrated through:

- A community needs assessment developed or accessed by the organization

- Documentation that demonstrated community need and/or a request from a public agency or community group was the basis for initiating or continuing the activity or program

- The involvement of unrelated, collaborative tax-exempt or government organizations as partners in the activity or program

Community benefit activities or programs must also seek to achieve objectives, including: improving access to health services, enhancing public health, advancing generalizable knowledge, and relief of government burden. This includes activities or programs that:

- Are available broadly to the public and serve low-income consumers

- Reduce geographic, financial, or cultural barriers to accessing health services, and if ceased to exist would result in access problems (e.g., longer wait times or increased travel distances)

- Address federal, state, or local public health priorities (such as eliminating disparities in healthcare among different populations)

- Leverage or enhance public health department activities (such as childhood immunization efforts)

- Otherwise would become the responsibility of government or another tax-exempt organization

- Advance generalizable knowledge through education or research that benefits the public

Examples of community health improvement services that should and should not be reported are shown in the next table.

ACTIVITY OR PROGRAM	REPORT	EXAMPLE RATIONALE
Immunization for low-income children	Yes	Public health priority, relief of government burden
Flu shots for employees	No	Cost of doing business, more benefit to organization than community
Health screening program in low-income community	Yes	Enhances access, health education

Health screening program in upscale mall	No	Probable marketing focus, therefore more benefit to organization than community
Health education regarding diabetes	Yes	Public health priority
Marketing material for diabetes program	No	Marketing focus, more benefit to organization than community
Outreach to help seniors remain independent in their homes	Yes	Public health priority
Discharge planning function	No	Represents the current standard of care, required for licensure
Taxi vouchers for low-income persons	Yes	Provides access to care for vulnerable people
Van service between wealthy retirement community and only the organization	No	Benefits the organization more than the community

Use Worksheet 4 from the instructions to calculate community health improvement service amounts. For more information on what counts and what does not count as community benefit, see www.chausa.org/whatcounts.

(v) LINE 7F (HEALTH PROFESSIONS EDUCATION)

Health professions education means educational programs that result in a degree, certificate, or training that is necessary to be licensed to practice as a health professional, as required by state law; or continuing education that is necessary to retain state license or certification by a board in the individual's health profession specialty. It does not include education or training programs available exclusively to the organization's employees and medical staff or scholarships provided to those individuals. However, it does include education programs if the primary purpose of such programs is to educate health professionals in the broader community, even if the organization's employees can and do attend. Costs for medical residents and interns may be included, even if they are considered "employees" for purposes of Form W-2 reporting.

Note that interns, residents, and fellows are generally employed by the hospital and such programs are generally available only to those persons (i.e., not available to the general public). While on its face this instruction appears to exclude intern, resident, and fellow programs, this clearly cannot be the intended result. These are precisely the types of programs that are to be included. Other parts of the instructions to Worksheet 5 (which calculates health profession education costs) make this clear. For example, the definition of *health professions education* includes degree and certificate programs, and the instructions clearly state that hospital's are to report intern, resident and fellow stipends as well as faculty salaries.

Education must primarily benefit the community rather than the organization. In other words, educational scholarships for community members would be included, but scholarships for hospital staff would not; CME provided to all physicians in the community would be included but CME provided only to the hospital's medical staff would not; nursing education would be included if graduates are free to seek employment anywhere but not if graduates must work at the hospital.

Examples of health professions education activities or programs that should and should not be reported are shown next.

ACTIVITY OR PROGRAM	REPORT	EXAMPLE RATIONALE
Scholarships for community members	Yes	More benefit to community than organization
Scholarships for staff members	No	More benefit to organization than community
Continuing medical education for community physicians	Yes	Accessible to all qualified physicians
Continuing medical education for own medical staff	No	Restricted to own medical staff members
Nurse education if graduates are free to seek employment at any organization	Yes	More benefit to community than organization
Nurse education if graduates are required to become the organization's employees	No	Program designed primarily to benefit the organization

Use Worksheet 5 from the instructions to calculate health professions education amounts. Include direct and indirect costs. See the instructions to Worksheet 5 for examples of includable direct and indirect costs. Also see the instructions for Part I, line 7(a) to (k), Column (c) for general direction on what constitutes includable direct and indirect costs. For more information on what counts and what does not count as community benefit, see www.chausa.org/whatcounts.

(vi) LINE 7G (SUBSIDIZED HEALTH SERVICES)

Subsidized health services mean clinical services provided despite a financial loss to the organization. The financial loss is measured after removing losses, measured by cost, associated with bad debt, charity care, Medicaid, and other means-tested government programs. Losses attributable to these items are not included when determining which clinical services are subsidized health services because they generate a financial loss to the organization. Losses attributable to these items are also excluded when measuring the losses generated by the subsidized health services. In addition, in order to qualify as a subsidized health service, the organization must provide the service because it meets an identified community need. For example, if the organization no longer offered the service, it would be unavailable in the community, the community's capacity to provide the service would be below the community's need, or the service would become the responsibility of government or another tax-exempt organization. (See the discussion for Part I, line 7e to determine what meets the definition of an identified community need.)

Subsidized health services generally include qualifying inpatient programs (such as neonatal intensive care and inpatient psychiatric units) and ambulatory programs (such as emergency and trauma services, satellite clinics, and home health programs). Subsidized health services generally exclude ancillary services (which support inpatient and ambulatory programs) such as anesthesiology, radiology, and laboratory departments. Subsidized health services include services or care provided by physician clinics and skilled nursing facilities if such clinics or facilities satisfy the general criteria for subsidized health services described in this section. An organization that includes any costs associated with physician clinics as subsidized health services in

Part I, line 7(g) must describe that it has done so and report in Part VI the amount of such costs included in Part I, line 7(g) (see § 15.2(i)(1)(j)).

Care should be taken with the preceding list, which is not exhaustive. In other words, there could be subsidized health services that are not on the list. Further, just because a service is on the list does not mean it is a subsidized health service if the hospital makes money providing the service. For example, some hospitals make money on neonatal intensive care, in which case it should not be reported on line 7g.

Although unreimbursed Medicare costs are *not* included on line 7b ("Unreimbursed Medicaid"), they can be included here if they are otherwise part of providing subsidized health services. The costs of providing the care would be reported in Column (c) and the Medicare reimbursement would be reported as a "Direct offsetting revenue" in Column (d). See the instructions for Part III, Section B, lines 5 and 8, and Worksheet B from the instructions, all of which indicate that reporting Medicare losses for subsidized health services is appropriate. However, if reported here, care should be taken to make sure such Medicare revenues are not again reported in Part III, Section B—this would result in double counting.

Examples of subsidized health services that should and should not be reported are shown next.

ACTIVITY OR PROGRAM	REPORT	EXAMPLE RATIONALE
Clinics for low-income persons	Yes	Enhances access
Prenatal classes for mostly insured persons	No	Current standard of care
Long-term care facility with high census and Medicaid patients	Yes	Responds to need and provides access for low-income consumers
Long-term care facility with low census that loses money	No	Need not established and likely to reflect poor business decision
Emergency room operated at a loss	Yes	Provides access to care for all patients, including low-income and uninsured patients
Cosmetic surgery and other elective care for which financial assistance is not available	No	Difficult to establish community need, and inaccessible for patients needing financial assistance

Use Worksheet 6 from the instructions to calculate subsidized health service amounts. For more information on what counts and what does not count as community benefit, see www.chausa.org/whatcounts.

(vii) LINE 7H (RESEARCH)

Research means any study or investigation that receives funding from a tax-exempt or governmental entity the goal of which is to generate generalizable knowledge that is made available to the public, such as: underlying biological mechanisms of health and disease; natural processes or principles affecting health or illness;

evaluation of safety and efficacy of interventions for disease such as clinical trials and studies of therapeutic protocols; laboratory-based studies; epidemiology, health outcomes and effectiveness; behavioral or sociological studies related to health, delivery of care, or prevention; studies related to changes in the health care delivery system; and communication of findings and observations (including publication in a medical journal).

Examples of costs of research include, but are not limited to: salaries and benefits of researchers and staff (including stipends for research trainees, either Ph.D. candidates or fellows); facilities (including research, data, and sample collection and storage, and animal facilities); equipment; supplies; tests conducted for research rather than patient care; statistical and computer support; compliance (e.g., accreditation for human subjects protection, biosafety, and Health Insurance Portability and Accountability Act); and dissemination of research results.

Only include the costs of internally funded research as well as research that is funded by a tax-exempt or government entity. The organization may not report in Part I, line 7(h) the direct or indirect costs of research that is funded by an individual or an organization that is not a tax-exempt or government entity. However, the organization may describe in Part VI any research it conducts that is not funded by tax-exempt or government entities, including the direct and indirect costs of such research, the identify of the funder, how the results of the research are made available to the public, if at all, and whether the results are made available to the public at no cost or nominal cost (see § 15.2(i)(1)(k)).

Note that although the definition is intended to prevent the reporting of industry-sponsored research (since pharmaceutical companies are neither tax-exempt nor governmental entities), there are examples where industry-sponsored research studies provide public benefit and generalizable knowledge. For example, the definition appears to prevent counting industry-sponsored research on orphan drugs, which is inconsistent with the Orphan Drug Act of 1983 (which was specifically adopted to encourage research for drugs affecting small populations when it would not otherwise be economically feasible). The conduct of orphan drug trials, while funded by for-profit pharmaceuticals, could arguably be reported as research on line 7h.

The IRS decided that direct offsetting revenue does *not* include research grants from private sources (e.g., individuals, foundations or endowments) or public sources (such as NIH grants or other grants from federal, state or local governments), regardless of whether such grants are earmarked or restricted to the specific research being calculated and reported. This is a tremendous benefit for academic medical centers and other teaching and research hospitals. They will be able to report significant community benefit because they will be able to report significant research costs in Column (c) (Total Community Benefit Expense) without having to offset the grants in Column (d) (Direct Offsetting Revenue), leaving a large net amount to be reported in Column (e) (Net Community Benefit Expense).

Use Worksheet 7 from the instructions to calculate research amounts. For more information on what counts and what does not count as community benefit, see www.chausa.org/whatcounts.

(viii) LINE 7I (CASH AND IN-KIND CONTRIBUTIONS)

Cash and in-kind contributions mean contributions made by the organization to healthcare organizations and other community groups that are restricted to one or more of the community benefit activities described in the Table in Part I, line 7 (or the work-sheets thereto). "In-kind contributions" include the cost of hours donated by staff to the community while on the organization's payroll, indirect cost of space donated to tax-exempt community groups (such as for meetings), and the financial value (generally measured at cost) of donated food, equipment, and supplies.

Report cash contributions and grants made by the organization to entities and community groups that share the organization's goals and mission. Do not report (a) cash or in-kind contributions contributed by employees, or emergency funds provided by the organization to employees; (b) loans, advances, or contributions to the capital of another organization; or (c) unrestricted grants or gifts to another organization that may, at the discretion of the grantee organization, be used other than to provide the type of community benefit described in the table.

If the organization makes a grant to a joint venture in which it has an ownership interest to be used to accomplish one or more of the community benefit activities listed in the table in Part I, line 7, report the grant on Part I, line 7(i). In order to avoid double counting, do not include elsewhere in the table in Part I, line 7 the organization's proportionate share of the amount spent by the joint venture on such activities.

To the extent that a cash or in-kind contribution is not for one of the activities described in Part I, line 7, or could be used by the grantee for an activity other than described in Part I, line 7 (because the hospital has not restricted the contribution to such purposes), the hospital should report such cash or in-kind contribution on the appropriate line in Part II, to the extent it meets the definition of one of the community-building activities described in Part II and is restricted to use for such purpose.

Do not include any contributions that were funded in whole or in part by a restricted grant, to the extent that such grant was from a related organization. The purpose of this rule is an anti-abuse measure to prevent churning. For example, if within a healthcare system of related of hospitals, Hospital A grants to Hospital B, Hospital B grants to Hospital C, and Hospital C regrants the same funds back to Hospital A, it would clearly be inappropriate for any of the three hospitals to report such grants on Part I, Line 7i of their Schedule H. This would be the community benefit equivalent of check kiting. Although the instructions have a blanket prohibition regarding restricted grants from related organizations ("do not include any contributions that were funded in whole or in part by a restricted grant, to the extent such grants was from a related organization"), the instructions provide several examples that soften the application of this rule, that is, which allow reporting of such contributions in some circumstances.

> **Example 1.** The filing organization (A) and its related foundation (B) are related organizations. B makes a grant to A that must be used by A to conduct a community needs assessment in a community served by A. A may report the cost of conducting the community needs assessment in Part I, line 7(e), Column (c) in the year it conducts the needs assessment, but A need not report the restricted grant from B in Part I, line 7(e), Column (d). The same result obtains if B is unrelated to A, or if the grant is unrestricted rather than required to be used by A to provide community benefit. (Note: Presumably the result is the same if both conditions are present, i.e., if B is unrelated to A and the grant is unrestricted.)

Example 2. Same facts as in Example 1, except A may also use the grant from B to make a grant to another organization (C), which must be used by C to provide community benefit. A makes such a grant to C. A may not report the grant to C in Part I, line 7(i) because it is funded by a related organization, but A need not report the grant from B in Part I, line 7, Column (d) for any line 7 item. This is the result regardless of whether B and C are related organizations. (Note: Presumably if the grant from B were unrestricted, then A could report the contribution to C in Part I, line 7(i)—it is only restricted grants from related organizations that cannot be reported as contributions if regranted.)

Example 3. The filing organization (A) is a related organization with respect to each of B, C, and D. Each of the organizations files a Form 990 and a Schedule H. A makes a restricted grant to B that is restricted to one or more of the community benefit activities described in the table in Part I (and the worksheets and instructions thereto). A's grant is not funded by a related organization. B makes a restricted grant to C that is funded by A's restricted grant. C makes an unrestricted grant to D that is funded by B's restricted grant. Under these circumstances, A may report the grant to B on A's Schedule H, Part I, line 7(i), but neither B nor C may report their respective grants to C and D on Part I, line 7(i) of their own Schedule H. If D uses the grant funds to make a grant that is restricted to one or more of the community benefit activities described in the table in Part I, D may report the grant in line 7(i).

Although these examples provide some useful clarification, they do leave some issues unanswered or, if answered, then answered unsatisfactorily. Specifically, Example 3 is limited to related organizations, all of which file a Schedule H. What answer would prevail if the organizations were related, but only some of them filed a Schedule H? For example, if a foundation gives a restricted grant to a related hospital for charity care, and the hospital gives it to a related outpatient clinic (organized under a separate corporation with a separate EIN) to provide free care to low-income patients, it would not seem inappropriate for the hospital to report the grant to the outpatient clinic on the hospital's Schedule H, Part I, line 7i. Neither the foundation nor the outpatient clinic files a Schedule H, so if the hospital does not report the community benefit, no one will report it. However, Example 2 seems to indicate that such reporting would not be permissible; the example says the same results obtain even if the organizations are related organizations (although it is silent about the impact on the result if some of the organizations file a Schedule H and some do not). Alternatively, the hospital could report the contribution in Part VI, line 7 where the hospital is allowed to describe community benefit activities of its affiliates, in this example the outpatient clinic.

Examples of cash and in-kind contributions that should and should not be reported are shown next.

Activity or Program	Report	Example Rationale
Donation to community clinic	Yes	Enhances access for vulnerable consumers
Donation to symphony	No	Unrelated to health/mission

Cost of staff working in a free clinic while on hospital payroll	Yes	Commitment of organization's resources to a community benefit program that enhances access
Value of staff time when volunteering on their own time	No	Benefit provided by the staff, not the organization
Equipment with remaining useful life donated to community clinic	Yes	Equipment has financial value, and donation results in net financial cost
Equipment that has been fully depreciated	No	Equipment has been fully expensed; only new cost to deliver the donated equipment should be reported
Emergency funds provided to individuals in the community	Yes	Benefits the community more than the organization
Emergency funds provided to employees	No	Benefits the organization more than the community

Use Worksheet 8 from the instructions to calculate cash and in-kind contribution amounts. For more information on what counts and what does not count as community benefit, see www.chausa.org/whatcounts.

(e) Part II (Community-Building Activities)

The IRS does not consider community-building activities to be in the same category as charity care and community benefit activities. Thus, they have to be reported separately from the table in Part I, line 7. Nevertheless, the IRS provides the filing organization an opportunity in Part VI, line 5 to describe how these community-building activities "promote the health of the community." It is important for filing organizations to provide a comprehensive response in Part VI, line 5 because (1) this can help make the argument that the community-building activity constitutes a form of community benefit, and (2) this helps the filing organization justify its tax-exempt status since "promoting the health of the community" is a basis for tax exemption. The discussion in the book at Part VI, line 5 includes some basic arguments to help the filing organization formulate its argument as to why its Part II community-building activities promote the health of the community.

For Columns (a) through (f), see the discussion for Part I, line 7, Columns (a) through (f) (§ 15.2(d)(7)(A)), and also see the accompanying IRS instructions for Part I, line 7, Columns (a) through (f).

As with Part I, line 7, all amounts in Part II should be reported at costs, not charges. In general, report in Part II the costs (not charges) of the organization's activities that it engages in during the tax year to protect or improve the community's health or safety and that are not reported in Parts I or III of Schedule H. If the organization makes a grant to an organization to be used to accomplish one of the community-building activities listed in Part II, then the organization should include the amount of the grant on the appropriate line of the table in Part II. If the organization makes a grant to a joint venture in which it has an ownership interest to be used to accomplish one or more of the community-building activities listed in Part II, it should report the grant on the appropriate line of Part II but, in order to avoid double counting, it should not include in Part II the organization's proportionate share of the amount spent by the joint venture on such activities. Do not include any contribution made by the organization that was funded in whole in part by a restricted grant to the extent that such grant was funded by a related organization. See § 15.2(d)(7)(B)(viii) for examples on how to report restricted grants from related organizations.

Examples of community-building activities that should and should not be reported are shown next.

ACTIVITY OR PROGRAM	REPORT	EXAMPLE RATIONALE
Housing for low-income seniors	Yes	Community need/access to housing
Housing for employees	No	Restricted to individuals affiliated with the organization
Violence prevention program	Yes	Public health/social need
Staff in-service education on domestic abuse	No	In-service education primarily benefits the organization, and is cost of doing business and standard of care
Advocacy on access to health care, public health, transportation	Yes	Community need
Advocacy for enhanced reimbursement	No	Benefits the organization
Physician recruitment in a medical shortage area	Yes	Community need
Physician recruitment to improve or sustain market share (clinicians for subsidized health services may be exceptions)	No	Benefits the organization more than the community

(1) Line 1 (Physical Improvements and Housing). *Physical improvements and housing* include, but are not limited to, the provision or rehabilitation of housing for vulnerable populations, such as removing building materials that harm the health of the residents; neighborhood improvement or revitalization projects; provision of housing for vulnerable patients upon discharge from an inpatient facility; housing for low-income seniors; and the development or maintenance of parks and playgrounds to promote physical activity.

For additional information on what counts and what does not count as community-building activities, see www.chausa.org/whatcounts.

(2) Line 2 (Economic Development). *Economic development* includes, but is not limited to, assisting small business development in neighborhoods with vulnerable populations and creating new employment opportunities in areas with high rates of joblessness.

For additional information on what counts and what does not count as community-building activities, see www.chausa.org/whatcounts.

(3) Line 3 (Community Support). *Community support* includes, but is not limited to, child care and mentoring programs for vulnerable populations or neighborhoods, neighborhood support groups, and disaster readiness and public health emergency activities, such as community disease surveillance or readiness training beyond what is required by accrediting bodies or government entities.

For additional information on what counts and what does not count as community-building activities, see www.chausa.org/whatcounts.

(4) Line 4 (Environmental Improvements). *Environmental improvements* include, but are not limited to, activities to address environmental hazards that affect community health, such as alleviation of water or air pollution, safe removal or treatment of garbage or other waste products, and other activities to protect the community from environmental hazards. The organization may not include on this line or in this part expenditures that it made to comply with environmental laws and regulations that apply to activities of (1) itself, (2) any of its disregarded entities, (3) any joint ventures in which it has an ownership interest, or (4) any member of a group exemption included in a group return of which the organization is also a member. Similarly, the organization may not include on this line or in this part expenditures that it made to reduce the environmental hazards caused by, or the environmental impact of, its own activities or those of its disregarded entities, joint ventures, or group exemption members.

For additional information on what counts and what does not count as community-building activities, see www.chausa.org/whatcounts.

(5) Line 5 (Leadership Development and Training). *Leadership development and training for community members* includes, but is not limited to, training in conflict resolution, civic, cultural or language skills, and medical interpreter skills for community residents.

For additional information on what counts and what does not count as community-building activities, see www.chausa.org/whatcounts.

(6) Line 6 (Coalition Building). *Coalition building* includes, but is not limited to, participation in community coalitions and other collaborative efforts with the community to address health and safety issues.

For additional information on what counts and what does not count as community-building activities, see www.chausa.org/whatcounts.

(7) Line 7 (Community Health Improvement Advocacy). *Community health improvement advocacy* includes, but is not limited to, efforts to support policies and programs to safeguard or improve public health, access to healthcare services, housing, the environment, and transportation.

For additional information on what counts and what does not count as community-building activities, see www.chausa.org/whatcounts.

(8) Line 8 (Workforce Development). *Workforce development* includes, but is not limited to, recruitment of physicians and other health professionals to areas designated as underserved, and collaboration with educational institutions to train and recruit health professionals needed in the community (other than the health professions education activities reported in Part I, line 7f).

For additional information on what counts and what does not count as community-building activities, see www.chausa.org/whatcounts.

(9) Line 9 (Other). *Other* refers to community-building activities that protect or improve the community's health or safety that are not captured in the categories listed in lines 1 to 8.

To the extent that a cash or in-kind contribution is not for one of the activities described in Part I, line 7, or could be used by the grantee for an activity other than described in Part I, line 7, the hospital should consider reporting such cash or in-kind contribution in this line if it meets the definition of a community-building activity or is otherwise for one of the activities described in Part II.

For additional information on what counts and what does not count as community-building activities, see www.chausa.org/whatcounts.

(f) Part III (Bad Debt, Medicare, and Collection Practices)

(1) Line 1 (HFMA Statement 15). This question asks whether the hospital complies with HFMA Principles and Practices Board Statement 15 (Statement 15) in calculating and reporting charity care and bad debt. A "no" answer could be misconstrued by someone reviewing the Form 990 as the hospital not complying with rules and requirements. The instructions clarify that the IRS does not require hospitals to report in accordance with Statement 15. Nevertheless, the filing organization should include an explanation in Part VI as to why it follows Statement 15 (or if not, why not) (see § 15.2(i)(1)(L)).

Hospitals are advised to study Statement 15 because it provides helpful clarifications regarding decision making and accounting for bad debt and charity care.

Additional resources on Statement 15 are available on the HFMA Web site: www.hfma.org.

(2) Line 2 (Bad Debt Expense). For organizations that have not adopted HFMA Statement 15, bad debt expense, like charity care, is to be calculated at costs, not charges. Costs can be determined using a cost accounting system or cost-to-charge ratio. The filing organization should use whatever methodology is most accurate. If the filing organization wants to use a cost-to-charge ratio, Worksheet 2 from the instructions can be used to calculate the ratio. Worksheet A from the instructions is used to calculate bad debt expense. Organizations should generally not change methodologies year to year, as doing so raises the question of whether they are using the most accurate costing methodology versus one that merely puts the organization in the best light.

The organization may want to explain in Part VI any discrepancies between the amount of bad debt expense reported on its audited financials and on Schedule H (see § 15.2(i)(1)(D)).

The organization should include its proportionate share of bad debt of any joint ventures in which it had an ownership interest during the year.

If the hospital is using Statement 15 to calculate bad debt, it should take into account these points:

- Organizations that have adopted Statement 15 for purposes of bad debt accounting (and/or charity care measurement and policies) should consider reporting "bad debt expense" without adjusting the expense to cost in line 2. Statement 15 requires reporting bad debt at the amount the payor was expected to pay (not charges or costs). Thus, reporting bad debt consistent with Statement 15 (i.e., at the amount the payor was expected to pay rather than at cost) is inconsistent with the IRS instructions (which require reporting at cost). Nevertheless, Statement 15 values bad debt conservatively, so the amount of "bad debt expense" for organizations that have adopted Statement 15 is a true representation of the actual financial loss those organizations incur (reporting the lost expected revenue rather than valuing bad debt expense at full charges or at cost).

- Statement 15 values bad debt differently because it responds to a concern expressed by AICPA, which "believes *healthcare providers inappropriately classify some items as bad debts that were never revenue in the first place.*" The statement indicates that revenue should be recognized only when "pervasive evidence exists of a payment agreement between the provider and the patient" and that "collectibility is reasonably assured." If these criteria are met, the organization should record as revenue the amount the patient is expected to pay—and if the patient does not pay, this same amount (expected revenue, not costs) should be classified as bad debt.

- For these reasons, organizations that follow Statement 15 have a good argument to report on Part III, line 2 the Statement 15 amount for bad debt (i.e., the amount the payor was expected to pay) rather than bad debt costs as the IRS instructions require.

(3) Line 3 (Bad Debt Expense Attributable to Charity Care). Provide an estimate of the amount of bad debt cost reported in line 2 that reasonably could be attributable to persons who would qualify for financial assistance under the hospital's charity care policy as reported in Part I, lines 1 to 4, but for whom sufficient information was not obtained to make a determination of their eligibility. *Do not include this amount in Part I, line 7.* Organizations may use any reasonable methodology to estimate this amount, such as record reviews, an assessment of charity care applications that were denied due to incomplete documentation, credit reports, analysis of demographics, or other analytical methods.

This question is one of the most challenging in Schedule H because it requires organizations that have not adopted Statement 15 to develop and apply a methodology for determining the portion of bad debt expense (at cost) that could be or is attributable to patients eligible under the organization's charity care policy.

The question requires developing a methodology for analyzing accounts with bad debt. Some methodologies to consider include:

- Analyzing accounts that have been denied financial assistance due to a lack of documentation

- Using medical credit scoring to estimate the portion of accounts with bad debt that is applicable to patients with an inability to pay

- Answering this question by reporting the charity care "portion" of accounts that have both a "bad debt" and a "charity" component

- Other reasonable methods

There are cases when a patient has been granted financial assistance and a payment plan has been established, and the patient later does not pay the prescribed amount. In these cases, the hospital has incurred bad debt for patients eligible for charity care. Write-offs for receivables created under payment plans or after financial assistance has been granted should be reported as one element of the answer to this question. Some hospitals are explicitly building another means tests into their revenue cycle to reassess patient means before writing these types of receivables off to bad debt. Such a procedure is allowed by Statement 15.

Organizations that have adopted Statement 15 generally can and should always report "$0" as their response to this question. Statement 15 requires that revenue and bad debt be reported at the amount the patient was able to pay and expected to pay. Revenue should not have been recorded for patients that might have qualified for financial assistance in the first place. By definition, then, bad debt as reported under Statement 15 includes only amounts for which the patient did not qualify for financial assistance. Accordingly, no part of bad debt, as defined by Statement 15, represents amounts attributable to patients eligible to receive financial assistance, and this line should be always reported as "$0" for Statement 15 organizations.

(4) Line 4 (Narrative Disclosures). In Part VI, line 1, the filing organization is supposed to provide the text of the footnote from its audited financial statements that describes bad debt, its costing methodology used to determine the amounts reported in lines 2 and 3, and its rationale for including the bad debt expense reported on line 3 as a community benefit expense. Describe how the organization accounts for discounts and payments on patient accounts in determining bad debt expense. Also describe the method the organization uses to determine the amount that reasonably could be attributable to patients who likely would qualify for financial assistance under the organization's charity care policy if sufficient information had been made available to make a determination of eligibility (e.g., some organizations use credit scores, zip codes, or other demographic data to determine if bad debt otherwise could have qualified for charity care discounts). If the organization does not believe that any of its bad debt should be considered a community benefit, that statement should be made in Part VI. For example, for organizations that comply with Statement 15, generally no portion of bad debt should be considered charity care, and this can be explained in Part VI.

If the organization has a rationale for considering all or a portion of bad debt to be community benefit, that rationale also should be stated in Part VI. Although rationales will vary from hospital to hospital, some of the common rationales include these:

- A number of patients are truly unable to pay their out-of-pocket liability but do not complete the process required to apply for financial assistance under the hospital's charity care policy. These patients would qualify for charity care if they completed the paperwork, so the bad debt expense associated with treating them should be treated as community benefit.

- The administrative requirements to determine whether patients who do not cooperate with the financial assistance process would have qualified for charity can be burdensome, particularly for small balances, so a reasonable estimate, based on broad demographic data, should be sufficient to justify community benefit treatment.

- Hospital revenue cycle operations are becoming quite efficient, so the argument that the bad debt problem is related to efficiency is becoming less well supported.

- Hospitals frequently continue serving patients even after the patients have generated significant bad debt, and this is evidence that the care is given for community benefit motivations.

- Hospitals cannot and do not refuse service to patients that generate bad debt, and this is evidence that the care is given for community benefit motivations.

In Part VI, provide the footnote from the organization's financial statements on bad debt expense, if applicable, or the footnotes related to accounts receivable, allowance for doubtful accounts or similar designations. If the footnote or footnotes address only the filing organization's bad debt expense—or accounts receivable, allowance for doubtful accounts, or similar designations—provide the footnote or footnotes verbatim. If the organization's financial statements include a footnote on these issues that also includes other information, report in Part VI only the relevant portions of the footnote. If the organization is a member of a group with consolidated financial statements, the organization may summarize that portion, if any, of the footnote or footnotes that apply to the organization. If the organization's financial statements do not include a footnote that discusses bad debt expense, accounts receivable, allowance for doubtful accounts, or similar designations, include a statement in Part VI that the organization's audited financial statements do not include a footnote discussing these issues, and explain how the organization's financial statements account for bad debt, if at all.

> With respect to Section B of Part III (lines 5–8), report (1) the organization's aggregate allowable costs to provide services reimbursed by Medicare, (2) aggregate Medicare reimbursements attributable to such costs, and (3) aggregate Medicare surplus or shortfall. Organizations are to include in Section B only those allowable costs and Medicare reimbursements that are reported in its Medicare Cost Report(s) for the year, including the organization's share of any such allowable costs and reimbursements from disregarded entities and joint ventures in which it has an ownership interest. The organization should describe what portion of its Medicare shortfall, if any, it believes should constitute community benefit and explain its rationale for its position in Part VI. The organization also may disclose in Part VI the amount of any Medicare revenues and costs not included on its Medicare Cost Report(s) for the year and may provide a reconciliation of the amounts reportable in Section B (including the surplus or shortfall reported on line 7) and the total revenues and costs attributable to all of the organization's Medicare programs. (See § 15.2(i)(1)(E).)

(5) Line 5 (Medicare Revenue).   Enter all net patient service revenue associated with allowable costs the organization reports in its Medicare Cost Report(s) for the year including payments for indirect medical education (IME) (except for Medicare Advantage IME), DSH (disproportionate share hospital, outliers, capital, bad debt, and any other amounts paid to the organization on the basis of its Medicare Cost Report(s). Do not include revenue related to subsidized health services as reported in Part I, line 7(g) and direct GME as reported in Part I, line 7(f). If the organization has more than one Medicare provider number, aggregate the revenue attributable to costs reported on the Medicare Cost Report(s) submitted under each provider number, and report the aggregate on line 5.

(6) Line 6 (Medicare Allowable Costs).   Enter all Medicare allowable costs reported in the organization's Medicare Cost Report. Do not report costs already reported in

Part I, line 7g (subsidized health services) and costs associated with direct GME already reported in Part I, line 7f (health professions education).

Filing organizations should use Worksheet B from the instructions to calculate this amount. The goal of the worksheet included in the Instructions is to eliminate all double-counting of Medicare revenue and cost between Parts I and III of Schedule H.

If the organization has more than one Medicare provider number, aggregate the revenue attributable to costs reported on the Medicare Cost Report(s) submitted under each provider number, and report the aggregate on line 6.

(7) Line 7 (Medicare Surplus or Shortfall). Report on this line the sum of line 5 minus line 7. If the result is negative, show the negative number (not zero).

(8) Line 8 (Narrative Disclosures). Check the box that best describes the costing methodology used to determine the Medicare allowable costs reported in the organization's Medicare Cost Report(s), as reflected on line 6. Describe this methodology in Part VI.

In Part VI, line 1, the filing organization is also supposed to provide its rationale for including the Medicare losses reported on line 7 as a community benefit expense. (Note: *Do not include this amount in Part I, line 7.*) Although rationales for treating Medicare losses as a community benefit expense will vary from hospital to hospital, some of the common rationales include:

- IRS Revenue Ruling 69-545, which established the community benefit standard for nonprofit hospitals, states that if a hospital serves patients with government health benefits, including Medicare, then this is an indication that the hospital operates to promote the health of the community. This implies that treating Medicare patients is a community benefit.

- For-profit specialty hospitals have been carving out certain high-margin services (such as cardiac, orthopedics, and oncology), leaving general acute care hospitals with lower-margin Medicare services. This indicates that Medicare losses can be a result of rendering these lower-margin services (which benefit the community) rather than inefficient operations.

- In some communities, Medicare is the largest payor, and hospitals must accept these patients regardless of whether they make a surplus or deficit from providing such services. If the Medicare participation is premised on this fact, then providing Medicare services promotes access to healthcare services, which is a community benefit.

- There are a number of low-income consumers receiving Medicare benefits.

- The elderly are often an underserved population who experience issues with access to healthcare services. Without tax-exempt hospitals providing Medicare services, CMS would bear the burden of directly providing services to the elderly.

- Medicare payment anomalies may be present in some states so even very efficient hospitals are unable to avoid losses. Thus, losses may not be indicative of inefficiency but rather provision of a community benefit.

Note: Lines 5, 6, and 7 do not include certain Medicare program revenues and costs, and thus may not reflect all of the organization's revenues and costs associated with its participation in Medicare programs. The organization may describe in Part VI the amounts of any Medicare revenues and costs that are not included in its Medicare Cost Report(s) for the year, including, for example, revenues and costs for freestanding ambulatory surgery centers, physician services billed by the organization, clinical laboratory services, and revenues and costs of Medicare Part C and Part D programs. The organization may report in Part VI a reconciliation of amounts reportable in Section B (including the surplus or shortfall reported on line 7) and all of the organization's total revenues and total expenses attributable to Medicare programs. If the organization received any prior-year settlements for Medicare-related services in the current taxable year, it may provide an explanation in Part VI. (See § 15.2(i)(1)(E).)

(9) Line 9 (Debt Collection Policy).   Each tax-exempt hospital *should* have a written, board-approved debt collection policy. If the organization answers "no," it should consider adopting a debt collection policy. Such policies commonly address a debtor's "bill of rights," a list of harassing or abusive practices that the hospital pledges not to utilize in collecting patient debt (e.g., phone calls at the patient's place of work, before a certain time in the morning, or after a certain time in the evening), pledges not to utilize certain legal collection options (e.g., bodily seizure, foreclosures against houses and cars, etc.), and certain internal review processes before accounts are referred to outside collection agencies and/or for legal action.

The debt collection policy should also address how the hospital will respond to new information regarding patient means obtained during the collection process. For example, if in the collection process a patient is subsequently determined to qualify for financial assistance, collection and legal activities should cease.

Many policies contain limitations on certain collection practices that apply to all patients (e.g., abusive phone calls or prohibitions on seizing houses or cars to pay hospital debts). Such practices are commonly prohibited for all patients, whether or not the patients receive charity care. If the filing organization's policy on collection activities applies equally to all patients, whether or not they receive charity care, such policies arguably "contain provisions on the collection practices to be followed for patients who are known to qualify for charity care or financial assistance," and the filing organization can presumably answer "yes" to line 9b. In other words, policies should not need to have special collection provisions applicable only to charity care patients in order for the organization to answer "yes" to line 9b.

On Part VI, line 1, the filing organization is also supposed to describe these collection practices applicable to charity care patients. Although neither line 9b nor the instructions to line 9b specifically state this, the instructions for Part VI, line 1 specify that these collection practices are to be described. (See the discussion for Part VI, line 1 in § 15.2(i)(1)(F).) Again, if the hospital has collection practices that apply equally to all patients (whether charity care or not), these are the practices that should be described in Part VI, line 1.

Information on collections practices can be found on the HFMA Patient Friendly Billing Web site at www.hfma.org/library/revenue/PatientFriendlyBilling/.

(g) Part IV (Management Companies and Joint Ventures)

List any joint venture or other separate entity (whether taxed as a partnership or a corporation), including any joint ventures outside of the United States, of which the organization is a partner or shareholder. Although the instructions speak in terms of partnerships and corporations (and share of profits in a partnership and stock of a corporation), presumably this includes joint ventures that operate as limited liability companies (LLCs).

Only include joint ventures (1) for which the following persons owned in the aggregate more than 10 percent of the share of partnership profits or stock in the corporation: (i) persons who were at any time during the organization's tax year officers, directors, trustees, key employees, and (ii) physicians who were employed as physicians by, or had staff privileges with, one or more of the organization's hospitals; and (2) that either (a) provided management services used by the organization in its provision of medical care, or (b) provided medical care, or owned or provided real, tangible personal, or intangible property used by the organization or by others to provide medical care. Again, despite the instruction's references to corporations and partnerships, presumably this includes LLCs if, say, a physician with staff privileges owns 10 percent of the membership interests of an LLC taxed as a corporation or 10 percent of the profits interest in an LLC taxed as a partnership.

For purposes of Part IV, the aggregated percentage share of ownership of officers, directors, trustees, key employees, and physicians who are employed by, or have staff privileges with, one or more of the organization's hospitals is measured as of the earlier of the close of the tax year of the filing organization or the last day the organization was a member of the joint venture.

Stock, whether common or preferred, is considered in determining ownership percentages, so presumably membership interests in an LLC with different voting and distribution rights would also be counted. What is not clear from the instructions is how such stock or membership interests with varying rights are to be included. For example, if a director owns 9 percent of the outstanding common stock and 1 percent of the outstanding preferred stock, does this meet the 10 percent threshold? What if the director owns 10 percent of the common stock but none of the outstanding preferred stock, or vice versa? Does the 10 percent apply to the number of shares, the number of votes represented by those shares, the value represented by those shares, or some combination thereof? Nor is it clear how to determine percentage amounts for more esoteric types of holdings such as options, convertible debentures, and similar interests. The IRS addresses none of these issues in the instructions. Organizations should use good faith in determining whether the 10 percent thresholds have been met, remembering that a conservative approach favors disclosure.

Only report the ownership of *current* (not former) officers, directors, trustees, and key employees. See the glossary to the instructions for the definition of "officer," "director," "trustee," and "key employee." Someone is "current" if they held the position at any time during the organization's tax year. (See page 5 of the instructions to the core form, Part VII, Section A.) Thus, if a person is an officer at any time during the tax year, the person is considered a current officer.

If a physician with an ownership interest is also a director, officer, trustee, or key employee, report such ownership on Column (d), not Column (e).

(h) Part V (Facility Information)

In Part V, the organization should report the name and address of each of the organization's facilities that, at any time during the tax year, was required to be licensed, registered, or similarly recognized as a healthcare facility under state law, whether such facility is operated directly by the organization or indirectly through a disregarded entity or joint venture taxed as a partnership. Check all boxes that apply to the facility (e.g., licensed hospital, children's hospital, teaching hospital, etc.).

The organization must list in Part VI the number of each type of facility, other than those that are required to be reported in Part V, for which the organization reports information on Schedule H (e.g., 2 rehabilitation clinics, 4 diagnostic centers, 3 skilled nursing facilities) (see § 15.2(i)(1)(H)).

Hospitals that are disproportionate share (DSH) hospitals for either Medicare or Medicaid reimbursement should consider reporting this in the "Other" column since DSH is not provided as a check-the-box category. Some states deem DSH hospitals as satisfying various criteria for state tax exemption. Other types of facilities that can be described in the "Other" column include, without limitation, outpatient physician clinics, long-term acute care facilities, diagnostic centers, rehabilitation clinics, and skilled nursing facilities.

(i) Part VI (Supplemental Information)

(1) Line 1 (Supplemental Narrative Descriptions)

(A) PART I, LINE 3c (DISCOUNT CRITERIA SUPPLEMENTAL DISCLOSURE)

Describe the income-based criteria for determining eligibility for free or discounted care under the organization's charity care policy if a measure other than FPGs is used. Also describe whether the organization uses an asset test or other threshold, regardless of income, to determine eligibility for free or discounted care.

Hospitals should consider including quotes from the actual financial assistance policy that was in effect during the tax year regarding the use of asset test or other thresholds and also the income-based criteria used for determining eligibility for financial assistance.

See the earlier discussion for Part I, line 3c (§ 15.2(d)(3)(C)) for a list of other possible tests, criteria, or thresholds the organization might use and which should be reported in response to this question.

(B) PART I, LINE 7 (COST CALCULATION DISCLOSURE)

The organization is required to provide an explanation of how it calculates costs for the purposes of reporting on Part I, line 7. Although the instructions to Part I, line 7 do not indicate this, nor for that matter the narrative on Part VI, line 1 of the Schedule, the instructions to Part VI, line 1 do clearly require this.

Provide an explanation of the costing methodology used to calculate the amounts reported in the table in Part I, line 7 ("Charity Care and Certain Other Community Benefits at Cost"). If a cost accounting system is utilized, indicate whether the cost accounting system addresses all patient segments (e.g., inpatient, outpatient, emergency room, private insurance, Medicaid, Medicare, uninsured or self-pay). Also, indicate whether a cost-to-charge ratio was used for any of the figures reported in the table. Describe whether this cost-to-charge ratio was derived from the attached Worksheet 2, Ratio of Patient Care Cost to Charges, and, if not, what kind of cost-to-charge ratio was used and how it was derived. If some other costing methodology was utilized besides a cost accounting system, cost-to-charge ratio, or a combination of the two, describe the method used.

(C) PART I, LINE 7, COLUMN (F) (BAD DEBT DISCLOSURES)

Part I, line 7, Column (f) requires calculation of "Percent of total expense" for each line item in line 7 by dividing "net community benefit expense" (Column (e)) by the amount in Part IX, line 25, Column (A) of the core Form 990. (Alternatively, organizations can use the percentages from the applicable worksheets.) The instructions to Column (f) require that any bad debt included in Part IX, line 25, Column (A) should be removed from the denominator and an explanation of the amount removed should be provided in Part VI (presumably in line 1 but the instructions do not say). The instructions to Part VI do not require this disclosure, but the instructions to Part I, line 7, Column (f) clearly do.

(D) PART III, LINE 4 (BAD DEBT SUPPLEMENTAL DISCLOSURE)

Provide the text of the footnote to the organization's financial statements that describes bad debt expense. Describe any discrepancies between bad debt reported on Schedule H and what is reported in the audited financials. (See § 15.2 (f)(2).) Also, describe the costing methodology used in determining the amounts reported on lines 2 and 3 of Part III and the organization's rationale and position regarding whether any portion of its bad debt expense should be regarded as community benefit.

See the discussion for Part III, line 4 (§ 15.2(f)(4)) for a list of possible rationales for why all or a portion of bad debt should be regarded as community benefit, and for additional information on what needs to be described in Part VI with respect to costing methodologies and financial statement footnotes.

(E) PART III, LINE 8 (MEDICARE SUPPLEMENTAL DISCLOSURE)

Describe the costing methodology used to determine the Medicare allowable costs reported in the Medicare Cost Report(s). Describe the extent to which any Medicare shortfall reported in Part III, line 7 should be treated as community benefit and the rationale for the organization's position. (Note that this may not include any Medicare amounts that were already included in Part I, line 7g under "subsidized health services" or GME amounts in Part I, line 7f under "health professions education.") Also report any revenue and costs associated with providing Medicare services that are not contained on the organization's Medicare Cost Report(s).

See the discussion for Part III, line 8 (§ 15.2(f)(8)) for a list of possible rationales for why all or a portion of Medicare losses should be treated as community benefit, as well as kinds of Medicare revenue and costs that are not included on the Medicare Cost Report(s) but that can be disclosed in Part VI.

(F) PART III, LINE 9B (COLLECTION PRACTICES SUPPLEMENTAL DISCLOSURE)

On Part VI, line 1, the filing organization is supposed to describe the debt collection practices applicable to charity care patients. Although neither Part III, line 9b nor the instructions to line 9b specifically state this, the instructions for Part VI, line 1 specify that these collection practices are to be described.

If the organization has a written debt collection policy and answered "yes" to Part III, line 9b, describe the collection practices set forth in the policy for patients who are known to qualify for financial assistance under its charity care policy.

Hospitals should consider including quotes from the actual financial assistance policy that was in effect during the tax year regarding collection practices.

As stated in the discussion to Part III, line 9b (§ 15.2(f)(9)), if the organization has collection practices that apply equally to all patients, both charity care and non–charity care patients, these should be described here on Part VI, line 1. Examples of such practices would be limitations on abusive phone calls or prohibitions on seizing houses or cars to pay hospital debts and how new information learned during the collections process regarding patient ability to pay is factored into the collection process (e.g., ceasing collection activities if evidence comes to light in the collection process that the patient qualifies for financial assistance).

(G) HOSPITALS AND FACILITIES LOCATED OUTSIDE THE UNITED STATES

As discussed in § 15.2(c), information about the organization's hospitals and facilities located outside the United States are not to be reported in Parts I through III or Part V of Schedule H. However, the organization may report such information in Part VI. Such information could include information that would be otherwise reported in Parts I through III if reporting foreign hospitals were permissible (e.g., charity care, subsidized health services, research and education, bad debt, and community-building activities provided by the foreign hospital). While the instructions to Part VI do not discuss this voluntary disclosure, it is permitted by the portion of the instructions regarding aggregation (see § 15.2(c)).

(H) PART V (FACILITIES NOT LICENSED OR REGISTERED UNDER STATE LAW)

The organization must disclose certain information in Part V for each of the organization's facilities that are licensed, registered, or similarly recognized as healthcare providers under state law (see § 15.2(h)). For facilities that are not licensed, registered, or similarly recognized under state law, the organization must report in Part VI summary information describing the number and types of such facilities whose information is included in Schedule H. For example, if Part I, line 7 of Schedule H includes charity care and other community benefits provided by 2 rehabilitation clinics, 4 diagnostic clinics, and 3 skilled nursing facilities operated by the hospital (which facilities are not required to be licensed under state law), this should be indicated in Part VI.

(I) PART I, LINE 6(A) (COMMUNITY BENEFIT REPORTS PREPARED BY RELATED ORGANIZATIONS)

If the organization's community benefit report is contained in a report prepared by a related organization, rather than in a separate report prepared by the organization, identify the related organization in response to Part I, line 6a.

(J) PART I, LINE 7(G) (PHYSICIAN CLINICS INCLUDED IN SUBSIDIZED HEALTH SERVICES)

If applicable, describe in Part VI whether the organization included as subsidized health services in Part I, line 7(g) any costs attributable to a physician clinic and report the amount of such costs the organization included in Part I, line 7(g)

(K) Part I, Line 7(h) (Certain Research)

Certain research, specifically research funded anyone other than tax-exempt and government entities, cannot be reported in Part I, line 7(h). However, such research can be reported in Part VI. See § 15.2(d)(7)(B)(vii) for a discussion of what can be reported in Part VI in this respect.

(L) GAAP Inconsistencies; HFMA Statement 15

In several places the Schedule H instructions require reporting in a manner that is inconsistent with GAAP. As a result, Schedule H may be inconsistent with the organization's financial statements. The organization may want to consider explaining these inconsistencies in Part VI. Schedule H requirements that are inconsistent with GAPP include: requiring the reporting of the pro rata portion of joint venture activities; not requiring reporting consistent with HFMA Statement 15 (HFMA Statement 15 is a recommended GAAP but not a mandatory GAAP); and the instruction's unique treatment of restricted grants received by related organizations. In addition, in response to Part III, line 1, regarding whether the organization reports consistently with HFMA statement 15, the organization should explain whether or not, and why, the organization reports pursuant to HFMA statement 15 (see § 15.2 (f)(1)).

(M) Prior-Year Revenue

Prior-year revenue received in the tax year being reported should be reported in Part I, line 7, column (d) pursuant to GAAP. If prior-year revenue results from a Medicare or Medicaid Cost Report settlement, this amount could be material and skew the net community benefit in column (e) or even cause a negative amount in column (e). In this event (and especially if the inclusion causes net community benefit to be a negative number), the organization should consider an explanation in Part VI.

(2) Line 2 (Description of Community Needs Assessment). Describe whether, and if so how, the organization assesses the health care needs of the community or communities it serves.

Describe any of these issues: if the hospital conducts its own needs assessments or needs surveys; if the hospital relies on assessments prepared by other entities (e.g., public health agencies or private organizations such as the United Way); if the hospital targets services to designated "Medically Underserved Areas" or "Medically Underserved Populations" or "Health Professional Shortage Areas"; or any other way in which the hospital attempts to discern the healthcare needs of the community and tailor services to meet those needs.

It is helpful for the hospital to demonstrate that senior leadership and/or board members have reviewed the findings of healthcare needs assessments and factored those findings into strategy and policy development.

Resources on community needs assessment include:

- Community Assessment Toolkit from the Association of Community Health Improvement. For instructions for accessing the toolkit, go to: www.communityhlth.org.

- "A Guide for Planning and Reporting Community Benefit from the Catholic Health Association." For instructions on obtaining the guide, go to: www .chausa.org/Pub/MainNav/ourcommitments/CommunityBenefits.

(3) Line 3 (Description of How Patients Are Informed of Eligibility for Financial Assistance).   Describe how the organization informs and educates patients and persons who may be billed for patient care about their eligibility for assistance under federal, state, or local government programs or under the organization's charity care policy. For example, state whether the organization (1) posts its charity care policy (or a summary thereof) and financial assistance contact information in admissions areas, emergency rooms, and other areas of the organization's facilities in which eligible patients are likely to be present; (2) provides a copy or summary of the policy and financial assistance contact information to patients as part of the intake process; (3) provides a copy or summary of the policy and financial assistance contact information to patients with discharge materials; (4) includes the policy or a summary of the policy, along with financial assistance contact information, in patient bills; and/or (5) discusses with the patient the availability of various government benefits, such as Medicaid or state programs, and assists the patient with qualification for such programs, where applicable.

Most patient rights advocates believe that patient-friendly summaries (not the charity care policy itself) should be posted and provided. If the hospital follows this practice, this should be disclosed.

Patient communication may include information provided at admission, through signs in admitting and waiting areas, through social workers and chaplains and other patient advocates, through billing agents, and through billing communications distributed with bills. All communications with patients should attempt to take into account language barriers. For example, if a large portion of the patient base is Hispanic, having signs and written brochures in Spanish would be helpful as well as a Spanish translator for front-line employees who would be communicating charity care policies to the patients. Every attempt should be made to communicate charity policies to patients as early as possible in the process, namely, as soon as an emergency patient is treated and stabilized or upon admission for other patients.

All staff with patient contact (admitting and billing clerks, nursing and medical staffs, social workers, chaplains, patient advocates, etc.) should be knowledgeable about the charity care policy. Staff should receive the necessary training about the policy and be able to refer any patient to the proper party to obtain more information.

Hospitals should consider:

- Developing scripts that patient registration staff and financial counselors follow when interacting with patients

- Signage, in easily understood language(s), at registration and high traffic areas

- Developing short brochures that summarize the financial assistance policies

- Indicating that financial assistance information is available on Web sites

- Including availability of financial assistance on patient statements

If the hospital has invested in software technologies to inform financial counselors and the business office regarding the patient ability to pay, these systems and investments also can be highlighted in response to this question.

(4) Line 4 (Description of Community Demographics). Describe the community or communities the organization serves, taking into account the geographic area (e.g., urban, suburban, rural), the demographics of the community or communities (e.g., population, average income, percentages of community residents with incomes below the federal poverty guideline, percentage of the hospital's and community's patients who are uninsured or Medicaid recipients), the number of other hospitals serving the community or communities, and whether one or more federally designated medically underserved areas or populations are present in the community.

For this question, the hospital should identify the geographic area that constitutes its primary and/or secondary service areas. The answer can describe the methodology used to specify the area served.

The hospital should not redefine its service area solely for purposes of filing Schedule H. The existing service area definition should be used if available.

If the community is a designated "Medically Underserved Area" or "Medically Underserved Population" or "Health Professional Shortage Area" or some similar designation, this should be indicated.

Teaching hospitals should emphasize that the community served by clinical endeavors varies from that served by education and research. Academic medical centers train health professionals for entire states or regions or the United States and often provide specialized healthcare services not otherwise available in the state or region. Research hospitals should indicate that knowledge obtained through research benefits everyone. All of these special attributes of teaching and research institutions should be emphasized.

(5) Line 5 (Description of How Part II Community-Building Activities Promote the Health of the Community). Describe how the organization's community-building activities, as reported in Part II, promote the health of the community or communities the organization serves.

Although the IRS has taken the position that community-building activities reported in Part II are not necessarily considered charity care or community benefit activities reported in Part I, this line gives the hospital the opportunity to make the argument that the hospital's community-building activities promote the health of the community. Hospitals should take every opportunity to make this argument.

Hospitals should begin by running each community-building activity through the definitions for "community health improvement services." (See discussion for Part I, line 7e (§ 15.2(d)(7)(B)(iv)). Many of the activities reported in Part II (housing, economic development, environmental improvements, community health improvement advocacy) would meet these criteria for community health improvement services (which are reported in Part I, line 7e):

- A request from a public agency or community group was the basis for initiating or continuing the activity or program

- Activities or programs that seek to achieve objectives, including: improving access to health services, enhancing public health, and relief of government burden

- Available to the public and serve low-income consumers

- Address federal, state, or local public health priorities

- Leverage or enhance public health department activities
- Otherwise would become the responsibility of government or another tax-exempt organization

To the extent the hospital's Part II community-building activities meet the criteria for Part I community health improvement activities, the hospital has a very good argument that the Part II community-building activities promote the health of the community.

In addition, several comments to the IRS regarding the draft Form 990 included very good arguments as to why Part II community-building activities should be considered promotion of community health. Hospitals should consider these arguments when making their own arguments. One notable example is the comments provided by the Catholic Health Association available at: www.chausa.org/NR/rdonlyres/ 2FB40592-AAFE-4BDB-836D-720E84DC5B10/0/070913_IRS990CHA.pdf. (other public comments on the draft Form and draft instruction are available at www .irs.gov.)

(6) Line 6 (Description of Other Ways Organization Promotes the Health of the Community).   Provide any other information important to describing how the organization's hospitals or other healthcare facilities further its exempt purpose by promoting the health of the community or communities, including but not limited to: (1) whether a majority of the organization's governing body is comprised of persons who reside in the organization's primary service area who are neither employees nor contractors of the organization, nor family members thereof; (2) whether the organization extends medical staff privileges to all qualified physicians in its community for some or all of its departments; and (3) whether and how the organization applies surplus funds to improvements in patient care, medical education, and research.

Other types of information that could be reported include:

- Whether the organization provides specialized services not otherwise available (e.g., a children's hospital, cancer hospital, rehabilitation hospital, inpatient psychiatric hospital, etc.)
- Whether the hospital operates an emergency room available to all regardless of ability to pay
- Whether the hospital engages in scientific or medical research
- Whether the hospital participates in education and training of healthcare professionals
- Whether the hospital participates in government-sponsored health programs
- Evidence of the organization's responsiveness to the community, such as opportunities for community involvement in governance and advisory groups
- Whether the organization is the sole community provider
- Advocacy activities on behalf of healthcare coverage for all persons and for improved public health
- Serving as a vehicle for attracting and effectively using donated funds

- Offering volunteer opportunities to members of the community
- Being a low-cost/low-charge provider

For additional information about how hospitals can further their exempt purposes by promoting the health of the community, refer to IRS Revenue Rulings 69-545 and 83-157.

(7) Line 7 (Description of How the Organization's Affiliates Promote the Health of the Community). If the organization is part of an affiliated healthcare system, describe the respective roles of the organization and its affiliates in promoting the health of the communities served by the system. For purposes of this question, an "affiliated health care system" is a system that includes affiliates that are under common governance or control or that cooperate in providing healthcare services to their community or communities.

Because the Form 990 and Schedule H are reported on an EIN-by-EIN basis, charity care and community benefit reported by entities within the system that have different EINs will not be included in Part I, line 7. Thus, this answer in Part VI, line 7 is the only place to describe the charity care and community benefit provided by other members of the system. The answer to this question should emphasize how the filing organization supports the overall charitable mission of the healthcare system, the breadth and depth of community benefits that are provided by affiliated organizations (e.g., medical school or foundation or research institute), and also how the organization itself provides community benefit that promotes the health of communities served.

The answer to this question is especially important for systems that provide non-hospital services through separate corporations with separate EINS. For example, if a system operates multiple hospitals through multiple EINs, even if the aggregate information is not reported here, at least each separate hospital is filing a separate 990 and a separate Schedule H, so the information is getting reported somewhere. However, if the system operates free health clinics, urgent care centers, ambulatory surgery centers, and other nonhospital facilities in separate corporations with separate EINs, if the charity care and community benefit provided by such organizations is not reported here it will not get reported anywhere because, although such organizations will file a separate 990, they will not file a Schedule H because they do not meet the definition of a hospital.

Programs and cash donations from foundations of system affiliates can also be reported here. This is especially important if the foundations have separate EINs because, although each such foundation would be filing its own 990, it would not file a Schedule H (because the foundation is not a hospital) and therefore would not otherwise have the opportunity to report its charity care and community benefit activities.

Hospitals that are part of systems should also report charity care provided by joint ventures in which system affiliates are partners if (1) the pro rata share of the joint venture items is not otherwise included in Schedule H (e.g., in Parts I, line 7 or Part II) or (2) the joint venture is required to use the charity policy of one of the system affiliates.

Hospitals that are part of, or affiliated with, academic medical centers should discuss how such clinical, teaching, and research affiliations promote the health of the community and provide community benefit, for example:

- Academic medical centers often have a clinical reach that extends beyond the local service area. For example, they may operate an NCI-designated Comprehensive Cancer Center or provide other highly specialized services that attracts patients from a multistate or national service area. Describe such unique clinical services.

- Teaching institutions should stress the numbers of medical students, residents, fellows, nurses, and allied health professionals they train. Describe the number of ACGME-accredited residencies in which the institution participates. Describe any regionally or nationally recognized specialty, subspecialty or fellowship programs the organization operates.

- Research institutions should give a thorough description of the types of research in which they are engaged, significant discoveries and breakthroughs and the impact on improving health, and significant honors or awards received by researchers. Describe the number of participants in important clinical trials and potential beneficiaries of a treatment or drug discovery.

See the discussion on the aggregation rules (§ 15.2(c)) for more information about affiliated health systems that should be reported in Part VI, line 7.

(8) Line 8 (Description of States Where Organization or Related Organization File Community Benefit Report). Identify all states with which the organization files (or a related organization files on its behalf) a community benefit report. Report only those states in which the organization's own community benefit report is filed, either by the organization itself or by a related organization on the organization's behalf.

If the organization posts such reports on its Web page, it may want to consider providing links to such reports.

The Catholic Health Association annually compiles information on states that require that a community benefit report be filed. That information is available on this Web site: www.chausa.org/Pub/MainNav/ourcommitments/CommunityBenefits/.

Along the left-hand side of the page there is a link called "Resources." Clicking on this link will expand the index and provide an additional link to "Advocacy and Public Policy." Clicking on this second link will open a page that has additional resources on state community benefit reporting requirements.

§ 15.3 NEW FORM 990 COMPLIANCE TASKS

In order to track and report the information the IRS is requesting on Schedule H, all hospitals should:

1. **Form work groups.** Form a work group of key departments (finance, legal, billing, community benefit/mission, compliance, communications, executive office).

2. **Assign 990 responsibilities to staff members.** Review 990 Schedule H questions and assign staff responsibility for drafting answers.

3. **Consult industry guidance.** Study and review industry reporting guidelines:

   • HFMA's Statement 15 (and determine whether or not the hospital will track and report charity care and bad debt in compliance with the Statement).

- CHA's Guide to Planning and Reporting Community Benefit (because the Schedule H accounting framework is based on the CHA Guide).

4. **Educate staff.** Hold educational sessions for staff who will contribute information.

5. **Inform officers and directors.** Brief the board and senior executives about Schedule H reporting requirements.

6. **Collect community benefit data.** Collect community benefit information:

   - Inventory community benefit services.

   - Review past community benefit reports.

7. **Summarize community benefit data.** Summarize financial and nonfinancial community benefit information.

8. **Incorporate community benefit data into Schedule H.** Complete 990 Schedule H with the information collected. Critically review draft: Are answers to any sections incomplete or inadequate? Is the hospital unable to answer certain questions (e.g., what portion of bad debt is allocable to patients who are unable to pay, or how does the hospital assess community needs)? Develop a corrective plan of action if needed.

9. **Seek additional resources.** Determine what additional resources (legal and accounting consultation, staff, software) will be needed to complete form.

10. **Review and revise key policies:.**

    - Charity care policy

    - Billing and collection policy

    - Community meeds assessment

    - Community benefit report

11. **Make practices fit policies.** Review practices to determine if practices are consistent with policies.

12. **Communicate effectively.** Develop a communications plan for the public, reporters, regulators, and legislators.

13. **Go the extra mile.** Decide whether to accept the option of submitting optional information to the IRS for tax year 2008.

CHAPTER SIXTEEN

Schedule I—Domestic Grantmaking

In addition to requesting detailed information concerning foreign grantmaking, the new Form 990 requires organizations that conduct domestic grantmaking to complete Schedule I reporting their activities in this regard. The purpose of Schedule I is to provide a concentrated image of a tax-exempt organization's grants and other assistance to governments, other organizations, and individuals within the United States.

Grants made to affiliates that are not separately organized from the filing organization or grants made to branch offices, accounts, or employees located in the United States are not considered grants for purposes of Schedule I. Grants made in the United States by a disregarded entity, or by a joint venture, partnership, limited liability company, or other entity taxed as a partnership, should be reported on Schedule I to the extent of the filing entity's ownership in the entity. Schedule I adopts a $5,000 grant amount filing threshold.

§16.1 LAW AND POLICY

As a general matter, public charities and other tax-exempt noncharitable entities may make grants in furtherance of their exempt purposes in the United States without being subject to extensive federal regulation and record-keeping requirements. Even so, tax-exempt organizations should make grants only if the grants are for causes, programs, activities, or expenses that are consistent with the organization's exempt purposes and if the grants are in conformity with the entity's organizational documents. As a matter of good management, organizations should adopt practices to ensure that their grants are being used in furtherance of their exempt purposes, are being spent efficiently, and are subject to return or redirection if the granting organization determines the funds are being misspent.

Schedule I requests a filing organization to provide information on grants and other assistance awarded to organizations, governments and individuals in the United States. For purposes of Schedule I reporting, the phrase *grants and other assistance* includes awards, prizes, allocations, stipends, scholarships, fellowships, research grants, and similar payments and distributions. *Grants and other assistance* does not include salaries or other compensation to employees, grants to affiliates that are not separately organized from the filing organization, or grants made to branch offices, accounts, or employees located in the United States. *Organizations in the United States* include nonprofit or other exempt organizations, partnerships, corporations, or other business entities that are created or organized in the United States or under the laws of the United States or of any state, the Commonwealth of Puerto Rico, the Commonwealth of the Northern Mariana Islands, and the territories and possessions of the United States (including Guam, American Samoa, and the United States Virgin Islands), and an estate or trust other than a foreign estate or trust. *Governments in the United States* include the U.S. government, and any state or political subdivisions of a state, including the District of Columbia and any possession of the United States. A grant to a U.S. government agency must be included on Schedule I regardless of where the agency is located or operated. The phrase *individuals in the United States* includes persons who are U.S. citizens or residents of the United States, but does not include U.S. citizens or residents of the United States living or residing in a foreign country. Grants to U.S. citizens or residents living or residing in a foreign country must be reported on Schedule F as grants to individuals outside the United States.

(a) Evaluating and Monitoring Grants

Grantmaking organizations should have a system for evaluating proposed grants and monitoring the grants it makes to determine the effectiveness of the grants. Most grantmaking organizations first identify causes or projects they wish to fund and make their grants only to organizations and individuals who will further these causes and projects. Grants are often made pursuant to a grant agreement, which details the intended purpose of the grant, requires reports to the granting entity regarding the use of the grant funds, and provides consequences in the event the grant is not expended in the designated manner. Although grant agreements are not generally required other than in specific situations, such as certain private foundation grants, they are a recommended practice.

(1) Grants to Organizations. The evaluation to be undertaken and the diligence to be expended by a tax-exempt organization when making grants to another entity, to ensure that its grant funds are being used for their intended purposes, is dependent on the classification of the entity to which the grants are made. If an exempt organization makes a grant to another organization with the same exempt status, and that status has been confirmed by the IRS and remains in effect, the organization can be reasonably assured that its grant will be used in furtherance of allowable purposes. For example, if a charitable entity makes a grant to another charitable entity for a specific charitable project or purpose, the granting entity can be realistically certain its grant will be used for charitable purposes. The same should hold true for a social welfare organization's grant to another social welfare entity for a specific social welfare project.

There are several methods a grantmaking organization can use to confirm the tax-exempt status of a grantee. The simplest method is to obtain a copy of the potential grantee organization's current IRS determination letter setting forth its exempt status. Because determination letters are typically dated many years prior to the year of the proposed grant, the grantor should confirm, by searching the IRS's Web site, that the organization's exempt status has not been revoked. If the intended grantee is a public charity, the grantor can confirm that the charity is listed in Publication 78, which also can be searched on the IRS Web site. Alternatively, a granting entity can research the potential grantee's exempt status by searching for the organization on www.Guidestar.org, which updates its site with information from the IRS not only for public charities but also for other types of tax-exempt organizations.

Where the grant is for a particular purpose or project, the granting entity will not want its funds expended for the general operating expenses of the grantee or for a different project conducted by the grantee. Thus, the granting organization should consider requiring the grantee entity to execute a grant agreement that details the intended purpose of the grant and provides consequences in the event the grant funds are not expended in the designated manner. Also, the granting organization should be certain that the grant funds will not be used in a manner that could jeopardize the grantee's tax-exempt status, such as use of funding in a manner that creates excessive lobbying issues for a charitable entity. Even when the funds are being granted for the general use of the grantee organization, the grantmaking organization should utilize a grant agreement or transmittal letter that (1) confirms the tax-exempt status of the grantee organization, (2) sets forth the approved use of the granted funds, and (3) sets forth the consequences if the funds are not used in the intended manner.

(2) Grants to Individuals. Grants made to individuals typically require more oversight to ensure their proper use. First, the grantmaking organization must make sure the individual receiving the grant is part of the class of individuals intended to be benefited. For example, if the granting organization is a disaster relief organization, it must determine that individuals receiving aid are, in fact, needy, whether on a short-term or long-term basis. A granting organization should consider having a written policy and using a written application process to document that the individual is part of the class intended to be benefited.

Second, the grantmaking entity should ensure that its selection of individual recipients is on an *objective and nondiscriminatory basis*. Although the rules regarding selection of recipients on this basis are applicable to private foundations, all organizations can meaningfully employ these rules in the individual grantmaking context. For a discussion of the award of grants on an objective and nondiscriminatory basis, see § 18.1(d).

Third, the grantmaking organization should exercise some degree of diligence in determining if the funds were spent for their proper use. One method for ensuring that a grant to an individual is being used for its intended purposes is to pay the expenses of the grantee directly. For example, the grantor can make a direct payment to a hospital or physician for the grantee's medical bills, or pay tuition directly to a college or university as a scholarship for an individual. Also, a grantmaking organization can make noncash grants, such as grants of food and clothing, to ensure that needy individuals are receiving the desired aid.

For grants to individuals, the monitoring of the use of grant funds can be performed by obtaining reports from the grantees on the manner in which the grant funds have been spent and the progress made toward achieving the purpose of the grant, or by securing other evidence of their proper purpose, such as grade or other academic reports in the case of scholarship grants. If a grantmaking organization receives information that leads it to believe grant funds may have been misspent or misdirected, it should investigate the grant, withhold future grant payments until it is satisfied the grant conditions are being fulfilled, and seek recovery of any funds that were diverted from their intended use.

Last, the grantmaking entity should keep records and case histories of the grants, including the names and addresses of the grant recipients, the amount distributed to each recipient (cash and the value of any noncash assistance), the purpose for which the grant was made, the manner in which the individual was selected, and the relationship, if any, between the recipient and the grant maker's insiders.

(3) Prohibited Grants to Individuals. Supporting organizations and donor-advised funds are subject to restrictions on their grants to individuals. A supporting organization cannot make grants to its substantial contributors or to its substantial contributors' families and 35-percent controlled entities. For example, a supporting organization cannot make a grant to the son of a substantial contributor. If a supporting organization makes such a grant, the grant is an automatic excess business transaction, and the entire grant amount is subject to the intermediate sanctions excise taxes (§ 6.1(b)) and must be repaid to the organization.

Donor-advised funds (§ 11.1(a)) are prohibited from making grants to natural persons. If a grant is made from a donor-advised fund to an individual, the grant is treated as a taxable expenditure of the fund, subject to a 20-percent excise tax. In addition, if a donor-advised fund makes a grant to a donor, donor-advisor, or a family member or 35-percent controlled entity of a donor or donor-advisor, the grant is an automatic excess benefit transaction (§ 6.1(b)), subject to excise taxes and repayment.

(b) Expenditure Responsibility Rules

Grantmaking organizations can look to the *expenditure responsibility rules* for guidance as to whether their grants are being used for their intended purposes. Although generally only private foundations are subject to the expenditure responsibility rules, other tax-exempt organizations can model their grantmaking diligence after these rules to ensure that their grants are being used in the anticipated manner.

If a private foundation makes grants to organizations other than governments or certain charitable entities, it must exercise *expenditure responsibility* over its grants to avoid classification of the grants as taxable expenditures, subject to excise taxes. The expenditure responsibility rules essentially require that the private foundation exert all reasonable efforts and establish adequate procedures to ascertain that the grant is spent solely for the purpose for which it was made, obtains full and complete reports from the grantee on how the funds are spent, and makes full and detailed reports with respect to such expenditures to the IRS. More specifically, the rules require

- A pregrant inquiry
- A written commitment/written grant agreement
- Annual reports to the grantor organization from the grantee, including a final report on the use of the funds
- Investigation of the diversion of funds
- Reporting to the IRS on the foundation's annual information return (Form 990-PF)
- Maintenance of records by the granting private foundation

Each of these requirements is discussed separately in the next sections.

(1) Pregrant Inquiry. Before making a grant to an organization, the grantor should conduct a limited inquiry directed at obtaining sufficient information to give a reasonable person assurance that the grantee will use the grant for the proper purposes. The inquiry should concern itself with matters such as (a) the identity, prior history, and experience (if any) of the grantee organization and its managers; and (b) any knowledge that the grantor has (based on prior experience or otherwise) of, or other information that is readily available concerning, the management, activities, and practices of the grantee organization. The scope of the inquiry may vary from case to case depending on the size and purpose of the grant, the period over which it is to be paid, and the prior experience that the grantor has had with respect to the capacity of the grantee to use the grant for the proper purposes.

(2) Terms of Grants. Under the expenditure responsibility rules, each grant must be made subject to a written commitment signed by an appropriate officer, director, or trustee of the grantee organization. Such commitment must include an agreement by the grantee

1. To repay any portion of the grant funds that are not used for the purpose of the grant.

2. To submit full and complete annual reports on the matter in which the funds are spent and the progress made in accomplishing the purposes of the grant.

3. To maintain records of the receipts and expenditures and to make its books and records available to the grantor at reasonable times.

4. Not to use any of the funds (a) to carry on propaganda, or otherwise to attempt to influence legislation, (b) to influence the outcome of any specific public election, or to carry on directly or indirectly any voter registration drive, (c) to make any grant to an individual or organization, or (d) to undertake any activity for any noncharitable purpose, to the extent that use of the funds would be a taxable expenditure if make directly by the granting private foundation.

Paragraph (4) above must be in a private foundation's grant agreement due to the restrictions on a private foundation's activities and expenditures. Tax-exempt organizations other than private foundations are not generally subject to these same prohibitions and can modify their grant agreements accordingly.

(3) Reports from Grantees. Except in the case of certain endowment grants, the expenditure responsibility rules require a grantor foundation to require reports on the use of the grant funds, compliance with the terms of the grant, and the progress made by the grantee toward achieving the purposes for which the grant was made. The grantee must make the reports as of the end of its annual accounting period within which the grant or any portion of it is received and all subsequent periods until the grant funds are expended in full or the grant is otherwise terminated. The reports must be furnished to the grantor within a reasonable period of time after the close of the annual accounting period of the grantee for which the reports are made. Within a reasonable period of time after the close of its annual accounting period during which the use of the grant funds is completed, the grantee must make a final report with respect to all expenditures made from the funds (including salaries, travel, and supplies) and indicating the progress made toward the goals of the grant. The grantor need not conduct any independent verification of the reports unless it has reason to doubt their accuracy or reliability.

(4) Diversion of Funds. If the granting organization determines that any part of a grant has been used for improper purposes, and the grantee has not previously diverted funds, the grantor must take all reasonable and appropriate steps to either recover the grant funds or to ensure the restoration of the diverted funds and the dedication of the other grant funds held by the grantee to the purposes being financed by the grant. In addition, the grantor must withhold any future payments to the grantee after the grantor becomes aware that a diversion may have taken place until it has received the grantee's assurances that future diversions will not occur, and require the grantee to take extraordinary precautions to prevent future diversions from occurring. In the case where the grantee has previously diverted funds received from a grantor foundation, and the grantor again determines that any part of a grant has again been used for improper purposes, then the grantor must (a) take all reasonable and appropriate reasonable and appropriate steps to either recover the grant funds or to insure the restoration of the diverted funds and the dedication of the other grant funds held by the grantee to the purposes being financed by the grant, except that if, in fact, some or all of the diverted funds are not so restored or recovered, then the foundation must take all reasonable and appropriate steps to recover all of the grant funds; and (b) withhold further payments until such funds are in fact so recovered or restored, obtain assurances from the grantee that future diversions will not occur, and require the grantee to take extraordinary precautions to prevent future diversions from occurring.

(5) Reporting to the IRS. The expenditure responsibility rules require a private foundation making grants pursuant to such rules to provide certain grant information on its Form 990-PF filed with the IRS. These reports must include the name and address of the grantee, the date and amount of the grant, the purpose of the grant, amounts expended by the grantee, whether the grantee has diverted any funds from the purpose of the grant, dates of any reports received from the grantee, and date and results of any verification of the grantee's reports undertaken by or at the direction of the grantmaking organization.

(6) Record Keeping by the Grantee. Under the expenditure responsibility rules, the grantmaking entity must keep, and make available to the IRS at the entity's principal office, a copy of the grant agreement, a copy of each report received during the taxable year from each grantee, and a copy of each report made by the grantor's personnel or independent auditors of any audits or other investigations made during the taxable year with respect to any expenditure responsibility grant.

§16.2 PREPARATION OF NEW FORM 990 SCHEDULE I

Schedule I of the new Form 990 requests an organization to provide information on grants or other assistance made by the filing organization during the tax year to organizations, governments, and individuals in the United States. On Schedule I, a filing organization should report activities conducted by the organization directly or indirectly through a disregarded entity or through a joint venture taxed as a partnership.

Thus, grants from a disregarded entity or from a joint venture, partnership, or limited liability company in which the filing organization is a partner or member should be reported on Schedule I, to the extent of the filing organization's interest in the entity.

(a)   Part I (General Information on Grants and Assistance)

Line 1 of Part I of Schedule I asks if the reporting organization maintains records to substantiate the amount of the grants or assistance, the grantee's eligibility for the grants or assistance, and the selection criteria used to award the grants or assistance (answer "yes" or "no"). As a matter of good management, a filing organization should keep records to substantiate its grants, including details on the amount of the grants, the eligibility of recipients for the grants, and the selection criteria used to award the grants. Selection criteria may include an application form, an independent selection committee, and objective criteria that is applied by the committee during the selection process.

Line 2 of Part I requests the organization to describe in Part IV of Schedule I the organization's procedures for monitoring the use of grants funds in the United States to ensure its grants are used for proper purposes and are not otherwise diverted from the intended use. Examples of methods of monitoring grants to organizations include requiring periodic reports from the grantee regarding use of the grant funds or field investigations conducted by the grantmaking entity. For grants awarded to individuals, monitoring the use of grant funds includes obtaining a report of a recipient's work for each academic period or a report from faculty members supervising the grantee in the case of a scholarship award, or a report from the grantee regarding his or her progress toward the objectives of the grant for other types of awards.

(b)   Part II (Grants and Other Assistance to Governments and Organizations in the United States)

Part II of Schedule I requests information about grants and other assistance to governments and organizations in the United States. Part II contains a table that must be completed if the reporting entity reports more than $5,000 as grants and other assistance to governments and organizations in the United States on Form 990, Part IX, line 1 and had any recipient that received over than $5,000. If the organization reports more $5,000 as grants and other assistance to governments and organizations in the United States, but no recipient received more than $5,000, the organization simply checks the box at the top of Part II but does not need to fill in the table. In completing the Part II table, the filing organization should report the details of each grantee organization on a separate line. In addition, if an organization receiving a grant or assistance is an interested person (§ 18.1(c)) or a related organization (see Chapter 21), the filing organization should consider whether it needs to disclose the grant or assistance on Schedule L (Transactions with Interested Persons) and/or Schedule R (Related Organizations and Unrelated Partnerships).

(1) Columns (a) through (c) (Name, Address, EIN, and IRC Code Section).   In Column (a), an organization reports the full legal name and mailing address of the recipient organization or governmental entity. In Column (b), the organization lists the recipient's employer identification number (EIN). For Column (c), an organization lists the Internal Revenue Code section under which the recipient organization is tax-exempt, if applicable. For example, for a grant to a charitable entity, the organization reports "501(c)(3)." If the recipient organization is a government entity, the filing organization should so indicate. If the recipient organization is neither a tax-exempt nor government entity, the filing organization should leave Column (c) blank.

(2) Column (d) (Amount of Cash Grant). In Column (d), the filing organization reports the amount of the cash grants it made to the recipient, which includes grants and allocations paid by cash, check, money order, electronic fund or wire transfer, and other charges against funds on deposit at a financial institution.

(3) Columns (e) through (g) (Noncash Assistance). Columns (e) through (g) are used to report information on noncash grants. An organization reports the fair market value of any noncash assistance it granted to a recipient organization in Column (e). In Column (f), the organization states the method of valuation of noncash assistance. Property with a readily determinable market value is reported using its fair market value. If an organization cannot readily determine the fair market value of the noncash assistance distributed, it should use an appraised or estimated value. If the grant includes marketable securities registered and listed on a recognized securities exchange, market value of the securities is to be measured by averaging the highest and lowest quoted selling prices or the average between the bona fide bid and ask prices on the date the property is distributed to the grantee. In Column (g), a reporting organization should provide a description of the noncash assistance, such as "medical supplies," "equipment," or "books."

(4) Column (h) (Purpose of the Grant or Assistance). In Column (h), an organization reports the purpose or ultimate use of the grant funds, using specific terms such as "payment for nursing services" or "grant for laboratory construction." The instructions state that organizations are not to use broad terms, such as "charitable" or "educational" but instead should use specific terms, such as general support, payments for nursing services, or laboratory construction. Organizations are instructed to specify the type of assistance, such as medical, dental, or hospital fees and charges to indigents. For disaster assistance, the reporting entity should include a description of the disaster and the assistance provided, such as "food, shelter, and clothing for the organization's assistance to Hurricane Katrina disaster victims."

Unlike with foreign grant reporting on Schedule F, which requires reporting by region without identification of the grantee organizations, Part II of Schedule I requires that each grantee organization or government be separately identified. The IRS allows for regional reporting on Schedule F in response to concerns for the safety of overseas workers if tax-exempt organizations were required to specifically identify the recipients of their foreign grants and assistance.

(5) Lines 2 and 3 (Total Number of Charitable and Government Organizations and Total Number of Other Organizations). Line 2 asks the organization to enter the total number of charitable organizations and governments reported on line 1. *Charitable organizations* include organizations that have been recognized as charitable organizations by the IRS and organizations that are not required to have their charitable status recognized, such as churches (including synagogues, temples, and mosques), integrated auxiliaries of churches, and conventions or associations of churches, and any organization that has gross revenues of not more than $5,000, unless the filing organization has knowledge that the organization does not qualify for exemption. See the discussion in § 16.1(a)(1) for methods to confirm the charitable status of a grantee entity.

Line 3 asks the organization to enter the total number of "other" grantee organizations, which includes tax-exempt organizations other than charitable organizations, such as social welfare organizations, trade associations, and social clubs.

(c) Part III (Grants and Other Assistance to Individuals in the United States)

Part III of Schedule I requests information on grants and other assistance to individuals in the United States, if the organization reports an aggregate amount of grants and other assistance to individuals in the United States of more than $5,000 on Form 990, Part IX, line 2. Part III does not require the filing organization to identify the recipients by name. Grants or other assistance provided to individuals through another organization or entity should be included in Part II, not Part III. For example, an organization's payment to a hospital to cover the medical expenses of a particular individual should be reported in Part III as a grant to an individual, but an organization's contribution to a hospital to provide service to the public or unspecified charity patients should be reported in Part II as a grant to an organization. If the grant is made to an interested person (§ 18.1(c)), the organization will need to disclose the grant on Schedule L (Transactions with Interested Persons).

(1) Column (a) (Type of Grant or Assistance). In Column (a), an organization reports the type of grant or assistance or the purpose of the grant. Examples include scholarships for students attending a particular school, the provision of books or other educational supplies, or the provision of food, clothing, and shelter for indigents. For specific disaster assistance, the filing organization should report the type of assistance and identify the type of disaster, such as "provision of food and supplies for victims of California earthquake."

(2) Column (b) (Number of Recipients). In Column (b), for each type of assistance, an organization reports the number of recipients or an estimate of the number of recipients. If the organization provides an estimate, it should provide an explanation of how the estimate was reached in Part IV of Schedule I.

(3) Column (c) (Amount of Cash Grant). Column (c) requires the filing organization to report the amount of its cash grants for each type of grant or assistance. *Cash grants* are those paid by cash, check, money order, electronic fund or wire transfer, or other charge against funds on deposit at a financial institution.

(4) Columns (d) through (f) (Noncash Assistance). In Column (d), an organization reports the fair market value of the noncash assistance it provided for each type of grant or assistance. Column (e) is used to report the method of valuation of noncash assistance. Property with a readily determinable market value is reported at its fair market value. If an organization cannot readily determine fair market value, it should use an appraised or estimated value. If the grant includes marketable securities registered and listed on a recognized securities exchange, market value of the securities is to be measured by averaging the highest and lowest quoted selling prices or the average between the bona fide bid and ask prices on the date the property is distributed to the grantee.

In Column (f), an organization provides a description of the noncash assistance it provided for each type of assistance or grants, listing all that apply. Examples include blankets, medical supplies, pharmaceuticals, books, food, shelter, and clothing.

(d)   Part IV (Supplemental Information)

Part IV of Schedule I provides an area for a reporting organization to disclose its response to Part I, line 2 (procedures for monitoring the use of grants funds in the United States) and any other information, narrative explanations and descriptions, such as the method used to estimate the number of individuals receiving grants reported in Part III. An organization should identify the specific part and line(s) to which the Part IV response relates.

§ 16.3   NEW FORM 990 COMPLIANCE TASKS

Organizations that make grants domestically need to be attending to these seven compliance tasks.

1. **Grant criteria.** Establish criteria pursuant to which the organization will make grants and select its grant recipients.

2. **Record keeping for grants to organizations.** For grants to governments, tax-exempt entities, and other organizations, keep detailed reports on the amounts of the grant, the purpose of the grant, how the organization determined the grant funds were used for the purposes intended to be financed with the grant, and how it handled any misuse of the grant funds.

3. **Grants to individuals on an objective and nondiscriminatory basis.** For grants to individuals, review the rules regarding awards made on an objective and nondiscriminatory basis.

4. **Record keeping for grants to individuals.** For grants to individuals, keep records regarding the information used to evaluate the qualification of potential grantees; the selection criteria used to select the grantees; copies of the application forms of the grantees, if any; the amount and purpose of each grant, including the value of any noncash assistance and the method used to value the noncash assistance; and copies of any progress reports and diversion investigation reports prepared by either the grantor or the grantee.

5. **Interested person grants.** Keep records and obtain the necessary information to determine if any of the organization's grant recipients are interested persons or related organizations for purposes of reporting on Schedule L and Schedule R.

6. **Grant agreements.** Consider using grant agreements for all grants made, whether to individuals or organizations, specifying the amount and purpose of the grant, the required reports on the grantee's progress made in achieving the

purposes of the grant, and the consequences in the event the grant funds are misused.

7. **Guidance using the expenditure responsibility rules.** Review the expenditure responsibility rules applicable to private foundations to determine if any of the expenditure responsibility procedures should be incorporated into the organization's grantmaking practices.

CHAPTER SEVENTEEN

Schedule K—Tax-Exempt Bonds

Charitable organizations generally are eligible to use tax-exempt bonds to finance the acquisition and construction of facilities and equipment used to further charitable purposes. Other exempt organizations are not eligible to use bond financing. Tax-exempt bond financing is attractive to charitable organizations as the interest rate paid by the charity on the bonds generally is less than it would pay with conventional financing. This is a case because the interest is tax-exempt to the holder of the bond. There are a number of rules governing tax-exemption. The rules apply at the time of bond issuance and throughout the life of the bonds.

Tax-exempt bond liabilities are reported on the current Form 990, but it does not require the submission of information to substantiate bond compliance. The IRS believes there is significant noncompliance in this area. To investigate the level of noncompliance, the IRS initiated a compliance check in 2007. The results of the compliance check indicated that only 15 percent of the organizations could verify conclusively that they actually implemented written procedures to ensure that the bonds were in compliance. New Schedule K requires reporting of information similar to the compliance check questions. This new schedule is not fully implemented until 2009. Only general information is required for 2008 filings. Many believe that the Schedule K instructions require more work. Further, gathering adequate information will be a challenge for charities. Consultation with bond counsel may be required in many cases.

§17.1 LAW AND POLICY

A number of rules must be satisfied for the bond to qualify for tax exemption. The primary rules include qualified use of proceeds, private business use limitations, arbitrage yield restrictions and rebate, hedge bonds and refunding. Although the proceeds are used by charities, the issuer of the bonds is typically a governmental organization. In some cases, however, nonprofit organization's issue bonds *on behalf of an issuer*. In this case, the governmental organization is viewed as the issuer, not the nonprofit organization and the bonds are considered obligations of the State or local government.

The IRS will issue an advance ruling in some circumstances that the obligations of a nonprofit corporation were issued on behalf of a State or local governmental unit. An on-behalf-of-issuer arrangement also includes bonds issued by a constituted authority organized by a state or local governmental unit specifically to issue tax-exempt bonds in order to further public purposes.

Separately issued bonds will be considered one bond issue in some cases. For example, two or more bonds will be considered one bond issue if they are: (1) sold at substantially the same time; (2) sold pursuant to the same plan of financing; and (3) payable from the same source of funds.

(a)   Qualified Use of Proceeds and Private Business Use

A qualified charitable bond must meet the ownership test and private business use test to be tax-exempt. The *ownership test* is met if the financed property is owned by either a charity or governmental unit. The *private business use* test is met if no more than 5 percent of the proceeds are used for private business use. In other words, at least 95 percent of the net proceeds must be used to further the charity's tax-exempt activities. The bond must also meet the private security or payment test to qualify. This test is met if not more than 5 percent of the payments of principal and interest are made or secured (directly or indirectly) by payments or property used or to be used for private business use.

All property financed by qualified charitable bonds must be owned by a charitable organization or governmental unit. The bonds must also be used for charitable purposes rather than for private purposes. The bonds will be treated as used for charitable purposes provided there is only minimal use by private parties. This private business use test is met for qualified bonds if no more than 5 percent of the issue's net proceeds are used for private business use. Generally, *private business use of tax-exempt bonds* means "use of the financed facility in a trade or business carried on by a private person." For this purpose, use as a member of the general public is not taken into account. Note, however, that the bond issuance costs, which may not exceed 2 percent, count toward the 5 percent limit on private business use, leaving only 3 percent of allowable private business use. Issuance costs generally include underwriter's discount, counsel fees, financial advisor fees, agency fees, trustee fees (agent fees from bond registrars, certification and altercation fees), accounting fees, printing costs for bonds and offering documents, public approval process costs, engineering and feasibility study costs, and guarantee fees other than for qualified guarantees.

Use of a bond-financed facility, whether through direct or indirect use, is treated as direct use of the bond proceeds. For this purpose, "any activity carried on by a person other than a natural person shall be treated as a trade or business." In determining whether private business use exists, both actual and beneficial use by a private person must be considered.

In most cases, private business use exists only if the private person has a *special legal entitlement* to use the *exempt facility* under an arrangement with the issuer or the activity is an unrelated business income activity. Special legal entitlements generally include ownership, leases, management contracts, output contracts, research agreements, and any other arrangement that conveys a comparable special legal entitlement. The next sections provide brief descriptions of various types of special legal entitlements.

(1) Ownership.   Generally, ownership for federal income tax purposes by a private person of exempt facility is private business use.

(2) Lease of Facility.   Any arrangement properly characterized as a lease for federal income tax purposes is treated as a lease for purposes of private use. Leasing an exempt facility by a private person will also cause private use. More specifically, an exempt facility is treated as being used for private business use if it is leased (1) to a private person and then subleased to a charity or (2) to a charity and then subleased to a private person, provided that in each case the private person is in a trade or business. In determining whether a contract is properly characterized as a lease, it is necessary to consider all the facts and circumstances, including (1) the degree of control over the exempt property that is exercised by a private person, and (2) whether a private person bears risk of loss of the exempt property. For example, a leasing arrangement would occur if a private person actually, or effectively, pays an occupancy fee for use of a research facility but conducts the research project on its own and retains some or all of the ownership in the intellectual property. In some cases, a lease arrangement can cause private business use even if the arrangement involves an organization that ordinarily could be viewed as a charity if the organization in question is *not* engaged in the same activity as the charity issuer.

(3) Management Contracts.   A management contract with respect to exempt property generally results in private business use of that property if the contract provides for compensation for services rendered, with compensation based, in whole or in part, on a share of net profits from operating the exempt facility. A management contract is the management, service, or incentive payment contract between a charity and a service provider under which the service provider provides services involving all, a portion of, or any function of exempt facility. However, these arrangements are generally not management contracts that result in private business use:

- Contracts for services that are solely incidental to the primary governmental function of an exempt facility (e.g., contracts for janitorial, office equipment repair, hospital billing, or similar services).

- The mere granting of admitting privileges by a hospital to a doctor, even if those privileges are conditioned on the provision of de minimis services, if those privileges are available to all qualified physicians in the area, consistent with the size and nature of its facilities.

- A contract to provide for the operation of a facility or system of facilities that consists predominantly of public utility property, if the only compensation is the reimbursement of actual and direct expenses of the service provider and reasonable administrative overhead expenses of the service provider.

- A contract to provide for services if the only compensation is the reimbursement of the service provider for actual and direct expenses paid by the service provider to unrelated parties.

The IRS provides a safe harbor for management contracts. The management contract will *not* result in private business use if certain rules are met. A management contract which gives a private person service provider an ownership or a leasehold interest in exempt facilities is not the only situation in which such a contract may result in private use. In general, the safe harbor requirements will be met if reasonable compensation is paid and no compensation is based in whole or in part on a share of net profits from operating the exempt facility. These arrangements generally will not be viewed as a "net profits arrangements": (a) a percentage of gross revenues (or adjusted gross revenue) of the exempt facility or a percentage of expenses from the exempt facility, but not both; (b) a capitation fee; or (c) a per-unit fee. Furthermore, permissible arrangements include:

- **95-percent periodic fixed fee arrangements.** If at least 95 percent of the compensation for services for each annual period during the term of the contract is based on a periodic fixed fee and the term of the contract, including all renewal options, does not exceed the lesser of 80 percent of the reasonably expected useful life of the exempt property or 15 years.

- **80-percent periodic fixed fee arrangements.** If the fixed fee portion is reduced to less than 95 percent but is at least 80 percent of the compensation for services for each annual period during the term of the contract, including all renewal options, the maximum term of the contract is reduced to the lesser of 80 percent of the reasonably expected useful life of the exempt property or 10 years.

- **50-percent periodic fixed fee arrangements.** If the fixed fee portion is reduced to less than 80 percent but is at least 50 percent of the compensation for services for each annual period during the term of the contract or all of the compensation for services is based on a capitation fee or combination of a capitation fee and a periodic fixed fee, the term of the contract, including all renewal options, must not exceed five years.

- **Percentage of revenue or expense fee arrangements in certain two-year contracts.** If all the compensation for services is based on the percentage of fees charged or a combination of per unit fee and a percentage of revenue or expense fee, the compensation may be based on the percentage of gross revenues, adjusted gross revenues, or expenses of the exempt facility. In this event, the term of the contract including all renewal options must not exceed two years. Further, the contract must be terminable by the charity on a reasonable notice, without penalty or cause, at the end of the first year of the contract term.

(4) Research Agreements. An agreement between a private person and a charity to sponsor research performed by the charity in an exempt facility may result in private business use of the exempt facility. This determination is made based on all the facts and circumstances. In general, sponsored research will result in private business use if the private person who sponsors the research is treated as the lessee or owner of the exempt facility for federal income tax purposes.

The IRS provides safe harbors for research agreements. It outlines two examples of research arrangements in a revenue procedure. For purposes of the safe harbor examples, a *sponsor* is any person other than a charity or a government organization as defined in the revenue procedure that supports or sponsors research under the contract (i.e., a private person). The two safe harbors are provided as Example 1 and Example 2.

> **Example 1.** An arrangement whereby any license or other use of resulting technology by a private person sponsor is permitted only on the same terms as the charity

would permit that use by an unrelated, nonsponsoring person (i.e., the private person sponsor must pay a competitive price for its use), with the price paid for that use determined when the license or other resulting technology is available for use. Although the charity need not permit persons other than the private person sponsor to use any license or other resulting technology, the price paid by the private person sponsor must be no less than the price that would have been paid by the nonsponsoring person for those same rights.

Example 2. A research agreement relating to property used pursuant to an industry or federally sponsored research arrangement if (1) a single sponsor or multiple sponsors agree to fund governmentally performed basic research; (2) the research to be performed and the manner in which it is to be performed (e.g., selection of the personnel to perform the research) is determined by the charity; (3) title to any patent or other product incidentally resulting from the basic research lies exclusively with the charity; and (4) the sponsor or sponsors are entitled to no more than a nonexclusive, royalty, free license to use the product of any of that research.

The revenue procedure also offers this guidance in applying the operating guidelines to federally sponsored research agreements referred to in Example 2:

In applying the operating guidelines on industry and federally sponsored research agreements of Example 2 to Federally sponsored research, the rights of the Federal Government and its agencies mandated by the Boyh-Dole Act will not cause a research agreement to fail to meet the requirements of Example 2, provided requirements (2) and (3) are met, and the license granted to any party other than the charity or governmental organization to use the product of the research is no more than a nonexclusive royalty-free license. Thus, to illustrate, the existence of the march-in rights or other special rights of the Federal Government or the sponsoring Federal agency mandated by the Boyh-Dole Act will not cause a research agreement to fail to meet the requirements of Example 2, provided that the charity or governmental organization determines the subject and manner of the research is in accordance with requirement (2) of Example 2, the charity or governmental organization retains exclusive title to any patent or other product of the research in accordance with requirement (3) of Example 2 and the nature of any license granted to the Federal Government or the sponsoring Federal agency (or any third-party nongovernmental person) to use the product of the research is no more than a nonexclusive, royalty-free license.

(5) Other Actual or Beneficial Use.   Other actual or beneficial use will be found in any arrangement that conveys special legal entitlements for the beneficial use of exempt property that are comparable to the other examples of special legal entitlements.

(6) Private Business Use of Non-Publicly Available Facilities Includes Special Economic Benefit.   For facilities not publicly available, private business use may also arise from providing, in addition to special legal entitlements, a "special economic benefit" to a private person based on consideration of all the facts and circumstances (even if the private person does not have any special legal entitlement). Factors to be considered in determining whether a special economic benefit exists include: (1) whether the exempt property is functionally related or physically proximate to property used in a private person's trade or business; (2) whether only a small number of private persons received the special economic benefit; and (3) whether any private person treats the exempt property's costs as depreciable.

(7) Unrelated Trade or Business. The use by a charity of bond proceeds in an unrelated trade or business activity is considered private use. An activity is an unrelated trade or business activity if it is (1) a trade or business, (2) regularly carried on, and (3) unrelated to the exempt activities of the charity.

(b) Arbitrage Yield Restrictions and Rebate Requirements

Tax-exempt charitable bonds lose their exempt status if they become arbitrage bonds. Arbitrage occurs when the gross proceeds of a bond issue are used to acquire investments that provide a yield materially higher than the yield on the bonds. Two rules are applied to determine whether the bonds in question have become arbitrage bonds: the yield restriction requirements and the rebate requirements.

(1) Yield Restriction Requirements. If the gross proceeds of a bond issue are invested in a yield materially higher than the yield of the bond issue, the bonds may become arbitrage bonds. Although certain exceptions apply, the term *materially higher* is generally applied to certain types of investments as shown in the next table.

TYPE OF INVESTMENT	MATERIALLY HIGHER
General rule for purpose and nonpurpose investments	$\frac{1}{8}$ of 1 percentage point
Investments in refunding escrow	1/1000 of 1 percentage point
Investment allocable to replacement proceeds	1/1000 of 1 percentage point
Program investments	$1\frac{1}{2}$ percentage points
Student loans	2 percentage points
General rule for investments in tax-exempt bonds	No yield limitation

There are three cases in which materially higher-yielding investments do not result in the bonds being treated as arbitrage bonds:

1. During a temporary period (i.e., generally three year temporary period for capital projects, and 13 months for restricted working capital expenditures)

2. As part of a reasonably required reserve or replacement funds

3. As part of a minor portion (an amount not exceeding the lesser of 5 percent of the sale proceeds of the issue or $100,000).

The determination of whether an issue consists of arbitrage bonds is based on the issuer's reasonable expectations as of the date of the issue. A deliberate or intentional act to earn arbitrage, however, will cause the bonds to become arbitrage bonds if that action, had it been reasonably expected on the issue date, would have caused the bonds to be arbitrage bonds. Intent to violate is not necessary for an action to be viewed as intentional.

(2) Rebate Requirements. If an excess yield is earned on the bonds, arbitrage can be avoided if it is rebated to the U.S. Department of Treasury. The arbitrage that must be rebated is based on the excess of the amount actually earned on nonpurpose investments over the amount that would have been earned if those investments had yield equal to the yield on the bond issue, plus any income attributable to such excess. The future values of all earnings received and payments made with respect to nonpurpose investments are included in determining the amount of the rebate due.

(i) EXCEPTIONS

The next table shows the spending exceptions to the rebate requirements.

SPENDING PERIOD	SPENDING EXCEPTION
6-month spending exception	Gross proceeds of the bond issue are allocated to expenditures for governmental or qualified purposes within 6 months up to the date of issuance
18-month spending exception	Gross proceeds of the bond issue are allocated to expenditures for governmental or qualified purposes incurred within this schedule: (1) 15 percent within 6 months; (2) 60 percent within 12 months; and (3) 100 percent within 18 months
2-year spending exception	Construction issues: When certain available construction proceeds are allocated to construction expenditures within this schedule: (1) 10 percent within 6 months; (2) 45 percent within 12 months; (3) 75 percent within 18 months; and (4) 100 percent within 24 months

(ii) FILING REQUIREMENTS

A form is filed with the IRS to make arbitrage rebate payments, including (1) yield reduction payments; (2) arbitrage rebate payments; (3) penalty in lieu of rebate payments; (4) the termination of the election to pay a penalty in lieu of arbitrage rebate; and (5) penalty for failure to pay arbitrage rebate on time.

A yield reduction payment and/or arbitrage rebate installment payment is required to be paid no later than 60 days after the end of the fifth bond year throughout the term of the bond issue. A payment must be equal to at least 90 percent of the amount due as of the end of the fifth bond year. Upon redemption of a bond issue, a payment of 100 percent of the amount must be paid no later than 60 days after the discharge date.

(c)   Treatment of Hedge Bonds

A bond issue will not qualify as tax-exempt if it is a *hedge bond*. A hedge bond is any part of a bond issue that meets these two elements:

1. The issuer reasonably expects that less than 85 percent of the net proceeds of the issue will be used to finance its qualified purpose within three years of the date the bonds are issued; and

2. Over 50 percent of the proceeds of the issue are invested in nonpurpose investments having a substantially guaranteed yield for four or more years.

There is an exception to the general definition of a hedge bond if at least 95 percent of the net proceeds of the issue are invested in tax-exempt bonds that are not subject to the alternative minimum tax. For this purpose, amounts held in either a bona fide debt service fund or for 30 days or less pending either reinvestment of the proceeds or bond redemption are treated as invested in tax-exempt bonds not subject to the alternative minimum tax. Additionally, a refunding bond issue does not generally consist of hedge bonds if the prior issue met the requirements for tax-exempt status and issuance of the refunding bonds furthers a significant governmental purpose (e.g., realize debt service savings but not to otherwise hedge against future increases in interest rates).

Even if an issue consists of hedge bonds, it will generally still be tax-exempt if two requirements are satisfied:

1. At least 95 percent of the reasonably expected legal and underwriting costs associated with issuing the bonds must be paid within 180 days after the issue date, *and* the payment of such costs must not be contingent on the disbursement of the bond proceeds.

2. The issuer must reasonably expect that the net proceeds of the issue will be allocated to expenditures for governmental or qualified purposes within this schedule:

   ○ 10 percent within one year after the date of issuance

   ○ 30 percent within two years after the date of issuance

   ○ 60 percent within three years after the date of issuance

   ○ 85 percent within five years after the date of issuance

(d) Refunding of Qualified Charitable Bonds

A refunding bond issue is an issue of obligations, the proceeds of which are used to pay principal, interest, or redemption price on another issue (a prior issue), including the issuance cost, accrued interest, capitalized interest on the refunding issue, a reserve or replacement fund, or similar cost, if any, properly allocable to that refunding issue.

Current and advance refunding issues are distinguishable in these ways:

- **Current refunding issue.** A refunding issue that is issued *not more* than 90 days before the last expenditure of any proceeds of the refunding issue for the payment of principal or interest (redemption) on the prior issue

- **Advance refunding issue.** A refunding issue that is issued *more* than 90 days before the final payment of principal or interest (redemption) on the prior issue

Qualified charitable bonds can be current or advance refunded. However, bonds issued after 1985 can only be advance refunded. Refunding bond issues derive their tax-exempt status from the original new money issues that they refund. As such, a refunding issue will generally not be tax-exempt if the refunded issue was not in full compliance with all applicable federal tax law requirements.

§17.2   PREPARATION OF FORM

The preparation of Schedule K is not fully implemented until tax years beginning in 2009. It is also expected that the Schedule K instructions may be revised because of the reporting complexity. For tax years beginning in 2008, only Part I of Schedule K must be completed. Every bond issue of $100,000 or more issued after December 31, 2002, is reported in Schedule K. The bond issues are separately reported in rows A through E in Part I, and information regarding each bond issue is reported in the corresponding Columns A through E in Parts II to IV. Multiple Schedule Ks should be used to account for all bond issues.

(a)   Part I (Bond Issues)

In Part I, report general information for all outstanding bond issues of the organization. The instructions define a *bond issue* as an issue of two or more bonds that are (1) sold at substantially the same time; (2) sold pursuant to the same plan of financing; and (3) payable from the same source of funds. This information can be gathered from Form 8038, Information Return for Tax-Exempt Private Activity Bond Issues. This form is filed at the time of the bond issue.

(1) Columns 1(a) and 1(b) (Issuer Name and EIN).   In Column (a), report the issuer of the bonds, and in Column (b) report the issuer's employer identification number (EIN). The issuer is the entity that issued the bonds, not the charity. Typically this is a state or local government unit. The instructions specify that the information provided in Columns (a) and (b) should be consistent with the corresponding information included on the Form 8038, Part I, lines 1 and 2.

(2) Column (c) (CUSIP—Committee on Uniform Securities Identification Procedures).   In Column (c), report the CUSIP number on the bond with the latest maturity. The CUSIP number should be identical to the number listed on Form 8038, Part I, line 8. The instructions indicate that if the bond issue is not publicly offered, and there is no assigned CUSIP number, then write "None."

(3) Column (d) (Issue Date).   In Column (d), report the issue date as listed on Form 8038, Part I, line 6. The instructions indicate that the issue date generally is the date on which the issuer receives the purchase price in exchange for delivery of the evidence of indebtedness. The instructions further provide that in no event is the issue date earlier than the first day on which interest begins to accrue on the bond for federal income tax purposes.

(4) Column (e) (Issue Price).   In Column (e), report the issue price listed on Form 8038, Part III, line 21(b). The instructions state that if the issue price reported is not identical to the issue price listed in Form 8038, use Schedule O to explain the difference.

(5) Column (f) (Description of Purpose).   In Column (f), report the general description of the bond issue in question. For example, possible entries would include to "construct a hospital," to "construct a research facility" or to "provide funds to refund a prior issue." In the case of a refund of a prior issue, the instructions direct the organization to enter the date of issue for each of the refunded issues (see § 17.1(d)). The instructions also indicate that if the issue is for multiple purposes, such multiple purposes should be included in the Column (f). If the issue financed various projects or activities corresponding to a related purpose, state the purpose only once. For example, if proceeds are used to acquire various items of office equipment, the amount of such expenditures should be aggregated and identified with the stated purpose of "office equipment." Alternatively, if proceeds are used to construct and equip a single facility, the expenditures should be aggregated and identified with the stated purpose of "construct and equip facility" where the identification of the facility is distinguishable from other bond-financed facilities, if any. Use Schedule O if additional space is needed to expand on the purpose.

(6) Column (g) (Defeasance or Refunding Escrow). In Column (g), indicate "yes" or "no" as to whether a defeasance or refunding escrow has been established to irrevocably defease the bond issue. The instructions define a defeasance escrow as an irrevocable escrow established to redeem the bonds on their earliest call date in an amount that, together with investment earnings, is sufficient to pay all of the principal of, and interest and call premiums on, the bonds from the date the escrow was established to the earliest call date. The instructions define a refunding escrow as one or more funds established as part of a single transaction or a series of related transactions, containing proceeds of a refunding issue and any other amounts to provide for payment of principal or interest on one or more prior issues.

(7) Column (h) (On Behalf of Issuer). In Column (h), indicate "yes" or "no" as to whether the organization acted as an "on behalf of issuer" in issuing the bond issue. Answer "no" if the organization only acted as the borrower of the bond proceeds pursuant to a conduit loan with the governmental unit issuing the bonds. The instructions define "on behalf of an issuer" as a situation in which a corporation organized under the general nonprofit corporate law of the state whose obligations are considered obligations of the state or local government unit. An "on behalf of an issuer" situation can also occur in the case of a state authority used specifically to issue tax-exempt bonds in order to further public purposes. In this situation, the filing organization has obligations that are considered obligations of the state or local government, not its own obligations. It appears that this would be an unusual case given that in most cases, the organizations just described would be exempt either as an integral part of the state or local government unit, an instrumentality of the state or local government unit, or otherwise exempt from federal income tax as a governmental entity rather than as a charity.

(b)   Part II (Proceeds) (Optional for 2008)

In Part II of Schedule K, report the allocation of bond proceeds. The allocation impacts a number of issues, including identification of the property owner and use of proceeds for private business use purposes, as well as arbitrage and other tax issues.

(1) Line 1 (Total Proceeds) and Line 2 (Gross Proceeds in Reserve Funds).   On line 1, report the total amount of bond proceeds reported as of the end of the 12-month period used in the Schedule. On line 2, report the gross bond proceeds deposited into the reasonably required reserve or replacement fund, sinking fund or pledged fund.

The term *proceeds* is defined in the instructions as the sale proceeds of an issue and (other than those sales proceeds used to retire bonds of the issue that are not deposited in a reasonably required reserve or replacement fund). Proceeds also include any investment proceeds from the investments that accrued during the project (net of rebate amounts attributable to the project period). There is some confusion as to whether including investment proceeds was proper for this purpose. Because the investment proceeds will vary year to year, the total proceeds number may vary until the project is complete. The instructions indicate that *gross proceeds* generally means any sale proceeds, investment proceeds, transfer proceeds, and replacement proceeds.

(2) Line 3 (Proceeds in Refunding or Defeasance Escrows). On line 3, report the amount of bond proceeds that are deposited into either a refunding or defeasance escrow. For this purpose, proceeds deposited into a refunding escrow are irrevocably pledged to refund a prior bond issue (refunded issue). Unless the amount of the proceeds of the bond issue used to currently or advance refund a prior issue exceeds the amount reported on Form 8038, Part IV, lines 27 and 28 filed with respect to the bond issue, the aggregate amount listed on these lines may be entered here. Also for this purpose, proceeds are typically used to fund the establishment of a defeasance escrow for the purpose of remediating nonqualified bonds. For the definition of a defeasance escrow, see § 17.2(a)(6).

(3) Line 4 (Other Unspent Proceeds). On line 4, report the amount of unspent bond proceeds other than those amounts identified in Part II, lines 2 and 3.

(4) Line 5 (Issuance Costs from Proceeds). On line 5, report bond issuance costs. This amount should include, but not be limited to, underwriter's discount, counsel fees, financial advisor fees, agency fees, trustee fees (agent fees from bond registrars, certification and altercation fees), accounting fees, printing costs for bonds and offering documents, public approval process costs, engineering and feasibility study costs and guarantee fees other than for qualified guarantees. The reporting of bond issuance costs relates to the 2 percent bond issuance limit and this amount is applied against the 5 percent private business use limitation (see § 17.1(a)).

(5) Line 6 (Working Capital Expenditures from Proceeds). On line 6, report the bond proceeds used to finance working capital. A working capital expenditure is any cost that is not a capital expenditure. For example, current operating expenses would be a working capital expenditure. Working capital expenditures are important in determining the proper use of bond proceeds due to minimum capital expenditure requirements for some bond issues (see § 17.2(b)(6)). This amount can also be relevant in the analysis of whether all of the bond proceeds have been spent. Unspent bond proceeds can cause perpetual arbitrage and other issues.

(6) Line 7 (Capital Expenditures from Proceeds). On line 7, report capital expenditures, including costs incurred to acquire, construct or improve land, buildings, and equipment. The level of capital expenditures relative to the working capital amounts is important to comply with minimum capital expenditure requirements depending on the type of bond issue. For example, a qualified small issue bond requires that 95 percent or more of the net proceeds are to be used to finance capital expenditures.

(7) Line 8 (Year of Substantial Completion). On line 8, report the year in which construction, acquisition, or rehabilitation of the financed project was substantially completed. The instructions indicate that a project may be treated as substantially completed when, based on all the facts and circumstances, the project has reached a degree of completion that would permit its operation at substantially its design level and it is, in fact, in operation as such. If the bond issue in question financed multiple projects, the year reported is the latest year in which construction, acquisition, or rehabilitation of each of the financed projects was substantially completed. If the bond issue financed working capital expenses, provide the latest year in which the proceeds of the issue are allocable to these expenditures. Note that it may not always be clear when a project has reached a degree of completion under the definition. In some cases the construction may be complete and all the bond proceeds spent but the project has still not reached an occupation level that permits operation at "substantially its design level."

(8) Line 9 (Current Refunding Issue). Beginning on line 9 and continuing through line 12, "yes/no" questions are asked. On line 9, indicate "yes" or "no" as to whether the bonds issued were part of a *current refunding issue*. The instructions define a *refunding issue* as an issue of obligations, the proceeds of which are used to pay principal, interest, or redemption price on another issue (a prior issue), including the issuance costs, accrued interests, capitalized interest on the refunding issue, a reserve or replacement fund or similar costs, if any, properly allocable to that refunding issue. A current refunding issue is a refunding issue that is issued not more than 90 days before the last expenditure of any proceeds of the refunding issue for the payment of principal or interest on the prior issue (see § 17.1(d)).

(9) Line 10 (Advance Refunding Issue). On line 10, indicate "yes" or "no" as to whether the bonds were part of an *advanced refunding issue*. An *advance refunding issue* is a refunding issue that is not a current refunding issue (see § 17.1(d)).

(10) Lines 11 and 12 (Allocation of Proceeds and Books and Records). On line 11, indicate "yes" or "no" as to whether a final allocation of proceeds has been made. On line 12, indicate "yes" or "no" as to whether the organization maintains adequate books and records to support the final allocation of proceeds. The final allocations impact the private business use analysis, use of funds analysis, and other issues. Maintaining adequate documentation of the allocation will be important in establishing use of proceeds and maintaining private business use at required levels. For example, the allocation will identify which portions of a facility are bond financed and which portions are not. If final allocations are not carefully prepared and documented, it will be difficult for the charity to claim that a portion of the facility can be used for private business use. For example, a portion of a hospital facility may be carved out of the bond financing so a joint venture with physicians can be conducted there.

(c) Part III (Private Business Use)

In Part III, Schedule K "yes/no" questions are asked and certain information is requested regarding the bond issues reported in Part I. Refunding bonds for a pre-January 1, 2003, issues are not reported in Part III. A refunding bond issue for this purpose also includes allocations and treatment of bonds of a multipurpose issue as a separate refunding issue. The ''yes/no'' questions relate to transactions that can result in private business use (see § 17.1(a)).

(1) Line 1 (Participation in Partnerships). On line 1, indicate ''yes'' or ''no'' as to whether the organization participated as a partner in a partnership or as a member in a limited liability company that owned bond-financed property. Participation in a partnership can result in private use depending on the activity of the partnership and whether the other partners are charities, governmental entities, or private persons. If a partnership has for-profit partners, private use will result; if the partnership conducts unrelated business income activities, private use will result.

(2) Line 2 (Lease Arrangements). On line 2, indicate ''yes'' or ''no'' as to whether the organization is involved in a lease arrangement that may result in private use. The instructions indicate that the answer to this question should be ''yes'' if the tenants are private parties rather than governmental organizations or charities. In some cases, private business use can result even if the property is leased to governmental organizations and/or charities.

(3) Line 3a (Management Agreements). On line 3a, indicate ''yes'' or ''no'' as to whether the organization has entered into any management or service contracts, effective at any time during the tax year with respect to bond-financed property. The instructions clarify that the answer should be ''yes'' even if it has determined that the management agreement meets the safe harbor available under the revenue procedure. The analysis of whether a management or service contract results in private business use is based on all the facts and circumstances. Generally, if compensation is rendered based, in whole or in part, on a share of net earnings, private business use will result. Compensation based in part on gross proceeds may be permissible in certain circumstances under IRS safe harbors (see § 17.1(a)(3)). In general, the longer the term of the management agreement, the smaller the portion of the management fee that can be tied to a percentage of gross proceeds.

(4) Line 3b (Research Agreements). On line 3b, indicate ''yes'' or ''no'' as to whether the organization has entered into any research agreements effective at any time during the tax year with respect to the bond-financed property that may result in private business use. For this purpose, answer ''yes'' even if the organization has determined that the contract meets the safe harbor under the revenue procedure. Like management contracts, this analysis is based on all the facts and circumstances. If the research agreement results in the sponsor treated as the leasee or owner of the financed property, private business use will result. Certain research agreements are permissible under IRS safe harbors. One example is an arrangement with a private sponsor whereby any license or the use of any resulting technology by a private sponsor is permitted only on the same terms as the charity would permit that use by an unrelated, nonsponsoring person (i.e., the private person sponsor must pay a competitive price for its use), with the price paid for that use determined when the license or other resulting technology is available for use (see § 17.1(a)(4)).

(5) Line 3c (Counsel Review of Agreements). On line 3c, indicate ''yes'' or ''no'' as to whether the organization requires bond counsel or other outside counsel to review management or service contracts or research agreements. The instructions state that if there are no such agreements enter "None". This reporting goes to whether the organization exercised due diligence in review of its agreements to ensure that it is compliant. This is another example of the IRS's encouragement of good governance and corporate best practices.

(6) Line 4 (Private Use Percentage). On line 4, report the average percentage of the bond-financed facility that was used by entities other than charities and governmental organizations. The average percentage should be reported to the nearest tenth of a percentage point (i.e., 8.9 percent). For this purpose, do not report use relating to a management contract or research agreement that meets a safe harbor provided in the respective revenue procedures (see § 17.1(a)(3) and (a)(4)). The percentage of private use may be very difficult to ascertain in some cases, and the reporting of the number for any one year could be misleading. For example, if both buildings and equipment are financed with bonds, how is the percentage reported if both assets are part of the same issue? Perhaps a blended percentage of private use should be inserted? Further, a reporting of private use in excess of 5 percent in any one year is not prohibited because private use is measured over the life of the bonds.

(7) Line 5 (Unrelated Trade or Business Activity). On line 5, report the average percentage of bond-financed property used in an unrelated trade or business activity carried on by the filing organization, another charity, or a state or local government. Report the percentage to the nearest tenth of a percentage point (e.g., 8.9 percent). For this purpose, do not report use relating to a management contract or research agreement that meets a safe harbor provided in the respective revenue procedures (see §§ 17.1(a)(3) and (a)(4)).

(8) Line 6 (Total Private Use Percentages). On line 6, the total of lines 4 and 5 is entered.

(9) Line 7 (Bond Compliance Policies). On line 7, indicate "yes" or "no" as to whether the organization has adopted management practices and procedures to ensure that the post-issuance compliance of its tax-exempt bonds. The instructions indicate that this question should be answered only with respect to the applicable tax year. Like the question in line 3c, this question is asked to encourage compliance, accountability, and good governance. Again, this is part of the IRS's encouragement of corporate best practices.

(d) Part IV (Arbitrage)

In Part IV, report information relative to whether the bonds result in prohibited arbitrage. Arbitrage occurs if the unused bond proceeds are invested at a yield higher than the yield paid on the bonds. If arbitrage occurs, it must be rebated back to the government.

(1) Line 1 (Filing of Form 8038-T). On line 1, indicate "yes" or "no" as to whether Form 8038-T, Arbitrage Rebate, Yield Restriction and Penalty in Lieu of Arbitrage

Rebate, has been filed with respect to the bond issue. This form is filed to remit rebate payments.

(2) Line 2 (Variable Rate Issue).   On line 2, indicate "yes" or "no" as to whether the bond is a variable rate issue. The instructions indicate that a variable rate issue is an issue that contains a bond that has a yield that is not fixed and determinable on the issue date.

(3) Lines 3a, 3b, and 3c (Hedge Bond).   On line 3a, indicate "yes" or "no" as to whether the charitable organization or the governmental issuer identified a hedge with respect to the bond issue on its books and records. In general, a hedge is a financial mechanism used to avoid the interest fluctuation risk on a variable rate bond. A hedge may be entered into before, at the same time, or after the date of issue. In general, payments made or received by a governmental issuer or borrower of bond proceeds under a qualified hedge are taken into account to determine the yield on the bond issue. The IRS requests this information because hedge arrangements can be abusive in some cases. If the answer to line 3a is "yes," enter the name of the provider of the hedge and the term of the hedge to the nearest tenth of a year (e.g., 2.4 years) on lines 3b and 3c.

(4) Lines 4a, 4b, 4c, and 4d (Gross Proceeds Invested in a GIC).   On line 4a, indicate "yes" or "no" as to whether the gross proceeds of the bond issue were invested in a guaranteed investment contract (GIC). A GIC includes any nonpurpose investment that has specifically negotiated withdrawal or reinvestment provisions and a specifically negotiated interest rate, and also includes any agreement to supply investments on two or more dates (i.e., a forward supply contract). In general, GICs are used to avoid arbitrage by fixing an investment rate. If the answer to line 4a is "yes," enter the name of the provider of the GIC on line 4b, the term of the GIC to the nearest tenth of a year on line 4c, and indicate whether the regulatory safe harbor for establishing fair market value is provided on line 4d. Like hedges, GICs are sometimes viewed as abusive arrangements.

(5) Line 5 (Investment of Gross Proceeds).   On line 5, indicate "yes" or "no" as to whether any gross proceeds were invested beyond a temporary period. The regulations provide certain exceptions known as the three-year temporary period allocable to proceeds spent on expenditures for capital projects or the 13-month temporary period applicable to proceeds spent on working capital expenditures (see § 17.1(b)(1)).

(6) Line 6 (Exceptions to Rebate).   On line 6, indicate "yes" or "no" as to whether the bond issue qualified for an exception to rebate. Exceptions to rebate include the 6-month, 18-month, or 2-year spending exceptions provided in the regulations (see § 17.1(b)(2)).

§ 17.3   SCHEDULE K COMPLIANCE TASKS

For purposes of preparing Schedule K, consider these 16 compliance tasks:

1. **Locate bond issue binder.** Locate bond binders containing all bond issue documents for all bond issues.

2. **Locate Form 8038s.** Locate all Forms 8038s, Information Return for Tax-Exempt Private Activity, filed for all bond issues. This is the information needed for Part I.

3. **Locate Form 8038-Ts.** Locate all annual forms filed for reporting of arbitrage rebates.

4. **Review management agreement and service provider agreements.** Review all management agreements and service provider agreements to ensure compliance.

5. **Develop a management agreement and service provider agreement policy.** Develop a management agreement and service provider agreement policy to conform agreement to the safe harbors of the revenue procedure.

6. **Review research agreements.** Review all research agreements to ensure compliance.

7. **Develop research agreement policy.** Develop a research agreement policy to conform to the safe harbors of the revenue procedure.

8. **Review hedges and guaranteed investment contracts.** Review all hedges and guaranteed investment contracts to ensure compliance.

9. **Identify allocation of proceeds.** Review allocation of proceeds for preparation of Schedule K and to identify which parts of the facilities are bond-financed for private use and other purposes.

10. **Develop bond compliance policy.** Develop policies and procedures to ensure compliance including private use and arbitrage provisions.

11. **Add bond provisions to document retention policy.** Document retention policies should include bond document retention provisions.

12. **Identify partnerships.** Identify all partnership arrangements to determine if any partnership activity is housed in a bond-financed facility.

13. **Add bond provisions to joint venture policy.** Joint venture policies should have checklist to ensure a bond-financed facility does not house a joint venture with private parties.

14. **Identify leases.** Identify all leases of bond-financed equipment and facilities. If lessees are not charities or governmental organizations, the leases may have to be restructured.

15. **Identify unrelated trade or business.** Identify all activities operated in the bond-financed facility that may be unrelated trades or businesses.

16. **Review investments of bond proceeds.** Review investments of bond proceeds to determine if arbitrage exists.

Schedule L—Transactions with Interested Persons

Schedule L of the new Form 990 requests information from tax-exempt organizations regarding their transactions with interested persons, which generally include its officers, directors, trustees, key employees, and substantial contributors. Schedule L is intended to provide a concentrated report of all of an exempt organization's transactions with interested persons. In addition, Schedule L is used in part to determine whether a member of the organization's governing body is an independent member for purposes of Form 990, Part VI, line 1b.

§ 18.1 LAW AND POLICY

Schedule L requires a tax-exempt organization to report information regarding its excess benefit transactions, loans to and from interested persons, grants or assistance benefitting interested persons, and business transactions involving interested persons. Each of these types of transactions is discussed in this chapter. In some instances, an interested person may also be a related party, in which case certain transactions would be reported on both Schedule L and Schedule R (Related Organizations and Unrelated Partnerships).

There are no filing thresholds on Schedule L for excess benefit transactions, loans with interested persons, and grants or assistance benefiting interested persons. Business transactions with interested persons are reportable only if the transactions are over certain thresholds set forth in § 18.1(d)(1). The definition of *interested person* varies depending on which part of Schedule L an organization is completing.

(a) Excess Benefit Transactions

The *intermediate sanctions* rules impose a series of excise taxes on *disqualified persons* (generally, the organization's insiders) who engaged in transactions with certain types of tax-exempt organizations in which the disqualified person impermissibly benefits from the transaction. The excise taxes are also imposed on certain managers of the organization who participated in the transaction knowing that it was improper.

Transactions to which the intermediate sanctions taxes are applied are called *excess benefit transactions*. In general, an excess benefit transaction is a transaction in which an economic benefit is provided by an applicable tax-exempt organization, directly or indirectly, to or for the use of a disqualified person, and the value of the economic benefit provided by the organization exceeds the value of the consideration (including the performance of services) received for providing the benefit. The difference between the value provided by the exempt organization and the consideration (if any) it received from the disqualified person is an *excess benefit*. The intermediate sanctions excise taxes are applied to the amount of the excess benefit derived by the disqualified person from the transaction. Examples of an excess benefit transaction are excessive compensation paid to an organization's chief executive and an above-market rental fee paid to a director.

The intermediate sanctions apply only to tax-exempt public charities and social welfare organizations, or such organizations that had this status any time during the five-year period ending on the date of the excess benefit transaction. The intermediate sanctions excise taxes are generally meant to be applied in lieu of revocation of the exempt status of these entities. The sanctions are called *intermediate* because they fall between the IRS's choices of revoking an organization's tax-exempt status and taking no action at all.

The intermediate sanctions rules entail an initial tax, which is 25 percent of the excess benefit, payable by the disqualified person or persons involved. Organizational managers who were knowingly involved in the transaction are subject to a 10 percent excise tax, unless the participation was not willful and was due to reasonable cause. The rules require that an excess benefit transaction be *corrected*. (See § 6.1(b)(9).) Correction involves placing the parties in the same economic position they were in before the transaction was entered into, which generally involves undoing the transaction. If the initial tax is not timely paid and the transaction is not timely and properly corrected, an additional tax equal to 200 percent of the excess benefit may be imposed.

For a more complete discussion of excess benefit transactions and the intermediate sanctions, see § 6.1(b).

(b) Loans with Interested Persons

Unlike private foundations, most public charities and tax-exempt noncharitable organizations generally are not prohibited from entering into loan transactions with its interested persons. Loans may be made, for example, in the employment setting to provide assistance to a nonprofit executive relocating from another area to perform services for the exempt entity. Loans of this nature are reportable on Schedule L but are generally not prohibited (except as provided in § 18.1(b)(1)), provided the terms of the loan are fair and reasonable to the exempt organization.

(1) Prohibitions on Loans to Interested Persons for Certain Organizations. Certain charitable organizations are restricted from making loans to their interested persons. Private foundations, by virtue of the self-dealing rules, are generally prohibited from engaging in loan transactions with their disqualified persons. Supporting organizations are barred from making loans to any substantial contributor to the organization, a member of the family of a substantial contributor, or an entity that is 35-percent controlled by a substantial contributor or the family of a substantial contributor. In addition, supporting organizations are prohibited from making loans to persons in a position to exercise substantial influence over the affairs of the organization, which include its directors, trustees, chief executive officer, and chief financial officer, and persons and entities related to these persons. Examples of prohibited loans are a supporting organization's loan to one of its directors or a salary advance to the organization's chief executive officer. If a supporting organization makes such a loan, the loan is treated as an automatic excess benefit transaction (see § 18.1(a)) and the entire loan amount is subject to the intermediate sanctions excise taxes.

Similarly, loans from a donor-advised fund to a person that is, with respect to the fund, a donor, donor-advisor, or a family member or 35-percent controlled entity of a donor or donor-advisor are prohibited. If amounts are loaned from a donor-advised fund in this manner, the loan is treated as an automatic excess benefit transaction (§ 18.1(a)), and the entire loan amount is subject to the intermediate sanctions excise taxes. In addition, many states have enacted laws that ban or limit loans from nonprofit organizations to their officers and directors.

(2) Entering into Loans with Interested Persons. Outside the private foundation, supporting organization, and donor-advised fund context, federal tax law allows tax-exempt organizations to enter into a loan transaction with an interested person, provided the terms of the loan are reasonable. An interested person may make a loan to a tax-exempt organization and the exempt organization can pay interest with respect to the loan, provided the interest rate is not excessive. If the interest rate on the loan is above market, the loan may result in private inurement (§ 6.1(a)). In addition, a loan with an excessive interest rate from an interested person to a public charity or social welfare organization is an excess benefit transaction (§ 18.1(a)), with the interested person benefitting from the above-market interest rate. An interested person generally may loan funds to an exempt organization at or below a market interest rate without running afoul of these rules. The interest rate on the loan, however, unless nominal, should be well documented to establish that it is not excessive.

A tax-exempt organization, unless specifically barred, generally may loan funds to an interested person. For example, an exempt organization may make a loan to an interested person as part of an executive compensation package. Loans of this nature need to bear interest at a market rate, so that the interested person is not benefiting from a below-market interest rate loan, or the exempt organization needs to treat the below-market interest rate as part of the interested person's compensation in exchange for services and contemporaneously document the compensatory element of the loan. Below-market interest rate loans from an exempt organization to an interested person may result in private inurement and/or an excess benefit transaction if not properly documented and reported, or if the circumstances surrounding the loan are not reasonable.

Prior to entering into a loan transaction with an interested person, charities and social welfare organizations should consider following the steps of the rebuttable presumption of reasonableness (§ 6.1(b)(8)) to help insulate the transaction from the intermediate sanctions. In addition, all tax-exempt organizations should determine whether the loan would be prohibited under state law.

For purposes of reporting loans on Schedule L, *interested persons* are an organization's current or former officers, directors, trustees, key employees, and five highest-compensated employees listed on Part VII, Section A of Form 990. For public charities and social welfare organizations, *interested persons* also include any person who was, at any time during the five-year period ending on the date of such transaction, in a position to exercise substantial influence over the affairs of the organization, and family members and 35-percent controlled entities of such persons. If the filing organization is a supporting organization, then its substantial contributors, their families, and their 35-percent controlled entities are also interested persons. For Form 990-EZ filers, interested persons are current officers, directors, trustees, and key employees listed in Part IV of Form 990.

A loan does not have to be subject to an agreement or otherwise be in writing to be classified as a loan. Thus, an undocumented advance, such as a salary advance, can be a loan. Loans to interested persons for Schedule L reporting purposes do not include excess benefit transactions, advances under an accountable plan, pledges receivable that would qualify as charitable contributions when paid, accrued but unpaid compensation owed by the organization, loans from a credit union made to an interested person on the same terms as offered to other members of the credit union, and receivables outstanding that were created in the ordinary course of the organization's business on the same terms as offered to the general public (such as receivables for medical services provided by a hospital to an officer of the hospital).

(3) Discouragement of Interested Person Loans by the IRS and Others.   The prevailing view of good governance principles is that tax-exempt organizations should not make loans to interested persons, even though such loans are not prohibited. The IRS, in its instructions to the first draft of the redesigned Form 990, stated that it was concerned that loan arrangements with insiders, although they may be permissible, "may be used to disguise compensation or [used] for improper purposes."

The Panel on the Nonprofit Sector, in its "Principles for Good Governance and Ethical Practice," states that a charitable organization should not provide loans (or loan equivalents such as loan guarantees, the purchase or transfer of ownership of a residence or office, or the relief of a debt or lease obligation) to directors, officers, or trustees. The Panel states that while there may be circumstances in which a charitable organization finds it necessary to offer loans to staff members, "there is no justification for making loans to board members." The Panel, in its 2005 report to Congress entitled "Strengthening Transparency, Governance, Accountability of Charitable Organizations," suggested that Congress enact legislation prohibiting charities from making loans to board members. Although Congress did not enact the suggested legislation, other than prohibiting certain loans by supporting organizations and donor-advised funds, the IRS and nonprofit watchdog organizations discourage these types of loans for all exempt organizations. In addition, many states have enacted laws to ban loans by nonprofit organizations to their officers, directors and others.

If a tax-exempt organization decides to engage in a loan transaction with an interested person, it should follow the procedures of its conflicts-of-interest policy in approving the loan. It should also provide documentation for the loan, in board minutes or otherwise, that evidences that the terms of the loan are reasonable and are fair to the exempt organization.

(c)   Grants or Assistance Benefiting Interested Persons

In the normal course of engaging in exempt activities, a tax-exempt organization may find that it wishes to give a grant or assistance to interested persons. Because of the person's relationship with the organization, transactions of this nature are subject to higher IRS scrutiny. Exempt organizations must ensure that the interested person is not receiving a grant or assistance from the organization because of the person's position with the organization or relationship to an individual affiliated with the organization. In addition, as discussed in § 18.1(c)(2), supporting organizations and donor-advised funds are prohibited from making grants to interested persons.

(1) Interested Persons. For purposes of reporting grants or assistance to interested persons on Schedule L to the Form 990, an *interested person* is an officer, director, trustee, or key employee listed in Form 990, Part VII, Section A, a substantial contributor, or a related person. For this purpose, a *substantial contributor* is a person who contributed at least $5,000 during the organization's tax year and is required to be reported by name in Schedule B. (See § 14.3(e).) A *related person* is

- A member of the organization's selection committee

- A family member of any of the organization's current or former officers, directors, trustees, or key employees listed in Part VII, Section A of the Form 990, substantial contributors, or members of the organization's selection committee

- A 35-percent controlled entity of any of the organization's current or former officers, directors, trustees, or key employees listed in Part VII, Section A of the Form 990, substantial contributors, or members of the organization's selection committee

- An employee (or child of an employee) of a substantial contributor or of a 35-percent controlled entity of a substantial contributor but only if the employee (or child of the employee) received the grant or assistance by the direction or advice of the substantial contributor or 35-percent controlled entity, or pursuant to a program funded by the substantial contributor that was intended primarily to benefit such employees or their children.

The phrase *grants or assistance benefiting interested persons* does not include excess benefit transactions, loans to or from interested persons, business transactions that do not contain any gift element and are engaged in to serve the direct and immediate needs of the organization, such as the payment of compensation (including taxable and nontaxable fringe benefits treated as compensation) to an employee or consultant in exchange for services of comparable value, or grants to employees (and their children) of a substantial contributor or 35-percent controlled entity of a substantial contributor, awarded on an objective and nondiscriminatory basis based on preestablished criteria and reviewed by a selection committee. (See § 18.1(c)(3).) The phrase also does not include certain grants and assistance awarded to an interested person as a member of the class of persons the organization is intended to benefit. See § 18.1(c)(4) for a discussion of this exception.

In the context of charitable organizations, the individuals who are to benefit from a charitable activity must be sufficiently large or indefinite to constitute a charitable class. Charitable status will be denied where a charity's activities are intended to benefit, for example, solely the relatives of its donors. Beneficiaries designated by geographic restriction or by age, such as children or the elderly, however, can be a charitable class. Whether or not a class is sufficiently large to constitute a charitable class is typically a matter of degree. It is not unusual for interested persons to be members of a charitable class. For example, a director whose daughter suffers from a particular affliction may serve as a director of a charity working to find a cure for the disease. In this instance, an interested person (the daughter of the director) is a member of the charitable class that the charity benefits. Even so, a grant to the director's daughter, in certain instances, may be excluded from Schedule L reporting. See § 18.1(c)(4) for a discussion of exceptions to reporting.

In determining whether to award a grant or assistance to an interested person, tax-exempt organizations must carefully document the selection process used to determine the interested person is part of the class intended to be benefited. In making this determination, any person related to the interested person should recuse himself or herself from the selection process that determines whether the interested person should receive a grant or assistance.

(2) Donor-Advised Fund and Supporting Organization Prohibition on Grants to Interested Persons. Following the enactment of the Pension Protection Act of 2006, donor-advised funds and supporting organizations are subject to new restrictions on their grants. Donor-advised funds may not make grants to natural persons. A grant to a natural person is treated as a taxable distribution from a donor-advised fund. In addition, a grant to a donor, a donor-advisor, or a family member or 35-percent controlled entity of a donor or donor-advisor is treated as an automatic excess benefit transaction (§ 18.1(a)), with the entire grant amount subject to the intermediate sanctions excise taxes. In addition, the grant would have to be *corrected*, which would involve repayment of the grant to the donor-advised fund. Similarly, supporting organizations may not make grants to a substantial contributor, a family member of a substantial contributor, or a business that is 35-percent controlled by a substantial contributor or members of the substantial contributor's family. Grants of this nature are also treated as automatic excess benefit transactions, with the grant subject to excise taxes and correction.

(3) Awarding Grants on an Objective and Nondiscriminatory Basis. In the private foundation context, there is a body of law regarding whether grants to individuals are made on *an objective and nondiscriminatory basis.* All tax-exempt organizations can meaningfully employ these rules to help avoid the appearance that grants or assistance from the organization favor interested persons. In addition, the Form 990 instructions specifically state that grants to a substantial contributor's employees and their children awarded under these rules are not considered grants to interested persons for purposes of Schedule L. Presumably, this exclusion is meant to apply to grants from charities that are, to a certain extent, employer-funded, such as scholarships or disaster relief grants from charities that are partially funded by an employer.

For grants to be considered awarded on an objective and nondiscriminatory basis, the selection of grantees must be from a group of individuals that are chosen on the basis of criteria that reasonably relates to the purpose of the grant and generally is from a group that is sufficiently broad to constitute a charitable class. Selection from a group, however, is not necessary where taking into account the purposes of the grant, one or several persons are selected because they are exceptionally qualified to carry out the organization's purposes or it is otherwise evident that the selection is particularly calculated to effectuate the purpose of the grant rather than to benefit particular persons or a particular class of persons. For example, the selection of a qualified research scientist, who is also an interested person, for a particular project should be allowable even though the organization selects him from a group of three scientists who are experts in the field.

In addition, the method of selecting the grantees must be related to the purpose of the grant. For example, in granting academic scholarships, an organization's selection criteria might include prior academic performance, performance on aptitude tests, recommendations from instructors, financial need, and the conclusion the committee has drawn from a personal interview as to the individual's motivation, character, ability, and potential. Last, the persons or group of persons who select recipients of the grants should not be in a position to derive a private benefit, directly or indirectly, if certain potential grantees are selected over others.

(4) Exemption for Benefits Received as a Member of the Benefited Class. The Form 990 instructions provide an exception to reporting interested person transactions for grants or assistance provided to an interested person as a member of the charitable class or other class (such as a member of a trade association or social club) that the organization intends to benefit in furtherance of its exempt purpose, if provided on similar terms as provided to other members of the class. For example, a grant from a charity to the child of a director for short-term disaster relief or trauma counseling is excludable from reporting if provided to the child as a member of the charitable class the organization intends to benefit in furtherance of its purposes and is made on similar terms as grants that are provided to other members of the class. If, however, the interested person receives a grant for travel, study, or other similar purposes, such as a grant to achieve a specific objective, produce a report or other similar product, or improve or enhance a literary, artistic, musical, scientific, teaching, or other similar capacity, skill, or talent of the grantee, then the grant is not excluded from being reported in Part III.

(5) Reasonable Effort to Determine Interested Person Grants and Assistance. The final Form 990 instructions add a reasonable effort provision for determining grants and other assistance awarded to interested persons. Pursuant to the instructions, an organization is not required to provide information about a grant or assistance if an interested person is unable to secure the information regarding interested person status after making a *reasonable effort* to obtain it. An example of a reasonable effort is for the tax-exempt organization to distribute a questionnaire annually to each interested person (see § 18.1(c)(1) for the definition of *interested person*) that includes the name, title, date, and signature of each person reporting information and contains the pertinent instructions and definitions for Part III of Schedule L.

Filing organizations are not expected to distribute the questionnaire to a substantial contributor (see § 18.1(c)(1)) or a related person to a substantial contributor, except (i) where the substantial contributor or the related person advises the organization as to the specific recipients of grants or assistance, or (2) with respect to programs of the organization intended primarily to benefit employees (or their children) of the substantial contributor or their 35-percent controlled entities. The IRS, in the Form 990 instructions, gives an example of this rule. In the example, a substantial contributor to a tax-exempt organization states that he would like Mr. X and Ms. Y to be beneficiaries of a grant. The organization asks the substantial contributor whether Mr. X and Ms. Y are interested persons with respect to the organization because of a family or business relationship they have with the substantial contributor (using the pertinent instructions and definitions). The substantial contributor replies in writing that the potential grantees are not interested persons. Whether Mr. X and Ms. Y are actually interested persons or not, the organization has made a reasonable effort in this situation. Thus, presumably, the IRS would not impose a penalty against the filing organization for failure to disclose the grant as an interested person grant in Part III of Schedule L to Form 990, even if the grant was, in fact, made to an interested person.

(d) Business Transactions with Interested Persons, Including Revenue-Sharing

Tax-exempt organizations often engage in business transactions with interested persons. Because of the interested person's affiliation with the organization, he or she may be best suited to provide services to the organization or may offer the best rate due to giving a discount to the organization. Because of the interested person's relationship with the organization, however, there is potential for the interested person to benefit from the transaction.

The new Form 990 requires increased reporting of business transactions with interested persons to give the IRS information regarding the circumstances surrounding these transactions. Because an interested person is typically in a position to influence the decisions of an exempt organization, business transactions with interested persons are subject to an increased level of IRS reporting.

Transactions with interested persons must be engaged in to further the purposes of the tax-exempt organization. Exempt organizations are not prohibited from engaging in business transactions with interested persons, but the transactions must be reasonable. The interested person cannot unduly benefit from the transaction, otherwise the transaction can result in private inurement (§ 6.1(a)) and/or cause an excess benefit transaction (§ 6.1(b)) to have occurred. An exempt organization should follow the procedures of its conflicts-of-interest policy in approving transactions with interested persons.

(1) Business Transactions and Reporting Threshold. For Form 990 reporting purposes, the phrase *business transactions with interested persons* includes, but is not limited to, contracts of sale, lease, license, and performance of services, whether initiated during the organization's tax year or ongoing from a prior year. Business transactions also include joint ventures, whether new or ongoing, in which the profits or capital interest of the organization and the interested person each exceeds 10 percent. An organization's charging of membership dues to its officers, directors, and other interested persons is not a business transaction, presumably because this transaction does not differ from the organization's transactions with its members who are not interested persons. Excess benefit transactions, loans, or grants and other assistance to or with interested persons are not *business transactions with interested persons* and should be reported elsewhere on Schedule L.

The draft instructions distinguished between a direct business transaction and an indirect business transaction. *Direct business transactions* occur directly between the interested person and the tax-exempt organization. Examples of direct business transactions are the lease by the exempt organization of office space in a building owned by an interested person or an exempt organization's contract with an interested person for the provision of goods or services to the exempt organization. *Indirect business transactions* are transactions between a tax-exempt organization and persons who are related to an interested person, and are therefore themselves considered interested persons. (See § 18.1(c)(2) for a definition of the term *interested person.*) In the final Form 990 instructions, the IRS eliminates the distinction between direct and indirect business transactions but retains the concept by the manner in which it defines *interested person.*

An organization is not required to report business transactions with interested persons if the dollar amount does not exceed the greater of $10,000 or 1 percent of the organization's total revenue for the organization's tax year, except in either of these two cases (in which case reporting is required):

1.   Total payments for all transactions between the parties during the organization's tax year exceeded $100,000 (regardless of the amount of the individual transactions).

2.   The transaction was the organization's payment of compensation to a family member of a current officer, director, trustee, or key employee of the organization (if payment of the compensation is greater than $10,000 for the organization's tax year).

If the payments under an arrangement exceed the organization's reporting threshold, the business transaction is reportable regardless of when the parties entered into the transaction. An exempt organization should treat all payments during the year between the parties under the same contract or transaction as a single reportable business transaction. For example, if a director of a tax-exempt organization is a greater than 5 percent partner of a law firm (or greater than 5 percent shareholder of a professional corporation) and the exempt organization pays the law firm an amount that is more than 1 percent of the organization's total revenue during the organization's tax year (and the amount exceeds $10,000) under a contract for a particular case or legal matter, the filing organization should treat all payments under the arrangement as a single reportable business transaction. A filing organization may choose to aggregate multiple individual transactions between the same parties or list them separately. If the organization chooses to aggregate the transactions, it must list the various types of transactions even though it may aggregate the amount of the transactions.

(2) Interested Persons.   *Interested persons* for purposes of reporting business transactions are the filing organization's current officers, directors, trustees, and key employees that are required to be listed in Part VII, Section A of Form 990. In addition, the term *interested person* includes family members of these interested persons and an entity that is more than 35 percent owned, directly or indirectly, individually or collectively, by interested persons and/or their family members. *Interested person* also includes an entity (other than a tax-exempt entity) of which a current or former officer, director, trustee, or key employee listed in Form 990, Part VII, Section A was serving at the time of the transaction as an officer, a director, a trustee, a key employee, a partner, or member with an ownership interest in excess of 5 percent if the entity is treated as a partnership, or a shareholder with an ownership interest in excess of 5 percent if the entity is a professional corporation.

Ownership is measured by stock ownership (either voting power or value, whichever is greater) of a corporation, profits or capital interest (whichever is greater) in a partnership or limited liability company, beneficial interest in a trust, or control of a nonprofit organization. Ownership includes indirect ownership, such as ownership in an entity that has ownership in the entity doing business with the organization, and there may be ownership through multiple tiers of entities. Constructive ownership rules apply for this purpose to attribute ownership by family members and related entities to an interested person. For example, stock owned by an interested person's parents is attributed to the interested person for purposes of determining the interested person's stock ownership in a corporation.

The draft Form 990 instructions contained a large board exception for determining an organization's interested persons. Under the exception, if an organization had more than 20 voting members of its governing body and delegated authority to an executive committee, it could disregard as interested persons all current and former directors and trustees who were not currently members of the executive committee or officers, key employees, or the highest-compensated employees of the organization. The final instructions omitted the large board exception in favor of a reasonable effort standard for determining interested persons. See § 18.1(d)(3) for a description of the reasonable effort standard.

The final instructions to Schedule L provide seven examples of business transactions with interested persons.

> **Example 1.** T, a family member of an officer of the organization, serves as an employee of the organization and receives during the organization's tax year compensation of $15,000, which is not more than 1% of the organization's total revenue. The organization is required to report T's compensation as a business transaction in Part IV of Schedule L because T's compensation to a family member of an officer exceeds $10,000, unless T's compensation was already reported in Part VII of Form 990.

> **Example 2.** X, the child of a current director who is an interested person, is a first-year associate at a law partnership. The filing organization pays $150,000 to the law firm during the organization's tax year. Because X has no ownership interest in the law firm and is not an officer, director, trustee, or key employee of the law firm, the organization is not required to report the business transaction.

> **Example 3.** Same facts as in Example 2, except that X is a partner of the law firm and has an ownership interest in the law firm of 5.25% of the profits. The organization must report the business transaction due to X's greater than 5% ownership interest in the law firm and because the dollar amount is in excess of the $100,000 threshold.

> **Example 4.** Same facts as in Example 3, except that the law firm entered into the transaction with the organization before X's parent became a director of the organization. The organization must report all payments made during its tax year to the law firm for the transaction.

> **Example 5.** Same facts as in Example 3, except that X is the child of a former director listed in Part VII, Section A of Form 990. The organization is required to report the business transaction because X, as a family member of a former director listed in Form 990, Part VII, is an interested person.

Example 6. Same facts as in Example 3, except that the organization pays $75,000 in total during the organization's tax year for 15 separate transactions to collect debts owed to the organization. None of the transactions involves payments to the law partnership in excess of $10,000. The organization is not required in this instance to report the business transaction, because the dollar amounts do not exceed either the $10,000 threshold or the $100,000 aggregate threshold.

Example 7. Same facts as in Example 6, except that the organization pays $105,000 instead of $75,000. Because the aggregate payments for the business transactions exceed $100,000, the organization must report all the business transactions, either on an aggregate basis or separately.

(3) Reasonable Effort for Identifying Business Transactions with Interested Persons.   As a practical matter, a tax-exempt organization may not have knowledge of all of its business transactions with interested persons. This may be especially true for indirect business transactions, which may involve

- A service contract between the exempt organization and a business entity in which an interested person, or a family member of an interested person, has a 35-percent or more ownership interest

- A sale transaction involving the exempt organization and a for-profit business for which one of the exempt organization's directors is also a director

- A lease transaction between the exempt organization and a limited liability company of which a director of the exempt organization is a more than 5 percent member

The IRS adopts a reasonable effort standard for obtaining information regarding interested person business transactions. The Form 990 instructions state that an exempt organization is not required to provide information regarding a business transaction with an interested person if it is unable to secure the information regarding interested person status after making a reasonable effort to obtain it. The instructions further provide, as an example, that an organization has made a reasonable effort if the organization distributes a questionnaire annually to each interested person that includes the name, title, date, and signature of each person reporting the information and contains the pertinent instructions and definitions. This questionnaire could be made part of the annual disclosure statement distributed as part of the organization's conflicts of interest policy. For a discussion of annual disclosure statements, see § 5.1(i)(1).

(4) Revenue Sharing.   Schedule L requests a tax-exempt organization to indicate if its business transactions with interested persons include *revenue sharing*. In some instances, tax-exempt organizations enter into revenue-sharing transactions with interested persons as a form of compensation to the interested person for their services. For example, an exempt organization may compensate an interested person for services performed with respect to a related or unrelated business activity of the exempt organization by giving the interested person a percentage of the gross revenues from the activity. For a discussion of revenue sharing and compensation, see §§ 6.1(a)(4) and 6.1(b)(5).

A revenue-sharing transaction is a type of joint venture. Revenue-sharing transactions usually involve sharing the gross or net profits from an activity with another tax-exempt entity, with one or more individuals, or with a for-profit business. The IRS's concern with revenue sharing is that an exempt organization may be allowing private persons to unduly benefit from the exempt organization's assets through the revenue-sharing arrangement. As a result, revenue-sharing transactions are subject to a great deal of scrutiny by the IRS and should be entered into cautiously, especially with interested persons. Exempt organizations should follow their conflicts-of-interest policies in approving revenue-sharing arrangements. In addition, they should build safeguards into the arrangement to protect the exempt status of the organization, such as having maximum levels of revenue that can be received by the individuals and nonexempt entities participating in the arrangement and ensuring the exempt organization maintains control of the decision making in the revenue-sharing arrangement. For a discussion of these safeguards, see § 5.1(i)(3).

§ 18.2 PREPARATION OF NEW FORM 990 SCHEDULE L

Schedule L is divided into four parts. Part I requests information on excess benefit transactions and is to be completed by charities and social welfare organizations only. Part II involves the disclosure of loans to and from interested persons. Part III requests information on grants or assistance benefiting interested persons. Part IV involves disclosure of business transactions involving interested persons. Transactions need to be disclosed only once on Schedule L and should be disclosed in the first applicable part. For example, if a loan transaction is an excess benefit transaction, it should be disclosed in Part I (Excess Benefit Transactions) but not Part II (Loans to and from Interested Persons). Similarly, a loan with an interested person should be disclosed in Part II (Loans), not Part IV (Business Transactions with Interest Persons). There is a different definition of *interested person* for each part of Schedule L.

Business transactions (Part IV) are reportable only if they exceed certain thresholds (see § 18.1(d)(1)). There is no minimum threshold for reporting transactions in Parts I, II, and III of Schedule L.

(a) Part I (Excess Benefit Transactions)

Only charities and social welfare organizations are subject to the intermediate sanction penalties on excess benefit transactions. Part I is to be completed by charities and social welfare organizations that answered "yes" on Form 990, Part IV, lines 25a or b, whereby they indicated that the organization engaged in an excess benefit transaction with a disqualified person during the year or that the organization become aware that it had engaged in an excess benefit transaction with a disqualified person from a prior year. As the IRS cautioned in the Form 990 draft instructions, characterization of a transaction as an excess benefit transaction may have serious consequences for the disqualified person involved in the transaction, organizational managers, and the exempt entity, and filing organizations should carefully considered its answer to this question.

(1) Line 1 (Information Regarding Excess Benefit Transactions).   If the organization is a public charity or social welfare organization and is engaged in an excess benefit transaction, the organization must disclose on line 1 the name of the disqualified person, the name(s) of any organizational managers who participated in the transaction, a description of the transaction, and indicate ("yes" or "no") whether the transaction has been corrected. See § 6.1(b)(9) for a discussion of the "correction" of an excess benefit transaction.

(2) Line 2 (Amount of Excise Tax). On line 2, the filing organization must enter the amount of tax imposed on the organization's managers or disqualified persons during the year under the intermediate sanctions rules. Note that the intermediate sanctions excise taxes are reported and paid on IRS Form 4720. For a discussion of the amount of the intermediate sanctions excise tax, see § 6.1(b)(4)

(3) Line 3 (Reimbursement of Excise Tax). A filing organization enters on line 3 the amount of tax, if any, on line 2 that was reimbursed by the organization. Filing organizations need to consider whether any income tax consequences and/or additional excess benefit transaction consequences arose from the reimbursement of the excise taxes on excess benefit transactions and whether the organization needs to contemporaneously substantiate the payment of the excise taxes (such as on a Form W-2 or 1099) to avoid further consequences.

(b) Part II (Loans to and from Interested Persons)

Part II of Schedule L must be completed by organizations that answered "yes" on Form 990, Part IV, line 26, indicating that a loan to or by a current or former officer, director, trustee, key employee, highly compensated employee, or disqualified person was outstanding as of the end of the organization's tax year. Loans between the reporting organization and an interested person that are not outstanding as of the last day of the organization's fiscal year do not need to be disclosed. For this purpose, a *loan* includes a salary advance and other advances and receivables. Loans to interested persons *do not* include:

- Excess benefit transactions
- Advances under an accountable plan
- Pledges receivable that would qualify as charitable contributions when paid
- Accrued but unpaid compensation owed by the organization
- Loans from a credit union made to an interested person on the same terms as offered to other members of the credit union
- Receivables outstanding that were created in the ordinary course of the organization's business on the same terms as offered to the general public (such as receivables for medical services provided by a hospital to an officer of the hospital)

In addition to reporting in Part II loans that initially are made between the organization and an interested person, a filing organization is instructed to report loans originally between the organization and a third party or between an interested person and a third party that were transferred so as to become a debt outstanding between the organization and an interested person.

(1) Column (a) (Name of Interested Person and Purpose of the Loan). In Column (a), the filing organization discloses the name of the interested person who is the debtor or creditor on the loan and the purpose of the loan, such as "compensation package."

(2) Column (b) (Debtor or Creditor). In Column (b), the filing organization indicates whether funds were loaned from the interested person to the organization or from the organization to the interested person.

(3) Columns (c) and (d) (Principal Amount of Loan and Year-End Balance). In Column (c), the organization states the original principal amount of the loan, meaning the original dollar amount borrowed. An organization states, in Column (d), the balance due on the loan at the end of its filing year. This amount includes outstanding principal, accrued interest, and any applicable penalties and collection costs. The sum total reported in this column must equal the total on the Form 990 Balance Sheet (Part X), lines 5 and 6 (amounts owed to the organization by interested persons) and line 22 (amounts owed by the organization to interested persons).

(4) Column (e) (Past Due Payments). Column (e) requires an organization to indicate, by checking "yes" or "no," whether any payment on the loan is past due as of the end of the organization's year or if the debtor is otherwise in default under the terms and conditions of the loan.

(5) Column (f) (Approval of Loan). An organization indicates in Column (f), by checking "yes" or "no," whether the loan was approved by the organization's governing body or a committee thereof.

(6) Column (g) (Written Agreement). In Column (g), an organization discloses whether or not the interested person loan is subject to a promissory note or other written agreement signed by the debtor.

(c) Part III (Grants or Assistance Benefiting Interested Persons)

Part III of Schedule L requests information regarding grants or assistance benefiting interested persons. Part III must be completed by organizations that answered "yes" to Form 990, Part IV, line 27, indicating that the organization provided a grant or other assistance to an officer, director, trustee, key employee, or substantial contributor or to a person related to such individual. For purposes of Part III, a substantial contributor is a person who contributed at least $5,000 during the organization's tax year and is required to be reported by name in Schedule B. (See § 14.3(e).) If an organization is not required to file Schedule B, it is not required to report transactions with substantial contributors and their related persons in Part III. See § 18.1(c)(1) for the definition of a *related person*.

In Part III, filing organizations are instructed to report each grant or similar economic assistance (including provision of goods, services, or use of facilities) provided by the organization to any interested person at any time during the organization's tax year. Examples of grants are scholarships, fellowships, internships, prizes, and awards. A grant also includes the gift portion of a part-gift, part-sale transaction.

Filing organizations are specifically instructed not to include in Part III any excess benefit transactions, loans to or from interested persons, business transactions that do not contain any gift element (i.e., for full and fair consideration) and that are engaged in to serve the direct and immediate needs of the organization, such as the payment of compensation to an employee or consultant (including taxable compensation and fringe benefits), or grants to a substantial contributor's employees (and their children) or a 35-percent controlled entity of a substantial contributor awarded on an objective and nondiscriminatory basis based on preestablished criteria and reviewed by a selection committee.

(1) Column (a) (Name of Interested Person). In Column (a), a filing organization lists the name of the interested person receiving the grant or assistance. If the interested person has this status because the person is a substantial contributor, a family member or 35-percent controlled entity of a substantial contributor, or an employee of a substantial contributor or 35-percent controlled entity of a substantial contributor, an organization should enter "substantial contributor" or "related to substantial contributor" in lieu of the interested person's name, for confidentiality reasons.

(2) Column (b) (Relationship between Interested Person and the Organization). In Column (b), the filing organization should describe the relationship between the interested person that benefited form the grant or assistance and the grantee organization. Examples of this are "spouse of Director John Smith" or "35-percent owned company of President Mary Jones." If the organization entered "substantial contributor" in Column (a) (for confidentiality reasons), then the organization should list "substantial contributor" in Column (b). If the interested person is related to a substantial contributor, then an organization should describe the relationship of the interested person to the substantial contributor in Column (b) without referring to specific names, such as "child of employee of 35-percent controlled entity of substantial contributor."

If a person has status as an interested person for Part III as both a substantial contributor (or related to a substantial contributor) and for other reasons, such as being an officer of the tax-exempt organization, then the filing organization should not make a reference to the substantial contributor status. For example, if grantee Jane Smith is both a substantial contributor (or related to a substantial contributor) and a spouse of Director John Smith, then she must be listed by name in Column (a) and the filing organization should state "spouse of Director John Smith" or make a similar disclosure in Column (b).

(3) Column (c) (Amount of Grant or Type of Assistance). In Column (c), a filing organization should state the total dollar amount of the grants provided to the interested person during the organization's tax year. Also, the organization should describe the type of assistance (such as scholarship or grant for research) and estimate the value of any noncash assistance. Although not stated in the Form 990 instructions, the amounts listed in Column (c) should be consistent with the amounts listed as grants and other assistance in other parts of Form 990, such as Schedule F (Statement of Activities Outside the United States) and Schedule I (Grants and Other Assistance to Organizations, Governments and Individuals in the United States).

(d) Part IV (Business Transactions Involving Interested Persons)

Part IV must be completed by organizations answering "yes" to Part IV, lines 28a, b, or c, which is a series of questions regarding whether or not the filing organization had an interested person who had a direct or indirect business relationship with the organization, had a family member with a direct or indirect business relationship with the organization, or who served as an officer, director, trustee, key employee, partner, or member of an entity (or shareholder of a professional corporation) doing business with the organization.

For Part IV, *interested persons* are the filing organization's current or former officers, directors, trustees, or key employees who are listed by the filing organization in Part VII, Section A of Form 990 and their related persons. For a definition of interested persons, see § 18.1(d)(2). Examples of business transactions with interested persons include the rental of property owned by an interested person, a vendor contract with a corporation that is more than 35-percent owned by an interested person, or the purchase of property from a partnership in which an interested person is a more than 5-percent partner. Business transactions also include joint ventures with interested persons if the profits or capital interests of the organization and the interest person each exceed 10 percent.

In reporting its business transactions with interested persons in Part IV of Schedule L, the organization is not required to report business transactions that did not exceed the applicable thresholds. See § 18.1(d)(1) for a discussion of these thresholds.

The organization may aggregate multiple individual transactions involving more than $10,000 between the same parties, or list them separately, in Part IV.

(1) Column (a) (Name of Interested Person). In Column (a), the filing organization must disclose the name of the interested person with whom the organization has engaged, directly or indirectly, in a business transaction. No other identifying information, such as tax identification number or address, is requested.

The draft Form 990 instructions stated that if an organization responded "yes" to Part IV, lines 28a, 28b, or 28c, but no business transactions are required to be reported in the Part IV table because they are at or below the applicable thresholds, the organizations should state: "All transactions are below reporting threshold" in Column (a) of the table.

(2) Column (b) (Relationship with Interested Person). In Column (b), a filing organization discloses the relationship between the organization and the interested person. For example, the organization may state "key employee," "family member of John Smith, director," or "entity owned more than 35 percent by John Smith, former director, and Cathy Jones, President" in Column (b).

(3) Column (c) (Amount of Transaction). The organization discloses, in Column (c), the amount of the business transaction with the interested person, which includes the cash and fair market value of other assets and services provided by the organization during the tax year, net of reimbursement of expenses. If aggregating transactions, an organization should report the aggregate amount in Column (c).

(4) Column (d) (Description of Transaction).   An organization should describe a transaction, for purposes of Column (d), by type, such as "independent contractor arrangement," "rental of property," or "sale of assets." If the organization reported an aggregate amount in Column (c), it should describe the various types of transactions (e.g., consulting and rental of real property) in Column (d). An organization should use Schedule O if additional space is needed.

(5) Column (e) (Revenue Sharing).   A filing organization should respond "yes" to Column (e) if all or part of the consideration paid by the organization is based on a percentage of revenues of the organization, such as a management fee that is based on a percentage of net or gross revenues, or the legal fee owed to outside attorneys by a public interest law firm is a percentage of the amount collected.

§18.3   NEW FORM 990 COMPLIANCE TASKS

Tax-exempt organizations should attend to these 11 compliance tasks with respect to its transactions with interested persons.

1. **Implement procedures.** Prior to entering into any compensation or business transactions, loans agreements, or grant awards that may be considered directly or indirectly with an interested person, implement appropriate strategies for determining such transactions are fair and reasonable to the organization by following the organization's conflicts-of-interest policy, invoking the rebuttable presumption of reasonableness under the intermediate sanctions rules, and establishing methods for awarding grants that are on an objective and nondiscriminatory basis.

2. **Review transactions.** Ascertain the transactions occurring during the filing year in which the exempt organization and interested persons were engaged, directly or indirectly, by reviewing the organization's loans, grants, and business transactions.

3. **Questionnaire.** Distribute and review a questionnaire completed by the organization's interested persons that solicits information regarding transactions with interested persons and satisfies the reasonable effort standards for grants and other assistance to interested persons and business transactions with interested persons.

4. **Documentation.** Contemporaneously document all transactions with interested persons and engage in all required IRS reporting with respect to the transactions.

5. **Excess benefit transactions.** Determine whether any transactions between an interested person, directly or indirectly, and the filing organization resulted in an excess benefit transaction, and if so, notify the interested person involved in the transaction as well as any organizational managers who were knowingly involved in the transaction.

6. **Correction.** Seek correction of any excess benefit transactions.

7. **Loans.** Document the terms and conditions of, and need for, any loans with interested persons outstanding during the filing year; ensure that the loan is

fair and reasonable to the exempt organization; and have a written agreement signed by the debtor substantiating the loan.

8. **Past-due loan amounts.** Strive to have no loan amounts past due as of the end of the filing year.

9. **Loan payoff.** To the extent possible, cause any outstanding loans to or from an interested person to be paid in full prior to year-end, to avoid disclosure of the loan on Schedule L.

10. **Interested person grants.** Ascertain whether any interested person received a grant or other assistance from the exempt organization during the year that is reportable on Schedule L by reviewing the organization's records and by requesting information from interested persons in satisfaction of the reasonable effort standard. See § 18.1(c)(5).

11. **Business transactions with interested persons.** Determine whether the exempt organization engaged in any business transactions with interested persons in excess of the reporting thresholds set forth in § 18.1(d)(1) by reviewing the organization's records and requesting information from interested persons that will allow the organization to meet the reasonable effort standard described in § 18.1(d)(3).

CHAPTER NINETEEN

Schedule M—Noncash Contributions

Congress, the Department of the Treasury, and the IRS have long been concerned about gifts of property (other than cash) to charities (and, to a much lesser extent, other tax-exempt organizations) because of situations where, in whole or substantial part, the donee cannot use or benefit from the noncash gift or because the donor to a charitable organization has claimed an inflated value in computing the charitable contribution deduction. To gain more information about noncash gifts and to help it combat abusive transactions, the IRS created Schedule M to accompany the new Form 990.

When the IRS initially formulated this schedule, it stated that the prior return "does not capture information about an organization's non-cash contributions, other than for certain contributions required to be reported on Schedule B." The agency added that "[s]ignificant tax compliance problems exist with respect to noncash contributions." The IRS continued: "In order to collect information regarding those organizations receiving significant amounts of noncash contributions, and specific types of such items," this schedule has been added to "collect aggregate annual information on the types of non-cash property an organization receives."

Schedule M requires tax-exempt organizations that receive over $25,000 in the form of aggregate noncash contributions, and certain other property irrespective of value, (see Form 990, Part IV, lines 29 and 30), to provide detail regarding various types of these contributed properties, including 17 specific categories of property (with some categories further subdivided, for a total of 24), plus "other" types of property. They are works of art, books and publications, clothing, household goods, vehicles, intellectual property, securities, conservation property, real estate, collectibles, food inventory, drugs and medical supplies, taxidermy, historical artifacts, scientific specimens, and archeological artifacts.

Two parts comprise this schedule; Part I is the main portion, and Part II is used to report certain additional information. Part I of the schedule includes four columns. Column (a) is a check-the-box column, requiring the organization to report receipt of certain types of property (even if quantity reporting is not required). Column (b) pertains to the number of contributions of types of property or the number of items contributed. Column (c) concerns situations where the property contribution is reported as revenue (Form 990, Part VIII, line 1g). Thus, reporting is restricted to "check-the-box" and "number of contributions" for museums and other organizations that do not report contributions as revenue. Column (d) requires reporting of the method of determining revenues. Part I also includes 24 specific questions in relation to the columns and 5 additional questions.

The instructions make it clear that (1) all tax-exempt organizations, not just charitable entities, must file this schedule, if they received noncash gifts; (2) a contribution is a noncash contribution irrespective of whether it is deductible as a charitable gift; and (3) gifts of donated services are not noncash gifts for purposes of the schedule. Public charities, however, will be the primary preparers and filers of Schedule M.

§19.1 LAW AND POLICY

Contributions may be made to charitable organizations by transfers of money (cash) and property; this property may be real or personal, tangible or intangible. For the most part, a federal income tax charitable contribution deduction is available for gifts. Charitable deductions may also be utilized in connection with the federal estate and/or gift taxes.

(a) Charitable Giving Rules in General

The basic concept of the federal income tax deduction for a charitable contribution is this: Corporations and individuals who itemize their deductions can deduct on their annual tax return, within certain limits, an amount equivalent to the amount contributed (money) or to the value of a contribution (property) to a qualified donee. A *charitable contribution* for income tax purposes is a gift to or for the use of one or more qualified donees.

Deductions for charitable gifts are also allowed under the federal gift tax and estate tax laws. Donors and the charitable organizations they support commonly expect gifts to be in the form of outright transfers of money or property. For both parties (donor and donee), a gift is usually a unilateral transaction, in a financial sense: the donor parts with the contributed item; the charity acquires it.

(1) Defining Charitable Gift. A fundamental requirement of the charitable contribution deduction law is that the cash or property transferred to a charitable organization must be transferred in the form of a *gift*. Just because money is paid or property is transferred to a charity does not necessarily mean that the payment or transfer is a gift. When a tax-exempt university's tuition, an exempt hospital's healthcare fee, or an exempt association's dues are paid, there is no gift and thus no charitable deduction for the payment.

Basically, a gift has two elements: It involves a transfer that is *voluntary* and is motivated by something other than *consideration* (something being received in return for a payment). Where payments are made to receive something in exchange (education, healthcare, etc.), the transaction is a purchase. The law places more emphasis on what is received by the payor than on the payment or transfer. The income tax regulations state that a transfer is not a contribution when made "with a reasonable expectation of financial return commensurate with the amount of the transfer." A single transaction, however, can be partially a gift and partially a purchase; when a charity is the payee, only the gift portion is deductible.

The U.S. Supreme Court, in a famous pronouncement, observed that a gift is a transfer motivated by "detached or disinterested generosity." The Court also characterized a gift as a transfer stimulated "out of affection, respect, admiration, charity, or like impulses." Thus, the focus in this area for the most part has been an objective analysis, comparing what the "donee" parted with and what (if anything) the "donor" received net in exchange.

Another factor, that of *donative intent*, is sometimes taken into consideration. A set of tax regulations states that, for any part of a payment made in the context of a charity auction to be deductible as a charitable gift, the patron must have donative intent. More broadly, a congressional committee report contains this statement:

> The term "contribution or gift" is not defined by statute, but generally is interpreted to mean a voluntary transfer of money or other property without receipt of adequate consideration and with donative intent. If a taxpayer receives or expects to receive a quid pro quo in exchange for a transfer to charity, the taxpayer may be able to deduct the excess of the amount transferred over the fair market value of any benefit received in return provided the excess payment is made with the intention of making a gift.

A federal court of appeals described the matter as to what is a gift this way: It is a "particularly confused issue of federal taxation." The statutory law on the subject, said this court, is "cryptic," and "neither Congress nor the courts have offered any very satisfactory definitions" of the terms *gift* and *contribution* (which are, for these purposes, basically synonymous).

(2) Qualified Donees. *Qualified donees* are charitable organizations (including educational, religious, and scientific entities), certain fraternal organizations, certain cemetery companies, and most veterans' organizations. Contributions to both private and public charities are deductible, but the law favors gifts to public charities.

Federal, state, and local governmental bodies are charitable donees. State or local law, however, may preclude a governmental entity from accepting charitable gifts. In most jurisdictions, a charitable organization can be established to solicit deductible contributions for and make grants to governmental bodies. This is a common technique for public schools, colleges, universities, and hospitals.

An otherwise nonqualifying organization may be allowed to receive a deductible charitable gift, where the gift property is used for charitable purposes or received by an agent for a charitable organization. An example of the former is a gift to a trade association that is earmarked for a charitable fund within the association. Examples of an agent for a charity is a title-holding company that holds a property for charitable purposes and a for-profit company that acquires and disposes of vehicles as part of a charity's used vehicle donation program.

(3) Limitations on Deductibility. The extent of charitable contributions that can be deducted for a particular tax year is limited to a certain amount, which for individuals is a function of the donor's *contribution base*—essentially, an amount equal to the individual's adjusted gross income. This level of allowable annual deductibility is determined by five percentage limitations. They are dependent on several factors, principally the nature of the charitable recipient and the nature of the property contributed. The examples used next assume an individual donor with an annual contribution base of $100,000.

The first three limitations apply to gifts to public charities and to private operating foundations.

First, there is a percentage limitation of 50 percent of the donor's contribution base for gifts of cash and ordinary income property. A donor with a $100,000 contribution base may, in a year, make deductible gifts of these items up to a total of $50,000. If an individual makes contributions that exceed the 50-percent limitation, the excess generally may be carried forward and deducted in one to five subsequent years. Thus, if this donor gave $60,000 to public charities in year 1 and made no other charitable gifts in that year, he or she would be entitled to a deduction of $50,000 in year 1 and the remaining $10,000 would be available for deductibility in year 2.

The second percentage limitation is 30 percent of the donor's contribution base for gifts of capital gain property. A donor thus may, in a year, contribute up to $30,000 of qualifying stocks, bonds, real estate, and like property, and receive a charitable deduction for that amount. Any excess (more than 30 percent) of the amount of these gifts is subject to the carryforward rule. If a donor gave $50,000 in capital gain property in year 1 and made no other charitable gifts that year, he or she would be entitled to a charitable contribution deduction of $30,000 in year 1 and the $20,000 would be available in year 2.

A donor who makes gifts of cash and capital gain property to public charities (and/or private operating foundations) in any one year generally is limited by a blend of these percentage limitations. For example, if the donor in year 1 gives $50,000 in cash and $30,000 in appreciated capital gain property to a public charity, his or her charitable deduction in year 1 is $30,000 of capital gain property and $20,000 of the cash (to keep the deduction within the overall 50 percent ceiling); the other $30,000 of cash would be carried forward to year 2 (or to years 2 through 5, depending on the donor's circumstances).

The third percentage limitation allows a donor of capital gain property to use the 50-percent limitation, instead of the 30-percent limitation, where the amount of the contribution is reduced by all of the unrealized appreciation in the value of the property. This election is usually made by donors who want a larger deduction in the year of the gift for an item of property that has not appreciated in value to a great extent. Once made, this election is irrevocable.

The fourth and fifth percentage limitations apply to gifts to private foundations and certain other charitable donees (other than public charities and private operating foundations). These donees are generally veterans' and fraternal organizations.

Under the fourth percentage limitation, contributions of cash and ordinary income property to private foundations and other entities may not exceed 30 percent of the individual donor's contribution base. The carryover rules apply to this type of gift. If the donor gives $50,000 in cash to one or more private foundations in year 1, his or her charitable deduction for that year (assuming no other charitable gifts) is $30,000, with the balance of $20,000 carried forward into subsequent years (up to 5).

The carryover rules blend with the first three percentage limitations. For example, if in year 1 a donor gave $65,000 to charity, of which $25,000 went to a public charity and $40,000 to a private foundation, his or her charitable deduction for that year would be $50,000: $30,000 for the gift to the private foundation and $20,000 for the gift to the public charity. The remaining $10,000 of the gift to the foundation and the remaining $5,000 of the gift to the public charity would be carried forward into year 2.

The fifth percentage limitation is 20 percent of the contribution base for gifts of capital gain property to private foundations and other charitable donees. There is a carryforward for any excess deduction amount. For example, if a donor gives appreciated securities, having a value of $30,000, to a private foundation in year 1, his or her charitable deduction for year 1 (assuming no other charitable gifts) is $20,000; the remaining $10,000 may be carried forward.

Deductible charitable contributions by corporations in any tax year may not exceed 10 percent of pretax net income. Excess amounts may be carried forward and deducted in subsequent years (up to five). For gifts by corporations, the federal tax laws do not differentiate between gifts to public charities and gifts to private foundations. As an illustration, a corporation that grosses $1 million in a year and incurs $900,000 in expenses in that year (not including charitable gifts) may generally contribute to charity and deduct in that year an amount up to $10,000 (10 percent of $100,000); in computing its taxes, this corporation would report taxable income of $90,000. If the corporation contributed $20,000 in that year, the numbers would remain the same, except that the corporation would have a $10,000 charitable contribution carryforward.

A corporation on the accrual method of accounting can elect to treat a contribution as having been made in a tax year if it is actually donated during the first 2½ months of the following year. Corporate gifts of property are generally subject to the deduction reduction rules, discussed next.

A business organization that is a *flow-through entity* generates a different tax result when it comes to charitable deductions. (These organizations are partnerships, other joint ventures, small business (S) corporations, and limited liability companies.) Entities of this nature, even though they may make charitable gifts, do not claim charitable contribution deductions. Instead, the deduction is passed through to the partners, members, or other owners on an allocable basis and they claim their share of the deduction on their tax return.

(4) Deduction Reduction Rules.   A donor (individual or corporation) who makes a gift of *ordinary income property* to a charitable organization (public or private) must confine the charitable deduction to an amount equal to the donor's cost basis in the property. The deduction is not based on the fair market value of the property; it must be reduced by the amount that would have been gain (ordinary income) if the property had been sold. As an example, if a donor gave to a charity an item of ordinary income property having a value of $1,000, for which he or she paid $600, the resulting charitable deduction would be $600.

Any donor who makes a gift of *capital gain property* to a public charity generally can compute the charitable deduction using the property's fair market value at the time of the gift, regardless of the basis amount and with no taxation of the appreciation (the capital gain inherent in the property). Suppose, however, a donor makes a gift of capital gain tangible personal property (such as a work of art) to a public charity and the use of the gift property by the donee is unrelated to its tax-exempt purposes. The donor must reduce the deduction by an amount equal to all of the long-term capital gain that would have been recognized had the donor sold the property at its fair market value as of the date of the contribution.

Generally, a donor who makes a gift of capital gain property to a private foundation must reduce the amount of the otherwise allowable deduction by all of the appreciation element (built-in capital gain) in the gift property. An individual, however, is allowed full fair market value for a contribution to a private foundation of certain publicly traded stock (known as *qualified appreciated stock*).

(b) Noncash Contribution Rules in General

Aside from the eligibility of the gift recipient (see § 19.1(a)(2)), the other basic element in determining whether a charitable contribution is deductible is the nature of the property given. Basically, the distinctions are between outright giving and planned giving, and between gifts of cash and gifts of property. In many instances, the tax law differentiates between personal property and real property, and tangible property and intangible property (securities).

The federal income tax treatment of gifts of property is dependent on whether the property is capital gain property. The tax law makes a distinction between *long-term capital gain* and *short-term capital gain*. Property that is not capital gain property is *ordinary income property*. These three terms are based on the tax classification of the type of revenue that would be generated on sale of the property. Short-term capital gain property is generally treated the same as ordinary income property. Therefore, the actual distinction is between capital gain property (really long-term capital gain property) and ordinary income property.

Capital gain property is a capital asset that has appreciated in value and, if sold, would give rise to long-term capital gain. To result in long-term capital gain, property must be held for at least 12 months. Most forms of capital gain property are securities and real estate.

The charitable deduction for capital gain property is often equal to its fair market value or at least is computed using that value. Gifts of ordinary income property generally produce a deduction equivalent to the donor's cost basis in the property. The law provides exceptions to this basis-only rule; an example is a gift by a corporation out of its inventory (see § 19.1(n)). A charitable deduction based on the full fair market value of an item of appreciated property (with no recognition of the built-in capital gain) is a critical feature of the federal tax law incentives for charitable giving.

(c) Property Valuation Basics

One of the first steps in determining a charitable contribution deduction for the gift of an item of property is to ascertain the fair market value of the property on the date of its contribution. *Fair market value* is the price that property would sell for on the open market; it is the price that would be agreed on between a willing buyer and a willing seller, with neither being required to act and both having reasonable knowledge of the relevant facts. If the donor places a restriction on the use of contributed property, the restriction is likely to affect (probably decrease) the fair market value of the property.

No single formula always applies when determining the value of a property. All of the pertinent facts and circumstances must be considered, such as the desirability, use, and scarcity of the property. The cost of the property incurred by its donor or the selling price received by the charitable organization may be the best indication of its fair market value. If it is worth it (or required by law), an appraisal may be the basis for the value. Conditions in the market change, so that the cost of a property or its sales price may have less weight if the property was not purchased or sold reasonably close to the date of contribution. The cost or selling price of a property is a good indicator of the property's value if (1) the purchase or sale occurred close to the valuation date in an open market, (2) the purchase or sale was at arm's length, (3) the buyer and seller knew all of the relevant facts, (4) the buyer and seller were not required to act, and (5) the market conditions did not materially change between the date of purchase or sale and the valuation date. As to the *open market* element, if a sale is made in a market that was artificially supported or stimulated, so as to not be truly representative, the price at which the sale was made will not be indicative of the property's fair market value. For example, a liquidation sale price usually does not indicate fair value; likewise, sales under unusual circumstances (such as sales of small lots, forced sales, and sales in a restricted market) may not represent fair market value.

Absent unusual circumstances, it is assumed that an increase or decrease in the value of a property, in relation to its cost, has been at a reasonable rate. For adjustments to accommodate the passage of time, an appraiser may consider published price indexes for information on general price trends, building costs, commodity costs, and items sold at auction.

An arm's-length offer to purchase a property close to the valuation date may help to prove its value if the person making the offer was willing and able to complete the transaction. To rely on such an offer, there should be proof of it and the specific amount to be paid. Offers to buy property other than the specific property being valued will help to determine value if the other property(ies) is or are reasonably similar to the specific property.

The sales prices of properties similar to a specific property are often important in determining the property's fair market value. The weight to be accorded each sale is dependent on the degree of similarity between the property sold and the specific property, the timing of the sale in relation to the valuation date, the circumstances of the sale (whether it was at arm's length with a knowledgeable buyer and seller, with neither being under any compulsion to act), and the conditions of the market in which the sale was made (perhaps causing an unusual inflation or deflation in value). The *degree of similarity* must, to reflect fair value, be sufficiently close so that the selling price would have been given consideration by reasonably well-informed buyers or sellers of the property.

The cost of buying, building, or manufacturing property similar to the specific item should be considered in determining the fair market value of an item of property. The *replacement cost* is the amount it would cost to replace the specific item of property on the valuation date. There must, however, be a reasonable relationship between the replacement cost and the fair value. Often there is no such relationship; if the supply of the item of property is more or less than the demand for it, the replacement cost becomes less important in determining value. To determine the replacement cost of an item of property, the *estimated replacement cost new* should be ascertained; from this cost figure an amount for depreciation due to the physical condition and obsolescence of the property is subtracted. The relationship between the depreciated replacement cost and the fair market value should be demonstrated, along with documentation as to how the estimated replacement cost new was calculated.

Generally, the weight given to an expert's opinion on matters such as the authenticity of a coin or a work of art, or the most profitable and best use of a parcel of real estate, depends on the knowledge and competence of the expert and the thoroughness with which the expert's opinion is supported by experience and facts. For an expert's opinion to deserve much weight, the facts must support the opinion.

Unexpected events happening after contribution of an item of property should not be considered in assessing the property's value. Only the relevant facts known at the time of the gift may be taken into account in determining fair market value. At the same time, past events may not fairly reflect a property's value.

(d) Contributions of Works of Art

Schedule M differentiates among contributions of historical treasures, contributions of fractional interests in art, and contributions of other types of works of art (Part I, lines 1–3).

(1) Contributions of Art in General. The IRS's instructions state that the term *works of art* includes "paintings, sculptures, prints, drawings, ceramics, antiques, decorative arts, textiles, carpets, silver, photography, film, video, installation and multimedia arts, rare books and manuscripts, historical memorabilia, and other similar objects." The term includes all contributions of art, other than historical treasures (see § 19 (d)(2)), in which the exempt organization received the donor's entire interest in the property. Thus, art in general does not include fractional interests in art (see § 19 (d)(3)). Also, art in general does not include *collectibles* (see § 19.1(m)).

(2) Contributions of Historical Treasures. The IRS's instructions state that the term *historical treasure* means a "building, structure, area, or [other] property with recognized cultural, aesthetic, or historical value that is significant in the history, architecture, archeology, or culture of a country, state, or city."

(3) Contributions of Fractional Interests in Art. A donor may take a deduction for a charitable contribution of a fractional interest in tangible personal property as long as the donor satisfies general law requirements for deductibility and, in subsequent years, makes additional charitable contributions of interests in the same property. There is recapture of the income and gift tax charitable contribution deduction under certain circumstances, such as where the donor's remaining interest in the property is not contributed to the same charitable donee within 10 years or if the donee does not timely take physical possession of the property or use the property for an exempt use. These rules are applicable for contributions, bequests, and gifts made after August 17, 2006.

The IRS's instructions state that a contribution of a *fractional interest* in art is a "contribution, not in trust, of an undivided portion of a donor's entire interest in a work of art." A contribution of a donor's *entire interest* "must consist of a part of each and every substantial interest or right the donor owns in such work of art and must extend over the entire term of the donor's interest in the property." These instructions state that a gift "generally is treated as a gift of an undivided portion of a donor's entire interest in property if the donee is given the right, as a tenant in common with the donor, to possession, dominion, and control of the property for a portion of each year appropriate to its interest in such property."

(4) Valuation.   A work of art may be valued using the cost or selling price of the donated property, sale of comparable properties, replacement cost, or the opinion of an expert. A charitable deduction for a contribution of a work of art should (unless the deduction does not exceed $5,000 (see § 19.1(u)) be supported by a written appraisal from a qualified and reputable source.

Important elements in the valuation of art, including antiques, are the property's physical condition and extent of restoration. These factors must be reflected in any appraisal. An antique in damaged condition may be worth much less than a similar piece in excellent condition.

More weight is usually given to an appraisal prepared by an individual specializing in the type and price range of the art being appraised. Certain art dealers or appraisers specialize, for example, in old masters, modern art, or bronze sculpture. Their opinions as to the authenticity and desirability of such art is usually accorded more significance than opinions of more generalized art dealers or appraisers. They can report more recent comparable sales in support of their opinions.

If a charitable deduction for a gift of art is claimed, where the deduction is $20,000 or more, the donor must attach a complete copy of the signed appraisal to the tax return (see § 19.1(u)). For individual objects valued at $20,000 or more, a photograph of a size and quality fully showing the object, preferably an 8 × 10-inch color photograph or a color transparency no smaller than 4 × 5 inches, must be provided to the IRS on request.

If there is a charitable contribution of an item of art that has been appraised at $50,000 or more, the donor can request a *statement of value* from the IRS. This request, which must be made before filing the tax return that supports the deduction, must include a copy of a qualified appraisal of the item, a completed Section B of Form 8283 (see § 19.1(u)), and a statement of the IRS territory that has examination responsibility for the return. The request must be accompanied by payment of a $2,500 user fee, applicable in the case of a request concerning as many as three items of art; this fee is increased by $250 for each additional item.

As to Form 990 reporting of contributions of works of art, see § 19.2, questions 1 to 3.

(e)   Contribution of Publications

Books and other publications are referenced in the schedule (Part I, line 4). These items may be contributed to charity, although the IRS requires contributions of rare books and manuscripts to be regarded separately. (These may be classified as *collections* (see § 19.1(m).) The number of these contributions for the filing year need not be reported.

Review of comparable sales and adjustment of the prices according to the differences between these sales and the item being evaluated is the usual way to determine the value of books. This undertaking is frequently the task of a specialized appraiser, such as a dealer who concentrates on certain areas (Americana, foreign imports, scientific books, etc.).

Some book collections may be of modest value (i.e., not requiring a written appraisal). In determining fair market value for this type of collection, it is necessary to remember that a book (or books) that is very old or very rare is not necessarily valuable. The condition of a book may have great influence as to its value; collectors are interested in items that are in fine, or at least good, condition (i.e., not torn, stained, or missing pages). Other factors affecting the value of a book are the type of its binding (leather, cloth, paper), page edges, and illustrations (drawings and photographs). Although collectors generally want first editions of books, other editions—because of changes or additions—may be worth as much as, or more than, the first edition.

As to manuscripts, autographs, diaries, and similar items, because they are (or can be) handwritten, or at least signed by famous individuals, they are often in demand and are valuable. The writings of unknown individuals also may be of value if they if they are of unusual historical or literary importance. Determining the value of this type of material is difficult. The appraiser determines a value in these cases by applying knowledge and judgment to factors such as comparable sales and conditions.

As to Form 990 reporting of contributions of publications, see § 19.2, question 4.

(f) Contributions of Clothing and Household Goods

Clothing and household gifts are to be reported on the schedule (Part I, line 5). The number of these contributions is not reported. *Household goods*, according to the IRS's instructions, includes "furniture, furnishings, electronics, appliances, linens, and other similar items." This term does not include food, objects of art (see § 19.1(d)), jewelry and gems (other than costume jewelry reportable as clothing) (see § 19.1(l)), and collectibles (see § 19.1(m)).

(1) General Rules. Generally, a charitable deduction for a gift of clothing or household item is not allowed unless the gift item is in good used condition or better. A deduction may be allowed for a charitable contribution of an item of clothing or household item that is not in good used condition or better if the amount claimed for the item is more than $500 and the donor includes with the tax return a qualified appraisal with respect to the property. These provisions are effective for contributions made after August 17, 2006.

(2) Valuation. The fair market value of used clothing and household goods is usually much lower than the price paid for the goods when they were new. This type of property may have little or no market value because of its worn condition. Also, property of this nature may be out of style or no longer useful. The price that buyers of used items actually pay in consignment stores or thrift shops is a good indication of value.

As to Form 990 reporting of contributions of clothing and/or household goods, see § 19.2, questions 5 and 6.

(g) Contributions of Vehicles

Contributions of motor vehicles, boats, airplanes, and the like to charitable organizations are to be reported on the schedule (Part I, lines 6 and 7). These types of gifts have vexed Congress and the IRS for many years. Although the principal concern has been and continues to be the matter of valuation, this aspect of charitable giving also potentially involves issues directly affecting the charitable donee: private inurement, private benefit, intermediate sanctions, and the unrelated business rules.

The focus in this context is on, in the words of the IRS's instructions, motor vehicles "manufactured primarily for use on public streets, roads, and highways." For reporting purposes in this context, the concept of vehicles does not encompass vehicles that are part of the "donor's stock in trade or property held by the donor primarily for sale to consumers in the ordinary course of a trade or business" (see § 19.1(n)).

(1) Background.   Although this subject considerably predates 2000, it is notable that in that year the IRS, analogizing to *A Tale of Two Cities* and the *Star Wars* epic, observed that "there is a dark side in the Exempt Organization Universe." Indeed, the agency on that occasion reflected its view that it was under siege because of evildoing in the realm of charitable giving: The IRS "in recent years has been confronted with a number of aggressive tax avoidance schemes." None of these sometimes abusive giving arrangements, however, has irked the IRS more than the matter of solicitation of contributions to charitable organizations of automobiles and other vehicles. This matter festered over the ensuing years, with Congress legislating on the subject in 2004.

(2) Statutory Regime.   The rules entail deductibility and substantiation requirements in connection with contributions to charity of motor vehicles, boats, and airplanes—collectively termed *qualified vehicles*. These requirements supplant the general gift substantiation rules (see § 14.1(i)(7)) where the claimed value of the contributed vehicles exceeds $500.

Pursuant to these rules, a federal income tax charitable contribution deduction is not allowed unless the donor substantiates the contribution by a contemporaneous written acknowledgment of it by the donee organization and includes the acknowledgment with the donor's income tax return reflecting the deduction. This acknowledgment must contain the name and taxpayer identification number of the donor and the vehicle identification number or similar number. If the gift is of a qualified vehicle that was sold by the donee charitable organization without any "significant intervening use or material improvement," the acknowledgment must also contain a certification that the vehicle was sold in an arm's-length transaction between unrelated parties, a statement as to the gross proceeds derived from the sale, and a statement that the deductible amount may not exceed the amount of the gross proceeds. If there is this type of use or improvement, the acknowledgment must include a certification as to the intended use or material improvement of the vehicle and the intended duration of the use and a certification that the vehicle will not be transferred in exchange for money, other property, or services before completion of the use or improvement. An acknowledgment is *contemporaneous* if the donee organization provides it within 30 days of the sale of the qualified vehicle or, in an instance of an acknowledgment including the foregoing certifications, of the contribution of the vehicle.

The amount of the charitable deduction for a gift of a qualified vehicle depends on the nature of the use of the vehicle by the donee organization. If the charitable organization sells the vehicle without any significant intervening use or material improvement of the vehicle by the organization, the amount of the charitable deduction may not exceed the gross proceeds received from the sale. Where there is a use or improvement, the charitable deduction is based on the fair market value of the vehicle.

The legislative history accompanying this law states that these two exceptions are to be strictly construed. To meet this *significant use* test, the organization must actually use the vehicle to substantially further the organization's regularly conducted activities and the use must be significant. The test is not satisfied if the use is incidental or not intended at the time of the contribution. Whether a use is *significant* also depends on the frequency and duration of use.

A *material improvement* includes major repairs to a vehicle or other improvements to the vehicle that improve its condition in a manner that significantly increases the vehicle's value. Cleaning the vehicle, minor repairs, and routine maintenance do not constitute a material improvement. Presumably this exception is available only when the donee charitable organization expresses its intent at the outset (at least in part by means of the certification) that the donee plans to materially improve the vehicle.

A donee organization that is required to provide an acknowledgment under these rules must also provide that information to the IRS. A penalty is imposed for the furnishing of a false or fraudulent acknowledgment, or an untimely or incomplete acknowledgment, by a charitable organization to a donor of a qualified vehicle.

(3) Regulatory Gloss. The IRS issued guidance concerning these rules for deductible charitable contributions of qualified vehicles. This guidance added third exception to these rules, which is for circumstances where the charity gives or sells the vehicle at a significantly below-market price to a needy individual, as long as the transfer furthers the charitable purpose of helping a poor or distressed individual who is in need of a means of transportation. The guidance also explains how the fair market value of a vehicle is determined.

(4) Form 1098-C. The IRS issued a form (Form 1098-C) to be used by donee charitable organizations to report to the IRS contributions of qualified vehicles and to provide the donor with a contemporaneous written acknowledgment of the contribution. A donor of a qualified vehicle must attach Copy B of this form to the donor's income tax return in order to take a deduction for the contribution of the vehicle where the claimed value is in excess of $500. Generally, the donee must furnish Copies B and C of the form to the donor either no later than 30 days after the date of sale or 30 days after the date of the contribution, depending on the circumstances. Copy A of this form is to be filed with the IRS, Copy C is for the donor's records, and Copy D is retained by the charitable donee.

(5) Valuation. Various commercial firms and trade organizations publish monthly or seasonal guides as to vehicles for different regions of the nation, containing complete dealer sale prices or dealer average prices for recent model years. Prices are reported for each make, model, and year. These guides also provide estimates for adjusting for unusual equipment, unusual mileage, and physical condition. Although these prices are not "official" and these publications do not rise to the level of an appraisal of any specific property, they provide clues for making an appraisal and suggest relative prices for comparison with current sales and offerings in particular geographical areas.

An acceptable measure of the fair market value of an automobile, boat, or airplane is an amount not in excess of the price listed in a used vehicle pricing guide for a private party sale, rather than the dealer retail value, of a similar vehicle. The fair market value may be less than that amount, however, if the vehicle has engine trouble, body damage, high mileage, or excessive wear. The fair market value of a vehicle is the same as the price listed in a used vehicle pricing guide for a private party sale only if the guide lists a sales price for a vehicle that is the same make, model, and year, sold in the same geographic area, in the same condition, with the same or similar options or accessories, and with the same or similar warranties.

Except for inexpensive boats, the valuation of these vehicles should be based on an appraisal by a marine surveyor because the physical condition of the boat is critical in ascertaining its value.

(6) Other Issues. *Appraisal.* If the value of the contributed vehicle is in excess of $5,000, the donor is obligated to obtain an independent appraisal of the value of the vehicle (see § 19.1(g)).

Penalties. Both parties are potentially liable for penalties for aiding and abetting understatements of tax liability, for preparation of false tax returns, and for promoting abusive tax shelters.

Unrelated Business Considerations. When vehicles are contributed to a charitable organization and the organization disposes of them, the charity may be perceived as being in the business of acquiring and selling the vehicles. Nonetheless, this activity is not considered an unrelated business, because of a *donated goods exception.* In some instances, payments to a charitable organization in the context of these programs may be characterized as tax-excludable royalties.

Contributions "to" Charity. To be deductible, a contribution must be to (or for the use of) a qualified charitable organization. To be *to* a charity, the gift must be made under circumstances where the donee has full control of the donated money or other property and full discretion as to its use. When a charitable organization utilizes the services of a for-profit company to receive and process donated vehicles, the gift may be deemed to be to the company, rather than the charity, in which case there is no charitable contribution deduction. This situation can be resolved, however, by denominating the company as the agent of the charity for this purpose.

Private Benefit Doctrine. The IRS has raised the issue of applicability of the private benefit doctrine. The agency posits situations in which an automobile dealer or some other third party is the true beneficiary of a transaction. If the private benefit is more than insubstantial, the charitable organization's tax-exempt status could be jeopardized.

Private Inurement Doctrine. The IRS has also raised the possibility of application, in this setting, of the private inurement doctrine. When such a third party is an insider with respect to the charitable organization, that doctrine could be implicated, thereby endangering the organization's exempt status.

Intermediate Sanctions. The intermediate sanctions rules are applicable when a transaction constitutes an *excess benefit transaction* and the charitable organization's dealings are with a *disqualified person* with respect to it. The IRS may also assess a penalty for willful and flagrant violation of these standards.

As to Form 990 reporting of contributions of vehicles, see § 21.2, questions 7 and 8.

(h)   Contributions of Intellectual Property

Intellectual property gifts are to be reported on the schedule (Part I, line 8). The IRS's instructions define the term *intellectual property* as any "patent, copyright [with some exceptions], trademark, trade name, trade secret, know-how, software [with an exception], or similar property."

The value of certain intellectual property contributed to charity can be speculative. An item of contributed intellectual property may prove to be worthless or the initial promise of worth may be diminished by subsequent inventions, marketplace competition, or other factors. Even if intellectual property has the potential for significant monetary benefit, this will not be the outcome if the charitable donee does not make the appropriate investment, have the necessary personnel and equipment, and/or have sufficient sustained interest to exploit the intellectual property. Valuation is made yet more difficult in the charitable contribution context because the transferee does not provide full, if any, consideration in exchange for the transferred property pursuant to arm's-length negotiations and there may not be a comparable sales market for the property to use as a benchmark for valuations.

Congress, in 2004, enacted legislation concerning charitable contributions of intellectual property. This legislation is predicated on the view that excessive charitable contribution deductions enabled by inflated valuations in this context are best addressed by confining the amount of the deduction for gifts of intellectual property to the donor's basis in the property (or, if less, the property's fair market value) while allowing for charitable contribution deductions thereafter if the contributed property generates income for the charitable organization.

(1) Statutory Regime.   Contributions of certain types of intellectual property have been added to the list of gifts that give rise to a charitable contribution deduction that is confined to the donor's basis in the property, although, as discussed later in this section, in instances of gifts of intellectual property, there may be one or more subsequent charitable deductions. Collectively, these properties are termed *qualified intellectual property* (except in instances when contributed to private foundations).

A person who makes this type of gift, denominated a *qualified intellectual property contribution,* is provided a charitable contribution deduction (subject to the annual percentage limitations) equal to the donor's basis in the property in the year of the gift and, in that year and/or subsequent years, a charitable deduction equal to a percentage of net income that flows to the charitable donee as the consequence of the gift of the property. For a contribution to be a qualified intellectual property contribution, the donor must notify the donee at the time of the contribution that the donor intends to treat the contribution as a qualified intellectual property contribution for deduction and reporting purposes. The net income involved is termed *qualified donee income.*

Thus, a portion of qualified donee income is allocated to a tax year of the donor, although this income allocation process is inapplicable to income received by or accrued to the donee after 10 years from the date of the gift; the process is also inapplicable to donee income received by or accrued to the donee after the expiration of the legal life of the property.

The amount of qualified donee income that materializes into a charitable deduction, for one or more years, is ascertained by the *applicable percentage*, which is a sliding-scale percentage determined by this table, which appears in the Internal Revenue Code:

Donor's Tax Year	Applicable Percentage
1st	100
2nd	100
3rd	90
4th	80
5th	70
6th	60
7th	50
8th	40
9th	30
10th	20
11th	10
12th	10

Thus, if, following a qualified intellectual property contribution, the charitable donee receives qualified donee income in the year of the gift, and/or in the subsequent tax year of the donor, that amount becomes, in full, a charitable contribution deduction for the donor (subject to the general limitations). If such income is received by the charitable donee eight years after the gift, for example, the donor receives a charitable deduction equal to 40 percent of the qualified donee income. As this table indicates, the opportunity for a qualified intellectual property deduction arising out of a qualified intellectual property contribution terminates after the 12th year of the donor ending after the date of the gift.

The reporting requirements rules, concerning certain dispositions of contributed property, were amended in 2004 to encompass qualified intellectual property contributions.

(2) Notification Requirement.   A donor satisfies the notification requirement if the donor delivers or mails to the donee, at the time of the contribution, a statement containing (1) the donor's name, address, and taxpayer identification number; (2) a description of the intellectual property in sufficient detail to identify it; (3) the date of the contribution; and (4) a statement that the donor intends to treat the contribution as a qualified intellectual property contribution. This filing is accomplished by means of Form 8899.

(3) Valuation.   The fair market value of a patent is determined by taking into account factors such as whether the patented technology has been made obsolete by other technology; any restrictions on the holders' use of, or ability to transfer, the patented technology; and the length of time remaining before the patent expires.

As to Form 990 reporting of contributions of intellectual property, see § 21.2, question 9.

(i) Contributions of Securities

Contributions of securities are reflected on the schedule (Part I, lines 9–12). A *security* is defined in the IRS's instructions as any "bond, debenture, note, or certificate or other evidence of indebtedness issued by a corporation or a government or political subdivision, share of stock, voting trust certificate, or any certificate of interest or participation in, certificate of deposit or receipt for, temporary or interim certificate for, or warrant or right to subscribe to or purchase, any of the foregoing."

(1) General Rules. The law distinguishes among *publicly traded securities*, which are defined in the IRS's instructions as securities "for which (as of the date of the contribution) market quotations are readily available on an established securities market"; *closely held stock*, which means "shares of stock issued by a corporation that is not publicly traded"; interests in a partnership, limited liability company, or trust which are not publicly traded; and other (miscellaneous) securities.

(2) Valuation. The value of a stock or a bond is the fair market value of the security on the valuation date. If there is an active market for the stocks or bonds, such as on a stock exchange or in an over-the-counter market, the fair market value of each share or bond is the average price between the highest and lowest quoted selling prices on the valuation date.

If there were no sales of the security on the valuation date, but there were sales within a reasonable period before and after the valuation date, the fair market value of a security is determined by taking the average price between the highest and lowest sales prices on the nearest date before and on the nearest date after the valuation date. Then the averages are weighted in inverse order by the respective number of trading days between the selling dates and the valuation date.

Stocks or bonds listed on more than one stock exchange are valued on the basis of the prices of the exchange on which they are principally dealt. This applies if these prices are published in a generally available listing or publication of general circulation. If this is not applicable, and the stocks or bonds are reported on a composite listing of combined exchanges in a publication of general circulation, the composite list should be used to determine value.

If there were no sales within a reasonable period before and after the valuation date, the fair market value of the security is the average price between the bona fide bid and asked prices on the valuation date.

If there were no prices available on the valuation date, fair market value of a security is determined by taking the average prices between the bona fide bid and asked prices on the closest trading date before and after the valuation date. Both dates must be within a reasonable period. Then these averages are weighted in inverse order by the respective number of trading days between the bid and asked dates and the valuation date.

If no selling prices or bona fide bid and asked prices are available on a date within a reasonable period before the valuation date, but are available on a date within a reasonable period after the valuation date, or if the reverse is the case, the average price between the highest and lowest of such available prices may be treated as the value.

When a large block of stock is put on the market, the selling price of the stock may be lowered if the supply exceeds the demand. Conversely, market forces may exist that will afford higher prices for large blocks of stock. Because of the many factors to consider, a determination of the value of large blocks of stock usually requires the assistance of experts specializing in underwriting large quantities of securities or in trading in the securities of the industry of which the particular issuing company is a part.

If selling prices or bid and asked prices are not available, or if securities of a closely held corporation are involved, the fair market value of the security is determined by consideration of these factors: (1) for bonds, the factors include the soundness of the security, the interest yield, and the date of maturity; (2) for shares of stock, the factors include the company's net worth, prospective earning power, and dividend-paying capacity.

Other relevant factors include the nature and history of the business, particularly its recent history; the goodwill of the business; the economic outlook in the particular industry; the company's position in the industry, its competitors, and its management; and the value of securities engaged in the same or similar business. For preferred stock, the most important factors are its yield, dividend coverage, and protection of its liquidation preference.

Some classes of stock cannot be publicly traded because of restrictions imposed by the Securities and Exchange Commission, by the corporate charter, or by a trust agreement. These *restricted securities* usually trade at a discount in relation to freely traded securities. Factors to be considered in ascertaining the fair market value of restricted securities include the resale provisions found in the restriction agreements, the relative negotiating strengths of the buyer and seller, and the market experience of freely traded securities of the same class as the restricted securities.

As to Form 990 reporting of contributions of securities, see § 19.2, questions 9 to 12.

(j)   Qualified Conservation Contributions

Qualified conservation contributions are to be reported on the schedule (Part I, lines 13 and 14). A *qualified conservation contribution* is a contribution of a qualified real property interest exclusively for conservation purposes. A *qualified real property interest* means any of these interests in real property: the entire interest of the donor, a remainder interest, or a restriction (such as an easement), granted in perpetuity, on the use that may be made of the real property. A *conservation purpose* means (1) the preservation of land areas for outdoor recreation by, or for the education of, the public; (2) the protection of a relatively natural habitat of fish, wildlife, plants, or similar ecosystems; (3) the preservation of open space (including farmland and forest land) where the preservation is for the scenic enjoyment of the public or is in accordance with governmental conservation policy; or (4) the preservation of an historically important land area or a certified historic structure.

A qualified real property interest may also entail a restriction with respect to the exterior of a certified historic structure. A *certified historic structure* is, according to the regulations, any "building or structure listed in the National Register as well as any building [that is] certified as being of historic significance to a registered historic district."

As to Form 990 reporting of qualified conservation contributions, see § 19.2, questions 13 and 14.

(k)   Contribution of Real Estate

Contributions of real estate are reflected on the schedule (Part I, lines 15–17). The law differentiates among residential real estate, commercial real estate, and other real estate interests. The term *personal residence* includes, according to the IRS's instructions, any "property used by the donor as a personal residence but is not limited to the donor's principal residence" and a dwelling represented by "stock owned by the donor as a tenant-stockholder in a cooperative housing corporation if the dwelling the donor is entitled to occupy as a tenant-stockholder is used by the donor as a personal residence." This also includes holdings "(not in trust) of a remainder interest in a personal residence which [is] not the donor's entire interest in the property."

Commercial real estate includes a commercial office building and a holding (not in trust) of a remainder interest in a farm that is not the donor's entire interest in the property. A *farm* is, according to the IRS's instructions, "land used for the production of crops, fruits, or other agricultural products or for the maintenance of livestock"; the term includes improvements located on the farm property.

As to Form 990 reporting of contributions of real estate, see § 19.2, questions 15 to 17.

(l) Contributions of Jewelry and Gems

Jewelry and gems are of such specialized nature that it is almost always necessary to obtain an appraisal by a knowledgeable appraiser. The appraisal should include a description of the style of the jewelry, the cut and setting of the gem, and whether the item is now in fashion. If it is not currently in fashion, the possibility of having the property redesigned, recut, or reset should be reported in the appraisal. The stone's coloring, weight, cut, brilliance, and flaws should be analyzed and reported. Sentimental value does not have an impact on the determination of fair value of jewelry or gems. The fact that an item of jewelry was owned or worn by a famous individual may increase the value of the item. Contributions of jewelry and gems may be reported as gifts of works of art (see § 19.1(d)) or as collectibles (see § 19.1(m)).

(m) Contributions of Collectibles

Collectibles are to be reported on the schedule (Part I, line 18). Many of the elements of valuation that apply with respect to works of art (see § 19.1(d)) apply to collections.

(1) General Rules. *Collectibles* include, according to the IRS's instructions, "autographs, sports memorabilia, dolls, stamps, coins, books [other than those referenced in § 19.1(e)], gems, and jewelry (other than costume jewelry)," but not art (see § 19.1(d)) or historical artifacts (see § 19.1(q)). Other items in this category are manuscripts, guns, phonograph records, and natural history items.

(2) Valuation. Valuation of a collection can be accomplished by use of catalogs, dealers' price lists, and specialized hobby periodicals. The most current edition of these types of reference materials, as of the contribution date, must be used. Nonetheless, these sources are not always reliable indicators as to fair market value (such as a dealer selling an item that has been unsold for some time at a discount or a rigged sale at an auction), and the value may need to be supported by other evidence.

For example, in the case of stamp collections, libraries have catalogs that report estimates of values (for postmarked and not postmarked stamps); stamp dealers generally are able to prepare satisfactory appraisals of valuable collections. Likewise, in connection with coin collections, many catalogs and other reference materials reflect opinion as to the value of coins on or near the date of the publication. Like many other collectors' items, the value of a coin depends on the demand for it, its age, its rarity, and its condition (mint or only good).

As to Form 990 reporting of contributions of collectibles, see § 19.2, question 18.

(n) Contributions of Inventory

Contributions of food inventory are reflected on the schedule (Part I, question 19). As a general rule, when a corporation makes a charitable gift of property from its inventory, the resulting charitable deduction cannot exceed an amount equal to the donor's cost basis in the donated property. In most instances, this basis amount is rather small, being equal to the cost of producing the property. Under certain circumstances, however, corporate donors can receive a greater charitable deduction for gifts out of their inventory. Where the tests are satisfied, the deduction can be equal to cost basis plus one-half of the appreciated value of the property. The charitable deduction may not, in any event, exceed an amount equal to twice the property's cost basis.

Five requirements have to be met for this twice-basis charitable deduction to be available:

1. The donated property must be used by the charitable donee for a related use.

2. The donated property must be used solely for the care of the ill, the needy, or infants.

3. The property may not be transferred by the donee in exchange for money, other property, or services.

4. The donor must receive a written statement from the donee representing that the use and disposition of the donated property will be in conformance with these rules.

5. Where the donated property is subject to regulation under the Federal Food, Drug, and Cosmetic Act, the property must fully satisfy the act's requirements on the date of transfer and for the previous 180 days.

For these rules to apply, the donee must be a public charity; that is, it cannot be a private foundation or a private operating foundation.

Any person engaged in a trade or business is eligible to claim an enhanced deduction for certain contributions of food inventory. For entities other than C corporations, the total deduction for contributions of food inventory in a tax year generally may not exceed 10 percent of the person's net income for the year from all sole proprietorships, S corporations, or partnerships (or other entity that is not a C corporation) from which contributions of apparently wholesome food are made.

The phrase *apparently wholesome food* means food intended for human consumption that meets all quality and labeling standards imposed by federal, state, and local laws, even though the food may not be readily marketable due to appearance, age, freshness, grade, size, surplus, or other conditions.

As to Form 990 reporting of contributions of food inventory, see § 19.2, question 19.

(o) Contributions of Drugs and Medical Supplies

Contributions of drugs, medical supplies, and similar items contributed by corporations and other businesses that manufactured or distributed the items are to be reported on the schedule (Part I, line 20).

As to Form 990 reporting of contributions of drugs and medical supplies, see § 19.2, question 20.

(p) Contributions of Taxidermy

Contributions of taxidermy are to be reported on the schedule (Part I, line 21). *Taxidermy property* is, according to the IRS's instructions, any "work of art that is the reproduction or preservation of an animal, in whole or in part; is prepared, stuffed, or mounted to recreate one or more characteristics of the animal, and contains a part of the body of the dead animal." The amount allowed as a deduction for charitable contributions of taxidermy property that is contributed by the person who prepared, stuffed, or mounted the property is the lesser of the taxpayer's basis in the property or its fair market value. Most associated indirect costs may not be included in basis. These rules apply to contributions made after July 25, 2006.

As to Form 990 reporting of contributions of taxidermy, see § 19.2, question 21.

(q) Contributions of Historical Artifacts

Contributions of historical artifacts are to be reported on the schedule (Part I, line 22). These properties include furniture, fixtures, textiles, and household items of a historic nature. Works of art and historical treasures are reported separately (see § 19.1(d)), as are archeological artifacts (see § 19.1(s)).

As to Form 990 reporting of contributions of historical artifacts, see § 19.2, question 22.

(r) Contributions of Scientific Specimens

Contributions of scientific specimens are to be reported on the schedule (Part I, line 23). Pursuant to the IRS's instructions, the term *scientific specimens* includes "living plant and animal specimens and objects or materials that are examples of natural and physical sciences, such as rocks and minerals, or that relate to, or exhibit, the methods or principles of science."

As to Form 990 reporting of contributions of scientific specimens, see § 19.2, question 23.

(s) Contributions of Archeological Artifacts

Contributions of archeological and ethnological artifacts are to be reported on the schedule (Part I, line 24). Works of art, historical treasures, and historical artifacts are reported separately (see § 19.1(d), (q)).

An *archeological artifact* is, as defined in the IRS's instructions, any "object that is over 250 years old and is normally discovered as a result of scientific excavation, clandestine or accidental digging for exploration on land or under water." *Ethnological artifacts* are, according to these regulations, "objects which are the product of a tribal or non-industrial society, and important to the culture heritage of a people because of its distinctive characteristics, comparative rarity or its contribution to the knowledge of the origins, development or history of that people."

As to Form 990 reporting of contributions of archeological or ethnological artifacts, see § 19.2, question 24.

(t) Other Types of Property

Other types of property (if any) need to be separately reported (see Part I, lines 25–28). This includes items that did not satisfy charitable deduction requirements applicable to the contribution of the type of property but which were contributed to the organization, such as clothing and household goods that were not in good used or better condition (see § 19.1(f)) and conservation easements that do not constitute qualified conservation contributions (see § 19.1(j)). Self-created items, such as personal papers and manuscripts, including archival records, must be separately listed.

According to the IRS's instructions, the term *archival records* means "materials of any kind created or received by any person, family, or organization in the conduct of their affairs [*sic*] that are preserved because of the enduring value of the information they contain or as evidence of the functions and responsibilities of their creator." Also, contributions of items used by the organization at a charitable auction (other than items sold by the charity at the auction), such as food served at the event or floral centerpieces, may be reported on these lines.

(u) Form 8283

Form 8283 is a form that must be filed with a donor's tax return if the claimed total deduction is over $500 for all contributed noncash property.

In Section A, Part I, of this form, the donor is required to list:

- Items (or groups of similar items) for which the donor claimed a charitable deduction of $5,000 or less
- Publicly traded securities even if the claimed deduction is more than $5,000

Each gift of property is assigned a letter (beginning with A).

Part I is comprised of eight columns requesting the name and address of the donee organization (Column (a)), a description of the donated property (Column (b)), the date of the contribution (Column (c)), the date the property was acquired by the donor (month and year) (Column (d)), how the property was acquired by the donor (Column (e)), the donor's cost or adjusted basis (Column (f)), the fair market value of the property (Column (g)), and the method used to determine the fair market value of the property (Column (h)). If the amount claimed by the donor as a charitable deduction for an item of property is $500 or less, the donor is not required to complete Columns (d) to (f).

Part II is to be completed if:

- The donor gave less than an entire interest in a property listed in Part I, and/or
- Conditions were placed on a contribution listed in Part I.

The donor must enter the letter from Part I that identifies the property as to which less than an entire interest was given; if Part II is applicable to more than one property, a separate statement is required for the other property(ies) (line 2a). The donor must report the total amount claimed as a deduction for the property listed in Part I for the tax year involved and for any prior tax years (line 2b). The name and address of each organization to which any such contribution was made in a prior year must be reported (if different from the address of the donee organization reported in Part I) (line 2c). For tangible property, the donor must report the place where the property is located or kept (line 2d). The donor must report the name of any person, other than the donee organization, having actual possession of the property (line 2e).

The donor must report whether a restriction, either temporary or permanent, was placed on the donee's right to use or dispose of the donated property ("yes" or "no") (line 3a). The donor must report whether the donor gave to anyone (other than the donee organization or another organization participating with the donee organization in cooperative fundraising) the right to the income from the donated property or to the possession of the property, including the right to vote donated securities, to acquire the property by purchase or otherwise, or to designate the person having this type of income, possession, or the right to acquire ("yes" or "no") (line 3b). The donor must report whether there is a restriction limiting the donated property to a particular use ("yes" or "no") (line 3c).

Section B of Form 8283 consists of four parts. In this section, the donor must list the items (or groups of similar items) for which the donor claimed a deduction of more than $5,000 per item or group (other than contributions of publicly traded securities (see § 19.1(i)). (Generally, an appraisal is required for property listed in this section.)

In Part I, the type of property donated must be reported (by checking a box): art (contribution of $20,000 or more), art (contribution of less than $20,000), collectibles, qualified conservation property, other real estate, intellectual property, equipment, securities, and other. Each of these gifts is assigned a letter (beginning with A). This part also consists of nine columns requesting a description of the donated property (Column (a)), a brief summary of the overall physical condition of the property (if tangible property) at the time of the gift (Column (b)), the appraised fair market value of the property (Column (c)), the date the property was acquired by the donor (Column (d)), the method of acquisition of the property by the donor (Column (e)), the donor's cost or adjusted basis in the property (Column (f)), the amount received by the donor (in the case of a bargain sale) (Column (g)), the amount claimed as a deduction (Column (h)), and (in the case of securities) the average trading price (Column (i)).

Part II consists of a donor statement, with the donor declaring that the item(s) in Part I has, to the best of the donor's knowledge and belief, an appraised value of no more than $500 per item. The donor is to attach a list of these items, accompanied by the identifying letter from Part I and a description of the specific item.

Part III is a declaration of the appraiser, with the appraiser declaring compliance with the qualified appraisal requirements and certifying understanding of the tax penalty law structure. Part IV is the donee acknowledgment, where the organization acknowledges that it is a qualified charitable organization and reports the date it received the donated property. The charitable donee affirms, by executing the form, that, in the event it sells, exchanges, or otherwise disposes of the gift property (or a portion of it) within three years after the date of receipt, it will file Form 8282 with the IRS and provide a copy of that form to the donor. The form states that this acknowledgment "does not represent agreement [by the charitable organization] with the claimed fair market value." The form requires the charity to report whether it intends to use the property for an unrelated use ("yes" or "no").

(v)   Form 8282

Form 8282 is filed by donee organizations to report information to the IRS and donors about dispositions of charitable deduction property made within three years after the donor contributed the property. *Charitable deduction property* is contributed property (other than money and publicly traded securities) if the claimed value exceeds $5,000 per item or group of similar items donated to one or more donee organizations. (This is the property referenced in Form 8283, Part B (see § 19.1(u).)

More specifically, original donees and successor donees generally must file Form 8282 if they sell, exchange, consume, or otherwise dispose of (with or without consideration) charitable deduction property (or a portion of it) within three years after the date the original donee received the property. Special rules apply in connection with dispositions of motor vehicles, airplanes, and boats.

There are two situations in which the Form 8282 does not have to be filed:

1. The organization does not have to file the form if, at the time the original donee signed Section B of Form 8283, the donor signed a statement on Form 8283 that the appraised value of the specific item was not more than $500. If Form 8283 contains reference to more than one item, this exception applies only to those items that are clearly identified as having a value of $500 or less. For purposes of the donor's determination of whether the appraised value of the item exceeds $500, however, all shares of nonpublicly traded stock, or items that form a set, are considered one item.

2. The organization does not have to file Form 8282 if an item is consumed or distributed, without consideration, in fulfillment of the organization's exempt purpose or function.

Part I of Form 8282 is used to report certain basic information about the original donor and the successor donee. Part II is used to report information on previous donees. Part III is used to provide information about the donated property. Part IV is a certification that may have to be executed by the donee involved.

(w)   Restrictions as to Donee Holding of Property

A donor may impose the requirement that the donee hold the property for at least three years from the date of the contribution, where the property is not obligated for use for exempt purposes.

(x)   Nonstandard Contributions

A *nonstandard contribution* includes, as stated in the IRS's instructions, a contribution of an item "that is not reasonably expected to be used to satisfy or further the organization's exempt purpose (aside from the need of such organization for income or funds) and for which (a) there is no ready market to which the organization may go to liquidate the contribution and convert it to cash and (b) the value of the item is highly speculative or difficult to ascertain."

For example, the contribution of a taxpayer's successor member interest is a nonstandard contribution. Essentially, in this type of transaction, a taxpayer acquires a successor member interest in a limited liability company that owns real estate, then transfers the interest more than one year after acquiring it to a charitable organization, claiming a charitable contribution deduction that is significantly greater than the amount the taxpayer paid to acquire the interest. In late 2007, the IRS launched an examination program pertain to these contributions, by means of a prototype letter and information document request that the charitable organization must answer.

(y) Substantiation and Reporting Requirements

The IRS, on August 6, 2008, issued four proposed regulations concerning the federal tax law substantiation and reporting requirements, and new definitions of *qualified appraisal* and *qualified appraiser*, in the charitable contribution context, to reflect law changes made in 2004 and 2006. These proposed regulations restate and incorporate a considerable amount of existing law.

(1) Noncash Contributions Substantiation Requirements. In general, a donor who claims an income tax charitable contribution deduction for a noncash charitable gift of less than $250 is required, under current law, to obtain a receipt from the donee or keep reliable records. The proposed regulations make it clear that, for such a gift by an individual, partnership, S corporation, or C corporation that is a personal service corporation or closely held corporation, there is no charitable deduction unless the donor maintains for each contribution a receipt from the charitable donee showing these five elements: the name and address of the donee, the date of the contribution, a description of the property in sufficient detail, and, if the gift is of securities, the name of the issuer, the type of security, and whether the securities are publicly traded.

If, however, it is impractical to obtain a receipt from the donee (such as when a donor deposits canned food at a charity's unattended drop site), the donor may satisfy the recordkeeping rules by maintaining reliable written records for the contributed property. The reliability of a written record is to be determined on the basis of all of the facts and circumstances of a particular case, including the contemporaneous nature of the writing evidencing the gift. Nonetheless, a *reliable written record* must include the five elements just cited, the fair market value of the property on the contribution date, the method used to determine the value, and, in the case of a contribution of clothing or a household item (see § 19.1(f)), the condition of the item.

An income tax charitable contribution deduction is not allowed for a noncash charitable contribution of $250 or more, but not more than $500, unless the donor substantiates the gift with a contemporaneous written acknowledgment (present law). This deduction is not allowed for a noncash charitable contribution of more than $500, but less than $5,000, unless the donor substantiates the contribution with a contemporaneous written acknowledgment and meets the Form 8283, Section A, completion and filing requirements (see § 19.1(u)). This latter rule is applicable to individuals, partnerships, S corporations, and C corporations that are personal service corporations or closely held corporations.

A completed Form 8283, Section A, includes the donor's name and taxpayer identification number, the name and address of the donee, the date of the contribution, and certain information about the contributed property. That information consists of (1) a description of the property in sufficient detail; (2) a statement as to the condition of the property; (3) in the case of securities, the name of the issuer, the type of security, and whether the securities are publicly traded; (4) the fair market value of the property on the contribution date; and (5) the method used in determining the property's value. This schedule also is to include information about the manner the property was acquired by the donor and the approximate date of acquisition (or substantial completion) of the property, the donor's basis in the property, and, in the case of tangible personal property, whether the donee has certified it for a use that is related to the donee's exempt purpose. In the case of a contribution of a vehicle, the donor must attach a copy of the acknowledgment to the Schedule A for the return on which the deduction is claimed.

Generally, there is no federal income tax charitable contribution deduction for a noncash charitable gift of more than $5,000 unless the donor substantiates the contribution with a contemporaneous written acknowledgment, obtains a qualified appraisal prepared by a qualified appraiser (see § 19.1(y)(3)), and completes and files Form 8283, Section B. Nonetheless, a qualified appraisal is not required, and a completed Form 8283, Section A, substitutes for a completed Form 8283, Section B, for contributions of publicly traded securities, inventory, vehicles, and intellectual property (see § 19.1(i), (n), (g), (h), respectively).

A completed Form 8283, Schedule B, includes the donor's name and taxpayer identification number; the donee's name, address, taxpayer identification number, and signature; the date signed by the donee and the date the donee received the property; the appraiser's name, address, taxpayer identification number, an appraiser declaration, signature, and the date signed by the appraiser; the fair market value of the contributed property, a description of the property and its condition; the manner of acquisition and the approximate date of acquisition (or substantial completion) of the property by the donor; the donor's basis in the property; and a statement explaining whether the charitable contribution was made by means of a bargain sale and, if so, the amount of consideration received by the donor for the transfer.

Generally, a federal income tax charitable contribution deduction is not allowed for a noncash charitable contribution of more than $500,000 unless the donor substantiates the contribution with a contemporaneous written acknowledgment, obtains a qualified appraisal prepared by a qualified appraiser, completes and files Section B of the Form 8283, and attaches a copy of the qualified appraisal of the property to the return on which the deduction is claimed. Again, a qualified appraisal is not required and a completed Form 8283, Section A, substitutes for a completed Form 8283, Section B, for contributions of publicly traded securities, intellectual property, vehicles, and inventory.

These rules as to substantiation documents that must be submitted with a tax return also apply to a return reflecting a carryover of the deduction. (See § 19.1(a)(3).)

This proposal also addresses the number of Forms 8283 that may be required, rules as to the Form 8283 for partners and S corporation shareholders, and determination of the deduction amount for purposes of the substantiation rules.

(2) Qualified Appraisal. Pursuant to a proposed regulation, a *qualified appraisal* is an appraisal document that is prepared by a qualified appraiser (see § 19.1(y)(3)) in accordance with generally accepted appraisal standards. These standards are the substance and principles of the Uniform Standards of Professional Appraisal Practice as developed by the Appraisal Standards Board of the Appraisal Foundation.

A qualified appraisal must include certain information about the contributed property, namely, a suitable description of the property, a statement of the condition of the property (other than securities), the valuation effective date (which is the date to which the value opinion applies), and the fair market value of the contributed property on that date. This appraisal must also reflect the terms of any agreement or understanding by or on behalf of the donor and donee that relates to the use, sale, or other disposition of the contributed property, such as a restriction on the donee as to use or disposition of the property, a reservation as to right to the income from or possession of the property, or an earmarking of the property for a particular use. The appraisal must also show the date (or expected date) of the contribution, certain information about the appraiser, the signature of the appraiser, the date the appraiser signed the appraisal, a declaration by the appraiser, a statement that the appraisal was prepared for income tax purposes, the method of valuation used, and the basis for the valuation.

A qualified appraisal must be signed and dated by the qualified appraiser no earlier than 60 days before the date of the contribution and no later than (1) the due date (including extensions) of the return on which the charitable deduction is first claimed, (2) the due date (including extensions) of the return on which the charitable deduction is first reported (where the donor is a partnership or S corporation), or (3) if the deduction is first claimed on an amended return, the date on which the amended return is filed.

An appraisal is not a qualified appraisal for a contribution, even if these requirements are satisfied, if a reasonable person would conclude that the donor failed to disclose or misrepresent facts that would cause the appraiser to overstate the value of the contributed property. The fee for a qualified appraisal cannot be based on the appraised value of the property. The donor must retain the qualified appraisal "for so long as it may be relevant in the administration of any internal revenue law." If the contributed property is a partial interest, the appraisal must be of that interest.

(3) Qualified Appraiser. Pursuant to a proposed regulation, a *qualified appraiser* is an individual with verifiable education and experience in valuing the type of property for which the appraisal is performed. An individual is treated as having the requisite education and experience if, as of the date of signing the appraisal, the individual has (1) successfully completed professional or college-level course work in valuing the type of property and has two or more years of experience in valuing the type of property or (2) earned a recognized appraisal designation for the type of property involved.

The course work must be obtained from a professional or college-level educational institution, a generally recognized professional appraisal organization that regularly offers educational programs in the principles of valuation, or an employer as part of an employee apprenticeship or educational program that is substantially similar to the preceding types of programs. A *recognized appraisal designation* is a designation awarded by a recognized professional appraiser organization on the basis of demonstrated competency. Education and experience in valuing the relevant type of property are *verifiable* if the appraiser specifies in the appraisal the appraiser's education and experience in valuing the type of property involved and the appraiser makes a declaration in the appraisal that, because of the appraiser's education and experience, the appraiser is qualified to make appraisals of the relevant type of property being valued.

These individuals cannot be qualified appraisers:

- An individual who receives a prohibited fee (as discussed earlier in this section)

- The donor of the property

- A party to the transaction in which the donor acquired the property, unless the property is contributed within two months of the date of its acquisition and the appraised value is not in excess of the acquisition price

- The donee of the property

- An individual who is (1) related to or an employee of any of the foregoing three categories of individuals or married to an individual who has a defined relationship with any of these individuals or (2) an independent contractor who is regularly used as an appraiser by any of the foregoing three categories of individuals and who does not perform a majority of his or her appraisals for others during the tax year

- An individual who is prohibited from practicing before the IRS at any time during the three-year period ending on the date the appraisal is signed by the individual

(4) Clothing and Household Items.   Generally, pursuant to a proposed regulation, a federal income tax charitable contribution deduction is not allowed for a contribution of clothing or a household item unless the item is in good used condition or better at the time of the contribution and the noncash substantiation requirements (see § 19.1(f)) are satisfied.

The rule requiring that the property be in good used condition or better is inapplicable to a contribution of a single item of clothing or a household item for which a charitable deduction of more than $500 is claimed, if the donor submits with the tax return on which the deduction is claimed a copy of a qualified appraisal (see § 19.1(y)(2)) of the property prepared by a qualified appraiser and a completed Form 8283, Section B.

§19.2   PREPARATION OF NEW FORM 990 SCHEDULE M

Schedule M consists of many questions pertaining to contributions to public charities and other categories of tax-exempt organizations of types of property other than money (*noncash contributions*). This schedule must be completed by exempt organizations that report, as revenue, more than an aggregate of $25,000 of noncash contributions on Form 990 (Part IV, line 1g). This schedule must also be filed by organizations that received during the year any contributions of art, historical treasures, or other similar assets, or qualified conservation contributions. At the top of this schedule, the filing organization must enter its name and employer identification number.

(a) Introduction

Organizations filing this schedule are likely to be *charitable* entities, namely, entities that may receive deductible noncash contributions:

- Charitable organizations (other than private foundations or organizations that test for public safety)
- Domestic fraternal organizations that use charitable contributions exclusively for charitable purposes
- Cemetery companies
- Qualified veterans' organizations

As noted, however, the Schedule M filing requirement is applicable to all exempt organizations that received one or more noncash gifts and does so irrespective of the availability of a charitable contribution deduction.

Questions 1 to 24 of Schedule M pertain to specific types of contributed property. Contributed items that are not identified on the schedule by category of property must be reported separately as *other* items beginning with line 25.

In Schedule M, Part I, Column (a), the filing organization must check each box that relates to the type of property referenced in the schedule (even if the number of contributions need not be reported).

In Schedule M, Part I, Column (b), the filing organization must enter, for each type of property received during the year, the number of contributions or the number of items, interests, collections, properties, and the like received during the year, determined in accordance with the organization's recordkeeping practices. The organization must explain in Schedule M, Part II, whether the organization is reporting the number of contributions or the number of items received.

For each security, the organization must treat each separate gift (rather than each share received) as an item for this purpose. For all other types of property, the organization must provide the number of items contributed to it. If precise numbers are not regularly kept by the organization, a good-faith estimate will suffice. This requirement, however, is inapplicable (because of the record-keeping burdens) with respect to contributions of books and publications, clothing, and household goods.

In Schedule M, Part I, Column (c), the organization must enter any revenue as reported elsewhere on the Form 990 (Part VIII, line 1g) for the appropriate type of property. Museums and other organizations, however, often do not report contributions of art, historical treasures, and similar items as revenue, as is permitted under generally accepted accounting principles. Organizations in this circumstance should enter "0" in Column (c). A museum, for example, may explain in Part II of Schedule M that a zero amount was reported because, as allowed by accounting principles, it does not capitalize its collections.

In Schedule M, Part 1, Column (d), the organization must describe the method it used to determine revenue amount (such as cost or selling price of the contributed property, sale of comparable properties, replacement cost, or an opinion of an expert). An organization that is permitted to enter "0" in Column (c) should leave the accompanying Column (d) blank.

The IRS's instructions provide two examples of these processes:

> **Example 1**. A used car in poor condition is donated to a high school for use by students studying car repair. A used car guide shows that the dealer retail value for this type of car in poor condition is $1,600. The guide, however, shows that the price for a private party sale of the car is $750. The fair market value of this car is considered by the donee to be $750; that is the amount the donee reported as revenue. In Column (c), the organization should report $750. In Column (d), the organization should enter "sale of comparable properties" or "opinion of expert" as the method used to determine the revenue amount.

> **Example 2**. An organization primarily receives bulk donations of clothing, household goods, and similar items, intended for resale. Under its permitted financial reporting practices, it does not recognize or record revenue at the time of receipt of the contribution but instead records these items in inventory and reports contribution revenues at the time of the sale based on prior inventory turnover experience. In Column (c), the organization may report the amount that represents the total estimated amount of annual sales revenue for each type of property received under its permitted financial reporting method. In Column (d), it reports "resale value" or "annual sales revenue" as the method of determining revenue.

(b)   Questions 1 to 3 (Works of Art)

Questions 1 to 3 of Schedule M pertain to contributions to tax-exempt organizations of types of works of art. These questions concern gifts of historical treasures, gifts of fractional interests in art, and all other types of art. Art does not include collectibles, which are reported on line 18 (see § 19.2(j)). For each of these types of art, the filing organization must check the box in Column (a) if applicable, and report the number of the work or works of art contributed (Column (b)), the amount of any of these gift(s) reported as revenue (Form 990, Part IV, line 1g) (Column (c)), and (if applicable) the method of determining revenues. (See § 19.1(d).)

In the case of a contribution of a fractional interest in a work of art, in the Column (b) reporting, the organization should report the fractional interest received in each year with respect to the underlying work of art.

It should be reiterated that the Form 990 inquires as to whether the filing organization maintains collections of works of art, historical treasures, or other similar assets for "public exhibition, education, or research in furtherance of public service rather than for financial gain" (Part VII, line 5). If the answer to this question is "yes," the filing organization must complete a portion of another schedule (Schedule D, Part X). In this schedule, the organization must: indicate whether it reported as revenue any contributions of art; indicate whether it capitalized any contributions of art in the reporting or prior years and reported those amounts on the Form 990 (Part VI); and provide the text of the footnote to the organization's audited financial statements that discusses the organization's holdings of art, historical treasures, and other similar assets.

(c) Question 4 (Books and Publications)

Question 4 of Schedule M pertains to contributions to tax-exempt organizations of books and publications. Books and other publications may be contributed to a charitable organization, and the gift may give rise to a charitable contribution deduction. Rare books and manuscripts are treated as works of art (see above); they may also be collectibles (see § 19.2(j)). For these contributions, the filing organization must check the line 4 box. The number of these contributions need not be reported. If applicable, the amount of the gift(s) reported as revenue (Form 990, Part VIII, line 1g) and the method of determining revenues must be reported. (See § 19.1(e))

(d) Question 5 (Clothing and Household Goods)

Question 5 of Schedule M pertains to contributions of clothing and/or household goods that were in good used condition or better. For these two categories of items, the filing organization must check the box. The number of these contributions need not be reported. If applicable, the organization must report the amount of the gift(s) reported as revenue (Form 990, Part VIII, line 1g) and the method of determining revenues. (See § 19.1(f).) Clothing items and/or household goods that were not in good used condition or better are reported as *other* (see § 19.2(b)(q)).

(e) Questions 6 and 7 (Vehicles)

Questions 6 and 7 of Schedule M concern contributions of vehicles, such as automobiles, boats, and airplanes. Vehicles that constitute inventory are to be reported as such (see below). For these types of vehicles, the filing organization must check the box and report the number of the vehicle or vehicles contributed, the amount of the gift(s) reported as revenue (Form 990, Part VIII, line 1g), and the method of determining revenues. (See § 19.1(g).)

The response to the question on line 6 should include only contributions of motor vehicles manufactured primarily for use on public streets, roads, and highways.

The organization is required to file Form 1098-C for certain of these contributions reported on these lines. See Form 990, Part V, line 7h.

(f) Question 8 (Intellectual Property)

Question 8 of Schedule M pertains to charitable and other contributions of intellectual property. For this type of property, the filing organization must check the box and report the number of the intellectual property or properties contributed, the amount of the gift(s) reported as revenue (Form 990, Part VIII, line 1g), and the method of determining revenues. (See § 19.1(h).)

Certain contributions of intellectual property may require the organization to file Form 8899 with the donor and the IRS with respect to the contribution. See Form 990, Part V, line 7g.

(g) Questions 9 to 12 (Securities)

Questions 9 to 12 of Schedule M pertain to charitable and other contributions of securities, differentiating among publicly traded securities, closely held stock, securities in the form of partnership or trust interests, and other types of securities. For each of these categories of securities, the filing organization must check the box and report the number of securities contributed, the amount of the gift(s) reported as revenue (Form 990, Part VIII, line 1g), and the method of determining revenues. For each security, the filing organization should treat each separate gift (rather than each share received) as a contribution for this purpose.

(h) Questions 13 and 14 (Qualified Conservation Contributions)

Questions 13 and 14 of Schedule M pertain to qualified conservation contributions, distinguishing between gifts involving historic structures and other conservation contributions. For each of these types of contributions, the filing organization must check the box and report the number of the property or properties contributed, the amount of the gift(s) reported as revenue (Form 990, Part VIII, line 1g), and the method of determining revenues.

On line 13, the filing organization should enter information about contributions of a qualified real property interest that is a restriction with respect to the exterior of a certified historic structure. Line 14 is used to report information about qualified conservation contributions other than those referenced in connection with line 13; this includes conservation easements to preserve land areas for outdoor recreation by or for the education of the public, to protect a relatively natural habitat or ecosystem, to preserve open space, or to preserve an historically important land area. (See § 19.1(j).)

(i) Questions 15 to 17 (Real Estate)

Questions 15 to 17 of Schedule M concern charitable and other contributions of real estate, differentiating among gifts of residential real estate, commercial real estate, and other categories of real estate. For each of these types of properties, the filing organization must check the box and report the number of the property or properties contributed, the amount of the gift(s) reported as revenue (Form 990, Part VIII, line 1g), and the method of determining revenues.

On line 15, the filing organization enters information about contributions of residential real estate. This entry should include any information about contributions (not in trust) of a remainder interest in a personal residence that was not the donor's entire interest in the property. On line 16, the organization enters information about contributions of commercial real estate, such as a commercial office building. This entry should include any information about contributions (not in trust) of a remainder interest in a farm that was not the donor's entire interest in the property. Line 17 is used to enter information about any real estate interests not reported on lines 15 or 16. (See § 19.1(k).)

(j) Question 18 (Collectibles)

Question 18 of Schedule M pertains to charitable and other contributions of collectibles. For this type of gift, the filing organization must check the box and report the number of the collectibles contributed, the amount of the gift(s) reported as revenue (Form 990, Part IV, line 1g), and the method of determining revenues. (See § 19.1(m).)

(k)   Question 19 (Food Inventory)

Question 19 of Schedule M pertains to charitable and other contributions of food items, including food inventory contributed by corporations and other businesses. For this type of gift, the filing organization must check the box and report the number of the inventory property contributed, the amount of the gift(s) reported as revenue (Form 990, Part VIII, line 1g), and the method of determining revenues. (See § 19.1(n).)

(l)   Question 20 (Drugs and Medical Supplies)

Question 20 of Schedule M concerns charitable and other contributions of drugs, medical supplies, and similar items contributed by businesses that manufactured or distributed these items. For this type of gift, the filing organization must check the box and rcport the number of the drugs or supplies contributed, the amount of the gift(s) reported as revenue (Form 990, Part VIII, line 1g), and the method of determining revenues. (See § 19.1(o).)

(m)   Question 21 (Taxidermy)

Question 21 pertains to contributions of taxidermy. For this type of gift, the filing organization must check the box and report the number of taxidermy items contributed, the amount of the gift(s) reported as revenue (Form 990, Part VIII, line 1g), and the method of determining revenues. (See § 19.1(p).)

(n)   Question 22 (Historical Artifacts)

Question 22 of Schedule M pertains to contributions of historical artifacts. For this type of gift, the filing organization must check the box and report the number of historical artifacts contributed, the amount of the gift(s) reported as revenue (Form 990, Part VIII, line 1g), and the method of determining revenues. This entry should not include works of art or historical treasures (see above) or archeological artifacts (see § 19.2(p)). (See § 19.1(q).)

(o)   Question 23 (Scientific Specimens)

Question 23 of Schedule M pertains to contributions of scientific specimens. For this type of gift, the filing organization must check the box and report the number of scientific specimens contributed, the amount of the gift(s) reported as revenue (Form 990, Part VIII, line 1g), and the method of determining revenues. (See § 19.1(r).)

(p)   Question 24 (Archeological Artifacts)

Question 24 of Schedule M pertains to contributions of archeological ethnological artifacts. For this type of gift, the filing organization must check the box and report the number of archeological artifacts contributed, the amount of the gift(s) reported as revenue (Form 990, Part VIII, line 1g), and the method of determining revenues.

This entry should not include information about works of art, historical treasures, or historical artifacts (see § 19.2(n)). (See § 19.1(s).)

(q)   Questions 25 to 28 (Other Types of Property)

Questions 25 to 28 of Schedule M enable the filing organization to report as to any other types of noncash contributions received. For each of these types of gift, the filing organization must check the box and report the number of the property(ies) contributed, the amount of the gift(s) reported as revenue (Form 990, Part VIII, line 1g), and the method of determining revenues.

(r)   Question 29 (Forms 8283)

The filing organization is required, pursuant to question 29 of Schedule M, to report the number of Forms 8283 that it received during the reporting year for contributions as to which the organization completed Part IV of the form(s). If the organization does not keep complete records of these forms, it should not provide an estimate but rather leave line 29 blank. (See § 19.1(u).)

(s)   Question 30 (Contribution Holding Period)

The filing organization must, in response to question 30a of Schedule M, report ("yes" or "no") whether, during the reporting year, it received a contribution of property, reported in Part I of the schedule, that it is required, by the terms of the gift or otherwise, to hold for at least three years from the date of the initial contribution, where it is not required that the property be used for exempt purposes for the entire holding period. If the answer to this question is "yes," the arrangement must be described in Schedule M, Part II (line 30b). (See § 19.1(w).)

Tax-exempt organizations should be cautious when considering acceptance of property with this condition. The IRS will assume that the purpose of the condition is to sidestep the three-year reporting requirement rule.

(t)   Question 31 (Gift Acceptance Policy)

The filing organization must, in response to question 31 of Schedule M, report ("yes" or "no") whether it has a gift acceptance policy that requires the review of any nonstandard contributions. (See § 19.1(x).)

(u)   Question 32 (Service Providers)

The filing organization must, in response to question 32a of Schedule M, report ("yes" or "no") whether it hired or otherwise used third parties or related organizations to solicit, process, or sell contributed noncash property. If the answer to this question is "yes," the matter must be described in Schedule M, Part II (line 32b). (See § 19.1(y).)

(v)   Question 33 (Explanation of Nonrevenue Treatment)

The filing organization must, if it did not report revenues in Part I, Column (c) for a type of property for which Column (a) is checked, explain the matter, in response to question 33 of Schedule M, in Schedule M, Part II.

§ 19.3 NEW FORM 990 COMPLIANCE TASKS

A tax-exempt organization that received during the reporting year one or more non-cash contributions should be attending to these 10 tasks:

1. **Revenue requiring reporting.** Determine whether the organization is or will be receiving more than an aggregate of $25,000 of noncash contributions (on Form 990, Part IV, line 29) (because, if it is, the filing of Schedule M is required).

2. **Assets requiring reporting.** Determine if the organization received or will be receiving any contributions of art, historical treasures, or other similar assets, or qualified conservation contributions (Form 990, Part IV, line 30) (because, if it is, the filing of Schedule M is required).

3. **Types of contributions.** Inventory the type or types of noncash contributions that will be reported for the year (so as to be able to check one or more boxes in Schedule M, Part I, Column (a)).

4. **Number of items.** Put a system in place to keep track of the number of items and the like received as contributions during the year (so as to be able to complete Schedule M, Part I, Column (b)).

5. **Recordation as revenue.** Put a system in place to record the receipt of these gifts as revenue when required (so as to be able to complete Schedule M, Part I, columns (c) and (d)).

6. **Forms 8283.** Put a system in place to keep track of the number of Forms 8283 received by the organization during the year for which Part IV was completed (so as to be able to correctly answer question 29 in Schedule M, Part I).

7. **Holding period.** Develop a policy as to whether the organization will accept a contribution of noncash property under the condition that the property will be held for at least three years from the date of the gift (see Form 990, Schedule M, Part I, line 30a).

8. **Gift acceptance policy.** Consider adoption of a gift acceptance policy (see Form 990, Schedule M, Part I, line 31).

9. **Service providers.** If the organization uses one or more entities to solicit, process, or sell contributed noncash property, carefully (particularly if an entity is a related party) prepare a description of the arrangement (see Form 990, Schedule M, Part I, line 32; Part II).

10. **Non–revenue reporting.** If the organization is not reporting as revenue the receipt, by contribution, of a type of noncash property, prepare an explanation for the practice (see Form 990, Schedule M, Part I, line 33; Part II).

CHAPTER TWENTY

Schedule N—Liquidation, Termination, Dissolution, or Significant Disposition of Assets

§ 20.1 LAW AND POLICY

Liquidations, dissolutions, terminations, mergers, and sales or other dispositions of significant assets are all significant transactions in the life cycle of a nonprofit entity that (1) require compliance with special state law processes, and (2) require certain disclosures on Schedule N of the Form 990. These transactions can often give rise to conversions—that is, the conversion of the nonprofit entity into a for-profit entity or the conversion of significant charitable assets from nonprofit ownership to for-profit ownership. Conversions raise unique issues under state law and under the Internal Revenue Code.

(a) Process Issues

Dissolution, merger, and disposition of significant assets all require compliance with certain steps required by state law. In general, these fall into two categories: special approval processes and special notice requirements. Approval processes vary from state to state but, depending on the state and/or the organization's articles or bylaws, some kind of enhanced approval process is generally required (e.g., more than the traditional approval of a majority of the organization's board at a meeting at which a quorum is present—the minimum necessary approval for an organization generally to take action). This enhanced approval could be at the board level (e.g., a majority or supermajority of all the directors in office, as opposed to those present at a meeting at which a quorum is present), approval by the members, and/or approval by a third party (e.g., a state official or regulator or perhaps a related nonprofit entity that is named in the organization's articles or bylaws). Some states (especially those that have adopted the Model Nonprofit Corporation Act) require that notice be given to the state attorney general before the organization consummates any of these transactions. These notice requirements often require a period of time to elapse after the notice so that the attorney general has the opportunity to investigate the transaction to determine that the charitable assets are not being put at risk (e.g., that a sale to a for-profit corporation is not at less than fair market value or that a nonprofit executive is not receiving an improper windfall as severance). Some of these notice requirements are coupled with disclosure requirements that require the organization to disclose certain information (similar to that disclosed on the Schedule N) to the attorney general.

With respect to dissolutions, organizations need to be aware of two issues. First, the organization needs to make sure it is distributing its assets in accordance with its articles of incorporation. As discussed in § 1.6(c) regarding the organizational test, exempt organizations are required to have a clause in their articles of incorporation that requires that all the organization's net assets be distributed upon dissolution to another (c)(3) organization or to a government entity for a public purpose. Some organizations have more specific clauses that name particular entities that will receive the assets upon dissolution. Whatever the dissolution clause states, the organization needs to comply with it. Second, the organization needs to comply with all donor restrictions. For example, if the organization has a fund that the donor has restricted to healthcare for the indigent, the organization cannot give the fund to the symphony.

In the case of disposition of significant assets, organizations need to be aware that thresholds under the Schedule N and state law may differ. Schedule N, as discussed more fully in § 20.2(b), requires the organization to fill out Part II if more than 25 percent of the organization's assets were disposed of by sale, exchange or other disposition. State law thresholds that require enhanced approval requirements or notice requirements may be higher. For example, many states require such approval and notice when there has been a "substantial" disposition of assets "not in the ordinary course of business." Courts vary but have often said that "substantial" can mean anything from 50 percent to 75 percent, much higher than the Schedule N threshold of 25 percent. A sale in the ordinary course of business is one that occurs frequently or regularly in the organization's operations, such as sales of inventory or investment portfolio assets. Sales not in the ordinary course of business are ones that occur infrequently or only once in the organization's operations, such as the sale of the organization's only asset or business line. Such events are characterized by a fundamental change in the organization's business or operations after the transaction.

Organizations engaged in any transaction reported on Schedule N should check local state law requirements (both statutes and case law) to make sure they are complying with all procedural requirements regarding approval and notice.

(b) Conversion Issues

Any of the Schedule N transactions can give rise to a "conversion"—the conversion of the organization from nonprofit to for-profit status or the conversion of the ownership of the nonprofit's assets to ownership by a for-profit entity. For example, the nonprofit can sell all of its assets to a for-profit entity or merge with a for-profit entity with the for-profit entity surviving and the nonprofit entity ceasing to exist. Conversions raise issues under both state law and the Internal Revenue Code. Because they give rise to the potential for private inurement, private benefit and/or excess benefit transactions (see § 6.1), they receive heightened scrutiny from the IRS and from state attorneys general. The questions on the Schedule N are intended to solicit information about certain "pressure points" in such transactions that the IRS and state attorneys general will scrutinize:

- Severance, change of control, golden parachute, and other improper windfalls or payments to the directors and officers of the nonprofit organization.

- Employment of the nonprofit directors and officers by the for-profit after the conversion transaction (one of the concerns being that the promise of subsequent employment may taint directors' and officers' judgments in determining whether the conversion transaction is in the best interests of the nonprofit).

- Use of sale proceeds by the nonprofit after the transaction (the concerns being that liquid cash proceeds may be easier to divert into large salaries or other insider transactions, that proceeds may be used for different purposes—e.g., that proceeds from the sale of a hospital may be used for the symphony—or that proceeds may be used in another state which could cause concern with the state attorney general).

- Concern whether a successor for-profit entity will provide the same benefits to the community as the nonprofit (most likely not), and whether sales proceeds can be used to mitigate the loss of the nonprofit operations to the community (e.g., while a for-profit company that buys a nonprofit hospital may not provide as much charity care as the nonprofit entity, the nonprofit entity may use the cash proceeds from the sale to help provide healthcare benefits to the community).

- Concern about sales to insiders—for example, a sale of the nonprofit assets to the directors and officers is certain to raise scrutiny with the IRS and the state attorney general.

The IRS can examine these and any other issues on audit. If improper activity has occurred, the IRS has the intermediate sanctions excise taxes (fines) and correction requirements as regulatory enforcement mechanisms (see § 6.1(b)). State attorneys general also have certain tools at their disposal to review conversion transactions and ensure they comply with state and federal law requirements. Many states have conversion statutes that require notice be given to the attorney general and that give the attorney general the right to review the transaction. In some cases the attorney general or other state official has the right to approve the transaction, in essence to block the transaction if they so desire. Even in states that do not give approval/blocking rights to the attorney general, conversion statutes generally give the attorney general the right to file suit to prevent the transaction, in which case a court would have to approve or block the transaction. If the state does not have a conversion statute, there is still often a statute requiring notice to the attorney general of the proposed conversion transaction, which provides the opportunity for the attorney general to file suit to stop the transaction under the attorney general's inherent power to safeguard charitable assets (sometimes referred to by its Latin name, parens patriae).

Whether attorneys general are acting under a conversion statute or their inherent powers, they will generally evaluate a conversion transaction based on three criteria: process, price, and proceeds.

1. Did the nonprofit board engage in the right process by, for example, determining that the conversion was the only or best way to achieve the nonprofit

mission, that the transaction was in the nonprofit's best interest, and that conflicts of interest (e.g., officer severance payments or sales to insiders) were
properly dealt with?

2. Did the nonprofit board ensure that a fair price was paid by the for-profit (e.g.,
   did the nonprofit obtain a qualified appraisal)?

3. Did the nonprofit board ensure that the proceeds would be used to continue to
   carry out the nonprofit's historical mission (e.g., are proceeds from the sale of a
   hospital used to provide healthcare benefits, or are proceeds from the sale of
   Web-based educational system used to continue to provide education benefits)
   and did the board obtain commitments from the for-profit buyer (e.g., that the
   for-profit owner will continue to provide charity care)?

Generally in conversion transactions, there are no unrelated business income consequences (see § 7.1(6)). For example, these are generally one-time sales that do not
meet the "regularly carried on" requirement and therefore capital gains are not considered taxable unrelated business income.

§ 20.2 PREPARATION OF NEW FORM 990 SCHEDULE N

(a) Part I (Liquidation, Termination, or Dissolution)

An organization must complete Part I of Schedule N if it ceased operations and has no
plans to continue any activities or operations in the future. This includes an organization that has dissolved, liquidated, terminated, or was a party to a merger where another entity was the surviving entity. Note: If the organization was a party to a
merger where the organization was the surviving entity, this gets reported in Part II.
The organization must provide evidence of its actions by attaching certified copies of
articles of dissolution, termination or merger; board resolutions; and plans of dissolution and merger. If the organization received any determination letter or private letter
ruling from the IRS regarding the dissolution or merger, these should also be
attached.

The IRS does not define the terms *dissolve, liquidate, terminate,* or *merge.* Presumably, organizations can rely on state law definition of these terms in corporation, partnership, or LLC statutes. For example, if the filing organization is a corporation that
has merged under the applicable state corporation code or an LLC that has dissolved
under the applicable state LLC act, then the organization will be completing Schedule
N, Part I.

Generally, the terms *dissolve, liquidate,* and *terminate* mean the same thing—dis-
continuing business operations and ceasing to exist. However, under many state
codes, there is a two-step process. Organizations first file articles of dissolution that
indicate that they have stopped doing business but will continue to exist for a "wind-
down" period during which they liquidate assets, pay debts, and distribute money to
their successors. After the wind-down, the second step is to file articles of termination
to cease existence. Which of these events (the filing of articles of dissolution or the
filing of articles of termination) triggers the filing of the Schedule N is unclear. If it all
happens in the same tax year, it makes no difference, but if dissolution occurs in one
year and termination occurs in a subsequent year, the IRS gives no direction. Generally, if an organization has filed articles of dissolution but not commenced the

distribution of assets, there would be nothing to report in Part I. If the distribution of assets occurred in a subsequent year, the reporting should occur in that year. If articles of dissolution are filed in one year and articles of termination in a subsequent year, then 990s will continue to be filed until the articles of termination are filed. In this instance, if the distribution of assets occurs in more than one year, Part I should be completed in each year that assets were distributed.

Some examples might be helpful.

> **Example 1.** Organization is a calendar-year taxpayer. Organization files articles of dissolution in 2008 but distributes no assets. In 2009 Organization distributes all of its assets and files its articles of termination. Organization would prepare Part I of Schedule N for 2009 but arguably not for 2008.

> **Example 2.** Organization is a calendar-year taxpayer. As part of a plan of dissolution, Organization begins distributing some of its assets in 2008. The distribution of assets continues to 2009, when Organization terminates and ceases to exist. Organization would arguably prepare Part I for Schedule N in both 2008 and 2009 reporting in each Schedule N only the assets that were distributed that year.

Note: Organizations that complete Part I do not have to complete Part II. For example, if an organization dissolves and distributes 100 percent of its assets, it would have to complete Part I. It would not also complete Part II because it disposed of more than 25 percent of its assets.

---

(1) Line 1, Columns (a) through (f)

(A) COLUMN (A)

(i) ASSET DISTRIBUTIONS

Report all assets distributed or transferred pursuant the liquidation, termination, dissolution, or merger. Assets can be grouped together by category rather than reporting every asset individually. Although the instructions do not say, the Balance Sheet in Part X of the core Form 990 would be a reasonable list of asset categories to guide in the preparation of Schedule N. As a practical matter, however, the categories of assets that get distributed will likely be fairly narrow: cash (and maybe investments), equipment, land, and buildings. Nevertheless, if other categories of assets are distributed (e.g., intellectual property), these should also be described.

(ii) TRANSACTION EXPENSES

Transaction expenses are also reported in Column (a). Each transaction expense of $10,000 or more must be listed separately. Transaction expenses are payments to a third party to assist for services to assist with the transaction or the winding down of the organization's activities, such as attorney or account fees. Broker fees should not be listed separately; instead the fees should be subtracted from the fair market value in Column (c) (see Column (c) discussion for an example).

(B) COLUMN (B)

Enter the date the asset was distributed or the transaction expense paid. This could present some problems if reporting by asset category and assets within the category were distributed on different dates. This could be remedied by grouping asset classes by date of distribution (e.g., all equipment distributed on March 1 as one asset category and all equipment distributed on June 1 as a second asset category). If there are numerous dates of distribution, the organization can consider putting a range in Column (b) (e.g., from March 1 through June 1).

(C) COLUMN (c)

Enter the fair market value of the asset distributed or the transaction expense paid. Generally, transaction expense will be in cash so it will be easy to value. Distributed assets may prove more difficult to value unless they are publicly traded assets. Non–publicly traded assets may require an appraisal. Broker fees are not to be listed separately but netted against fair market value. Thus, if an organization merges with another entity, and the other entity survives, and the organization is valued at $1 million and a broker fee of $100,000 is paid, fair market value is reported in Column (c) as $900,000. The problem is that the broker fee often has to be allocated across every class of asset. The instructions do not describe how to do this, but a pro rata allocation would seem reasonable. Thus, in the event of a merger, if land is appraised at $750,000 and equipment is value at $250,000, and the broker fee is $100,000, it would seem reasonable to report the fair market value of the land at $675,000 ($750,000 − $75,000) and the equipment at $225,000 ($250,000 − $25,000).

(D) COLUMN (d)

Enter the method to determine fair market value. Methods include appraisals, comparables, book value, actual cost (with or without depreciation), outstanding offers, and, presumably, stock exchanges and other public exchanges if the asset is a publicly traded asset. For transaction expense, list the method for determining the amount of the expense (e.g., hourly fee or fixed fee). If the method for determining the fee is a percentage of transaction amount, it is probably a broker fee that should be netted against the fair market value of the asset in Column (c) (see discussion for Column (c) for an example).

(E) COLUMNS (e) AND (f)

Enter the name, address, and employer identification number (EIN) of each recipient of assets or transaction expense. For transfers to members, each individual member does not have to be listed; rather, listing members as a category (with separate categories for each class of membership) is sufficient. Presumably, in the case of a merger where an entity other than the organization is the survivor, listing the name, address, and EIN of the surviving entity is sufficient.

(F) COLUMN (g)

If the recipient is tax-exempt, list the section under the Code that describes the organization (e.g., 501(c)(3), (4), (6), etc.). For entities that are not tax-exempt, enter the type of entity. Examples include C corporation, S corporation, limited liability company (LLC), partnership, government entity, individual, and so on.

(2) Line 2. Report whether any director, officer, trustee, or key employee of the organization listed in the core Form 990, Part VII, Section A is (or is expected to become) involved in a successor or transferee organization through a governing relationship (e.g., director or officer), a controlling relationship (e.g., a majority shareholder), or a financial relationship (e.g., receiving any payments as an employee, independent contractor, or otherwise).

In lines 2a through 2e, the organization is required to disclose whether a director, officer, trustee, or key employee of the organization listed in the core Form 990, Part VII, Section A is (or is expected to become):

- A director or trustee of the successor or transferee organization (line 2a)

- An employee or independent contractor of the successor or transferee organization (line 2b)

- A direct or indirect owner of the successor or transferee organization (line 2c)

- A recipient of compensation or other payments as a result of the organization's liquidation, termination, or dissolution (line 2d) (such as severance, change of control payments, or other payments that would not have been made but-for liquidation, termination or dissolution—this could presumably include acceleration of deferred compensation payments, which often occurs in these circumstances)

If the organization answers "yes" on lines 2a through 2d, the organization must provide in Part III the name of the person involved, the relationship with the successor or transferee organization (e.g., director, officer, employee, independent contractor, member, stockholder, etc.), and the type of benefit received or to be received (e.g., compensation, stock options, severance payment, etc.).

(3) Line 3. Answer "yes" if the assets were distributed in accordance with the organization's governing instruments. For example, the articles of incorporation for most nonprofit corporations specify what happens to assets upon dissolution of the organization (distribution to a 501(c)(3) organization, distribution to members, etc.). If the distribution was consistent with the governing instruments, answer "yes." If the distribution was not consistent with the governing instruments, answer "no" and explain in Part III. Neither Part III nor the instructions to Part III require this disclosure, but line 3 and the instructions to line 3 clearly do.

(4) Line 4. Answer "yes" if the organization requested or received a determination letter from the IRS that the exempt status was terminated. Attach the request and, if available, the determination letter. Provide the date of the letter in line 4b.

(5) Line 5. Answer "yes" in line 5a if the organization is required to provide notice to the state attorney general or other state official of the organization's intent to dissolve, liquidate, or terminate. Many state statutes have such a notification requirement. (Note: Many state statutes also have a notification requirement for merger and if the organization is reporting a merger in Part I in which it is not the surviving entity, and if such a merger notification exists under the organization's state law, line 5a should be answered "yes.") Report in line 5 whether such a notification, if required, was in fact given.

(6) Line 6. Answer "yes" if the organization discharged or paid all of its liabilities in accordance with state law. Most states have laws applicable to corporations, partnerships, and LLCs that specify how, and in what order, liabilities are to be satisfied in the event of dissolution. Answer "yes" if these state law requirements are complied with.

(7) Line 7. Answer "yes" in line 7a if the organization had any tax-exempt bonds outstanding during the tax year. Answer "yes" in line 7b if these tax-exempt bond liabilities were discharged or defeased during the tax year. Bonds are discharged when they are paid and the bonds surrendered or retired. Bonds are defeased when the bondholders retain the bonds but an escrow account is established to continue to pay the interest and principal amounts over the life of the bonds as they mature. Either discharge or defeasance is an acceptable way to pay off bond liabilities. Which option is chosen is usually determined by the terms of the bonds (e.g., some bonds cannot be paid off early and must be defeased). The organization must describe in Part III the how the discharge, defeasance, or other settlement occurred and if it was consistent with the Code and state law. If the organization avoided the need for a defeasance of bonds, such as through the transfer of assets to another Section 501(c)(3) entity, the organization should in Part III provide the name of the transferees of such assets, the CUSIP number of the bond issue, and a description of the terms of such arrangements.

(b) Part II (Sale, Exchange, Disposition, or Other Transfer of More than 25 Percent of the Organization's Assets)

An organization must complete Part II of Schedule N if it has undergone a significant disposition of net assets during the year. This includes a sale, exchange, disposition, or other transfer of more than 25 percent of the fair market value of its net assets during the year, regardless of whether the organization received fair market value and regardless of whether the transferee was for-profit or nonprofit. For example, a transfer without consideration or payment by the organization of more than 25 percent of its assets to another organization described in 501(c)(3) would get reported in Part II, as would be the case if the transferee (c)(3) paid fair market value.

A significant disposition includes a series of dispositions that amount, in the aggregate, to more than 25 percent of the fair market value of the net assets of the organization, including a series of dispositions that are spread over more than one tax year. This includes:

- One or more dispositions during the tax year amounting to more than 25 percent of the fair market value of the organization's net assets as of the beginning of its tax year; and

- One or more of a series of related dispositions or events commenced in a prior year that, when combined, comprise more than 25 percent of the fair market value of the net assets of the organization as of the beginning of the tax year when the first disposition in the series was made. Whether a significant disposition occurred through a series of related dispositions or events depends on the facts and circumstances in each case. For example, an agreement entered into with a transferee to sell 20 percent of the organization's assets in one year, with an option in the transferee to buy an additional 20 percent of the organization's assets in a subsequent tax year, would appear to be a series of related transactions. However, a sale by the organization of 20 percent of its assets to one transferee in one tax year followed three years later by a sale of another 20 percent of its assets to a different transferee would not appear to be a series of related dispositions. Even two or more sales to the same transferee, if separated by enough time and circumstance, may be an unrelated series of dispositions. At some point, the trail becomes "old and cold," and the last disposition is not "related" to the first disposition.

For purposes of Part II of Schedule N, *net assets* means total assets less total liabilities. The determination of a significant disposition of net assets is made by reference to the fair market value of the organization's net assets at the beginning of the tax year (or in the case of a series of related dispositions that commenced in a prior year, at the beginning of the tax year during which the first disposition was made).

The directions do not specify the measuring date for the assets that are being disposed. Because the asset might not be held on the first day of the year when the fair market value of net assets is measured, it makes sense to measure the fair market value of the disposed assets as of the date of disposition. Consider this example:

> A calendar-year organization has net assets with a fair market value of $1 million on January 1. On February 1 the organization buys a piece of real estate for $200,000. On December 1, the organization sells the property for $300,000. The organization presumably has had a significant disposition of assets. ($300,000 divided by $1 million is 30 percent, which exceeds the 25-percent threshold.) Although, arguably, there has only been a disposition of 20 percent ($200,000 divided by $1 million) which would not require a disclosure, a conservative approach (which surely the IRS would adopt) would favor disclosure.

Consider the same example but with the values reversed: On February 1 the organization purchases the real estate for $300,000 and sells it on December 1 for $200,000. A consistent methodology (valuing as of the date of disposition) would not require disclosure because there has only been a 20-percent disposition ($200,000 divided by $1 million). Again, however, a conservative approach may value the disposition at 30 percent of the net assets ($300,000 divided by $1 million). In light of this uncertainty, organizations and their advisors will have to make good-faith judgments regarding disclosure, knowing that one of the stated purposes of the Form 990 redesign is transparency and disclosure.

All this, of course, belies a fundamental valuation issue. Most organizations do not establish the fair market value of their net assets on the first day of each year. Many (or most) assets are carried at book value and not fair market value. When a significant disposition has occurred, this will require the organization to establish fair market value as of a date in the past, perhaps several years in the past if a series of related dispositions has been spread over multiple tax years. Although not impossible, determining fair market value of sometimes hard-to-value assets as of a date several years in the past may not be a simple exercise.

The instructions also leave some matters unresolved with respect reporting a series of related transactions when the transaction in the first year does not exceed the 25-percent threshold but a related disposition in a subsequent year pushes the aggregate over the 25-percent threshold. Consider the next example:

A calendar-year organization has net assets with a fair market value of $ 1 million on January 1 of year Y. During year Y, the organization enters into an agreement to sell a piece of real estate and a building to Buyer for $200,000. The organization also gives Buyer an option to buy an adjoining piece of real estate for $100,000 in year Y+1. In year Y+1, Buyer exercises the option and pays $100,000 for the adjoining real estate. On January 1 of year Y+1, the fair market value of the organization's net assets is $2 million.

Part II of Schedule N would not be prepared for year Y because there has only been a disposition of 20 percent of the net assets ($200,000 divided by $1 million). Part II of Schedule N would be prepared for tax year Y+1, the year in which the aggregate value of the related dispositions exceeds the 25-percent threshold ($300,000 divided by $1 million). Note that although the total disposition of $300,000 is less than 25 percent of the fair market value of the net assets as of January 1 of year Y+1 ($300,000 divided by $2 million is only 15 percent), the instructions are clear that the proper measuring amount and date is the $1 million as of January 1 of year Y.

What is not clear in the instructions is whether in year Y+1 just the transaction in year Y+1 is reported (the sale of the adjoining real estate for $100,000), or whether the original sale of the real estate and building for $200,000 from year Y would also be reported since it was not previously reported in year Y. If asked, the IRS would probably answer in favor of more, rather than less, disclosure—again, one of the primary reasons for the Form 990 redesign being enhanced transparency and disclosure. For this reason, organizations should consider reporting all transactions that have not been previously reported, even if they occur in a prior year. This could be explained in Part III.

> *Note:* As indicated, the instructions are not clear about certain issues. The examples just given utilize a consistently applied rationale and, it is hoped, would be acceptable to the IRS.

The types of dispositions required to be reported in Part II include any significant disposition or series of related dispositions, such as:

- Taxable or tax-free sales or exchanges of exempt assets for cash or other consideration (such as other property or ownership interests)—a sale may be tax-free because capital gains incurred by a nonprofit are generally tax-free because they are generally excluded from the definition of unrelated trade or business income (see § 7.1(b)). Certain mergers and reorganizations may also be tax free under the Internal Revenue Code.

- Sales, contributions, or other transfers of assets to establish, maintain, or capitalize a partnership, LLC, corporation (whether for-profit or nonprofit), or joint venture, regardless of whether such sale or transfer is taxable or tax-free under Code Sections 351 or 721, and regardless of whether or not the transferor organization receives an ownership interest in return for the contribution (e.g., capital contributions to a subsidiary or joint venture may or may not come with additional ownership interests accruing to the transferor organization).

- Sales or transfers of assets by a partnership or joint venture in which the organization has an ownership interest. Although the instructions do not say, presumably the organization would take into account only its pro rata share of the assets sold or transferred by the partnership or joint venture. (This is the position stated in Appendix F of the Form 990 instructions.) For example, if the organization owns 50 percent of a joint venture, then the organization would take 50 percent of the assets that were sold or transferred by the joint venture and compare that to 25 percent of the fair market value of the organization's net assets as of the beginning of the year to determine if a significant disposition has occurred. How the joint venture assets are valued (fair market value, book value, etc.) is not clear. Organizations will have to settle on a reasonable methodology based on the circumstances. Further—and again the instructions are silent here—presumably this applies only to assets sold by a partnership or a joint venture taxed as a partnership. Activities of a partnership are generally attributable to the organization, and it makes sense to include the pro rata share of a partnership's sales and transfers. However, the activities of a corporation or entity taxed as a corporation (e.g., an LLC taxed as a corporation) generally are not attributable to the organization, so sales or transfers of an entity taxed as a corporation should not be considered a significant disposition by the organization. This, however, is not settled one way or the other by the instructions. The conservative position, of course, is to report sales by an entity taxed as a corporation (and in which the organization has an ownership interest), if the organization's pro rata share of sales and transfers by the corporation meet the 25-percent significant disposition threshold. (Of course, the valuation problems mentioned earlier would be an issue here as well—namely, are the corporation's sales and transfers valued at market, book, or some other method.)

- Transfers of assets pursuant to a reorganization in which the organization is a surviving entity. The instructions do not define what this means, but it would presumably include a merger in which the organization is the surviving entity. It would also presumably include a situation where the organization transfers in excess of 25 percent of its assets to one or more related organizations that the organization directly or indirectly controls. For example, a nonprofit hospital organization may go through a reorganization where it transfers its hospital into one controlled subsidiary, its pharmacy into another controlled subsidiary, and its physician clinics into another controlled subsidiary. The organization survives as the parent organization of all three newly created subsidiaries. If these three transfers constitute more than 25 percent of the organization's assets, this is the kind of reorganization in which the organization is a surviving entity and which would presumably be reported in Part II.

- A contraction of net assets resulting from a grant or charitable contribution of assets to another organization described in Section 501(c)(3).

The instructions clarify that certain changes in the fair market value of the organization's net assets do not have to be reported in Part II, even if such changes exceed the 25-percent threshold. These changes include:

- A change in the composition of publicly traded securities held in the organization's passive investment portfolio

- Asset sales in the ordinary course of business, such as gross sales of inventory

- A decrease in the value of net assets due to market fluctuations in the value of assets held by the organization

- Transfers to disregarded entities of which the organization is the sole member

The table in Part II is generally identical to the table in Part I. For line-by-line and column-by-column instructions for Part II, refer to the instructions and commentary for Part I in § 20.2(a).

(c) Part III (Supplemental Information)

Use Part III to provide these explanations.

(1) Parts I and II, Line 2e. Line 2 in both Parts I and II asks an identical series of "yes/no" questions designed to ferret out if there are potential transactions that could give rise to private inurement, private benefit or excess benefit transactions (Did any directors and officers receive severance or change of control payments?; will any directors or officers be employees, independent contractors, owners, directors or officers of the successor entity?; etc.). To the extent the organization answers "yes" to any of these questions, it is supposed to name the director or officer at issue and provide an explanation in Part III. The explanation should include data about fair market value (Was an appraisal obtained to determine the sales price or a compensation consultant engaged to determine the reasonableness of a severance package?), steps taken to mitigate conflicts of interest (e.g., Did the directors of the organization who would take a role (director, officer, employee, etc.) or receive a benefit (compensation or ownership interest) in the successor organization recuse themselves from the vote?), and the steps the organization took to ensure that its exempt purposes would be fulfilled (see discussion of price, proceeds, and process in § 20.1(b)).

(2) Part I, Line 3. Line 3 in Part I asks if the assets were distributed in accordance with the organization's governing instruments. For example, the articles of incorporation for most nonprofit corporations specify what happens to assets upon dissolution of the organization (distribution to a 501(c)(3) organization, distribution to members, etc.). If the distribution was consistent with the governing instruments, answer "yes." If the distribution was not consistent with the governing instruments, answer "no" and explain in Part III. Neither Part III nor the instructions to Part III require this disclosure, but line 3 of Part I and the instructions to line 3 clearly do.

Generally, an organization should distribute its assets upon dissolution in accordance with its articles of incorporation, and there will generally be no satisfactory answer for failing to do so. There always being an exception to the rule, however, one can imagine situations. For example, if the articles of incorporation call for the organization to distribute its assets to an organization that no longer exists, or no longer qualifies as a charity under Section 501(c)(3), then the organization could not distribute its assets in accordance with its articles. In this case, the organization should distribute its assets in a manner that best accomplishes its exempt purposes (or the purposes of the transferee organization stated in the articles and explain accordingly in Part III.

(3) Part I, Line 7.   Line 7 in Part I asks several questions about whether an organization that is dissolving has outstanding tax-exempt bond liabilities and, if so, how such liabilities are discharged or defeased. In Part III, the organization should describe how the liabilities were settled (e.g., discharge or defeasance) and whether the settlement was consistent with state law and the Internal Revenue Code. If the settlement was not consistent with the Code (which is not an enviable position for the organization to find itself), then this also must be explained in Part III.

(d)   Special Rules for Group Exemptions, Joint Ventures, and Disregarded Entities

Appendices E and F to the Form 990 instructions contain some special rules regarding reporting on Schedule N (and other schedules) if the organization is operating under a group exemption or has ownership interests in joint ventures or disregarded entities. The rules applicable to Schedule N are described next.

- If the Form 990 is a consolidated 990 for a group of subordinate members under a group exemption, answer these lines on Schedule N "no" if any one subordinate member can answer the question "no": Part I, lines 3, 5b, 6, and 7b. All "no" answers will require supplemental explanations in Schedule O (e.g., describing which subordinate member answered "no"). Note: Although Appendix E says to make the supplemental disclosure in Schedule O, a more reasonable place would be Part III of Schedule N.

- Explain in Schedule N, Part III which of the subordinate members have undergone a liquidation, termination, dissolution, or significant disposition of assets. With respect to a significant distributions of assets, Appendix E is not clear whether that is 25 percent of the subordinate organization's net assets or 25 percent of the consolidated group's net assets, but presumably the former.

- Do not report a termination, liquidation, or dissolution of a disregarded entity if the organization continues to operate. Do not report transfers between the organization and any of its disregarded entities. However, any transfers by a disregarded entity to any person or entity other than the organization are taken into account to determine if the organization exceeds the 25-percent threshold. (In other words, all transfers by the disregarded entity are to be treated as transfers by the organization itself.)

- With respect to joint ventures, take into account the organization's share of the joint venture's transfers. (See the discussion in § 20.2(b).)

§ 20.3   NEW FORM 990 COMPLIANCE TASKS

If an organization engages in a Schedule N transaction, it should:

1. **Know state law.** Determine what state law requirements are regarding approval (by board, members, and/or others) and notice (e.g., to the state attorney general).

2. **Scrutinize sweetheart deals.** Take appropriate safeguards if directors, officers, trustees, or key employees will receive any benefit from the Schedule N transaction. Benefits include serving as a director, officer, trustee, employee, independent contractor, or owner of the successor organization. Get appraisals to support fair market value consideration if there are transactions with insiders (e.g., a sale of charitable assets to a director or officer), and obtain the opinion of a compensation consultant to ensure that any compensatory benefits to directors, officers, and key employees are reasonable (e.g., severance payments, change-of-control payments, golden parachutes, acceleration of deferred compensation benefits, compensation from or ownership interests in transferee organizations, etc.)

3. **Promote charitable purpose.** Ensure that charitable purpose will continue through the successor organization or with sales proceeds. For example, if the successor organization will not be fulfilling the organization's exempt purposes, make sure that the sales proceeds are used to do so.

4. **Focus on price, process, and proceeds.** Price should represent fair market value and compensation should be reasonable. The process should include steps taken by the organization to ensure that the transaction fulfills the organization's exempt purpose. The proceeds should be used for the same purposes for which the organization exists and consistent with the intent of the original donors, and should generally be used in the same community that the organization serves.

CHAPTER TWENTY-ONE

Schedule R—Related Organizations and Unrelated Partnerships

The use of related organizations to conduct both exempt and for-profit activities is more prevalent today than in past years. The current Form 990 asks many questions about related organizations, including information about for-profit subsidiaries, joint ventures, and disregarded entities. The questions address compensation paid by related organizations to key personnel, transactions between the organization and the related organizations, and other matters.

The new Form 990, Schedule R, consolidates and expands the reporting requirements for related organizations. It also requires information from certain unrelated partnerships. Related organizations include disregarded entities, related exempt organizations, and related for-profit organizations. The related organizations are first identified in Schedule R, then detailed information is reported on transactions between the filing organization and the related organizations. The additional information is requested so that the IRS is better equipped to analyze various issues on both an individual organization basis and a group basis. There is some potential reporting overlap with Schedule L as to indirect transactions with organizations controlled by insiders and with Schedule I as to reporting of grants.

§ 21.1 LAW AND POLICY

The existence of related organizations raises a number of legal issues. Private inurement and excess benefit transactions can occur not only in direct transactions between the organization and insiders/disqualified persons but also in indirect transactions with a related organization controlled by insiders/disqualified persons (see § 6.1((a)(5)). Unfair transactions with these related organizations may result in private inurement and/or excess benefit. In addition, compensation from all related organizations must be considered in determining whether excessive compensation occurs (see § 6.1(a)(3)). Private benefit often arises from the interaction of for-profit organizations with exempt organizations, especially if the organizations are commonly controlled. Joint ventures involving for-profit organizations can also cause private benefit issues (see § 6.1(c)). Unrelated business income is recognized by parent exempt organizations if they receive payments of interest, rent, or royalties from their controlled subsidiaries. Items of unrelated business income, lobbying, and political activities flow through to the exempt organization on its Form 990 from both related and unrelated entities taxed like partnerships, including limited liability companies, general partnerships, and limited partnerships (see Chapters 9 and 10). Further, if related organizations are not separately operated, the related organization's activities may be attributed to the exempt organization, causing exempt status issues.

(a) Corporation Entity Tax versus Flow-through of Tax Items

Organizations such as limited liability companies, limited partnerships, and general partnerships generally are taxed under the partnership flow-through rules. S corporations also are taxed under similar flow-through rules. Corporations (other than S corporations), however, pay their own entity-level tax, and there is no flow-through of tax items to its owners. Under the flow-through regime, all items of income, deduction, and credits flow-through to owners of the organization and are treated as if the owner conducted the activity itself to the extent of the owner's share of income. Passive income, such as interest, certain rents, royalties, and dividends, also flows through to the owners and retains its character. Activities conducted by flow-through entities that are unrelated to the organization's exempt purposes flow through as unrelated business income activities to the exempt organization, and passive income flows through as exempt passive income. Further, political and lobbying activities of a flow-through organizations are treated as political and lobbying activities of the exempt organization to the extent of its ownership percentage. (See §§ 9.1 and 10.1.) The income and deductions that flow-through are combined with the other income and deductions of the filing organization for purposes of applying the various tax rules applicable to exempt organizations. One of the most significant exemption issues in this regard is whether the exempt organization's primary purpose remains exempt when combined with the flow-through activities of the partnership. Income, deductions, and credits of organizations taxed as corporations (other than S corporations) are taxed at the entity level and do not flow-through to the exempt organization or other owners, provided the subsidiary is separately operated from the exempt organization. (See § 21.1(b).)

(b) Attribution of Subsidiary Activities to Exempt Parent

A taxable C corporation is often used to separate unrelated activities from the organization's exempt activities. This is a common planning mechanism when the unrelated activities transferred to the subsidiary are significant relative to the exempt activities. The substantial unrelated activity is separated from the exempt activity to avoid a challenge to the organization's exempt status under the primary purpose rule. If the organization is established with a bona fide business purpose and has real and substantial business functions, its existence generally will not be disregarded for tax purposes. However, if the subsidiary is, in reality, an arm, agent, or integral part of the parent, it will be ignored and all activities of the subsidiary will be attributed to the exempt parent organization. This determination is made based on all the facts and circumstances of the arrangement. At a minimum, corporate formalities must be adhered to, including separate board meetings and minutes, separate accounting, and separate bank accounts. Some of the other important factors in the analysis include the relative overlap of officers, directors, and employees as well as whether the parent and subsidiary share facilities, equipment, mailing lists, and service providers. One significant focus of the IRS in the analysis is whether the exempt organization is deemed to be involved in a day-to-day management of the subsidiary. A favorable fact in this regard is if the key officer of the subsidiary in charge of the day-to-day subsidiary operations is not the same officer in charge of the day-to-day operations of the exempt parent. Many of the transactions that impact the attribution analysis between related parties are addressed in Schedule R. (See § 21.2(e).)

(c)   Attribution of Related Exempt Organization

The attribution of activities from one organization to another can also occur between exempt organizations. A common situation is where a social welfare organization and a charity work together in a policy initiative. The charity may be conducting the education activity for a particular policy issue like stem cell research or the environment, and the social welfare organization may be conducting lobbying activities. A political action committee may also be involved to conduct political campaign activities in this regard. Often the charity and the social welfare organizations are controlled by the same persons. If this occurs, the charity reports the related social welfare organization on its Schedule R. Like the exempt parent with the for-profit subsidiary, a charity's relationship with the exempt social welfare organization will be scrutinized by the IRS, and the social welfare activities can sometimes be attributed to the charity. Because the social welfare organization's activities may involve substantial lobbying activity and perhaps some political campaign activity, the attribution of these activities to the charity could cause the charity to lose its tax-exempt status because the lobbying activities are more than insubstantial (see § 9.1) or because of the prohibition on political campaign activities (see § 10.1).

(d)   Private Inurement and Excess Benefit Transactions

Transactions between related organizations can result in private inurement and/or excess benefit transactions. This can occur when the related organization in question is considered an "insider" or "disqualified person" under the respective rules. Generally an insider or disqualified person would include an organization in which a disqualified person or persons holds more than 35-percent ownership interest. If the insiders collectively had an ownership interest in an organization that reaches more than 50 percent, then the organization would be a related organization. As such, all transactions between the filing organization and the related organization, reported on Schedule R, would be scrutinized under the private inurement and excess benefit transaction doctrines. An organization could also be an insider where, through the terms and conditions of management and other agreements, the organization contracting with the filing organization has substantial influence over the operations of the filing organization. (See § 6.1(b).) In this case, the transaction would not be reported on Schedule R but would be disclosed in Part VI, line 3.

(e) Private Benefit—Generally

The usual IRS inquiry when investigating the involvement of private parties in a charity's activities is whether the insiders are receiving unreasonable compensation or whether the sale of goods and services between the charity and the insiders, or controlled entities of the insiders, are fair and reasonable. The excess benefit provisions of the intermediate sanctions also are considered in the analysis and can be imposed as an alternative, or in addition to, private inurement. If an unfair transaction is entered into by the "insider" and "disqualified person," respectively, the organization's exempt status can be lost and/or the intermediate sanctions can be imposed on the individuals involved.

Unlike private inurement and excess benefit transactions, private benefit involves a much broader analysis. Whether an organization's activities serve private interests more than incidentally is a factual determination that generally involves an analysis of the relationships between the charity and one or more for-profit entities as a whole, not just a single transaction.

In the context of reporting on the Form 990, transactions are scrutinized under the private benefit doctrine not only in the compensation context (see § 6.1) but also transactions reported on Schedule L (see § 18.1) relative to direct business transactions between a current or former officer, director, trustee, or key employee, and/or their family members and the filing organization (other than as an officer, director, trustee, or employee) or an indirect business relationship with the filing organization through ownership by these individuals and/or their family members of more than a 35-percent interest in another entity (individually or collectively with the persons just listed). The other area where private benefit is found is in the context of related organizations. The classic case is when a management company has majority overlap of its directors with the charity or other exempt organization that it manages. For a detailed discussion of the private benefit doctrine, see § 6.1(c)).

(f) Private Benefit and Joint Ventures

The analysis of joint ventures between for-profit entities and charities has evolved over many years. Joint ventures are reported on Schedule R if the filing organization holds more than a 50-percent profits or capital interest in the partnership. They are also reported on Schedule R, if the joint venture conducts more than 5 percent of its exempt activities through the partnership. Prior to 1982, the IRS's general position was that a charity could not be a general partner in a joint venture. The proposition was that a charity could not operate "exclusively" for charitable purposes and be involved in a partnership with a for-profit partner. The IRS later changed that position and adopted a two-prong test to determine whether a joint venture between a charity and a for-profit entity threatened the charity's tax exempt status. The two-prong test required that (1) the activities furthered charitable purposes, and (2) the structure of the partnership insulated the charity from potential conflicts between its charitable purposes and its general partnership obligations and minimized the likelihood that the arrangement would generate private benefit. The first prong is simply an analysis of whether the activities generally further charitable, educational, or other exempt purposes. For example, if the activity is charitable by relieving the poor and distressed or educational because the program advances education, this first prong is met. The second prong involves are more difficult analysis.

Factors indicating that an organization's assets are protected from conflicts and the joint venture is protected from impermissible private benefit and private inurement include:

- The exempt partner has control of joint venture.

- The exempt partner has limited contractual liability.

- There is no obligation on the part of the exempt partner to return the limited partner's capital contribution from the exempt partner's funds.

- There are no inequitable guarantees by the exempt partner protecting the for-profit partner's investments.

The most significant joint venture ruling in recent years was in 1998. This ruling triggered the avalanche of joint venture discussions, rulings, and cases over the past several years. It applied the two-prong test to a whole-hospital joint venture arrangement. The ruling involved a "good" example and a "bad" example. The good example involved a transfer by an exempt organization of all of its hospital assets to a limited liability company (LLC) formed with a for-profit entity. The for-profit entity also contributed assets and the parties received proportionate ownership interests in return for their asset transfers. The only substantive difference between the good example and the bad example was that the charity named three of the five members of the governing board in the good example. In the bad example, the charity named three members of the governing board and the for-profit named three members. The conclusion was that assuming the activities were otherwise related activities, having majority control of the joint venture was the key to protecting exempt status and avoiding unrelated business income.

For several years after the ruling, the issue of control was paramount in structuring both joint ventures involving all of a charity's assets and joint ventures where only a portion of the charity's assets was involved. For many this was a fiction. While control certainly should be an issue in the analysis, it should not be determinative of exempt status revocation.

The ruling was followed by a number of cases involved a charity's contributions of its entire activity. In one case a joint venture entity formed with for-profit individuals. The activity in this case was an ambulatory surgery center. Like the bad example of 1998 ruling, the charity and the for-profit each had the right to name the same number of members to the governing body, so the charity did not have majority control over the joint venture activities. Further, the governing documents did not require that charitable purposes trumped all other joint venture purposes. The court concluded, therefore, that there was neither an expressed nor an implied obligation to place charitable objectives first and that the charity had effectively conceded control of the surgery center to private parties, thus conferring impermissible private benefit.

In another case, board control was split 50/50. The joint venture partner was a for-profit health system. All parties agreed that the joint venture performed substantial charity care and met the community benefit standard. Again, control was the issue. The lower court ruled in favor of the charity, but the appeals court found that there were genuine issues of material fact left undecided so it reversed the lower court and remanded the case back for jury trial. The appeals court expanded the analysis of the 1998 ruling and other cases. It held that the charity does not have to retain formal control of the partnership if it has effective control over the major decisions of the partnership. The appeals court stated that the charity should retain effective control including the right to dissolve the partnership, if charitable activities are not furthered. The appeals court instructed the jury to consider the totality of the circumstances in deciding whether the partnership's operations were primarily for charitable purposes. The jury ultimately found in favor of the charity.

A 2004 ruling addressed the tax impact of an ancillary joint venture. Prior to this ruling, the primary authority all involved whole-entity joint ventures. The ruling adopted the refined control analysis. The facts of ruling involved a tax-exempt university and a for-profit company. The university and the for-profit entity each owned a 50-percent share of the joint venture LLC and each had equal representation on the LLC's board of directors. The for-profit was responsible for arranging and conducting all administrative details, regarding the video training seminars for teachers. The university, however, had the exclusive right to approve the curricula, training materials, instructors, and standards of completion of the seminar. The for-profit had the exclusive right to send video-training technicians to locations. All other decisions were made jointly by the members under the operating agreement. The two issues analyzed were: (1) whether an organization continues to qualify for exemption as a charity when it contributes a portion of its assets to and conducts a portion of its activities through an LLC formed with a for-profit corporation; and (2) whether the organization is subject to unrelated business income tax on its distributive share of the LLC's income.

The assumptions in the ruling were: (1) the joint venture activities are an "insubstantial" part of the university's total activities; (2) all transactions are conducted at "arm's length"; and (3) all contracted transaction prices are at "fair market value." The ruling provided that some control could be ceded to the for-profit provided that exempt organization controls the substantive "charitable" aspects of the arrangement. In defining *ancillary,* the facts of the ruling indicate that the activity involved was an "insubstantial" part of the university's overall activities in the educational joint venture. If effective control of the joint venture arrangement is ceded to the for-profit partner, the activity could be viewed as an unrelated business income activity. The exempt status of the organization should not be affected, however, as long as the activity is insubstantial. The key to the analysis is that the assumption that the activity is "insubstantial." If control is conceded in a substantial activity, excessive private benefit will result in the loss of tax-exempt status. The IRS is implicitly saying that the business of the joint venture is thereby converted to an unrelated business, even though the business remains inherently related.

(g) Passive Income from Controlled Subsidiaries

Items of passive income, such as dividends, interest, certain rents, and royalties, are generally exempt from taxation as unrelated business income. One exception to this rule if the passive income (other than dividends) is received from a controlled subsidiary or other controlled entities (greater than 50 percent of the voting power or value of stock). This exception applies, however, only if the controlled entity takes a deduction for the income paid to the exempt parent. The rule exists to avoid a double tax benefit (i.e., a deduction and an exemption).

(h) Disregarded Entities

An entity that is wholly owned by the organization and has not elected to be taxed as a corporation is a disregarded entity. The most common example is a single-member limited liability company. Such an entity does not exist for federal income tax purposes. It is often used as a planning vehicle to limit liability or to separate governance and management focus from the organization's other activities.

Because the entity is disregarded, all of its income and all of its assets are reported directly on the Form 990 of the filing organization. Although single-member LLCs are disregarded for federal income tax purposes, they are not always disregarded for state and local purposes. The most common example is the treatment of disregarded entities for state and local property taxes. In many states, a single-member LLC will have to pay property taxes on property it holds even though such property is used for exempt purposes and would be exempt from property taxes if held directly by the filing organization. Thus, while this is an effective planning tool for liability and governance purposes, it can cause state and local tax issues.

(i) Supporting Organizations and Automatic Excess Benefit Transactions

If a supporting organization makes a grant, loan, payment of compensation, or similar payment (such as an expense reimbursement) to a substantial contributor or related person of the supporting organization, the substantial contributor is regarded, for purposes of the intermediate sanction rules, as a disqualified person. This type of payment is treated as an automatic excess benefit transaction. As such, the entire amount of the payment is treated as an excess benefit. If this were to occur, a substantial contributor would be subject to the initial intermediate sanctions excess tax on the amount of the payment. Further, the organization manager who knowingly participated in the making of the payment is also subject to the excise tax. The second-tier taxes under the other intermediate sanctions rules are also applicable to these payments. For example, loans by a supporting organization to a substantial contributor with respect to the supporting organization are treated as excess benefit transactions. The entire amount of this loan is regarded as an excess benefit and is reported in Schedule L. An automatic excess benefit transaction also can occur between related parties if an organization is a substantial contributor to a related organization and it engages in certain transactions with the related organization. For example, if a social welfare organization has a supporting organization and it becomes a substantial contributor to the supporting organization, any payment back to the social welfare organization, such as an expense reimbursement, could be an automatic excess benefit transaction. Similarly, if one supporting organization becomes a substantial contributor to a related supporting organization, any payments to the contributor by the recipient supporting organization may be an excess benefit transaction. These types of transactions would be reported in Schedule R, and if they result in excess benefit transactions, they would also be reported in Schedule L.

§21.2 PREPARATION OF FORM

Schedule R asks for information on related organizations, including disregarded entities, related tax-exempt entities, related corporations (including S corporations) and related organizations taxed as partnerships. It also requires the reporting of the relationships with certain unrelated organizations taxed as partnerships. Once the related organizations are identified, the form requires the reporting of certain transactions between the filing organization and each of the related organizations.

Central organizations and subordinate organizations of a group exemption are not required to be listed as related organizations in Schedule R, Part II. All other related organizations of the central organization or of a subordinate organization are required to be listed in Schedule R. Thus:

- An organization that is a central or subordinate organization in a group exemption (whether filing an individual return or a group return) is not required to list any of the subordinate organizations of the group in Schedule R, Part II.

- In the case of a group return, the central organization must attach a list of the subordinate organizations included in the group return in response to Form 990, page 1, item H(b). The central organization must list in Schedule R the related organizations of each subordinate organization other than (1) related organizations that are included within the group exemption, or (2) related organizations that the central organization knows to be included in another group exemption. If an organization is not listed because it is known to be included in another group exemption, the central organization must explain in Schedule O the relationship between its own group and members and the related organization known to be included in another group exemption (but need not include the names of such related organizations).

- An organization that is not included in a group exemption is not required to list a related organization that is included in a group exemption. Similarly, an organization that is included in a group exemption is not required to list a related organization that is included in another group exemption. In either case, the organization must explain in Schedule O the relationship between it and the related organization included in another group exemption (but need not include the names of such related organizations).

Even if a related organization is not required to be listed in Part II, however, the organization must report its transactions with the related organization in Part V, as required by the Part V instructions (e.g., transactions over the applicable $50,000 reporting threshold for line 2), including listing the name of the related organization in Part V, line 2, Column (A) for transactions that must be reported in line 2.

Control can be indirect. For example, if the filing organization controls Entity A, which in turn controls (under the definition of "control" discussed later in this section) Entity B, the organization will be treated as controlling Entity B. Rules under Section 318 (relating to constructive ownership of stock) apply for purposes of determining constructive ownership of a corporation. Similar rules apply for determining constructive ownership of other entities, such as a partnership or trust.

If Entity B controls an entity taxed as a partnership by being one of three or fewer members or partners as discussed later in this section, then the organization that controls Entity B also controls the partnership. The instructions provide three other examples:

> **Example 1.** B, an exempt organization, wholly owns (by voting power) C, a taxable corporation. C holds a 51% profits interest in D, a partnership. Under the principles of Section 318, B is deemed to own 51% of D (100% of C's 51% interest in D)). Thus, B controls both C and D, which are therefore both related organizations with respect to B.

> **Example 2.** X, an exempt organization, owns 80% (by value) of Y, a taxable corporation. Y holds a 60% profits interest as a limited partner of Z, a limited partnership. Under the principles of Section 318, X is deemed to own 48% of Z (80% of Y's 60% interest in Z). Thus, X controls Y. X does not control Z through X's ownership in Y. Y is a related organization with respect to X, and (absent other facts) Z is not.

> **Example 3.** Same facts as in Example 2, except that Y is also one of three general partners of Z. Because Y controls Z through means other than ownership percentage, and X controls Y, in these circumstances Z is a related organization with respect to X. The other general partners of Z (if organizations) are not related organizations with respect to X, absent other facts.

The reporting of all organizations indirectly controlled by the filing organizations will be cumbersome. In complex hospital settings, for example, reporting will be required of second- and third-tier subsidiaries and partnerships if there is a more than 50-percent ownership string through the tiers.

(a) Part I—Identification of Disregarded Entities

In Part I, report all of the organization's disregarded entities. Disregarded entities are organizations wholly owned by the filing organization that did not elect to be taxed as corporations. The most common example is a limited liability company in which the filing organization is its sole member. Disregarded entities are treated as related organizations (subsidiaries of the filing organization) for purposes of reporting in Schedule R, Part I, but not for purposes of reporting transactions with related organizations in Part V or otherwise in Form 990, such as in Part VII relative to reporting compensation. Rather, the income and assets of a disregarded entity are treated as income and assets of the filing organization and not income and assets of a separate entity.

(1) Column (A) (Name, Address, EIN). In Column (A), report the name, address, and employer identification number (EIN) of every disregarded entity. The instructions clarify that the full legal name and mailing address of the disregarded entity should be provided. The EIN should be provided as well, if it has one. In some cases, a disregarded entity will not have an EIN. Generally, the EIN of the sole member will be the EIN of the disregarded entity. There is an exception for this in the case of employment taxes. The instructions indicate that on or after January 1, 2009, the disregarded entity must file separate employment tax returns and use its own EIN number on such returns. The instructions clarify that if there is insufficient room in Part I to report all of the organization's disregarded entities, that additional information can be provided on Schedule R-1, Part I.

(2) Columns (B) and (C) (Primary Activity and Domicile). In Column (B), report the primary activity of the disregarded entity. Legal domicile is reported in Column (C). This is the U.S. state (or possession) or foreign country in which the disregarded entity is organized.

(3) Columns (D) and (E) (Total Income and Total Assets). In Column (D), report the total income of the disregarded entity. This number should match up with the revenue reported on Part VIII, Statement of Revenue attributable to the disregarded entity. In Column (E), report the disregarded entity's total assets. This item should match the total assets reported on Part X, Balance Sheet, attributable to the disregarded entity. Because the entity is disregarded, its activities are treated as if they are performed by the filing organization. Thus, if the activity is related to the filing organization's exempt purpose, its revenue is exempt program service revenue, but if the activity is unrelated to the filing organization's exempt purposes, the income is unrelated business income.

(4) Column (F) (Direct Controlling Entity). In Column (F), report the organization that is in direct control of the disregarded entity, if control is owned indirectly, then the name of the entity that directly controls should be reported.

> **Example.** If the filing organization is the sole member of A, a disregarded entity, and A is the sole member of B, a disregarded entity, the filing organization would include both A and B on Schedule R. As to A, the filing organization would report itself as the organization with direct control of A. As to B, it would report A as the organization with direct control of B in Column (F).

(b) Part II—Identification of Related Tax-Exempt Organizations

In Part II, report information for all related tax-exempt organizations.

A parent/subsidiary control relationship exists between nonprofit organizations if (1) there is a power to remove and replace (or to appoint or elect, if such power includes a continuing power to appoint or elect periodically or in event of vacancies) a majority of a related organization's directors or trustees, and (2) organizations with a management overlap where a majority of the subsidiary's directors or trustees are trustees, directors, officers, employees, or agents of the parent. In the case of brother/sister relationships between nonprofit organizations, a control relationship exists if the same persons constitute a majority of the members of the governing body of both organizations.

One example is the supporting organization/supported organization relationship. A related exempt organization would be an organization that is (or claims to be) at any time during the organization's tax year (i) a supporting organization of the filing organization within the meaning of Section 509(a)(3), if the filing organization is a supported organization within the meaning of Section 509(f)(3), or (ii) a supported organization, if the filing organization is a supporting organization.

(1) Column (A) (Name, Address, and EIN). In Column (A), report the full legal name, mailing address, and EIN of the related tax-exempt organization.

(2) Columns (B) and (C) (Primary Activity and Legal Domicile). In Column (B), report the organization's primary activity and in Column (C), report the related exempt organization's legal domicile. List the U.S. state (or U.S. possession) or foreign country in which the related organization is organized. For a corporation, enter the state of incorporation (country of incorporation for a foreign corporation formed outside the United States). For a trust or other entity, enter the state whose law governs the organization's internal affairs (the foreign country whose law governs for a foreign organization other than a corporation).

(3) Columns (D) and (E) (Exempt Code Section and Public Charity Status). In Column (D), report the exempt Code section for the related exempt organization. For example, if a social welfare organization is the related exempt organization, "Section 501(c)(4)" would be inserted here. In Column (E), report the public charity status of the organization. Use the line number (line 1–line 11(d)) corresponding to public charity status indicated in Schedule A for this purpose. For example, a school would be line 2 and a church would be line 1. In the case of a private foundation, the designation "PF" should be used. In the case of a supporting organization, the type of supporting organization must also be indicated for Type I, Type II, Type III functionally integrated, or Type III other.

(4) Column (F) (Direct Controlling Entity). In Column (F), report the direct controlling entity of the related organization. If the filing organization is indirectly in control of the related organization, the organization directly in control is reported. Otherwise state "NA."

(c) Part III—Identification of Related Organizations Taxable as a Partnership

In Part III, report information on all related partnerships and other entities taxed as partnerships. A related entity includes:

- Ownership of more than 50 percent of the profits or capital interest in a partnership

- Ownership of more than 50 percent of the profits or capital in a limited liability company (LLC), regardless of the designation under state law of the ownership interests as stock, membership shares, or otherwise under state law

- Being a managing partner or managing member in a partnership or LLC that has three or fewer managing partners or managing members (regardless of which partner or member has the most actual control)

- Being a general partner in a limited partnership that has three or fewer general partners (regardless of which partner has the most actual control)

The instructions indicate that if the partnership is related to the filing organization by reason of being its parent or brother/sister and the filing organization is not a partner or member in the partnership, then complete only Columns (A), (B), and (C) and state "NA" in Columns (D), (E), (F), (G), (H), (I), and (J).

Some of the information requested next is derived from Schedule K-1 of Form 1065 issued to the organization. If the Schedule K-1 is not available, provide a reasonable estimate of the required information.

(1) Column (A) (Name, Address, EIN). In Column (A), report the full name, mailing address, and EIN of the related partnership.

(2) Columns (B) and (C) (Primary Activity and Legal Domicile). In Column B, report the organization's primary activity. In Column (C) report the organization's legal domicile. List the state (or U.S. possession) or foreign country in which the related partnership is organized (i.e., the state or foreign country whose law governs the related parties internal affairs).

(3) Column (D) (Direct Control). In Column (D), report the direct controlling entity of the partnership if the filing organization indirectly controls the partnership. Otherwise state "NA."

> **Example.** The filing organization owns a 90% profits interest in A, a limited liability company taxed as a partnership. A owns a 80% profits interest in B, a limited liability company taxed as a partnership, which owns a 80% profits interest in C, a limited partnership. The filing organization includes A, B and C in Schedule R. With respect to A, the filing organization is in direct control and it would indicate "NA" in Column (D) because it is the organization in direct control. With respect to B it owns a 72% indirect interest (90% $\times$ 80%) and it would indicate A as the organization in direct control; with respect to C, it owns a 57.6% interest (72% $\times$ 80%) and it would indicate B as the organization in direct control.

(4) Column (E) (Predominant Income). In Column (E), report the predominant income of the related partnership. The primary categories of income are related, unrelated, or investment or other income excluded from tax under Section 512, 513, or 514. It is related income if the partnership's primary activities furthers the filing organization's exempt purpose. It is unrelated income if the partnership's primary activity does not further the filing organization's exempt purposes. It is investment income or other excludable income if the partnership primarily generates dividends, interest, rents, royalties or other excludable income. Examples of other excludable income include donated merchandise and receipts from bingo games (see § 7.2).

(5) Column (F) (Share of Total Income). In Column (F), report the organization's share of the partnership's total income in accordance with the organization's profit interests for the related partnership's tax year ending with or within the filing organization's tax year. For example, if the filing organization has a 51-percent profits and capital interest in the partnership, it would report 51 percent of the income items of the partnership as shown on the partnership tax return. Use the total amount listed on Schedule K-1 of Form 1065 provided to the partner by the partnership for the partnership's year ending with or within the filing organization's tax year (total of Schedule K-1, Part III, lines 1–11, plus line 18).

(6) Column (G) (Share of Total Assets). In Column (G), report the filing organization's distributable share of the related partnership's end-of-year total assets, in accordance with the organization's capital interest as specified by the partnership or limited liability company agreement for the partnership's tax year ending with or within the filing organization's tax year. If Schedule K-1 of Form 1065 for the partnership's year ending with or within the partnership's tax year is available, determine this amount by adding the organization's ending capital account to the organization's share of the partnership's liabilities at year-end reported on the Schedule K-1.

(7) Column (H) (Disproportionate Allocations). In Column (H), indicate "yes" or "no" as to whether disproportionate allocations exist for the partnership. Indicate "yes" if any item of income, gain, loss, deduction, or credit or any right to distributions was disproportionate to the filing organization's investment in such partnership at any time during the year.

(8) Column (I) (UBI Amount). In Column (I), state the dollar amount, if any, listed as the Code V amount (unrelated business taxable income (UBI)) in Box 20 of Schedule K-1 to Form 1065 received from the related partnership for the partnership's tax year ending with or within the filing organization's tax year. If no Code V amount is listed in Box 20, state "NA."

(9) Column (J) (General or Managing Partner). In Column (J), indicate "yes" or "no" as to whether the filing organization is a general partner of the related limited partnership or is a managing partner or managing member of a related general partnership, limited liability company, or other entity taxed as a partnership at any time during its tax year. The position as a general partner or managing partner may make the organization a related organization if there are three or fewer general partners or managing members, respectively. This relationship can also determine control over the partnership for purposes of the private benefit analysis (see § 21.1(f)).

(d) Part IV—Identification of Related Organizations Taxable as a Corporation or a Trust

In Part IV, report a corporation or trust, respectively, if the filing organization controls the corporation or trust. If the corporation or trust is related to the filing organization as its parent or as a brother/sister organization, and the filing organization does not have an ownership interest in the corporation or trust, then complete only Columns (A), (B), (C) and (E) and state "NA" in Columns (D), (F), (G), and (H). Do not report a trust described within Section 401(a). Section 401(a) applies to qualified profit-sharing plans.

Some of the relationships that will make the organization a related organization include:

- Parent—an organization that controls the filing organization.
- Subsidiary—an organization controlled by the filing organization.
- Brother/Sister—an organization controlled by the same person or persons that control the filing organization.

In the case of stock corporations and other organizations with owners or persons having beneficial interests, whether such organization is taxable or tax-exempt, "control" means:

- Ownership of more than 50 percent of the stock (by voting power or value) of a corporation

- Ownership of more than 50 percent of the beneficial interests in a trust

Some of the information requested next is derived from Schedule K-1 of Form 1041 or 1120S issued to the organization. If the Schedule K-1 is not available, provide a reasonable estimate of the required information.

(1) Column (A) (Name, Address, and EIN). In Column (A), report the related organization's full name, mailing address, and EIN.

(2) Columns (B) and (C) (Primary Activity and Legal Domicile). In Column (B), report the related organization's primary activity and, in Column (C), the related organization's legal domicile. List the U.S. state (or U.S. possession) or foreign country in which the related organization is organized. For a corporation, enter the state of incorporation (or the country of incorporation for a foreign corporation formed outside the United States). For a trust or other entity, enter the state whose law governs the organization's internal affairs (or the foreign country whose law governs for a foreign organization other than a corporation).

(3) Column (D) (Direct Controlling Entity). In Column (D), report the entity with direct control of the corporation or trust. If the filing organization has direct control, indicate "NA" in Column (D).

> **Example:** The filing organization owns 100% of the stock of Corporation A, and Corporation A owns 51% of the stock of Corporation B. Both Corporation A and B would be reported in Schedule R. As to Corporation A, the filing organization is the direct owner so "NA" is indicated in Column (D). As to Corporation B, report Corporation A as the direct owner.

(4) Column (E) (Type of Entity). In Column (E), report the type of related corporation (indicate C for a corporation or association taxed under subchapter C, S for a corporation or association taxed under subchapter S, or T for a trust taxable under subchapter J).

(5) Column (F) (Share of Total Income). In Column (F), report the related organization's share of total income. For a related organization that is a C corporation, state the dollar amount of the organization's hypothetical share of the C corporation's total income. To calculate the share, multiply the total income by this fraction: the value of the filing organization's shares of all classes of stock in the C corporation, divided by the value of all outstanding shares of all classes of stock in the C corporation. The total income is for the related organization's tax year ending with or within the filing organization's tax year. For a related organization that is an S corporation, state the filing organization's allocable share of the S corporation's total income. Use the amount as set forth in Schedule K-1 of Form 1120S for the S Corporation's tax year ending with or within the filing organization's tax year, if available (K-1, Part III, lines 1–10). For a related organization that is a trust, state the total income and gains reported on Part

III, lines 1 to 8 of Schedule K-1 of Form 1041 issued to the filing organization for the trust's tax year ending with or within the filing organization's tax year, if available.

Please note that if a charity is an S corporation shareholder, it must treat all allocations of income from the S corporation as unrelated business income, including gain on the disposition of the stock.

(6) Column (G) (Share of Total Assets). In Column (G), report the dollar amount of the filing organization's allocable share of the related organization's total assets as of the end of the related organization's tax year ending with or within the filing organization's tax year. For related corporations, this amount is determined by multiplying the corporations end-of-year total assets by the fraction described in Column (F). For a related trust, this amount corresponds to the filing organization's percentage ownership in the trust.

(7) Column (H) (Percentage Ownership). In Column (H), report the reporting organization's percentage ownership in the related organization. For a related organization taxable as a corporation, state the filing organization's percentage of stock ownership in the corporation (total combined voting power or total value of all outstanding shares, whichever is greater). For a related S corporation, use the percentage reported on Schedule K-1 of Form 1120S for the year ending with or within the filing organization's tax year, if available. For a related organization taxable as a trust, state the filing organization's percentage of beneficial interest. In each case, the percentage interest is as of the end of the related organization's tax year ending with or within the filing organization's tax year.

(e) Part V—Transactions with Related Organizations

For all organizations reporting in Parts II, III, or IV, a number of different questions are asked relative to transactions with related organizations listed in Parts II to IV. A transfer includes a conveyance of funds or property not included in lines 1a to 1p, whether or not for consideration, such as a merger with a related organization. Transactions between the filing organization and related organizations will be scrutinized to various degrees depending on the type of entity involved. Clearly with charities and social welfare organizations, the greatest scrutiny will be imposed due to the private inurement and excess benefit prohibitions. Even when insiders/disqualified persons are not involved, the transaction may be scrutinized under the private benefit proscription. Transactions between related exempt organizations can also be suspect, especially if the transaction is between a charity and an exempt organization that is not a charity.

(1) Line 1a (Receipt of Interest, Annuities, Royalties or Rent from a Controlled Entity). On line 1a, the filing organization indicates "yes" or "no" as to whether it received interest, annuities, royalties, or rent from a controlled entity. If "yes" is answered, more detail is required on line 2. Like the current Form 990, the IRS asks for specific reporting of passive income from controlled subsidiaries. Interest, annuities, royalties or rent generally are exempt from unrelated business income except when received from a controlled entity (see § 21.1(g)).

(2) Lines 1b and 1c (Gift, Grant, or Capital Contribution). On line 1b, indicate "yes" or "no" as to whether a gift, grant, or capital contribution was made to the related organization by the filing organization. On line 1c, indicate "yes" or "no" as to whether a gift, grant, or capital contribution was made by the related organization to the filing organization. Examples of transactions of this type that would invite IRS scrutiny include capital contributions to related for-profit entities and grants made by charities to other related exempt organizations. A capital contribution would be more scrutinized in the case of an exempt organization that owned a controlling interest in a related for-profit organization but did not own 100 percent of the related organization. If a contribution is made to a related organization that is also owned, in part, by private persons, the IRS would want to know whether the private persons made a proportionate contribution to the related entity. If not, private inurement, excess benefit, and/or private benefit could result. In the case of a for-profit related organization that is wholly owned by the exempt organization, the scrutiny would be substantially less because the exempt organization would continue to indirectly own the money or property contributed. Grants made to other exempt organizations may also be suspect if the other exempt organizations are not charities. For example, a grant to a social welfare organization may constitute a lobbying or political campaign expenditure. In some cases, a charity will make a grant to a social welfare organization of its maximum lobbying expenditure allocable under the expenditure test (see § 9.1(e)). Grants made to a supporting organization by another supporting organization or by exempt organizations (other than certain public charities) could cause an automatic excess benefit transaction if the contributor received something back from the supporting organization (see § 21.1(i)).

(3) Lines 1d and 1e (Loans or Loan Guarantee). On line 1d, indicate "yes" or "no" as to whether a loan was made, or guarantee provided, by the filing organization to or for the related organization. On line 1e, report "yes" or "no" as to whether a loan was made, or guarantee provided, by the related organization to or for the filing organization. Loans are carefully scrutinized, especially loans made by a charity to a related organization, whether the related organization is a for-profit organization or other exempt organization (not a charity). This is especially the case if the related organization is an insider and the filing organization is a charity or social welfare organization (see § 6.1(a)(1)). The making of loans is sometimes restricted by state nonprofit corporation law and governing documents.

(4) Line 1f (Sale of Assets). On line 1f, indicate "yes" or "no" as to whether the filing organization sold assets to the related organization. The sale of assets to a related organization is scrutinized to ensure that a fair market value sales price is paid. This is especially the case with charities and social welfare organizations. If the related organization is an insider/disqualified person, the rebuttable presumption of reasonableness procedure should be followed (see § 6.1(b)(8)).

(5) Line 1g (Purchase of Assets). On line 1g, indicate "yes" or "no" as to whether the filing organization purchased assets from the related organization. The purchase of assets is also scrutinized for fair market value purposes and structure. This is especially the case with charities and social welfare organizations. The rebuttable presumption of reasonableness procedure should be followed if the related organization is an insider/disqualified person (see § 6.1(b)(8)).

(6) Line 1h (Exchange of Assets). On line 1h, indicate "yes" or "no" as to whether there was an exchange of assets between the filing organization and the related organization. Like the purchase and sale of assets between the filing organization and the related organization, an exchange of assets also will be carefully scrutinized by the IRS. This is especially the case with charities and social welfare organizations. The organization should follow the rebuttable presumption of reasonableness procedure if the related organization is an insider (see § 6.1(b)(8)).

(7) Lines 1i and 1j (Lease of Facilities, Equipment, or Other Assets). On line 1i, indicate "yes" or "no" whether facilities, equipment, or other assets were leased to the related organization by the filing organization. On line 1j, indicate "yes" or "no" as to whether the related organization leased facilities, equipment, or other assets to the filing organization. Whenever a transaction occurs between the related organization and the filing organization, steps must be taken to insure that fair market value rent is paid and that the transaction is properly documented. The rebuttable presumption of reasonableness procedure should be followed to ensure fairness. When the for-profit related organization is leasing from the filing organization, at least fair market value must be paid. A rental arrangement where less than fair market value is paid would be more acceptable if the exempt organization pays less than fair market value rent to a for-profit related organization. If both organizations are charities, a rental arrangement of less than fair market value may be acceptable in some cases. The leasing of facilities is also one of the factors the IRS will look to in determining whether a related subsidiary or sister exempt organization is separately operated for purposes of the attribution rules (see §§ 21.1(b) and (c)).

(8) Lines 1k and 1l (Performance of Services or Fundraising). On line 1k, indicate "yes" or "no" as to whether the filing organization performed services or provided membership or fundraising solicitations support for the related organization and on line 1l, indicate "yes" or "no" as to whether the related organization performed services or provided membership or fundraising solicitations support for the filing organization. The provision of services or fundraising assistance between related organizations will be scrutinized in a manner similar to the exchange, purchase, or sale of assets. The primary issue is whether fair market value is paid and whether proper procedures were followed to determine fair market value. Depending on the status of the two parties involved and the direction of the flow of money, the IRS scrutiny will vary. Whenever the arrangement involves a charity and another exempt organization or for-profit organization, the charity must always receive fair market value for services it performs for the related organization. The performance of services may also cause an unrelated business income issue for the charity in some cases if the services are administrative in nature, even if the services are provided to another charity. If the charity receives more than fair market value, the excess likely would be viewed as a contribution. If the charity receives less than fair market value, private inurement, excess benefit and/or private benefit may result, depending on the relationship (see § 6.1). The performance of services between related organizations also impacts the attribution analysis. To the extent significant interaction between related organizations occur, including exchange of services and leasing and sharing of facilities, the risk of attribution increases (see § 21.1(b) and (c)).

(9) Line 1m (Sharing of Facilities, Equipment, Mailing Lists, or Other Assets). On line 1m, indicate "yes" or "no" as to whether the filing organization and related organization shared facilities, equipment, mailing lists, or other assets. The same fair market value issues discussed in § 21.2(e)(8) and attribution issues discussed in § 21.1(b) and (c) apply here.

(10) Line 1n (Sharing of Paid Employees). On line 1n, indicate "yes" or "no" as to whether the filing organization and related organization shared employees. The same fair market value issues discussed in § 21.2(e)(8) and attribution issues discussed in § 21.1(b) and (c) apply here.

(11) Lines 1o and 1p (Expense Reimbursement). On line 1o, indicate "yes" or "no" as to whether the filing organization reimbursed the related organization for expenses. On line 1p, indicate "yes" or "no" as to whether the related organization reimbursed the filing organization for expenses. The same fair market value issues discussed in §21.2(e)(8) and the attribution issues discussed in §21.1(b) and (c) apply here.

(12) Lines 1q and 1r (Other Transfer of Cash or Property). On line 1q, indicate "yes" or "no" as to whether the filing organization made other transfers of cash or property to the related organization. On line 1r, indicate "yes" or "no" as to whether the filing organization received other transfers of cash or property from the related organization.

(13) Line 2 (Receipt of Income from Controlled Entity). On line 2, report the following transactions with a controlled entity defined in Section 512(b)(13). An organization will be a controlled entity under this definition if the filing organization: (1) owns more than 50 percent of the stock (by voting power or value) of a corporation, (2) owns more than 50 percent of the profits or capital interests in a partnership, or (3) owns more than 50 percent of the profits or capital interest in a limited liability company, or (4) in any other case, owns more than 50 percent of the beneficial interests in the entity. These transactions with controlled entities must be reported:

- The receipt of interest, annuities, royalties, or rent from a controlled entity (line 1a)
- A loan made to a controlled entity (line 1d)
- Any other transfer of funds between the organization and the controlled entity

In addition, a Section 501(c)(3) organization and a 4947(a)(1) trust must report transactions with related exempt organizations not described in Section 501(c)(3) (including, but not limited to, Section 527 political organizations).

A separate line should be indicated for each type of transaction with the particular organization. If there are multiple transactions of the same type with a particular organization, the transaction should be aggregated for reporting purposes. For each transaction, list the name of the controlled entity in Column (A). The full legal name should be used. In Column (B), report the transaction type (lines (a)(i)–(r)). In Column (C), report the amount involved. The fair market value of the services, cash, and other assets should be used, using any reasonable method of valuation.

Disregard transactions described in line (a)(i) to line (a)(r) between two organizations where the aggregate amounts involved during the tax year do not exceed $50,000, except for receipt of interest, annuities, royalties, or rent from a controlled entity, which are to be reported regardless of amount. Thus, if there is a lease arrangement for annual rent of $25,000 between the filing organization and the related organization, it is not reported on line 2 unless it is a rental relationship with a controlled entity defined in Section 512(b)(13).

(f)   Part VI—Unrelated Organizations Taxed as Partnerships

In Part VI, report information on organizations that are not related to the filing organization but meet these conditions: (1) the unrelated organization is treated as a partnership for federal tax purposes, (2) the filing organization was a partner or member of the unrelated partnership during the organization's tax year, and (3) the filing organization conducts more than 5 percent of its activities, as measured by its total assets as of the end of its tax year or gross revenue for its tax year (whichever percentages, total assets or total revenue, is greater), through the unrelated partnership.

In determining the percentage of the filing organization's activities as measured by its total assts, use the amount reportable on Part X, line 16 as the denominator and the filing organization's ending capital account balance for the partnership tax year ending with or within the filing organization's tax year as the numerator. (The amount reported on Schedule K-1 may be used.) In determining the percentage of the filing organization's activities as measured by its gross revenue, use the amount reportable on Part VIII, line 12 as the denominator and the filing organization's proportionate share of the partnership's gross revenue for the partnership tax year ending with or within the filing organization's tax year as the numerator.

The instructions provide this example:

> **Example.** X, a § 501(c)(3) organization, is a partner of Y, a partnership which conducts an activity that constitutes an unrelated trade or business with respect to X. X's proportionate share of Y's gross revenue is $20,000 for Y's tax year ending with or within X's tax year. X has an ending capital account balance in Y of $200,000 as reported on Schedule K-1. X's gross revenue and total assets for its tax year are $500,000 and $2,000,000, respectively. X conducts 4% of its activities through Y as measured by X's gross revenues ($20,000 ÷ $500,000), and 10% as measured by X's total assets ($200,000 ÷ $2,000,000). Because at least one of these percentages exceeds 5%, X conducted more than 5% of its activities through Y for X's tax year and must identify Y in Schedule R, Part VI, and provide the required information.

Unrelated partnerships that meet both of these conditions should be disregarded for purposes of Schedule R Part VI reporting:

- 95 percent or more of the filing organization's gross income from the partnership for the partnership's tax year ending with or within the filing organization's tax year is described in §§ 512(b)(1)–(3) and (5), such as interest, dividends, royalties, rents, and capital gains (including unrelated debt-financed income).

- The primary purpose of the filing organization's investment in the partnership is the production of income or appreciation of property and not the conduct of the Section 501(c)(3) charitable activity, such as a program-related investment.

(1) Column (A) (Name, Address, and EIN). In Column (A), report the partnership's full legal name, address, and EIN.

(2) Column (B) (Primary Activity). In Column (B), report the primary business activity conducted or product or service provided by the unrelated partnership.

(3) Column (C) (Legal Domicile). In Column (C), report the U.S. state (or possession) or foreign country in which the unrelated partnership is organized. The law of the jurisdiction designated governs the internal affairs of the partnership.

(4) Column (D) (Section 501(c)(3) Partners). In Column (D), indicate "yes" or "no" as to whether all of the partners of the unrelated partnership (or members of the limited liability company) are Section 501(c)(3) organizations or governmental units (or wholly owned subsidiaries of either). This information will help the IRS identify joint ventures with for-profit organizations to apply the private inurement and private benefit analysis. (See § 6.1.)

(5) Column (E) (Share of End-of-Year Assets). In Column (E), report the dollar amount of the filing organization's distributable share of the unrelated partnership's total assets, in accordance with the filing organization's capital interest as specified by the partnership or limited liability company agreement as of the end of the partnership's tax year ending with or within the filing organization's tax year. Use the ending capital account reported on Schedule K-1 of Form 1065 for the year ending with or within the filing organization's tax year, if available.

(6) Column (F) (Disproportionate Allocations). In Column (F), indicate "yes" or "no" as to whether any item of income, gain, loss, deduction, or credit is disproportionately allocated to any owner or whether any right to distributions is disproportionate to the organization's investment in such partnership or limited liability company at any time during the year.

(7) Column (G) (Code V UBI). In Column (G), report the amount, if any, listed as a Code V amount (unrelated business taxable income) in box 20 of Schedule K-1 to Form 1065 received from the unrelated partnership for the partnership's tax year ending with or within the filing organization's tax year. If no Code V amount is listed in box 20, state "NA."

(8) Column (H) (General or Managing Partner). In Column (H), indicate "yes" or "no" if the filing organization is a general partner of an unrelated limited partnership or is a managing partner or managing member of an unrelated general partnership, limited liability company, or any other entity taxable as a partnership at any time during its tax year. Status as such will be important in determining whether the filing organization is in "control" of the partnership under the private benefit analysis. (See § 21.1(e).)

§ 21.3 SCHEDULE R COMPLIANCE TASKS

For purposes of preparing Schedule R, consider these 14 compliance tasks.

1. **Prepare director/trustee questionnaires.** Director/trustee questionnaires should be developed and distributed asking each director or trustee to list the organizations in which he or she serves as a director, trustee, officer, or key employee and organizations in which ownership interests are held. This information should be compiled to determine common control. This list is also necessary for other schedules and parts of the new Form 990. (See §§ 5.3 and 18.3.)

2. **Prepare officer and key employee questionnaires.** Officer and key employee questionnaires should be developed and distributed, asking each officer or key employee to list the organizations in which he or she serves as a director, trustee, officer, or key employee and organizations in which ownership interests are held. This information should be compiled to determine common control. This list is necessary for other schedules and parts of the new Form 990. (See §§ 5.3 and 18.3.)

3. **Identify disregarded entities.** Identify all disregarded entities. Prepare information including name, address, and EIN, primary activity, legal domicile, total income, end-of-year assets, and direct controlling entity.

4. **Prepare disregarded entity policy.** Consider the development of a policy for determining whether the use of single-member entities treated as "disregarded entities" is advisable. Consider the state and local consequences of the use of a disregarded entity.

5. **Identify investments in corporations.** Identify all investments in corporations. If the stock (value or vote) is more than 50 percent, a list should be made including name, address, EIN, primary activity, legal domicile, type of corporation, percentage ownership, percentage share of income, and percentage share of assets.

6. **Consider conversion of S corporations to C corporations.** Consider converting S corporations to C corporation status due to the flow-through of UBI.

7. **Prepare for-profit subsidiary policy.** Consider developing a policy for investing in a for-profit subsidiary. If the subsidiary is wholly owned, the policy should include an operations check list to ensure that the subsidiary is separately operated to the extent possible, including adherence to corporate formalities and proper structuring of board of directors, officers, sharing of facilities, employees, cost reimbursement, shared services, and other functions. It should also cover planning to minimize taxable passive income.

8. **Identify partnerships.** Identify whether the filing organization holds any partnership interests. Identify whether the interest is a general partner interest or managing member interest. Identify the percentage ownership of the partnership in both its profits and capital. If more than a 50-percent profits or capital

interest is held, gather information including name, address, and EIN, primary activity, legal domicile, direct controlling entity, predominant income, share of total income, share of year-end assets, whether income is disproportionately allocated, and amount of UBI. Similar information should be gathered if the partnership is owned less than 50 percent by the filing organization but more than 5 percent of the filing organization's exempt activities are operated through the partnership.

9. **Prepare joint venture policy.** Consider establishing a joint venture policy to be followed when the filing organization enters into any joint venture arrangement to avoid issues under the private benefit doctrine relative to control and ensuring that organization's exempt purposes are furthered. (See § 5.3.)

10. **Identify related exempt organizations.** Identify all exempt organizations in which the filing organization names a majority of their directors. Identify in item 1 and 2 above exempt organizations controlled by the insiders of the filing organization. The information gathered for these organizations would include name, address, and EIN of the related exempt organization, primary activity, legal domicile, exempt code section, public charity status, and direct controlling entity.

11. **Identify related party transactions .** Once related organizations are identified, as discussed, identify all transactions between related organizations, including:

    ○ Gifts, grants, or capital contributions

    ○ Loans or loan guarantees

    ○ Sale, purchase, or exchange of assets

    ○ Lease of facilities, equipment, or other assets

    ○ Performance of services or membership or fundraising solicitations

    ○ Sharing of facilities, equipment, mailing lists, or other assets

    ○ Sharing of paid employees

    ○ Reimbursement of expenses

    ○ Other transfers of cash or property

12. **Identify related parties as insiders/disqualified persons.** Identify all organizations that are controlled by one or more insiders/disqualified persons of the filing organization from items 1 and 2 above.

13. **Use rebuttable presumption of reasonableness.** Develop a policy/procedure requiring the use of the rebuttable presumption of reasonableness in transactions between related organizations and organizations controlled by insiders/ disqualified persons. (See §§ 5.3 and 6.3.)

14. **Prepare related exempt organizations policy.** Similar to the for-profit subsidiary policy, if the organization has related exempt organizations, a separateness policy should be followed.

APPENDIX A

Form 990 (2008)

Form **990**	**Return of Organization Exempt From Income Tax**	OMB No. 1545-0047
	Under section 501(c), 527, or 4947(a)(1) of the Internal Revenue Code (except black lung benefit trust or private foundation)	**2008**
Department of the Treasury Internal Revenue Service(77)	▶ The organization may have to use a copy of this return to satisfy state reporting requirements.	**Open to Public Inspection**

A For the 2008 calendar year, or tax year beginning _____ , 2008, and ending _____ , 20 ___

B Check if applicable:	Please use IRS label or print or type. See Specific Instruc- tions.	**C** Name of organization _____		**D** Employer identification number
☐ Address change		Doing Business As _____		
☐ Name change		Number and street (or P.O. box if mail is not delivered to street address) / Room/suite		**E** Telephone number ( )
☐ Initial return				
☐ Termination		City or town, state or country, and ZIP + 4		**G** Enter gross receipts $
☐ Amended return				
☐ Application pending		**F** Name and address of Principal Officer:		**H(a)** Is this a group return for affiliates? ☐ Yes ☐ No
				H(b) Are all affiliates included? ☐ Yes ☐ No If "No," attach a list. (See instructions)

I Tax-exempt status: ☐ 501(c) ( )◀ (insert no.) ☐ 4947(a)(1) or ☐ 527

J Website: ▶ _____   H(c) Group Exemption Number ▶ _____

K Type of organization: ☐ Corporation ☐ trust ☐ association ☐ Other ▶   **L** Year of Formation: _____   **M** State of legal domicile: _____

Part I   Summary

1 . Briefly describe the organization's mission or most significant activities: _____

_____

2 Check this box ☐ if the organization discontinued its operations or disposed of more than 25% of its assets.

	Activities & Governance	
3 Enter the number of voting members of the governing body (Part VI, line 1a) . . .	**3**	
4 Enter the number of independent voting members of the governing body (Part VI, line 1b) . .	**4**	
5 Enter the total number of employees (Part V, line 2a).	**5**	
6 Enter the total number of volunteers (estimate if necessary)	**6**	
7a Enter total gross unrelated business revenue from Part VIII, line 12, column (C)	**7a**	
b Enter net unrelated business taxable income from Form 990-T, line 34	**7b**	

	Revenue	Prior Year	Current Year
8 Contributions and grants (Part VIII, line 1h)		
9 Program service revenue (Part VIII, line 2g)		
10 Investment income (Part VIII, lines 3, 4, and 7d, column (A))		
11 Other revenue (Part VIII, lines 5, 6d, 8c, 9c, and 10c of column (A), and 11e)		
12 Total revenue—add lines 8 through 11 (must equal Part VIII, line 12, column (A))		

	Expenses		
13 Grants and similar amounts paid (Part IX, lines 1–3, column (A))		
14 Benefits paid to or for members (Part IX, line 4, column (A)) . . .		
15 Salaries, other compensation, employee benefits (Part IX, lines 5–10, column (A))		
16a Professional fundraising fees (Part IX, line 11e, column (A))		
b (Enter total fundraising expenses, Part IX, line 25, column (D) _____)		
17 Other expenses (Part IX, lines 11a–11d, 11f–24f, column (A))		
18 Total expenses—add lines 13–17 (must equal Part IX, line 25, column (A)). .		
19 Revenue less expenses—line 12 minus line 18		

	Net Assets or Fund Balances	Beginning of Year	End of Year
20 Total assets (Part X, line 16)		
21 Total liabilities (Part X, line 26)		
22 Net assets or fund balances, line 20 minus line 21		

Part II   Signature Block

Under penalties of perjury, I declare that I have examined this return, including accompanying schedules and statements, and to the best of my knowledge and belief, it is true, correct, and complete. Declaration of preparer (other than officer) is based on all information of which preparer has any knowledge.

Please Sign Here	▶ Signature of officer _____	Date _____
	▶ Type or print name and title _____	

Paid Preparer's Use Only	Preparer's signature ▶	Date	Check if self-employed ▶ ☐	Preparer's PTIN (See Gen. Inst.)
	Firm's name (or yours if self-employed), address, and ZIP + 4 ▶		EIN ▶	
			Phone no. ▶ ( )	

May the IRS discuss this return with the preparer shown above? (See instructions) . . . . ☐ Yes ☐ No

For Privacy Act and Paperwork Reduction Act Notice, see the separate instructions.   Cat. No. 11282Y   Form **990** (2008)

APPENDIX A

Part III	Statement of Program Service Accomplishments (See the instructions.)

1   Briefly describe the organization's mission:

----

2   Did the organization undertake any significant program services during the year which were not listed on
the prior Form 990 or 990-EZ? . . . . ☐ Yes ☐ No
If "Yes," describe these new services on Schedule O.

3   Did the organization cease conducting or make significant changes in how it conducts any program
services? . . . . ☐ Yes ☐ No
If "Yes," describe these changes on Schedule O.

4   Describe the exempt purpose achievements for each of the organization's three largest program services by expenses.
Section 501(c)(3) and (4) organizations and 4947(a)(1) trusts are required to report the amount of grants and allocations to
others, the total expenses, and revenue, if any, for each program service reported.

4a (Code: _____) (Expenses $ _____ including grants of $ _____) (Revenue $ _____)

4b (Code: _____) (Expenses $ _____ including grants of $ _____) (Revenue $ _____)

4c (Code: _____) (Expenses $ _____ including grants of $ _____) (Revenue $ _____)

4d Other program services. (Describe in Schedule O.)
(Expenses $ _____ including grants of $ _____) (Revenue $ _____)

4e **Total program service expenses $** _____   *Must equal Part IX, Line 25, column (B).*

Form **990** (2008)

Part IV	**Checklist of Required Schedules**		Yes	No
1	Is the organization described in section 501(c)(3) or 4947(a)(1) (other than a private foundation)? *If "Yes," complete Schedule A*	**1**		
2	Is the organization required to complete Schedule B, Schedule of Contributors?	**2**		
3	Did the organization engage in direct or indirect political campaign activities on behalf of or in opposition to candidates for public office? *If "Yes," complete Schedule C, Part I*	**3**		
4	*501(c)(3) organizations.* Did the organization engage in lobbying activities? *If "Yes," complete Schedule C, Part II*	**4**		
5	*501(c)(4), 501(c)(5), and 501(c)(6) organizations.* Is the organization subject to the section 6033(e) notice and reporting requirement and proxy tax? *If "Yes," complete Schedule C, Part III*	**5**		
6	Did the organization maintain any donor advised funds or any accounts where donors have the right to provide advice on the distribution or investment of amounts in such funds or accounts? *If "Yes," complete Schedule D, Part I*	**6**		
7	Did the organization receive or hold a conservation easement, including easements to preserve open space, the environment, historic land areas, or historic structures? *If "Yes," complete Schedule D, Part II*	**7**		
8	Did the organization maintain collections of works of art, historical treasures, or other similar assets? *If "Yes," complete Schedule D, Part III*	**8**		
9	Did the organization report an amount in Part X, line 21; serve as a custodian for amounts not listed in Part X; or provide credit counseling, debt management, credit repair, or debt negotiation services? *If "Yes," complete Schedule D, Part IV*	**9**		
10	Did the organization hold assets in term, permanent, or quasi-endowments? *If "Yes," complete Schedule D, Part V*	**10**		
11	Did the organization report an amount in Part X, lines 10, 12, 13, 15, or 25? *If "Yes," complete Schedule D, Parts VI, VII, VIII, IX, or X as applicable*	**11**		
12	Did the organization receive an audited financial statement for the year for which it is completing this return that was prepared in accordance with GAAP? *If "Yes," complete Schedule D, Parts XI, XII, and XIII*	**12**		
13	Is the organization operating a school as described in section 170(b)(1)(A)(ii)? *If "Yes," complete Schedule E*	**13**		
14a	Did the organization maintain an office, employees, or agents outside of the U.S.?	**14a**		
b	Did the organization have aggregate revenues or expenses of more than $10,000 from grantmaking, fundraising, business, and program service activities outside the U.S.? *If "Yes," complete Schedule F, Part I*	**14b**		
15	Did the organization report on Part IX, line 3, more than $5,000 of grants or assistance to any organization or entity located outside the United States? *If "Yes," complete Schedule F, Part II*	**15**		
16	Did the organization report on Form 990, Part IX, line 3, more than $5,000 of aggregate grants or assistance to individuals located outside the United States? *If "Yes," complete Schedule F, Part III*	**16**		
17	Did the organization report more than $15,000 on Part IX, line 11e? *If "Yes," complete Schedule G, Part I*	**17**		
18	Did the organization report more than $15,000 total on Part VIII, lines 1c and 8a? *If "Yes," complete Schedule G, Part II*	**18**		
19	Did the organization report more than $15,000 on Part VIII, line 9a? *If "Yes," complete Schedule G, Part III*	**19**		
20	Did the organization operate one or more hospitals? *If "Yes," complete Schedule H*	**20**		
21	Did the organization report more than $5,000 on Part IX, line 1? *If "Yes," complete Schedule I, Parts I and II*	**21**		
22	Did the organization report more than $5,000 on Part IX, line 2? *If "Yes," complete Schedule I, Parts I and III*	**22**		
23	Did the organization answer "Yes" to questions 3, 4, or 5, Part VII, Section A? *If "Yes," complete Schedule J*	**23**		
24a	Did the organization have a tax-exempt bond issue with an outstanding principal amount of more than $100,000 as of the last day of the year, that was issued after December 31, 2002? *If "Yes," answer 24b–24d and complete Schedule K. If "No," go to question 25.*	**24a**		
b	Did the organization invest any proceeds of tax-exempt bonds beyond a temporary period exception?	**24b**		
c	Did the organization maintain an escrow account other than a refunding escrow at any time during the year to defease any tax-exempt bonds?	**24c**		
d	Did the organization act as an "on behalf of" issuer for bonds outstanding at any time during the year?	**24d**		
25a	*501(c)(3) and 501(c)(4) organizations.* Did the organization engage in an excess benefit transaction with a disqualified person during the year? *If "Yes," complete Schedule L, Part I*	**25a**		
b	Did the organization become aware that it had engaged in an excess benefit transaction with a disqualified person from a prior year? *If "Yes," complete Schedule L, Part I*	**25b**		
26	Was a loan to or by a current or former officer, director, trustee, key employee, highly compensated employee, or disqualified person outstanding as of the end of the organization's tax year? *If "Yes," complete Schedule L, Part II*	**26**		
27	Did the organization provide a grant or other assistance to an officer, director, trustee, key employee, or substantial contributor, or to a person related to such an individual? *If "Yes," complete Schedule L, Part III*	**27**		

Form **990** (2008)

APPENDIX A

Part IV	Checklist of Required Schedules *(Continued)*		
		Yes	No
28	During the tax year, did any person who is a current or former officer, director, trustee, or key employee:		
a	Have a direct business relationship with the organization (other than as an officer, director, trustee, or employee), or an indirect business relationship through ownership of more than 35% in another entity (individually or collectively with other person(s) listed in Part VII, Section A)? *If "Yes," complete Schedule L, Part IV* · 28a		
b	Have a family member who had a direct or indirect business relationship with the organization? *If "Yes," complete Schedule L, Part IV* · · · · · · · · · · · · · · · 28b		
c	Serve as an officer, director, trustee, key employee, partner, or member of an entity (or a shareholder of a professional corporation) doing business with the organization? *If "Yes," complete Schedule L, Part IV* 28c		
29	Did the organization receive more than $25,000 in non-cash contributions? *If "Yes," complete Schedule M* 29		
30	Did the organization receive contributions of art, historical treasures, or other similar assets, or qualified conservation contributions? *If "Yes," complete Schedule M* · · · · · · · · · · 30		
31	Did the organization liquidate, terminate, or dissolve and cease operations? *If "Yes," complete Schedule N, Part I* · 31		
32	Did the organization sell, exchange, dispose of, or transfer more than 25% of its net assets or undergo a substantial contraction? *If "Yes," complete Schedule N, Part II* · · · · · · · · · 32		
33	Did the organization own 100% of an entity disregarded as separate from the organization under Regulations section 301.7701-2 and 301.7701-3? *If "Yes," complete Schedule R, Part I* · · · · · · 33		
34	Was the organization related to any tax-exempt or taxable entity? *If "Yes," complete Schedule R, Parts II, III, IV, and V, line 1* · 34		
35	Is any related organization a controlled entity within the meaning of section 512(b)(13)? *If "Yes," complete Schedule R, Part V, line 2* · · · · · · · · · · · · · · · · · · 35		
36	*501(c)(3) organizations.* Did the organization make any transfers to an exempt non-charitable related organization? *If "Yes," complete Schedule R, Part V, line 2* · · · · · · · · · · 36		
37	Did the organization conduct more than 5% of its exempt activities through an entity that is not a related organization and that is taxed as a partnership? *If "Yes," complete Schedule R, Part VI* · · · · · 37		

Form **990** (2008)

APPENDIX A

Part V Statements Regarding Other IRS Filings and Tax Compliance

		Yes	No
1a Enter the number reported in Box 3 of Form 1096, *Annual Summary and Transmittal of U.S. Information Returns*. Enter -0- if not applicable	**1a**		
b Enter the number of Forms W-2G included in line 1a. Enter -0- if not applicable . .	**1b**		
c Did the organization comply with backup withholding rules for reportable payments to vendors and reportable gaming (gambling) winnings to prize winners?	**1c**		
2a Enter the number of employees reported on Form W-3, *Transmittal of Wage and Tax Statements* filed for the calendar year ending with or within the year covered by this return	**2a**		
b If at least one is reported in 2a, did the organization file all required federal employment tax returns? .	**2b**		
Note: *If the sum of lines 1a and 2a is greater than 250, you may be required to e-file this return.*			
3a Did the organization have unrelated business gross income of $1,000 or more during the year covered by this return?	**3a**		
b If "Yes," has it filed a Form 990-T for this year? *If "No," provide an explanation in Schedule O*	**3b**		
4a At any time during the calendar year, did the organization have an interest in, or a signature or other authority over, a financial account in a foreign country (such as a bank account, securities account, or other financial account)?	**4a**		
b If "Yes," enter the name of the foreign country: _____			
See the instructions for exceptions and filing requirements for **Form TD F 90-22.1**, *Report of Foreign Bank and Financial Accounts.*			
5a Was the organization a party to a prohibited tax shelter transaction at any time during the tax year? . .	**5a**		
b Did any taxable party notify the organization that it was or is a party to a prohibited tax shelter transaction?	**5b**		
c If "Yes," to 5a or 5b, did the organization file Form 8886-T, *Disclosure by Tax-Exempt Entity Regarding Prohibited Tax Shelter Transaction?*.	**5c**		
6a Did the organization solicit any contributions that were not tax deductible?	**6a**		
b If "Yes," did the organization include with every solicitation an express statement that such contributions or gifts were not tax deductible?.	**6b**		
7 *Organizations that may receive deductible contributions under section 170(c).*			
a Did the organization provide goods or services in exchange for any contribution of $75 or more? . . .	**7a**		
b If "Yes," did the organization notify the donor of the value of the goods or services provided?	**7b**		
c Did the organization sell, exchange, or otherwise dispose of tangible personal property for which it was required to file Form 8282?	**7c**		
d If "Yes," indicate the number of Forms 8282 filed during the year	**7d**		
e Did the organization, during the year, receive any funds, directly or indirectly, to pay premiums on a personal benefit contract?	**7e**		
f Did the organization, during the year, pay premiums, directly or indirectly, on a personal benefit contract?	**7f**		
g For all contributions of qualified intellectual property, did the organization file Form 8899 as required? .	**7g**		
h For contributions of cars, boats, airplanes, and other vehicles, did the organization file a Form 1098-C as required?.	**7h**		
8 *501(c)(3) and other sponsoring organizations maintaining donor advised funds and 509(a)(3) supporting organizations.* Did the supporting organization, or a fund maintained by a sponsoring organization, have excess business holdings at any time during the year?	**8**		
9 *501(c)(3) and other sponsoring organizations maintaining donor advised funds.*			
a Did the organization make any taxable distributions under section 4966?	**9a**		
b Did the organization make a distribution to a donor, donor advisor, or related person?.	**9b**		
10 *501(c)(7) organizations.* Enter:			
a Initiation fees and capital contributions included on Part VIII, line 12.	**10a**		
b Gross receipts, included on Form 990, Part VIII, line 12, for public use of club facilities	**10b**		
11 *501(c)(12) organizations.* Enter:			
a Gross income from members or shareholders	**11a**		
b Gross income from other sources (Do not net amounts due or paid to other sources against amounts due or received from them.)	**11b**		
12a *4947(a)(1) non-exempt charitable trusts.* Is the organization filing Form 990 in lieu of Form 1041? . .	**12a**		
b If "Yes," enter the amount of tax-exempt interest received or accrued during the year .	**12b**		

Part VI Governance, Management, and Disclosure *(Sections A, B, and C request information about policies not required by the Internal Revenue Code.)*

Section A. Governing Body and Management

			Yes	No
	For each "Yes" response to lines 2–7 below, and for a "No" response to lines 8 or 9b below, describe the circumstances, process, or changes in Schedule O. See instructions.			
1a	Enter the number of voting members of the governing body **1a**			
b	Enter the number of voting members that are independent **1b**			
2	Did any officer, director, trustee, or key employee have a family relationship or a business relationship with any other officer, director, trustee, or key employee?	**2**		
3	Did the organization delegate control over management duties customarily performed by or under the direct supervision of officers, directors or trustees, or key employees to a management company or other person? .	**3**		
4	Did the organization make any significant changes to its organizational documents since the prior Form 990 was filed?	**4**		
5	Did the organization become aware during the year of a material diversion of the organization's assets?	**5**		
6	Does the organization have members or stockholders?	**6**		
7a	Does the organization have members, stockholders, or other persons who may elect one or more members of the governing body?	**7a**		
b	Are any decisions of the governing body subject to approval by members, stockholders, or other persons? . .	**7b**		
8	Did the organization contemporaneously document the meetings held or written actions undertaken during the year by the following:			
a	the governing body?	**8a**		
b	each committee with authority to act on behalf of the governing body?	**8b**		
9a	Does the organization have local chapters, branches, or affiliates?	**9a**		
b	If "Yes," does the organization have written policies and procedures governing the activities of such chapters, affiliates, and branches to ensure their operations are consistent with those of the organization?	**9b**		
10	Was a copy of the Form 990 provided to the organization's governing body before it was filed? All organizations must describe in Schedule O the process, if any, the organization uses to review the Form 990	**10**		
11	Is there any officer, director or trustee, or key employee listed in Part VII, Section A, who cannot be reached at the organization's mailing address? If "Yes," provide the names and addresses in Schedule O	**11**		

Section B. Policies

			Yes	No
12a	Does the organization have a written conflict of interest policy? *If "Yes":*	**12a**		
b	Are officers, directors or trustees, and key employees required to disclose annually interests that could give rise to conflicts?	**12b**		
c	Does the organization regularly and consistently monitor and enforce compliance with the policy? If "Yes," describe in Schedule O how this is done	**12c**		
13	Does the organization have a written whistleblower policy?	**13**		
14	Does the organization have a written document retention and destruction policy?	**14**		
15	Did the process for determining compensation of the following persons include a review and approval by independent persons, comparability data, and contemporaneous substantiation of the deliberation and decision:			
a	The organization's CEO, Executive Director, or top management official?	**15a**		
b	Other officers or key employees of the organization?	**15b**		
	Describe the process in Schedule O.			
16a	Did the organization invest in, contribute assets to, or participate in a joint venture or similar arrangement with a taxable entity during the year?	**16a**		
b	If "Yes," has the organization adopted a written policy or procedure requiring the organization to evaluate its participation in joint venture arrangements under applicable Federal tax law, and taken steps to safeguard the organization's exempt status with respect to such arrangements?	**16b**		

Section C. Disclosure

17 List the States with which a copy of this Form 990 is required to be filed. _____

18 IRC Section 6104 requires an organization to make its Form 1023 (or 1024 if applicable), 990, and 990-T (501(c)(3)s only) available for public inspection. Indicate how you make these available. Check all that apply.

☐ own website ☐ another's website ☐ upon request

19 Describe in Schedule O whether (and if so, how), the organization makes its governing documents, conflict of interest policy, and financial statements available to the public.

20 State the name, physical address, and telephone number of the person who possesses the books and records of the organization: _____

APPENDIX A

| **Part VII** | Compensation of Officers, Directors, Trustees, Key Employees, Highest Compensated Employees, and Independent Contractors |

Section A   Officers, Directors, Trustees, Key Employees, and Highest Compensated Employees

1a Complete this table for all persons required to be listed. Use Schedule J-2 if additional space is needed.

* List all of the organization's **current** officers, directors, trustees (whether individuals or organizations) and key employees regardless of amount of compensation. Enter -0- in columns (D), (E), and (F) if no compensation was paid.

* List the organization's five **current** highest compensated employees (other than an officer, director, trustee, or key employee) who received reportable compensation (Box 5 of Form W-2 and/or Box 7 of Form 1099-MISC) of more than $100,000 from the organization and any related organizations.

* List all of the organization's **former** officers, key employees, or highest compensated employees who received more than $100,000 of reportable compensation from the organization and any related organizations.

* List all of the organization's **former directors or trustees** that received, in the capacity as a former director or trustee of the organization, more than $10,000 of reportable compensation from the organization and any related organizations.

List persons in the following order: individual trustees or directors; institutional trustees; officers; key employees; highest compensated employees; and former such persons.

☐ Check this box if the organization did not compensate any officer, director, trustee, or key employee.

(A) Name and Title	(B) Average hours per week	(C) Position (check all that apply)						(D) Reportable compensation from the organization (W-2/1099-MISC)	(E) Reportable compensation from related organizations (W-2/1099-MISC)	(F) Estimated amount of other compensation from the organization and related organizations
		Individual trustee or director	Institutional trustee	Officer	Key employee	Highest compensated employee	Former			

Form **990** (2008)

APPENDIX A

Form 990 (2008)

Page 8

Part VII Continued

1b Total ▶

2 Total number of individuals (including those in 1) who received more than $100,000 in reportable compensation from the organization ▶

		Yes	No
3	Did the organization list any **former** officer, director or trustee, key employee, or highest compensated employee in Section A? If "Yes," complete Schedule J for such individual **3**		
4	For any individual listed in Section A, is the sum of reportable compensation and other compensation from the organization and related organizations greater than $150,000? If "Yes," complete Schedule J for such individual. **4**		
5	Did any person listed in Section A receive or accrue compensation from any unrelated organization for services rendered to the organization? If "Yes," complete Schedule J for such person **5**		

Section B. Independent Contractors

1 Complete this table for your five highest compensated independent contractors that received more than $100,000 of compensation from the organization.

(A) Name and business address	(B) Description of services	(C) Compensation

2 Total number of independent contractors (including those in 1) who received more than $100,000 in compensation from the organization   ▶

Form **990** (2008)

■ 545 ■

Part VIII   Statement of Revenue

			(A) Total Revenue	(B) Related or Exempt Function Revenue	(C) Unrelated Business Revenue	(D) Revenue Excluded from Tax under IRC 512, 513, or 514
Contributions, gifts, grants and other similar amounts	**1a** Federated campaigns	**1a**				
	b Membership dues	**1b**				
	c Fundraising events	**1c**				
	d Related organizations	**1d**				
	e Government grants (contributions)	**1e**				
	f All other contributions, gifts, grants. and similar amounts not included above	**1f**				
	g Noncash $ _____					
	h Total (lines 1a–1f). ▶					
Program Service Revenue			Business Code			
	2a _____					
	b _____					
	c _____					
	d _____					
	e _____					
	f All other program service revenue					
	g Total ▶ $					
Other Revenue	**3** Investment income (including dividends, interest and other similar amounts) ▶					
	4 Income from investment of tax-exempt bond proceeds ▶					
	5 Royalties ▶					
		(i) Real	(ii) Personal			
	6a Gross Rents					
	b Less: rental expenses					
	c Rental income or (loss)					
	d Net rental income or (loss) ▶					
		(i) Securities	(ii) Other			
	7a Gross amount from sales of assets other than inventory					
	b Less: cost or other basis and sales expenses					
	c Gain or (loss)					
	d Net gain or (loss) ▶					
	8a Gross income from fundraising events (not including $_____ of contributions reported on line 1c). See Part IV, line 18. **a**					
	b Less: direct expenses **b**					
	c Net income or (loss) from fundraising events ▶					
	9a Gross income from gaming activities. See Part IV, line 19. **a**					
	b Less: direct expenses. **b**					
	c Net income or (loss) from gaming activities ▶					
	10a Gross sales of inventory, less returns and allowances **a**					
	b Less: cost of goods sold **b**					
	c Net income or (loss) from sales of inventory ▶					
	Miscellaneous Revenue	Business Code				
	11a _____					
	b _____					
	c _____					
	d All other revenue					
	e Total ▶ $					
	12 Total Revenue. Add lines 1h, 2g, 3, 4, 5, 6d, 7d, 8c, 9c, 10c, and 11e ▶					

Form **990** (2008)

Form 990 (2008)

Part IX Statement of Functional Expenses

501(c)(3) and (4) organizations must complete all columns.

All other organizations must complete column (A) but are not required to complete columns (B), (C), and (D).

Do not include amounts reported on lines 6b, 7b, 8b, 9b, and 10b of Part VIII.	(A) Total expenses	(B) Program service expenses	(C) Management and general expenses	(D) Fundraising expenses
1 Grants and other assistance to governments and organizations in the U.S. See Part IV, line 21				
2 Grants and other assistance to individuals in the U.S. See Part IV, line 22				
3 Grants and other assistance to governments, organizations, and individuals outside the U.S. See Part IV, lines 15 and 16				
4 Benefits paid to or for members				
5 Compensation of current officers, directors, trustees, and key employees . . .				
6 Compensation not included above, to disqualified persons (as defined under section 4958(f)(1)) and persons described in section 4958(c)(3)(B) . .				
7 Other salaries and wages				
8 Pension plan contributions (include section 401(k) and section 403(b) employer contributions) . .				
9 Other employee benefits				
10 Payroll taxes				
11 Fees for services (non-employees):				
a Management				
b Legal				
c Accounting				
d Lobbying				
e Professional fundraising. See Part IV, line 17				
f Investment management fees				
g Other				
12 Advertising and promotion				
13 Office expenses				
14 Information technology				
15 Royalties				
16 Occupancy				
17 Travel				
18 Payments of travel or entertainment expenses for any Federal, state, or local public officials				
19 Conferences, conventions, and meetings .				
20 Interest				
21 Payments to affiliates				
22 Depreciation, depletion, and amortization .				
23 Insurance				
24 Other expenses—Itemize expenses not covered above (Expenses grouped together and labeled miscellaneous may not exceed 5% of total expenses shown on line 25 below.)				
a				
b				
c ..:................................				
d				
e				
f All other expenses				
25 Total functional expenses. Add lines 1 through 24f				
26 Joint Costs. Check ☐ if following SOP 98-2. Complete this line only if the organization reported in column (B) joint costs from a combined educational campaign and fundraising solicitation				

Form **990** (2008)

Part X	Balance Sheet			

			(A) Beginning of year	(B) End of year
Assets	1	Cash—non-interest-bearing	1	
	2	Savings and temporary cash investments	2	
	3	Pledges and grants receivable, net	3	
	4	Accounts receivable, net	4	
	5	Receivables from current and former officers, directors, trustees, key employees, or other related parties. *Complete Part II of Schedule L*	5	
	6	Receivables from other disqualified persons (as defined under section 4958(f)(1)) and persons described in section 4958(c)(3)(B). *Complete Part II of Schedule L*	6	
	7	Notes and loans receivable, net	7	
	8	Inventories for sale or use	8	
	9	Prepaid expenses and deferred charges	9	
	10a	Land, buildings, and equipment: cost basis | 10a		
	b	Less: accumulated depreciation. *Complete Part VI of Schedule D* | 10b	10c	
	11	Investments—publicly traded securities	11	
	12	Investments—other securities. *Complete Part VII of Schedule D*	12	
	13	Investments—program-related. *Complete Part VIII of Schedule D*	13	
	14	Intangible assets	14	
	15	Other assets. *Complete Part IX of Schedule D*	15	
	16	**Total assets.** *Add Columns A and B, lines 1 through 15 (must equal line 34)*	16	
Liabilities	17	Accounts payable and accrued expenses	17	
	18	Grants payable	18	
	19	Deferred revenue	19	
	20	Tax-exempt bond liabilities	20	
	21	Escrow account liability. *Complete Part IV of Schedule D*	21	
	22	Payables to current and former officers, directors, trustees, key employees, highest compensated employees, and disqualified persons. *Complete Part II of Schedule L*	22	
	23	Secured mortgages and notes payable to unrelated third parties	23	
	24	Unsecured notes and loans payable	24	
	25	Other liabilities. *Complete Part X of Schedule D*	25	
	26	**Total liabilities.** *Add lines 17 through 25*	26	
Net Assets or Fund Balances		**Organizations that follow SFAS 117, check here ▶ ☐ and complete lines 27 through 29, and lines 33 and 34.**		
	27	Unrestricted net assets	27	
	28	Temporarily restricted net assets	28	
	29	Permanently restricted net assets	29	
		Organizations that do not follow SFAS 117, check here ▶ ☐ and complete lines 30 through 34.		
	30	Capital stock or trust principal, or current funds	30	
	31	Paid-in or capital surplus, or land, building, or equipment fund	31	
	32	Retained earnings, endowment, accumulated income, or other funds	32	
	33	Total net assets or fund balances	33	
	34	Total liabilities and net assets/fund balances	34	

Part XI	Financial Statements and Reporting		

		Yes	No
1	Accounting method used to prepare the Form 990: ☐ cash ☐ accrual ☐ other		
2a	Were the organization's financial statements compiled or reviewed by an independent accountant?	2a	
b	Were the organization's financial statements audited by an independent accountant?	2b	
c	If "Yes" to 2a or 2b, does the organization have a committee that assumes responsibility for oversight of the audit, review, or compilation of its financial statements and selection of an independent accountant?	2c	
3a	As a result of a federal award, was the organization required to undergo an audit or audits as set forth in the Single Audit Act and OMB Circular A-133?	3a	
b	If "Yes," did the organization undergo the required audit or audits?	3b	

Form **990** (2008)

APPENDIX A

SCHEDULE A
(Form 990 or 990-EZ)

Department of the Treasury
Internal Revenue Service

Public Charity Status and Public Support

To be completed by all section 501(c)(3) organizations.

See instructions.

Name of the organization

Employer identification number

Part I   Reason for Public Charity Status (to be completed by all organizations) (See instructions)

The organization is not a private foundation because it is: (Please check only **one** applicable box.)

1. ☐ A church, convention of churches, or association of churches. **Section 170(b)(1)(A)(i).**
2. ☐ A school. **Section 170(b)(1)(A)(ii).** (Attach Schedule E.)
3. ☐ A hospital or a cooperative hospital service organization. **Section 170(b)(1)(A)(iii).** (Attach Schedule H.)
4. ☐ A medical research organization operated in conjunction with a hospital. **Section 170(b)(1)(A)(iii).** Enter the hospital's name, city, and state: _____
5. ☐ An organization operated for the benefit of a college or university owned or operated by a governmental unit. **Section 170(b)(1)(A)(iv).** (Complete the *Support Schedule* in Part II.)
6. ☐ A federal, state, or local government or governmental unit. **Section 170(b)(1)(A)(v).**
7. ☐ An organization that normally receives a substantial part of its support from a governmental unit or from the general public. **Section 170(b)(1)(A)(vi).** (Complete the *Support Schedule* in Part II.)
8. ☐ A community trust. **Section 170(b)(1)(A)(vi).** (Complete the *Support Schedule* in Part II.)
9. ☐ An organization that normally receives: (1) more than 33⅓ % of its support from contributions, membership fees, and gross receipts from activities related to its exempt functions—subject to certain exceptions, and (2) no more than 33⅓ % of its support from gross investment income and unrelated business taxable income (less section 511 tax) from businesses acquired by the organization after June 30, 1975. **Section 509(a)(2).** (Complete the *Support Schedule* in Part III.)
10. ☐ An organization organized and operated exclusively to test for public safety. **Section 509(a)(4).** (See instructions.)
11. ☐ An organization organized and operated exclusively for the benefit of, to perform the functions of, or to carry out the purposes of one or more publicly supported organizations described in section 509(a)(1) or section 509(a)(2). **Section 509(a)(3).** Check the box that describes the type of supporting organization and complete lines 11e through 11h.

     a ☐ Type I   b ☐ Type II   c ☐ Type III–Functionally Integrated   d ☐ Type III–Other

     e ☐ By checking this box, I certify that the organization is not controlled directly or indirectly by one or more disqualified persons other than foundation managers and other than one or more publicly supported organizations described in section 509(a)(1) or section 509(a)(2).

     f   If the organization received a written determination from the IRS that it is a Type I, Type II or Type III supporting organization, check this box . . . . ☐

     g   Since August 17, 2006, has the organization accepted any gift or contribution from any of the following persons?

		Yes	No
(i) a person who directly or indirectly controls, either alone or together with persons described in (ii) and (iii) below, the governing body of the supported organization?	11g(i)		
(ii) a family member of a person described in (i) above?	11g(ii)		
(iii) a 35% controlled entity of a person described in (i) or (ii) above?	11g(iii)		

     h   Provide the following information about the organizations the organization supports.

(i) Name of Supported Organization	(ii) EIN	(iii) Type of organization (described on lines 1–9 above or IRC section.)	(iv) Is the organization in (i) listed in your governing document?		(v) Did you notify the organization in (i) of your support?		(vi) Is the organization in (i) organized in the U.S.?		(vii) Amount of support
			Yes	No	Yes	No	Yes	No	
Total									

For Paperwork Reduction Act Notice, see the Instructions for Form 990.   Cat. No. 11285F   Schedule A (Form 990 or 990-EZ) 2008

Part II   Support Schedule for Organizations Described in IRC 170(b)(1)(A)(iv) and 170(b)(1)(A)(vi)
(Complete only if you checked the box on line 5, 7, or 8 of Part I.)

Public Support

Calendar year (or fiscal year beginning in)	(a) 2004	(b) 2005	(c) 2006	(d) 2007	(e) 2008	(f) Total
1 Gifts, grants, contributions, and membership fees received. (Do not include any "unusual grants.")						
2 Tax revenues levied for the organization's benefit and either paid to or expended on its behalf						
3 The value of services or facilities furnished by a governmental unit to the organization without charge						
4 **Total**						
5 Amounts included on line 1 from each person (other than a governmental unit or publicly supported organization) whose total payments for the years in columns (a) through (e) exceeded 2% of the amount shown on line 11 column (f)						
6 **Public Support** (line 4 minus line 5)						

Total Support

Calendar year (or fiscal year beginning in)	(a) 2004	(b) 2005	(c) 2006	(d) 2007	(e) 2008	(f) Total
7 Amounts from line 4						
8 Gross income from interest, dividends, payments received on securities loans, rents, royalties and income from similar sources						
9 Net income from unrelated business activities, whether or not the business is regularly carried on						
10 Other income. (Explain in Part IV.) Do not include gain or loss from the sale of capital assets						
11 **Total Support** (Add lines 7 through 11)						

12   Gross receipts from related activities, etc. (See instructions.) .... | 12 |

13   **First Five Years:** If the Form 990 is for the organization's first, second, third, fourth, or fifth tax year as a 501(c)(3) organization, check this box and **stop here** .... ▶ ☐

Computation of Public Support Percentage

14   Public Support Percentage for 2008 (line 6 column (f) divided by line 11 column (f)) ... | 14 | % |

15   Public Support Percentage from 2007 Schedule A, Part IV-A, line 26f .... | 15 | % |

16a   33⅓ % **Test - 2008:** If the organization did not check the box on line 13, and line 14 is 33⅓ % or more, check this box and **stop here.** The organization qualifies as a publicly supported organization .... ▶ ☐

   b   33⅓ % **Test - 2007:** If the organization did not check a box on line 13 or 16a, and line 15 is 33⅓ % or more, check this box and **stop here.** The organization qualifies as a publicly supported organization .... ▶ ☐

17a   10% **Facts and Circumstances Test - 2008:** If the organization did not check a box on line 13, 16a or 16b, and line 14 is 10% or more, and if the organization meets the "facts and circumstances" test, check this box and **stop here.** Describe in Part IV how the organization meets the "facts and circumstances" test. The organization qualifies as a publicly supported organization .... ▶ ☐

   b   10% **Facts and Circumstances Test - 2007:** If the organization did not check a box on line 13, 16a, 16b or 17a, and line 15 is 10% or more, and if the organization meets the "facts and circumstances" test, check this box and **stop here.** Describe in Part IV how the organzation meets the "facts and circumstances" test. The organization qualifies as a publicly supported organization .... ▶ ☐

18   **Private Foundation:** If the organization did not check a box on line 13, 16a, 16b, 17a or 17b, check this box and see instructions .... ▶ ☐

APPENDIX A

Part III Support Schedule for Organizations Described in IRC 509(a)(2)
(Complete only if you checked the box on line 9 of Part I.)

Public Support

Calendar year (or fiscal year beginning in)	(a) 2004	(b) 2005	(c) 2006	(d) 2007	(e) 2008	(f) Total
1 Gifts, grants, contributions, and membership fees received. (Do not include any "unusual grants.")						
2 Gross receipts from admissions, merchandise sold or services performed, or facilities furnished in any activity that is related to the organization's tax-exempt purpose						
3 Gross receipts from activities that are not an unrelated trade or business under section 513						
4 Tax revenues levied for the organization's benefit and either paid to or expended on its behalf						
5 The value of services or facilities furnished by a governmental unit to the organization without charge						
6 Total						
7a Amounts included on lines 1, 2, and 3 received from disqualified persons						
7b Amounts included on lines 2 and 3 received from other than disqualified persons that exceed the greater of 1% of line 13 for the year or $5,000						
7c Total of lines 7a and 7b						
8 **Public Support** (line 6 minus line 7c)						

Total Support

Calendar year (or fiscal year beginning in)	(a) 2004	(b) 2005	(c) 2006	(d) 2007	(e) 2008	(f) Total
9 Amounts from line 6						
10a Gross income from interest, dividends, payments received on securities loans, rents, royalties and income from similar sources						
10b Unrelated business taxable income (less section 511 taxes) from businesses acquired after 6/30/75						
10c Total of lines 10a and 10b						
11 Net income from unrelated business activities not included in line 10b, whether or not the business is regularly carried on						
12 Other income. (Explain in Part IV.) Do not include gain or loss from the sale of capital assets						
13 Total Support (Add lines 9, 10c, 11 and 12)						

14 **First Five Years:** If the Form 990 is for the organization's first, second, third, fourth, or fifth tax year as a 501(c)(3) organization, check this box and **stop here** . . . . ▶ ☐

Computation of Public Support Percentage

15 Public Support Percentage for 2008 (line 8 column (f) divided by line 13 column (f))	**15**	%
16 Public Support Percentage from 2007 Schedule A, Part IV-A, line 27g	**16**	%

Computation of Investment Income Percentage

17 Investment Income Percentage for **2008** (line 10c column (f) divided by line 13 column (f))	**17**	%
18 Investment Income Percentage from **2007** Schedule A, Part IV-A, line 27h	**18**	%

19a **33⅓ % Tests - 2008:** If the organization did not check the box on line 14, and line 15 is more than 33⅓ % and line 17 is not more than 33⅓ %, check this box and **stop here.** The organization qualifies as a publicly supported organization . ▶ ☐

b **33⅓ % Tests - 2007:** If the organization did not check a box on line 14 or line 19a, and line 16 is more than 33⅓ % and line 18 is not more than 33⅓ %, check this box and **stop here.** The organization qualifies as a publicly supported organization . ▶ ☐

20 **Private Foundation:** If the organization did not check a box on line 14, 19a or 19b, check this box and see instructions ▶ ☐

Schedule A (Form 990 or 990-EZ) 2008

Page **4**

Part IV **Supplemental Information.** Complete this part to provide the information required by Part II, line 17a or 17b, the explanation for Part II, line 10, or Part III, line 12, and any other additional information.

Schedule A (Form 990 or 990-EZ) 2008

 Printed on recycled paper

Schedule B
(Form 990, 990-EZ, or 990-PF)

Department of the Treasury
Internal Revenue Service

Schedule of Contributors

▶ Attach to Form 990, 990-EZ, and 990-PF.
▶ See separate instructions.

OMB No. 1545-0047

2008

Name of the organization

Employer identification number

Organization type (check one):

Filers of:

Section:

Form 990 or 990-EZ

☐ 501(c)( ) (enter number) organization

☐ 4947(a)(1) nonexempt charitable trust **not** treated as a private foundation

☐ 527 political organization

Form 990-PF

☐ 501(c)(3) exempt private foundation

☐ 4947(a)(1) nonexempt charitable trust treated as a private foundation

☐ 501(c)(3) taxable private foundation

Check if your organization is covered by the **General Rule** or a **Special Rule. (Note.** Only a section 501(c)(7), (8), or (10) organization can check boxes for both the General Rule and a Special Rule. See instructions.)

General Rule

☐ For organizations filing Form 990, 990-EZ, or 990-PF that received, during the year, $5,000 or more (in money or property) from any one contributor. Complete Parts I and II.

Special Rules

☐ For a section 501(c)(3) organization filing Form 990, or Form 990-EZ, that met the 33⅓% support test of the regulations under sections 509(a)(1)/170(b)(1)(A)(vi), and received from any one contributor, during the year, a contribution of the greater of **(1)** $5,000 or **(2)** 2% of the amount on Form 990, Part VIII, line 1h or 2% of the amount on Form 990-EZ, line 1. Complete Parts I and II.

☐ For a section 501(c)(7), (8), or (10) organization filing Form 990, or Form 990-EZ, that received from any one contributor, during the year, aggregate contributions or bequests of more than $1,000 for use *exclusively* for religious, charitable, scientific, literary, or educational purposes, or the prevention of cruelty to children or animals. Complete Parts I, II, and III.

☐ For a section 501(c)(7), (8), or (10) organization filing Form 990, or Form 990-EZ, that received from any one contributor, during the year, some contributions for use *exclusively* for religious, charitable, etc., purposes, but these contributions did not aggregate to more than $1,000. (If this box is checked, enter here the total contributions that were received during the year for an *exclusively* religious, charitable, etc., purpose. Do not complete any of the parts unless the **General Rule** applies to this organization because it received nonexclusively religious, charitable, etc., contributions of $5,000 or more during the year.)   .   .   .   .   ▶ $ ....

Caution. Organizations that are not covered by the General Rule and/or the Special Rules do not file Schedule B (Form 990, 990-EZ, or 990-PF), but they **must** answer "No" on Part IV, line 2 of their Form 990, or check the box in the heading of their Form 990-EZ, or on line 2 of their Form 990-PF, to certify that they do not meet the filing requirements of Schedule B (Form 990, 990-EZ, or 990-PF).

For Paperwork Reduction Act Notice, see the Instructions for Form 990. These instructions will be issued separately.

Cat. No. 30613X

Schedule B (Form 990, 990-EZ, or 990-PF) (2008)

APPENDIX A

Schedule B (Form 990, 990-EZ, or 990-PF) (2008)

Page _____ of _____ of **Part I**

Name of organization	Employer identification number

Part I   **Contributors** (see instructions)

(a) No.	(b) Name, address, and ZIP + 4	(c) Aggregate contributions	(d) Type of contribution
....		$........................	Person ☐ Payroll ☐ Noncash ☐ (Complete Part II if there is a noncash contribution.)
......		$........................	Person ☐ Payroll ☐ Noncash ☐ (Complete Part II if there is a noncash contribution.)
......		$........................	Person ☐ Payroll ☐ Noncash ☐ (Complete Part II if there is a noncash contribution.)
......		$........................	Person ☐ Payroll ☐ Noncash ☐ (Complete Part II if there is a noncash contribution.)
......		$........................	Person ☐ Payroll ☐ Noncash ☐ (Complete Part II if there is a noncash contribution.)
......		$........................	Person ☐ Payroll ☐ Noncash ☐ (Complete Part II if there is a noncash contribution.)

Schedule B (Form 990, 990-EZ, or 990-PF) (2008)

■ 554 ■

Schedule B (Form 990, 990-EZ, or 990-PF) (2008)

Page _____ of _____ of **Part I**

Name of organization	Employer identification number

Part I Contributors (see instructions)

(a) No.	(b) Name, address, and ZIP + 4	(c) Aggregate contributions	(d) Type of contribution
......		$ _____	Person ☐ Payroll ☐ Noncash ☐ (Complete Part II if there is a noncash contribution.)

(a) No.	(b) Name, address, and ZIP + 4	(c) Aggregate contributions	(d) Type of contribution
......		$ _____	Person ☐ Payroll ☐ Noncash ☐ (Complete Part II if there is a noncash contribution.)

(a) No.	(b) Name, address, and ZIP + 4	(c) Aggregate contributions	(d) Type of contribution
......		$ _____	Person ☐ Payroll ☐ Noncash ☐ (Complete Part II if there is a noncash contribution.)

(a) No.	(b) Name, address, and ZIP + 4	(c) Aggregate contributions	(d) Type of contribution
......		$ _____	Person ☐ Payroll ☐ Noncash ☐ (Complete Part II if there is a noncash contribution.)

(a) No.	(b) Name, address, and ZIP + 4	(c) Aggregate contributions	(d) Type of contribution
......		$ _____	Person ☐ Payroll ☐ Noncash ☐ (Complete Part II if there is a noncash contribution.)

(a) No.	(b) Name, address, and ZIP + 4	(c) Aggregate contributions	(d) Type of contribution
......		$ _____	Person ☐ Payroll ☐ Noncash ☐ (Complete Part II if there is a noncash contribution.)

Schedule B (Form 990, 990-EZ, or 990-PF) (2008)

Schedule B (Form 990, 990-EZ, or 990-PF) (2008)

Page _____ of _____ of **Part I**

Name of organization

Employer identification number

Part I Contributors (see instructions)

(a) No.	(b) Name, address, and ZIP + 4	(c) Aggregate contributions	(d) Type of contribution
....		$	Person ☐ Payroll ☐ Noncash ☐ (Complete Part II if there is a noncash contribution.)
....		$	Person ☐ Payroll ☐ Noncash ☐ (Complete Part II if there is a noncash contribution.)
....		$	Person ☐ Payroll ☐ Noncash ☐ (Complete Part II if there is a noncash contribution.)
....		$	Person ☐ Payroll ☐ Noncash ☐ (Complete Part II if there is a noncash contribution.)
....		$	Person ☐ Payroll ☐ Noncash ☐ (Complete Part II if there is a noncash contribution.)
....		$	Person ☐ Payroll ☐ Noncash ☐ (Complete Part II if there is a noncash contribution.)

Schedule B (Form 990, 990-EZ, or 990-PF) (2008)

APPENDIX A

Page _____ of _____ of Part II

Name of organization

Employer identification number

| **Part II** | Noncash Property (see instructions) | | |

(a) No. from Part I	(b) Description of noncash property given	(c) FMV (or estimate) (see instructions)	(d) Date received
		$	/ /
		$	/ /
		$	/ /
		$	/ /
		$	/ /
		$	/ /

■ 557 ■

APPENDIX A

Page ____ of ____ of Part II

Name of organization

Employer identification number

Part II Noncash Property (see instructions)

(a) No. from Part I	(b) Description of noncash property given	(c) FMV (or estimate) (see instructions)	(d) Date received
......		$	......./......./.........
......		$	......./......./.........
......		$	......./......./.........
......		$	......./......./.........
......		$	......./......./.........
......		$	......./......./.........

■ 558 ■

Schedule B (Form 990, 990-EZ, or 990-PF) (2008)   Page _____ of _____ of Part III

Name of organization	Employer identification number

Part III   *Exclusively* religious, charitable, etc., individual contributions to section 501(c)(7), (8), or (10) organizations aggregating more than $1,000 for the year. Complete columns (a) through (e) and the following line entry.

For organizations completing Part III, enter the total of *exclusively* religious, charitable, etc., contributions of **$1,000 or less** for the year. (Enter this information once. See instructions.) ▶ $

(a) No. from Part I	(b) Purpose of gift	(c) Use of gift	(d) Description of how gift is held
....	....	....	....

(e) Transfer of gift	
Transferee's name, address, and ZIP + 4	Relationship of transferor to transferee
....	....

(a) No. from Part I	(b) Purpose of gift	(c) Use of gift	(d) Description of how gift is held
....	....	....	....

(e) Transfer of gift	
Transferee's name, address, and ZIP + 4	Relationship of transferor to transferee
....	....

(a) No. from Part I	(b) Purpose of gift	(c) Use of gift	(d) Description of how gift is held
....	....	....	....

(e) Transfer of gift	
Transferee's name, address, and ZIP + 4	Relationship of transferor to transferee
....	....

(a) No. from Part I	(b) Purpose of gift	(c) Use of gift	(d) Description of how gift is held
....	....	....	....

(e) Transfer of gift	
Transferee's name, address, and ZIP + 4	Relationship of transferor to transferee
....	....

Schedule B (Form 990, 990-EZ, or 990-PF) (2008)

Schedule B (Form 990, 990-EZ, or 990-PF) (2008)   Page _____ of _____ of **Part III**

Name of organization	Employer identification number

Part III   *Exclusively* religious, charitable, etc., individual contributions to section 501(c)(7), (8), or (10) organizations aggregating more than $1,000 for the year. Complete columns (a) through (e) and the following line entry.

For organizations completing Part III, enter the total of *exclusively* religious, charitable, etc., contributions of **$1,000 or less** for the year. (Enter this information once. See instructions.) ▶ $

(a) No. from Part I	(b) Purpose of gift	(c) Use of gift	(d) Description of how gift is held
. . . .			

(e) Transfer of gift

Transferee's name, address, and ZIP + 4	Relationship of transferor to transferee

(a) No. from Part I	(b) Purpose of gift	(c) Use of gift	(d) Description of how gift is held
. . . .			

(e) Transfer of gift

Transferee's name, address, and ZIP + 4	Relationship of transferor to transferee

(a) No. from Part I	(b) Purpose of gift	(c) Use of gift	(d) Description of how gift is held
. . . .			

(e) Transfer of gift

Transferee's name, address, and ZIP + 4	Relationship of transferor to transferee

(a) No. from Part I	(b) Purpose of gift	(c) Use of gift	(d) Description of how gift is held
. . . .			

(e) Transfer of gift

Transferee's name, address, and ZIP + 4	Relationship of transferor to transferee

Schedule B (Form 990, 990-EZ, or 990-PF) (2008)

SCHEDULE C	**Political Campaign and Lobbying Activities**	OMB No. 1545-0047
(Form 990 or 990-EZ)		2008
	For Organizations Exempt From Income Tax Under section 501(c) and section 527	
Department of the Treasury Internal Revenue Service	To be completed by organizations described below.	**Open to Public Inspection**

If the organization answered "Yes," to Form 990, Part IV, line 3, or Form 990-EZ, Part VI, line 46 (Political Campaign Activities)
- Section 501(c)(3) organizations: complete Parts I-A and B. Do not complete Part I-C.
- Section 501(c) (other than section 501(c)(3)) organizations: complete Parts I-A and C below. Do not complete Part I-B.
- Section 527 organizations: complete Part I-A only.

If the organization answered "Yes," to Form 990, Part IV, line 4, or Form 990-EZ, Part VI, line 47 (Lobbying Activities)
- Section 501(c)(3) organizations that have filed Form 5768 (election under section 501(h)) complete Part II-A. Do not complete Part II-B.
- Section 501(c)(3) organizations that have NOT filed Form 5768 (election under section 501(h)): complete Part II-B. Do not complete Part II-A.

If the organization answered "Yes," to Form 990, Part IV, line 5 (Proxy Tax)
- Section 501(c)(4), (5), or (6) organizations: complete Part III.

Name of organization	Employer identification number

Part I-A To be completed by all organizations exempt under section 501(c) and section 527 organizations. (See Schedule C Instructions for details.)

1 Provide a description of the organization's direct and indirect political campaign activities in Part IV.
2 Political expenditures . . . . $ _____
3 Volunteer hours . . . . _____

Part I-B To be completed by all organizations exempt under section 501(c)(3). (See Schedule C Instructions for details.)

1 Enter the amount of any excise tax incurred by the organization under section 4955 . . . . $ _____
2 Enter the amount of any excise tax incurred by organization managers under section 4955 . $ _____
3 If the organization incurred a section 4955 tax, did it file Form 4720 for this year? . . . . . ☐ Yes ☐ No
4a Was a correction made? . . . . ☐ Yes ☐ No
 b If "Yes," describe in Part IV.

Part I-C To be completed by all organizations exempt under section 501(c), except section 501(c)(3). (See Schedule C Instructions for details.)

1 Enter the amount directly expended by the filing organization for section 527 exempt function activities . . . . $ _____
2 Enter the amount of the filing organization's own internal funds contributed to other organizations for section 527 exempt function activities . . . . $ _____
3 Total of direct and indirect exempt function expenditures. Add lines 1 and 2 and enter here and on Form 1120-POL, line 17b . . . . $ _____
4 Did the filing organization file **Form 1120-POL** for this year? . . . . ☐ Yes ☐ No
5 State the names, addresses and Employer Identification Number (EIN) of all section 527 political organizations to which payments were made. Enter the amount paid and indicate if the amount was paid from the filing organization's own internal funds or were political contributions received and promptly and directly delivered to a separate political organization, such as a separate segregated fund or a political action committee (PAC). If additional space is needed, provide information in Part IV.

(a) Name	(b) Address	(c) EIN	(d) Amount paid from filing organization's own internal funds. If none, enter -0-	(e) Amount of political contributions received and promptly and directly delivered to a separate political organization. If none, enter -0-

For Paperwork Reduction Act Notice, see the instructions for Form 990.   Cat. No. 50084S   Schedule C (Form 990 or 990-EZ) 2008

APPENDIX A

Part II-A To be completed by organizations exempt under section 501(c)(3) that filed Form 5768 (election under section 501(h)). (See Schedule C Instructions for details.)

A Check ☐ if the filing organization belongs to an affiliated group.

B Check ☐ if the filing organization checked box A and "limited control" provisions apply.

Limits on Lobbying Expenditures— (The term "expenditures" means amounts paid or incurred.)	(a) Filing Organization's Totals	(b) Affiliated Group Totals
1a Total lobbying expenditures to influence public opinion (grass roots lobbying)		
b Total lobbying expenditures to influence a legislative body (direct lobbying)		
c Total lobbying expenditures (add lines a and b)		
d Other exempt purpose expenditures		
e Total exempt purpose expenditures (add lines c and d)		
f Lobbying nontaxable amount. Enter the amount from the following table in both columns—		

If the amount on line e is—	The lobbying nontaxable amount is—
Not over $500,000	20% of the amount on line e
Over $500,000 but not over $1,000,000	$100,000 plus 15% of the excess over $500,000
Over $1,000,000 but not over $1,500,000	$175,000 plus 10% of the excess over $1,000,000
Over $1,500,000 but not over $17,000,000	$225,000 plus 5% of the excess over $1,500,000
Over $17,000,000	$1,000,000

	(a) Filing Organization's Totals	(b) Affiliated Group Totals
g Grassroots nontaxable amount (enter 25% of line f)		
h Subtract line g from line a. Enter -0- if line g is more than line a		
i Subtract line f from line c. Enter -0- if line f is more than line c		

j If there is an amount other than zero on either line h or line i, did the organization file Form 4720 reporting section 4911 tax for this year? .... ☐ Yes ☐ No

4-Year Averaging Period Under Section 501(h)
(Some organizations that made a section 501(h) election do not have to complete all of the five columns below. See the instructions for lines a through f on page xx of the instructions.)

Lobbying Expenditures During 4-Year Averaging Period

Calendar year (or fiscal year beginning in)	(a) 2005	(b) 2006	(c) 2007	(d) 2008	(e) Total
2a Lobbying non-taxable amount					
b Lobbying ceiling amount (150% line 2a, column(e))					
c Total lobbying expenditures					
d Grassroots non-taxable amount					
e Grassroots ceiling amount (150% of line d, column (e))					
f Grassroots lobbying expenditures					

Part II-B   To be completed by organizations exempt under section 501(c)(3) that have NOT filed Form 5768 (election under section 501(h)). (See Schedule C Instructions for details.)

		(a)		(b)
		Yes	No	Amount
1	During the year, did the filing organization attempt to influence foreign, national, state or local legislation, including any attempt to influence public opinion on a legislative matter or referendum, through the use of:			
a	Volunteers			
b	Paid staff or management (include compensation in expenses reported on lines c through i) . . .			
c	Media advertisements			
d	Mailings to members, legislators, or the public			
e	Publications, or published or broadcast statements			
f	Grants to other organizations for lobbying purposes			
g	Direct contact with legislators, their staffs, government officials, or a legislative body . . .			
h	Rallies, demonstrations, seminars, conventions, speeches, lectures, or any other means . .			
i	Other activities. If "Yes," describe in Part IV			
j	Total lines c through i			
2a	Did the activities in line 1 cause the organization to be not described in section 501(c)(3)?			
b	If "Yes," enter the amount of any tax incurred under section 4912			
c	If "Yes," enter the amount of any tax incurred by organization managers under section 4912 .			
d	If the filing organization incurred a section 4912 tax, did it file Form 4720 for this year? .			

Part III-A   To be completed by all organizations exempt under section 501(c)(4), section 501(c)(5), or section 501(c)(6). (See Schedule C Instructions for details.)

			Yes	No
1	Were substantially all (90% or more) dues received nondeductible by members?	1		
2	Did the organization make only in-house lobbying expenditures of $2,000 or less?	2		
3	Did the organization agree to carryover lobbying and political expenditures from the prior year? . .	3		

Part III-B   To be completed by all organizations exempt under section 501(c)(4), section 501(c)(5), or section 501(c)(6) if BOTH Part III-A, questions 1 and 2 are answered "No" OR if Part III-A, question 3 is answered "Yes." (See Schedule C Instructions for details.)

1	Dues, assessments and similar amounts from members	
2	Section 162(e) non-deductible lobbying and political expenditures (do not include amounts of political expenses for which the section 527(f) tax was paid).	
a	Current year	
b	Carryover from last year	
c	Total	
3	Aggregate amount reported in section 6033(e)(1)(A) notices of nondeductible section 162(e) dues.	
4	If notices were sent and the amount on line 2c exceeds the amount on line 3, what portion of the excess does the organization agree to carryover to the reasonable estimate of nondeductible lobbying and political expenditure next year?	
5	Taxable amount of lobbying and political expenditures (line 2c total minus 3 and 4)	

Part IV   Supplemental Information

Complete this part to provide the descriptions required for Part I-A, line 1, Part I-B, line 4, Part I-C, line 5, and Part II-B, line 1i. Also, complete this part for any additional information.

....

....

....

....

....

....

....

APPENDIX A

Part IV   **Supplemental Information** *(Continued)*

 Printed on recycled paper

SCHEDULE D
(Form 990)

Supplemental Financial Statements

OMB No. 1545-0047

2008

Department of the Treasury
Internal Revenue Service

▶ Attach to Form 990. To be completed by organizations that
answered "Yes," to Form 990, Part IV, line 6, 7, 8, 9, 10, 11, or 12.

**Open to Public
Inspection**

Name of the organization	Employer identification number

Part I Organizations Maintaining Donor Advised Funds or Other Similar Funds or Accounts. Complete if the organization answered "Yes" to Form 990, Part IV, line 6.

	(a) Donor advised funds	(b) Funds and other accounts
1 Total number at end of year		
2 Aggregate Contributions to (during year)		
3 Aggregate Grants from (during year)		
4 Aggregate value at end of year . . .		

5 Did the organization inform all donors and donor advisors in writing that the assets held in donor advised funds are the organization's property, subject to the organization's exclusive legal control? . . . . . ☐ Yes ☐ No

6 Did the organization inform all grantees, donors, and donor advisors in writing that grant funds may be used only for charitable purposes and not for the benefit of the donor or donor advisor or other impermissible private benefit? . . . . ☐ Yes ☐ No

Part II Conservation Easements. Complete if the organization answered "Yes" to Form 990, Part IV, line 7.

1 Purpose(s) of conservation easements held by the organization (check all that apply).
☐ Preservation of land for public use (e.g., recreation or pleasure) ☐ Preservation of an historically importantly land area
☐ Protection of natural habitat ☐ Preservation of certified historic structure
☐ Preservation of open space

2 Complete lines 2a–2d if the organization held a qualified conservation contribution in the form of a conservation easement on the last day of the tax year.

		Held at the End of the Year
a Total number of conservation easements	2a	
b Total acreage restricted by conservation easements	2b	
c Number of conservation easements on a certified historic structure included in (a)	2c	
d Number of conservation easements included in (c) acquired after 8/17/06	2d	

3 Number of conservation easements modified, transferred, released, extinguished, or terminated by the organization during the taxable year ▶ ------------------

4 Number of states where property subject to conservation easement is located ▶ ------------------

5 Does the organization have a written policy regarding the periodic monitoring, inspection, violations, and enforcement of the conservation easements it holds? . . . . ☐ Yes ☐ No

6 Staff or volunteer hours devoted to monitoring, inspecting, and enforcing easements during the year ▶ ------------------

7 Amount of expenses incurred in monitoring, inspecting, and enforcing easements during the year ▶ $ ------------------

8 Does each conservation easement reported on line 2(d) above satisfy the requirements of section 170(h)(4)(B)(i) and section 170(h)(4)(B)(ii)? . . . . ☐ Yes ☐ No

9 In Part XIV, describe how the organization reports conservation easements in its revenue and expense statement, and balance sheet, and include, if applicable, the text of the footnote to the organization's financial statements that describes the organization's accounting for conservation easements.

Part III Organizations Maintaining Collections of Art, Historical Treasures, or Other Similar Assets. Complete if the organization answered "Yes" to Form 990, Part IV, line 8.

1a If the organization elected, as permitted under SFAS 116, not to report in its revenue statement and balance sheet works of art, historical treasures, or other similar assets held for public exhibition, education, or research in furtherance of public service, provide, in Part XIV, the text of the footnote to its financial statements that describes these items.

b If the organization elected, as permitted under SFAS 116, to report in its revenue statement and balance sheet works of art, historical treasures, or other similar assets held for public exhibition, education, or research in furtherance of public service, provide the following amounts relating to these items:
(i) Revenues included in Form 990, Part VIII, line 1 . . . . ▶ $ ------------------
(ii) Assets included in Form 990, Part X . . . . ▶ $ ------------------

2 If the organization received or held works of art, historical treasures, or other similar assets for financial gain, provide the following amounts required to be reported under SFAS 116 relating to these items:
a Revenues included in Form 990, Part VIII, line 1 . . . . ▶ $ ------------------
b Assets included in Form 990, Part X . . . . ▶ $ ------------------

For Paperwork Reduction Act Notice, see the Instructions for Form 990. Cat. No. 50058W Schedule D (Form 990) 2008

APPENDIX A

Part III   Organizations Maintaining Collections of Art, Historical Treasures, or Other Similar Assets *(continued)*

3   Using the organization's accession and other records, check any of the following that are a significant use of its collection items (check all that apply):

a   ☐   Public exhibition   d   ☐   Loan or exchange programs

b   ☐   Scholarly research   e   ☐   Other _____

c   ☐   Preservation for future generations

4   Provide a description of the organization's collections and explain how they further the organization's exempt purpose in Part XIV.

5   During the year, did the organization solicit or receive donations of art, historical treasures, or other similar assets to be sold to raise funds rather than to be maintained as part of the organization's collection?   ☐ Yes   ☐ No

Part IV   Trust, Escrow and Custodial Arrangements. Complete if organization answered "Yes" to Form 990, Part IV, line 9, or reported an amount on Form 990, Part X, line 21.

1a   Is the organization an agent, trustee, custodian or other intermediary for contributions or other assets not included on Form 990, Part X?   ☐ Yes   ☐ No

b   If "Yes," explain why in Part XIV and complete the following table:

		Amount
c	Beginning balance	1c
d	Additions during the year	1d
e	Distributions during the year	1e
f	Ending balance	1f

2a   Did the organization include an amount on Form 990, Part X, line 21?   ☐ Yes   ☐ No

b   If "Yes," explain the arrangement in Part XIV.

Part V   Endowment Funds. Complete if organization answered "Yes" to Form 990, Part IV, line 10.

	(a) Current year	(b) Prior year	(c) Two years back	(d) Three years back	(e) Four years back
1a Beginning of year balance					
b Contributions					
c Investment earnings or losses					
d Grants or scholarships					
e Other expenditures for facilities and programs					
f Administrative expenses					
g End of year balance					

2   Provide the estimated percentage of the year end balance held as:

a   Board designated or quasi-endowment ▶ _____ %

b   Permanent endowment ▶ _____ %

c   Term endowment ▶ _____ %

3a   Are there endowment funds not in the possession of the organization that are held and administered for the organization by:

		Yes	No
(i) unrelated organizations	3a(i)		
(ii) related organizations	3a(ii)		
b If "Yes" to 3a(ii), are the related organizations listed as required on Schedule R?	3b		

4   Describe in Part XIV the intended uses of the organization's endowment funds.

Part VI   Investments—Land, Buildings, and Equipment. See Form 990, Part X, line 10.

Description of investment	(a) Cost or other basis (investment)	(b) Cost or other basis (other)	(c) Depreciation	(d) Book value
1a Land				
b Buildings				
c Leasehold improvements				
d Equipment				
e Other				

Total. Add lines 1a–1e. *(Column (d) should equal Form 990, Part X, column (B), line 10(c).)*   ▶

Part VII Investments—Other Securities. See Form 990, Part X, line 12.

(a) Description of security or category (including name of security)	(b) Book value	(c) Method of valuation: Cost or end-of-year market value
Financial derivatives and other financial products . .		
Closely-held equity interests		
Other -----------------------------------		
--		
--		
--		
--		
--		
--		
--		
Total. *(Column (b) should equal Form 990, Part X, col. (B) line 12.)* ▶		

Part VIII Investments—Program Related. See Form 990, Part X, line 13.

(a) Description of investment type	(b) Book value	(c) Method of valuation: Cost or end-of-year market value
Total. *(Column (b) should equal Form 990, Part X, col. (B) line 13.)* ▶		

Part IX Other Assets. See Form 990, Part X, line 15.

(a) Description	(b) Book value
Total. *(Column (b) should equal Form 990, Part X, col. (B) line 15.)* . . . . ▶	

Part X Other Liabilities. See Form 990, Part X, line 25.

(a) Description of liability	(b) Amount	
Federal income taxes		
Total. *(Column (b) should equal Form 990, Part X, col. (B) line 25.)* ▶		

In Part XIV, provide the text of the footnote to the organization's financial statements that reports the organization's liability for uncertain tax positions under FIN 48.

Schedule D (Form 990) 2008   Page **4**

Part XI	**Reconciliation of Change in Net Assets from Form 990 to Financial Statements**		
1	Total revenue (Form 990, Part VIII, column (A), line 12)	**1**	
2	Total expenses (Form 990, Part IX, column (A), line 25)	**2**	
3	Excess or (deficit) for the year. Subtract line 2 from line 1	**3**	
4	Net unrealized gains (losses) on investments	**4**	
5	Donated services and use of facilities	**5**	
6	Investment expenses	**6**	
7	Prior period adjustments	**7**	
8	Other (Describe in Part XIV)	**8**	
9	Total adjustments (net). Add lines 4–8	**9**	
10	Excess or (deficit) for the year per financial statements. Combine lines 3 and 9	**10**	

Part XII	**Reconciliation of Revenue per Audited Financial Statements With Revenue per Return**			
1	Total revenue, gains, and other support per audited financial statements		**1**	
2	Amounts included on line 1 but not on Form 990, Part VIII, line 12:			
a	Net unrealized gains on investments	**2a**		
b	Donated services and use of facilities	**2b**		
c	Recoveries of prior year grants	**2c**		
d	Other (Describe in Part XIV)	**2d**		
e	Add lines **2a** through **2d**		**2e**	
3	Subtract line **2e** from line **1**		**3**	
4	Amounts included on Form 990, Part VIII, line 12, but not on line **1**:			
a	Investment expenses not included on Form 990, Part VIII, line 7b	**4a**		
b	Other (Describe in Part XIV)	**4b**		
c	Add lines **4a** and **4b**		**4c**	
5	Total revenue. Add lines **3** and **4c**. (This should equal Form 990, Part I, line 12.)		**5**	

Part XIII	**Reconciliation of Expenses per Audited Financial Statements With Expenses per Return**			
1	Total expenses and losses per audited financial statements		**1**	
2	Amounts included on line 1 but not on Form 990, Part IX, line 25:			
a	Donated services and use of facilities	**2a**		
b	Prior year adjustments	**2b**		
c	Losses reported on Form 990, Part IX, line 25	**2c**		
d	Other (Describe in Part XIV)	**2d**		
e	Add lines **2a** through **2d**		**2e**	
3	Subtract line **2e** from line 1		**3**	
4	Amounts included on Form 990, Part IX, line 25, but not on line **1**:			
a	Investment expenses not included on Form 990, Part VIII, line 7b	**4a**		
b	Other (Describe in Part XIV)	**4b**		
c	Add lines **4a** and **4b**		**4c**	
5	Total expenses. Add lines **3** and **4c**. (This should equal Form 990, Part I, line 18.)		**5**	

Part XIV	**Supplemental Information**

Complete this part to provide the descriptions required for Part II, line 9; Part III, lines 1a and 4; Part IV, lines 1b and 2b; Part V, line 4; Part X; Part XI, line 8; Part XII, lines 2d and 4b; and Part XIII, lines 2d and 4b.

Schedule D (Form 990) 2008

Schedule D (Form 990) 2008   Page **5**

Part XIV   **Supplemental Information** *(continued)*

Schedule D (Form 990) 2008

 Printed on recycled paper

APPENDIX A

Schools

► Attach to Form 990 or Form 990-EZ. To be completed by organizations that answer "Yes" to Form 990, Part IV, line 13, or Form 990-EZ, Part VI, line 48.

OMB No. 1545-0047

2008

Open to Public Inspection

Name of the organization

Employer identification number

		YES	NO
1	Does the organization have a racially nondiscriminatory policy toward students by statement in its charter, bylaws, other governing instrument, or in a resolution of its governing body?	**1**		
2	Does the organization include a statement of its racially nondiscriminatory policy toward students in all its brochures, catalogues, and other written communications with the public dealing with student admissions, programs, and scholarships?	**2**		
3	Has the organization publicized its racially nondiscriminatory policy through newspaper or broadcast media during the period of solicitation for students, or during the registration period if it has no solicitation program, in a way that makes the policy known to all parts of the general community it serves? If "Yes," please describe. If "No," please explain	**3**		

4	Does the organization maintain the following?		
a	Records indicating the racial composition of the student body, faculty, and administrative staff? . . .	**4a**	
b	Records documenting that scholarships and other financial assistance are awarded on a racially nondiscriminatory basis?	**4b**	
c	Copies of all catalogues, brochures, announcements, and other written communications to the public dealing with student admissions, programs, and scholarships?	**4c**	
d	Copies of all material used by the organization or on its behalf to solicit contributions?	**4d**	
	If you answered "No" to any of the above, please explain. (If you need more space, attach a separate statement.)		

5	Does the organization discriminate by race in any way with respect to:		
a	Students' rights or privileges?	**5a**	
b	Admissions policies?	**5b**	
c	Employment of faculty or administrative staff?	**5c**	
d	Scholarships or other financial assistance?	**5d**	
e	Educational policies?	**5e**	
f	Use of facilities?	**5f**	
g	Athletic programs?	**5g**	
h	Other extracurricular activities?	**5h**	
	If you answered "Yes" to any of the above, please explain. (If you need more space, attach a separate statement.)		

6a	Does the organization receive any financial aid or assistance from a governmental agency?	**6a**	
b	Has the organization's right to such aid ever been revoked or suspended?	**6b**	
	If you answered "Yes" to either line 6a or line 6b, please explain using an attached statement.		
7	Does the organization certify that it has complied with the applicable requirements of sections 4.01 through 4.05 of Rev. Proc. 75-50, 1975-2 C.B. 587, covering racial nondiscrimination? If "No," attach an explanation.	**7**	

For Paperwork Reduction Act Notice, see the Instructions for Form 990.   Cat. No. 50085D   Schedule E (Form 990 or 990-EZ) 2008

 Printed on recycled paper

APPENDIX A

Schedule F (Form 990)

Department of the Treasury
Internal Revenue Service

Statement of Activities Outside the United States

▶ Attach to Form 990. Complete if the organization answered "Yes" to Form 990, Part IV, line 14b.

OMB No. 1545-0047

2008

Open to Public Inspection

Name of the organization

Employer identification number

Part I **General Information on Activities Outside the United States.** Complete if the organization answered "Yes" to Form 990, Part IV, line 14b.

1 **For grantmakers.** Does the organization maintain records to substantiate the amount of the grants or assistance, the grantees' eligibility for the grants or assistance, and the selection criteria used to award the grants or assistance? . . . . ☐ Yes ☐ No

2 **For grantmakers.** Describe in Part IV the organization's procedures for monitoring the use of grant funds outside the United States.

3 Activities per Region. (Use Schedule F-1 (Form 990) if additional space is needed.)

(a) Region	(b) Number of offices in the region	(c) Number of employees or agents in region	(d) Activities conducted in region (by type) (i.e., fundraising, program services, grants to recipients located in the region)	(e) If activity listed in (d) is a program service, describe specific type of service(s) in region	(f) Total expenditures in region
Totals ▶					

For Paperwork Reduction Act Notice, see the Instructions for Form 990.   Cat. No. 50082W   Schedule F (Form 990) 2008

Part II **Grants and Other Assistance to Organizations or Entities Outside the United States.** Complete if the organization answered "Yes" to Form 990, Part IV, line 15, for any recipient who received more than $5,000. Check this box if no one recipient received more than $5,000 . . . . . ▶ ☐ Use Schedule F-1 (Form 990) if additional space is needed.

1	(a) Name of organization	(b) IRS code section and EIN (if applicable)	(c) Region	(d) Purpose of grant	(e) Amount of cash grant	(f) Manner of cash disbursement	(g) Amount of non-cash assistance	(h) Description of non-cash assistance	(i) Method of valuation (book, FMV, appraisal, other)

2 Enter total number of organizations that are recognized as charities by the foreign country or for which the grantee or counsel has provided a section 501(c)(3) equivalency letter . . . . ▶

3 Enter total number of other organizations or entities . . . . ▶

Part III **Grants and Other Assistance to Individuals Outside the United States.** Complete if the organization answered "Yes" to Form 990, Part IV, line 16.
Use Schedule F-1 (Form 990) if additional space is needed.

(a) Type of grant or assistance	(b) Region	(c) Number of recipients	(d) Amount of cash grant	(e) Manner of cash disbursement	(f) Amount of non-cash assistance	(g) Description of non-cash assistance	(h) Method of valuation (book, FMV, appraisal, other)

Part IV Supplemental Information

Complete this part to provide the information required in Part I, line 2, and any other additional information.

Printed on recycled paper

APPENDIX A

SCHEDULE G
(Form 990 or 990-EZ)

Department of the Treasury
Internal Revenue Service

Supplemental Information Regarding Fundraising or Gaming Activities

▶ Attach to Form 990 or Form 990-EZ. Must be completed by organizations that answer "Yes" to Form 990, Part IV, lines 17, 18, or 19, and by organizations that enter more than $15,000 on Form 990-EZ, line 6a.

OMB No. 1545-0047

2008

Open To Public Inspection

Name of the organization

Employer identification number

Part I   Fundraising Activities. Complete if the organization answered "Yes" to Form 990, Part IV, line 17.

1   Indicate whether the organization raised funds through any of the following activities. Check all that apply.

a ☐ Mail solicitations   e ☐ Solicitation of non-government grants
b ☐ Email solicitations   f ☐ Solicitation of government grants
c ☐ Phone solicitations   g ☐ Special fundraising events
d ☐ In-person solicitations

2a   Did the organization have a written or oral agreement with any individual (including officers, directors, trustees or key employees listed in Form 990, Part VII) or entity in connection with professional fundraising services? ☐ Yes ☐ No

b   If "Yes," list the ten highest paid individuals or entities (fundraisers) pursuant to agreements under which the fundraiser is to be compensated at least $5,000 by the organization. Form 990-EZ filers are not required to complete this table.

(i) Name of individual or entity (fundraiser)	(ii) Activity	(iii) Did fundraiser have custody or control of contributions?		(iv) Gross receipts from activity	(v) Amount paid to (or retained by) fundraiser listed in col. (i)	(vi) Amount paid to (or retained by) organization
		Yes	No			
Total . . . . . . ▶						

3   List all states in which the organization is registered or licensed to solicit funds or has been notified it is exempt from registration or licensing.

For Paperwork Reduction Act Notice, see the Instructions for Form 990.   Cat. No. 50083H   Schedule G (Form 990 or 990-EZ) 2008

Schedule G (Form 990 or 990-EZ) 2008 — Page **2**

Part II — **Fundraising Events.** Complete if the organization answered "Yes" to Form 990, Part IV, line 18, or reported more than $15,000 on Form 990-EZ, line 6a. List events with gross receipts greater than $5,000.

		(a) Event #1 _____ (event type)	**(b)** Event #2 _____ (event type)	**(c)** Other Events _____ (total number)	**(d)** Total Events (Add col. **(a)** through col. **(c)**)
Revenue	1 Gross receipts				
	2 Less: Charitable contributions				
	3 Gross revenue (line 1 minus line 2)				
Direct Expenses	4 Cash prizes				
	5 Non-cash prizes				
	6 Rent/facility costs . . .				
	7 Other direct expenses .				

8 Direct expense summary. Add lines 4 through 7 in column (d) . . . . ▶ (_____)
9 Net income summary. Combine lines 3 and 8 in column (d) . . . . ▶

Part III — **Gaming.** Complete if the organization answered "Yes" to Form 990, Part IV, line 19, or reported more than $15,000 on Form 990-EZ, line 6a.

		(a) Bingo	**(b)** Pull tabs/Instant bingo/progressive bingo	**(c)** Other gaming	**(d)** Total gaming (Add col. **(a)** through col. **(c)**)
Revenue	1 Gross revenue				
Direct Expenses	2 Cash prizes				
	3 Non-cash prizes . . .				
	4 Rent/facility costs . .				
	5 Other direct expenses .				
	6 Volunteer labor . . .	☐ Yes _____ % ☐ No	☐ Yes _____ % ☐ No	☐ Yes _____ % ☐ No	

7 Direct expense summary. Add lines 2 through 5 in column (d) . . . . ▶ (_____)

8 Net gaming income summary. Combine lines 1 and 7 in column (d) . . . . ▶

		Yes	No
9	Enter the state(s) in which the organization operates gaming activities: _____		
a	Is the organization licensed to operate gaming activities in each of these states?	9a	
b	If "No," Explain: _____		
10a	Were any of the organization's gaming licenses revoked, suspended or terminated during the tax year?	10a	
b	If "Yes," Explain: _____		
11	Does the organization operate gaming activities with nonmembers?	11	
12	Is the organization a grantor, beneficiary or trustee of a trust or a member of a partnership or other entity formed to administer charitable gaming?	12	

Schedule G (Form 990 or 990-EZ) 2008

APPENDIX A

		Yes	No

13 Indicate the percentage of gaming activity operated in:

a The organization's facility . . . . **13a** %

b An outside facility . . . . **13b** %

14 Provide the name and address of the person who prepares the organization's gaming/special events books and records:

Name ▶ ....

Address ▶ ....

15a Does the organization have a contract with a third party from whom the organization receives gaming revenue? **15a**

b If "Yes," enter the amount of gaming revenue received by the organization ▶ $ .... and the amount of gaming revenue retained by the third party ▶ $ ....

c If "Yes," enter name and address:

Name ▶ ....

Address ▶ ....

16 Gaming manager information:

Name ▶ ....

Gaming manager compensation ▶ $ ....

Description of services provided ▶ ....

☐ Director/officer ☐ Employee ☐ Independent contractor

17 Mandatory distributions:

a Is the organization required under state law to make charitable distributions from the gaming proceeds to retain the state gaming license? **17a**

b Enter the amount of distributions required under state law distributed to other exempt organizations or spent in the organization's own exempt activities during the tax year ▶ $

SCHEDULE H
(Form 990)

Department of the Treasury
Internal Revenue Service

Hospitals

▶ Attach to Form 990. To be completed by organizations that
answer "Yes" to Form 990, Part IV, line 20.

OMB No. 1545-0047

2008

**Open to Public
Inspection**

Name of the organization

Employer identification number

Part I	Charity Care and Certain Other Community Benefits at Cost *(Optional for 2008)*

		Yes	No
1a	Does the organization have a charity care policy? If "No," skip to question 6a . . .	**1a**	
b	If "Yes," is it a written policy?	**1b**	
2	If the organization has multiple hospitals, indicate which of the following best describes application of the charity care policy to the various hospitals.		

☐ Applied uniformly to all hospitals ☐ Applied uniformly to most hospitals
☐ Generally tailored to individual hospitals

3 Answer the following based on the charity care eligibility criteria that applies to the largest number of the organization's patients.

a	Does the organization use Federal Poverty Guidelines (FPG) to determine eligibility for providing *free* care to low income individuals? If "Yes," indicate which of the following is the family income limit for eligibility for free care:	**3a**	

☐ 100% ☐ 150% ☐ 200% ☐ Other _____ %

b	Does the organization use FPG to determine eligibility for providing *discounted* care to low income individuals? If "Yes," indicate which of the following is the family income limit for eligibility for discounted care:	**3b**	

☐ 200% ☐ 250% ☐ 300% ☐ 350% ☐ 400% ☐ Other _____ %

c If the organization does not use FPG to determine eligibility, describe in Part VI the income based criteria for determining eligibility for free or discounted care. Include in the description whether the organization uses an asset test or other threshold, regardless of income, to determine eligibility for free or discounted care.

4	Does the organization's policy provide free or discounted care to the "medically indigent"?	**4**	
5a	Does the organization budget amounts for free or discounted care provided under its charity care policy?	**5a**	
b	If "Yes," did the organization's charity care expenses exceed the budgeted amount?	**5b**	
c	If "Yes" to line 5b, as a result of budget considerations, was the organization unable to provide free or discounted care to a patient who was eligible for free or discounted care?	**5c**	
6a	Does the organization prepare an annual community benefit report?	**6a**	
b	If "Yes," does the organization make it available to the public?	**6b**	

Complete the following table using the worksheets provided in the Schedule H instructions. Do not submit these worksheets with the Schedule H.

7 Charity Care and Certain Other Community Benefits at Cost

Charity Care and Means-Tested Programs	(a) Number of activities or programs (optional)	(b) Persons served (optional)	(c) Total community benefit expense	(d) Direct offsetting revenue	(e) Net community benefit expense	(f) Percent of total expense
a Charity care at cost (from *worksheets 1 and 2*)						
b Unreimbursed Medicaid (from *worksheet 3, column a*) . .						
c Unreimbursed costs—other means-tested government programs (from *worksheet 3, column b*) . .						
d **Total** Charity Care and Means-Tested Programs . . .						
Other Benefits						
e Community health improvement services and community benefit operations (from worksheet 4) .						
f Health professions education (from worksheet 5)						
g Subsidized health services (from worksheet 6)						
h Research (from worksheet 7) . .						
i Cash and in-kind contributions to community groups (from worksheet 8)						
j **Total** Other Benefits						
k Total (line 7d and 7j)						

For Paperwork Reduction Act Notice, see the Instructions for Form 990.   Cat. No. 50192T   Schedule H (Form 990) 2008

APPENDIX A

Part II Community Building Activities Complete this table if the organization conducted any community building activities. *(Optional for 2008)*

		(a) Number of activities or programs (optional)	(b) Persons served (optional)	(c) Total community building expense	(d) Direct offsetting revenue	(e) Net community building expense	(f) Percent of total expense
1	Physical improvements and housing						
2	Economic development						
3	Community support						
4	Environmental improvements						
5	Leadership development and training for community members						
6	Coalition building						
7	Community health improvement advocacy						
8	Workforce development						
9	Other						
10	Total						

Part III Bad Debt, Medicare, & Collection Practices *(Optional for 2008)*

Section A. Bad Debt Expense

			Yes	No
1	Does the organization report bad debt expense in accordance with Healthcare Financial Management Association Statement No. 15?	1		
2	Enter the amount of the organization's bad debt expense (at cost)	**2**		
3	Enter the estimated amount of the organization's bad debt expense (at cost) attributable to patients eligible under the organization's charity care policy.	**3**		
4	Provide in Part VI the text of the footnote to the organization's financial statements that describes bad debt expense. In addition, describe the costing methodology used in determining the amounts reported on lines 2 and 3, or rationale for including other bad debt amounts in community benefit.			

Section B. Medicare

5	Enter total revenue received from Medicare (including DSH and IME)	**5**		
6	Enter Medicare allowable costs of care relating to payments on line 5	**6**		
7	Enter line 5 less line 6—surplus or (shortfall)	**7**		
8	Describe in Part VI the extent to which any shortfall reported in line 7 should be treated as community benefit and the costing methodology or source used to determine the amount reported on line 6, and indicate which of the following methods was used:			

☐ Cost accounting system   ☐ Cost to charge ratio   ☐ Other

Section C. Collection Practices

9a	Does the organization have a written debt collection policy?	9a	
b	If "Yes," does the organization's collection policy contain provisions on the collection practices to be followed for patients who are known to qualify for charity care or financial assistance? Describe in Part VI . . .	9b	

Part IV Management Companies and Joint Ventures *(Optional for 2008)*

	(a) Name of entity	(b) Description of primary activity of entity	(c) Organization's profit % or stock ownership %	(d) Officers, directors, trustees, or key employees' profit % or stock ownership %	(e) Physicians' profit % or stock ownership %
1					
2					
3					
4					
5					
6					
7					
8					
9					
10					
11					
12					
13					
14					

Schedule H (Form 990) 2008

Part V	Facility Information *(Required for 2008)*									
Name and address		Licensed hospital	General medical & surgical	Children's hospital	Teaching hospital	Critical access hospital	Research facility	ER–24 hours	ER–other	Other (Describe)

Schedule H (Form 990) 2008

APPENDIX A

Part VI   **Supplemental Information** *(Optional for 2008)*

Complete this part to provide the following information.

1 Provide the description required for Part I, line 3c; Part I, line 7; Part III, line 4; Part III, line 8; and Part III, line 9b.

2 **Needs Assessment.** Describe how the organization assesses the health care needs of the communities it serves.

3 **Patient Education of Eligibility for Assistance.** Describe how the organization informs and educates patients and persons who may be billed for patient care about their eligibility for assistance under federal, state, or local government programs or under the organization's charity care policy.

4 **Community Information.** Describe the community the organization serves, taking into account the geographic area and demographic constituents it serves.

5 **Community Building Activities.** Describe how the organization's community building activities, as reported in Part II, promote the health of the communities the organization serves.

6 Provide any other information important to describing how the organization's hospitals or other health care facilities further its exempt purpose by promoting the health of the community (e.g., open medical staff, community board, use of surplus funds, etc.).

7 If the organization is part of an affiliated health care system, describe the respective roles of the organization and its affiliates in promoting the health of the communities served.

8 If applicable, identify all states with which the organization, or a related organization, files a community benefit report.

Schedule H (Form 990) 2008

 Printed on recycled paper

SCHEDULE I
(Form 990)

Department of the Treasury
Internal Revenue Service

Grants and Other Assistance to Organizations, Governments and Individuals in the U.S.

Complete if the organization answered "Yes," on Form 990, Part IV, lines 2, for any recipient who received more than $5,000.

OMB No. 1545-0047

2008

Open to Public Inspection

Name of the organization

Employer identification number

Part I General Information on Grants and Assistance

1 Does the organization maintain records to substantiate the amount of the grants or assistance, the grantees' eligibility for the grants or assistance, and
the selection criteria used to award the grants or assistance? ☐ Yes ☐ No

2 Describe in Part IV the organization's procedures for monitoring the use of grant funds in the United States.

Part II Grants and Other Assistance to Governments and Organizations in the United States. Complete if the organization answered "Yes" on Form 990, Part IV, line 21 for any recipient that received more than $5,000. Check this box if no one recipient received more than $5,000. Use Schedule I-1 if additional space is needed ▲ ☐

1 (a) Name and address of organization or government	(b) EIN	(c) IRC Code section if applicable	(d) Amount of cash grant	(e) Amount of non-cash assistance	(f) Method of valuation (book, FMV, appraisal, other)	(g) Description of non-cash assistance	(h) Purpose of grant or assistance

2 Enter total number of 501(c)(3) and government organizations . . . . ▲
3 Enter total number of other organizations . . . . ▲

For Paperwork Reduction Act Notice, see the Instructions for Form 990. Cat. No. 50055P Schedule I (Form 990) 2008

Page **2**

Part III **Grants and Other Assistance to Individuals in the United States.** Complete if the organization answered "Yes" on Form 990, Part IV, line 22.
Use Schedule I-1 if additional space is needed.

(a) Type of grant or assistance	**(b)** Number of recipients	**(c)** Amount of cash grant	**(d)** Amount of non-cash assistance	**(e)** Method of valuation (book, FMV, appraisal, other)	**(f)** Description of non-cash assistance

Part IV Supplemental Information. Complete this part to provide the information required in Part I, line 2, and any other additional information.

Printed on Recycled Paper

■ 583 ■

<table>
<tr><td>SCHEDULE J
(Form 990)

Department of the Treasury
Internal Revenue Service</td><td colspan="2">**Compensation Information**
For certain Officers, Directors, Trustees, Key Employees, and Highest
Compensated Employees
▶ Attach to Form 990. To be completed by organizations
that answered "Yes" to Form 990, Part IV, line 23.</td><td>OMB No. 1545-0047

20**08**

**Open to Public
Inspection**</td></tr>
</table>

Name of the organization	Employer identification number

Part I Questions Regarding Compensation

		Yes	No
1a	Check the appropriate box(es) if the organization provided any of the following to or for a person listed in Form 990, Part VII, Section A, line 1a. Complete Part III to provide any relevant information regarding these items.		

    ☐ First-class or charter travel   ☐ Housing allowance or residence for personal use
    ☐ Travel for companions   ☐ Payments for business use of personal residence
    ☐ Tax indemnification and gross-up payments   ☐ Health or social club dues or initiation fees
    ☐ Discretionary spending account   ☐ Personal services (e.g., maid, chauffeur, chef)

b	If line 1a is checked, did the organization follow a written policy regarding payment or reimbursement or provision of all of the expenses described above? If "No," complete Part III to explain	**1b**		
2	Did the organization require substantiation prior to reimbursing or allowing expenses incurred by all officers, directors, trustees, and the CEO/Executive Director, regarding the items checked in line 1a?	**2**		
3	Indicate which, if any, of the following the organization uses to establish the compensation of the organization's CEO/Executive Director. Check all that apply.			

    ☐ Compensation committee   ☐ Written employment contract
    ☐ Independent compensation consultant ☐ Compensation survey or study
    ☐ Form 990 of other organizations   ☐ Approval by the board or compensation committee

4	During the year, did any person listed in Form 990, Part VII, Section A, line 1a:			
a	Receive a severance payment or change of control payment?	**4a**		
b	Participate in, or receive payment from, a supplemental nonqualified retirement plan?	**4b**		
c	Participate in, or receive payment from, an equity-based compensation arrangement?	**4c**		
	If "Yes" to any of lines 4a–c, list the persons and provide the applicable amounts for each item in Part III.			

501(c)(3) and 501(c)(4) organizations only must complete lines 5–8.

5	For persons listed in Form 990, Part VII, Section A, line 1a, did the organization pay or accrue any compensation contingent on the revenues of:			
a	The organization?	**5a**		
b	Any related organization?	**5b**		
	If "Yes" to line 5a or 5b, describe in Part III.			
6	For persons listed in Form 990, Part VII, Section A, line 1a, did the organization pay or accrue any compensation contingent on the net earnings of:			
a	The organization?	**6a**		
b	Any related organization?	**6b**		
	If "Yes" to line 6a or 6b, describe in Part III.			
7	For persons listed in Form 990, Part VII, Section A, line 1a, did the organization provide any non-fixed payments not described in lines 5 and 6? If "Yes," describe in Part III	**7**		
8	Were any amounts reported in Form 990, Part VII, paid or accrued pursuant to a contract that was subject to the initial contract exception described in Regs. section 53.4958-4(a)(3)? If "Yes," describe in Part III	**8**		

For Privacy Act and Paperwork Reduction Act Notice, see the separate instructions.   Cat. No. 50053T   Schedule J (Form 990) 2008

Part II **Officers, Directors, Trustees, Key Employees, and Highest Compensated Employees.** Use Schedule J-1 if additional space is needed.

For each individual whose compensation must be reported in Schedule J, report compensation from the organization on row (i) and from related organizations, described in the instructions, on row (ii). Do not list any individuals that are not listed on Form 990, Part VII.

Note. The sum of columns (B)(i)–(iii) must equal the applicable column (D) or column (E) amounts on Form 990, Part VII, line 1a.

(A) Name		(B) Breakdown of W-2 and/or 1099-MISC compensation			(C) Deferred compensation	(D) Nontaxable benefits	(E) Total of columns (B)(i)–(D)	(F) Compensation reported in prior Form 990 or Form 990-EZ
		(i) Base compensation	(ii) Bonus & incentive compensation	(iii) Other compensation				
	(i)							
	(ii)							
	(i)							
	(ii)							
	(i)							
	(ii)							
	(i)							
	(ii)							
	(i)							
	(ii)							
	(i)							
	(ii)							
	(i)							
	(ii)							
	(i)							
	(ii)							
	(i)							
	(ii)							
	(i)							
	(ii)							
	(i)							
	(ii)							
	(i)							
	(ii)							
	(i)							
	(ii)							
	(i)							
	(ii)							
	(i)							
	(ii)							
	(i)							
	(ii)							

Part III **Supplemental Information**

Complete this part to provide the information, explanation, or descriptions required for Part I, lines 1a, 1b, 4c, 5a, 5b, 6a, 6b, 7, and 8. Also complete this part for any additional information.

SCHEDULE K
(Form 990)

Department of the Treasury
Internal Revenue Service

Supplemental Information on Tax Exempt Bonds

To be completed by organizations that answered "Yes" to Form 990, Part IV, line 24a.
Provide descriptions, explanations, and any additional information in Schedule O.

OMB No. 1545-0047

2008

Open to Public
Inspection

Name of the organization

Employer identification number

Part I Bond Issues (Required for 2008)

	(a) Issuer Name	(b) Issuer EIN	(c) CUSIP #	(d) Date Issued	(e) Issue Price	(f) Description of Purpose	(g) Defeased		(h) On Behalf of Issuer	
							Yes	No	Yes	No
A										
B										
C										
D										
E										

Part II Proceeds (Optional for 2008)

		A		B		C		D		E	
1	Total Proceeds of Issue										
2	Gross Proceeds in Reserve Funds										
3	Proceeds in Refunding or Defeasance Escrows										
4	Other Unspent Proceeds										
5	Issuance Costs from Proceeds										
6	Working Capital Expenditures from Proceeds										
7	Capital Expenditures from Proceeds										
8	Year of Substantial Completion										
		Yes	No	Yes	No	Yes	No	Yes	No	Yes	No
9	Were the bonds issued as part of a current refunding issue?										
10	Were the bonds issued as part of an advance refunding issue?										
11	Has the final allocation of proceeds been made?										
12	Does the organization maintain adequate books and records to support the final allocation of proceeds?										

Part III Private Business Use (Optional for 2008)

		A		B		C		D		E	
		Yes	No	Yes	No	Yes	No	Yes	No	Yes	No
1	Was the organization a partner in a partnership, or a member of an LLC, which owned property financed by tax-exempt bonds?										
2	Are there any lease arrangements with respect to the financed property which may result in private business use?										

For Paperwork Reduction Act Notice, see the Instructions for Form 990.

Cat. No. 50193E

Schedule K (Form 990) 2008

587

Part III Private Business Use *(Continued)*

	A		B		C		D		E	
	Yes	No	Yes	No	Yes	No	Yes	No	Yes	No
3a Are there any management or service contracts with respect to the financed property which may result in private business use?										
3b Are there any reseach agreements with respect to the financed property which may result in private business use?										
3c Does the organization routinely engage bond counsel or other outside counsel to review any management or service contracts or research agreements relating to the financed property?										
4 Enter the percentage of financed property used in a private business use by entities other than a 501(c)(3) organization or a state or local government . .										
5 Enter the percentage of financed property used in a private business use as a result of unrelated trade or business activity carried on by your organization, another 501(c)(3) organization, or a state or local government .										
6 Total of lines 4 and 5										
7 Has the organization adopted management practices and procedures to ensure the post-issuance compliance of its tax-exempt bond liabilities?										

Part IV Arbitrage *(Optional for 2008)*

	A		B		C		D		E	
	Yes	No	Yes	No	Yes	No	Yes	No	Yes	No
1 Has a Form 8038-T been filed with respect to the bond issue?										
2 Is the bond issue a variable rate issue?										
3a Has the organization or the governmental issuer identified a hedge with respect to the bond issue on its books and records?										
b Name of provider.										
c Term of hedge										
4a Were gross proceeds invested in a GIC?										
b Name of provider.										
c Term of GIC										
d Was the regulatory safe harbor for establishing the fair market value of the GIC satisfied?										
5 Were any gross proceeds invested beyond an available temporary period?										
6 Did the bond issue qualify for an exception to rebate?										

Printed on recycled paper

Schedule K (Form 990) 2008

SCHEDULE L (Form 990 or 990-EZ) Department of the Treasury Internal Revenue Service	**Transactions With Interested Persons** ▶ Attach to Form 990 or Form 990-EZ. ▶ To be completed by organizations that answered "Yes" on Form 990, Part IV, line 25a, 25b, 26, 27, 28a, 28b, or 28c, or Form 990-EZ, Part V, line 38a or 40b.	OMB No. 1545-0047 2008 **Open To Public Inspection**

Name of the organization	Employer identification number

Part I   Excess Benefit Transactions (section 501(c)(3) and section 501(c)(4) organizations only).
To be completed by organizations that answered "Yes" on Form 990, Part IV, line 25a or 25b, or Form 990-EZ, Part V, line 40b.

1	(a) Name of disqualified person	(b) Description of transaction	(c) Corrected?	
			Yes	No

2   Enter the amount of tax imposed on the organization managers or disqualified persons during the year
under section 4958 . . . . ▶ $ _____

3   Enter the amount of tax, if any, on line 2, above, reimbursed by the organization . . . . ▶ $ _____

Part II   Loans to and/or From Interested Persons.
To be completed by organizations that answered "Yes" on Form 990, Part IV, line 26, or Form 990-EZ, Part V, line 38a.

(a) Name of interested person and purpose	(b) Loan to or from the organization?		(c) Original principal amount	(d) Balance due	(e) In default?		(f) Approved by board or committee?		(g) Written agreement?	
	To	From			Yes	No	Yes	No	Yes	No

Total . . . . ▶ $

Part III   Grants or Assistance Benefitting Interested Persons.
To be completed by organizations that answered "Yes" on Form 990, Part IV, line 27.

(a) Name of interested person	(b) Relationship between interested person and the organization	(c) Amount of grant or type of assistance

Part IV   Business Transactions Involving Interested Persons.
To be completed by organizations that answered "Yes" on Form 990, Part IV, line 28a, 28b, or 28c.

(a) Name of interested person	(b) Relationship between interested person and the organization	(c) Amount of transaction	(d) Description of transaction	(e) Sharing of organization's revenues?	
				Yes	No

For Paperwork Reduction Act Notice, see the Instructions for Form 990.   Cat. No. 50056A   Schedule L (Form 990 or 990-EZ) 2008

Printed on recycled paper

SCHEDULE M (Form 990) Department of the Treasury Internal Revenue Service	**Non-Cash Contributions** To be completed by organizations that answered "Yes" on Form 990, Part IV, lines 29 or 30.	OMB No. 1545-0047 2008 Open To Public Inspection
Name of the organization		Employer identification number

Part I   Types of Property

		(a) Check if applicable	(b) Number of Contributions	(c) Revenues reported on Form 990, Part VIII, line 1g	(d) Method of determining revenues
1	Art—Works of art				
2	Art—Historical treasures . .				
3	Art—Fractional interests . .				
4	Books and publications . .				
5	Clothing and household goods				
6	Cars and other vehicles . .				
7	Boats and planes				
8	Intellectual property				
9	Securities—Publicly traded .				
10	Securities—Closely held stock .				
11	Securities—Partnership, LLC, or trust interests				
12	Securities—Miscellaneous .				
13	Qualified conservation contribution (historic structures)				
14	Qualified conservation contribution (other)				
15	Real estate—Residential . .				
16	Real estate—Commercial . .				
17	Real estate—Other				
18	Collectibles				
19	Food inventory				
20	Drugs and medical supplies .				
21	Taxidermy				
22	Historical artifacts				
23	Scientific specimens . . .				
24	Archeological artifacts . . .				
25	Other (describe ....)				
26	Other (describe ....)				
27	Other (describe ....)				
28	Other (describe ....)				

29	Number of Forms 8283 received by the organization during the tax year for contributions for which the organization completed *Part IV, Donee Acknowledgement*	29	

			Yes	No
30a	During the year, did the organization receive by contribution any property reported in Part I that it must hold for at least three years from the date of the initial contribution, and which is not required to be used for exempt purposes for the entire holding period?	30a		
b	If "Yes," describe the arrangement in Part II.			
31	Does the organization have a gift acceptance policy that requires the review of any non-standard contributions?	31		
32a	Does the organization hire or use third parties or related organizations to solicit, process, or sell non-cash contributions?	32a		
b	If "Yes," describe in Part II.			
33	If the organization did not report revenues in Column (c) for a type of property for which Column (a) is checked, describe in Part II.			

For Paperwork Reduction Act Notice, see the Instructions for Form 990.   Cat. No. 51227J   Schedule M (Form 990) 2008

Schedule M (Form 990) 2008   Page **2**

Part II   **Supplemental Information.** Complete this part to provide the information required by Part I, lines 30b, 32b, and 33. Also complete this part for any additional information.

Schedule M (Form 990) 2008

 Printed on recycled paper

SCHEDULE N
(Form 990 or 990-EZ)

Department of the Treasury
Internal Revenue Service

Liquidation, Termination, Dissolution, or Significant Disposition of Assets

- To be completed by organizations that answer "Yes" to Form 990, Part IV, lines 31 or 32; or Form 990-EZ, line 36.
▶ Attach certified copies of any articles of dissolution, resolutions, or plans.
▶ Attach to Form 990 or 990-EZ.

Name of the organization | Employer identification number

Part I **Liquidation, Termination, or Dissolution.** Complete this part if the organization answered "Yes" to Form 990, Part IV, line 31, or Form 990-EZ, line 36. Use Schedule N-1 if additional space is needed.

1 (a) Description of asset(s) distributed or transaction expenses paid	(b) Date of distribution	(c) Fair market value of asset(s) distributed or amount of transaction expenses	(d) Method of determining FMV for asset(s) distributed or transaction expenses	(e) EIN of recipient	(f) Name and address of recipient	(g) IRC Code section of recipient(s) (if tax-exempt) or type of entity

		Yes	No
2	Did or will any officer, director, trustee, or key employee of the organization:		
a	Become a director or trustee of a successor or transferee organization?	2a	
b	Become an employee of, or independent contractor for, a successor or transferee organization?	2b	
c	Become a direct or indirect owner of a successor or transferee organization?	2c	
d	Receive, or become entitled to, compensation or other similar payments as a result of the organization's liquidation, termination, or dissolution?	2d	
e	If the organization answered "Yes" to any of the questions in this line, provide the name of the person involved and explain in Part III.		

For Paperwork Reduction Act Notice, see the Instructions for Form 990.   Cat. No. 50087Z   Schedule N (Form 990 or 990-EZ) 2008

Part I Liquidation, Termination, or Dissolution (continued)

Note. If the organization distributed all of its assets during the tax year, then Form 990, Part X, column (B) should equal -0-.

		Yes	No
3	Did the organization distribute its assets in accordance with its governing instruments? If "No," describe in Part III . . .	3	
4a	Did the organization request or receive a determination letter from EO Determinations that the organization's exempt status was terminated? . .	4a	
b	(If "Yes," provide the date of the letter._____)		
5a	Is the organization required to notify the attorney general or other appropriate state official of its intent to dissolve, liquidate, or terminate? . .	5a	
b	If "Yes," did the organization provide such notice? . . .	5b	
6	Did the organization discharge or pay all liabilities in accordance with state laws? . . .	6	
7a	Did the organization have any tax-exempt bonds outstanding during the year? . . .	7a	
b	Did the organization discharge or defease tax-exempt bond liabilities in accordance with the Internal Revenue Code and state laws? . .	7b	
c	If "Yes," describe in Part III how the organization defeased or otherwise settled these liabilities. If "No," explain in Part III.		

Part II Sale, Exchange, Disposition, or Other Transfer of More Than 25% of the Organization's Assets. Complete this part if the organization answered "Yes" to Form 990, Part IV, line 32, or Form 990-EZ, line 36. Use Schedule N-1 if additional space is needed.

1	(a) Description of asset(s) distributed or transaction expenses paid	(b) Date of distribution	(c) Fair market value of asset(s) distributed or amount of transaction expenses	(d) Method of determining FMV for asset(s) distributed or transaction expenses	(e) EIN of recipient	(f) Name and address of recipient	(g) IRC Code section of recipient(s) (if tax-exempt) or type of entity

		Yes	No
2	Did or will any officer, director, trustee, or key employee of the organization:		
a	Become a director or trustee of a successor or transferee organization? . . .	2a	
b	Become an employee of, or independent contractor for, a successor or transferee organization? . . .	2b	
c	Become a direct or indirect owner of a successor or transferee organization? . . .	2c	
d	Receive, or become entitled to, compensation or other similar payments as a result of the organization's significant disposition of assets? . .	2d	
e	If the organization answered "Yes" to any of the questions in this line, provide the name of the person involved and explain in Part III.		

APPENDIX A

Part III	**Supplemental Information.** Complete this part to provide the information required by Part I, lines 2e, 7c; or Part II, line 2e; and any additional information.

 Printed on recycled paper

SCHEDULE O
(Form 990)

Department of the Treasury
Internal Revenue Service

Supplemental Information to Form 990

► Attach to Form 990. To be completed by organizations to provide additional information for responses to specific questions for the Form 990 or to provide any additional information.

OMB No. 1545-0047

2008

Open to Public Inspection

Name of the organization

Employer identification number

For Paperwork Reduction Act Notice, see the Instructions for Form 990.

Cat. No. 51056K

Schedule O (Form 990) 2008

Schedule O (Form 990) 2008   Page **2**

Name of the organization	Employer identification number

Schedule O (Form 990) 2008

 Printed on recycled paper

Related Organizations and Unrelated Partnerships

▶ Attach to Form 990. To be completed by organizations that answered "Yes" to Form 990, Part IV, line 33, 34, 35, 36, or 37.
▶ See separate instructions.

OMB No. 1545-0047

2008

Open to Public Inspection

Name of the organization

Employer identification number

Part I   Identification of Disregarded Entities

(A) Name, address, and EIN of disregarded entity	(B) Primary activity	(C) Legal domicile (state or foreign country)	(D) Total income	(E) End-of-year assets	(F) Direct controlling entity

Part II   Identification of Related Tax–Exempt Organizations

(A) Name, address, and EIN of related organization	(B) Primary activity	(C) Legal domicile (state or foreign country)	(D) Exempt Code section	(E) Public charity status (if section 501(c)(3))	(F) Direct controlling entity

For Paperwork Reduction Act Notice, see the Instructions for Form 990.

Cat. No. 50135Y

Schedule R (Form 990) 2008

Part III Identification of Related Organizations Taxable as a Partnership

(A) Name, address, and EIN of related organization	(B) Primary activity	(C) Legal domicile (state or foreign country)	(D) Direct controlling entity	(E) Predominant income (related, investment, **unrelated**)	(F) Share of total income	(G) Share of end-of-year assets	(H) Disproportionate allocations?		(I) Code V—UBI amount on Box 20 of K-1	(J) General or managing partner?	
							Yes	No		Yes	No

Part IV Identification of Related Organizations Taxable as a Corporation or Trust

(A) Name, address, and EIN of related organization	(B) Primary activity	(C) Legal domicile (state or foreign country)	(D) Direct controlling entity	(E) Type of entity (C corp, S corp, or trust)	(F) Share of total income	(G) Share of end-of-year assets	(H) Percentage ownership

Part V **Transactions With Related Organizations**

Note. Complete line 1 if any entity is listed in Parts II, III, or IV.

		Yes	No
1	During the tax year, did the organization engage in any of the following transactions with one or more related organizations listed in Parts II–IV?		
a	Receipt of **(i)** interest **(ii)** annuities **(iii)** royalties **(iv)** rent from a controlled entity **1a**		
b	Gift, grant, or capital contribution to other organization(s) **1b**		
c	Gift, grant, or capital contribution from other organization(s) **1c**		
d	Loans or loan guarantees to or for other organization(s) **1d**		
e	Loans or loan guarantees by other organization(s) **1e**		
f	Sale of assets to other organization(s) **1f**		
g	Purchase of assets from other organization(s) **1g**		
h	Exchange of assets **1h**		
i	Lease of facilities, equipment, or other assets to other organization(s) **1i**		
j	Lease of facilities, equipment, or other assets from other organization(s) **1j**		
k	Performance of services or membership or fundraising solicitations for other organization(s) . . . **1k**		
l	Performance of services or membership or fundraising solicitations by other organization(s) . . . **1l**		
m	Sharing of facilities, equipment, mailing lists, or other assets **1m**		
n	Sharing of paid employees **1n**		
o	Reimbursement paid to other organization for expenses **1o**		
p	Reimbursement paid by other organization for expenses **1p**		
q	Other transfer of cash or property to other organization(s) **1q**		
r	Other transfer of cash or property from other organization(s) **1r**		
2	If the answer to any of the above is "Yes," see the instructions for information on who must complete this line, including covered relationships and transaction thresholds.		

(A) Name of other organization(s)	**(B)** Transaction type (a–r)	**(C)** Amount involved
(1)		
(2)		
(3)		
(4)		
(5)		
(6)		

Part VI Unrelated Organizations Taxable as a Partnership

Provide the following information for each entity taxed as a partnership through which the organization conducted more than five percent of its activities (measured by total assets or gross revenue) that was not a related organization. See instructions regarding exclusion for certain investment partnerships.

(A) Name, address, and EIN of entity	(B) Primary activity	(C) Legal domicile (state or foreign country)	(D) Are all partners section 501(c)(3) organizations?		(E) Share of end-of-year assets	(F) Disproportionate allocations?		(G) Code V—UBI amount on Box 20 of K-1	(H) General or managing partner?	
			Yes	No		Yes	No		Yes	No

Schedule R (Form 990) 2008

 Printed on recycled paper

■ 600 ■

A P P E N D I X   B

Supplemental Instructions Information

§ B.1 CHAPTER 6 PART VII AND SCHEDULE J

(a) Compensation table for reporting on Part VII, Section A or Schedule J, Part II. The following table may be useful in determining how and where to report items of compensation in Part VII, Section A and in Schedule J, Part II. The list is not comprehensive but covers most items for most organizations. Many items of compensation may or may not be taxable or currently taxable, depending on the plan or arrangement adopted by the organization and other circumstances. The list attempts to take into account these varying facts and circumstances. The list is merely a guideline to report amounts for those persons required to be listed. In all cases, items included in Box 5 of Form W-2 and Box 7 of Form 1099-MISC are required to be reported in Part VII, Section A and, for applicable persons, Schedule J, Part II, column B. Items marked with an asterisk (''*'') instead of an ''x'' are excludible from Form 990, Part VII, Section A, column (F) if below $10,000.

	WHERE TO REPORT				
	FORM 990, PART VII, SECTION A, COL. (D) OR (E)			FORM 990, PART VII, SECTION A, COL. (F)	
	SCHEDULE J, PART II, COL.				
TYPE OF COMPENSATION	B(I)	B(II)	B(III)	COL. C	COL. D
Base salary/wages/fees paid	x				
Base salary/wages/fees deferred (taxable)	x				
Base salary/wages/fees deferred (nontaxable)				x	
Bonus paid (including signing bonus)		x			
Bonus deferred (taxable in current year)		x			
Bonus deferred (not taxable in current year)				x	
Incentive compensation paid		x			
Incentive compensation deferred (taxable in current year)		x			
Incentive compensation deferred (not taxable in current year)				x	
Severance or change of control payments made			x		

(Continued)

	WHERE TO REPORT				
	FORM 990, PART VII, SECTION A, COL. (D) OR (E)			FORM 990, PART VII, SECTION A, COL. (F)	
	SCHEDULE J, PART II, COL.				
TYPE OF COMPENSATION	B(I)	B(II)	B(III)	COL. C	COL. D
Sick pay paid by employer	x				
Third party sick pay			x		
Other compensation amounts deferred (taxable in current year)		x			
Other compensation amounts deferred (not taxable in current year)				x	
Tax gross-ups paid			x		
Vacation/sick leave cashed out			x		
Stock options at time of grant				x	
Stock options at time of exercise			x		
Stock awards paid by taxable organizations substantially vested			x		
Stock awards paid by taxable organizations not vested				x	
Stock equivalents paid by taxable organizations substantially vested			x		
Stock equivalents paid by taxable organizations not vested				x	
Loans—forgone interest or debt forgiveness			x		
Contributions (employer) to qualified retirement plan				x	
Contributions (employee deferrals) to 401 (k) plan			x		
Contributions (employee deferrals) to 403(b) plan			x		
Qualified or nonqualified retirement plan defined benefit accruals (reasonable estimate of increase in actuarial value)				x	
Qualified or nonqualified retirement defined contribution plan investment earnings (no reportable or other compensation)					
Taxable distributions from qualified retirement plan (reported on Form 1099-R)—no reportable or other compensation					
Distributions from nongovernmental 457(b) plan—no reportable or other compensation					
Amounts includible in income under 457(f)			x		
Amounts deferred (plus earnings) under 457(b) plan (vested)			x		
Amounts deferred (plus earnings) under 457(b) plan (nonvested)				x	
Contributions to nonqualified plans (vested)			x		
Contributions to nonqualified plans (nonvested)				x	
Increase in earnings of nonqualified plan			x		

Scholarships and fellowship grants (taxable)	X	
Health benefit plan premiums (taxable)	X	
Health benefit plan premiums (nontaxable)		X
Medical reimbursement and flexible spending programs (taxable)	X	
Medical reimbursement and flexible spending programs (nontaxable)		X
Other health benefits (taxable)	X	
Other health benefits (nontaxable)		X
Life, disability, or long-term-care insurance (taxable)	X	
Life, disability, or long-term-care insurance (nontaxable)		*
Split-dollar life insurance (see Notice 2002-8)	X	
Housing provided by employer(taxable)	X	
Housing provided by employer (nontaxable)		*
Personal legal services (taxable)	X	
Personal legal services (nontaxable)		*
Personal financial services (taxable)	X	
Personal financial services (nontaxable)		*
Dependent care assistance (taxable)	X	
Dependent care assistance (nontaxable)		*
Adoption assistance (taxable)	X	
Adoption assistance (nontaxable)		*
Tuition assistance for family (taxable)	X	
Tuition assistance for family (nontaxable)		*
Cafeteria plans (taxable)	X	
Cafeteria plans (nontaxable health benefit)		X
Cafeteria plans (nontaxable benefit other than health)		*
Liability insurance (taxable)	X	
Employer-provided automobile (taxable)	X	
Employer-subsidized parking (taxable)	X	
Travel (taxable)	X	
Moving (taxable)	X	
Meals and entertainment (taxable)	X	
Social club dues (taxable)	X	
Spending account (taxable)	X	

§B.2   CHAPTER 9: SCHEDULE C

(a) Part III-B, Line 2 of Schedule C Form 990.

The IRS provides these allocation methods for reporting on Part III-B, line 2.

Allocation of costs to lobbying activities and influencing legislation. An organization that is subject to the lobbying disclosure rules of section 6033(e) must use a reasonable allocation method to determine its total costs of its direct lobbying activities; that is, costs to influence:

- Legislation
- The actions of a covered executive branch official through direct communication (e.g., president, vice president, or cabinet-level officials, and their immediate deputies) (sections 162(e)(1)(A) and (D))

Reasonable methods of allocating costs to direct lobbying activities include, but are not limited to:

- The ratio method
- The gross-up and alternative gross-up methods
- A method applying the principles of section 263A

See Regulations sections 1.162-28 and 1.162-29 and the special rules and definitions for these allocation methods given below.

An organization that is subject to the lobbying disclosure rules of section 6033(e) must also determine its total costs of:

De minimis in-house lobbying,

Grassroots lobbying, and

Political campaign activities.

There are no special rules related to determining these costs.

All methods. For all the allocation methods, include labor hours and costs of personnel whose activities involve significant judgment with respect to lobbying activities.

Special rules:

Ratio and gross-up methods

1. May use even if volunteers conduct activities
2. May disregard labor hours and costs of clerical or support personnel (other than lobbying personnel) under the ratio method

Alternative gross-up method

- Disregard labor hours
- Disregard costs of clerical or support personnel (other than lobbying personnel)

Third-party costs are those paid to:

- Outside parties for conducting lobbying activities
- Dues paid to another membership organization that were declared to be nondeductible lobbying expenses
- Travel and entertainment costs for lobbying activities

Direct contact lobbying. Treat all hours spent by a person in connection with direct contact lobbying as labor hours allocable to lobbying activities.

Do not treat the hours spent by a person who engages in research and other background activities related to direct contact lobbying, but who makes no direct contact with a legislator, or covered executive branch official, as direct contact lobbying.

De minimis rule. If less than 5 percent of a person's time is spent on lobbying activities, and there is no direct contact lobbying, an organization may treat that person's time spent on lobbying activities as zero.

Purpose for engaging in an activity is based on all the facts and circumstances. If an organization's lobbying communication was for a lobbying and a nonlobbying purpose, the organization must make a reasonable allocation of costs to influencing legislation.

Correction of prior-year lobbying costs. If in a prior year, an organization treated costs incurred for a future lobbying communication as a lobbying cost to influence legislation, but after the organization filed a timely return, it appears the lobbying communication will not be made under any foreseeable circumstance, the organization may apply these costs to reduce its current year's lobbying costs, but not below zero. The organization may carry forward any amount of the costs not used to reduce its current year's lobbying costs to subsequent years.

Example: Ratio method. X Organization incurred:

1. 6,000 labor hours for all activities
2. 3,000 labor hours for lobbying activities (three employees)
3. $300,000 for operational costs
4. No third-party lobbying costs

X Organization allocated its lobbying costs in this way:

Lobbying Labor hrs.					
3,000 6,000 Total labor hrs	x	$300,000 Total costs of operations	+	0 Allocable third-party costs	=	$150,000 Costs allocable to lobbying activities

Examples: Gross-up method and alternative gross-up method.

A and B are employees of Y Organization.

1. A's activities involve significant judgment with respect to lobbying activities.
2. A's basic lobbying labor costs (excluding employee benefits) are $50,000.
3. B performs clerical and support activities for A.

4. B's labor costs (excluding employee benefits) in support of A's activities are $15,000.

5. Allocable third-party costs are $100,000.

If Y Organization uses the gross-up method to allocate its lobbying costs, Y multiplies 175 percent times its basic labor costs (excluding employee benefits) for all of the lobbying of its personnel and adds its allocable third-party lobbying costs as follows:

175% Basic lobbying labor costs of A + B	x	$65,000	+	$100,000 Allocable third-party costs	=	$213,750 Costs allocable to lobbying activities

If Y Organization uses the alternative gross-up method to allocate its lobbying costs, Y multiplies 225 percent times its basic labor costs (excluding employee benefits) for all of the lobbying hours of its lobbying personnel and adds its third-party lobbying costs as follows:

225% Basic lobbying labor costs of A	x	$50,000	+	$100,000 Allocable third-party costs	=	$212,500 Costs allocable to lobbying activities

(b) Part III-B, Line 5 of Form 990.
The IRS instructions provide these examples and assumptions for reporting on Part III-B, line 5.

Organization A, B, and C:

1. Reported on a calendar-year basis.

2. Incurred only grassroots lobbying expenses (did not qualify for the under 2,000 in house lobbying exception).

3. Allocated dues to tax year in which received.

For Organization A—Dues, assessments, and similar amounts received in 2008 were greater than its lobbying expenses for 2008.

WORKPAPERS (FOR **2008 FORM 990**)—ORGANIZATION A

1. Total dues, assessments, etc., received	$800	
2. Lobbying expenses paid or incurred		$600
3. Less: Total nondeductible amount of dues notices	100	100
4. (Subtract line 3 from both lines 1 and 2)	$700	$500
5. Taxable amount of lobbying expenses (smaller of the two amounts on line 4)		$500

> *TIP:* The amounts on lines 1, 2, 3, and 5 of the workpapers were entered on lines 1, 2c, 3, and 5 of the 2008 Form 990, Schedule C, Part III-B.
> Because dues, etc., received were greater than lobbying expenses, there is no carry-over of excess lobbying expenses to PART III-B, line 2b of the year 2008 Form 990. See the instructions for Part III-B, line 5 for the treatment of the $500.
>
> **For Organization B**—Dues, assessments, and similar amounts received in 2008 were less than its lobbying expenses for 2008.
>
> **WORKPAPERS (FOR 2008 FORM 990)—ORGANIZATION B**
> | | | |
> |---|---|---|
> | 1. Total dues, assessments, etc., received | $400 | |
> | 2. Lobbying expenses paid or incurred | | $600 |
> | 3. Less: Total nondeductible amount of dues notices | 100 | 100 |
> | 4. (Subtract line 3 from both lines 1 and 2) | $300 | $500 |
> | 5. Taxable amount of lobbying expenses (smaller of the two amounts on line 4) | $300 | |

> *TIP:* The amounts on lines 1, 2, 3, and 5 of the workpapers were entered on lines 1, 2c, 3, and 5 of the 2008 Form 990, Schedule C, Part III-B.

Examples

Because dues, etc., received were less than lobbying expenses, excess lobbying expenses of $200 must be carried forward to PART III-B, line 2b of the next year Form 990 Schedule C (excess of $600 of lobbying expenses over $400 dues, etc., received). The $200 will be included along with the other lobbying and political expenses paid or incurred in 2009 reporting year.

> **For Organization C**—Dues, assessments, and similar amounts received in 2008 were greater than its lobbying expenses for 2008 and the organization agreed to carry over a portion of its excess lobbying and political expenses to the next year.
>
> **WORKPAPERS (FOR 2008 FORM 990)—ORGANIZATION C**
> | | | |
> |---|---|---|
> | 1. Total dues, assessments, etc., received | $800 | |
> | 2. Lobbying expenses paid or incurred | | $600 |
> | 3. Less: Total nondeductible amount of dues notices | 100 | 100 |
> | 4. Less: Amount agreed to carryover | 100 | 100 |
> | 5. (Subtract lines 3 and 4 from both lines 1 and 2) | $600 | $400 |
> | 6. Taxable amount of lobbying expenses (smaller of the two amounts on line 5) | | $400 |

> TIP: The amounts on lines 1, 2, 3, 4, and 5 of the workpapers were entered on lines 1, 2c, 3, 4 and 5 of the 2008 Form 990, Schedule C, Part III-B.

See the instructions for Part III-B, line 5 for the treatment of the $300.

See the instructions for Part III-B, line 5 for the treatment of the $400.

INDEX